The Sourcebook
of Nonverbal Measures

Going Beyond Words

The Sourcebook
of Nonverbal Measures

Going Beyond Words

Edited by

VALERIE MANUSOV
University of Washington

LAWRENCE ERLBAUM ASSOCIATES, PUBLISHERS
2005   Mahwah, New Jersey   London

Lawrence Erlbaum Associates, Inc., Publishers
10 Industrial Avenue
Mahwah, New Jersey 07430

Cover design by Kathryn Houghtaling Lacey

Library of Congress Cataloging-in-Publication Data

The sourcebook of nonverbal measures : going beyond words / edited by
    Valerie Manusov.
      p. cm.
    Includes bibliographical references and index.
    ISBN 0-8058-4746-4 (cloth : alk. paper)
    ISBN 0-8058-4747-2 (pbk. : alk. paper)
    1. Nonverbal communication. 2. Interpersonal relations. I. Manusov,
      Valerie.
    P99.5.S58   2004
    302.2'22—dc22   2003049545
                                                                  CIP

Books published by Lawrence Erlbaum Associates are printed on acid-
free paper, and their bindings are chosen for strength and durability.

Printed in the United States of America
10 9 8 7 6 5 4 3 2 1

Contents

Coding and Rating

Preface

Valerie Manusov
University of Washington

A few years ago, a bold graduate student in communication, Jack Sargent (now a faculty member and contributor to this book) asked me, and several other experienced researchers who study nonverbal behavior, to be part of a conference panel. At that time, Jack was interested in doing a study that used coding and rating techniques to measure nonverbal cues, and he could not find a current published source to help him. So he gathered us together in Denver, Colorado, and asked us a series of questions. It was useful for Jack but also for those of us on the panel—and hopefully for the audience as well. All of us realized that much of the work we had been doing involved creating and re-creating measures to assess the aspects of nonverbal behavior in which we were most interested. We all concurred that having a more cohesive discussion of research choices specifically for the investigation of nonverbal phenomena seemed important. That is the primary aim of this book.

All of us who study—or wish to include—nonverbal cues in their scholarship know the myriad ways that nonverbal behavior can be conceptualized. Depending on how we think about the nature, functions, and meanings of nonverbal cues, we are likely to go about investigating them in a certain way. The complexity and ambiguity of nonverbal processes and products allows for a plethora of research opportunities. It also provides for so much variety that it may be difficult sometimes to compare research findings. An additional aim of this volume, then, is to encapsulate some of the primary means by which researchers assess nonverbal cues with the hope that these may be used by others as well.

The particular selection of chapters to include in this volume was strategic. My hope was to include some well-known and repeatedly validated assessment measures alongside some novel approaches just beginning their research "journeys." I also wanted specifically to include research and researchers from a number of disciplines, as nonverbal behavior is one of those research topics that spans an array of scholarly interests. Additionally, and although the term "measurement" entails, typically, an orientation toward quantitative assessment, I hoped that this book would show qualitative means through which nonverbal cues can be illustrated and understood. It is my good fortune that most of the potential contributors I contacted said "yes," and this volume has taken much of the shape I hoped it would.

It has also been expanded farther than my original intentions, and I am glad of this. Specifically, in addition to measures that can be used by other researchers with an interest in nonverbal cues, much of the book also orients around broader issues involved in doing this research. Several of the chapters, for example, provide discussion of larger research "paradigms" into which a particular measure may be placed. Other chapters are devoted more to strategies that researchers have available to them to help answer their questions. The latter includes discussions meant to help researchers think through the array of choices available to them and to show the strong connection between the type of answers one seeks and the means through which she or he may seek them.

The book is limited necessarily to those measures that, for the most part, can "fit" into these pages. Important, but "larger," well-known assessments, such as Rosenthal's Profile of Nonverbal Sensitivity, and Paul Ekman's Facial Action Coding System, were too big for this book but are available elsewhere (Judith Hall, a contributor to this book, can be contacted for PNS, and Ekman can be contacted for FACs and several other very useful assessments). We hope, however, that having most of the measures actually printed in this volume will make it a particularly useful sourcebook.

The authors of these chapters and I hope that this book will be useful to its audience. We encourage each reader to read it in the manner that works best for his or her individual needs. Some people may read only those chapters that have specific relevance to a particular study they are planning. Others, especially those who wish to become researchers of nonverbal processes and/or those taking classes in nonverbal behavior, may benefit most from reading all parts of the book to look at how these authors made the choices they did. Whatever form of help this book takes, I am glad of it.

I am also glad to have this chance to thank a few people for this book's creation. In addition to Jack Sargent, whom I mentioned previously, and another colleague, Kimo Ah Yun, who also lamented on the difficulty of finding a range of methods easily for studying nonverbal cues, I thank the other authors for their willingness to write these excellent chapters. Most specifically, thanks to Kory Floyd for allowing me to use his chapter as an exemplar to entice others to join the project. I also thank Lane Akers at Lawrence Erlbaum Associates for calling me back excitedly the first morning he received my proposal, Linda Bathgate, also at LEA, who lived up to the extremely positive rumors about her character and competence, and Sara Scudder, a senior book production editor at LEA who was the consumate copy editor. Thanks also to my colleagues in the Department of Communication at the University of Washington, who always provide encouragement for the work that I do. Finally, my love and thanks to my son, Cameron, and my husband, Chuck, who provide ample opportunities to see the importance of nonverbal cues in the everyday of our lives together.

I. INTRODUCTION TO NONVERBAL COMMUNICATION RESEARCH

Researcher Choices and Practices in the Study of Nonverbal Communication

Cindy H. White
University of Colorado

Jack Sargent
Kean University

INTRODUCTION

There is sometimes a temptation to believe that a book like this provides researchers with ready-made approaches for examining interaction and answering research questions. So, we begin this chapter with a caution that fulfilling such a belief is unlikely because ready-made research solutions are rare. A book like this one can, however, be a great asset to researchers, because such volumes *allow researchers to see clearly what others are doing and to make thoughtful decisions about how to examine nonverbal behavior.* Decisions about measurement, whether the measures involve self- (or other-) reports, coding, rating, or physiological measures are theoretical acts (Bakeman & Gottman, 1997). They are the researchers' assessments of what is important in the interaction and what will have relevance to the theory being tested or the context being examined. It makes sense, then, to begin this book with a discussion of some of the decisions that researchers face as they begin to examine nonverbal cues.

Once a researcher makes that first decision to study nonverbal behavior, he or she is put on a path that requires many other decisions. These decisions include *who* is going to be studied, *what* type of interaction will be studied, *where* the study will take place, *how* the study will be designed, *which* behavior will be examined, and *how long* the behavior will be observed (Scherer & Ekman, 1982, see Cappella, this volume and Dunbar & Burgoon, this volume). Some of these decisions are easy because they are indicated clearly by the behavior or situation being studied (for in-

3

stance, if a researcher wants to study affection displays during airport departures, he or she has to go to the airport as Heslin & Boss, 1980, did). But many of these choices are decisions the researcher must make along the way as he or she considers how to best capture the elements of interaction that are important and meaningful (e.g., should he or she study touch during departure or facial expressions or both, across what time frame, and among which passengers?). Moreover, each of these choices has implications for the others, so that the researcher is faced not with discrete choices but with a set of interrelated judgments.

In the sections that follow, we examine the advantages and disadvantages of some selected research choices related to the study of nonverbal communication. We first discuss the potential uses and limitations of self-reports for the study of nonverbal behavior. Then we explore in depth the decisions related to categorization of observations, because oftentimes the nature and the practical enactment of coding or rating schemes are somewhat undetectable once a study comes to publication. Specifically, we examine choices researchers make about the type of observational system to employ (type of observation scheme, coding versus rating), decisions regarding where to collect data (field or laboratory settings), and issues related to the nature of the interaction being examined (coding individuals versus dyads/groups, examining interaction events or coding slices of time). We then discuss briefly when a researcher may choose physiological measures. Our goal is to provide readers with an introduction to some of the issues nonverbal researchers grapple with and to highlight chapters in this volume where readers can see that choice in action.

Self-Reports of Nonverbal Behavior

One choice researchers have is whether to use self-report measures in their studies. Self-report tools rely on participants' own perspectives (or, occasionally, the perspectives of others who are connected to the one observed), rather than the views of independent observers, to not only determine what specific behaviors were enacted but also delineate their meanings and significance. These measures are often used to gather information about microbehaviors, naturally occurring social interactions, meanings assigned by observers to behaviors, or to assess numerous communication-related skills and abilities across a variety of contexts (see Riggio, this volume; Riggio & Riggio, this volume). For instance, in a number of studies, Stanley Jones has used the self-report *Touch Log Record* to record the touching behavior of individuals. In his chapter in this book, he describes work by Jones and Yarbrough (1985), who were interested in the meanings associated with specific touching behaviors. Their study identified 12 mutually exclusive meanings associated with specific touching behaviors, and the self-report coding system generated in their work is one available framework. In another example, Palmer and Simmons (1995) used a self-report method that asked research confederates to record in an open-ended questionnaire the specific behaviors they used to convey liking to their interaction partner. Later these responses were content analyzed. This allowed the authors to compare participants' understanding of the behaviors they had used with observer assessments of that behavior.

The advantages of nonverbal self-reports are many. They are easy and inexpensive to administer (see Duke & Nowicki, this volume), the costs may be lower than for typical behavioral observation, and they provide access to a wide variety of interactions that may not be available any other way (see Keeley, this volume, and Floyd & Mikkelson, this volume). In addition, because participants are not required to report to a research site, they may be more willing to participate. Finally, many self-report measures have strong reliability (see Andersen & Andersen, this volume; Riggio & Riggio, 2001) and are correlated positively with independent observer rating tests.

Despite the benefits of using self-report measures to examine nonverbal communication, a number of limitations to their use also exist. These types of measures can be less precise than coders' observations and more prone to response biases, such as social desirability. Additionally, participants may recall their own behaviors more accurately than they recall the behavior of the person with whom they are interacting (Metts, Sprecher, & Cupach, 1991; Riggio & Riggio, 2001). Some researchers even question if self-report measures record only "impressionistic" rather than the "actual" nonverbal behaviors (Metts et al., 1991). Furthermore, participants may be overwhelmed by the amount of recording that is required from them. Jones (this volume) points out that participants need to be "motivated to record events conscientiously" but that this can be remedied through training. Participants, also, need to understand what specific behaviors or proximal cues the researcher is looking for, as well as the differences in the various constructs that the participant is expected to measure.

Numerous self-report measures of nonverbal behavior exist—particularly measures of emotional expressiveness—a number of which are discussed in this book. For a more thorough review of a number of these measures, as well as their internal and construct validity, see the section on self reports in PART II.

Observer Assessments of Nonverbal Behavior

Although we can learn much about human interaction by asking communicators to reflect on their own behavior and the behavior of others, such reflections cannot always provide detailed information about the myriad behaviors that are actually enacted as people communicate. If a researcher wants to learn how the behavior of one person influences another or observe differences in how interaction in managed (see Cappella's discussion of coding, this volume), for example, he or she may need to examine interaction as it occurs.

Observational studies of nonverbal behavior provide insight into a number of communication and relational processes. Researchers have demonstrated, among other things, the ways in which deceptive interactions are shaped jointly by both participants in a deceptive conversation (e.g., Burgoon, Buller, White, Afifi, & Buslig, 1999; see Burgoon, this volume), the way interaction between relational partners is impacted by their respective attachment styles (e.g., Guerrero, 1996), the differences in nonverbal behavior that can distinguish couples whose relationships are successful from those who are not (e.g., Gottman & Levenson, 1992; Manusov, 1995), and the importance of nonverbal behavior in adult–infant bonding and interaction (Bernieri & Rosenthal, 1991; Cappella, 1981). Observational studies focus the attention of researchers on the actual behavior of participants and provide an opportunity for researchers to explore how meanings and feelings are manifest in interaction. Although it is clear that observational studies can reveal many interesting aspects of interaction, the decision to observe behavior is not a simple one.

A researcher who decides to observe behavior is faced with a number of choices about what to observe and how to catalog observations in an observational system. Although it might seem that *what* to observe would be clear once a researcher has decided on a research question or identified a focus of the study, the decision about what to code actually entails many judgments about what constitutes communicative action and how social interaction is organized (see Bakeman, this volume).

Bakeman and Gottman (1997) noted that coding schemes could be thought to exist along a continuum, with one end anchored by physically based schemes that reflect the organism's physiology, and the other end anchored by socially based schemes "that deal with behavior whose very classification depends far more on the mind of the investigator (and others) than on the mechanisms of the body" (p. 18). In the discussion that follows, we focus on what we consider to be socially based schemes; that is, observational systems that examine behaviors or messages that have more to do with social categories of interaction (such as smiling or involvement) than with physiological elements of behavior (such as amplitude; for more on physiological measures, however, see Kinney, this volume; Tusing, this volume).

Socially Based Measurement Schemes

One very important decision that researchers make when examining nonverbal communication via a socially based coding scheme is the level of measurement. By this term we mean that researchers make choices about the amount of behavior they will examine within an interaction and the extent to which the assessment involves more concrete indicators of the behavior's occurrence or more abstract assessments of the social meaning of the behavior. Burgoon and Baesler (1991) discussed this choice as one of micro versus macro levels of measurement. Specifically, they argue that micro level measurement "involves single, concrete behaviors," whereas macro level measurement involves "larger samples of a given behavior or collection of behaviors" (p. 59). They also noted that macro level measurement typically entails more abstract terms and larger time intervals than does micro level measurement (see Cappella, this volume, on time choices), but they distinguish the level of measurement from the abstractness of what is measured.

In nonverbal research, it is typical for coding of larger amounts of behavior to also involve perceptual judgments that entail interpretation by coders. Likewise, micro level coding tends to involve more concrete assessments of single behaviors. For instance, assessment of involvement typically involves coders' assessments of the extent to which the relational message is displayed based on examination of a number of behaviors that are used to convey involvement (see Guerrero, 1996, this volume); this choice can be contrasted with coding that assesses the occurrence of a specific behavior such as smiling (Julien, this volume; Segrin, 1992). Thus, we discuss this distinction as one of rating versus coding.

Rating. Rating entails having coders attend to a set of behaviors that comprise the meaning or message conveyed within an interaction. For instance, a number of deception researchers have examined the involvement displayed in interaction (Burgoon et al., 1999; White & Burgoon, 2001). Ratings of involvement reflect observers' assessments of the degree of involvement displayed (i.e., the meaning), but such assessments are based on careful observation of a set of behaviors that are related to involvement (e.g., eye contact, forward lean, body orientation). Similarly, Knobloch and Solomon (this volume) trained coders to rate the level of conversational equality displayed in interaction based on verbal contributions and nonverbal elements of interaction that contribute to equality of the conversation (such as eye contact, volume/rate of speaking, and gestures).

One advantage of rating is that it tends to make effective use of raters' time by asking them to make more comprehensive judgments of larger chunks of behavior. Another advantage of this type of coding is that it reflects what Burgoon and Baesler (1991) refer to as isomorphism between the "coder's [or rater's] task and the phenomenological experience of communicators" (pp. 60–61). In others words, these types of judgments are similar to the types of judgments made by communicators during interaction, and they take advantage of the ability of raters to understand how behaviors work together to convey social messages. Finally, rating is often sufficient for research projects that seek to understand how social meaning relates to aspects of the relationship or interaction task (see Koenig Kellas & Trees, this volume; Manusov, this volume) or how it influences interaction outcomes (see Buller, this volume; Roberts & Noller, this volume; Trees, this volume).

Rating does, however, limit researchers' understanding of interaction in important ways. First, ratings require considerable inference on the part of raters; this means that the perceptual judgment being made by the raters must be elaborated clearly, the observers must be well trained, and the reliability of their perceptions must be checked and recalibrated throughout the entire rating process. Additionally, rating does not provide insight into the extent to which specific behaviors contribute to interaction processes (Burgoon & Baesler, 1991). Finally, when behaviors are changing frequently across an interaction, rating may be ineffective because raters cannot capture the dynamic nature of the interaction effectively.

Coding.   Coding, on the other hand, provides a level of precision and accuracy that may be very useful when researchers wish to understand how micromomentary actions contribute to interaction dynamics (see Aune, this volume; Chovil, this volume). This type of assessment has been used successfully in research on marital dyads (Buehlman, Carrère, & Siler, this volume; Doohan, Carrère, & Taylor, this volume; Jones, Carrère, & Gottman, this volume; Noller, this volume), mother–infant interaction (Cappella, 1981), initial interaction (Palmer & Simons, 1995), and couples' communication (see Afifi & Johnson, this volume; Dillard & Solomon, this volume).

One advantage of coding is that it often yields high levels of reliability because single behaviors are examined, and their presence or absence is relatively easy to identify. When a number of separate behaviors are coded, researchers also have the opportunity to combine behaviors in their analyses so that they can examine the influence of individual behaviors and sets of behavior as they co-occur as well as the individual variance contributed by each behavior vis-à-vis the other cues. Finally, when assessments of a behavior are made across time, coding is a good way to capture if and how behaviors change across an interaction.

The disadvantages of coding relate to the fact that typically it does not address the social meaning of a behavior (i.e., the focus is on the behavior's occurrence). As a result, coded behavior may not predict interaction outcomes as well as rated behavior does. Additionally, coding of behavior is often more time and cost intensive than is rating (Burgoon & Baesler, 1991). Also, although coding specific behaviors allows researchers to combine behaviors for analysis, it is unclear how this should be accomplished, as it seems certain that the impact of different behaviors is not directly "additive." As a result, the combinations of behaviors that researchers examine may not have relevance to the experience of communicators in interaction.

Choosing Rating or Coding.   Cappella (1991) argued that coding and rating (as well as participant judgments and untrained observer assessments) provide "different frames of reference" (p. 111) from which to view what is happening in interaction. He asserted that although each approach yields data that are somewhat different, information from each approach can be reconciled if researchers take into account the differences in point of view that influence what is captured by each approach (see Bernieri, this volume; Dunbar & Burgoon, this volume). Such a view of rating and coding is useful because it reminds us that choosing to rate or code is really a decision about the point of view from which we will see things. Coding provides a tighter focus, fixing our view on specific behaviors, whereas rating shifts our gaze to a wider angle, encouraging us to see the social features of interaction. Researchers' decisions about which form of observational assessment to use should reflect the aspects of interaction they wish to describe. Of course, the type of communication situations we are studying and the nature of the data we have collected can affect the point of view we select for our analyses.

Selecting and Training Raters/Coders.   The issue of coder/rater selection and training has received little attention in writings about nonverbal research. Researchers involved in observational research, however, are aware that coder selection and training is an important aspect of the research process. Although there is not space here to provide a complete overview of issues related to rater/coder selection/training, we mention some of the decisions that researchers must make as they begin to work with coders/raters.

In terms of selection, coders/raters need to be skilled observers of interaction. That is, they need to be able to discern what behavior is being displayed and, in some cases, to make a judgment of the message conveyed by the behavior. The substantial research on nonverbal sensitivity and decoding skill (see Riggio, this volume) suggests that, in many cases, female coders/raters are likely to be more effective than male coders/raters, although we know of no research that explores this specifically. Additionally, the "effectiveness" of coders might depend on the nature of the coding system being applied and the nature of the interaction being observed. Coders/raters who have experience with the type of interaction being examined may make different judgments than coders who know little about the interaction setting or the experience of the interaction situation (Woolfolk, 1981).

Coders/raters can provide an insider or outsider perspective on the interaction. Which is more valuable depends on whether the researcher assumes that the coding/rating system is largely objective and requires only careful observation of the behavior displayed or if the researcher assumes that the meaning of the behavior displayed is informed by an understanding of interaction dynamics and the situation. In short, selecting coders requires researchers to think carefully about their assumptions regarding the way communication is conducted.

Some researchers employ a number of coders/raters to watch an interaction and provide a holistic assessment of the interaction. This type of assessment, although useful, relies on observers' intuitive assessments of interaction, and trained coders or raters receive instruction in how to understand and apply an observational system. Additionally, it is worthwhile to consider issues of coder/rater training and the management of coders/raters throughout the project. Guerrero (this volume) provides a number of helpful suggestions for such training. She also provides suggestions for ways to make observers' tasks more manageable.

We simply add to her discussion the idea that when researchers train coders/raters, they are, in a sense, provided with an opportunity to see how their concepts and observational systems intersect with people's understandings of interaction. The observational system that coders/raters use to examine interaction is a way of making sense of the interaction. Training provides a way to learn if the system is coherent enough for coders to apply it. Additionally, the demonstration of coder/rater reliability initially, after training, and throughout the coding process provides a way for researchers to determine if their observational system can be applied in a consistent way (see Bakeman, this volume, for discussion of assessment of interrater reliability). In sum, coder/rater selection and training can be treated by researchers as an opportunity to reflect on the assumptions inherent in the observational system they have developed. Such reflection may provide researchers great conceptual insight into the work that they are doing.

Choices Regarding Where to Collect Data

Imagine that a researcher decides he or she would like to know how nonverbal cues of politeness influence the way others respond to a request. Because requests occur in many settings, the researcher has numerous options for studying this process. He or she can monitor requests for help at a local library, watch what happens when people ask for directions at a gas station, or spend time observing mishaps at a local ice skating rink (see LeBaron, this volume). Alternately, he or she could train confederates to ask for assistance in any of these settings and watch what occurs, or bring participants into a lab setting, creating a situation where confederates ask participants for help (see Guerrero & Le Poire, this volume).

The decision of where and how to study nonverbal behavior is important because it has implications for the specific aspects of behavior that can be observed, the extent to which the behavior occurs in a context of ongoing interaction, and the way that behavior can be captured for analysis. In some cases, the nature of the behavior being studied dictates the context in which it must be observed. For instance, one cannot study wedding behavior in the laboratory (we hope!). But, in other cases, researchers can choose to observe behavior in the field or transport it into the laboratory. Both settings have advantages and disadvantages that the researcher needs to consider in the design of the study.

Field Study Environments.   When nonverbal researchers discuss conducting their studies in field environments, they are referring to the physical setting in which the communication event or behavior occurs, such as in bowling alleys, living rooms, classrooms, and shopping malls. Coding in naturalistic settings is advantageous when little is known about a specific behavior because these venues provide a better understanding of how behavior is exhibited (Scherer & Ekman, 1982; see Roberts, this volume, for a discussion about making "naturalistic" laboratory observations). In fact, some researchers have argued that an understanding of nonverbal behavior can only really be garnered by studying interaction that occurs within natural contexts because communication is part of the social and physical context in which it is used (Jones & LeBaron, 2002). Although we recognize that behavior is situated, for most researchers, the decision of whether or not to study nonverbal behavior in the field is tied to the extent to which the behavior can be examined and understood adequately in the field. In this section, we consider the advantages of studies that involve observation of naturally occurring behavior and then examine situations where a manipulation of behavior is introduced in a field setting.

The decision to study nonverbal communication in a field setting is often made because a researcher wants to retain the spontaneity and "situatedness" of the behavior. If a researcher chooses simply to observe behavior in the field (which Hecht & Guerrero, 1999, called naturalistic observation), he or she does not attempt to influence the behavior in any way. For example, a researcher may be interested in studying the immediacy behaviors of romantic partners departing on international flights at airports. In this situation, the researcher codes the couple's behaviors as they occur naturally.

The advantages of observing behavior in this way are many (see Buck, this volume, and Patterson, this volume, for discussion of useful observation methods). The behavior is enacted and motivated by the needs of the communicators; it is responsive to a real situation and is likely to reveal how social norms and contexts influence interaction. Additionally, as Scherer and Ekman (1982) note, some events such as weddings or political rallies *must* be observed in the field in order to understand the nature of communication within the event.

Of course, naturalistic observation also poses a number of challenges. It may be difficult to observe a large number of naturally occurring interactions that are similar in nature, and such coding typically offers the researcher only limited access to the thoughts and reactions of participants, things that are often of interest to researchers. Moreover, until recently this type of research required that researchers rely on the observations of trained coders, because no record of the interaction could be obtained easily via videotape. Advances in the size and nature of video equipment have made it more feasible to record field situations relatively unobtrusively, which may provide an opportunity for researchers to capture and review communication events observed in the field. This additional ability does not, however, provide researchers the chance to examine the *effects* of particular communication behaviors on interaction events as well possible ethical concerns arise in unobtrusive recordings.

There are situations, however, in which the behavior being examined in the field allows researchers to introduce some type of manipulation into the study environment. These studies are often called field experiments or field studies (Hecht & Guerrero, 1999). This type of design not only has the advantage of allowing the researcher to observe behaviors in a naturalistic setting, but it also allows researchers to observe the behaviors repeatedly and to have greater control over the specific manner and setting of the behavior. Field experiments also allow researchers to examine how behaviors occur differently under varying natural environments.

When introducing a manipulation, researchers often ask participants to engage in certain behaviors and then observe the behavioral reactions of the study participant or another person within the interaction. Field experiments have the advantage of situating behaviors in a context and reducing the likelihood that participants are stylizing their communication in reaction to the laboratory setting.

When studying communication in natural settings, scholars face a number of challenges that exist simply as a result of the venue. One of the most difficult issues researchers encounter in examining communication behaviors within this environment is seeing the behavior occur with enough frequency and strength to study.

In other words, observing similar, repeated occurrences of the desired behavior can be difficult. Researchers may have to wait long periods of time to observe specific behaviors, and then these behaviors may occur only fleetingly (Patterson, Webb, & Schwartz, 2002). The lack of control of over the frequency of behavior and the nature of individuals engaging in the communication behavior must be weighed early on in the research process in deciding where to observe the communication. Choices such as the ones described earlier will have significant effects on the systematic study of the behavior.

Laboratory Settings.   Researchers also have the option of conducting their studies in a laboratory. Laboratory-based studies provide the greatest amount of control over a behavior and can lead to increases in internal validity: Various settings can be created and behaviors observed with greater detail (see Roberts, this volume). Scherer and Ekman (1982) suggest that when the specific event under study is "problematic," laboratory-type experiments may yield the greatest reliability due to the difficulty of observing behaviors under similar conditions in more naturalistic environments. Furthermore, researchers may wish to use a laboratory if they are interested in videotaping the behaviors of their participants. By reviewing videotapes in a controlled setting, researchers may be able to increase the accuracy of aggregating data across individuals and situations. Videotaping is advantageous when studying the microbehaviors of individuals, such as eye blinks or participants' eyebrows raises, and it provides the researcher the opportunity to reexamine the data, asking different questions.

Laboratory studies allow researchers to manipulate the behavior or intentions of the participants, the situation/context or task, or some combination of these. For instance, the researcher can ask the participant to engage in a specific role or behavior, either emphasizing or deemphasizing it during the interaction. Burgoon, Olney, and Coker (1987) used this approach when they had one participant increase or decrease nonverbal involvement during mock employment interviews. Alternately, Palmer and Simmons (1995) gave participants the goal (intention) of conveying liking, and then examined what behaviors participants used in a conversation with a stranger. Other studies have explored how deception is enacted (Burgoon et al., 1999) or how nonverbal cues are related to accounts of failure events (Manusov & Trees, 2002).

As we have noted, not all environments or interactions can be recreated in the laboratory. Despite this, many behavioral interactions between individuals in a laboratory are a good diagnostic of behavior as it occurs in the natural settings, because the interactional resources that communicators have at their disposal are present in the laboratory just as they are in everyday interaction (Bavelas, 1995).

Nonetheless, when researchers use the laboratory as a site for interaction, there are a number of issues to consider. Researchers need to have participants engage in familiar behaviors that they feel comfortable enacting. If participants are asked to engage in a behavior or action that they believe is irrelevant for the situation, then it is likely their behaviors will be contrived and unnatural (Scherer & Ekman, 1982). Additionally, participants may not have much of a stake or investment when conversing with individuals with whom they share no past or any possible future (such as confederates or strangers). As a result, their behavior may be different from what it would be with those whom they know or with whom they have some relational investment; this can be modified if the researcher chooses to use relational partners or friends in laboratory studies, but needs to be considered. Finally, the environment or situation chosen needs to have some relevance to participants' frame of reference. If a researcher creates a situation for participants that is unfamiliar or that they feel is inappropriate, then unless the researcher is looking purposely for some specific effect, participants' resultant behaviors may be very different from what would happen in a naturally occurring interaction.

In sum, whether a researcher chooses to conduct his or her study in either the field or laboratory, there are a number of decisions that go hand-in-hand with this choice, such as whether to manipulate a behavior, employ a confederate, or videotape the interaction. Ultimately, the study's research questions or hypotheses should drive which context the researcher selects. Once the researcher has selected a venue for the study, he or she must consider if examination of the data involves focusing on individuals or exploring the aspects of interaction that are jointly produced by all participants. The chapters in Part III of this book, on "Paradigms and Practices" provide additional discussion of these choices.

The Nature of Data: Coding the Individual Versus the Interaction, Relationship, or the Group

One important decision about the nature of data concerns how the behavior that is produced in the interaction. Although some research, such as work on person perception, focuses on how individuals assess another's nonverbal display, most research on nonverbal communication involves situations where two or more individuals are interacting. Scherer and Ekman (1982) argue that in such situations, the behavior of all participants should be sampled and measured. But decisions about sampling and measurement are fairly complicated.

We see two decisions as important in this area. First, researchers must decide if they will code/rate the behavior of each participant separately or if they will code/rate a feature of the interaction that reflects the joint behavior of both participants. Second, researchers must decide how to treat behavior in analyses. The advantage of assessing the behavior of individuals is that such coding allows researchers to determine, at least to some degree, how the behavior of one person affects the behavior of another. For instance, Jones, Carrère, and Gottman (this volume) use the Specific Affect Coding System to examine the emotional displays of each marital partner and then to consider how the emotion of one partner influences the reactions of the other.

Likewise, a researcher might be interested in determining if a decrease in involvement on the part of one participant has an effect on the involvement level of another interaction participant (e.g., White & Burgoon, 2001). In order to assess this, the researcher must code/rate the involvement of each participant separately and then must examine change in involvement of each participant across the interaction (see Julien, this volume). This type of coding also has the advantage of allowing researchers to examine how individual characteristics of participants (such as goals or personality characteristics) are related to the behavior of an individual in the interaction.

Researchers may also choose to examine a feature of the interaction that is jointly produced. In this case, the assumption is that the feature of interaction being examined can only be understood by examining the combined behavior of participants; such work typically seeks to reveal how features of interaction distinguish particular types of dyads or groups from one another. For instance, Knobloch and Solomon (this volume) describe a system for rating conversational equality: Conversational equality is a feature of the interaction that is revealed by examining communicators conversing together. It cannot be assessed for an individual. Cappella (this volume) describes ratings systems for assessing adaptation between partners, which reflects the fit of partners' behaviors with one another. Similarly, Koenig Kellas and Trees (this volume) describe a system that assesses the engagement and coherence of a jointly produced family story. The aspects of storytelling they code reflect the nature of the storytelling endeavor as a whole rather than the contributions of specific participants.

The advantage of this type of coding is that it provides an assessment of features of the interaction that could not be determined by coding the individual behavior of participants. Coding individual behavior does not, of course, preclude coding behavior related to the interaction (and vice versa). The decision about coding individuals or an interaction reminds researchers that they need to think carefully about their assumptions regarding the impact of participants' behavior on one another and the way aspects of interaction may emerge from the contributions of multiple participants.

Coding Practices

We have been discussing rather broad choices that reflect decisions about different ways to design a study or different ways to look at the interaction. We now turn to issues that are more narrowly focused and that reflect specific techniques used in examining nonverbal communication. We discuss these to provide a sense of the reasoning behind each coding practice. The use of each practice is more fully explained in other chapters in this volume.

Selecting a Coding Unit.   Even after researchers have made many important decisions about how to collect and treat their data, they are faced with an important choice regarding what Bakeman and Gottman (1997) call the coding unit. The coding unit refers to the decision researchers make about when to code within the interaction and the length of time observation lasts. This decision is related to assessing either a behavioral event or assessing intervals of time within the interaction (Bakeman & Gottman, 1997; also see Bakeman, this volume). In attempting to determine whether to use event or interval coding, researchers need to consider a number of issues, such as the level of accuracy of the data they desire, the complexity of their coding scheme, and how frequently the behavior occurs (Bakeman & Gottman, 1997).

Event Coding.   A researcher who decides to code events within an interaction (i.e., a temper tantrum, an instance of parallel play, or a self-disclosure), may be interested in examining several things, including how frequently a behavioral event occurs, the order in which different events happen, or the duration of an event (Bakeman & Gottman, 1997; Cappella, this volume). These assessments of events reflect different coding strategies. The first type of coding strategy measures how frequently an enacted behavior occurs. In this type of event coding, the researcher looks for the behavioral event and simply records whether it occurred or not. For instance, if a researcher is interested in the number of hugs enacted between young siblings, any time one sibling hugged the other, it would be recorded.

A second type of event coding records the enactment of multiple behavioral events and the sequence in which they occurred. For instance, a researcher may be interested in not only hugging between siblings, but also other expressions of caring, such as kissing, patting, or holding hands. This type of event coding would not only record the specific expression of care, but in what order the behaviors occurred. This is similar to Bakeman and Gottman's (1997) sequential analysis.

Finally, a third type of event coding records the length of time the behavioral event occurred—in other words, the duration of time participants devote to enacting a specific behavioral event. Again, using the previous example, a researcher may be interested in the length of time toddler siblings hold hands or how long they hug each other (Bakeman & Gottman, 1997). The length of time a behavior is enacted is what is most important here.

Interval Coding.   When researchers use the term *interval coding*, they are describing typically those portions or segments of an interaction from which they will sample and code nonverbal behaviors. In this research strategy, the entire interaction is divided into predetermined brief units of time or intervals in which coders/raters observe and code/rate behaviors (Bakeman & Gottman, 1997). In other words, researchers restrict the sampling of nonverbal behaviors to segments or slices within the communication interaction that are of specific interest (Ambady & Conner, 1999; Ambady & Gray, 2002). For instance, a researcher may be interested in coding the immediacy behaviors of close relational partners during indirect self-disclosures to one another. The researcher will specifically select intervals of disclosure within the interaction and code only those slices of behavior (e.g., Sargent, 2000).

Once researchers elect to code intervals within the interaction, depending on the purpose of the study, they must decide on the number of intervals to use within the interaction and the length of each interval. In making these decisions, researchers need to consider the frequency with which the behavior is likely to occur, how long it takes participants to enact a behavior, and the number of behaviors to be coded/rated in each interval. If the particular behavior of interest occurs only occasionally during the interaction, the researcher may consider coding all of the intervals in which the behavior is found, but if the behavior is seen repeatedly during the interaction, the researcher may elect to code fewer intervals (Scherer & Ekman, 1982).

Once this choice is made, the researcher decides whether the placement of the intervals should be defined by the communication event or positioned in the interaction by fixed time intervals, such as 1 minute of coding for every 5 minutes of interaction. (Bakeman & Gottman, 1997, called this systematic observation). For example, if the focus of a study is on the affection cues displayed as parents drop off children at preschool, the event itself will define the coding interval naturally. By making this choice, the researcher allows the event to determine the placement of the coding interval. In contrast, when the particular behavior of interest occurs regularly within an interaction, there are more opportunities to place coding intervals throughout the interaction. For instance, if a researcher is interested in examining politeness cues exhibited during a baby shower, the researcher can more easily select fixed points in the interaction to place the intervals. Depending on the frequency of the politeness cues, a researcher could decide to code 2 minute intervals within every 5 minutes of interaction. An advantage of fixed intervals in coding sequence is that the behavior is observed consistently throughout the interaction, allowing for a more accurate reflection of how it is represented in the data.

Researchers can also be somewhat less "systematic" in their placement of coding intervals. For example, behaviors could be coded for 2 minutes at the beginning of the first 10 minutes of an interaction, 2 minutes in the middle of the second 10 minutes of an interaction, and 2 minutes at the end of a third 10 minutes of interaction, with this system repeated until the interaction has ended. For example, Guerrero and Andersen (1994) coded the initiation of touching between individuals waiting in movie theater and zoo lines. They defined their coding interval as the first 2 minutes of interaction between couples as soon as they started standing at the end of the line.

There are clear and important differences between event and interval coding strategies. One distinction between the two is that event coding may be more "objective" than interval coding. According to Bakeman and Gottman (1997), event coding can result in "more accurate data" (p. 38) by requiring less observer inference. In event coding, observers are not required to determine the degree to which a behavior is enacted or the intention or function of a specific behavior. Also, event coding may allow researchers to observe the enactment of more complete patterns of behaviors, providing a clearer relationship between a behavior and its function (Scherer & Ekman, 1982).

Despite the strengths of event coding, interval coding has advantages as well. Interval coding allows researchers to examine the occurrence of microbehaviors, such as eye movements, smiles, or fluctuations in eyebrows. This strategy also provides researchers the ability to isolate and examine extremely small, but meaningful, changes in a single behavior as well as precise differences between different behaviors. Additionally, if a researcher has videotaped participants, it is often easier at a later time to reexamine and code for more global impressions or meanings. Choosing to event or interval code is an important decision and one that will significantly impact the outcome of the study. As such, researchers need to carefully consider the purpose of their study as well as the strengths and weaknesses of both approaches before settling on one.

Combined or Separate Assessments of Verbal/Nonverbal Channels

Another choice that researchers face concerns whether to examine verbal and nonverbal behavior together or whether to attempt to determine their separate effects by modifying one of these channels during the research process or coding process. Given that Noller (this volume) provides a nice discussion of the standard content method, which seeks to control the verbal channel so that the effects of nonverbal behavior can be more clearly understood, we focus here on the choices researchers make when they code communication behavior that includes *both* verbal and nonverbal interaction.

Early research (e.g., Mehrabian & Ferris, 1967) sought to reveal the power and importance of nonverbal behavior; typically, it involved coding that restricted access to the verbal content (by having coders/raters view interaction without audio) or used data that had been altered (such as speech that had been content filtered) to reveal the impact of paralinguistic cues (Krauss, 1981). More recently, however, researchers have acknowledged that the meaning of nonverbal behavior is often tied to the verbal content of interaction, and so coders/raters have been asked to use both verbal content and nonverbal cues to make assessments of the interaction (e.g., Ebesu Hubbard, 2000; Guerrero, 1996). Additionally, both sets of cues are used in some self-reports (e.g., Floyd & Mikkleson, this volume).

The key advantages of coding based on access to both verbal communication and nonverbal behavior are related to (a) the isomorphism of the coding task with real interaction, and (b) contextualization of meaning. Observers who make ratings based on access to all aspects of the interaction are likely making judgments that are similar to the types of assessments made in day-to-day interaction. Moreover, assessments of any specific behavior will reflect the meaning of the behavior within the stream of other behaviors (verbal and nonverbal) that are occurring.

The decision to combine verbal and nonverbal behavior in assessments of an interaction is particularly useful when researchers want to assess aspects of interaction, such as involvement, that are affected by many behaviors or when researchers want to examine aspects of the interaction that are produced jointly by participants. The cost of coding in this way is that researchers cannot make claims about the influence of a particular behavioral channel on the interaction, and researchers are not able to determine how interpretation of the interaction would vary if certain channels of communication are modified.

The decision to limit coder access, or to modify a channel of interaction (e.g., standard content method, Noller, this volume), is usually made with one of the following goals in mind. Modifying a channel of communication (for instance, making the verbal content of interaction ambiguous) allows researchers to assess communicator competence and to determine the impact of a particular channel of communication on interaction outcomes. Coding that limits access to a particular channel (for instance, asking coders to make ratings without access to the audio portion of an interaction) may produce more fine-tuned assessments of particular behaviors. Additionally, when different channels are coded separately, it may be possible to identify inconsistencies between channels that would not be evident to coders who have access to all channels and to find a way to reconcile them or access the combined effects of different channels.

Having noted these opportunities, however, this type of coding also has the potential to produce highly artificial results because the actual or full meaning of behavior in interaction is likely to be the result of combined verbal and nonverbal channels (Burgoon, Buller, Hale, & deTurck, 1984). Additionally, when channels are coded separately and researchers seek to combine them, it is unclear how this should be done: As we mentioned in our discussion of level of measurement, it seems unlikely that simply adding these codes together is an appropriate way to sum their effects.

It should be clear that the practice of combining or separating is tied to differences in the types of issues researchers want to examine. One approach seeks to examine how different channels of behavior influence meaning; the other asks questions about what meaning is conveyed when both verbal and nonverbal aspects of interaction are examined. It is important to notice that these practices are related to the researcher's view of behavior; it is easy to believe that coding practices such are just that: practices. But, practices have at their roots assumptions about how interaction is enacted, understood, and managed. These assumptions are also evident when researchers choose use physiological measures to assess nonverbal behavior.

Physiological Measures

At times, researchers may consider measuring the physiological responses of participants. By examining physical responses such as heart rates, skin conductivity, body temperature, and hormonal fluctuations, researchers may be able to tap into the intensity levels of some emotional and social states that cannot necessarily be detected by observer coders or by participants themselves with self-report measures. Because these emotional or social states may not be manifested overtly, physiological measures could yield additional insights into the nature of certain behaviors.

Often, researchers correlate physiological responses with communication behaviors or perceptions. For instance, in a study by Gottman and Levenson (2002), couples were connected to devices that measured heartbeat, skin conductance level, body movement, and finger pulse. Once connected, couples were asked to discuss three different topics specifically designed to elicit physiological reactions. While conversing, couple members' physiological responses to the conversation they were having with their partner were measured, allowing researchers to examine how the different conversations influenced each partner's physiological states. In another example, Tusing and Dillard (2000) tested the effects of varying vocal cues on perceptions of dominance and influence. They found that vocal amplitude was positively associated with dominance judgments, but speech rate was negatively correlated with judgments. In later chapters, both Kinney (this volume) and Tusing (this volume) discuss further the merits of physiological coding and measures and argue that physiological assessments have been greatly underutilized in nonverbal research.

CONCLUSION

The study of nonverbal communication can be simultaneously one of the most rewarding and most challenging of research endeavors. One needs only to examine a small portion of the nonverbal research literature—including what is included in this volume—to see the large number of decisions that go into the design of a study. It cannot be emphasized enough, though, that the choices researchers make will influence the study—for good or ill. Despite the numerous decisions that are required, we hope that researchers will see these choices as opportunities to consider how nonverbal behavior can best be studied and understood.

REFERENCES

Ambady, N., & Conner, B. (1999). Accuracy of judgments of sexual orientation from thin slices of behavior. *Journal of Personality and Social Psychology, 77,* 538–548.

Ambady, N., & Gray, H. M. (2002). On being sad and mistaken: Mood effects on the accuracy of thin-slice judgments. *Journal of Personality and Social Psychology, 83,* 947–962.

Bakeman, R., & Gottman, J. M. (1997). *Observing interaction: An introduction to sequential analysis.* Cambridge, UK: Cambridge University Press.

Bavelas, J. B. (1995). Quantitative versus qualitative? In W. Leeds-Hurwitz (Ed.), *Social approaches to communication* (pp. 49–62). New York: Guilford.

Bernieri, F. J., & Rosenthal, R. (1991). Interpersonal coordination: Behavioral matching and interactional synchrony. In R. S. Feldman & B. Rime (Eds.), *Fundamentals of nonverbal behavior* (pp. 401–432). Cambridge: Cambridge University Press.

Burgoon, J. K., & Baesler, E. J. (1991). Choosing between micro and macro nonverbal measurement: Application to selected vocalic and kinesic nonverbal indices. *Journal of Nonverbal Behavior, 15,* 57–78.

Burgoon, J. K., Buller, D. B., Hale, J., & deTurck, M. (1984). Relational messages associated with nonverbal behavior. *Human Communication Research, 10,* 351–378.

Burgoon, J. K., Buller, D. B., White, C. H., Afifi, W., & Buslig, A. (1999). The role of conversational involvement in deceptive interpersonal interactions. *Personality and Social Psychology Bulletin, 25,* 669–706.

Burgoon, J. K., Olney, C. A., & Coker, R. A. (1987). The effects of communicator characteristics on patterns of reciprocity and compensation. *Journal of Nonverbal Behavior, 11,* 146–165.

Cappella, J. N. (1981). Mutual influence in expressive behavior: Adult–adult and infant–adult dyadic interaction. *Psychological Bulletin, 89,* 101–132.

Cappella, J. N. (1991). Mutual adaptation and relativity of measurement. In B. M. Montgomery & S. Duck (Eds.), *Studying interpersonal interaction* (pp. 103–117). New York: Guilford.

Ebesu Hubbard, A. S. (2000). Interpersonal coordination in interactions: Evaluations and social skills. *Communication Research Reports, 17,* 95–104.

Gottman, J. M., & Levenson, R. W. (1992). Marital processes predictive of later dissolution: Behavior, physiology, and health. *Journal of Personality and Social Psychology, 63,* 221–233.

Gottman, J. M., & Levenson, R. W. (2002). A two-factor model for predicting when a couple will divorce: Exploratory analyses using 14-year longitudinal data. *Family Process, 41,* 83–96.

Guerrero, L. K. (1996). Attachment style difference in intimacy and involvement: A test of the four-category model. *Communication Monographs, 63,* 269–292.

Guerrero, L. K., & Andersen, P. A. (1994). Patterns of matching and initiation: Touch behavior and touch avoidance across romantic relationship stages. *Journal of Nonverbal Behavior, 18,* 137–153.

Harvey, J. H., Hendrick, S. S., & Tucker, K. (1988). Self-report methods in studying personal relationships. In S. W. Duck (Ed.), *Handbook of personal relationships* (pp. 99–113). New York: John Wiley & Sons.

Hecht, M. L., & Guerrero, L. K. (1999). Perspectives on nonverbal research methods. In L. K. Guerrero, J. A. DeVito, & M. L. Hecht (Eds.), *The nonverbal communication reader: Classic and contemporary readings* (2nd ed., pp. 24–41). Prospect Heights, IL: Waveland Press.

Heslin, R., & Boss, D. (1980). Nonverbal intimacy in airport arrival and departure. *Personality and Social Psychology Bulletin, 6,* 248–252.

Jones, S. E., & LeBaron, C. D. (2002). Research on the relationship between verbal and nonverbal communication: Emerging interactions. *Journal of Communication, 52,* 499–521.

Jones, S. E., & Yarbrough, A. E. (1985). A naturalistic study of the meanings of touch. *Communication Monographs, 52,* 19–56.

Krauss, R. M. (1981). Verbal, vocal, and visible factors in judgments of another's affect. *Journal of Personality and Social Psychology, 40,* 312–320.

Manusov, V. (1995). Reacting to changes in nonverbal behaviors: Relational satisfaction and adaptation patterns in romantic dyads. *Human Communication Research, 21,* 456–477.

Manusov, V., & Trees, A. R. (2002). "Are you kidding me?": The role of nonverbal cues in the verbal accounting process. *Journal of Communication, 52,* 640–656.

Mehrabian, A., & Ferris, S. R. (1967). Inferences of studies from nonverbal communication in two channels. *Journal of Consulting Psychology, 31,* 248–252.

Metts, S., Sprecher, S., & Cupach, W. R. (1991). Retrospective self-reports. In B. M. Montgomery & S. Duck (Eds.), *Studying interpersonal interaction* (pp. 162–178). New York: Guilford.

Palmer, M. T., & Simmons, K. B. (1995). Communicating intentions through nonverbal behaviors: Conscious and nonconscious encoding of liking. *Human Communication Research, 22,* 128–160.

Patterson, M. L., Webb, A., & Schwartz, W. (2002). Passing encounters: Patterns of recognition and avoidance in pedestrians. *Basic and Applied Social Psychology, 24,* 57–66.

Riggio, R., E., & Riggio H. R. (2001, July). *Using self-report methods to measure nonverbal communication skill.* Paper presented at the International Network on Personal Relationships, Prescott, AZ.

Sargent, J. (2000). *Nonverbal boundaries: An examination of the immediacy behaviors in explicit and implicit disclosures.* Unpublished doctoral dissertation, The University of Nebraska, Lincoln.

Scherer, K. R., & Ekman, P. (1982). Methodological issues in studying nonverbal behavior. In K. R. Scherer & P. Ekman (Eds.), *Handbook of methods in nonverbal behavior research* (pp. 1–44). Cambridge, UK: Cambridge University Press.

Segrin, C. (1992). Specifying the nature of social skill deficits associated with depression. *Human Communication Research, 19,* 89–123.

Tusing, K. J., & Dillard, J. P. (2000). The sounds of dominance: Vocal precursors of perceived dominance during interpersonal influence. *Human Communication Research, 26,* 148–171.

White, C. H., & Burgoon, J. K. (2001). Adaptation and communicative design: Patterns of interaction in truthful and deceptive conversations. *Human Communication Research, 25,* 9–37.

Woolfolk, A. E. (1981). The eye of the beholder: Methodological considerations when observers assess nonverbal communication. *Journal of Nonverbal Behavior, 5,* 199–204.

II. NONVERBAL MEASURES

The Social Skills Inventory (SSI): Measuring Nonverbal and Social Skills

Ronald E. Riggio
Claremont McKenna College

INTRODUCTION

The measurement of individual differences in nonverbal and social skills is, in many ways, rooted in research on intelligence, particularly the early work by Thorndike (1920) and others (Moss, Hunt, Omwake, & Ronning, 1927) in measuring social intelligence (i.e., the ability to understand and manage people and to act wisely in human relations). Researchers of social intelligence (e.g., Chapin, 1942; O'Sullivan, 1983; O'Sullivan & Guilford, 1975) realized that the ability to read or decode the feelings and intentions of others, and to decode and understand social interactions and social settings, were critical components of social intelligence. Guilford (1967), in his *structure of intellect* model and in the development of measures of multiple intelligences, included several nonverbal tests of social intelligence (O'Sullivan & Guilford, 1976).

Whereas the "intelligence" line of research represents attempts to define and measure individual differences in social interaction skills, it was the pioneering research of Robert Rosenthal and his colleagues in measuring nonverbal decoding skills (see Rosenthal, 1979) that led to the first performance-based measures of nonverbal ability. One such measure, the Profile of Nonverbal Sensitivity (PONS; Rosenthal, Hall, DiMatteo, Rogers, & Archer, 1979), was used widely in research on individual differences in nonverbal skill. Another measure of both verbal and nonverbal decoding skill—one that is closely linked to notions of social intelligence—is Archer and Akert's (1977) work with the Social Interpretations Task (SIT), a performance-based measure of ability to decode and interpret social situations. The SIT evolved into the updated Interpersonal Perception Task (IPT; Costanzo & Archer, 1993).

25

This chapter, however, presents The Social Skills Inventory (SSI; Riggio, 1986, 1989; Riggio & Carney, 2003). The SSI is a 90-item, self-report instrument that measures basic skill in nonverbal/emotional communication as well as verbal/social skills that are related to social competence. The inventory was derived from multidisciplinary research focusing on the development of nonverbal, emotional, and interpersonal skills. This research included groundbreaking work for measuring nonverbal encoding and decoding skills (Archer & Akert, 1977; Friedman, 1979; Rosenthal et al., 1979; Zuckerman & Larrance, 1979), Snyder's (1974, 1987) research on assessing skill in impression management/self-monitoring, and Guilford's and O'Sullivan's (O'Sullivan, 1983; O'Sullivan & Guilford, 1975) scholarship for measuring social intelligence.

THE SOCIAL SKILLS INVENTORY

Drawing on a basic communication model, the SSI framework breaks down basic communication skills into three types: skill in encoding, or *expressivity*; skill in decoding, or *sensitivity*; and skill in regulation, or *control*, over communication. These three basic communication skills operate in two domains: the nonverbal, or *emotional*, and the verbal, or *social*. Table 1 provides an illustration of the SSI model and brief description of each of the six SSI subscales along with sample items from the SSI. Information on obtaining the SSI is provided at the end of the chapter.

The three SSI emotional skill subscales are tied to nonverbal communication skill most directly. Emotional Expressivity (EE) is a measure of emotional expressiveness, related closely to other self-report measures of the same construct (see Riggio & Riggio, this volume). The Emotional Sensitivity (ES) scale is a self-report measure of nonverbal decoding skill. The SSI Emotional Control (EC) scale is an assessment of ability to monitor and control one's own emotional expressions. It is also linked theoretically to posed nonverbal/emotional encoding, because emotionally controlled individuals need to regulate their facial expressions in order to mask felt emotions, either by appearing stoic, or by using a conflicting emotional state as a mask (e.g., putting on a happy face to cover felt sadness or anger). Research suggests, however, that it is a combination of Emotional Control and Emotional Expressivity that contributes to posed emotional sending/encoding ability (Tucker & Riggio, 1988).

Summed, these three emotional skills can form an index of general emotional/nonverbal skill competence. Indeed, the recent surge of interest in the construct of emotional intelligence has much in common with the SSI emotional skill framework. In fact, Mayer and Salovey's (1997) *ability model* of emotional intelligence includes abilities to identify/decode others' emotions, express/encode one's own emotions accurately, and monitor and regulate felt emotional states. The Social Skills Inventory assesses these three core dimensions of emotional intelligence. Moreover, in psychometric terms, the SSI compares favorably to some of the existing self-report measures of emotional intelligence (see Ciarrochi,

TABLE 1

The Social Skills Inventory (SSI) Framework, Scale Definitions, and Sample Items from the SSI

Nonverbal/Emotional Domain (Emotional Skills) [related to Emotional Intelligence]	*Verbal/Social Domain (Social Skills)* [related to Social Intelligence]
Emotional Expressivity (EE) Skill in nonverbal encoding. Ability to accurately express felt emotional states.	*Social Expressivity (SE)* Skill in verbal encoding and ability to engage others in social interaction. Associated with verbal fluency.
• I am able to liven up a dull party. • I have been told that I have expressive eyes.	• When telling a story, I usually use a lot of gestures to help get the point across. • I usually take the initiative to introduce myself to strangers.
Emotional Sensitivity (ES) Skill in nonverbal decoding. Being attentive to subtle emotional cues; being empathic.	*Social Sensitivity (SS)* Skill in verbal decoding. Sensitivity to and understanding of norms governing appropriate social behavior. Ability to decode social situations.
• I sometimes cry at sad movies. • I am often told that I am a sensitive, understanding person.	• I'm generally concerned about the impression I'm making on others. • Sometimes I think that I take things other people say to me too personally.
Emotional Control (EC) Skill in regulating and controlling emotional expressions. Hiding felt emotions behind an emotional "mask."	*Social Control (SC)* Skill in social role-playing and social self-presentation. Social adeptness and tact. "Savoir-faire."
• I am easily able to make myself look happy one minute and sad the next. • I am very good at maintaining a calm exterior even if I am upset.	• I am usually very good at leading group discussions. • I can easily adjust to being in just about any social situation.

Chan, Caputi, & Roberts, 2001), such as those developed by Bar-On (1997) and Schutte et al. (1998).

Although there may appear to be little direct connection between research in nonverbal communication and the social skill subscales of the SSI, the skill of Social Expressivity (SE) involves verbal speaking skill and the ability to engage others in social interaction. This is, in many ways, a complement to Emotional Expressivity and suggests skill in initiating interpersonal interactions. The SSI dimension of Social Sensitivity (SS), although primarily related to verbal decoding skill (i.e., listening), also involves ability to decode and interpret social situations, a skill that is very important in decoding tasks as represented in measures such as the Interpersonal Perception Task (IPT; Costanzo & Archer, 1993). In fact, the SSI-SS scale is significantly and positively correlated with scores on the IPT (Riggio & Carney, 2003).

The skill of Social Control (SC) is linked to ability to manage impressions—similar to the construct of self-monitoring—but more recently equated with the construct of savoir-faire: the ability to know how to act in social situations (Eaton, Funder, & Riggio, 2002). Taken together, these three social skill dimensions—SE, SS, and SC—can be considered an index of social intelligence (Riggio, Messamer, & Throckmorton, 1991). Thus, researchers of nonverbal behavior and interpersonal processes may be interested not only in the nonverbal skill scales of the SSI but also in the entire scale.

Psychometric Properties of the SSI

Scale Reliability. The SSI scales have shown good test–retest reliability, ranging from .81 to .96 for a 2-two week interval ($N = 40$). Cronbach's *alpha* coefficients ranging from .65 to .88 were obtained from a sample of 549 employed adults recruited from a number of work organizations across the United States. *Alpha* coefficients from a group of 389 undergraduate students ranged from .64 to .89. These findings suggest that the various SSI scales have acceptable to good internal consistency (see Riggio & Carney, 2003).

Scale Intercorrelations and Sex Differences. The SSI subscales are positively correlated, with some notable exceptions. For instance, Emotional Expressivity and Emotional Control are somewhat negatively correlated, as are Social Sensitivity and Social Control. The actual relationships among the various SSI dimensions are quite complex (see Riggio & Carney, 2003).

Consistent with expectations, however, women tend to be more expressive and sensitive than are men, with women obtaining typically higher scores on Emotional Expressivity, Social Expressivity, Emotional Sensitivity, and Social Sensitivity. Men tend to score significantly higher on Emotional Control, with no significant differences on Social Control. These sex differences are consistent for both samples of adults and college students (Riggio & Carney, 2003).

Factor Structure.   Confirmatory factor analyses have supported the basic subscale structure of the SSI. The factor structure has held up both in tests of the SSI in English and in other cultures/languages, such as Italian (Galeazzi, Franceschina, & Holmes, 2002; Riggio, 1986).

Convergent and Discriminant Validity.   The SSI scales have demonstrated very good convergent validity with other self-report measures of nonverbal skill-related constructs, such as measures of emotional expressiveness, emotional reactivity, and emotional empathy. There is also evidence from a study using undergraduate students that SSI Emotional Sensitivity correlates significantly with performance-based measures of emotional decoding skill (see Riggio & Carney, 2003) such as the Profile of Nonverbal Sensitivity (PONS; Rosenthal et al., 1979), the Diagnostic Analysis of Nonverbal Accuracy (DANVA; Nowicki & Duke, 1994; Duke & Nowicki, this volume), and an emotional decoding subscale of the Multifactor Emotional Intelligence Scale (MEIS-Pictures; Mayer, Salovey, & Caruso, 1997).

A study of undergraduate students conducted by Tucker and Riggio (1988) explored the relationships between the SSI scales and both posed and spontaneous emotional encoding, the latter using the Buck slide-viewing paradigm (see Buck's chapter, this volume). As predicted, SSI-Emotional Expressivity was related to both posed and spontaneous emotional encoding. Emotional Control, as one might suspect, was significantly negatively correlated with spontaneous emotional expression while viewing emotion-eliciting slides, but was, contrary to prediction, unrelated to posed emotional encoding (although a combination of EE and EC was significantly positively correlated to posed sending). SSI-Social Control was, however, significantly positively related to posed sending, further suggesting that SC is an important social acting skill.

An important concern to many researchers is the use of self-report measures to assess nonverbal skill, with critics suggesting that individuals do not have the insight or the unbiased perspective to make accurate assessments of their nonverbal communication skills. However, validity evidence demonstrating significant relationships between self-report measures of nonverbal skill and performance-based assessments of skill suggest that the self-report methodology is valuable, useful, and a cost-effective alternative to more time-consuming and costly performance measures (see Riggio & Riggio, 2001). In addition to evidence of convergent validity, there is good evidence demonstrating the discriminant validity of the SSI scales. For example, although Emotional and Social Expressivity are theoretically and empirically linked to personality constructs such as extraversion, evidence suggests that they are distinct constructs (see Friedman, 1983; Riggio & Riggio, 2002). Additionally, there has been little concern about socially desirable responding for the SSI scales (see Riggio, 1986; Riggio & Carney, 2003).

The SSI and Research in Nonverbal Communication

The SSI has been used widely in research on nonverbal behavior. One line of research examined the impact of emotional expressiveness and global nonverbal/social skills on impressions made in initial encounters and in initial attractiveness. Consistent with past research (e.g., Friedman, Riggio, & Casella, 1988; Riggio & Friedman, 1986; Riggio & Woll, 1984; Sabatelli & Rubin, 1986), emotionally and socially expressive persons (high scores on EE and SE), and persons with high overall SSI scores, were rated as more likable and attractive than persons scoring low on these SSI dimensions in initial encounters, even after controlling for static cues of physical attractiveness (Riggio, 1986; Riggio, Widaman, Tucker, & Salinas, 1991). These studies included undergraduate students as well as adult members of a videodating organization (Riggio & Woll, 1984).

Nonverbal social skills have also been investigated in the context of deception by undergraduate students. An important finding is that nonverbally skilled communicators, as measured by the SSI, are more successful deceivers primarily because they have a more "honest" overall demeanor–emitting cues that are stereotypically associated with truthfulness–than are persons lacking these important nonverbal skills (Riggio, Tucker, & Throckmorton, 1987; Riggio, Tucker, & Widaman, 1987). Likewise, nonverbal social skills, as represented by the SSI framework, have been shown to be important in relationship formation and maintenance and in the ability to garner social support from these relationships to cope effectively with everyday stress (Riggio, 1992; Riggio & Zimmerman, 1991). Moreover, the SSI has important implications for evaluating the quality of communication in marriages (both young adult marriages and marriages of more than 50 years) and interpersonal relationships (see Riggio & Carney, 2003).

Most recently, the SSI has been used to study the nonverbal and social behavior of leaders in small groups and persons in managerial or business leadership positions. For instance, the SSI was found to correlate positively and significantly with observer ratings of participants' communication skills in a managerial assessment center conducted for students in a university school of business (Riggio, Aguirre, Mayes, Belloli, & Kubiak, 1997). In addition, scores on the SSI predicted group members' satisfaction with their leaders in simulated work groups, and were related to followers' ratings of leader effectiveness in the fire service (Riggio, Riggio, Salinas, & Cole, 2003). An exciting line of research explores the role that nonverbal social skills play in contributing to a leader's charisma and extends some of the ideas presented in Friedman et al. (1988) and Riggio (1987). In an additional study, the SSI predicted performance evaluations of hospice workers (Riggio & Taylor, 2000), and SSI scores correlated negatively with indices of loneliness, depression, and social maladjustment in student populations (Riggio, Watring, & Throckmorton, 1993; Segrin & Flora, 2000).

An important line of research investigates the role of nonverbal skills and nonverbal skill imbalances (e.g., wide variations such as high scores on Emotional Control coupled with very low scores on Emotional Expressivity) in predicting psychopathology in outpatients from mental hospitals (Perez & Riggio, 2003; Perez, Riggio, & Kopelowicz, 2003). Although wide discrepancies in scores on the various subscales of the Social Skills Inventory are hypothesized to be indicative of social skill "imbalances" that may suggest an overall social skill deficit, more work needs to be done looking at how different combinations of high and low scores on the SSI subscales relate to social performance and psychosocial adjustment.

FUTURE DIRECTIONS

Future research on the SSI can investigate the role of nonverbal behavior skills in leadership and in contributing to effective management in work organizations, as well as additional research on how specific nonverbal and social skills impact relationship formation and relationship quality. Besides its use as a research tool for assessing nonverbal and social skills, the SSI can also be used to get baseline assessments of possession of communication skills or to measure the development of skills over time. This can be important for individual development or for larger scale nonverbal/social skill development and training programs. The Social Skills Inventory is available to researchers for a nominal fee at www.mindgarden.com

REFERENCES

Archer, D., & Akert, R. M. (1977). Words and everything else: Verbal and nonverbal cues in social interpretation. *Journal of Personality and Social Psychology, 35,* 443–449.
Bar-On, R. (1997). *Bar-On Emotional Quotient Inventory: Technical manual.* Toronto, ON: Multi-Health Systems.
Chapin, F. S. (1942). Preliminary standardization of a social insight scale. *American Sociological Review, 7,* 214–225.
Ciarrochi, J., Chan, A., Caputi, P., & Roberts, R. (2001). Measuring emotional intelligence. In J. Ciarrochi, J. P. Forgas, & J. D. Mayer (Eds.), *Emotional intelligence in everyday life: A scientific inquiry* (pp. 25–45). Philadelphia, PA: Psychology Press.
Costanzo, M. A., & Archer, D. (1993). Interpreting the expressive behavior of others: The Interpersonal Perception Task (IPT). *Journal of Nonverbal Behavior, 13,* 225–245.
Eaton, L. G., Funder, D. C., & Riggio, R. E. (2003). Skill in social role-playing: The essence of savior faire. Manuscript submitted for publication.
Friedman, H. S. (1979). The concept of skill in nonverbal communication: Implications for understanding social interaction. In R. Rosenthal (Ed.), *Skill in nonverbal communication* (pp. 2–27). Cambridge, MA: Oelgeschlager, Gunn, & Hain.
Friedman, H. S. (1983). On shutting one's eyes to face validity. *Psychological Bulletin, 94,* 185–187.
Friedman, H. S., Riggio, R. E., & Casella, D. F. (1988). Nonverbal skill, personal charisma, and initial attraction. *Personality and Social Psychology Bulletin, 14,* 203–211.
Galeazzi, A., Franceschina, E., & Holmes, G. R. (2002). Factor analysis of Social Skills Inventory responses of Italians and Americans. *Psychological Reports, 90,* 1115–1121.
Guilford, J. P. (1967). *The nature of human intelligence.* New York: McGraw-Hill.
Mayer, J. D., & Salovey, P. (1997). What is emotional intelligence? In P. Salovey & J. D. Sluyter (Eds.), *Emotional development and emotional intelligence* (pp. 3–34). New York: Basic Books.
Mayer, J. D., Salovey, P., & Caruso, D. (1997). *Multifactor Emotional Intelligence Test (MEIS).* Needham, MA.
Moss, F. A., Hunt, T., Omwake, K. T., & Ronning, M. M. (1927). *Social intelligence test.* Washington, DC: George Washington University.

Nowicki, S., & Duke, M. P. (1994). Individual differences in the nonverbal communication of affect: The Diagnostic Analysis of Nonverbal Accuracy Scale. *Journal of Nonverbal Behavior, 18*, 9–35.

O'Sullivan, M., & Guilford, J. P. (1976). *Four factor tests of social intelligence (behavioral cognition): Manual of instructions and interpretations.* Orange, CA: Sheridan Psychological Services.

O'Sullivan, M. (1983). Measuring individual differences. In J. M. Wiemann & R. P. Harrison (Eds.), *Nonverbal interaction* (pp. 243–270). Beverly Hills, CA: Sage.

O'Sullivan, M., & Guilford, J. P. (1975). Six factors of behavioral cognition: Understanding other people. *Journal of Educational Measurement, 12*, 255–271.

Perez, J. E., & Riggio, R. E. (2003). Nonverbal social skills and psychopathology. In P. Philippot, E. J. Coats, & R. S. Feldman (Eds.), *Nonverbal behavior in clinical settings* (pp. 17–44). New York: Oxford University Press.

Perez, J. E., Riggio, R. E., & Kopelowicz, A. (2003). *Social skill imbalances as indicators of psychopathology: An exploratory investigation.* Manuscript submitted for publication.

Riggio, H. R., & Riggio, R. E. (2002). Emotional expressiveness, extraversion, and neuroticism: A meta-analysis. *Journal of Nonverbal Behavior, 26,*

Riggio, R. E. (1986). Assessment of basic social skills. *Journal of Personality and Social Psychology, 51*, 649–660.

Riggio, R. E. (1987). *The charisma quotient.* New York: Dodd, Mead.

Riggio, R. E. (1989). *Manual for the Social Skills Inventory: Research edition.* Palo Alto, CA: Consulting Psychologists Press.

Riggio, R. E. (1992). Social interaction skills and nonverbal behavior. In R. S. Feldman (Ed.), *Applications of nonverbal behavioral theories and research* (pp. 3–30). Hillsdale, NJ: Lawrence Erlbaum Associates.

Riggio, R. E., Aguirre, M., Mayes, B. T., Belloli, C., & Kubiak, C. (1997). The use of assessment center methods for student outcome assessment. *Journal of Social Behavior and Personality, 12*, 273–288.

Riggio, R. E., & Carney, D. R. (2003). *Social Skills Inventory manual: Second edition.* Redwood City, CA: MindGarden.

Riggio, R. E., & Friedman, H. S. (1986). Impression formation: The role of expressive behavior. *Journal of Personality and Social Psychology, 50*, 421–427.

Riggio, R. E., Messamer, J., & Throckmorton, B. (1991). Social and academic intelligence: Conceptually distinct but overlapping constructs. *Personality and Individual Differences, 12*, 695–702.

Riggio, R. E., & Riggio, H. R. (2001). Self-report measurement of interpersonal sensitivity. In J. A. Hall & F. J. Bernieri (Eds.), *Interpersonal sensitivity: Theory and measurement* (pp. 127–142). Mahwah, NJ: Lawrence Erlbaum Associates.

Riggio, R. E., Riggio, H. R., Salinas, C., & Cole, E. J. (2003). The role of social and emotional communication skills in leader emergence and effectiveness. *Group Dynamics: Theory, Research, and Practice, 7*, 83–103.

Riggio, R. E., & Taylor, S. J. (2000). Personality and communication skills as predictors of hospice nurse performance. *Journal of Business and Psychology, 15*, 347–355.

Riggio, R. E., Tucker, J., & Throckmorton, B. (1987). Social skills and deception ability. *Personality and Social Psychology Bulletin, 13*, 568–577.

Riggio, R. E., Tucker, J., & Widaman, K. F. (1987). Verbal and nonverbal cues as mediators of deception ability. *Journal of Nonverbal Behavior, 11*, 126–145.

Riggio, R. E., Watring, K., & Throckmorton, B. (1993). Social skills, social support, and psychosocial adjustment. *Personality and Individual Differences, 15*, 275–280.

Riggio, R. E., Widaman, K. F., Tucker, J. S., & Salinas, C. (1991). Beauty is more than skin deep: Components of attractiveness. *Basic and Applied Social Psychology, 12*, 423–439.

Riggio, R. E., & Woll, S. B. (1984). The role of nonverbal cues and physical attractiveness in the selection of dating partners. *Journal of Social and Personal Relationships, 1*, 347–357.

Riggio, R. E., & Zimmerman, J. A. (1991). Social skills and interpersonal relationships: Influences on social support and support seeking. In W. H. Jones & D. Perlman (Eds.), *Advances in personal relationships* (Vol. 2, pp. 133–155). London: Jessica Kingsley Press.

Rosenthal, R. (Ed.). (1979). *Skill in nonverbal communication.* Cambridge, MA: Oelgeschlager, Gunn, & Hain.

Rosenthal, R., Hall, J. A., DiMatteo, M. R., Rogers, P. L., & Archer, D. (1979). *Sesnsitivity to nonverbal communications: The PONS test.* Baltimore, MD: Johns Hopkins University Press.

Sabatelli, R. M., & Rubin, M. (1986). Nonverbal expressiveness and physical attractiveness as mediators of interpersonal perceptions. *Journal of Nonverbal Behavior, 10*, 120–133.

Schutte, N. S., Malouff, J. M., Hall, L. E., Haggerty, D. J., Cooper, J. T., Golden, C. J., & Dornheim, L. (1998). Development and validation of a measure of emotional intelligence. *Personality and Individual Differences, 25,* 167–177.

Segrin, C., & Flora, J. (2000). Poor social skills are a vulnerability factor in the development of psychosocial problems. *Human Communication Research, 26,* 489–514.

Snyder, M. (1974). The self-monitoring of expressive behavior. *Journal of Personality and Social Psychology, 30,* 526–537.

Snyder, M. (1987). *Public appearances/private realities: The psychology of self-monitoring.* New York: W.H. Freeman.

Thorndike, E. L. (1920). Intelligence and its uses. *Harper's Magazine, 140,* 227–235.

Tucker, J. S., & Riggio, R. E. (1988). The role of social skills in encoding posed and spontaneous facial expressions. *Journal of Nonverbal Behavior, 12,* 87–97.

Zuckerman, M., & Larrance, D. (1979). Individual differences in perceived encoding and decoding abilities. In R. Rosenthal (Ed.), *Skill in nonverbal communication* (pp. 171–203). Cambridge, MA: Oelgeschlager, Gunn, & Hain.

The Emory Dyssemia Index

Marshall Duke
Stephen Nowicki, Jr.
Emory University

INTRODUCTION

For more than two decades, we have been examining the relationship between social/interpersonal difficulties and nonverbal language deficits in children and adults (Nowicki & Duke, 1992, 1994, 2002, 2003; Duke, Nowicki, & Walker, 1996). Over this time, we and others (e.g., Elfenbein & Ambady, 2002; Feldman & Thayer, 1980) have established a significant link between these two variables. As a result, a variety of assessment and intervention procedures have emerged that are directed at improving social/interpersonal relationships via the strengthening of expressive and/or receptive nonverbal abilities (Feldman, Philippot, & Custrini, 1991). To remediate nonverbal language problems successfully, however, it is first necessary to diagnose them reliably.

Whereas the extensive battery of expressive and receptive scales gathered under the rubric of the Diagnostic Analysis of Nonverbal Accuracy (DANVA; Nowicki & Duke, 2003) is suitable for research and for individualized clinical application, we believed that there was a need for a method by which larger numbers of people could be screened by psychologists and nonpsychologists with limited time available. Hence, to complement the more time-consuming DANVA, we developed an easy-to-use checklist, The Emory Dyssemia Index (EDI; Love, Duke, & Nowicki, 1994).

The EDI, described here, is modeled after other widely used and effective screening checklist measures such as the Achenbach Child Behavior Checklist (CBCL; Achenbach 1991). We selected a similar format for two reasons. First, due to their familiarity with the widely used CBCL, teachers would have little difficulty learning to use the EDI. Second, such checklists can be submitted easily to procedures to establish their reliability, validity, and usefulness in screening large numbers of people with minimal time requirements. This chapter outlines the development of and uses for the EDI.

35

NEED FOR THE EMORY DYSSEMIA INDEX

Although children may develop nonverbal expressivity problems for a variety of reasons, there can be both biological and social causes for these difficulties. For example, children may be born with or acquire damage to the neural processing systems necessary for interpreting, translating, and expressing nonverbal cues. The limbic system or structures associated with the amygdale are most often implicated as crucial to the proper processing of nonverbal information.

Whereas neural difficulties play a significant role in some relationship problems—especially serious ones—associated with nonverbal cues, we believe that most nonverbal expressivity problems result from simple failures to learn. By this we mean that, although children may be perfectly capable of learning the appropriate means of communicating nonverbally, they may not have had the opportunity to observe how others express themselves nonverbally and/or be reinforced for showing correct expressions. If it is assumed that children learn proper nonverbal expressivity within their families, it likely is that most parents and others around the children may not show the full range and intensity of emotions nonverbally that children need to see and hear in order to learn. If not corrected with school experience, then children's nonverbal problems may continue or perhaps worsen as their social problems increase.

For these reasons, the early detection—usually within the education system—of such inappropriate use of nonverbal expressive behavior becomes important. In that the DANVA and other more extensive measures of expressive and receptive nonverbal abilities typically require extended training in their use as well as significant amounts of time and equipment, the EDI was developed in hopes of providing a reasonably reliable and valid method for teacher-based assessment of nonverbal language capacity in large groups of children or in children who appear to have some social/interpersonal difficulties. Researchers and social workers must always be aware of the degree to which they may interrupt ongoing school activities when they are working with children, and maximum effectiveness appears to be related to minimum intrusion coupled with maximum input from teachers. Easy-to-use checklists seem to fit these criteria quite well.

Development of the Emory Dyssemia Index

The development of the EDI followed traditional test-development guidelines. First, a sample of 20 teachers was drawn from a variety of public and private schools ranging from elementary through high school. The teachers were asked to generate statements describing the behavior of children whom they knew to have social difficulties in the form of higher rates of conflict with others, isolation, neglect by others, rejection by others, or difficulty establishing and maintaining friendships. Among them, teachers generated more than 300 descriptive phrases, such as "touches others when they don't want to be touched" and "speaks too loudly."

A group of psychologists and psychology graduate students ($n = 8$) familiar with nonverbal channels were asked to select from among the teacher-generated phrases all those items that dealt with one or more nonverbal cues (e. g., touch, facial expression, postures, gestures, clothing/jewelry, and paralanguage). The result of this selection process produced a list of 112 items. The 112 items were then grouped according to general nonverbal categories (e.g., kinesics, paralanguage, facial expression). Each item was placed next to a rating scale. The rating scale ranged from 1 to 4 on the basis of frequency of occurrence of these behaviors in a child (1 = never; 2 = rarely [once in 2 or more weeks]; 3 = sometimes [weekly]; 4 = often [daily] and 5 = very often [several times daily]). This "Beta" form of the EDI was then given to a sample of 104 teachers who were taking summer continuing education courses and volunteered to help develop the measure. The teachers were asked to think of one child they had known who had significant social/interpersonal difficulties and one child that was an interpersonal "star." They then completed an EDI-Beta for each of these children. Items that were in found to be chosen in common by 80% of the teachers in each group were selected to be studied further.

The selection process resulted in a 96-item form of the EDI, which comprised 10 groupings of seven or eight items each. As before, each item was scored from 1 to 5, which produced ten cluster scores as well as a total EDI score. The 96-item form was then subjected to two item validation procedures. In the first, a sample of teachers ($n = 20$) was asked to complete EDIs on several children in their class that had been rated independently for social efficacy by other, more time-consuming means (e.g., child and parent interviews, child observation). In the second procedure, validation took place in a psychological clinic specializing in working with children with social/interpersonal difficulties. In addition to the standard battery of tests (which included the full administration of the DANVA), each child, who was seen over a 1-year period, was administered the EDI (a total of more than 200 children). Based on these procedures, and with input from both researchers and practitioners (Jones & Heimann, personal communication, 2002), a 42-item form of the EDI was produced. Six items that had survived the item validation procedures represented each of the six major nonverbal channels. Termed the EDI-C, it is the instrument that is used presently with children and adolescents.

Upon completion of the EDI-C, we set out recently to extend its use to adults in hopes of being able to identify and address the degree to which their nonverbal abilities may be contributing to interpersonal/social difficulties. The result of this attempt was the EDI-A. The EDI-A is an 85-item rating scale that follows a somewhat similar format as the EDI-C. The main difference is that the behaviors described include more adult-like nonverbal patterns such as conversational activities and business-related behaviors. Rather than using teachers as our source of descriptive items, in this case the participants were a group of business workers, consultants, personnel specialists, and mental health professionals working primarily with adults. The generation, selection, and cross validation of the items was similar to the process used for the EDI-C. Both measures are included in the appendix for this chapter.

Research Applications

Research with the EDI measures has focused primarily on development and refinement. In an ongoing long-term study of the efficacy of the measure, Jones and Heimann (2003) and their colleagues at the Beyond Words Center for Social Skills in Atlanta have administered the EDI to several hundred children ranging from 5 to 8 years of age. The EDI was given as part of a larger battery of tests that included the DANVA (Nowicki & Duke, 1994) and that serves as a validity criterion for the EDI. The DANVA is an extensive set of measures comprising eight subtests that assess expressive and receptive nonverbal language usage abilities. In the expressive subtests, children are shown photos of various postures, facial expressions, and gestures, and then they listen to tapes of various voice tones. The children's nonverbal abilities are indicated not only by the number of errors they make but the *sorts* of errors (e.g., labeling a face as angry when it is sad). Expressive nonverbal abilities (those assessed by the EDI) are determined via judgments of children's capacities to encode emotion facially, gesturally, posturally (videotaped), and paralinguistically (audiotape).

Preliminary analysis of Jones and Heimann's (personal communication, 2003) data indicates significant relationships (Pearson r ranging from .56 to .78) between EDI scores, as provided by teachers, and DANVA scores. These data suggest preliminarily that the EDI can serve as an effective screening measure for the identification of expressive nonverbal language deficits (and their associated social difficulties). Further analyses indicate that EDI scores also correlate significantly with teacher ratings of social problems in school settings. Interestingly, but predictably, the correlations between EDI scores and unstructured social interactions (playground, transitions from classroom to cafeteria, school buses) are much stronger than those between EDI scores and structured, classroom activities. This supports our theoretical argument that social deficits are more likely to manifest themselves in situations in which children need to provide their own structure (Nowicki & Duke, 1994).

One aspect of the EDI makes it necessary to urge users of the instrument to carry out limited validation studies of their own. Although it has been possible to establish norms for the instrument (e.g., what scores can be expected in children with adequate to good social relationships, what scores in those with moderate difficulty, etc.), we have found that what is considered acceptable or "normal" nonverbal behavior varies from place to place. We have even found noteworthy variations among different schools in the same large city. Therefore, it appears that users will need to establish local norms for their schools or areas. To do this, they will need to gather data within a more or less standardized research design.

In one possible design, teachers should be asked to provide two sorts of data about children in their classes. First, they should be asked to complete an EDI on each child. Some weeks later, they should be asked to rate the child's social behaviors and interpersonal capacities using a standardized measure acceptable to the school. A good example would be the Achenbach Child Behavior Checklist, which is very widely used. Finally, school records may be examined to determine the degree to which prior teachers or counselors describe each child as having social/interpersonal difficulties. Through the application of simple descriptive and inferential statistics, local norms can be established and used with some caution in assessing children thereafter.

The EDI is a relatively new addition to the set of measures available for the assessment of social skills (see Riggio & Riggio, this volume). It has the advantage of being easy and quick and of being able to provide data on large numbers of children in a population. Early data suggest that it can be very useful in the right setting and in the right hands. We urge further research with the instrument to determine the fuller extent of its efficacy. Caution is appropriate in the use of this (and all) tests; no single test should ever be used as the sole basis for diagnosis, planning, or decision making.

Clinical Applications

The EDI-C and the EDI-A may be used in a variety of ways in a number of settings. The EDI-C is particularly well-suited for use by clinicians interested in assessing the nonverbal behavioral patterns of children who are experiencing social difficulties in both school and nonschool settings. We have found that teachers, coaches, youth leaders, and the like are willing to take the few minutes necessary to complete it. Furthermore, the EDI-C may be used as a measure of treatment or intervention efficacy because, with its being nontime-consuming, teachers are usually able to complete follow up assessments on a regular basis.

Once gathered from several sources, professionals may use the EDI-C data to isolate areas of expressive or receptive nonverbal usage that need remediation. Specially tailored activities may then be developed to address specific needs. It has been our experience that when teachers can see a clear connection between their input and the intervention programs proposed by mental health professionals, they are more likely to comply with treatment regimens. Furthermore, given its straightforwardness and ease of understanding, many teachers have found the EDI-C to be a useful device for identifying areas in need of emphasis and practice for large segments of their classes. This has resulted in the development of special curricular units dealing with the importance of nonverbal cues in general (for more information, contact the authors).

In contrast with the EDI-C, which is used primarily by mental health professionals and teachers, we have found that the EDI-A can be used effectively by adults who, themselves, are experiencing social problems that they cannot explain. In a recent book (Nowicki & Duke, 2002), we described the use of the EDI-A in a program designed to help adults identify and remediate their own nonverbal problems and to improve thereby their interpersonal success. In this program, the EDI-A is completed not by teachers but by a "coach" or a number of trusted colleagues or peers whose help is sought by an individual. With its adult orientation and focus on workplace as well as social behaviors, the EDI-A can be an effective tool for helping people to help themselves. Because the major use of the EDI-A thus far has been individual, and because clinical and empirical data attesting to its construct validation are currently being gathered, however, it should be used carefully.

Other uses of the EDI that have emerged since its introduction include its administration in clinical settings as a specific component of a battery in which other, more individually based assessment devices cannot be used due to time or insurance-based limitations. Also, the EDI-C makes possible studies of large numbers of children over a wide age range, thereby allowing for the development of local norms that were difficult to establish for longer procedures such as the DANVA or the PONS. Finally, the EDI can be used to monitor ongoing progress in clinical settings because it is short and easy to complete over intervals of months or even weeks.

CONCLUSION

Children with nonverbal processing difficulties can be significantly handicapped as they face the daunting task of attempting to develop relationships with peers and adults alike. They believe that they are communicating appropriately with others when, in actuality, they are not. Furthermore, they typically are not aware that they are the source of the problems occurring with others. The existence of reliable and valid rating scales can lead to the accurate identification of children with expressivity difficulties. Such identification can then lead to their obtaining early help before their problems become worse. For adults, however, even "late" assessment may still provide an opportunity to remediate social skill concerns. We offer the EDI as one possible instrument that might help in these endeavors.

REFERENCES

Achenbach, T. (1991). *Manual for the Child Behavior checklist/4–18 and 1991 Profile.* Burlington VT: University Department of Psychiatry.
Duke, M. P., Nowicki, S., Jr., & Walker, E. (1996). *Teaching your child the language of social success.* Atlanta: Peachtree Publishers.
Elfenbein, H. A., & Ambady, N. (2002). Predicting workplace outcomes from the ability to eavesdrop on feelings. *Journal of Applied Psychology, 48,* 123–140.
Feldman, M., & Thayer, S. (1980). A comparison of three measures of nonverbal decoding ability. *Journal of Social Psychology, 112,* 91–97.
Feldman, R. S., Philippot, P., & Custrini, R. J. (1991). Social competence and nonverbal behavior. In R. S. Feldman & B. Rime (Eds.), *Fundamentals of nonverbal behavior* (pp. 329–350). New York: Cambridge University Press.
Jones, J., & Heimann, L. (2003). *Use of the Emory Dyssemia Index in children with social skills difficulties.* Unpublished study, Beyond Words Social Skills Center, Atlanta, GA.

Love, E., Duke, M., & Nowicki, S., Jr. (1994). The Emory Dyssemia Index. *Journal of General Psychology*, *128*, 703–705.

Nowicki, S., Jr., & Duke, M. P. (1992). *Helping the child who doesn't fit in.* Atlanta: Peachtree Publishers.

Nowicki, S., Jr., & Duke, M. P. (1994). Individual differences in the nonverbal communication of affect: The Diagnostic Analysis of Nonverbal Accuracy Scale. *Journal of Nonverbal Behavior, 18,* 9–35.

Nowicki, S., Jr., & Duke, M. P. (2002). *Will I ever fit in?* New York: The Free Press.

Nowicki, S., Jr., & Duke, M. P. (2003). *Manual and reference list for the Diagnostic Analysis of Nonverbal Accuracy.* Atlanta, GA: Emory University.

APPENDIX

The Emory Dyssemia Indices

EMORY DYSSEMIA INDEX-REVISED (EDI-C)
(Copyright, 1999; B. Love, M. Duke, S. Nowicki, Jr., & J. Jones)

DIRECTIONS: Please indicate the frequency of each of the following behaviors according to the four-point scale below.

1	2	3	4	5
NEVER	RARELY	SOMETIMES	OFTEN	VERY OFTEN

SECTION A: Gaze and eye contact

1 2 3 4 5: (1) Fails to look at others when addressed
1 2 3 4 5: (2) Fails to look at others when speaking
1 2 3 4 5: (3) Avoids eye contact with others
1 2 3 4 5: (4) Fails to look up when called by name
1 2 3 4 5: (5) Hangs head when listening to others
1 2 3 4 5: (6) Stares at the floor when talking with others

A SCORE _____

SECTION B: Space and touch

1 2 3 4 5: (7) Seeks attention by inappropriate touching
1 2 3 4 5: (8) Stands too close to others when interacting
1 2 3 4 5: (9) Stands too distant from others when interacting
1 2 3 4 5: (10) Fails to keep hands to self
1 2 3 4 5: (11) Pulls back when approached by others
1 2 3 4 5: (12) Grabs others to get attention

B SCORE _____

SECTION C: Paralanguage

1 2 3 4 5: (13) Speaks too softly to be heard easily
1 2 3 4 5: (14) Tone of voice does not fit emotional state
1 2 3 4 5: (15) Mumbles when speaking
1 2 3 4 5: (16) Speaks in a monotone
1 2 3 4 5: (17) Speaks with "baby talk"
1 2 3 4 5: (18) Fails to alter speech volume to fit situation

C SCORE _____

SECTION D: Facial expression

1 2 3 4 5: (19) Facial expressions do not fit emotional state
1 2 3 4 5: (20) Uses inappropriate facial expressions
1 2 3 4 5: (21) Face is blank when discussing emotional topics
1 2 3 4 5: (22) Usual facial expression is negative (e.g., sad)
1 2 3 4 5: (23) Fails to smile back to other's smile
1 2 3 4 5: (24) Fails to look interested

D SCORE _____

SECTION E: Objectics/Fashion

1 2 3 4 5: (25) Shows inadequate personal hygiene
1 2 3 4 5: (26) Shows inadequate grooming (e.g., hair combed)
1 2 3 4 5: (27) Clothing is not fastened correctly
1 2 3 4 5: (28) Interests seem out of "sync" with peers
1 2 3 4 5: (29) Uses poor manners when eating or drinking
1 2 3 4 5: (30) Seems unaware of fads/styles within peer group

E SCORE _____

SECTION F: Social rules/norms

1 2 3 4 5: (31) Has difficulty understanding rules and sequences of games
1 2 3 4 5: (32) Makes embarrassing behavioral mistakes
1 2 3 4 5: (33) Lacks "common sense" in peer interactions
1 2 3 4 5: (34) Seems tactless
1 2 3 4 5: (35) Has difficulty saying funny things or telling jokes successfully
1 2 3 4 5: (36) Seems to lack social "maturity"

F SCORE _____

SECTION G: Nonverbal receptivity

1 2 3 4 5: (37) Misreads the intentions or feelings of others
1 2 3 4 5: (38) Perseveres in action or comment regardless of adverse impact
1 2 3 4 5: (39) Seems insensitive to others' feelings
1 2 3 4 5: (40) Seems hypersensitive to others' feelings
1 2 3 4 5: (41) Behavior is out of "sync" with demands of situation
1 2 3 4 5: (42) Fails to respond appropriately or at all to greetings

G SCORE _____

TOTAL SCORE _____

Scoring and Interpreting the EDI-C

Used in the simplest way, the higher the score, the more likely it is suggested that the child has some difficulty nonverbally. However, the source of the higher score is also important to consider clinically. For example, a score of 9 could be obtained by ratings of one for each of the three items and of two for the other items of a particular scale or by a score of 4 for one of the scales and 1s for the other 5. Therefore, it is suggested that while total scores for each item and total score across all items are important, users should also pay special attention to items that are rated as 3s and 4s.

Normative studies completed on public school children produced the following findings, which can be used as tentative guidelines when interpreting the EDI-C scale and total scores. Data gathered from 300 elementary students from a suburban county school system revealed the following findings:

SECTION A: Score above 15 suggests adjustment difficulty
SECTION B: Score above 12 suggests adjustment difficulty
SECTION C: Score above 13 suggests adjustment difficulty
SECTION D: Score above 11 suggests adjustment difficulty
SECTION E: Score above 13 suggests adjustment difficulty
SECTION F: Score above 7 suggests adjustment difficulty

TOTAL SCORE ABOVE 71 SUGGESTS ADJUSTMENT DIFFICULTY

Emory Dyssemia Index—Adult Form (EDI-A)

DIRECTIONS: Please circle the frequency of each of the following behaviors according to the four-point scale below.

1	2	3	4	5
NEVER	RARELY	SOMETIMES	OFTEN	VERY OFTEN

SECTION A: Gaze and eye contact

1 2 3 4 5: Fails to look at people in conversations
1 2 3 4 5: Fails to look at others when speaking to groups
1 2 3 4 5: Avoids eye contact when walking by people
1 2 3 4 5: Fails to look up when addressed
1 2 3 4 5: Hangs head when listening to people
1 2 3 4 5: Stares at the floor when talking with people
1 2 3 4 5: Watches people out of corner of his/her eye
1 2 3 4 5: Stares excessively at people

A SCORE _____ (Max =40)

SECTION B: Space and touch

1 2 3 4 5: Touches people inappropriately
1 2 3 4 5: Stands too close to people when interacting
1 2 3 4 5: Stands too distant from people when interacting
1 2 3 4 5: Seeks excessive physical contact with people
1 2 3 4 5: Pulls back when approached by people
1 2 3 4 5: Grabs people to get their attention
1 2 3 4 5: Spreads materials beyond his "area" when working
1 2 3 4 5: Makes people uncomfortable with his physical positioning
1 2 3 4 5: Enters offices without knocking or seeking recognition/permission
1 2 3 4 5: Sits down in office without invitation to do so

B SCORE _____ (Max =50)

SECTION C: Paralanguage

1 2 3 4 5: Speaks too softly to be heard easily
1 2 3 4 5: Speaks too loudly for situation
1 2 3 4 5: Uses vocabulary inappropriate to listeners or situation
1 2 3 4 5: Tone of voice does not fit emotional state
1 2 3 4 5: Tone of voice does not fit situation
1 2 3 4 5: Mumbles when speaking
1 2 3 4 5: Speaks in a monotone
1 2 3 4 5: Speaks with "baby talk"
1 2 3 4 5: Fails to alter speech volume to fit situation

C SCORE _____ (Max =45)

SECTION D: Facial expression

1 2 3 4 5: Facial expressions do not fit emotional state
1 2 3 4 5: Uses inappropriate facial expressions
1 2 3 4 5: Face is blank when discussing emotional topics
1 2 3 4 5: Usual "resting" facial expression is negative (e.g., sad or angry)
1 2 3 4 5: Does not smile back when smiled at
1 2 3 4 5: Looks disinterested or bored
1 2 3 4 5: Facial expressions are hard to "read"
1 2 3 4 5: Facial expressions are exaggerated

D SCORE _____ (Max =40)

SECTION E: Objectics/Fashion

1 2 3 4 5: Shows inadequate personal hygiene
1 2 3 4 5: Shows inadequate grooming (e.g., hair combed, teeth cared for)
1 2 3 4 5: Clothing appears uncared for
1 2 3 4 5: Clothing inappropriate for situation (over- or under-dressed)
1 2 3 4 5: Uses excessive perfume or cologne
1 2 3 4 5: Uses poor manners when eating or drinking
1 2 3 4 5: Seems unaware of styles within peer group
1 2 3 4 5: Choice of accessories (e.g., jewelry) provokes undue negative attention

E SCORE _____ (Max =40)

SECTION F: Hands and hand gestures

1 2 3 4 5: Hands "give off" nervousness or confusion
1 2 3 4 5: Hand gestures are too intense for situation
1 2 3 4 5: Fidgets with rings or other jewelry; "plays" with pens or pencils
1 2 3 4 5: Cracks knuckles when with others or drums fingers "unconsciously"
1 2 3 4 5: Hides hands in pockets or behind back
1 2 3 4 5: Does not attend to grooming of hands and fingernails
1 2 3 4 5: Hand gestures are poorly "timed" with speech content
F SCORE _____ (Max =35)

SECTION G: Social rules/norms

1 2 3 4 5: Has difficulty understanding social rules and "etiquette"
1 2 3 4 5: Makes embarrassing behavioral mistakes
1 2 3 4 5: Lacks "common sense" in peer interactions
1 2 3 4 5: Seems tactless
1 2 3 4 5: Has difficulty saying funny things or telling jokes successfully
1 2 3 4 5: Seems to lack social "maturity"
1 2 3 4 5: Does not seem to follow office or professional "etiquette"
1 2 3 4 5: Raises conversation topics "out of nowhere"
G SCORE _____ (Max =40)

SECTION H: Nonverbal receptivity

1 2 3 4 5: Misreads the intentions or feelings of others
1 2 3 4 5: Perseveres in action or comment regardless of adverse impact
1 2 3 4 5: Seems insensitive to others' feelings
1 2 3 4 5: Seems hypersensitive to others' feelings
1 2 3 4 5: Behavior is out of "sync" with demands of situation
1 2 3 4 5: Fails to respond appropriately or at all to greetings
1 2 3 4 5: Doesn't seem to "sense" interpersonal "trouble"
1 2 3 4 5: Appears unaware of things going on around him or her
1 2 3 4 5: Does not "check" self in mirrors or in window reflections
H SCORE _____ (Max =45)

SECTION I: Conversational skills

1 2 3 4 5: Starts talking before others finish
1 2 3 4 5: Does not read cues regarding desire of other people to converse or not
1 2 3 4 5: Does not pick up "your turn" signals
1 2 3 4 5: Speaks too fast for situation
1 2 3 4 5: Speaks to slowly for situation
1 2 3 4 5: Uses "y'know" or other noncontributing phrases excessively
1 2 3 4 5: Doesn't seem to listen to what others are saying
1 2 3 4 5: Choice of conversation topics is inappropriate to situation
I SCORE _____ (Max =40)

SECTION J: Chronemics and the use of time

1 2 3 4 5: Arrives late for meetings
1 2 3 4 5: Leaves meetings too early or at inappropriate times
1 2 3 4 5: Stays well beyond time needed to complete "business"
1 2 3 4 5: Walks too fast for situation
1 2 3 4 5: Walks too slowly for situation
1 2 3 4 5: Does not wait for people appropriate amounts of time
1 2 3 4 5: Finishes eating long after or long before others
1 2 3 4 5: Makes people feel pressured to move more quickly
1 2 3 4 5: Checks time too frequently
1 2 3 4 5: "Bolts" to leave as soon as workday is over

J SCORE_____ (Max =50)

TOTAL SCORE_____ (Sum of scores on A - J) Maximum = 425

The Affectionate Communication Index

Kory Floyd
Alan C. Mikkelson
Arizona State University

INTRODUCTION

Researchers have long recognized the communication of affection for its importance in social interaction (e.g., Bowlby, 1953; Burgoon & Hale, 1984; Frank, 1973; Koch; 1959; Rotter, Chance, & Phares, 1972). Besides influencing relationship maintenance, affectionate behavior contributes to everything from physical health (Komisaruk & Whipple, 1998) and mental well-being (Downs & Javidi, 1990) to academic performance (Steward & Lupfer, 1987) and individual happiness (Floyd, 2002). Despite the fact that affectionate communication characterizes a broad range of positive human relationships and is associated with a number of individual and relational benefits, it is capable of producing negative effects. Many of these potential negative outcomes result from the tenuous relationship between the experience of an emotion and its expression. As with other emotional states, one can feel affection toward another without actually expressing it. Similarly, however, one can express affection to another without really feeling it, and research indicates that both men and women routinely do so as a means of manipulating or persuading others (see Floyd, in press, for review).

That affectionate communication could be associated with negative outcomes for individuals or their relationships is somewhat counterintuitive, given the extent to which affectionate behavior is prized in relationships and the fact that closer, more intimate relationships also tend to be more affectionate than are relationships that are less close or intimate. Although several theories might be used to explain this apparent paradox in part, Affection Exchange Theory (AET; Floyd, 2001, 2002; Floyd & Morman, 2001, in press; Floyd & Ray, 2003) explains it with reference to humans' constant, and often competing, motivations toward viability and fertility.

47

According to AET, affectionate communication can act both to advance and to in-hibit these goals and, as a result, can produce positive effects in one instance while producing negative effects in another.

Despite recent integrations of theory, historically, efforts at studying affection-ate communication have been plagued by inconsistencies in the way the construct is operationally defined. These inconsistencies were addressed in Floyd and Morman's (1998) development of their Affectionate Communication Index (ACI). In this chapter, we review the rationale behind the development of the ACI and the processes described by which the scale was developed and validated initially. We then describe the six major datasets that have used the ACI since its publication. Finally, we discuss the strengths and limitations of the scale and how researchers might utilize it.

Measurement Strategies for Affectionate Communication

Prior to development of the ACI, studies of affectionate communication tended to take one of three approaches to measurement. The first involves coding behavior without *a priori* specification of the behaviors to be coded as affection. For in-stance, Noller (1978) examined videotapes of parent–child interaction and re-corded "the number of instances of interactive behavior that would normally be regarded as affectionate" (p. 317; see also Walters, Pearce, & Dahms, 1957). A sec-ond approach entails coding behavior according to a prespecified list of referents. Twardosz, Schwartz, Fox, and Cunningham (1979), for example, developed an ex-tensive coding scheme for analysis of affectionate behavior in preschool and day-care environments (see also Twardosz et al., 1987). Others have developed similar, although less extensive, coding schemes for measuring affectionate behavior, ei-ther live or from videotapes (e.g., Acker, Acker, & Pearson, 1973; Acker & Marton, 1984; Lovaas, Schaeffer, & Simmons, 1965).

Because of the nature of affectionate behavior, there are times when coding schemes are limited as a form of assessment in that they require the behavior to be observed, either live or via videotape. Affectionate behavior often occurs in relative privacy, however, making it difficult to observe even in naturalistic settings. For this reason, Floyd and Morman (1998) introduced a third approach to measuring affec-tion by developing the ACI, a self-report measure of affectionate communication behavior. Self-report measures, although often maligned, are extremely useful measurement tools, primarily because they are efficient, cost-effective, and allow for the measurement of behaviors that researchers may not be able to observe di-rectly. The ACI was developed to capitalize on these advantages.

Development and Validation of the ACI

In developing the measure, Floyd and Morman (1998) adopted a grounded theory approach to generating referents for affectionate communication in order to increase the ecological validity of those referents. A large initial pool of respondents was asked to think of one close relationship and to respond to the question, "How do you communicate your affection for each other? That is, how do you let each other know that you like and care about each other?" Respondents provided a list of 67 unique items, which was subsequently reduced to 34 items after a second panel eliminated items lacking face validity. Later administrations of these items were factor analyzed for their underlying structure, and the present 19-item scale was produced.

The ACI consists of three subscales measuring different forms of affectionate communication. The first subscale, measuring verbal expressions of affection, includes items such as saying "I love you" and expressing the importance of the relationship verbally. The second subscale, measuring direct nonverbal expressions of affection, includes items such as hugging, holding hands, sitting close, and kissing on the cheek. The third subscale, measuring affectionate social support behaviors, includes items such as giving compliments, helping with problems, and sharing private information. For scholars interested only in nonverbal cues, the second subscale can be employed on its own. A copy of the scale appears in the appendix.

Floyd and Morman (1998) reported acceptable internal and test–retest reliability for all three subscales and subjected the scale to numerous tests of convergent and discriminant validity. The ACI has been used in six major datasets, each of which has focused primarily on communication in family relationships. A separate paper (Floyd & Mikkelson, 2002) used the data from these six projects to perform additional psychometric tests of the ACI and found strong support for its structure, reliability, and validity. Specifically, all three subscales had high internal, split-half, and test–retest reliability, and convergent, discriminant, and predictive validity.

The scale reliably discriminates between high-affection and low-affection relationships, and it corresponds to actual affection behavior displayed in laboratory settings. Across several studies, the subscales each demonstrate convergent validity through their correlations with a number of relevant indices, such as relationship closeness, love, liking, communication satisfaction, and relationship satisfaction. They are also unrelated to measures of social desirability. Finally, the scales demonstrate predictive validity by predicting communication satisfaction, liking, love, closeness, and relationship satisfaction in romantic, platonic, and familial relationships over a six-month period. In sum, the ACI and its individual subscales demonstrate all forms of psychometric adequacy.

Previous Applications

Following are some of the specific studies in which the ACI has been applied. We discuss findings from the first two datasets in detail, and then provide summary information for the remaining studies.

Morman and Floyd, 1999.   The study examined the individual and relational correlates to affectionate behavior in adult paternal relationships. Included in the study were 55 pairs of adult men and their biological fathers. Participants, who were primarily from the midwestern United States, completed a written questionnaire about affection, closeness, communication satisfaction, and self-disclosure in their father–adult son relationship. Internal reliabilities for the ACI subscale were as follows: verbal (.85 for fathers and .82 for sons), nonverbal (.68 for fathers and .72 for sons), and support (.82 for fathers and .75 for sons).

As hypothesized, fathers communicated more affection to their sons through supportive activities (M = 5.47, SD = 1.00) than through direct verbal (M = 3.43, SD = 1.25) or nonverbal expressions (M = 3.26, SD = 0.89). Likewise, sons communicated more affection to their fathers through supportive activity (M = 5.07, SD = 1.05) than through verbal (M = 2.55, SD = 1.18) or nonverbal expressions (M = 2.75, SD = 0.81). Moreover, fathers reported communicating significantly more verbal, nonverbal, and supportive affection to their sons than the sons reported communicating to the fathers. In addition, both fathers' and sons' affection scores were linearly associated with relational closeness, self-disclosure, and communication satisfaction. Specifically, fathers' nonverbal affection was significantly associated with fathers' and sons' closeness, disclosure, and communication satisfaction. Sons' nonverbal affection was significantly related with fathers' and sons' disclosure, sons' closeness, and fathers' communication satisfaction.

Floyd and Morman, 2000.   This dataset involved 622 adult men who are fathers of at least one son aged 12 or older, and 181 of those sons. Roughly half of the participants were recruited from the midwestern United States, whereas the remaining half was recruited from throughout the rest of the geographic United States. Participants completed written questionnaires about their affection, closeness, communication satisfaction, and relationship satisfaction. Results from this dataset appear in Floyd and Morman (2000, 2001, 2003).

Because this is the largest of the datasets to use the ACI since its publication, we used it to examine the stability of the factor structure. We conducted confirmatory factor analysis (CFA) on the ACI items, with three factors (verbal, nonverbal, support) identified. Covariances were .67 between the verbal and support subscales, .69 between the verbal and nonverbal subscales, and .25 between the nonverbal and support subscales. Reported next are results that appear in Floyd and Morman (2000) and Floyd and Morman (2001). Each of these studies used portions of the dataset, and both investigated different aspects of affectionate communication.

Floyd and Morman's (2000) study proposed that men's affectionate communication with their sons is predicted by the affectionate communication the men received from their own fathers. Specifically, the researchers predicted a U-shaped curvilinear relationship, such that men who communicated the most affection to their sons are those whose own fathers were either highly affectionate or highly disengaged. Participants were 506 adult men who were fathers of at least one son. Affectionate communication was measured using the ACI's composite score, rather than its individual subscale scores. Participants reported on their affection with their son (affection given; α = .90) and the affection they received from their father (affection received; α = .94). As predicted, a U-shaped curvilinear relationship was identified between affection received and affection given. The authors proposed that men who received a great deal of affection from their own fathers modeled this communication behavior with their sons, whereas men who received little affection from their fathers compensated for this behavior by being more affectionate with their own sons. The study also reported that fathers' affection with their sons was linearly related to the positive involvement, relational satisfaction, and closeness characterizing those relationships, a finding that replicates that identified by Morman and Floyd (1999).

Floyd and Morman's (2001) investigation examined differences in the amount of affection men communicate to their biological sons, adopted sons, and stepsons. They hypothesized that fathers are more affectionate with biological and adopted sons than with stepsons. The two studies reported in Floyd and Morman (2001) involved a total of 384 males. Internal reliability coefficients for the ACI subscales were as follows: verbal (.85 for Study 1 fathers, .82 for Study 2 fathers, and .86 for Study 2 sons), nonverbal (.84 for Study 1 fathers, .74 for Study 2 fathers, and .87 for Study 2 sons), and support (.76 for Study 1 fathers, .76 for Study 2 fathers, and .74 for Study 2 sons).

The first study involved 182 adult males who were fathers of least one son (79 reported on a relationship with a biological son, 78 on a relationship with a stepson, and 25 on a relationship with an adopted son). As predicted, fathers communicated more affection to biological and adopted sons than to stepsons using verbal statements ($M_{biological}$ = 4.81, SD = 1.47; $M_{adopted}$ = 4.51, SD = 1.48; M_{step} = 3.51, SD = 1.42); nonverbal gestures ($M_{biological}$ = 3.55, SD = 1.41; $M_{adopted}$ = 3.45, SD = 1.44; M_{step} = 2.70, SD = 1.02); and supportive activities ($M_{biological}$ = 5.77, SD = .89; $M_{adopted}$ = 5.63, SD = 1.07; M_{step} = 5.37, SD = 0.99). Moreover, verbal, nonverbal, and supportive affection were linearly related to closeness, relational satisfaction, and relational involvement, a finding that replicates results in earlier studies.

The procedure in Study 2 was identical to that of Study 1 except that father–son dyads were used. Participants were 202 males comprised of 101 father–son dyads (44 dyads included a biological son, 41 included a stepson, and 16 included an adopted son). Fathers reported communicating more affection to both biological and adopted sons than to stepsons using verbal ($M_{biological}$ = 4.88, SD = 1.26; $M_{adopted}$ = 4.29, SD = 1.45; M_{step} = 3.86, SD = 1.63) and nonverbal forms ($M_{biological}$ = 3.24, SD = 0.84; $M_{adopted}$ = 3.12, SD = 1.06; M_{step} = 2.90, SD = 1.02). Similarly, biological and adopted sons reported receiving more affection than did stepsons; this was true for verbal statements ($M_{biological}$ = 4.56, SD = 1.36; $M_{adopted}$ = 3.89, SD = 1.61; M_{step} = 3.56, SD = 1.72) and nonverbal gestures ($M_{biological}$ = 3.10, SD = 1.22; $M_{adopted}$ = 2.71, SD = 1.03; M_{step} = 2.41, SD = 0.93). Fathers' nonverbal affection was linearly related to fathers' and sons' involvement, satisfaction, and closeness. Moreover, sons' nonverbal affection was associated with both fathers' and sons' involvement, satisfaction, and closeness.

Summary of Additional Studies

Floyd, 2002. This dataset involved 179 adults, recruited primarily from the southern and southwestern United States, who reported on their affectionate communication with three different targets: their mothers, their fathers, and one of their siblings. They also reported on their closeness with the sibling, and on a number of intrapsychic variables, including their happiness, stress, level of depression, level of social engagement, and general mental health. Results from this dataset are reported in Floyd (2002).

Floyd and Tusing, 2002. This study, which involved both a laboratory experiment and a longitudinal data collection, included 23 pairs of opposite-sex adults who were platonic friends, romantic partners, or biological siblings. Participants reported on their affection, closeness, liking, love, communication satisfaction, relationship satisfaction, and gender role orientations when they took part in the laboratory experiment. Six months later, they again reported on their affection, closeness, liking, love, communication satisfaction, and relationship satisfaction.

Hess, 2003. This study, which corresponded to the development and validation of a self-report measure of distancing behavior, included 209 adults who reported either on an ongoing relationship or on a previously terminated relationship. The nature of the relationships varied: 61% were friendships or social relationships, 34% were romantic or formerly romantic relationships, and 5% were familial relationships. Participants came primarily from the midwestern United States.

Floyd and Morr, in press. This study involved 109 triads consisting of a married couple and the sibling of one of the spouses. The triads, therefore, represented three dyadic relationships: a marriage, a sibling relationship, and a sibling-in-law relationship. All three participants in each triad completed questionnaires asking about the affection, closeness, and satisfaction of their relationships. Participants were recruited primarily from the south and southwest.

DISCUSSION

In this chapter, we discussed the development and use of the Affectionate Communication Index, a self-report measure that assesses nonverbal expressions of affection as well as verbal expressions and supportive gestures. This measure has proved useful in a number of studies about various aspects of affectionate communication, and with continued attention to its psychometric properties it can serve as a primary measurement tool for researchers interested in the dynamics of affectionate relational behavior. Nonverbal communication scholars, like all social scientists, must be cognizant of the psychometric adequacy of measurement tools used in research they conduct or even in research they cite. A lack of attention to such issues can lead to an accumulation of contradictory findings and impede the systematic progress of discovery.

Limitations and Implications for Usage

Self-report measures are commonly maligned on several grounds, some of which have merit but are offset by equally important benefits (see White & Sargent, this volume). One common concern is the extent to which self-report measures are susceptible to social desirability biases. This is a valid concern in that any method in which participants are aware that they are being studied is susceptible to social desirability biases. A second criticism concerns the lack of isomorphism between self-reports of behavior and actual behavior due to either recall bias or perception bias. The former bias concerns participants' abilities to remember their behaviors, and the latter concerns their abilities to be cognizant of them in the first place. These, too, are important concerns, and they highlight even more clearly the need for extensive validation of any self-report measure. In particular, these concerns call for research establishing the association between self-reports of behavior and actual, observed behavior. Floyd and Morman (1998) reported such research, and additional tests in this vein are certainly warranted.

Despite these and other criticisms, self-reports are enormously useful measurement tools. They bring a number of advantages over other methods, the first being their practicality. Compared to face-to-face interviews or observational methods, self-report measures are easier, faster, and less expensive to administer and require considerably less labor in the way of coding and entering data. A second, equally important advantage, at least when compared to observational methods, is that self-report measures allow for the study of behaviors that either occur so infrequently that it is difficult to observe them in great number or occur so privately that researchers rarely have entrée to observe them at all. Often, affectionate behavior falls into both categories, making self-report measures like the ACI the only viable option for measuring such behavior. The best option is often to triangulate methods, either within a given study or across a research program. When self-report measures are to be used in research on affection, however, the extant evidence supports strongly the ACI as the most psychometrically sound alternative.

REFERENCES

Acker, L. E., Acker, M. A., & Pearson, D. (1973). Generalized imitative affection: Relationship to prior kinds of imitation training. *Journal of Experimental Child Psychology, 16*, 111–125.

Acker, L. E., & Marton, J. (1984). Facilitation of affectionate-like behaviors in the play of young children. *Child Study Journal, 14*, 255–269.

Bowlby, J. (1953). *Maternal care and the growth of love.* London: Penguin.

Burgoon, J. K., & Hale, J. L. (1984). The fundamental topoi of relational communication. *Communication Monographs, 51*, 193–214.

Downs, V. C., & Javidi, M. (1990). Linking communication motives to loneliness in the lives of older adults: An empirical test of interpersonal needs and gratifications. *Journal of Applied Communication Research, 18*, 32–48.

Floyd, K. (2001). Human affection exchange: I. Reproductive probability as a predictor of men's affection with their adult sons. *Journal of Men's Studies, 10,* 39–50.

Floyd, K. (2002). Human affection exchange: V. Attributes of the highly affectionate. *Communication Quarterly, 50,* 135–154.

Floyd, K. (in press). *Communicating affection: Interpersonal behavior and social context.* Cambridge, UK: Cambridge University Press.

Floyd, K., & Mikkelson, A.C. (2002, November). *Psychometric properties of the affectionate communication index.* Paper presented to National Communication Association, New Orleans, LA.

Floyd, K., & Morman, M. T. (1998). The measurement of affectionate communication. *Communication Quarterly, 46,* 144–162.

Floyd, K., & Morman, M. T. (2000). Affection received from fathers as a predictor of men's affection with their own sons: Tests of the modeling and compensation hypotheses. *Communication Monographs, 67,* 347–361.

Floyd, K., & Morman, M. T. (2001). Human affection exchange: III. Discriminative parental solicitude in men's affectionate communication with biological and nonbiological sons. *Communication Quarterly, 49,* 310–327.

Floyd, K., & Morman, M. T. (2003). Human affection exchange: II. Affectionate communication in father–son dyads. *Journal of Social Psychology, 143,* 599–612.

Floyd, K., & Morr, M. C. (in press). Human affection exchange: VII. Affectionate communication in the sibling/spouse/sibling-in-law triad. *Communication Quarterly.*

Floyd, K., & Ray, G. B. (2003). Human affection exchange: IV. Vocalic predictors of perceived affection in initial interactions. *Western Journal of Communication, 67,* 56–73.

Floyd, K., & Tusing, K. J. (2002, July). *"At the mention of your name": Affect shifts induced by relationship-specific cognitions.* Paper presented to International Communication Association, Seoul, South Korea.

Frank, J. D. (1973). *Persuasion and healing: A comparative study of psychotherapy.* Baltimore, MD: Johns Hopkins University Press.

Hess, J. A. (2003). Measuring distance in personal relationships: the relational Distance Index. *Personal Relationships, 10,* 197–216.

Koch, S. (1959). *Psychology: A study of science* (Vol. 3). New York: McGraw-Hill.

Komisaruk, B. R., & Whipple, B. (1998). Love as sensory stimulation: Physiological consequences of its deprivation and expression. *Psychoneuroendocrinology, 23,* 927–944.

Lovaas, O. I., Schaeffer, B., & Simmons, J. Q. (1965). Experimental studies in childhood schizophrenia: Building social behavior in autistic children by use of electric shock. *Journal of Experimental Research in Personality, 1,* 99–109.

Morman, M. T., & Floyd, K. (1999). Affectionate communication between fathers and young adult sons: Individual- and relational-level correlates. *Communication Studies, 50,* 294–309.

Noller, P. (1978). Sex differences in the socialization of affectionate expression. *Developmental Psychology, 14,* 317–319.

Rotter, J. B., Chance, J. E., & Phares, E. J. (1972). *Applications of a social learning theory of personality.* New York: Holt, Rinehart & Winston.

Steward, A. L., & Lupfer, M. (1987). Touching as healing: The effect of touch on students' perceptions and performance. *Journal of Applied Social Psychology, 17,* 800–809.

Twardosz, S., Botkin, D., Cunningham, J. L., Weddle, K., Sollie, D., & Schreve, C. (1987). Expression of affection in day care. *Child Study Journal, 17,* 133–151.

Twardosz, S., Schwartz, S., Fox, J., & Cunningham, J. L. (1979). Development and evaluation of a system to measure affectionate behavior. *Behavioral Assessment, 1,* 177–190.

Walters, J., Pearce, D., & Dahms, L. (1957). Affectional and aggressive behavior of preschool children. *Child Development, 28,* 15–26.

APPENDIX

Affectionate Communication Index

We would like you to think about how you express love or affection to this person. That is, how do you let this person know that you love him or her? To what extent would you say that you do each of the following things *as a way to express affection to him or her*? Indicate your response by writing the appropriate number on the line preceding each item, according to the scale below.

1	2	3	4	5	6	7
Never or Almost Never Do This					Always or Almost Always Do This	

_____ Help him or her with problems

_____ Say "I love you"

_____ Kiss on lips

_____ Acknowledge his or her birthday

_____ Say how important he or she is to you

_____ Hug him or her

_____ Praise his or her accomplishments

_____ Wink at him or her

_____ Say he or she is one of your best friends

_____ Hold his or her hand

_____ Share private information

_____ Say "I care about you"

_____ Kiss on cheek

_____ Give him or her compliments

_____ Say he or she is a good friend

_____ Put your arm around him or her

_____ Sit close to him or her

_____ Give him or her a massage or backrub

The Touch Avoidance Measure

Peter A. Andersen
San Diego State University

INTRODUCTION

Among the many forms of nonverbal communication, few people would argue that *touch* is central to the communication of immediacy (Andersen, 1985; Andersen & Andersen, this volume), affection (see Floyd & Mikkelson, this volume), intimacy (Morris, 1971), love (Montagu, 1971), and warmth (Andersen & Guerrero, 1998). Touch is a critical aspect of relationships, from the initial handshake between strangers to the embrace of close friends to sexual intimacy. The extent to which people are predisposed to approach versus avoid touch also seemingly affects virtually every type of interpersonal and relational behavior. This chapter reports on the origins of touch avoidance research, discusses the dimensionality and reliability of the Touch Avoidance Measure, examines evidence for its validity, and discusses the relationship between touch avoidance and other important variables.

The Touch Avoidance Construct

The construct of touch avoidance emerged at the confluence of two streams of research: the abundant literature on communication avoidance (see McCroskey, 1982) and the literature on the importance of tactile communication in human relationships from infants to the elderly (Frank, 1957; Morris, 1971). Conceptually, Jourard (1966; Jourard, & Rubin, 1968) discussed that men and women show a consistent trait of more or less "touchability" that is an important communication predisposition and affects the nature of their interpersonal relationships. Until the mid-1970s, no measure was available to investigate touch avoidance systematically when Andersen and Leibowitz (1978; Leibowitz & Andersen, 1976) began to investigate and measure the construct.

From its inception, researchers have conceptualized touch avoidance as a communication predisposition (Andersen & Leibowitz, 1978; Leibowitz & Andersen, 1976).
Specifically, touch avoidance has been defined consistently as "an individual nonverbal
predisposition to generally approach or avoid touch in interpersonal interactions"
(Andersen & Sull, 1985, p. 62). According to Andersen, Andersen, and Lustig (1987),

> [T]ouch Avoidance is a trait or individual difference measure of a person's *atti-*
> *tude toward touch.* The touch avoidance construct is not a direct index of how
> much a person actually touches or avoids being touched. Instead it is an index of a
> person's affect toward touch. (p. 90)

Dimensionality and Reliability of the Touch Avoidance Construct

In its original conceptualization and operationalization, touch avoidance was expected to have two dimensions: a sender/receiver dimension and an opposite-sex/
same-sex dimension. A series of factor analyses by Andersen and Leibowitz (1978)
on an original matrix of 55 items that specified same- or opposite-sex touch
crossed with sending, receiving, or simultaneous touch, however, revealed only a
same-sex/opposite-sex dimension subsequently called the *touch avoid measure one*
(TAM1), indexing predispositions toward same-sex touch, and the *touch avoidance measure two* (TAM2) indexing predispositions toward opposite-sex touch.
Subsequent confirmatory factor analysis of the Touch Avoidance Measure likewise revealed a two-factor solution consisting of opposite- and same-sex touch
avoidance (Remland & Jones, 1988).

Internal Cronbach *alpha* reliability estimates for the TAM1 have demonstrated
its consistent reliability across a number of diverse populations. Studies of undergraduates have produced estimates of internal reliability in the .82 to .86 range
(Andersen & Leibowitz, 1978). In Lower's (1980) study of student nurses, internal
reliability for the TAM1 was .75. Estimates of internal reliability for the eight-item
TAM2 have ranged from .74 to .87, suggesting adequate internal consistency for the
measurement of opposite-sex touch. These estimates have shown that the internal
reliability of the TAM2 is stable across a set of widely diverse samples. The simple
18-item TAM1 and TAM2 are integrated together in the appendix.

Studies of undergraduates at 41 universities (Andersen et al., 1987; Andersen &
Leibowitz, 1978) have shown reliability estimates in the .86 to .87 range. Lower's
(1980) study of touch avoidance in nurses produced an internal reliability estimate of
.74. A study of the touch avoidance of elementary and secondary teachers produced
an estimate of .87 for the TAM2 measure (Leibowitz & Andersen, 1976). Likewise, a
field study of adult couples waiting in line at the movie theater and zoo line produced
an individual internal reliability estimate of .80 for the TAM2 (Guerrero & Andersen,
1991). Test–retest reliability analyses conducted by Andersen and Leibowitz (1978)
revealed that the TAM1 had a test–retest reliability of .61, which increased to .75 when
correcting for attenuation. Similarly the TAM2 measure had a test–retest reliability of
.56, which increased to .69 when correcting for attenuation.

Validity of the Touch Avoidance Instrument

Substantial evidence for the validity of the touch avoidance measure now exists. As predicted, touch avoidance is associated with interpersonal distance, with reactions to touch, and with actual touch. In a laboratory setting, Andersen and Sull (1985) found that observed interpersonal distance associated highly with both TAM1 and TAM2 scores particularly for female confederates. Specifically, TAM1 scores for female participants explained 11% of the variance in distance from female confederates. Males' TAM2 scores predicted 33% of the variance in males' distance from female confederates. These findings suggest that touch avoidance is part of a larger construct of interpersonal avoidance or nonimmediacy.

An imaginative laboratory study by Sorensen and Beatty (1988) found that touch avoiders respond negatively to actual touch by a confederate, whereas touch approachers responded more positively to touch. The brief touch, a handshake and a pat on the shoulder by the experimenter, made high touch avoiders act more negatively in the touch as opposed to the no-touch condition, whereas a handshake and a touch on the shoulder made low touch avoiders act more positively in the touch than in the no-touch condition. This study is perhaps the most direct validation of touch avoidance as an attitudinal predisposition toward touch.

Larsen and LeRoux (1984) established construct validity for the TAM1 measure. As predicted, TAM1 showed a negative correlation of $-.71$ with the Same Sex Touching Scale, a measure of comfort with and liking for same-sex touch. Several studies have shown that touch avoidance is related to actual, observed touch. Most notably, Guerrero and Andersen (1991) found that TAM2 scores were associated with actual tactile behavior as observed in lines outside movie theatres and the zoo. After opposite-sex couples were observed unobtrusively, they were approached, consented, separated, and given a questionnaire that included the TAM2 instrument.

Results showed that TAM2 scores were linearly related to amount of observed touch and accounted for 5% of the variance in observed touch. Moreover, this relationship was significant at both relational stages and accounted for 7% of the variance in touch in initial and intermediate relationship stages but was not predictive of touch in long-term relationships (Guerrero & Andersen, 1991). In longer term relationships, however, the relationship accounts for virtually all the variance in touch. Guerrero and Andersen (1994) reported that intradyadic correlation for actual touch in married relationships was .98, accounting for 96% of the variance in observed touch and leaving little variation remaining for communication predispositions or other variables to explain.

Age and Touch Avoidance

What are the correlates and causes of people's predisposition to approach or avoid touch? A series of studies examined demographic, psychological, gender, cultural, and other variables in an effort to better understand the touch avoidance relationship. Opposite-sex touch avoidance was found to be positively associated with age, although the extent to which this finding was a maturation effect or a cohort effect is not clear. Andersen and Leibowitz (1978) reported a significant positive association, r = .30, between TAM2 and age in a study of primary and secondary teachers. Lower (1980) found a significant positive correlation of .14 in her study of professional nurses. It may be that relatively younger people, who are more driven by sex hormones, are less likely to avoid opposite-sex touch than are older people. Alternatively, Americans or at least those in the studies, may be becoming less and less socially conservative, permitting more opposite-sex touch in each subsequent generation. Studies of same-sex touch avoidance have failed to find an association with age (Andersen & Leibowitz, 1978; Lower, 1980). The fact that age is positively associated with opposite-sex touch avoidance but not same-sex touch avoidance also suggests a hormonal explanation: Younger people in their prime reproductive years appear more likely to approach opposite-sex touch.

Touch Avoidance and Self-Esteem

The available evidence from a series of studies suggests that touch avoidance is negatively but weakly related to self-esteem. Andersen and Leibowitz (1978), in their sample of schoolteachers, originally found only one significant relationship between TAM1 and four dimensions of self-esteem, a correlation of −.21 between TAM1 and anxiety dimension of self-esteem. They found no significant relationship between TAM2 and any of four dimensions of self-esteem. Other more comprehensive studies suggest such a relationship exists. In their study of nearly 4,000 undergraduates at 40 American universities, Andersen et al. (1987) found a statistically significant negative relationship between self-esteem and TAM2 at 32 of the 40 universities sampled, with correlations in the −.07 to −.37 range. The overall relationship between self-esteem and TAM2 was −.19 across all 40 samples. Although a common stereotype exists that high self-esteem individuals may be standoffish, aloof, and snobby, these results suggest the opposite: People who are comfortable with themselves appear to be more comfortable with touch.

Sex and Gender Differences

A consistent finding across all the touch avoidance literature is that males are more avoidant of same-sex touch, and females are more avoidant of opposite-sex touch (i.e., people are more likely to avoid touching males). It is possible that the greater threat value of males makes them less approachable as tactile interactants. The original studies by Andersen and Leibowitz (1978) reveal that males have significantly higher TAM1 scores, and females have significantly higher TAM2 scores. The study of nurses by Lower (1980) reported that male nurses had significantly higher TAM1 scores than female nurses. In Andersen et al.'s (1987) research from 40 American universities, females had higher TAM2 scores than did mates in 39 of the 40 samples, 32 of these differences were statistically significant. Overall, the gender effect for TAM2 scores was about a half a standard deviation and accounts for about 7% of the variation, indicating a moderate effect size. In a study by Guerrero and Andersen (1994) of randomly selected individuals at the zoo and outside movie theatres, women reported higher TAM2 scores than men, accounting for about 11% of the variance.

Research on American, Mediterranean, Near Eastern, and Far Eastern respondents (Remland & Jones, 1988) corroborated the finding that men reported more same-sex touch avoidance than do women, suggesting this may be a transcultural or biological difference. For opposite-sex touch avoidance, gender and culture produced interactive effects on touch avoidance. Only Far-Eastern participants manifested more opposite-sex touch avoidance for women than for men. Surprisingly, no differences in TAM2 scores were observed between American men and women. Crawford (1994) also found that men had significantly higher TAM1 scores than did women, with biological sex accounting for 20% of the variance, successfully replicating earlier findings. Women did not have higher TAM2 scores than men, however, in Crawford's study.

Touch avoidance is more than just based in biological sex, however. Crawford (1994) found that gender also played a role, with androgynous men having significantly lower TAM1 scores and androgyny accounting for about 11% of the variance in touch avoidance. For women, however, androgyny was not correlated with TAM1 scores. For men, androgyny did not relate to their TAM2 score, but androgynous women had lower TAM2 scores, accounting for about 3% of the variance. Eman, Dierks-Stewart, and Tucker (1978) also found that androgynous and masculine individuals reported less touch avoidance than feminine individuals reported, especially in opposite-sex touch. This suggests that more masculine individuals may be socialized to engage in opposite-sex touch consistent with the gender stereotypes about the initiation of touch.

Cultural Differences in Touch Avoidance

The predisposition to avoid touch is probably a function of both biology and culture. Certainly cultural variables like religion are associated with touch avoidance. Studies of both teachers and nurses found that Protestants had the highest level of same-sex touch avoidance, Catholics had intermediate levels, and both Jewish and nonreligious respondents had the lowest levels of touch avoidance (Andersen & Leibowitz, 1978; Lower, 1980). Similarly, both the aforementioned studies found Protestants to have higher levels of opposite-sex touch avoidance than other groups. Likewise, significant U.S. regional differences have been observed in opposite-sex touch avoidance: Sunbelt universities tend to have significantly lower touch avoidance scores than frost-belt universities (Andersen et al., 1987; Andersen, Lustig, & Andersen, 1990). This difference, however, may be attributable to sunlight, which is known to have significant effects on communication behavior (Andersen, Lustig, & Andersen, 1990), or to the greater availability of skin in the Sunbelt.

Whereas cultural role variables have been found to influence touch avoidance, Remland and Jones (1988) found no international cultural differences in same-sex touch avoidance scores. For opposite-sex touch avoidance, however, culture had some effect on opposite-sex touch avoidance scores. Far Eastern women reported more touch avoidance than any other cultural group. American men and women were the least same-sex touch-avoidant of any of the sex-by-culture groups.

Touch Avoidance and Other Communication Variables

Touch avoidance has been found to be related consistently, if weakly, to other communication predispositions. Andersen and Leibowitz (1978) reported touch avoidance is positively correlated (TAM1 = .15; TAM2 = .18) with communication apprehension (CA), suggesting that touch approach and avoidance is significantly but faintly related to CA (McCroskey, 1982). Likewise, in a national study of 3,877 undergraduates simultaneously conducted at 40 universities, Andersen et al. (1987) found a significant overall relationship between both TAM measures and several verbal communication predispositions. The mean correlation across the 40 universities between TAM1 and communication apprehension was .21, and 39 of the 40 schools had correlations between TAM1 and CA in the predicted direction, with 30 of the 40 statistically significant. Similarly, as predicted, the relationship between predispositions toward verbal behavior was $-.20$, with 39 of the 40 correlations in the predicted direction, and 29 of the 40 samples reporting a statistically significant relationship.

Research has also shown that touch avoidance is negatively related to some dimensions of self-disclosure, suggesting a small but significant avoidance of intimate verbal communication (Andersen & Leibowitz, 1978). Both TAM1 and TAM2 showed significant negative correlations with positivity, and control of self-disclosure ranging from $-.16$ to $-.22$. Research on a similar construct indicated that openness (Norton, 1984) was negatively related to TAM2 scores (Andersen et al., 1987); results showed a significant relationship ($r = -.16$) but a small effect size ($r^2 = .03$).

CONCLUSION

The touch avoidance measure consists of two reliable and valid dimensions: avoidance of same-sex touch and avoidance of opposite-sex touch. The measure has been shown to predict interpersonal distance, reactions to touch, and actual touch behavior. Same-sex touch avoidance is generally higher among men than among women, whereas opposite-sex touch avoidance is higher among women than among men. It is associated negatively with self-concept, positive predispositions toward verbal behavior, openness, self-disclosure, intimacy, and living in the American culture. It is associated positively with age, Protestant religious training, femininity, communication apprehension, and Asian cultural orientation. Future research should utilize this measure as an index of relational well-being and satisfaction and other clinical applications.

REFERENCES

Andersen, J. F., Andersen, P. A., & Jensen, A. D. (1979). The measurement of nonverbal immediacy. *Journal of Applied Communication Research, 7,* 153–180.

Andersen, J. F., Andersen, P. A., & Lustig, M. W. (1987). Opposite-sex touch avoidance: A national replication and extension. *Journal of Nonverbal Behavior, 11,* 89–109.

Andersen, P. A. (1985). Nonverbal immediacy in interpersonal communication. In A. W. Siegman & S. Feldstein (Eds.), *Multichannel integrations of nonverbal behavior* (pp. 1–36). Hillsdale, NJ: Lawrence Erlbaum Associates.

Andersen, P. A., & Guerrero, L. K. (1998). The bright side of relational communication: Interpersonal warmth as a social emotion. In P. A. Andersen & L. K. Guerrero (Eds.), *Handbook of communication and emotion: Research, theory, applications and contexts* (pp. 303–324). San Diego, CA: Academic Press.

Andersen, P. A., & Leibowitz, K. (1978). The development and nature of the construct touch avoidance. *Environmental Psychology and Nonverbal Behavior, 3,* 89–106.

Andersen, P. A., Lustig, M. W., & Andersen, J. F. (1990). Changes in latitude, changes in attitude: The relationship between climate and interpersonal communication predispositions. *Communication Quarterly, 38,* 291–311.

Andersen, P. A., & Sull, K. K. (1985). Out of touch, out of reach: Tactile predispositions as predictors of interpersonal distance. *The Western Journal of Speech Communication, 49,* 57–72.

Crawford, C. B. (1994). Effects of sex and sex roles on avoidance of same- and opposite-sex touch. *Perceptual and Motor Skills, 79,* 107–112.

Eman, V. A., Dierks-Stewart, K. J., & Tucker, R. K. (1978, November). *Implications of sexual identity and sexually identified situations on nonverbal touch.* Paper presented at the annual meeting of the Speech Communication Association, Minneapolis, MN.

Frank, L. K. (1957) Tactile communication. *Genetic Psychology Monographs, 56,* 209–255.

Guerrero, L. K., & Andersen, P. A. (1991). The waxing and waning of relational intimacy: Touch as a function of relational stage, gender and touch avoidance. *Journal of Social and Personal Relationships, 8,* 147–165.

Guerrero, L. K., & Andersen, P. A. (1994). Patterns of matching and initiation: Touch behavior and avoidance across romantic relationship stages. *Journal of Nonverbal Behavior, 18,* 137–153.

Jourard, S. M. (1966). An exploratory study of body-accessibility. *British Journal of Social and Clinical Psychology, 5,* 221–231.

Jourard, S. M., & Rubin, J. E. (1968). Self-disclosure and touching: A study of two modes of interpersonal encounter and their inter-relation. *Journal of Humanistic Psychology, 8,* 39–48.

Larsen, K. S., & LeRoux, J. (1984). A study of same sex touching attitudes: Scale development and personality predictors. *The Journal of Sex Research, 20,* 264–278.

Leibowitz, K., & Andersen, P. A. (1976, December). *The development and nature of the construct touch avoidance.* Paper presented at the annual meeting of the Speech Communication Association, San Francisco, CA.

Lower, H. M. (1980). Fear of touching as a form of communication apprehension in professional nursing students. *Australian Scan: Journal of Human Communication, 7–8,* 71–78.

McCroskey, J. C. (1982). Oral communication apprehension: A reconceptualization. *Communication Yearbook, 6,* 136–170.

Mehrabian, A. (1971). *Silent messages.* Belmont, CA: Wadsworth.

Montagu, A. (1971). *Touching: The human significance of the skin.* New York: Columbia University Press.

Morris, D. (1971). *Intimate behavior.* New York: Random House.

Norton, R. (1984) *Communicator style: Theory, applications, and measures.* Beverly Hills, CA: Sage.

Remland, M. S., & Jones, T. S. (1988). Cultural and sex differences in touch avoidance. *Perceptual and Motor Skills, 67,* 544–546.

Sorensen, G., & Beatty, M. J. (1988). The interactive effects of touch and touch avoidance on interpersonal perceptions. *Communication Research Reports, 5,* 84–90.

APPENDIX

The Touch Avoidance Measure (TAM1 and TAM2)

DIRECTIONS: This instrument is composed of 18 statements concerning general feelings about touching other people and being touched. Please indicate the degree to which each statement applies to you by circling whether you: (1) Strongly Agree; (2) Agree; (3) Are Undecided; (4) Disagree; (5) Strongly Disagree with each statement. While some of these statements may seem repetitious, take your time and try to be as honest as possible.

sa	a	un	d	sd	
1	2	3	4	5	1. A hug from a same sex friend is a true sign of friendship.
1	2	3	4	5	2. Opposite sex friends enjoy it when I touch them.
1	2	3	4	5	3. I often put my arm around friends of the same sex.
1	2	3	4	5	4. When I see two people of the same sex hugging it revolts me.
1	2	3	4	5	5. I like it when members of the opposite sex touch me.
1	2	3	4	5	6. People shouldn't be so uptight about touching people of the same sex.
1	2	3	4	5	7. I think it is vulgar when members of the opposite sex touch me.
1	2	3	4	5	8. When a member of the opposite sex touches me I find it unpleasant.
1	2	3	4	5	9. I wish I were free to show emotions by touching members of the same sex.
1	2	3	4	5	10. I'd enjoy giving a message to an opposite sex friend.
1	2	3	4	5	11. I enjoy kissing a person of the same sex.
1	2	3	4	5	12. I like to touch friends that are the same sex as I am.
1	2	3	4	5	13. Touching a friend of the same sex does not make me uncomfortable.
1	2	3	4	5	14. I find it enjoyable when my date and I embrace.
1	2	3	4	5	15. I enjoy getting a back rub from a member of the opposite sex.
1	2	3	4	5	16. I dislike kissing relatives of the same sex.
1	2	3	4	5	17. Intimate touching with members of the opposite sex is pleasurable.
1	2	3	4	5	18. I find it difficult to be touched by a member of my own sex.

Touch Avoidance Scoring

1. Label each question as an A, B, X, or Y in this manner.

1=Y	10=B
2=B	11=Y
3=Y	12=Y
4=X	13=Y
5=B	14=B
6=Y	15=B
7=A	16=X
8=A	17=B
9=Y	18=X

2. Total your responses for all A questions, all B questions, all X questions, and all Y questions. This should give you a total A score, a total B score, a total Y score, and a total X score.

3. Plug those four scores into the following formula.

TAM 1= $15 + Y - X$ This is your same sex touch avoidance score
TAM 2= $10 + B - A$ This is your opposite sex touch avoidance score

The Touch Log Record:
A Behavioral Communication Measure

Stanley E. Jones
University of Colorado, Boulder

INTRODUCTION

Researchers have long known that touch is essential to the physical, psychological, and social development of young children (Bell & Ainsworth, 1972; Frank, 1957; Montagu, 1971; Spitz, 1946). Somewhat more recently, evidence has also accumulated to suggest that touch is important for humans throughout the life cycle. For example, research with adult populations shows that people generally desire to receive more touching than they believe they get (Mosby, 1978) and that touch is related to self-esteem (Silverman, Pressman, & Bartel, 1973) and to social self-confidence (Jones & Brown, 1996). Beyond early childhood, however, access to the touching people need and want depends on their abilities to use a complex code (Jones & Yarbrough, 1985), and studies reveal there are considerable individual differences in the mastery of such ability (e.g., Jones & Brown, 1996).

Despite widespread interest in this subject, the task of measuring touch-as-behavior in a way that is consistent with its complexity has proven to be daunting for scholars. In early studies, it was assumed routinely that people could recollect their touch experiences accurately, so paper-and-pencil measures were employed extensively (e.g., Andersen & Leibowitz, 1978; Deethardt & Hines, 1983; Jourard, 1966). Notably, Andersen and Leibowitz's (1978; Andersen, this volume) Touch Avoidance Measure (TAM) and Fromme et al.'s (1986) Touch Test have been shown to be good predictors of interpersonal distance, a behavior presumably related to inclinations toward touching (Andersen & Sull, 1985; Fromme et al., 1986, 1989). And the opposite-sex dimension of TAM has been found in a field observational study to correlate with touch among couples (Guerrero & Andersen, 1991). The degree to which such measures generally predict actual touching is not clear, however, and some authors have acknowledged that the touch questionnaire measures they have developed are designed not to test how people touch but rather how they feel about touch (Andersen, Andersen, & Lustig, 1987; Fromme et al., 1986).

The Touch Log Record

The method described here was designed to deal with the need for a behavioral communication measure that allows for the recording of detailed information about each event involving touch, facilitates the study of individual differences by providing samples of each person's touch experiences over time, and also permits the examination of trends across individuals. The log recording method (Jones & Yarbrough, 1985) meets these criteria. Specifically, the approach involves training study participants to record their own touch experiences over a series of days, using one of several standardized forms. A copy of the Touch Observation Form, utilized in the initial studies in this program of research, is found in the appendix. The most important advantage of this coding scheme is that it yields considerable information about each event, as inspection of the recording form shows. Although most of the items on the form are self-explanatory, a more detailed explanation of the content of each category can be found in Jones and Yarbrough (1985, pp. 22–24).

The chief disadvantages of the method are that it is labor intensive for participants, requiring that they be motivated to record events conscientiously, and that fairly extensive training in the use of the log form prior to recording activities is desirable. The motivational issue is dealt with in part by the administration of the training itself, which assures participants that they can record events competently. In addition, motivation can be enhanced by telling participants that they will learn a great deal about their own touch experiences by doing the recordings, a promise that was verified by the testimony of those who took part in the studies reported in this chapter. The training procedure involves explanation and demonstration of the items on the form, practice in making recordings based on viewing of a naturalistic documentary film of a family where numerous touches are observable (Family, produced by the N.I.H.; a similar type film can be used), and a field-based exercise in which participants make recordings for one day of their actual touches and return to a training session to discuss their experiences.

Validity and Reliability of the Log Method

Although the log record is a type of self-report measure, it is a self-report with a difference. As Stier and Hall (1984) noted, diary or log methods have greater face validity for the measurement of touch than do questionnaires because recordings are made immediately after each event. Although it is not feasible to follow each participant around in the field to check on the accuracy of his or her recordings, it is possible to test whether participants could use the form in a consistent manner, the assumption being that if judges were able to agree on recordings, their observations were probably accurate. In support of this, a study (Jones & Yarbrough, 1985) was conducted in which a separate sample of subjects received the explanation and demonstration of the items on the form, made some practice observations of touch incidents in the Family film, and then recorded observations of 19 additional touch incidents from the film. This last activity provided the data for the reliability study. The film was stopped after each observable touch to allow for recording. Only items that required technical training were tested for reliability across the subjects.

Results showed that agreement on the modal response in each category ranged from 90% to 100% for recordings of who initiated each touch, the timing of verbalizations (commencing before, during, or after the touch), and whether each touch was accepted or rejected. The lowest amount of agreement—69%—was found for type of touch, which involved judges making a choice out of a large number of possibilities (see item 8, subitems A–K). As for recordings of body parts touched, Pearson correlations were performed for randomly paired sets of judges on how many body parts were recorded for each incident; the correlations ranged from .91 to .98. In general, whereas this study does not assess whether participants in the field study were accurate in recording events, it does suggest that they were capable of using the coding form effectively.

One other study provided partial evidence for the test–retest reliability of log recordings (Jones, 1986). Eighteen males and nineteen females recorded touches for 2 days in similar (university) environs. Day-to-day reliability correlations ranged from .41 to .46—each significant beyond the .006 level—for a variety of indices of touch, including total touches, received touches, total opposite-sex touches, and touches initiated to the opposite sex. Only same-sex total and initiated touch reliabilities were low and nonsignificant, owing perhaps to the fact that quantities of same-sex touches were low.

Studies of Touch Meanings, Rules, Individual Differences, and Measures

The Touch Log Record method was utilized in each of the six studies described in the remainder of this chapter. Except where otherwise noted, the Touch Observation Form was employed.

Touch Meanings. The purpose of the first study (Jones & Yarbrough, 1985) was to discover meanings-in-context of touches reported in logs kept for a series of days by volunteers from university classes. Participants were instructed to select days when they expected to be with a variety of persons, and, by design, most people recorded incidents both in the school environment and at home during vacation periods. Over 1,500 touch incidents were reported.

The data were analyzed both qualitatively and quantitatively, using only those incidents where touches were accepted by the recipient and not repaired by an apology from the initiator. Initially, incidents were placed in separate categories based on apparent similarities of meanings, using the participants' translations of touches into verbal equivalents (item 6 on the recording form) as a guide, employing the constant comparative method of analysis (Glaser & Strauss, 1967), and resolving disagreements between the investigators by discussion and consensus. Behavioral and contextual factors associated with incidents within each meaning category were then compiled and counted. This established *key features:* those characteristics that would be present ordinarily for clear communication of the meaning (in at least 85% of the incidents), while also identifying subsets of incidents within each category in which certain combinations of factors conveyed a given meaning in a distinctive way.

The results showed that the type of touch and body parts involved were seldom sufficient to explain meanings. Rather, meanings were conveyed in "packages" of behavioral and situational factors. Ultimately, 12 rather distinct and unambiguous meanings or messages were identified: support, appreciation, sexual interest, affection, playful affection, playful aggression, compliance with requested action, attention-getting, announcing a response (requesting sharing of emotion), greetings, and departures. In addition, there were several kinds of *hybrid* touches, conveying two or more of these meanings at once, and four distinct but potentially *ambiguous* touches that could convey mixed messages (e.g., touching a body part or item of apparel and commenting on it, conveying possible liking or flirtation).

Touch Prohibitions.   In a second study, reported in Jones (1994), log records of touches that were either rejected by the recipient or repaired by an apology from the initiator were analyzed in order to discover informal prohibitive rules about touch. In a manner similar to the meanings-in-context study already described, incidents were placed initially in categories, this time according to the apparent rule that was violated by the touch, and judges' reliabilities for placement in categories were established. Behavioral and contextual features associated with each type of rule violation were calculated and compared with similar appearing incidents where no rejection or repair occurred in order to identify exceptional circumstances where a generally objectionable touch would be accepted. For example, most touches between strangers, even accidental contacts, were prohibited generally; but they were *permitted for certain purposes,* notably when strangers were being introduced to one another or when a minimal touch such as a brief attention-getter was used to request help from a stranger. In all, seven informal rules were identified.

In an additional study concerning prohibitive rules of touch, this time in the workplace and also reported in Jones (1994), a version of the Touch Observation Form was used as a recall measure. Business and professional people attending communication seminars were asked to recall details of incidents where they were the recipient of an objectionable touch in the workplace. Although it was a deviation from usual practice to ask participants to recall rather than to log incidents, a study with a separate sample had provided evidence that people can remember incidents involving rejected touches with more accuracy than cases of accepted touch (see Jones, 1994). Collected records of incidents were described in paragraph form on cards, which another separate sample of subjects was asked to group into categories according to the apparent similarities in the nature of the violations. These data were then cluster analyzed, while still another separate sample of subjects rated the degree of appropriateness or inappropriateness of each touch incident. The final product was the delineation of 10 rules or "taboos" of workplace touch, with a hierarchy of seriousness of violations established for four different groups of rule violations.

Sex Differences in Touch.   The purposes of a fourth study (Jones, 1986) were to test inferences about sex differences in touch drawn from previous studies that were based on questionnaire data and to supplement other available behavioral research on this topic (e.g., Willis & Rinck, 1983). Testing Henley's (1973) hypothesis—that males tend to initiate more touches in opposite-sex interactions than do females as a way of displaying their position of dominance—was a matter of special interest. Twenty males and twenty females logged their touch experiences for a series of days. Additional information on individual differences was also available from participant scores on the Predispositions toward Verbal Behavior (PVB) scale (Mortensen, Arntson, & Lustig, 1977) and the control dimension of Schutz's (1958) FIRO-B scale.

The findings that females reportedly engaged in more total touching than did males and that both males and females engaged in more opposite-sex than same-sex touches were not especially surprising. Of greater interest was the finding that women reported about twice as many opposite-sex touches per day as men, contrary to Henley's (1973) hypothesis. Furthermore, in a more direct test of the hypothesis, females were found to report engaging in more opposite-sex control touches than did males, with control touches defined as those requesting attention, action, or sharing of feelings by the other person. In supplemental analyses, it was also discovered that females who were more talkative (as measured on the PVB scale) and more control-oriented (as indicated on the FIRO-B scale) were more active initiators of touch. The results suggest that touch is one form of communication that is particularly likely to be used by women as a mode of influence.

Jourard's Body-Accessibility Questionnaire.   This study (Jones, 1991) was designed to test Jourard's assertion that his questionnaire is a behavioral measure of body accessibility (Jourard, 1966; Jourard & Rubin, 1968). The scale requires subjects to make eight different judgments, recollecting body parts they contacted and were touched on in interactions with four target persons: mother, father, best same-sex friend, and best opposite-sex friend. The method employed in Jones (1991) involved three stages of data collection, each separated by a 10-day interval. The 53 participants first filled out the body-accessibility questionnaire, anticipating contacts they would initiate and receive on a regular basis, then logged their touches for a 2-week period just before and during a vacation break. They then again completed the body-accessibility questionnaire, this time recalling the body parts contacted with each target person during the logging period. Data for analysis consisted of the total numbers of body parts anticipated, logged, or recalled. Correlations were computed for each of the eight initiation–reception/relationship categories across the three types of measures.

Positive and mostly significant correlations (ranging from .37 to .68) were found for log records and recalled touches and for recalled and anticipated touches. Correlations between log records and anticipated touches, although positive, were low (ranging from .08 to .21) and nonsignificant, however. Comparisons of the mean numbers of body parts reported showed that anticipated and recalled touch scores were quite similar and consistently higher than the log record scores, at a statistically significant level in most cases. Taken together, the findings suggest that recollections were tainted by how much contact was anticipated. Considering that the act of recording touches prior to recalling them would likely inflate accuracy of recall, the evidence for the validity of the body-accessibility questionnaire is not impressive. It was concluded that the scale is best regarded as a perceptual rather than a behavioral measure, reflecting beliefs about what amounts of contact with different target persons would be appropriate or perhaps desired.

Touch Measures and Social Self-Confidence.

The purpose of the final study reported here (Jones & Brown, 1996) was to examine relationships among four paper-and-pencil touch measures, log records, and an index of social self-confidence. In a preliminary session, 116 participants filled out Andersen and Leibowitz's (1978) Touch Avoidance Measure (TAM; see Andersen's chapter, this volume), Deethardt and Hines' (1983) TACTYPE measure, Fromme et al.'s (1986) Touch Test, a Recollection of Early Childhood Touch scale (see appendix) adapted from a previous measure by Gladney and Barker (1979), and a short form of Helmreich and Ervin's (1974) Texas Social Behavior Inventory (TSBI; Helmreich, Stapp, & Ervin, 1974), a behaviorally validated measure of social self-confidence. Participants then received training in the use of a shortened version of the Touch Observation Form (see appendix) and recorded their touches for a one-week period. Log record scores were calculated on a per-day average basis, as not all participants recorded for the full 7-day period.

The TAM, TACTYPE, and Touch Test measures, deemed to register attitudes toward touch, and also the childhood recollection measure, all correlated positively and significantly with one another (correlations ranging from .25 to .53). These paper-and-pencil tests were, however, generally not predictive of quantities of actual touch as indicated in the log records. The log record and three of the questionnaire measures (excluding the TACTYPE scale), on the other hand, each correlated positively and significantly with the TSBI measure ($r = .35$ for logs, .23 to .29 for questionnaires). A series of listwise regression analyses, pitting each of the three questionnaires against log records, revealed that both kinds of measures make separate contributions to the prediction of social self-confidence. Jones and Brown

(1996) concluded that, whereas touch questionnaires primarily measure attitudes rather than behaviors, both liking for touch and active touching are associated with self-esteem in social situations.

CONCLUSIONS

The various studies reported here demonstrate the distinctiveness of the touch log record as compared with other self-report measures in providing a behavioral index of touch. It is also suggested that this measure has some advantages over other behavioral approaches in that it can be used to trace individual differences in touch over time and that it yields rich information about communication incidents involving touch, some information not being readily ascertainable by a nonparticipant observer. A simpler version of the recording form could be used in studies where only frequencies of touch are of interest, although the more complex versions allow checking on how conscientiously study participants appear to have recorded information, and *post hoc* analyses on a variety of dimensions are also possible with the more complete record.

The Recollection of Early Childhood Touch scale presented here (see appendix) has also acceptable internal reliability (Jones & Brown, 1996), has not been published before, and may be useful to scholars interested in this subject. Like other touch questionnaires, it may reflect attitudes or wishes about touch rather than actual behaviors experienced, and validation with behavioral criteria does not seem feasible. Nevertheless, Jones and Brown have suggested that the "stimulated recall" methodology might be applied just after respondents have completed the questionnaire to assess whether they rely in their answers on visualizations of early experiences or general feelings about warmth expressed by caretakers. This approach might shed light on the validity of the measure as an index of remembrances of early touch experiences.

REFERENCES

Andersen, J. F., Andersen, P. A., & Lustig, M. W. (1987). Opposite-sex touch avoidance: A national replication and extension. *Journal of Nonverbal Behavior, 11*, 89–109.

Andersen, P. A., & Leibowitz, K. (1978). The development and nature of the construct touch avoidance. *Environmental Psychology and Nonverbal Behavior, 3*, 89–106.

Andersen, P. A., & Sull, K. K. (1985). Out of touch, out of reach: Tactile predispositions as predictors of interpersonal distance. *Western Journal of Speech Communication, 49*, 57–72.

Bell, S. M., & Ainsworth, M. D. S. (1972). Infant crying and maternal responsiveness. *Child Development, 43*, 1171–1190.

Deethardt, J. F., & Hines, D. (1983). Tactile communication and personality differences. *Journal of Nonverbal Behavior, 8*, 143–156.

Frank, L. K. (1957). Tactile communication. *Genetic Psychology Monographs, 56*, 209–255.

Fromme, D. K., Fromme, M. L., Brown, S., Daniell, J., Taylor, D. K., & Rountree, J. R. (1986). Attitudes toward touch: Cross-validation and the effects of gender and acquaintanceship. *Rassengna di Psicologia, 3*, 49–63.

Fromme, D. K., Jaynes, W. E., Taylor, D. K., Hanold, E. G., Daniell, J., Rountree, J. R., & Fromme, M. L. (1989). Nonverbal behavior and attitudes toward touch. *Journal of Nonverbal Behavior, 13*, 3–14.

Gladney, K., & Barker, L. (1979). The effects of tactile history on attitudes toward and frequency of touching behavior. *Sign Language Studies, 24,* 231–252.

Glaser, B. G., & Strauss, A. L. (1967). *The discovery of grounded theory: Strategies for qualitative research.* Chicago: Aldine.

Guerrero, L. K., & Andersen, P. A. (1991). The waxing and waning of relational intimacy: Touch as a function of relational stage, gender and touch avoidance. *Journal of Social and Personal Relationships, 8,* 147–165.

Helmreich, R., & Stapp, J. (1974). The Texas social behavior inventory (TSBI): An objective measure of self-esteem or social competence. *Journal Supplement Abstract Service. Catalog of Selected Documents in Psychology, 4,* 79.

Helmreich, R., Stapp, J., & Ervin, C. (1974). Short forms of the Texas social behavior inventory (TSBI): An objective measure of self-esteem. *Bulletin of the Psychonomic Society, 4,* 473–475.

Henley, N. M. (1973). Status and sex: Some touching observations. *Bulletin of the Psychonomic Society, 2,* 91–83.

Jones, S. E. (1986). Sex differences in touch communication. *Western Journal of Speech Communication, 50,* 227–241.

Jones, S. E. (1991). Problems of validity in questionnaire studies of nonverbal behavior: Jourard's tactile body-accessibility scale. *Southern Communication Journal, 56,* 83–95.

Jones, S. E. (1994). *The right touch: Understanding and using the language of physical contact.* Cresskill, NJ: Hampton Press.

Jones, S. E., & Brown, B. C. (1996). Touch attitudes and behaviors, recollections of early childhood touch, and social self-confidence. *Journal of Nonverbal Behavior, 20,* 147–163.

Jones, S. E., & Yarbrough, A. E. (1985). A naturalistic study of the meanings of touch. *Communication Monographs, 52,* 19–56.

Jourard, S. M. (1966). An exploratory study of body-accessibility. *British Journal of Social and Clinical Psychology, 5,* 221–231.

Jourard, S. M., & Rubin, J. E. (1968). Self-disclosure and touching: A study of two modes of interpersonal encounter and their inter-relation. *Journal of Humanistic Psychology, 8,* 39–48.

Mortensen, C. D., Arntson, P. H., & Lustig, M. (1977). The measurement of verbal predispositions: Scale development and application. *Human Communication Research, 3,* 146–158.

Montagu, M. F. A. (1971). *Touching: The human significance of the skin.* New York: Columbia University Press.

Mosby, K. D. (1978). *An analysis of actual and ideal touching behavior as reported on a modified version of the body accessibility questionnaire.* Unpublished doctoral dissertation, Virginia Commonwealth University, Richmond, VA.

Schutz, W. C. (1958). *FIRO-B: A three dimensional theory of interpersonal behavior.* New York: Rinehart.

Silverman, A. F., Pressman, M. E., & Bartel, H. W. (1973). Self-esteem and tactile communication. *Journal of Humanistic Psychology, 13,* 73–77.

Spitz, R. A. (1946). Anaclitic depression. *Psychoanalytic Study of the Child, 2,* 313–342.

Stier, D. S., & Hall, J. A. (1984). Gender differences in touch: An empirical and theoretical review. *Journal of Personality and Social Psychology, 47,* 440–459.

Willis, F. N., & Rinck, C. M. (1983). A personal log method for investigating interpersonal touch. *Journal of Psychology, 113,* 119–122.

APPENDIX

TOUCH OBSERVATION FORM

Name _____ Date _____

Use arrows to link entries which are part
of the same interaction. Ex. 1.
                               2.

Indicate where applicable: BM—Best Male Friend;
BF—Best Female Friend; MO—Mother; FA—Father

1.
Initiator of touch
A. Me
B. Other
C. Mutual
D. Unclear
(1 letter)

1. ____
2. ____
3. ____

2a.
*Parts of body when ini-
tiated*
(1 or more letters @
blank: note 2-handed
touches)
Initiator / Receiver
touched / touched
with: / on:

2b.
*Parts of body when mu-
tual or unclear*
(1 or more letters per
blank)
Me: / Other:

3.
Place
A. Mine
B. Other's
C. Neutral
(Specify bldg. and
room)

4.
Time of day
(Include a.m. or
p.m.)

5.
Accompanying verbal statement
(Paraphrase if necessary)
When:
A. Immediately prior to touch
B. Immediately after touch
C. During
By: (M) Me; (O) Other

1. ____
2. ____
3. ____

6.
*Touch translated into verbal state-
ment*
(Make into short sentence if possible;
note voice tone or facial expression if
critical to meaning)

7.
(Mark "Psych" for touches you reject
internally only)
Acceptance/Rejection
A. Touch accepted by me
B. Touch rejected by me
C. Touch accepted by other
D. Touch rejected by other
(Spec. with letter; explain how & why
t. is rejected)

1. ____
2. ____
3. ____

8.
Type of touch
A. Caressing / holding
B. Feeling / Caressing
C. Prolonged holding
D. Holding / pressing ag.
E. Spot touching
F. Accidental brushing
G. Handshake
H. Pat I. Squeeze J. Punch
K. Pinch L. Other
(1 or more letters)

1.
2.
3.

9.
Purpose of participants
A. Give / get info (spec.)
B. Ask / give favor
C. Persuading
D. Persuaded
E. Casual talk
F. Deeptalk
G. Greeting
H. Departing
I. Any other (specify)
Me   Other

1.
2.
3.

10.
Others present
(Male & / or female)
(Specify relation to you us-
ing letters from Category
11)

11.
Relationship to other
A. Relative (spec.)
B1. Close Friend
B2. Not close friend
C. Acquaintance
D. Co-worker
E. Superior
F. Subordinate
G. Stranger
H. Other (spec.)
Spec. if intimate

12.
*Nature of social occa-
sion*
A. Work
B. Class
C. Party
D. Informal meeting
E. Other (spec.)
For public places, spec-
ify function (bar, etc.)

1.
2.
3.

13.
Status of other
A. Higher 1. Formal
B. Lower 2. Informal
C. Equal
(1 letter and 1 no.)

1.
2.
3.

14.
Age of other
(Approximate)

15.
Sex of other
(M / F)

16.
Race of other
A. Anglo
B. Black
C. Chicano
D. Asian
E. Other (spec)

17.
Standing or sitting
Me: Other:

1.
2.
3.

18.
Any other contextual factors you think influenced your touches:

77

Touch Observation Short Form

<u>TOUCH CHART</u>   <u>DATE:</u>_____

LAST 4 DIGITS OF STUDENT #:_____

Initials or name of other_____   OR name unknown_____
                                   Recorded touch previously for
                                   this person: YES NO

CHECK ONE:
____A. One touch   ____B. Multiple touches (consecutive)
                # of people:_____

INITIATED TOUCH: **TYPE OF RELATIONSHIP:**
                            (check one or more)
____A. Me   ____A. Intimate(s)
____B. Other   ____B. Close friend(s)
____C. Mutual   ____C. Friend(s)
____D. Accidental   ____D. Acquaintance(s)
____E. Combination ____E. Stranger(s)
     (indicate above)   ____F. Relative(s)

SEX OF OTHER(S):   _____Male   _____Female

DESCRIBE BODY PART(S) CONTACTED ON EACH PERSON:
         YOU: _____

_____

         OTHER:_____

_____

TOUCH WAS: (circle one)   Accepted   Rejected

TYPE OF TOUCH:
___A. Frontal hug   ___E. Holding hands   ___L. Pat
___B. Side hug   ___F. Hold   ___J. Punch
___C. Caress/feel   ___G. Spot touch   ___K. Other:(specify):
___D. Kiss   ___H. Handshake   _____

TOUCH WAS: (check one or more)
____A. Comforting   ____F.Accidental
____B. Friendly   ___G. Exclamatory ("be happy with me")
____C. Togetherness   ___H. Persuasive
___D. Playful   ____I. Other meaning (provide own
____E. Flirtatious   translation):

CONTEXT:

____PUBLIC (mall, party, school, work, etc.)
____PRIVATE (home, friends house, etc.)

Touch Observation Short Form Instructions

INSTRUCTIONS FOR FILLING OUT TOUCH CHART:
*(These are for you to refer to if you have a problem filling out one of the categories on the chart).
*(Each stapled packet contains 10 charts, be sure to take at least two with you per day incase you need extras).
(1). REMEMBER to make note of the DATE and the LAST 4 DIGITS of your student #.
(2). EXCLUDE touches leading to sexual intimacy.
(3). INITIATOR: whoever approaches or touches first
    MUTUAL: if approach or touch at same time
(4). AREAS CONTACTED: parts of each person contacted; hand/hand, shoulder/hand, hand/thigh, knee/knee, etc.
(5). REJECTION: one/both person pulls back, negative response
(6). MEANINGS OF TOUCH:
    A. Comforting: reassuring, trying to make person feel better when hurt or troubled.
    B. Friendly: greeting, departure, affectionate, thanks
    C. Togetherness: continuous touch: "we are together" "I'm enjoying being with you", etc.
    D. Playful: joking with touch; mock hugs, etc.; mock fighting or "I was only kidding."
    E. Flirtatious: touching to imply attraction or sexual interest
    F. Accidental: brushes, light bumps, etc; unintentional.
    G. Exclamatory: touching to express a feeling-"you made a clever remark", "I'm surprised",etc; complement or comment on appearance "Nice shirt", etc.; congratulating or mutual congratulations-handslap, etc.
    H. Persuasive(influencing): touching to get someone to do something; get attention; or influence an attitude or feeling, e.g., "I'm excited-get excited too!" ,"Be happy with me".
(7). PUBLIC: restaurants, bars, school, street, does not allow for privacy, intimacy, etc.
    PRIVATE: home, apartment, etc.

Recollections of Early Childhood Touch Scale

Directions:

Using the following five categories (0–4), please estimate the amount of touch you remember engaging in as a child, from earliest recollection (probably age 4–5, perhaps early primary grades). Please read each statement carefully and take sufficient time to recall past events or get a clear image of a touch which occurred before responding. Strive for as accurate an estimate as possible.

The five categories have been defined as follows:
0   Cannot ever recall event occurring
1   Recall event occurring, but not regularly
2   Occasionally, from time to time with some regularity
3   Occurred regularly, but not daily or nightly
4   Occurred with regularity, almost every day or every night.

For each statement answer accordingly for both principle female caretaker and principle male caretaker. In most cases this would be the mother and father. However, in instances of death, travel, divorce, parent living in different home, etc., the principle male and/or female caretaker may be a nanny, relative living in the home, older brother or sister, stepparent, etc. The principle caretaker for each gender needs to be the individual you had the closest contact with and who lived in the home during your early childhood. If there was no male or female caretaker please leave those parts of the answers blank and indicate yes or no on the line below.

Principle male caretaker _____
Principle female caretaker _____

1. Caretaker kissed or hugged you goodnight at bedtime.

| Female | 0 | 1 | 2 | 3 | 4 |
| Male | 0 | 1 | 2 | 3 | 4 |

2. Engaged in play activities involving touch with caretaker (wrestling, jostling, patty cake, etc.).

| Female | 0 | 1 | 2 | 3 | 4 |
| Male | 0 | 1 | 2 | 3 | 4 |

3. Caretaker kissed or hugged you when he/she returned home from a brief absence of a day or less (home, work, etc.).

Female	0	1	2	3	4
Male	0	1	2	3	4

4. Caretaker gave you a back rub or other soothing touch while you were going to sleep.

Female	0	1	2	3	4
Male	0	1	2	3	4

5. Sat in caretaker's lap while doing some activity (watching TV, reading, talking, etc.).

Female	0	1	2	3	4
Male	0	1	2	3	4

6. Caretaker kissed or hugged you before you left for school or a day outing.

Female	0	1	2	3	4
Male	0	1	2	3	4

7. Caretaker held your hand while out in public places (shopping, etc.).

Female	0	1	2	3	4
Male	0	1	2	3	4

8. Caretaker laid down and held you when you were going to sleep.

Female	0	1	2	3	4
Male	0	1	2	3	4

9. Caretaker tickled you.

Female	0	1	2	3	4
Male	0	1	2	3	4

10. Caretaker would pick you up and hold you while involved in some activity (talking on the phone, light household work, talking with visitor, etc.).

Female	0	1	2	3	4
Male	0	1	2	3	4

Measuring Live Tactile Interaction: The Body Chart Coding Approach

Peter A. Andersen
San Diego State University

Laura K. Guerrero
Arizona State University

INTRODUCTION

Of the five human senses, touch develops first (Montagu, 1978). Perhaps this is why touch is essential for emotional and psychological well-being. Early research conducted in orphanages suggests that if babies do not receive adequate amounts of touch, they are at risk for both physical and psychological problems (Montagu, 1978; Spitz, 1946). More recent research suggests that children who receive an abundance of positive touch likely grow up to be warm, affectionate, and self-confident adults (Burgoon, Buller, & Woodall, 1996; Jones, 1994; Jones & Brown, 1996; Weiss, 1990) and that touch has health benefits such as reducing stress, eliciting positive emotion, and lowering blood pressure for adults (Fanslow, 1990; Reite, 1990).

Tactile communication also plays an important role in developing and maintaining various types of relationships. As Andersen (1999) put it:

> The embrace of a close friend, the stroke of a lover's hand, the firm handshake of a business associate, and the warm hug of a family member in a time of bereavement all communicate with an intensity that other forms of communication lack. Perhaps no mode of human interaction has the same potential to communicate love, warmth, and intimacy as actual body contact. (pp. 45–46)

Of course, touch can also convey powerful *negative* messages through behaviors such as hitting, pushing someone away, or inappropriately touching someone (see Jones, this volume).

83

As a powerful—physically and emotionally—and important form of communication, tactile interaction is certainly worthy of scholarly attention. Yet touch is difficult to measure. If a researcher asks, people to tell him or her how much touch they use, they may be able to give the researcher a rough estimate, but they are unlikely to remember exactly how many times they touched someone or were touched during a given interaction. In addition, simply counting the number of times touch occurs only provides a partial glimpse into the nature of tactile interaction. Being able to pinpoint body location in addition to frequency provides a more complete picture. The body chart system discussed in this chapter was designed to measure frequency, location, and, to a lesser extent, duration of touch. Before discussing our body chart system, we turn to a discussion of other related methods.

APPROACHES TO MEASURING TACTILE INTERACTION

Aside from utilizing observations of actual tactile interaction, researchers most often use one of two disparate operationalizations of touch. First, they use self-report measures of actual touch such as Jourard's (1966) widely reported body accessibility scale. Second, researchers employ self-reports of attitudes toward touch.

Self-Reports of Behavior

A quick and easy way to collect data on nonverbal interaction is for subjects to self-report the behaviors they engage in across or within various situations and relationships. The two most widely reported self-report measures of tactile behavior are body accessibility measures (e.g., Jourard, 1966) and projective and quasi-projective techniques of measuring proxemic behavior ranging from tactile contact through a range of interpersonal distances. Unfortunately, the two most widely used self-report methods of tactile behavior provide poor indices of actual behavior and have never been successfully validated using actual tactile interaction (for discussion, see Jones, 1991; Jones & Aiello, 1979).

Jourard's (1966) body accessibility measure consists of a series of questions asking subjects to recall where certain significant others (mother, father, closest same-sex friend, closest opposite-sex friends) touched them. This measure is widely reported in many textbooks on nonverbal communication and was cited by other researchers 72 times between 1972 and 1990 (see Jones, 1991). Unfortunately, not a single one of those studies ever reported validity data such as a correlation between the body accessibility measure and actual tactile interaction. Similarly, projective measures such a diagram and felt-boards are poorly correlated with actual tactile and proxemic behavior (Jones & Aiello, 1979) and thus are not valid measures of actual spatial or tactile behavior.

Self-Reports of Attitudes

Although self-reports are not a very valid index of actual behavior, they are the preferred method for measuring attitudes and other internal cognitive states. Measures of attitudes toward touch such as Andersen's (this volume) touch avoidance measure are highly predictive of behavior but a poor choice in representing behavior itself. For example, whereas the touch avoidance measure is highly correlated with interpersonal distance, reactions to being touched, and touch itself (Andersen, this volume), it is a much better measure of tactile attitudes than of touch behavior.

Diary Studies

Greater success has been obtained with diary studies, which correlate reasonably well with actual tactile behavior (Jones, 1994, this volume; Jones & Yarborough, 1985). Participants are asked to complete a diary recalling their recent touch behavior after a fixed period of time, usually once or more per day. One of the major advantages of this approach is that it is perhaps the best method of obtaining data on private and sexual touch that is not observable readily. Although respondents learn to be fairly accurate in recording these recollections, the diary method still does not measure actual tactile behavior directly. Two types of forgetting occur in diary studies: failure to remember to record the data and inaccuracies regarding the actual tactile behavior in which they engaged. Moreover, as Jones and Yarborough (1985) pointed out, diaries do not permit detailed inspection of the actual behaviors that are available in videotaped tactile interactions (but see Jones, this volume, for other advantages of the diary method).

Videotaped Interaction

A good method of recording actual tactile behavior is to make a videotape of interaction. For example, Guerrero (1996, 1997) had dyads report to a research laboratory where they were told they would be videotaped while talking about a commonly discussed conversational topic. Later, a variety of nonverbal behaviors were coded from the videotapes, including touch frequency and touch duration. This method affords the researcher a great degree of control. For instance, in Guerrero's studies, the environment (a comfortable living-room type setting) and the length of interaction were constant across all interactions. Videotaping in a research laboratory also allows the researcher to control camera settings so that behaviors can easily be seen. In addition, coders can rewind videotapes if they are unsure about the number, duration, and location of any particular touch, which increases their coding or rating accuracy.

Despite these advantages, videotaping in laboratory settings has two major drawbacks. First, when participants are aware of videotaping, they may alter their behavior or perform for the camera. Second, and relatedly, the artificiality of the environment may lead to unnatural behavior. Although these concerns are lessened by employing strategies such as creating a comfortable environment and having participants engage in familiar activities and/or talk about frequently discussed topics, laboratory observations are certainly less ecologically valid than are unobtrusive field observations.

From both a pragmatic and an ethical standpoint, however, unobtrusive video-taping is problematic in most field settings. In many field settings it is nearly impossible to obtain unobtrusive data on videotape because people are constantly moving, making it difficult to adjust the camera without being noticed. If the camera is placed in a corner where it is less likely to be seen, the researcher cannot control who and what types of behavior are captured on videotape. Furthermore, ethics require a challenging process of obtaining consent either before or after the taping occurs. If consent is obtained before videotaping, the observations are no longer unobtrusive with people possibly altering their behavior because they know they are being taped. If consent is obtained after videotaping, the researcher risks having to destroy data that have been collected and introduces bias into the observed sample (i.e., only some participants' tapes will be analyzed).

Live coding of tactile interaction provides an avenue of data collection that is unobtrusive and ethical. Human subjects boards typically do not require researchers to secure subject consent when making pen-and-paper observations of behavior that are clearly visible in public settings. Without videotaping, subjects are anonymous and do not perform for the camera. Instead, they are observed during natural interaction in the field. Thus, although this method affords less control than laboratory observations, live coding of tactile behavior in the field provides ecologically valid data (see Patterson's chapter, this volume, for an approach to studying gaze and face in the field).

THE BODY CHART APPROACH

To obtain a system for real-time coding of tactile interaction in the field, Andersen, Guerrero, and Andersen created the body chart approach. This approach has been used successfully in a series of studies to obtain reliable and valid data on touch in live human interaction and in an unobtrusive manner. Indeed, across a series of studies all subjects who were approached after data collection reported being unaware that they had been observed.[1]

The Procedure

To use this procedure, two trained coders are stationed in an unobtrusive location. In Guerrero and Andersen's (1991, 1994) studies, subjects were observed in theater lines through a window from inside a fast food restaurant and in bus lines at the zoo from a roof-top restaurant. In studies conducted at airports (which, in recent years, has become restricted) researchers observed tactile departure rituals (McDaniel & Andersen, 1998) or tactile greeting rituals (Sjoberg, Townsley, & Andersen, 1996) from unobtrusive areas near airport gates, jetways, or at screening points.

---

[1]The body chart system was developed in conjunction with Laura Guerrero's master's thesis at San Diego State University, which was directed by Peter and Janis Andersen. The idea of using body charts was first offered by Janis Andersen. Laura Guerrero and Peter Andersen then refined the mechanics of using the charts for research.

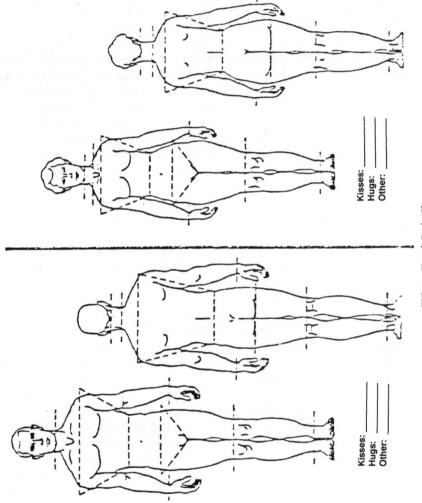

Kisses: _____
Hugs: _____
Other: _____

Kisses: _____
Hugs: _____
Other: _____

FIG. 1   Touch Body Chart.

87

Once a couple is identified, touch is recorded for a period of time, usually 2 minutes, on body charts that show 13 areas of the human body (see Fig. 1). The two coders record touch in 10-second intervals. A third member of the team indicates each 10-second interval verbally. Two spaces for mutual touches, including mutual hugs and mutual kisses, are also included on the coding form. In Guerrero and Andersen's (1991, 1994) studies, touch that was sustained for more than 10 seconds received a second tally in that area of the chart. Therefore, along with recording the body location where touch occurred, both the duration and frequency of touch were taken into account.

For example, if a couple held hands for the entire 2 minutes of observation, they would receive 12 tally marks on each of their body charts, one for each 10 seconds they touched. By contrast, if a woman briefly touched her husband's arm twice and he put his arm around her waist for 18 seconds, the pair would receive four tally marks, one for each of the wife's discrete touches and two for the husband's more prolonged touch. All of the first couple's touches would be marked as mutual touches in the hand area. For the second couple, two tally marks would be placed in the arm region of the husband's body chart, and two tally marks would be placed in the waist region of the wife's body chart.

Reliability and Validity

Reliability data suggest that trained undergraduates can accurately assess live tactile interaction. For the aggregate data on total touch behavior, interrater reliability has been extremely high, ranging from above .99 (Guerrero & Andersen, 1991, 1994) to .88 (Sjoberg et al., 1996). Reliability coefficients can be computed for each of the 13 areas and are equally impressive ranging from a low of .90 for the neck to a high of 1.0 for the head (Andersen & Guerrero, 1991, 1994). Given the high level of reliability obtained in these early studies, McDaniel and Andersen (1998) had teams of two observers work collaboratively to record live tactile behavior, and their results replicated earlier findings.

Some evidence also points to the validity of the body chart approach. For example, if this approach yields valid data, we might expect there to be at least a small correlation between attitudes toward touch and actual tactile behavior as recorded using the body charts. Indeed, research shows that touch avoidance (i.e., a negative disposition toward touch) shares a significant inverse relationship with actual touch behavior as recorded using this system (Guerrero & Andersen, 1991). Evidence for convergent validity also comes from studies showing that data collected using self-report measures (Emmers & Dinida, 1995) and other forms of observational coding (Willis & Briggs, 1992) produce similar findings to those found using the body chart approach. For example, results from Emmers and Dindia (1995) and Guerrero and Andersen (1991) suggest that there is a curvilinear relationship between touch and relationship development, such that touch is used most frequently in escalating (rather than casual or fully committed) relationships. Results from both Willis and Briggs (1992) and Guerrero and Andersen (1994) suggest that men tend to touch more in the beginning stages of relationships, whereas women tend to touch more in married relationships. These and other findings, which are elaborated on next, also demonstrate the predictive validity of the body chart approach.

Salient Findings

Studies employing the body chart have produced a series of interesting findings that both have significance for communication theory and demonstrate the validity of the body chart methods. Perhaps the most significant finding is that touch shows a curvilinear relationship with relational stage such that opposite-sex touch is lower in the beginning and long-term stages of a relationship and peaks at the intermediate stages. This finding has been reported in studies of theatre and zoo lines (Guerrero & Andersen, 1991) and in studies of international airline departures for an intercultural sample from 26 nations (McDaniel & Andersen, 1998). As noted previously, the curvilinear nature of touch across relational stages has also been successfully replicated for private touch using self-report methodology (Emmers & Dindia, 1995).

Perhaps the second most important finding is that touch in relationships is highly reciprocal. Andersen and Guerrero (1994) reported an intracouple correlation in tactile behavior of .89 in theatre and zoo lines, and Sjoberg et al. (1996) reported a .71 intracouple correlation in tactile behavior during airport greetings. A related finding is that romantic partners appear to engage in increasingly similar amounts of touch as their relationships develop. Guerrero and Andersen (1994) reported that even casually dating couples show a high level ($r = .81$) of tactile reciprocity, that seriously dating couples show an even higher level ($r = .88$) of tactile reciprocity, and married couples show extremely high ($r = .98$) levels of tactile reciprocity. This high level of tactile reciprocity suggests that relational partners may select each other on the basis of similarity in tactile behavior and that the relationship may be a more important generator of behavior than personality or situation.

A third important finding from body chart studies is that substantial cultural differences exist in public touch. Based on their observations of couples departing at an airline terminal for international flights, McDaniel and Andersen (1998) found that nationality explained 50% of the variance in tactile behavior. Contrary to prior findings, people from the United States exhibited relatively high levels of public touch. Consistent with other research (see Andersen, 1999), Asians, particularly northeast Asians, exhibited extremely little public touch.

Fourth, the finding that sex differences in touch are moderated by relational stage is important. Rather than simply finding that men touch more than women in relationships, or conversely, that women touch more than men in relationships, Guerrero and Andersen (1994) noted that men touched more in casually dating relationships, whereas women touched more than men in marriages. This finding, which corroborated Willis and Briggs's (1992) earlier results, shed light on some of the inconsistencies found in past research. Men may touch more in the initial stages of a relationship because they are taught to be more sexually assertive than women and because they are expected to "make the first move" (Blumstein & Schwartz, 1983; Byers, 1996). Women may touch more in marriages because they are taught, generally, to be more relationally oriented than are men and therefore may use touch as a way to show intimacy and maintain the relationship (Guerrero & Andersen, 1994).

Finally, data from body chart studies suggest some new findings regarding location of public touch for opposite-sex dyads. First and surprisingly, contact with virtually every area of the body has been observed in each of studies discussed here. For example, in Guerrero and Andersen's (1991) study, touch on the buttocks was observed in 13.5% of couples in the initial relational stage and by 16.4% in the intermediate relational stage. Although we may not notice it during normal public behavior, couples do touch highly intimate areas of the body. Additionally and perhaps less surprisingly, location of public touch interacts with relational stage for touch in some areas of the body such that most touching of the hands and waist occurs in intermediate relational stages. Touch on the buttocks and shoulder shows a different pattern with no difference in initial and intermediate stages but a significant decline in these locations of touch in long-term relationships. These findings underscore the importance of location of touch as well as type, frequency, and duration.

CONCLUSION

The body chart approach to coding tactile communication has produced some interesting findings and has been shown to be a reliable and valid method for studying live tactile interaction. The method takes into account body location, frequency, and duration of touch. Because the approach uses duration to modify gross frequency counts, this system is most appropriate when researchers are interested in obtaining an overall estimate of the level of touch that occurs during a given interaction. However, the system can be modified somewhat depending on a researcher's focus. For example, researchers who are interested in pinpointing the number of discrete touches that occur can use the system without incorporating duration. In this case, relational partners who held hands during an entire 2-minute interaction would only receive one tally mark in the hand region of their body charts. Researchers who are interested in pinpointing the duration of touch could time the length of touches and put these times in the appropriate places on the body chart.

Other aspects of touch are not incorporated into the body chart approach. For example, the intensity of touch may be important to consider. Gently squeezing a relational partner's arm is obviously very different from pinching her or his arm. The function of the touch is also important. Was the couple holding hands to show affection, or was one person leading the other person somewhere? Finally, the instrument of touch can make a difference. Did the wife touch her husband's knee with her hand, a pen, or her foot? Or did she rest her head on his knee? Researchers interested in these facets of touch would need to rely on more detailed descriptions than the body touch system supplies.

Nonetheless, the body chart coding system is a particularly helpful approach for coding live interaction in public settings. When researchers want to record naturally occurring touch behavior in the field, and when they are interested in obtaining a good overall measure of the level of touch occurring in a given interaction or situation, the body chart coding system presents a viable option for operationalizing touch.

REFERENCES

Andersen, P. A. (1999). *Nonverbal communication: Forms and functions.* Mountain View, CA: Mayfield.

Blumstein, P., & Schwartz, P. (1983). *American couples: Money, work, sex.* New York: Morrow.

Burgoon, J. K., Buller, D. B., & Woodall, W. G. (1996). *Nonverbal communication: The unspoken dialogue* (2nd ed.). New York: McGraw-Hill.

Byers, E. S. (1996). How well does the traditional sexual script explain sexual coercion? Review of a program of research. *Journal of Psychology and Human Sexuality, 8,* 7–25.

Emmers, T. M., & Dindia, K. (1995). The effect of relational stage and intimacy on touch: An extension of Guerrero and Andersen. *Personal Relationships, 2,* 225–236.

Fanslow, C. A. (1990). Touch and the elderly. In K. E. Barnard & B. T. Brazelton (Eds.), *Touch: The foundation of experience* (pp. 541–557). Madison, CT: International Universities Press.

Guerrero, L. K. (1996). Attachment-style differences in intimacy and involvement: A test of the four-category model. *Communication Monographs, 63,* 269–292.

Guerrero, L. K. (1997). Nonverbal involvement across interactions with same-sex friends, opposite-sex friends, and romantic partners: Consistency or change? *Journal of Social and Personal Relationships, 14,* 31–59.

Guerrero, L. K., & Andersen, P. A. (1991). The waxing and waning of relational intimacy: Touch as a function of relational stage, gender and touch avoidance. *Journal of Social and Personal Relationships, 8,* 147–165.

Guerrero, L. K., & Andersen, P. A. (1994). Patterns of matching and initiation: Touch behavior and avoidance across romantic relationship stages. *Journal of Nonverbal Behavior, 18,* 137–153.

Jones, S. E. (1991). Problems of validity in questionnaire studies of nonverbal behavior: Jourard's tactile body-accessibility scale. *Southern Communication Journal, 56,* 83–95.

Jones, S. E. (1994). *The right touch: Understanding and using the language of physical contact.* Cresskill, NJ: Hampton Press.

Jones, S. E., & Aiello, J. R. (1979). A test of the validity of projective and quasi-projective measures of interpersonal distance. *Western Journal of Speech Communication, 43,* 143–152.

Jones, S. E., & Brown, B. C. (1996). Touch attitudes and touch behaviors: Recollections of early childhood touch and social self-confidence. *Journal of Nonverbal Behavior, 20,* 147–163.

Jones, S. E., & Yarbrough, E. (1985). A naturalistic study of the meanings of touch. *Communication Monographs, 52,* 19–56.

Jourard, S. M. (1966). An exploratory study of body-accessibility. *British Journal of Social and Clinical Psychology, 5,* 221–231

McDaniel, E., & Andersen, P. A. (1998) Intercultural patterns of tactile communication: A field study. *Journal of Nonverbal Behavior, 22,* 59–76.

Montagu, A. (1978). *Touching: The human significance of the skin.* New York: Harper & Row.

Reite, M. (1990). Touch, attachment, and health: Is there a relationships? In K. E. Barnard & B. T. Brazelton (Eds.), *Touch: The foundation of experience* (pp. 195–225). Madison, CT: International Universities Press.

Sjoberg, S. L., Townsley, N., & Andersen, P. A. (1996, February). *Touch, relational stage, and matching: A study of airport arrival encounters.* Paper presented at the annual convention of the Western States Communication Association, Pasadena, CA.

Spitz, R. A. (1946). Hospitalism: A follow-up report. *Psychoanalytic Study of the Child, 2,* 113–117.

Weiss, S. J. (1990). Parental touching: Correlates of a child's body concept and body sentiment. In K. E. Barnard & B. T. Brazelton (Eds.), Touch: *The foundation of experience* (pp. 425–459). Madison, CT: International Universities Press.

Willis, F. N., Jr., & Briggs, L. F. (1992). Relationship and touch in public settings. *Journal of Nonverbal Behavior, 16,* 55–63.

The Nonverbal Perception Scale

Maureen P. Keeley
Texas State University-San Marcos

[Every time my best friend begins to whistle, I know that he is stressed out and is about to "blow," but anyone else looking at him would think that he is feeling good and that he is relaxed... No one knows him like I do.   —Mary]

INTRODUCTION

Nonverbal cues are an integral part of communication within close relationships, revealing (or perceived to reveal) people's thoughts, feelings, and attitudes (Allan, 1989; Gottman, 1994; Noller & Fitzpatrick, 1993). Nonverbal acts are enacted commonly within close relationships, creating a foundation of knowledge from which people draw to aid in their decoding process. Indeed, people in close relationships could be considered "experts" in decoding their partners' nonverbal behaviors because of the frequency in which people engage in noting and interpreting one another's nonverbal actions, although certainly they may often be inaccurate in their interpretations. Research conducted on relational communication does not often, however, take into consideration the participants' perceptions (Surra & Ridley, 1991). The Nonverbal Perception Scale (NVPS) was thus created as a way to take advantage of people's perspective on their partners' nonverbal communication.

This chapter discusses the development and testing of a measurement that enables researchers to tap into participants' realities. The chapter begins with a discussion regarding the value of participants' interpretation of their partners' nonverbal behaviors within close relationships in naturalistic contexts. Second, an overview of the three phases of the development and testing of the NVPS is provided. Finally, some general and practical concerns regarding the NVPS are discussed.

Participants' Private Realities

The human brain does not record information in the same way as a snapshot or video camera. People's perceptions of actual behaviors are filtered. These perceptions, however, become reality for the perceivers and are the outcomes of the interaction that are acted on. The consequences of relational messages are important because people act and react, not to their partner's actual behaviors, but according to their own perceptions of how those behaviors are functioning in their interaction and/or relationship and to the meaning that is assigned to those perceptions.

Manusov and Rodriguez (1989) substantiated that receivers attribute intent to nonverbal cues and assign meaning based, at least in part, on their perceptions of nonverbal cues. Thus, actual behaviors may have little inherent meaning: It is often peoples' perceptions of actual behaviors that are meaningful and of consequence to the interaction and relationship. It is therefore valuable to sometimes take a receiver's perspective when examining nonverbal behaviors in close relationships, because perceivers assign meaning and label others' behaviors, potentially impacting the ongoing interaction as well as future communication attempts between the interactants (Sillars, 1980).

Numerous theorists cite the importance of examining a receiver's perspective on an interaction. Laing (1967), for example, stated that a person's communication behavior is shaped largely by his or her perception of the relationship he or she has with the other communicator. Laing's perspective on relationships highlights the fact that people are not machines that simply record observable behavior that occurs within an interaction; rather, they "experience" (i.e., perceive) the action within the context of their relationship.

How one behaves toward another is a function of the perception of the other person's behavior and the experience of the relationship (Laing, 1967). Laing's foundational theory of "perspectives" includes the observation and interpretation of behavior that occurs within relationships, incorporates the process of inferring what the other person is feeling or thinking as a pathway to understanding within the relationship, and demonstrates the importance of accounting for the perceptions of the interactants within a relationship (Littlejohn, 1992).

Similarly, Watzlawick, Beavin, and Jackson's (1967) now-famous axiom "one cannot not communicate" (p. 51) emphasizes that any perceivable behavior is potentially communicative. The attempt to avoid an action, for example, may communicate a great deal of meaning to the receiver. Duck (1994) asserts "[m]eaning is not simply a magical assignment of content to concept but represents a choice of something and a simultaneous rejection of something else" (p. 55). More specifically, nonverbal cues often have a range of meanings that may be applied to them depending on the context and relationship (Stewart, 1996).

Manusov (2001) argues that nonverbal cues have symbolic meanings that communicate "about and within relationships through a shared set of meanings created within the relational, and larger, culture" (p. 4). Specifically, people in close relationships become very adept at interpreting and assigning meaning to behaviors that are exhibited within their relationships because of their experience with one another. Thus, to understand the meaning of nonverbal behaviors within participants' lives, researchers must find ways to assess these alternative, private realities. To that end, the Nonverbal Perception Scale (NVPS) was developed.

Context Matters

The perception of nonverbal behaviors is likely to change a great deal in respect to the context in which the behaviors occur as well as with the nature of the relationship (Dindia, Fitzpatrick, & Attridge, 1989). Yet, research exploring nonverbal behaviors in relationships does not often capture the influence of context (e.g., the time, place, situation, power structure, etc.) on the interpretation of nonverbal behaviors as they occur in naturalistic settings (Knapp, 1983; Kruglanski, 1989; Millar & Rogers, 1987). Nonetheless, the interpretation of nonverbal behaviors is heavily dependent on the context or field for accurate decoding. A research method that allows for data collection in the field immediately following a naturally occurring interaction and that takes context into account would be beneficial for nonverbal scholars. The NVPS was developed so that researchers may more easily explore nonverbal behaviors, particularly within personal relationships in naturalistic settings.

NONVERBAL PERCEPTION SCALE (NVPS)

The NVPS uses a structured report form on which participants record their perceptions of their partner's nonverbal behaviors (see appendix). The NVPS is designed with the same basic premise as other diary reports in that self-reports of interactions are completed immediately following an interaction to avoid largely the problems of retrospective recall and intrusiveness of other measures of social participation (Duck, Rutt, Hurst, & Strejc, 1991). Qualitative and quantitative methodologies were used in the development and testing of the NVPS.

Phase I: Instrument Development

Development of the NVPS began with participants ($N = 35$) keeping recording logs of their partners' nonverbal behaviors. Participants recorded their observations of their partners' nonverbal behavior following a dyadic interaction that lasted a minimum of 10 minutes. Participants were asked to record their observations at least twice a week, and logs were kept for a total of 6 weeks. Once the logs were turned in to the researcher, they were followed up with interviews concerning the participants' impressions of their 6-week observations and logs.

In the second part of the development of the scale, the researcher had participants use a specific version of the NVPS for a 6-week period. Three groups ($N = 75$,

25 per group) used consecutive (and improved) versions of the NVPS (i.e., original NVPS, second draft of the NVPS, and the final draft of the NVPS). Following each 6-week testing period, participants were asked, during focus group discussions, for extensive feedback and were prompted to clarify details regarding a number of relevant factors. Specifically, participants were interviewed regarding the wording of the items, the complexity of the Likert scale, their ability to focus on specific nonverbal cues within each code, and the overall ease or difficulty of the scale. A total of 110 participants (59 females and 51 males) collaborated in the development phase of the NVPS during a 1-year period.

The specific items for the NVPS were chosen based on a number of criteria: (a) their importance in describing the nonverbal behaviors of the interaction; (b) their similarity to items commonly used in experimental studies by trained coders; (c) their clarity; (d) ease of use; and (e) self-explanatory power. Items that were found to be too difficult for participants to assess were dropped. Additionally, questions were phrased to elicit the participants' perceptions of their partners' nonverbal behaviors (as opposed to traditional self-reports that focus on participant's own behaviors). The unit of analysis is midlevel or intermediate (e.g., intensities rather than counts). Lastly, the items focus on participants' *perceptions* of behaviors rather than on actual nonverbal behaviors. The final draft of the NVPS presented in the appendix was examined against and met the aforementioned criteria.

Phase II: "Known Groups" Validity Check

Once the development of the NVPS was completed, an initial validity check was conducted. Before the NVPS could be tested for its relevance outside of the lab and utilizing participants in developed relationships, the researcher wanted to confirm the degree to which the NVPS assessed and distinguished between nonverbal behaviors using naïve and untrained participants. Singleton, Strait, and Straits (1993) stated that a comparison of two different groups is an effective source of validating evidence. Therefore, a study was created utilizing the "differences among known groups" (p. 128). Given the research on the importance of involvement and immediacy on personal relationships (Andersen & Andersen, this volume; Burgoon, 1994; Cappella, 1983; Guerrero, this volume; Manusov, 1991), the test focused on the differences of high and low involvement levels as communicated through the nonverbal channel.

The key question of the initial validity check focused on whether untrained participants ($N = 100$) could use the NVPS and come up with the same results as those found in past studies that utilized trained coders using traditional methods. Although the NVPS is designed to tap the perceptions of individuals with a relational history, the participants in this validity check were strangers. If untrained, naïve strangers could use the scale successfully to detect nonverbal differences among known groups, then it seemed reasonable to assume that relational partners could use it within their own relationships across a variety of different situations. Confederates were trained to behave with high involvement or low involvement nonverbal cues.

Four dyads of same-sex friend confederates were videotaped while participating in a 10-minute conversation regarding upcoming vacation plans. One male dyad and one female dyad were instructed to behave with a great deal of involvement and immediacy; another male dyad and another female dyad were instructed to behave with very low involvement and immediacy. Fifty participants observed a high involvement interaction, and fifty participants observed a low involvement interaction (i.e., the two known groups: high involvement interaction and low involvement interaction). Both male and female participants were in each of the four observing groups, and no participant saw more than one interaction. After watching the 10-minute interaction, the participants completed the NVPS.

The participants who viewed the videotape focused on one person in the videotape. Participants answered the questions on the NVPS as if they had participated in the interaction with the person who was the main focus of the videotape. Both confederates could be seen in the videotape in the lower left hand of the screen. This enabled participants to answer questions regarding the use of other-oriented proxemics and haptics. Untrained participants used the NVPS successfully for discriminating differences between high and low involvement nonverbal cues (see Table 2).

These findings provide validating evidence that the NVPS is effective for discriminating differences in nonverbal behaviors between groups and is a useful tool for examining untrained coders' perceptions of nonverbal behaviors within their personal relationships.

Phase III: Quantitative Test of the NVPS

The reliability and validity of the NVPS were tested further by comparing the findings from previous lab-based studies that utilized traditional objective, third-party observations with an additional new study utilizing participants' observations of their partners' nonverbal behaviors during natural interactions. "One of the standard ways in which new tests are validated is by comparison with the best of existing tests" (Trimboli & Walker, 1993, p. 62). This follows Burgoon and her associates' (Burgoon, Buller, Hale, & DeTurk, 1984; Burgoon & Hale, 1987; Burgoon, Kelley, Newton, & Keeley-Dyreson, 1989) method of using numerous experimental studies conducted within the laboratory setting to provide tests for comparison.

Participants ($N = 475$) were adults with existing same-sex friendships (i.e., someone that they identify as a friend) with whom they interact frequently (e.g., at least once a week). The survey was comprised of three instruments: The Relational Communication Scale (RCS; Burgoon & Hale, 1984, 1987; see Hale, Burgoon, & Householder, this volume), the Iowa Communication Record (ICR; Duck, Rutt, Hurst, & Strejc, 1991), and the Nonverbal Perception Scale (NVPS). The surveys were collected over a 4-week period. Participants returned the surveys within 1

TABLE 2

Known Groups Validity Check For Nonverbal Items
On The NVPS As Distinguished Between High And Low Levels Of Involvement

Nonverbal Item #	Level of Involvement	Mean	T
1. How Lively	Low	1.31	
	High	4.72	−30.58***
2. Head Nod (Yes)	Low	2.20	
	High	3.94	−8.11***
3. Head Shake (No)	Low	2.04	
	High	2.96	−4.56***
4. Tense Posture	Low	3.68	
	High	4.13	−1.98*
5. Eye Gaze	Low	1.58	
	High	3.74	−12.62***
6. Facial Pleasantness	Low	2.36	
	High	4.58	−12.16***
7. Frequency of Smile	Low	1.88	
	High	4.18	−11.96***
8. How Close	Low	2.94	
	High	4.48	−11.86***
9. Direct Orientation	Low	3.00	
	High	4.52	−7.91***
10. Positive Touch	Low	1.02	
	High	3.92	−17.32***
11. Negative Touch	Low	4.44	
	High	4.22	0.87 NS
12. Self Touch	Low	3.84	
	High	3.00	3.34**
13. Varied Tone of Voice	Low	1.50	
	High	4.20	−16.39***
14. Loudness	Low	2.5	
	High	3.82	−8.09***
15. Rate of Speech	Low	2.06	
	High	3.76	−14.04***
16. Pause Frequency	Low	3.88	
	High	2.30	8.76***
17. Overall Vocal Impression	Low	2.52	
	High	3.86	−6.49***
18. Frequency of Interruption	Low	1.90	
	High	3.18	−6.61***

19. Overall Inferred Interactant Interest	Low	1.68	
	High	4.30	−15.57***
20. Overall Inferred Partner Composure	Low	3.12	
	High	3.40	−1.37 NS
21. Overall Inferred Partner Animation	Low	1.38	
	High	4.48	−18.57***
22. Overall Inferred Partner Relaxation	Low	3.34	
	High	3.96	−2.36*

Note: * $p < .05$; ** $p < .01$; *** $p < .001$.

week of receiving them. Participants were asked to complete the diary immediately following an interaction with a same-sex friend. The interactions had to have lasted a minimum of 10 minutes.

Assessment of Reliability.   The data indicated that the NVPS has moderately strong internal consistency. The NVPS yielded a Cronbach's *alpha* of .74. The three factors were also relatively internally consistent with the following *alphas*: immediacy .62, animation .71, and composure .72. Focusing on specific relational contexts (e.g., conflict situations or power-oriented relationships) may reveal additional factors in future tests of the NVPS.

Face and Construct Validity.   There are three ways that face and construct validity of the NVPS have been substantiated. First, the creation of the NVPS was theoretically driven, focusing on foundational research highlighting the relevance and importance of taking a receiver's perspective (e.g., Laing, 1967; Manusov, 2001; Watzlawick et al., 1967). Second, the infrastructure of the scale revolved around the four dynamic nonverbal codes (kinesic, vocalic, proxemic, and haptic) that have been the focus across studies for the past two decades (Baeseler & Burgoon, 1987). Third, the correlations of the specific items on the NVPS with each other demonstrate that the nonverbal behaviors that associated with each other were logically, theoretically, and empirically reasonable and justifiable. The NVPS detected similar relationships between nonverbal cues as those found in past nonverbal research that utilized trained objective coders, whereas the NVPS allows researchers to "tap" the actual participant's perception.

Convergent Validity.   Singleton, Straits, and Straits (1993) state that there should be consistency between different measures of the same concept (in this case, nonverbal behaviors) if a particular instrument is valid. The comparison between the NVPS and the RCS demonstrated that there *was* a consistency between the two measures (see Table 3). Specifically, the items in the first factor of the NVPS called *immediacy* (i.e., head nods, eye gaze, physical closeness, body orientation, and posi-

TABLE 3

Convergent Validity Assessment: Pair-Wise Correlations Between Nonverbal Factors
(Immediacy, Animation, Composure) And Factors of Relational Messages
(Intimacy, Similarity, Trust, Equality)

	Immediacy	Animation	Composure
Relational Intimacy	0.57***	0.35***	0.40***
	N = 465	N = 467	N = 460
Relational Similarity	0.48***	0.20***	0.31***
	N = 468	N = 469	N = 463
Relational Trust	0.48***	0.18***	0.40***
	N = 472	N = 474	N = 467
Relational Equality	0.34***	0.16***	0.36***
	N = 470	N = 472	N = 465

Note: ***$p < .001$

tive touch) are consistent with those nonverbal behaviors that have been identified
in research conducted within a lab setting (Andersen, 1999; Burgoon & Hale, 1987;
see Guerrero, this volume). The items in the second NVPS factor of *animation* (i.e.,
lively gestures, tone and loudness of voice, rate of speech, and partner animation)
are consistent with lab-based research findings that indicate that these nonverbal
behaviors communicate involvement in the interaction (Andersen, 1999; Burgoon
& Hale, 1987). The items in the third NVPS factor of *composure* (i.e., posture, facial
and vocal pleasantness, and partner relaxation) are consistent with past research establishing that these nonverbal behaviors often communicate interpersonal
warmth and positive affect (Andersen, 1999; Burgoon & Hale, 1987). The significant correlations between the two measures of the RCS and the NVPS support the
contention of convergent validity for this new instrument.

Predictive Validity.   The results from the test demonstrate that the instrument is effective for identifying differences in nonverbal behaviors and that the
NVPS does have predictive validity. The NVPS accounted for 33% of the variance
in relational quality. This is consistent with Keeley and Hart's (1994) argument
that nonverbal behaviors are important to the overall perception of quality communication. The results of the pair-wise correlations suggest that perceptions of
nonverbal behaviors do have an impact on the overall impression of quality communication (see Table 4).

The nonverbal factor of *immediacy* (i.e., eye gaze, close proximity, direct orientation, positive touch, head nods, and general interest) may be akin to Montgomery's (1988) ideal of intimacy. The immediacy factor of the NVPS reflects openness,
a willingness to reveal oneself to another, and a certain amount of vulnerability. Immediacy behaviors are often perceived to be spontaneous and honest messages of
intimacy (Gottman, 1979). The NVPS factor of *animation* (i.e., lively gestures,

TABLE 4

Predictive Validity Test: A Forced-Entry Regression Analysis of Nonverbal Factors
(Immediacy, Animation, Composure) on Quality of Interaction

Analysis of Variance

Source:	DF	Sum of Squares	Mean Square	F Value	Prob > F
Model	3	4616.76	153.9	76.59	0.001
Error	457	9182.57	20.09		
C Total	460	13799.33			
	Root MSE	4.48	R-Square	0.33	
	Dep. Mean	42.18	Adj. R-Sq	0.33	
	C.V.	10.63			

Parameter Estimates

Variable	DF	Parameter Estimates	Standard Error	T for HO: Parameter = 0	Prob > |T|	Variable Label
Intercep	1	19.53	1.66	11.73	0.001	Intercept
Immediacy	1	0.50	0.06	7.92	0.001	NONVERBAL IMMEDIACY
Animation	1	0.04	0.07	0.51	0.609	NONVERBAL ANIMATION
Composure	1	0.73	0.07	9.97	0.001	NONVERBAL COMPOSURE

pleasant tone of voice, loudness, a fast rate of voice, and an overall impression of animation) may be touching on Montgomery's (1988) ideal of positivity. Nonverbal behaviors that communicate animation may be associated with excited, happy, and positive exchanges.

The NVPS factor of *composure* (relaxed posture, facial and vocal pleasantness, and partner relaxation) appears to be associated with Montgomery's (1988) discussion of control. The ideal of control focuses on people's desire to be in control of their relationships and more specifically, in control of specific kinds of interactional patterns (Montgomery, 1988). Keeley and Hart (1994) posited that both partners must feel that their own nonverbal behaviors are synchronized and coordinated with those of their partner's to have a sense of control within a given interaction. People's perceptions of their partner's nonverbal behaviors as being composed could lead to the conclusion that they are at ease, in control of their interactional patterns, and ultimately in control of their relationship. Each of the nonverbal factors of the NVPS seems to provide a logical fit with Montgomery's (1988) ideals of quality communication. These findings are an important first step toward understanding the role of nonverbal behaviors on the perception of quality communication within a relationship.

DISCUSSION

Knapp (1983) observed that more nonverbal communication research must focus on participants with relational histories if the field is going to advance. The NVPS provides this perspective. The NVPS (using the perceptions of naïve, untrained participants for identifying nonverbal behaviors) corresponds with findings based on traditional methods (which use trained coders in lab settings with videotapes). The ability to conduct nonverbal research using the participants' perceptions allows us to investigate the potential impact of relational partners' expertise and interpretation of that behavior on the relationship. The participants' perspectives take into account the sometimes hidden understandings that are created over time within a relationship.

Additionally, all of the interactions reported in studies that have used the NVPS occurred in natural settings, during typical, everyday activities. These conditions are most likely quite different from the standard laboratory experimental setting (but see Roberts, this volume). NVPS offers an opportunity to increase ecological validity by exploring nonverbal behaviors during real and naturally occurring interactions.

REFERENCES

Allan, G. (1989). *Friendship: Developing a sociological perspective.* Great Britian: Hemel Hempstead, Harvester Wheatsheaf.

Andersen, P. A. (1999). *Nonverbal communication: Forms and functions.* Mountain View, CA: Mayfield Publishing Co.

Baesler, E. J., & Burgoon, J. K. (1987). Measurement and reliability of nonverbal behavior. *Journal of Nonverbal Behavior, 11,* 205–233.

Burgoon, J. K. (1994). Nonverbal signals. In M. L. Knapp & G. R. Miller (Eds.), *Handbook of interpersonal communication* (2nd ed., pp. 229–285). Thousand Oaks, CA: Sage.

Burgoon, J. K., Buller, D. B., Hale, J. L., & deTurck, M. A. (1984). Relational messages associated with nonverbal behaviors. *Human Communication Research, 10,* 351–378.

Burgoon, J. K., & Hale, J. L. (1984). The fundamental topoi of relational communication. *Communication Monographs, 51,* 193–214.

Burgoon, J. K., & Hale, J. L. (1987). Validation and measurement of the fundamental themes of relational communication. *Communication Monographs, 54,* 19–41.

Burgoon, J. K., Kelley, D. L., Newton, D. A., & Keeley-Dyreson, M. P. (1989). The nature of arousal and nonverbal indices. *Human Communication Research, 16,* 217–255.

Cappella, J. N. (1983). Conversational involvement: Approaching and avoiding others. In J. M. Wiemann & R. P. Harrison (Eds.) *Nonverbal interaction* (pp. 113–148). Beverly Hills, CA: Sage.

Dindia, K., Fitzpatrick, M. A., & Attridge, M. (1989, November). *Gaze and mutual gaze: A social relations analysis.* Paper presented at the annual convention of the Speech Communication Association, San Francisco, CA.

Duck, S. W. (1994). *Meaningful relationships: Talking sense and relating.* Thousand Oaks, CA: Sage.

Duck, S. W., Rutt, D., Hurst, M., & Strejc, H. (1991). Some evident truths about conversation in everyday relationships: All communications are not created equal. *Human Communication Research, 18,* 228–267.

Gottman, J. M. (1979). *Marital interaction: Experimental investigations.* New York: Academic Press.

Gottman, J. M. (1994). *Why marriages succeed or fail.* New York: Fireside, Simon & Schuster.

Keeley, M. K., & Hart, A. J. (1994). Nonverbal behavior in dyadic interactions. In S. Duck (Ed.), *Dynamics of relationships* (pp. 135–162). Thousand Oaks, CA: Sage.

Knapp, M. L. (1983). Dyadic relationship development. In J. M. Wiemann & R. P. Harrison (Eds.), *Nonverbal interaction* (pp. 179–207). Beverly Hills, CA: Sage.

Kruglanski, A. W. (1989). The psychology of being "right." The problem of accuracy in social perception and cognition. *Psychological Bulletin, 106,* 395–409.

Laing, R. D. (1967). *The politics of experience.* New York, NY: Pantheon Books.

Littlejohn, S. W. (1992). *Theories of human communication* (4th ed.). Belmont, CA: Wadsworth.

Manusov, V. (1991). Perceiving nonverbal messages: Effects of immediacy and encoded intent on receiver judgments. *Western Journal of Speech Communication, 55,* 235–253.

Manusov, V. (2001, June). *Discerning couples' meaning for nonverbal behaviors: A diary to access the degree of symbolism in the perception of nonverbal messages.* Paper presented to the International Network on Personal Relationships/International Society for the Study of Personal Relationships Joint Conference, Prescott, AZ.

Manusov, V., & Rodriquez, J. S. (1989). Intentionality behind nonverbal messages: A perceiver's perspective. *Journal of Nonverbal Behavior, 13,* 15–24.

Millar, F. E., & Rogers, L. E. (1987). Relational dimensions of interpersonal dynamics in M. E. Roloff & G. R. Miller (Eds.), *Interpersonal processes: New directions in communication research* (pp. 117–139). Beverly Hills, CA: Sage.

Montgomery, B. M. (1988). Quality communication in personal relationships. In S. W. Duck (Ed.), *Handbook of personal relationships* (pp. 343–366). New York: John Wiley & Sons.

Noller, P., & Fitzpatrick, M. A. (1993). *Communication in family relationships.* Englewood Cliffs, NJ: Prentice Hall.

Sillars, A. L. (1980). Attributions and communication in roommate conflict. *Communication Monographs, 47,* 180–200.

Singleton, R. A., Straits, B. C., & Straits, M. (1993). *Approaches to social research.* New York: Oxford University Press.

Stewart, J. (1996). *Beyond the symbol model: Reflections on the representational nature of language.* Albany, NY: State University of New York Press.

Surra, C. A., & Ridley, C. A. (1991). Multiple perspectives on interaction: Participants, peers, and observers. In B. M. Montgomery & S. W. Duck (Eds.), *Studying interpersonal interactions* (pp. 35–55). New York: Guilford Press.

Trimboli, A., & Walker, M. (1993). The Cast Test of nonverbal sensitivity. *Journal of Language and Social Psychology, 12,* 49–65.

Watzlawick, P., Beavin, J., & Jackson, D. (1967). *Pragmatics of human communication: A study of interactional patterns, pathologies, and paradoxes.* New York, NY: Norton.

Self-Report Measures of Emotional and Nonverbal Expressiveness

Ronald E. Riggio
Heidi R. Riggio
Claremont McKenna College

INTRODUCTION

The construct of nonverbal or emotional expressiveness has received a great deal of research interest in the past three decades; so much so, there are now more than a half dozen self-report instruments that assess nonverbal/emotional expressiveness and closely related constructs. These measures are "trait-like" in their approach and purport to assess individual differences in the generation and/or expression of emotions. Unlike measures of nonverbal emotional encoding ability, such as testing an individual's ability to pose basic emotional expressions on cue (e.g., Buck, 1975; Zuckerman, Lipets, Koivumaki, & Rosenthal, 1975) or performance measures of spontaneous emotional expressiveness (see, for example, Buck, this volume), self-report measures of emotional expressiveness assess a more general tendency to display affect spontaneously and across a wide range of situations.

This chapter reviews several of the more widely researched measures of nonverbal and emotional expressiveness and discusses briefly a few closely related measures that may be of interest to nonverbal communication researchers. It differs from some of the other chapters in this section in that it does not include the scales themselves. It does, however, provide information about how to access the measures.

Affective Communication Test

The Affective Communication Test, or ACT, (Friedman, Prince, Riggio, & DiMatteo, 1980) was one of the first self-report measures of nonverbal expressiveness. Nonverbal expressiveness, as measured by the ACT, assesses individual differences in the ability to transmit emotions and "to use nonverbal cues to move, lead, inspire, or captivate others" (Friedman et al., 1980, p. 333). This expression of affect occurs through facial expressions, tone of voice, gestures, and body movement, and has been described as a critical core element of "personal charisma" (Friedman, Riggio, & Casella, 1988). The ACT is a 13-item self-report measure with a 9-point response scale ranging from −4 to +4, with scale anchors of "not at all true of me" and "very true of me." Sample items include "When I hear good dance music, I can hardly keep still," and "I usually have a neutral facial expression" (reverse scored item).

The initial validation studies for the ACT (Friedman et al., 1980) demonstrated good internal consistency, with an *alpha* coefficient of .77 for the 13-item scale and 2-month and 1-week test–retest correlations of .90 and .91, respectively. The ACT was only slightly positively correlated with a measure of social desirability. As is the case with several measures of expressiveness, women tend to score significantly higher on the ACT than do men. All of the initial validity studies for the ACT were done with college students, but the ACT has been used successfully with nonstudent populations as well.

In regard to construct validity, scores on the ACT were positively correlated with a number of activities that are linked theoretically to expressive persons, including experience in politics and public speaking, acting experience, and working as a salesperson (Friedman et al., 1980). Scores on the ACT were only associated marginally with posed emotional encoding ability, but the ACT is more theoretically related to spontaneous, rather than posed, emotional sending. Subsequent studies have found the ACT to be associated more strongly with expressive nonverbal behavior in less restricted communication settings (DePaulo, Blank, Swaim, & Hairfield, 1992; Friedman & Miller-Herringer, 1991). It is important to note, however, that sex differences may play an important part in how nonverbal expressiveness is displayed. For example, in one study where participants were speaking spontaneously, scores on the ACT correlated significantly with incidences of facial expressions, body movements, and gestural fluency for women, whereas the ACT correlated significantly with speech rate for men, but not significantly with the nonverbal cues (Riggio & Friedman, 1986).

To understand how expressiveness may relate to traditional personality dimensions, patterns of correlations between the ACT and personality instruments suggest that nonverbally expressive persons tend to be extraverted, affiliative, dominant, and exhibitionistic, but the ACT is negatively correlated with measures of neuroticism. In fact, a recent meta-analysis, using a variety of self-report measures of expressiveness, suggests that there is a strong and consistent positive relationship between expressiveness and extraversion and a consistent negative relationship between expressiveness and neuroticism (Riggio & Riggio, 2002). This finding is consistent with the notion that expressive individuals may have better psychosocial adjustment than nonverbally unexpressive persons (Friedman, 1991; Riggio, 1992).

The Affective Communication Test can be obtained from Dr. Howard S. Friedman, Department of Psychology, University of California, Riverside, CA 92521; Friedman@citrus.ucr.edu. It is also published in Friedman et al. (1980).

Emotional Expressivity Scale

Kring, Smith, and Neale (1994) define emotional expressiveness as "the outward display of emotion, regardless of valence (positive or negative) or channel (facial, vocal, or gestural)" (p. 934). The Emotional Expressivity Scale (EES) presents emotional expressiveness as a trait-like construct reflecting the degree to which individuals express their emotions. Moreover, it is presumed that this expression of affect is consistent across situations and across communication channels. The EES is a 17-item self-report scale with a 6-point response scale, with scale anchors of "never true" (1) to "always true" (6). Sample items include "I display my emotions to other people" and "Even when I'm experiencing strong feelings, I don't express them outwardly" (reverse scored).

Kring et al.'s initial validation studies for the EES involved undergraduate students primarily and a small sample of adults drawn from the community. Internal consistency of the EES, however, is very good, with an average Cronbach's *alpha* coefficient of .91. Test–retest correlation with a 4-week interval between administrations was also very good, with a correlation of .90. As on many measures of expressiveness, women score significantly higher than men do typically on the EES (see also Kring & Gordon, 1998). Importantly, the EES was not significantly correlated with a measure of social desirability.

Construct validity of the EES is very good and is reported in Kring et al. (1994). For example, the EES had a significant correlation of .45 ($N = 77$ undergraduates) with the Affective Communication Test (ACT; Friedman et al., 1980), suggesting that these two measures are related but may be measuring different forms of expressiveness. Like the ACT, the EES is positively correlated with extraversion (or *surgency*), emotional stability, and the Satisfaction with Life Scale (Diener, Emmons, Larsen, & Griffin, 1985). Using a spontaneous emotional encoding task, involving having participants watch emotion-inducing film clips while being videotaped, the EES was positively and significantly correlated with overall facial expressiveness made by raters, even when participants' level of experienced/induced emotion was statistically controlled. Interestingly, the ACT was also included in this study and showed similar positive correlations with overall facial expressiveness. In an additional validation study, mothers ($N = 37$) filled out the EES for their undergraduate children, and students' scores on the EES correlated .49 with their mothers' "ratings." The EES is published in Kring et al. (1994).

Berkeley Expressivity Questionnaire

The Berkeley Expressivity Questionnaire (BEQ; Gross & John, 1995) was derived from a theoretical model that viewed emotional expressivity as a trait-like construct composed of the strength of an individual's emotional reactivity, what the authors refer to as "the inner emotional impulse," (p. 556) and the direct expression of emotional behavior, or the "expression of certain emotions." Moreover, Gross and John (1995) suggest that the expression of positive emotions is somewhat distinct from negative emotional expressivity. The BEQ, therefore, has three subscales: Negative Expressivity, Positive Expressivity, and Impulse Strength. These three subscales all contribute to a General Emotional Expressivity factor.

The BEQ is a 16-item self-report instrument with a 7-point response scale with scale anchors "strongly disagree" (1) to "strongly agree" (7). Four items assess the Positive Expressivity factor, six items measure Negative Expressivity, and six items assess the Impulse Strength factor. Sample items include "When I'm happy, my feelings show" (Positive Expressivity), "Whenever I feel negative emotions, people can easily see exactly what I am feeling" (Negative Expressivity), and "I experience my emotions very strongly" (Impulse Strength).

Internal consistency of the BEQ scales is good, with Cronbach *alpha* reliabilities ranging from .71 to .76 (Gross & John, 1995). Test-retest correlations with a 2-month interval between administrations range from .71 to .82 for the subscales and .86 for the full scale. In addition, intercorrelations among the three subscales are approximately .50, suggesting that the three subscales can indeed be combined into a general expressivity scale (Gross & John, 1995). None of the BEQ subscales, or the total score, is significantly correlated with a measure of social desirability.

Construct validation for the BEQ included examination of correlations between BEQ scores and peer evaluations using a modified form of the BEQ. Similar to the validation studies for the EES, participants were administered the BEQ and then shown emotion-inducing video clips. As expected, scores on the BEQ correlated significantly with participants' emotionally expressive behavior while viewing the video clips. Moreover, the negative and positive expressivity scales correlated significantly with emotional expressiveness only during the viewing of positive emotional expressions (i.e., amusement) or negative emotional expressions (i.e., sadness) segments, respectively (Gross & John, 1997). The BEQ is published in Gross and John (1995).

Emotional Expressivity Questionnaire

The Emotional Expressivity Questionnaire (EEQ) was developed as an alternative to the Affective Communication Test, and was, according to the authors (King & Emmons, 1990), more narrowly focused on emotional expressiveness. The EEQ was developed along with the Ambivalence Over Emotional Expressiveness Questionnaire (AEQ), which is described as a measure of "ambivalent emotional strivings" (p. 864) and reflects the notion that there are individual differences in people's tendencies to repress or inhibit the expression of felt emotions (see also the notion of Emotional Control; Riggio, this volume). The AEQ is printed, along with the EEQ, in King and Emmons (1990).

The EEQ is a 16-item self-report measure, with a 7-point response scale, indicating agreement with the item (1 = "does not agree at all" to 7 = "strongly agree"). Sample items include "Watching television or reading a book can make me laugh out loud," and "I always express disappointment when things don't go as I'd like them to." Although factor analysis suggested the presence of three factors (expression of positive emotion, expression of negative emotion, and expression of intimacy), the EEQ has been used primarily as a unitary scale. Validation studies for the EEQ have used undergraduate students. The EEQ shows good internal consistency with an *alpha* reliability of .78. As expected, women scored higher on the EEQ than did men. The EEQ was significantly negatively correlated with a measure of social desirability, suggesting that social desirability is not a problem for the scale. Rather, persons scoring high on the EEQ are slightly less likely to respond in a socially desirable manner.

Initial validity studies for the EEQ focused primarily on the measure's relationships to other expressiveness measures and to measures of psychological and physical well-being. The EEQ was significantly positively correlated with peer ratings of expressiveness, and with a measure of expressiveness in the respondent's home, the Family Expressiveness Questionnaire (Halberstadt, 1986). The EEQ was not significantly correlated with the ACT ($N = 48$, $r = .19$), nor was the EEQ consistently related to measures of psychological or physical well-being. In another study of married couples, the EEQ was significantly and positively related to husbands' marital satisfaction, but not wives' satisfaction (King, 1993).

Additional Self-Report Measures of Nonverbal and Emotional Communication

In addition to the four measures reviewed earlier, there are a number of other self-report measures of emotional/nonverbal expressiveness. For example, the Emotional Expressivity scale of the Social Skills Inventory (see Riggio, this volume) is similar to the measures reviewed here. In addition, an older instrument, the Test of Attentional and Interpersonal Style (TAIS; Nideffer, 1976; available at www.enhanced-performance.com), has two subscales that measure negative and positive affective expression, respectively, similar to the BEQ and EEQ subscales.

Another type of measure assesses the intensity of emotional expression. The most popular of these is the Affect Intensity Measure (AIM; Larsen & Diener, 1985, 1987). This 40-item, self-report measure assesses "emotional reactivity and variability" (Larsen & Diener, 1987, p. 1). Research has demonstrated that individuals scoring high on the AIM have more intense emotional reactions to emotional stimuli (Larsen, Diener, & Emmons, 1986). The AIM is printed in Larsen et al. (1986) as an appendix.

The Emotional Intensity Scale (EIS; Bachorowski & Braaten, 1994) is similar to the AIM, but the 30-item EIS has subscales separately measuring the intensity of positive and negative emotions, as well as an overall score. The EIS scales are significantly and positively correlated with the AIM ($rs = .37 - .48$). The EIS is printed in Bachorowski and Braaten (1994).

CONCLUSIONS

There is considerable interest in individual differences in the experience and expression of emotion, in general, and in tendencies to display emotions nonverbally. The nonverbal behavior researcher interested in expressiveness has a variety of measures to choose from. In general, these instruments are more alike than they are different. In fact, many of the items used in these various self-report scales are quite similar. Validation work suggests that self-report measures of nonverbal/emotional expressiveness are indeed related to actual nonverbal displays of emotions, so they are useful and valid tools for the nonverbal researcher (Riggio & Riggio, 2001). For the most part, these measures are relatively brief and could be included easily in studies of nonverbal communication processes to provide another dimension: that of exploring consistent individual differences in nonverbal/emotional expressive style. Individual differences in regulating nonverbal expressions are closely associated with nonverbal expressiveness, as shown by the research of King and Emmons (1990) with the AEQ, the more recent work of Gross (1999) on emotion regulation, the earlier work by Snyder (1974, 1987) on the self-monitoring of emotional expression, and Riggio's work (1986; Riggio & Carney, 2003) on emotional control.

REFERENCES

Bachorowski, J., & Braaten, E. B. (1994). Emotional intensity: Measurement and theoretical implications. *Personality and Individual Differences, 17,* 191–199.

Buck, R. (1975). Nonverbal communication of affect in children. *Journal of Personality and Social Psychology, 31,* 644–653.

DePaulo, B. M., Blank, A. L., Swaim, G. W., & Hairfield, J. G. (1992). Expressiveness and expressive control. *Personality and Social Psychology Bulletin, 18,* 276–285.

Diener, E., Emmons, R. A., Larsen, R. J., & Griffin, S. (1985). The Satisfaction With Life Scale. *Journal of Personality Assessment, 49,* 71–75.

Friedman, H. S. (1991). *The self-healing personality: Why some people achieve health and others succumb to illness.* New York: Henry Holt.

Friedman, H. S., & Miller-Herringer, T. (1991). Nonverbal display of emotion in public and private: Self-monitoring, personality, and expressive cues. *Journal of Personality and Social Psychology, 61,* 766–775.

Friedman, H. S., Prince, L. M., Riggio, R. E., & DiMatteo, M. R. (1980). Understanding and assessing nonverbal expressiveness: The Affective Communication Test. *Journal of Personality and Social Psychology, 39,* 333–351.

Friedman, H. S., Riggio, R. E., & Casella, D. F. (1988). Nonverbal skill, personal charisma, and initial attraction. *Personality and Social Psychology Bulletin, 14,* 203–211.

Gross, J. J. (1999). Emotion regulation: Past, present, future. *Cognition & Emotion, 13,* 551–573.

Gross, J. J., & John, O. P. (1995). Facets of emotional expressivity: Three self-report factors and their correlates. *Personality and Individual Differences, 19,* 555–568.

Gross, J. J., & John, O. P. (1997). Revealing feelings: Facets of emotional expressivity in self-reports, peer ratings, and behavior. *Journal of Personality and Social Psychology, 72,* 435–448.

Halberstadt, A. (1986). Family socialization of emotional expression and nonverbal communication of styles and skills. *Journal of Personality and Social Psychology, 51,* 827–836.

King, L. A. (1993). Emotional expression, ambivalence over expression, and marital satisfaction. *Journal of Social and Personal Relationships, 10,* 601–607.

King, L. A., & Emmons, R. A. (1990). Conflict over emotional expression: Psychological and physical correlates. *Journal of Personality and Social Psychology, 58,* 864–877.

Kring, A. M., & Gordon, A. H. (1998). Sex differences in emotion: Expression, experience, and physiology. *Journal of Personality and Social Psychology, 74,* 686–703.

Kring, A. M., Smith, D. A., & Neale, J. M. (1994). Individual differences in dispositional expressiveness: Development and validation of the Emotional Expressivity Scale. *Journal of Personality and Social Psychology, 66,* 934–949.

Larsen, R. J., & Diener, E. (1985). A multitrait–multimethod examination of affect structure: Hedonic level and emotional intensity. *Personality and Individual Differences, 6,* 631–636.

Larsen, R. J., & Diener, E. (1987). Affect intensity as an individual difference characteristic: A review. *Journal of Research in Personality, 21,* 1–39.

Larsen, R. J., Diener, E., & Emmons, R. A. (1986). Affect intensity and reactions to daily life events. *Journal of Personality and Social Psychology, 51,* 803–814.

Nideffer, R. M. (1976). Test of Attentional and Interpersonal Style. *Journal of Personality and Social Psychology, 34,* 394–404.

Riggio, H. R., & Riggio, R. E. (2002). Emotional expressiveness, extraversion, and neuroticism: A meta-analysis. *Journal of Nonverbal Behavior, 26,* 195–218.

Riggio, R. E. (1986). Assessment of basic social skills. *Journal of Personality and Social Psychology, 51,* 649–660.

Riggio, R. E. (1992). Social interaction skills and nonverbal behavior. In R. S. Feldman (Ed.), *Applications of nonverbal behavioral theories and research* (pp. 3–30). Hillsdale, NJ: Lawrence Erlbaum Associates.

Riggio, R. E., & Carney, D. R. (2003). *Social Skills Inventory manual: Second Edition.* Redwood City, CA: MindGarden.

Riggio, R. E., & Friedman, H. S. (1986). Impression formation: The role of expressive behavior. *Journal of Personality and Social Psychology, 50,* 421–427.

Riggio, R. E., & Riggio, H. R. (2001). Self-report measurement of interpersonal sensitivity. In J. A. Hall & F. J. Bernieri (Eds.), *Interpersonal sensitivity: Theory and measurement* (pp. 127–142). Mahwah, NJ: Lawrence Erlbaum Associates.

Snyder, M. (1974). The self-monitoring of expressive behavior. *Journal of Personality and Social Psychology, 30,* 526–537.

Snyder, M. (1987). *Public appearances/private realities: The psychology of self-monitoring.* New York: W. H. Freeman.

Zuckerman, M., Lipets, M., Koivumaki, J., & Rosenthal, R. (1975). Encoding and decoding nonverbal cues of emotion. *Journal of Personality and Social Psychology, 32,* 1068–1076.

Measurements of Perceived Nonverbal Immediacy

Peter A. Andersen
Janis F. Andersen
San Diego State University

INTRODUCTION

Arguably the most central function of nonverbal communication is the communication of immediacy: the exchange of warm, involving, affiliative behaviors (Andersen, 1984, 1999; Andersen & Guerrero, 1998). The term *immediacy* characterizes messages that convey warmth, closeness, and involvement among interactants (Mehrabian, 1971). Andersen (1985) described four definitional attributes of immediacy behaviors: (a) immediacy behaviors are characterized by approach as opposed to avoidance in interaction; (b) immediacy behaviors signal availability as opposed to unavailability for interaction; (c) immediacy behaviors induce stimulation and physiological arousal in a receiver; and (d) in virtually all relationships, except those with a history or expectation of conflict, immediacy behaviors are perceived as warm messages that convey interpersonal closeness to another interactant (Andersen, 1985).

Although immediacy can also be communicated verbally, this chapter focuses on the perception of immediacy via nonverbal cues. The power and relational significance of nonverbal immediacy is, in part, the result of the multichannelled nature of nonverbal communication. Whereas verbal communication generally occupies a single channel, nonverbal communication is typically multichannelled (Andersen, 1999). The multiple messages convey moods, states, and relationship simultaneously and create messages that are compelling, redundant, and seemingly authentic. The following section highlights some of the most notable nonverbal cues associated with immediacy.

CHANNELS OF NONVERBAL COMMUNICATION

Numerous studies reveal that nonverbal immediacy is conveyed through a host of discrete yet interdependent channels. Considerable evidence suggests that nonverbal communication cues are processed as a gestalt that results in global perceptions of nonverbal immediacy (see Andersen, 1985, 1999). Nonverbal immediacy, likewise, is typically conveyed through proxemic, haptic, oculesic, kinesic, vocalic, and chronemic behavior simultaneously. Although they tend to occur together, each of these channels is discussed separately to show their potential contribution to perceptions of immediacy.

Proxemics

Immediacy can be signaled through several proxemic or spatial channels. Most primary is interpersonal distance (i.e., proxemics). Closer distances can be both an indication and a cause of closer interpersonal relationships. Indeed, Hall (1959) suggested that interaction distances define the very nature of relationships. A host of studies have found that closer interpersonal distances convey greater warmth, friendship, and agreement (Egland, Stelzner, Andersen, & Spitzberg, 1997; Jensen & P. Andersen, 1979; Mehrabian & Ksionsky, 1970; Priest & Sawyer, 1967), especially when communicated by a rewarding communicator (Burgoon, Manusov, Mineo, & Hale, 1985).

Other space-based cues are important contributors to immediacy judgments. Body angle or orientation, for example, can communicate immediacy, with a face-to-face position between interactants usually signaling the most interest, availability, and warmth (Coker & Burgoon, 1987; Patterson, 1973, 1977); conversely, a side-to-side position often gives an interactant "the cold shoulder." Warmth and availability are enhanced typically as well if one interactant does not "tower" over the other. The metaphor "seeing eye to eye" suggests that the same physical plane is associated with greater agreement and acquiescence. Adults often tower over children; tall men sometimes loom over shorter women; disabled individuals in wheelchairs have to crane their neck and strain their ears to interact with a standing adult (Andersen, 1985, 1999). Finally, immediacy is communicated via forward leans. Leaning forward during interaction conveys interest and facilitates interaction. A number of researchers have found that forward leans often convey immediacy (e.g., Burgoon, Buller, Hale, & deTurck, 1984; Coker & Burgoon, 1987; Trout & Rosenfeld, 1980).

Haptics

Haptic, or tactile, communication is, perhaps, the most immediate form of communication (see Jones, this volume). Although touch can be used in a variety of ways to comfort, love, sexually arouse, tease, and hurt, the most typical types of touch in interpersonal interaction send messages of immediacy, warmth, and availability (Andersen, 1999). A host of studies show that individuals who touch more are generally more self-confident, warmer people who enjoy more intimacy and physical closeness (see Andersen's touch avoidance chapter, this volume).

Oculesics

Several oculesic behaviors, including eye contact, gaze, and pupil dilation, can convey immediacy in interpersonal communication. Eye contact or mutual gaze, the most important and most studied form of oculesic behavior, has been called an invitation to communicate. Eye contact is at the heart of the immediacy construct, as it can signal interest, approach, involvement, warmth, and connection simultaneously (Andersen, 1999; Burgoon et al., 1985). It is also represented on virtually every behavioral measure of immediacy (see Guerrero, this volume). Relatively higher levels of gaze and eye contact are associated with more positive perceptions (Burgoon et al., 1985).

Kinesics

A variety of kinesic behaviors may communicate warmth and intimacy, including smiling, nodding, general facial expressiveness, bodily relaxation, increased gestural behavior, and interactional synchrony (Andersen, 1984, 1999). Smiling is another central nonverbal immediacy cue and is represented in most behavioral measures of immediacy (e.g., Andersen, Andersen, & Jensen, 1979; Coker & Burgoon, 1987). Smiles have a biological basis as warm, non-aggressive behaviors and tend to be perceived cross-culturally as a sign of friendship, warmth, and positive affect (Andersen, 1999; Gutsell, 1979). Head nods, particularly by interactants while listening, are examples of important components of nonverbal immediacy. Increased facial expressiveness and gestural behavior are also associated with perceptions of involvement, warmth, and immediacy. Interactional synchrony has been shown similarly to be an immediacy behavior (Andersen, 1984, 1999; Trees, this volume).

Vocalics and Chronemics

Several elements of the voice can also be components of nonverbal immediacy. At the molar level, voices that are enthusiastic, optimistic, and warm are likely to convey the most immediacy (Andersen, 1999). At the molecular level, vocal variations in pitch, volume, and rate are associated with greater immediacy (Andersen, 1985). Listener behaviors such as "ah-huh" and "um-hmm," for instance, have been shown across a number of studies to enhance immediacy (Andersen, 1985; Mehrabian, 1971).

A number of chronemic behaviors may likewise play an important role in the communication of immediacy. Chief among these is spending time with another person (Burgoon & Aho, 1982; Egland et al., 1997). On-time arrival, not seeming rushed, being in the present, appropriate pauses and silences, and sharing talk time are all potentially important chronemic immediacy behaviors (Andersen, 1999).

MEASURES OF NONVERBAL IMMEDIACY

To facilitate the study of nonverbal immediacy in both instructional and interpersonal contexts, we created a series of (typically) self-report measures of nonverbal immediacy (Andersen, 1979; Andersen, Norton, & Nussbaum, 1981; Andersen & Coussoule, 1980; Coussoule & Andersen, 1979; Jensen & Andersen, 1979). These are summarized in J. Andersen, P. Andersen, and Jensen (1979). One way to measure nonverbal immediacy is to code carefully each nonverbal behavior (e.g., Andersen, Guerrero, Buller, & Jorgensen, 1998; Le Poire & Burgoon, 1994). Although such a method of coding actual immediacy behaviors has obvious advantages (see White & Sargent, this volume; Bakeman, this volume), it has disadvantages as well: It is inordinately time-consuming to videotape and code multiple channels of nonverbal behavior, and there is no assurance that each behavior is perceived, salient, or meaningful for actual interactions.

To complement behavioral coding of actual interaction, or sometimes in its place, Andersen et al. (1979) devised three alternative measurement schemes: (a) The Behavioral Indicants of Immediacy Scale (BII), which measures an interactant's perception of a partner's immediacy (see Appendixes 1 and 3), (b) The Generalized Immediacy Scale (GI), a gestalt measure of general immediacy (see Appendixes 2 and 4), and (c) The Rater's Perception of Immediacy Scale (RI) that is used by a trained observer to assess immediacy (see Appendix 5).

The Behavioral Indicants of Immediacy Scale (BII)

The BII is a comparative, perceptually based measure of 15 nonverbal immediacy behaviors that mirror those discussed earlier in this chapter. The version of the BII used in instructional settings was originally a 28-item instrument but was reduced to a more parsimonious, factor-based, Likert-type instrument that measures perceptions of 15 immediacy/nonimmediacy behaviors (see Appendix 1). The interpersonal version of the BII is a 20-item, factor-based, Likert scale that measures receiver perceptions of 20 immediacy or nonimmediacy behaviors (see Appendix 3)

Reliability of the BII. The instructional version of the 15-item BII has yielded consistently high reliability coefficients that ranged from .86 to .95, with a mean of .91 across the entire series of studies (Allen & Shaw, 1990; Andersen, 1979; Andersen et al., 1979; Andersen et al, 1981; Giglio & Lustig, 1987; Sorensen, 1989). Likewise, these studies revealed a test–retest reliability ranging from .74 to .80, suggesting the high stability of both the immediacy behaviors and their measurement. The 20-item interpersonal version of the BII scale, consisting of a diverse set of behaviors, has yielded split-half internal reliability coefficients ranging from .70 to .78, with a mean internal reliability of .74 (Andersen et. al., 1979; Jensen & Andersen, 1979; Gutsell, 1979).

Validity of the BII. The instructional version of the BII has demonstrated considerable concurrent validity with other measure of measures of immediacy. The BII correlated .67 with the GI in two studies (Andersen, 1979; Andersen et al., 1981) and correlated .92 with the RI, a rating of immediacy by an outside observer (Andersen, 1979). The BII has been shown to be a moderate predictor of more positive student attitudes toward course content, quality overall communication in the course, positive affect toward the course, behavioral commitment to what was taught, perceived relational solidarity with the instructor, and the probability of enrolling in a related course (Andersen, 1979; Andersen et al., 1981; Giglio & Lustig, 1987). The BII is also highly predictive of overall students' affect toward an instructor (Andersen, 1979; Giglio & Lustig, 1987).

In addition, the BII is correlated strongly with instructor openness, friendliness, communication image, animation, impression leaving, relaxation, attentiveness, and interpersonal drama. Sorensen (1989) reported a substantial correlation between teacher competence and teacher immediacy using a version of the BII. The BII also was found to significantly predict supervisor ratings of affective learning and general teacher effectiveness (Allen & Shaw, 1990). The interpersonal version of the BII was found to be a significant predictor of interpersonal credibility, attraction, homophily, solidarity, and opinion leadership (Jensen & Andersen, 1979).

The Generalized Immediacy Scale (GI)

The generalized immediacy scale assesses a person's gestalt global impressions of a person's nonverbal immediacy. Typically it has been used to assess the immediacy of an instructor (see Appendix 2) or an interpersonal interactant (see Appendix 4).

Reliability of the GI. Internal reliability estimates for the nine-item instructional version of the GI are extremely high, ranging from .95 to .98, with a mean internal reliability estimate across studies of .96 (Allen & Shaw, 1990; Andersen, 1979; Andersen et al., 1979; Andersen & Withrow, 1981; Carrell & Menzel, 2001; Giglio & Lustig, 1987). Several studies revealed a test–retest reliability ranging from .81 to .84, indicating both the trait-like nature of instructional immediacy and considerable stability for the scales (e.g., Andersen, 1979; Andersen et al., 1979). A shorter 5-item version of the GI yielded internal reliability estimates that ranged from .89 to .96 (Kearney, Plax, & Wendt-Wasco, 1985). The nine-item interpersonal version of the GI scale has been found to have consistently high coefficient *alpha* reliability estimates between .94 and .97, with a mean across six studies of .96 (Andersen et al., 1979; Gutsell, 1979; Jensen & Andersen, 1979).

Validity of the GI.   The instructional version of the GI has demonstrated con-current validity with other measures of immediacy. The GI had a .67 correlation with the BI in two studies (Andersen, 1979; Andersen et al., 1981). The GI has also shown considerable predictive validity across a number of studies. The GI has been shown to be highly predictive of more positive student attitudes toward course content, affective learning, quality overall communication in the course, positive affect toward the instructor, positive affect toward the course, behavioral commitment to what was taught, perceived relational solidarity with the instructor, and the probability of enrolling in a related course (Andersen, 1979; Andersen et al., 1981; Andersen & Withrow, 1981; Giglio & Lustig, 1987). These findings have held for both face-to-face and mediated instructional environments (Andersen, 1979; Andersen & Withrow, 1981; Carrell & Menzel, 2001). Research using the GI has shown that face-to-face lectures are a more immediate form of communication than are video lectures that, in turn, were seen as more immediate than a Power-point presentation (Carrell & Menzel, 2001).

The GI has significant positive correlations with a number of instructor characteristics including openness, friendliness, communicator image, animation, impression leaving, relaxation, attentiveness, and dramatic style (Andersen et al., 1981). The GI has also been found to be related to perceived student learning (Allen & Shaw, 1990) but not to actual student learning (Andersen, 1979). The GI has been found to significantly predict supervisor ratings of affective student learning, student behavioral commitment, and general teacher effectiveness (Allen & Shaw, 1990). Using a shortened version of the GI, Kearney et al. (1985), for example, found a relationship between immediacy and a host of instructional effectiveness variables including positive affect toward the course, improved course content, instructor ratings engaging in practices recommended in the course, and enrolling in another, similar course. These findings held in both people-oriented and technically oriented classes. Likewise, Jensen and Andersen (1979) reported that the interpersonal version of the GI scale is highly associated with a number of interpersonal perceptions of credibility, attraction, homophily, opinion leader-ship, and interpersonal solidarity, demonstrating its predictive validity.

Raters' Perception of Immediacy Scale (RI)

The RI was designed to be used by observers in an instructional context to measure the nonverbal immediacy behaviors of teachers (see Appendix 5).

Reliability of the RI.   The original studies of the 11-item RI conducted in instructional context showed interrater reliability coefficients that ranged from .79 to .97, and the split-half reliability coefficient was .82 (Andersen, 1979; Andersen et al., 1979). In one study, modifications of the BII and GI for use by raters yielded reliability estimates for each scale of .93 (Kay & Christophel, 1995).

Validity of the RI.   The RI demonstrated considerable concurrent validity with other measures of nonverbal immediacy. The independently assessed RI correlated .92 with student perceptions of nonverbal immediacy as assessed by the BII (Andersen, 1979). A version of BII and GI for use by raters found that nonverbal immediacy of managers significantly predicted motivation by employees (Kay & Christophel, 1995).

CONCLUSION

Although developed nearly 25 years ago, the five measures reported in this study are still among the most reliable and valid measures of perceived nonverbal immediacy available. The BII is an excellent measure of gestalt perceptions of immediacy and is the most reliable measure of its type. It has been used with great success in studies of instructional immediacy. The interpersonal version of the BII has acceptable reliabilities and is one of several good choices available to researchers to assess interpersonal immediacy. The GI is an outstanding measure of gestalt perceptions of nonverbal immediacy, with mean reliability estimates of .96 across studies in both instructional and interpersonal contexts. Both the instructional and interpersonal GI have established validity and continue to be excellent measures of gestalt impression of nonverbal immediacy.

REFERENCES

Allen, J. L., & Shaw, D. H. (1990). Teachers' communication behaviors and supervisors' evaluation of instruction in elementary and secondary classrooms. *Communication Education, 39,* 308–322.

Andersen, J. F. (1979). Teacher immediacy as a predictor of teaching effectiveness. In D. Nimmo (Ed.), *Communication yearbook 3* (pp. 543–559). New Brunswick, NJ: Transaction Books.

Andersen, J. F., Andersen, P. A., & Jensen, A. D. (1979). The measurement of nonverbal immediacy. *Journal of Applied Communication Research, 7,* 153–180.

Andersen, J. F., Norton, R. W., & Nussbaum, J. F. (1981). Three investigations exploring relationships between perceived teacher communication behaviors and student learning. *Communication Education, 30,* 377–392.

Andersen, J. F., & Withrow, J. G. (1981). The impact of lecturer nonverbal expressiveness on improving mediated instruction. *Communication Education, 30,* 342–353.

Andersen, P. A. (1984, April). *An arousal-valence model of nonverbal immediacy exchange.* Paper presented to the Central States Speech Association Convention, Chicago, IL.

Andersen, P. A. (1985). Nonverbal immediacy in interpersonal communication. In A. W. Siegman & S. Feldstein (Eds.), *Multichannel integrations of nonverbal behavior* (pp. 1–36). Hillsdale, NJ: Lawrence Erlbaum Associates.

Andersen, P. A. (1999). *Nonverbal communication: Forms and functions.* Boston, MA: McGraw Hill.

Andersen, P. A., & Coussoule, A. R. (1980). The perceptual world of the communication apprehensive: The effect of communication apprehension and interpersonal gaze on interpersonal perception. *Communication Quarterly, 28,* 44–54.

Andersen, P. A., & Guerrero, L. K. (1998). The bright side of relational communication. Interpersonal warmth as a social emotion. In P. A. Andersen & L. K. Guerrero (Eds.), *Communications and Emotion* (pp. 305–331). San Diego, CA: Academic Press.

Andersen, P. A., Guerrero, L. K., Buller, D. B., & Jorgensen, P. F. (1998). An empirical comparison of three theories of nonverbal immediacy exchange. *Human Communication Research, 24,* 501–535.

Burgoon, J. K., & Aho, L. (1982). Three field experiments on the effects of violations of conversational distance. *Communication Monographs, 49,* 71–88.

Burgoon, J. K., Buller, D. B., Hale, J. L., & deTurck, J. L. (1984). Relational messages associated with immediacy behaviors. *Human Communication Research, 10,* 351–371.

Burgoon, J. K., Manusov, V., Mineo, P., & Hale, J. L. (1985). Effects of gaze on hiring, credibility, attraction, and relational message interpretation. *Journal of Nonverbal Behavior, 9,* 133–146.

Carrell, L. J., & Menzel, K. E. (2001). Variations in learning, motivation, and perceived immediacy between live and distance education classrooms. *Communication Education, 50,* 230–240.

Coker, D. A., & Burgoon, J. K. (1987). The nature of conversational involvement and nonverbal encoding patterns. *Human Communication Research, 13,* 463–494.

Coussoule, A. R., & Andersen, P. A. (1979, November). *The perceptual world of the communication apprehensive: The effect of communication apprehension and interpersonal gaze on interpersonal perception.* Paper presented to the Speech Communication Association, San Antonio, TX.

Egland, K. L., Stelzner, M. A., Andersen, P. A., & Spitzberg, B. H. (1997). Perceived understanding, nonverbal communication, and relational satisfaction. In J. Aitken & L. Shedletsky (Eds.), *Intrapersonal communication processes* (pp. 386–395). Annandale, VA: The Speech Communication Association.

Giglio, K., & Lustig, M. W. (1987, February). *Teacher immediacy and student expectations as predictors of learning.* Paper presented to the Western Communication Association, Salt Lake City, UT.

Gutsell, L. M. (1979). *Perceptual and behavioral responses to smiling.* Unpublished masters thesis, West Virginia University, Morgantown, WV.

Hall, E. T. (1959). *The silent language.* New York: Doubleday.

Jensen, A. D., & Andersen, P. A. (1979, May). *The relationship among communication traits, communication behaviors, and interpersonal perception variables.* Paper presented at the International Communication Association, Philadelphia, PA.

Kay, B., & Christophel, D. M. (1995). The relationships among manager communication openness, nonverbal immediacy, and subordinate motivation. *Communication Research Reports, 12,* 200–205.

Kearney, P., Plax, T. G., & Wendt-Wasco, N. J. (1985). Teacher immediacy for affective learning in divergent college classes. *Communication Quarterly, 33,* 61–74.

Le Poire, B. A., & Burgoon, J. K. (1994). Two contrasting explanations of involvement violations: Expectancy violations theory versus discrepancy arousal theory. *Human Communication Research, 20,* 590–591.

Mehrabian, A. (1971). *Silent messages.* Belmont, CA: Wadsworth.

Mehrabian, A., & Ksionsky, S. (1970). Models for affiliative and conformity behavior. *Psychological Bulletin, 74,* 110–126.

Patterson, M. L. (1973). Stability of nonverbal immediacy behaviors. *Journal of Experimental Social Psychology, 7,* 97–101.

Patterson, M. L. (1977). Interpersonal distance, affect, and equilibrium theory. *Journal of Social Psychology, 101,* 205–214.

Priest, R. F., & Sawyer, J. (1967). Proximity and peership: Bases of balance in interpersonal attraction. *The American Journal of Sociology, 72,* 633–649.

Sorensen, G. (1989). The relationships among teachers' self-disillusive statements, students' perceptions and affective learning. *Communication Education, 38,* 259–279.

Trout, D. L., & Rosenfeld, H. M. (1980). The effect of postural lean and body congruence on the judgment of psychotherapeutic rapport. *Journal of Nonverbal Behavior, 4,* 176–190.

APPENDIX A

Behavioral Indicants Of Immediacy (BII) Scale:
Instructional Context

Please mark these scales to indicate how you perceive your instructor in the teaching role. Please mark the following statements to indicate whether you: (7) strongly agree; (6) agree; (5) moderately agree; (4) are undecided; (3) moderately disagree; (2) disagree; or (1) strongly disagree. Please record the number of your response in the spaces provided beside each statement. There is no correct answer. Simply record your perceptions. Some of the questions may seem similar, but this is necessary.

_____ *1. This instructor engages in more eye contact with me when teaching than most other instructors.

_____ 2. Students discuss less in this class than in most other classes.

_____ *3. This instructor has a more tense body position while teaching than most other instructors.

_____ *4. This instructor gestures more while teaching than most other instructors.

_____ *5. This instructor engages in less movement while teaching than most other instructors.

_____ 6. This instructor sits in a student desk less than most other instructors when teaching.

_____ 7. This instructor touches students less than most other instructors when teaching.

_____ *8. This instructor has a more relaxed body position while teaching than most other instructors.

_____ *9. This instructor directs his/her body position more toward students while teaching than most other instructors.

_____ 10. This instructor stands in front of the classroom less than most other instructors while teaching.

_____ *11. This instructor smiles more during class than most other instructors.

_____ 12. This instructor dresses less informally than most other instructors when teaching.

_____ *13. This instructor engages in less eye contact with me when teaching than most.

_____ 14. This instructor spends less time with students before and after class than most instructors.

_____ 15. This instructor touches students more than most other instructors when teaching.

_____ 16. Students discuss more in this class than in most other classes.

_____ *17. This instructor is more vocally expressive while teaching than most other instructors.

_____ *18. This instructor is more distant from students while teaching than most other instructors.

_____	*19. This instructor directs his/her body position less toward students while teaching than most other instructors.
_____	*20. This instructor gestures less while teaching than most other instructors.
_____	*21. This instructor engages in more movement while teaching than most other instructors.
_____	22. This instructor sits in a student desk more often than most other instructors while teaching.
_____	23. This instructor dresses more informally than most other instructors when teaching.
_____	24. This instructor stands in front of the classroom more than most other instructors while teaching.
_____	*25. This instructor is less vocally expressive while teaching than most other instructors.
_____	*26. This instructor smiles less during class than most other instructors.
_____	27. This instructor is less distant from students than most other instructors while teaching.
_____	28. This instructor spends more time with students before and after class than most other instructors.

Scoring Instructions

* These items constitute the 15-item behavioral indicants of immediacy scale. To obtain an immediacy score, use this formula:

1. Total the subject's response for the following scale items: 1, 4, 8, 9, 11, 17, 21. Call this X.
2. Total the subject's response for the following scale items: 3, 5, 13, 18, 19, 20, 25, 26. Call this Y.
3. Immediacy score = X − Y + 56.

APPENDIX B

Generalized Immediacy (GI) Scale:
Instructional Context

Immediate behaviors are those communication behaviors that reduce distance between people. Immediate behaviors may actually decrease the physical distance, or
they may decrease the psychological distance. The more immediate a person is, the
more likely he/she is to communicate at close distances, smile, engage in eye contact, use direct body orientations, use overall body movement and gestures, touch
others, relax and be vocally expressive. In other words, we might say that an immediate person is perceived as overtly friendly and warm.

Please place an "X" in *each* of the following scales to indicate your agreement
with the following statement:

In your opinion, the teaching style of your instructor is very immediate.

agree	___:___:___:___:___:___	disagree
false	___:___:___:___:___:___	true
incorrect	___:___:___:___:___:___	correct
wrong	___:___:___:___:___:___	right
yes	___:___:___:___:___:___	no

Please place an "X" in *each* of the following scales to indicate the word that best describes the teaching style of your instructor:

immediate	___:___:___:___:___:___	not immediate
cold	___:___:___:___:___:___	warm
unfriendly	___:___:___:___:___:___	friendly
close	___:___:___:___:___:___	distant

Scoring Instructions

1. Number each subject's response by numbering each scale from left to right
   (1–7).
2. Total the subject's response for the following scales: false/true, wrong/right,
   cold/warm, and unfriendly/friendly. Call this X.
3. Total the subject's response for the other five scales. Call this Y.
4. Generalized immediacy score = X – Y + 40.

APPENDIX C

Behavioral indicants Of Immediacy (BII) Scale:
Interpersonal Context

Directions

Please complete the following scales to indicate how you see the relationship between you and the other person. Please mark the following statements to indicate whether you: (7) strongly agree; (6) agree; (5) moderately agree; (4) are undecided; (3) moderately disagree; (2) disagree; or (1) strongly disagree. Please record the number of your response in the spaces provided beside each statement. There is no correct answer. Simply record your perceptions. Some of the questions may seem similar, but this is necessary.

_____	1. This person engages in more eye contact with me than most other people.
_____	2. This person's body is more tense than most other people.
_____	3. This person gestures more than most other people.
_____	4. This person engages in less movement than most other people.
_____	5. This person touches me less than most other people usually do.
_____	6. This person has a more relaxed body position than most other people.
_____	7. This person directs his/her body position more toward me than most other people usually do.
_____	8. This person smiles more than most other people do.
_____	*9. This person dresses more formally than most other people.
_____	10. This person engages in less eye contact with me than most other people.
_____	11. This person seems eager to spend time talking with me.
_____	12. This person touches me more than most other people.
_____	13. This person is more vocally expressive than most other people.
_____	14. This person seems more distant from me than most other people.
_____	15. This person directs his/her body position less toward me than most
_____	16. This person gestures less than most other people.
_____	17. This person engages in more movement than most other people.
_____	*18. This person dresses more informally than most other people.
_____	19. This person is less vocally expressive than most other people.
_____	20. This person smiles less than most other people.
_____	21. This person seemed less distant from me than most other people.
_____	22. This person seemed reluctant to spend time talking to me.

* Dropped from scale because of failure to load above 40.

Scoring Instructions

1. Total the subject's response for the following scale items: 1, 3, 6, 7, 8, 11, 12, 13, 17, 21. Call this X.
2. Total the subject's response for the following scale items: 2, 4, 5, 10, 14, 15, 16, 19, 20, 22. Call this Y.
3. Immediacy score = X – Y + 80.

APPENDIX D

Generalized Immediacy (GI) Scale:
Interpersonal Context

Immediate behaviors are those communication behaviors that reduce distance between people. Immediate behaviors may actually decrease the physical distance, or they may decrease the psychological distance. The more immediate a person is, the more likely they are to communicate at close distance, smile engage in eye contact, use direct body orientations, use overall body movement and gestures, touch others, relax, and be vocally expressive. In other words, we might say that an immediate person is perceived as overtly friendly and warm.

Is, in your opinion, the conversational style of the other person is very immediate? Please place and "X" in *each* of the following scales to indicate your agreement with the above statement.

agree	___:___:___:___:___:___	disagree
false	___:___:___:___:___:___	true
incorrect	___:___:___:___:___:___	correct
wrong	___:___:___:___:___:___	right
yes	___:___:___:___:___:___	no

Please place an "X" in *each* of the following scales to indicate the word that best describes the conversational style of the other person:

immediate	___:___:___:___:___:___	not immediate
cold	___:___:___:___:___:___	warm
unfriendly	___:___:___:___:___:___	friendly
close	___:___:___:___:___:___	distant

Scoring Instructions

1. Number each subject's response by numbering each scale from left to right (1–7).
2. Total the subject's response for the following scales: false/true, wrong/right, cold/warm, and unfriendly/friendly. Call this X.
3. Total the subject's response for the other five scales. Call this Y.
4. Generalized immediacy score = X – Y + 40.

The Relational Communication Scale

Jerold L. Hale
University of Georgia

Judee K. Burgoon
University of Arizona

Brian Householder
University of Georgia

INTRODUCTION

Individuals define the nature of their relationships with others as communication episodes are transacted. That is, the process of defining relationships occurs by sending and receiving relational messages. Relational messages are verbal and nonverbal expressions that indicate how two or more people regard each other, regard their relationship, or regard themselves within the context of the relationship (Burgoon & Saine, 1978). This relational function of interaction can be distinguished from the "report" or content function of communication (Watzlawick, Beavin, & Jackson, 1967).

Early works related to interpersonal behavior and communication fostered the view that interpersonal behavior occurred along a limited number of dimensions. That work, reviewed by Burgoon and Hale (1984), typically includes a dominance–submission or relational *control* dimension (see, also, Dillard & Solomon, this volume), an *inclusion* dimension that concerns the degree to which an individual establishes and maintains relationships with a satisfying number of other people, and an *affection* dimension that relates to establishing psychologically intimate relationships with others (see, also, Floyd & Mikkelson, this volume). According to those seminal works, relational messages serve to define relationships and relational participants along a limited and narrow set of dimensions.

Burgoon and Hale (1984, 1988) took the position, however, that the parsimony achieved in seminal writings on interpersonal behavior masked a more complete understanding of relational message content. We reviewed diverse bodies of litera-

127

ture including classic studies from anthropology and psychotherapy, studies of biological displays, semantic meaning, interpersonal evaluations, relational definition and development, and dimensions of social interaction. The three traditionally recognized dimensions of control, inclusion, and affection were represented consistently across disciplinary perspectives, theories, and lines of empirical inquiry, but there was also compelling evidence that relational definitions and relational messages included many more dimensions or themes. In all, 12 relational message themes emerged in our review with regularity and are as follows: (a) dominance–submission, (b) emotional arousal, (c) composure–noncomposure, (d) similarity–dissimilarity, (e), formality–informality, (f) task orientation–social orientation, (g) intimacy and subcomponents related to intimacy including (h) depth (or familiarity), (i) affection (attraction and liking), (j) inclusion–exclusion, (k) trust, and (l) intensity of involvement.

ORIGINS OF THE RELATIONAL COMMUNICATION SCALE

Much of the literature supporting the relational communication schema Burgoon and Hale (1984) proposed came from empirical investigations, but the schema had not been validated in their entirety. To corroborate the proposed schema and construct a measure that more thoroughly captured relational message themes, Burgoon and Hale (1987) created the Relational Communication Scale (RCS). The original RCS included a series of Likert items and tapped the participant's perceptions of relational messages communicated by a conversational partner. The results of a series of measurement studies provided compelling evidence that the RCS was a reliable and valid measure of most of the message themes Burgoon and Hale (1984) proposed.

ISSUES OF RELIABILITY AND VALIDITY

Relational Communication Themes

As noted, twelve conceptually distinct but interrelated relational message themes have been identified consistently. There is a global or superordinate intimacy–nonintimacy dimension, which includes involvement–noninvolvement, affection–hostility (also labeled liking or attraction), depth–superficiality, trust–distrust, receptivity–nonreceptivity (rapport), and similarity–dissimilarity. Three relatively orthogonal dimensions are dominance–submission, formality–informality, and task orientation–social orientation. Two closely related final dimensions are composure–noncomposure (often equated with relaxation) and emotional arousal (which includes both positive and negative forms of arousal). Factor analytic research has shown that several of these themes can be combined into message composites. The RCS has been widely used, and the most commonly employed subscales, along with subscale reliabilities, are shown in Table 5.

TABLE 5
Relational Communication Dimensions and Reliability Coefficients

Dimension	Reliability Estimates
1. Global intimacy/similarity	.81, .86, .70, .77, .86, .99
a. Involvement/affection	.81, .46, .79, .74, .78, .83, .70, .86, .78, .97, .97
b. Similarity/inclusion/depth	.77, .69, .73, .58, .95, .61, .93, .86
c. Receptivity/trust	.76, .80, .86, .44, .97, .77, .97, .84, .77, .76
d. Affection/depth	.75
e. Similarity/trust/equality	.77, .81, .74
f. Immediacy	.76, .82, .89, .83, .81, .86
g. Affection	.81, .78, .85, .83, .79
2. Dominance	.66, .76, .60, .52, .90, .65, .69, .60, .76, .68, .76, .75, .57, .55, .72, .78, .74, .88, .78
3. Composure/arousal	.80, .73, .80, .89, .82, .87, .68, .77, .86, .73, .89, .86, .78, .81, .89
4. Formality	.74, .83, .55, .92, .76, .80, .67, .48, .43, .89, .80, .63
5. Task v. social orientation	.42, .41, .34

Note: Reliability coefficients are from the original validation studies (Burgoon & Hale, 1987) and several subsequent investigations (e.g., Burgoon & Hale, 1988; Hale, Lundy, & Mongeau, 1989; Walther & Burgoon, 1992).

Communication Contexts and the RCS

The RCS has been used to study relational messages in several communication contexts. With regard to nonverbal behaviors specifically, the RCS has measured relational meanings associated with immediacy behaviors, expectancy violations, conflict behaviors, deceptive cues, reticence cues, and reciprocal and compensatory behavior patterns. More generally, the RCS was used in studies of physician–patient interaction, marital satisfaction, computer-mediated interaction, and relational development. Table 6 lists RCS studies by communication contexts, and a few examples are noted in more detail next.

Immediacy Behaviors and Relational Meanings. After laying the conceptual and empirical groundwork for the relational communication scale, Burgoon and her associates completed several studies to determine whether nonverbal cues communicated relational meanings. Burgoon, Buller, Hale, and deTurck (1984) conducted the first of those studies. In their work, the authors constructed a series of videotapes in which confederates varied proximity, eye contact, body lean, and touch while an opposite-sex confederate engaged in normative behaviors. Two levels of each immediacy cue were enacted, i.e., close and far distance, high and low eye contact, forward and backward lean, and touch

TABLE 6

Studies Using the Relational Communication Scale Broken Down by Communication Context and Measurement Perspective

	Measurement Perspective		
CONTEXT	P	SR	O
Relational Messages and Immediacy Behaviors			
Burgoon (1991)	X		
Burgoon, Buller, Hale, & deTurck, (1984)			X
Burgoon & Dillman (1995)			X
Burgoon & Hale (1988)	X		
Burgoon, Manusov, Mineo, & Hale (1985)	X		
Burgoon & Newton (1991)	X		X
Burgoon, Walther, & Baesler (1992)	X		
Floyd & Voloudakis (1999)	X		
Hale & Burgoon (1984)	X		X
Coker & Burgoon (1987)			X
Relational Messages of Nonverbal Expectancy Violations			
Burgoon (1991)	X		
Burgoon, Coker, & Coker (1986)	X		
Burgoon & Hale (1988)	X		
Burgoon & Le Poire (1993)			X
Burgoon & Newton (1991)	X		X
Burgoon, Newton, Walther, & Baesler (1989)	X		
Burgoon & Walther (1990)			X
Burgoon, Walther, & Baesler (1992)	X		
Coker & Burgoon (1987)			X
Le Poire & Burgoon (1991)	X		X
Physician-Patient Relational Communication			
Burgoon, Pfau, Parrott, Birk, Coker, & Burgoon, (1987)			X
Relational Communication and Marital Satisfaction			
Kelley & Burgoon (1991)		X	
Kelley (2000)		X	
Relational Messages During Conflict			
Newton & Burgoon (1990)		X	
Relational Messages Associated with Deception			
Burgoon & Buller (1994)	X		
Burgoon Buller, Dillman, & Walther (1995)	X		
Relational Messages and Computer-Mediated Interaction			
Walther & Burgoon (1992)	X		
Relational Messages and Reticence Behaviors			
Burgoon, & Koper (1984)	X		
Burgoon, Pfau, Birk, & Manusov (1987)	X		

Reciprocal and Compensatory Interaction Patterns		
Burgoon, Le Poire, & Rosenthal (1995)		X
Burgoon, Olney, & Coker (1988)	X	
Floyd & Burgoon (1999)	X	
Guerrero & Burgoon (1996)	X	
Hale & Burgoon (1984)	X	X

present or touch absent. A design with cues in all combinations was not possible because touch could not be enacted from the far distances. Twenty videotaped segments with varying cue combinations were made for both a male and a female confederate. Research participants watched two of the videotaped segments, and using the RCS, were asked to evaluate what messages the confederate was communicating. The results showed that each of the nonverbal immediacy cues conveyed strong and unequivocal relational messages. Table 2 lists several studies that report relational meanings associated with nonverbal cues.

Relational Messages of Expectancy Violations. Research using the RCS has examined the impact of nonverbal expectancy violations on relational meanings. For example, Burgoon, Coker, and Coker (1986) compared a social meaning model to an expectancy violations model of nonverbal behaviors. The social meaning model holds that nonverbal behaviors communicate clear and unambiguous relational meanings. The nonverbal expectancy violations model (e.g., Burgoon & Hale, 1988) holds that unexpected nonverbal behaviors have meanings that are ambiguous and mediated by whether the behavior is very rewarding or very non-rewarding.

Burgoon, Coker, and Coker (1986) tested the social meaning and expectancy violations models with respect to gaze behaviors. They had participants engage in mock job interviews with confederates. The confederates varied their levels of eye gaze (high, normal, low) during the interviews. The job credentials of the confederates were also varied (weak, strong). After the interviews were completed participants rated the confederates on a number of qualities including perceived credibility, suitability for the job, and the perceived relational messages they conveyed. As predicted by the expectancy violations model, the relational meanings of differential amounts of eye gaze were mediated by the reward value (job credentials) of the confederates.

Reciprocal and Compensatory Interaction Patterns. Research from several traditions focuses on how individuals' actions influence one another's behaviors (see Cappella, this volume). Behaviors in response to another person's cues may be reciprocal (i.e., similar or matching), or they may be compensatory (i.e., dissimilar or complementary). Hale and Burgoon (1984) examined patterns of reciprocity and compensation among friends and strangers in dyadic interactions. Two pairs of friends reported to research sessions together. One member of each pair was enlisted as a confederate and trained to vary his or her nonverbal immediacy (low, high). In a control condition, one participant was only nominally a confederate, and no instructions or training were given regarding his or her interaction behaviors. Participants then engaged in two conversations, one with a confederate stranger and the other with a confederate friend.

The RCS scales were employed as a dependent measure in three ways. Confederates rated the relational messages communicated by the participant. In turn, participants rated the relational messages communicated by the confederates. Trained observers also rated the relational messages conveyed by the participants in response to the confederate's behaviors. Hale and Burgoon (1984) reported mostly reciprocal behaviors. For example, as confederates' perceived immediacy (as rated by the participant) increased, so did participants' perceived immediacy. As the confederate's perceived immediacy increased, the perceived detachment of the participant (as rated by the confederate) decreased. Observer ratings of the relational messages sent by the confederate and participants showed similar patterns of reciprocal communication.

USING THE RELATIONAL COMMUNICATION SCALE

Participant Observations, Self-Reports, and Observer Ratings

One attractive feature of the RCS is its flexibility and ability to assess relational message content from various perspectives. The instrument uses a Likert format, typically with seven response intervals. The number of items included in the scale varies across studies; occasionally 60 or more items have been included, but some quantity nearer 30 items is typical. The RCS has been used to measure relational message content from three perspectives: (a) a participant observation perspective where the participant reports on the messages conveyed by a conversational partner, (b) a self-report perspective where the participant indicates what messages he or she communicated to others, or (c) a nonparticipant observer reports on the messages sent by others. The RCS studies listed in Table 2 are broken down by whether the study employed participant observations, self-reports, or observer ratings of relational messages. The RCS written for use as a participant observation measure appears in the appendix.

With minor modifications, RCS items can be used as a self-report of relational communication (i.e., what relational messages the respondent believed he or she was conveying to one or more others). To assess one's self-reported relational message content, the wording of the items would be changed from, for example, "He/she dominated the conversation" to "I dominated the conversation," and "S/he was interested in what I had to say" to "I was interested in what he/she had to say." In the same way, minor modifications to the RCS allow the researcher to tap the perceptions of nonparticipant observers. To assess the perceptions of nonparticipant observers, the wording of the items would be changed to "Person A dominated the conversations with Person B," and "Person A was interested in what Person B had to say."

Number and Scoring of Items

The reliability of measures is sensitive to the number of items that comprise each scale. If each item is of equal quality, including more items increases the reliability of measurement, and fewer items decreases the reliability of measurement. If an abbreviated form of the RCS is used, researchers should still use multiple items to measure each dimension. As well, each dimension of the RCS includes positively and negatively worded items. If an abbreviated form is used, researchers should include both positively and negatively worded items. The score for each dimension of the RCS should be represented as a mean value. Scores on items measuring each dimension of the RCS should therefore be summed after reflecting or reverse scoring negatively worded items and then divided by the number of items. Items needing to be reverse-scored are noted in the appendix with an asterisk.

DISCUSSION

For 20 years the RCS has been used in a variety of ways and has shown to be a useful measure of relational message content. The measure was created after a review spanning several scholarly disciplines and bodies of literature (Burgoon & Hale, 1984). It was scrutinized in a series of initial measurement studies. Those studies yielded similar dimensions and the dimensions were reliably assessed across studies (Burgoon & Hale, 1987). The initial factor structure has been replicated in several subsequent studies (e.g., Burgoon, Coker, & Coker, 1986; Hale, Lundy, & Mongeau, 1989; Mongeau, Yeazell, & Hale, 1994; Walther & Burgoon, 1992). The RCS has proven to be quite versatile. Its applications have varied from studies of the most intimate relationships (e.g., Kelly, 2000; Kelly & Burgoon, 1991) to the most casual ones (Walther & Burgoon, 1992). The RCS has been used extensively to study nonverbal behaviors. Studies have explored the relational meanings associated with nonverbal cues, nonverbal expectancy violations, patterns of behavioral adaptation, nonverbal cues of deception, and nonverbal behaviors during episodes of interpersonal conflict, and related to nonverbal reticence cues (see Table 6). Research into each of those subject areas continues, and the RCS can certainly make useful contributions to the knowledge generated in future studies.

Applications of the RCS have also included contexts and issues quite apart from the study of nonverbal behaviors. For example, the RCS has been used to study communication in personal relationships, physician–patient communication, and computer-mediated communication (see Table 6). Each of those contexts of communication continues to generate considerable inquiry, and the RCS will usefully contribute to those research efforts. Two qualities make the RCS especially useful across communication contexts. The RCS may be adapted to study communication from several perspectives. It has been used as a participant observation measure, a self-report measure, and by nonparticipant observers. The RCS has also been used as a check of experimental controls (e.g., Floyd & Burgoon, 1999; Burgoon & Le Poire, 1993), an independent variable (e.g., Hale & Burgoon, 1984), and extensively as a dependent variable or outcome measure (e.g., Burgoon, 1991; Burgoon, Buller, Hale, & deTurk, 1984; Floyd & Voloudakis, 1999).

The dimensions of relational communication are well established. Recently Kam, Burgoon, and Bacue (2002) have begun to explore alternative means for measuring the fundamental themes of relational messages identified by Burgoon and Hale (1984). They suggested two alternatives. One was a Gestalt measure using a quadrant coding system. The quadrant coding could be part of a participant observation, self-report, or non-participant observation, where a person's relational messages would be coded into bi-polar quadrants based on message content and the valence of the message content. For example, if the dominance dimension of relational content were being assessed, quadrants would include a dominant-positive quadrant, a dominant-negative quadrant, a submissive-positive quadrant, and a submissive-negative quadrant. The same format could be repeated for each of the dimensions of relational communication content.

Kam, Burgoon, and Bacue (2002) also discuss the possibility of measuring relational communication content by directly coding nonverbal behaviors. Several of the studies discussed earlier established clear relational meanings associated with nonverbal cues. If the cues convey consistent relational meanings then one way to measure message content is to directly code the behaviors. This idea is an intriguing one, but the same nonverbal cues can convey multiple relational meanings. As a result, using the direct coding of nonverbal cues as the only measure of relational communication content may be unadvisable. Kam et al. (2002) suggest using multiple methods, based on the RCS, to measure relational communication content. Whether by itself, or as part of a multiple measures approach, the RCS should retain a leading role in the assessment of the fundamental themes of relational communication.

REFERENCES

Burgoon, J. K. (1991). Relational message interpretations of touch, conversational distance, and posture. *Journal of Nonverbal Behavior, 15,* 233–258.

Burgoon, J. K., & Buller, D. B. (1994). Interpersonal deception: III. Effects of deceit on perceived communication and nonverbal behavior dynamics. *Journal of Nonverbal Behavior, 18,* 155–184.

Burgoon, J. K., Buller, D. B., Dillman, L., & Walther, J. (1995). Interpersonal deception: IV. Effects of suspicion on perceived communication and nonverbal behavior dynamics. *Human Communication Research, 22,* 163–196.

Burgoon, J. K., Buller, D. B., Hale, J. L., & deTurck, M. (1984). Relational messages associated with nonverbal behaviors. *Human Communication Research, 10,* 351–378.

Burgoon, J. K., Coker, D. A., & Coker, R. A. (1986). Communicative effects of gaze behavior: A test of two contrasting explanations. *Human Communication Research, 12*, 495–524.

Burgoon, J. K., & Dillman, L. (1995). Gender, immediacy and nonverbal communication. In P. J. Kalbfleisch & M. J. Cody (Eds.), *Gender, power, and communication in human relationships* (pp. 63–81). Hillsdale, NJ: Lawrence Erlbaum Associates.

Burgoon, J. K., & Hale, J. L. (1984). The fundamental topoi of relational communication. *Communication Monographs, 51*, 19–41.

Burgoon, J. K., & Hale, J. L. (1987). Validation and measurement of the fundamental themes of relational communication. *Communication Monographs, 54*, 19–41.

Burgoon, J. K., & Hale, J. L. (1988). Nonverbal expectancy violations: Model elaboration and application to immediacy behaviors. *Communication Monographs, 55*, 58–79.

Burgoon, J. K., & Koper, R. J. (1984). Nonverbal and relational communication associated with reticence. *Human Communication Research, 10*, 601–626.

Burgoon, J. K., & Le Poire, B. A. (1993). Effects of communication expectancies, actual communication, and expectancy disconfirmation on evaluations of communicators and their communication behavior. *Human Communication Research, 20*, 75–107.

Burgoon, J. K., Le Poire, B. A., & Rosenthal, R. (1995). Effects of preinteraction expectancies and target communication on perceiver reciprocity and compensation in dyadic interaction. *Journal of Experimental Social Psychology, 31*, 287–321.

Burgoon, J. K., Manusov, V., Mineo, P., & Hale, J. L. (1985). Effects of eye gaze on hiring, credibility, attraction and relational message interpretation. *Journal of Nonverbal Behavior, 9*, 133–146.

Burgoon, J. K., & Newton, D. A. (1991). Applying a social meaning model to relational messages of conversational involvement: Comparing participant and observer perspectives. *Southern Communication Journal, 56*, 96–113.

Burgoon, J. K., Newton, D. A., Walther, J. B., & Baesler, E. J. (1989). Nonverbal expectancy violations and conversational involvement. *Journal of Nonverbal Behavior, 13*, 97–120.

Burgoon, J. K., Olney, C. A., & Coker, R. (1988). The effects of communicator characteristics on patterns of reciprocity and compensation. *Journal of Nonverbal Behavior, 11*, 146–165.

Burgoon, J. K., Pfau, M., Birk, T., & Manusov, V. (1987). Nonverbal communication performance and perceptions associated with reticence: Replications and classroom implications. *Communication Education, 36*, 119–130.

Burgoon, J. K., Pfau, M., Parrott, R., Birk, T., Coker, R., & Burgoon, M. (1987). Relational communication, satisfaction, compliance-gaining strategies and compliance in communication between physicians and patients. *Communication Monographs, 54*, 307–234.

Burgoon, J. K., & Saine, T. J. (1978). *The unspoken dialogue: An introduction to nonverbal communication.* Boston: Houghton-Mifflin.

Burgoon, J. K., & Walther, J. B. (1990). Nonverbal expectancies and the consequences of violations. *Human Communication Research, 17*, 232–265.

Burgoon, J. K., Walther, J. B., & Baesler, E. J. (1992). Interpretations and consequences of interpersonal touch. *Human Communication Research, 19*, 237–263.

Coker, D. A., & Burgoon, J. K. (1987). The nature of conversational involvement and nonverbal encoding patterns. *Human Communication Research, 13*, 463–494.

Floyd, K., & Burgoon, J. K. (1999). Reacting to nonverbal expressions of liking: A test of interaction adaptation theory. *Communication Monographs, 66*, 219–239.

Floyd, K., & Voloudakis, M. (1999). Affectionate behavior in adult platonic friendships: Interpreting and evaluating expectancy violations. *Human Communication Research, 25*, 341–369.

Guerrero, L. K., & Burgoon, J. K. (1996). Attachment styles and reactions to nonverbal involvement change in romantic dyads: Patterns of reciprocity and compensation. *Human Communication Research, 22*, 335–370.

Hale, J. L., & Burgoon, J. K. (1984). Models of reactions to changes in nonverbal immediacy. *Journal of Nonverbal Behavior, 8*, 287–314.

Hale, J. L., Lundy, J. C., Jr., & Mongeau, P. A. (1989). Perceived relational intimacy and relational message content. *Communication Research Reports, 6*, 94–99.

Kam, K. Y., Burgoon, J. K., & Bacue, A. (2002). *A comprehensive approach to the observational coding of relational messages.* Paper presented to the International Network on Personal Relationships, Prescott, AZ.

Kelley, D. L. (2000). Relational expectancy fulfillment as an explanatory variable for distinguishing couple types. *Human Communication Research, 25,* 420–442.

Kelley, D. L., & Burgoon, J. K. (1991). Understanding marital satisfaction and couple type as functions of relational expectations. *Human Communication Research, 18,* 40–69.

Le Poire, B. A., & Burgoon, J. K. (1991). *Participant and observer perceptions of relational messages associated with nonverbal involvement and pleasantness.* Paper presented to the annual meeting of the Speech Communication Association, Atlanta.

Mongeau, P. A., Yeazell, M., & Hale, J. L. (1994). Sex differences in relational message interpretations on male- and female-initiated first dates: A research note. *Journal of Social Behavior and Personality, 9,* 731–742.

Newton, D. A., & Burgoon, J. K. (1990). The use and consequences of verbal influence strategies during interpersonal disagreements. *Human Communication Research, 16,* 477–518.

Walther, J. B., & Burgoon, J. K. (1992). Relational communication in computer-mediated interaction. *Human Communication Research, 19,* 50–88.

Watzlawick, P., Beavin, J., & Jackson, D. (1967). *Pragmatics of human communication: A study of interactional patterns, pathologies, and paradoxes.* New York, NY: Norton.

APPENDIX

Relational Communication Scale for Participant Observation

Following are a number of statements about the interchange (you just completed). For each, I would like you to use a 1 to 7 scale to indicate whether you agree or disagree with the statement. Please circle 1, 2, 3, 4, 5, 6 or 7, depending on your opinion. A 7 means you strongly agree, a 6 means you agree, a 5 means you agree somewhat, a 4 means you are neutral or unsure, a 3 means you disagree somewhat, a 2 means you disagree, and a 1 means you strongly disagree.

He/she [Intimacy: Involvement]	Strongly Disagree					Strongly Agree	
1. was highly involved in the conversation.	1	2	3	4	5	6	7
2. showed enthusiasm while talking with me.	1	2	3	4	5	6	7
*3. was not fully engaged in the conversation.	1	2	3	4	5	6	7
*4. acted bored by the conversation.	1	2	3	4	5	6	7
5. was interested in what I had to say.	1	2	3	4	5	6	7
*6. created a sense of distance between us.	1	2	3	4	5	6	7
*7. was detached during the conversation.	1	2	3	4	5	6	7
He/she [Intimacy: Affection]							
1. acted like he/she was enjoying the conversation.	1	2	3	4	5	6	7
2. displayed pleasantness toward me.	1	2	3	4	5	6	7
*3. seemed to dislike me.	1	2	3	4	5	6	7
*4. communicated coldness rather than warmth.	1	2	3	4	5	6	7
5. conveyed that he/she me attractive.	1	2	3	4	5	6	7
6. showed affection toward me.	1	2	3	4	5	6	7

He/she [Intimacy: Receptivity/Trust]	Strongly Disagree					Strongly Agree	
*1. was unreceptive to what I had to say.	1	2	3	4	5	6	7
2. tried to win my trust.	1	2	3	4	5	6	7
3. was open to my ideas.	1	2	3	4	5	6	7
4. appeared honest and truthful when communicating with me.	1	2	3	4	5	6	7
*5. was unwilling to listen to me.	1	2	3	4	5	6	7
6. was sincere in communicating with me.	1	2	3	4	5	6	7
*7. didn't care what I thought.	1	2	3	4	5	6	7
8. tried to establish rapport with me.	1	2	3	4	5	6	7

He/she
[Intimacy: Depth]

1. tried to move the conversation to a deeper level.	1	2	3	4	5	6	7
*2. showed no desire for further interaction with me.	1	2	3	4	5	6	7
3. created an air of familiarity between us.	1	2	3	4	5	6	7
4. tried to create a more personal relationship with me.	1	2	3	4	5	6	7
*5. kept the conversation at an impersonal level.	1	2	3	4	5	6	7
6. acted like we were good friends.	1	2	3	4	5	6	7
*7. made the conversation seem superficial.	1	2	3	4	5	6	7

He/she
[Intimacy: Similarity/Inclusion]

1. made me feel we were similar.	1	2	3	4	5	6	7
2. tried to establish common ground with me.	1	2	3	4	5	6	7
*3. made differences between us evident.	1	2	3	4	5	6	7
*4. made me feel like we didn't have a lot in common.	1	2	3	4	5	6	7
*5. acted like he/she was more powerful than me.	1	2	3	4	5	6	7
6. treated me like an equal.	1	2	3	4	5	6	7

He/she
[Dominance]

*1. let me take the lead in the conversation.	1	2	3	4	5	6	7
2. attempted to persuade me.	1	2	3	4	5	6	7
3. took the initiative in directing the conversation.	1	2	3	4	5	6	7
*4. was very submissive toward me.	1	2	3	4	5	6	7
5. dominated the conversation.	1	2	3	4	5	6	7
*6. didn't try to influence me.	1	2	3	4	5	6	7
*7. was not very assertive with me.	1	2	3	4	5	6	7
8. took control of the conversation.	1	2	3	4	5	6	7
9. had the upper hand in the conversation.	1	2	3	4	5	6	7
10. made his/her presence felt.	1	2	3	4	5	6	7
11. did more talking than listening.	1	2	3	4	5	6	7
12. was very skillful in managing the conversation.	1	2	3	4	5	6	7

(continued on next page)

He/she [Dominance] *(continued)*	Strongly Disagree					Strongly Agree	
*13. was influenced by me.	1	2	3	4	5	6	7
14. was completely self-confident when interacting with me.	1	2	3	4	5	6	7
*15. was more of a follower than a leader during the conversation.	1	2	3	4	5	6	7
*16. was not very smooth verbally.	1	2	3	4	5	6	7
*17. showed a lot of poise during the interaction.	1	2	3	4	5	6	7
18. was responsible for keeping the conversation going.	1	2	3	4	5	6	7
19. had a dramatic way of interacting.	1	2	3	4	5	6	7
*20. had trouble thinking of things to talk about.	1	2	3	4	5	6	7
21. was very expressive during the conversation.	1	2	3	4	5	6	7

He/she
[Composure/Emotional (Non)arousal]

1. was calm and poised with me.	1	2	3	4	5	6	7
*2. expressed annoyance with me.	1	2	3	4	5	6	7
*3. revealed feelings of tension while talking with me.	1	2	3	4	5	6	7
4. appeared to be comfortable talking with me.	1	2	3	4	5	6	7
5. acted relaxed and at ease while talking with me.	1	2	3	4	5	6	7
*6. acted frustrated with me.	1	2	3	4	5	6	7
7. was energized and active while interacting with me.	1	2	3	4	5	6	7
*8. seemed nervous in my presence.	1	2	3	4	5	6	7

He/she
[Formality]

1. kept the interaction at a formal level.	1	2	3	4	5	6	7
*2. tried to make the conversation informal.	1	2	3	4	5	6	7
3. tried to keep the conversation very businesslike.	1	2	3	4	5	6	7
*4. tried to make the interaction easygoing and relaxed.	1	2	3	4	5	6	7
*5. took a casual approach to the conversation.	1	2	3	4	5	6	7

He/she
[Task versus Social Orientation]

*1. was as interested in building a good relationship as in completing the task at hand.	1	2	3	4	5	6	7
2. wanted to stick to the main purpose of the discussion.	1	2	3	4	5	6	7
3. was very work-oriented.	1	2	3	4	5	6	7
*4. was more interested in having a social conversation than completing the assigned task.	1	2	3	4	5	6	7

Scoring Key: Items with an asterisk should be reverse-scored (i.e., 7 = 1, 6 = 2, 5 = 3, 3 = 5, 2 = 6, 1 = 7). Add together all the items belonging to a given dimension or composite (e. g., involvement/affection), then divide by number of items. Global intimacy/similarity includes the first five sets of items. Higher scores represent greater intimacy, similarity, dominance, composure and nonarousal, formality, and task orientation.

Behavioral Coding
of Visual Affect Behavior

Patricia Noller
University of Queensland

INTRODUCTION

Both positive and negative emotions are important aspects of close relationships (Feeney, Noller, & Roberts, 1998; Noller & Roberts, 2002; Roberts & Noller, this volume). We also tend to react most intensely in the context of our close personal relationships, particularly, as Bowlby (1973) noted, if those relationships are at risk. For these reasons, affective behavior is of great interest to many researchers. The best way to study the expression of affect in close relationships (as against peoples' experience of affect) is by using observational methods and coding systems that allow us to explore the actual behaviors used by relational partners when discussing emotional issues.

There are many ways to categorize nonverbal affective behavior, but a frequently used method is to code the presence or absence of particular behaviors. In this chapter, I describe a system for coding particular nonverbal behaviors that was developed by Noller and Gallois (1986). The coding system was developed for use in studies of marital communication, and it relates only to visual behaviors such as smiles, eyebrow raises, and eyebrow flashes. It is important, however, to keep in mind that paralinguistic cues are also important in marital (and other) communication (Noller, 1985). Using a sample of 48 videotaped couple interactions, including those described later in this chapter, Noller found that negative messages were coded negative in the vocal channel more frequently than in the verbal or visual channels. Despite this, visual behaviors are also important to many research projects, and thus this present chapter offers guidance as to how such coding can be accomplished.

Development of the Coding System

The coding scheme discussed in this chapter was developed by Noller and Gallois (1986). Because we were primarily focusing on the communication of emotion, and because our primary interest was in the behaviors associated with positive and negative affect, we first selected behaviors shown in previous research to be related to the expression of emotion (Ekman & Friesen, 1975; Ekman, Friesen, & Ellsworth, 1972; Ekman & Oster, 1979). One of the coders then worked through the videotapes of the standard content messages used by Noller (1980; see also Noller, this volume) and added any behaviors that were not part of the original list. In this way, 28 discrete behaviors were included in our list.

When each of these behaviors had been coded for each message by a trained coder, blind to the hypotheses of the study, we found that some of these behaviors occurred in fewer than 5% of the messages overall, and so these behaviors were dropped from the study, leaving 16 behaviors that made up the coding system. Table 7 includes these behaviors, the operational definition of each behavior, and the reliability estimates obtained when a second coder worked through 25% of the messages. As can be seen, all of these behaviors can be coded reliably. In the study discussed here (Noller & Gallois, 1986), each participant was given a score for the number of times a particular behavior occurred on each message. These scores were

TABLE 7

Nonverbal Behaviors Used by Spouses Sending Standard Content Messages

Behavior	Operational Definition	Reliability
Gaze	Encoder's eyes in direction of partner's face	.88
Stare	Sustained gaze at partner and eyes widened	.97
Open smile	Smile with teeth exposed	.95
Closed smile	Smile with lips closed	.92
Eyebrow flash	Eyebrows briefly raised and lowered (no pause)	.86
Eyebrow raise	Eyebrows raised and held	.75
Eyebrow furrow	Eyebrows drawn down and in	.86
Frown	Lips turned downward	.85
Head tilt	Lateral tilt of the head	.95
Head up	Sagittal tilt forward, with chin raised	.82
Head down	Sagittal tilt forward, chin down	.79
Forward lean	Upper torso tilted forward, with back away from chair	.98
Head nod	Continuous up–down movement of the head in the sagittal plane	.86
Head shake	Continuous left–right movement of the head in the transverse plane	1.00
Head turn	Head turned and held in the transverse plane	.88
Hand gesture	Any movement of the hand and wrist	.95

Note: Reliabilities represent percentage agreement between the two coders.

then combined within message-type to provide a score for each participant on each behavior for positive, neutral, and negative messages separately. So, for example, if an individual used an open smile on all of her nine positive messages, she would receive a score of nine.

Message-Type Differences.   Our first question for analysis concerned the extent to which these 16 behaviors discriminated successfully between the different types of message (i.e., positive, neutral, and negative). This issue was important for establishing the validity of the coding system. To answer this question, we carried out a discriminant analysis, with scores on the 16 behaviors as the dependent variables and type of message as the grouping variable. A significant multivariate effect was found for message-type, with two significant functions being obtained.

The first function discriminated among all three types of messages, with positive messages being characterized by open and closed smile, eyebrow raise, and forward lean. Negative messages, on the other hand, were characterized by frown and eyebrow furrow. The second function distinguished between neutral and negative messages, with neutral messages being characterized by a lack of certain behaviors, specifically open smile, frown, and stare. See Table 8 for the results of the discriminant function analysis. This table contains the correlations with each discriminant function, and the results of the univariate *F*-tests, assessing differences between message-types.

Sex Differences.   We were also interested in sex differences, and particularly in exploring the question of why, in Noller's (1980) study, wives proved to be better encoders than husbands. To answer this question, we carried out three discriminant analyses comparing husbands and wives on (a) positive messages, (b) negative messages, and (c) neutral messages. For positive messages, four behaviors (open smile, closed smile, head down, and head tilt) occurred more frequently for women than for men, and the three behaviors of eyebrow raise, eyebrow flash, and head up occurred more frequently for men.

TABLE 8

Behaviors of Couples Significantly Associated With the Discriminant Functions on Type of Message for Standard Content Task

Behavior	Correlation with function 1	Correlation with function 2	$F (2, 141)$
Open smile	0.71	0.41	35.9***
Closed smile	0.48	0.14	11.65***
Frown	-0.54	0.41	19.17***
Eyebrow raise	0.44	-0.12	9.32***
Eyebrow furrow	-0.52	0.26	15.06***
Forward lean	0.26	0.10	3.18*
Stare	-0.07	0.36	5.49**

Note: $p < .05^*$; $p < .01^{**}$; $p < .001^{***}$

For negative messages, wives were more likely to frown than were husbands, and husbands were more likely to use eyebrow raise and eyebrow flash than were wives. These findings suggest that the reason that women's messages are able to be decoded more accurately than those of men is because women tend to use the behaviors that are characteristic of that type of message (i.e., smiles on positive messages and frowns on negative messages), and because women discriminate more clearly between their positive messages and their negative messages. Finally, as would be expected given the earlier finding, there were no differences between the sexes for neutral messages.

Using the Coding System in a Free Interaction Situation

In another study (Noller & Gallois, 1988), we coded the same couples used in the earlier study as they engaged in a free interaction (see Noller, 1982, for more detail about this task). The interactions had been coded previously (see Noller, 1982), using thought units that were categorized as positive, neutral, or negative in various channels. The codes used by Noller and Gallois (1988), however, were those that involved all channels (the verbal channel in terms of the content, the vocal channel or tone of voice, and the visual channel). The interactions were coded every 15 seconds for the presence or absence of particular behaviors. A slightly different set of behaviors was used from that in the standard content study discussed earlier, particularly to account for the fact that the interaction involved couples discussing their responses to a questionnaire with one another, and referring to the questionnaire from time to time (see Table 9 for the variations in behaviors and definitions). This need to include other behaviors because of the different context should be kept in mind by researchers wanting to carry out research involving the microcoding of actual nonverbal behaviors.

In the same way as in the earlier study, we obtained scores for each participant on each of the behaviors, summed separately for segments of the interaction that had previously been coded positive, neutral, or negative. In this case, because the length of utterances was not matched, we divided scores by the number of utterances of that particular message-type. For example, if an individual used an open smile on 14 positive utterances, and did not use an open smile on the other seven utterances, his score for open smile on positive messages would be 14 divided by 21 (.67). Two discriminant analyses were then carried out to compare positive, neutral, and negative utterances—for speakers and listeners separately—to see which, if any, behaviors discriminated between them. For speakers, positive messages tended to be characterized by head move to partner and open smile (but particularly open smile), and negative messages tended to be characterized by facing partner, head shake, and eye widen (or stare), although the proportion of messages on which head shake was used did not differ between message-types, according to a univariate ANOVA. (See Table 10 for the results of the discriminant analysis between the three message-types).

TABLE 9

Behaviors of Couples Coded From the Free Interaction Task

Behavior	Operational definition
Facing partner	Nose and chin pointed in direction of partner's face
Facing questionnaire	Nose and chin pointed in direction of own or partner's questionnaire
Facing away	Nose and chin pointed away from both partner and questionnaire
Head move to partner	Head moves to position of facing partner
Head move to questionnaire	Head moves to position of facing questionnaire
Head nod	Rapid, continuous up-and-down movement of head
Head shake	Rapid, continuous left-to-right head movement
Other head move	Head moves (up, down, tilt, turn) other than those above
Open smile	Smile showing upper teeth
Closed smile	Smile with lips closed
Eyebrow raise	Rapid or sustained up-and-down movement of one or both eyebrows
Eye widen	Contraction of eyelids exposing more white around iris
Speech-related gesture	Hand movement clearly related to speech (emblem or illustrator)
Other gesture	Hand movement not related to speech
Body movement	Movement of entire body torso

TABLE 10

Behaviors of Couples Discriminating Between Message-types for Free Interaction

Behavior	Correl Function 1	Correl Function 2	Positive mean	Neutral mean	Negative mean	Significance
Face partner		0.48	0.43	0.27	0.49	.01
Head to partner	0.38		0.31	0.18	0.29	.001
Open smile	0.88		0.29	0.07	0.11	.01
Eye widen		0.36	0.02	0.04	0.08	.001

In Noller and Gallois (1988), which involved a more natural interaction than was involved in the study by Noller and Gallois (1986) where standard content messages were used, the behavior "eyebrow raise" did not discriminate between the different types of messages as it did in the standard content study. Perhaps this behavior was used in the less natural situation, especially by husbands, to stress particular words and hence change the meaning of messages. It also seems clear that the structured, as compared to the free, interactions involved more of the behaviors typically associated with positivity and negativity. It is important, however, to keep in mind that the free interaction study involved only 10 couples, and hence only tentative conclusions can be drawn. There were no differences for listener behaviors as a function of type of message.

To explore sex and message-type differences in the use of these behaviors, the four behaviors that discriminated between the three types of message (i.e., face partner, head to partner, open smile, eye widen) were used as the dependent variables in a series of 2 (male or female) by 3 (positive, neutral, or negative) ANOVAS. Both males and females faced the partner more when uttering positive or negative messages, rather than neutral messages, and wives faced more than husbands did. Open smiles were used more frequently on positive than on other types of messages, and there was a trend for females to use more open smiles than males. Eye widen (or stare) was used more by females than males, and on negative messages more than on other types of messages. Results of these analyses are presented in Table 11. It is interesting to note that eye widen was hardly used at all by males. Overall, the findings for the free interaction task tend to suggest that differences between males and females are attenuated in that task.

Study Applying This Methodology to Demanding and Withdrawing Behaviors

Noller and Christensen (cited in Feeney, Noller, Sheehan, & Peterson, 1999) carried out a study using a similar coding system to that used in the study of structured interaction described previously. In this particular study, we were interested in which nonverbal behaviors were most clearly related to demanding and withdrawing behavior in married couples, and also whether the frequency of those behaviors would be affected by whose issue (husband's or wife's) was being discussed, the sex of the person doing the demanding and withdrawing, and the marital adjustment level of the couple. Christensen and his colleagues (Christensen & Heavey, 1990; Heavey, Layne, & Christensen, 1993) have shown that demanding

TABLE 11

Means for Each Sex on Speaker Behaviors Discriminating Between Types of Message

Behavior	Sex	Positive	Neutral	Negative
Facing partner	Males	0.34	0.18	0.40
	Females	0.52	0.35	0.59
Head to partner	Males	0.24	0.10	0.30
	Females	0.38	0.26	0.29
Open smile	Males	0.23	0.04	0.09
	Females	0.34	0.10	0.14
Eye Widen	Males	0.00	0.01	0.02
	Females	0.04	0.07	0.13

and withdrawing behaviors are related to whose issue is being discussed (the husband's issue or the wife's issue), and we were interested in whether related differences in nonverbal behavior would be evident.

Each couple from a sample of 29 married couples (19 high in marital adjustment, and 10 low in marital adjustment) engaged in two conflict interactions as suggested by Christensen and Heavey (1990): one initiated by the wife and the other by the husband, with the issues being discussed in counterbalanced order. The videotaped interactions were coded for the presence or absence of the behaviors defined in Table 9. Behaviors were coded every 15 seconds by a group of coders, with husbands and wives being coded on different passes through the tape. Ratings of demanding and withdrawing behaviors were made by an independent set of coders, using the relevant scales from the Conflict Rating System (Heavey et al., 1993). Each dimension was rated on a 9-point scale according to the extent to which the behavior was used across the whole 6-minute interaction. Correlations were calculated between the frequency of each nonverbal behavior and the ratings of demanding and withdrawing for each issue.

For discussion of the husband's issue, there were significant correlations between his withdrawal and his head down ($r = .44$), his wife's head down ($r = .52$), and her head shake ($r = .41$); there were also correlations between her withdrawal and her head down ($r = .37$) and his open gestures ($r = .47$); her demanding was significantly negatively correlated with his closed gestures ($r = -.48$), and his demanding was positively correlated with his head shake ($r = .38$). Thus, when they are withdrawing during discussion of the husband's issue, both husband and wife tend to have their heads down, and she tends to shake her head, perhaps in frustration. He tends to shake his head when he is demanding, perhaps as a way of denying her arguments. She seems to respond to his open gestures, presumably used when he presents his arguments, by withdrawing. Neither pattern seems likely to aid in the resolution of their issues.

For discussion of the wife's issue, the correlations were all with the husband's behavior; his withdrawal was positively correlated with his head down ($r = .68$) and his head turn ($r = .43$) and negatively correlated with his open gestures ($r = -.38$) and his gaze ($r = .52$); in addition, his demanding was significantly negatively correlated with his closed smile ($r = -.38$). In other words, the husband's withdrawal is characterized by head down and head turn (presumably away from his wife), lack of gaze, and lack of open gestures, and when the husband is being demanding, he tends not to smile.

We also looked at the correlations, for both husbands and wives, between behavior across the two different issues. For husbands, there was a strong correlation between his withdrawal on his wife's issue and his withdrawal on his own issue ($r = .70$), and moderate correlations between his demanding on his own issue and on his wife's issue ($r = .49$), between his withdrawal on his wife's issue and her demanding on his issue ($r = .40$) and between his withdrawal on his own issue and his demanding on her issue ($r = -.45$).

Overall, these findings support the validity of the behaviors included in these scales for discriminating demanding and withdrawing behaviors, despite the fact that the scales were designed for coding more general couple communication. The strongest pattern of results was for the husband's behavior on the wife's issue, where his nonverbal behavior suggested a classic withdrawal pattern of head down, head turn, and a lack of gaze and open gestures. These findings fit with the finding that the most common pattern for couples is wife demand and husband withdraw (Christensen, 1988; Noller & White, 1990), particularly in couples low in satisfaction. No particular nonverbal behaviors were related to the wife's demanding, but it is likely that most of this negativity was carried by the vocal channel (Noller, 1985). It should be noted, however, that there were some problems with the reliability of the coding of the behaviors in this study, particularly for behaviors such as gaze and other behaviors that may have occurred a number of times in any 15-second period.

Study Applying This Methodology to the Interactions of Parents and Adolescents

In a further study (Noller & Callan, 1989), we coded family interactions involving mother, father, and an adolescent engaged in two discussion tasks: one where they discussed problems with the adolescent's behavior, and one where they had to decide what rule they would choose for their family if they could only have one. These interactions had been rated previously by the family members on four scales: strong–weak, involved–uninvolved, friendly–unfriendly, and anxious–calm. The videotape of the interaction was stopped every 15 seconds so that family members could make these four ratings. On each pass through the videotape, each family member was rating a different family member. Only the middle 3-minute segment of the 5-minute interaction was rated.

The main goal of this particular part of the study was to look at the associations between the family members' ratings (that is, insider ratings) and the nonverbal behavior of family members as coded by a trained coder, using the behaviors listed in Table 9. Again, only the middle 3 minutes of the 5-minute interaction was coded every 15 seconds so that the ratings by family members and the behavioral coding could be directly related to one another. Of the behaviors coded, three were not used in the analyses because they occurred rarely. These behaviors were stare, eyebrow furrow, and frown. Across the behaviors, interrater reliabilities tended to be high, ranging from .85 to 1.00. Family members were categorized as high or low in terms of the ratings they received on the four adjective scales (involved, anxious, strong, friendly) on the basis of median splits. Family role (mother, father, adolescent) was also included in the analysis. The dependent variables for this MANOVA analysis were the number of 15-second segments on which a particular behavior occurred.

For mothers' ratings of adolescents, there were significant effects for involvement and strength. For fathers' ratings of adolescents, the only significant effect was for involvement. Interestingly, mothers and fathers seemed to rely on different behaviors in their ratings of high involvement. Adolescents who were rated by their mothers as more involved tended to use more head up movements and head nods, whereas adolescent rated by their fathers as more involved tended to gaze and smile more. Those adolescents who were rated by their mothers as stronger also tended to engage in more head movements, including more head up, head down, and head nods. Finally, for adolescents' ratings of mothers, the only effect was for involvement, with mothers who gazed more and also used more head down movements being rated as more involved. There were no significant effects for adolescents' ratings of fathers. It is interesting that most significant relations were for involvement ratings. Cappella (1982) has argued that nonverbal behaviors are more useful for indicating how involved people are in an interaction than for indicating how they are feeling.

CONCLUSION

Although the coding of actual nonverbal behaviors can be very time consuming, this methodology can provide important information about participants' observable reactions in a range of situations. As we have seen, this methodology can increase our understanding of sex differences in nonverbal behavior, for example, why women tend to be easier to decode than are men (Noller & Gallois, 1986, 1988) and how men and women behave when they withdraw in situations of marital conflict (Feeney et al., 1999). I have also shown that these behaviors are useful for coding behavior in relationships other than marriage and for increasing our understanding of global ratings and the behaviors likely to be seen as relevant to those ratings.

REFERENCES

Bowlby, J. A. (1973). *Attachment and loss: Vol. 2. Separation, anxiety and anger.* New York, NY: Basic Books.
Cappella, J. N. (1982). Conversational involvement: Approaching and avoiding others. In J. Wiemann & R. Harrison (Eds.), *Nonverbal interaction* (pp. 113–148). Beverly Hills, CA: Sage.
Christensen, A. (1988). Dysfunctional interaction patterns in couples. In P. Noller & M. A. Fitzpatrick (Eds.) *Perspectives on marital interaction* (pp. 31–52). Clevedon & Philadelphia: Multilingual Matters.
Christensen, A., & Heavey, C. L. (1990). Gender, power, and marital conflict. *Journal of Personality and Social Psychology, 59,* 73–85.
Ekman, P., & Friesen, W. V. (1975). *Unmasking the face: A guide to recognizing emotions from facial cues.* Oxford, UK: Prentice-Hall.
Ekman, P., & Friesen, W. V., & Ellsworth, P. (1972). *Emotion in the human face: Guidelines for research and an integration of findings.* New York: Pergamon.
Ekman, P., & Oster, H. (1979). Facial expressions of emotion. *Annual Review of Psychology, 30,* 527–554.
Feeney, J. A., Noller, P., & Roberts, N. D. (1998). Emotion, attachment and satisfaction in close relationships. In P. A. Andersen, & L. K. Guerrero (Eds.), *Handbook of communication and emotion: Research, theory, applications and context* (pp. 474–501). San Diego, CA: Academic Press.
Feeney, J. A., Noller, P., Sheehan, G., & Peterson, C. (1999). Conflict issues and conflict strategies as contexts for nonverbal behavior in close relationships. In P. Philippot, R. S. Feldman, & E. J. Coats

(Eds.), *The social context of nonverbal behavior* (pp. 348–371). Cambridge: Cambridge University Press.

Heavey, C. L., Layne, C., & Christensen, A. (1993). Gender and conflict structure in marital interaction: A replication and extension. *Journal of Consulting and Clinical Psychology, 61*, 16–27.

Noller, P. (1980). Misunderstandings in marital communication: A study of couples' nonverbal communication. *Journal of Personality and Social Psychology, 39*, 1135–1148.

Noller, P. (1982). Channel consistency and inconsistency in the communications of married couples. *Journal of Personality and Social Psychology, 43*, 732–741.

Noller, P. (1985). Negative communication in marriage. *Journal of Social and Personal Relationhips, 2,* 289–301,

Noller, P., & Callan, V. J. (1989). Nonverbal communication in families with adolescents. *Journal of Nonverbal Behavior, 13*, 47–64.

Noller, P., & Gallois, C. (1986). Sending emotional messages in marriage: Nonverbal behaviour, sex and communication clarity. *British Journal of Social Psychology, 25*, 287–297.

Noller, P., & Gallois, C. (1988). Understanding and misunderstanding in marriage: Sex and marital adjustment differences in structured and free interaction. In P. Noller & M. A. Fitzpatrick (Eds.) *Perspectives on marital interaction* (pp. 53–77). Clevedon & Philadelphia: Multilingual Matters.

Noller, P., & Roberts, N. D. (2002). The communication of couples in violent and non-voilent relationships: Temporal associations with own and partner's anxiety/arousal and behavior. In P. Noller & J. A. Feeney (Eds.), *Understanding marriage: Developments in the study of couple interaction* (pp. 348–378). Cambridge, UK: Cambridge University Press.

Noller, P., & White, A. (1990). The validity of the Communication Patterns Questionnaire. *Psychological Assessment: A Journal of Consulting and Clinical Psychology, 2*, 478–482

Patterson, M. L. (1983). *Nonverbal behavior: A functional perspective.* New York: Springer-Verlag.

Assessing Display Rules in Relationships

Krystyna S. Aune
University of Hawaii

INTRODUCTION

Emotions are central features of human interaction. Specifically, development and maintenance of relationships are based on the experience and expression of emotions (Berscheid, 1987; Metts & Bowers, 1994). Emotions are *not* typically expressed to the same degree as they are felt, however (Clark, Pataki, & Carver, 1996). Feeling rules (Hochschild, 1979) and display rules (Ekman & Friesen, 1975) are learned beginning in early childhood and often govern the appropriateness of emotion experience and expression, respectively. For example, people learn throughout the socialization process to minimize, enhance, and replace certain emotions according to situational constraints (Zivin, 1985). The realization of these emotions in interaction is often in the form of nonverbal cues.

Whereas emotion education in childhood teaches cultural and sociological feeling and display rules, the process of emotion education is further developed and refined within close relationships through what Buck (1989) describes as a "social biofeedback process" (p. 145). As relationships develop, partners develop an idiosyncratic rule structure that governs the emotion experiences and expressions of the partners within the context created by cultural and subcultural emotion rules (Aune, Buller, & Aune, 1996; Buck, 1989; Miller & Steinberg, 1975; Perlman & Fehr, 1987; Stearns, 1993). Despite the increase in theoretical and empirical attention paid to emotions in the context of close relationships (e.g., Berscheid, 1987; Gottman & Levinson, 1986; Lewis & Haviland, 1993; Notarius & Johnson, 1982), the process of nonverbal and verbal display rule development in adult relationships remains elusive, largely due to conceptual and methodological challenges (Fitness & Strongman, 1991). The difficulty in assessing display rules is compounded by the conceptual and operational difficulties inherent in measuring emotions.

There are several general ways to measure emotion (Lewis & Michalson, 1983). Emotions have been defined traditionally as comprised of a combination of physiological arousal and the interpretation of that arousal. Emotion, from this view, is a phenomenological or internal mental event that must be obtained from the individual (Kemper, 1993; Lewis & Michalson, 1983). Introspection is, therefore, essential to measure the *experience* of emotion. On the other hand, the *expression* of emotion may be assessed by the individual (e.g., Shimanoff, 1985a), the relationship partner (e.g., Guthrie & Noller, 1988), or a third-party observer (e.g., Shimanoff, 1985a, 1985b). *Perceptions* of individuals and their partners are particularly relevant to the process of display rule negotiation within the context of personal relationships.

Feeling and display rules, the focus of this chapter, can also be measured in a number of ways. One method of assessing these rules is to calculate the frequency of felt/experienced and expressed emotions (e.g., Shimanoff, 1985a). Another method is to calculate discrepancies between the intensity of the experience and expression of an emotion and infer that display rules prescribe control of the emotion. A third method of assessing feeling and display rules is to assess the perceived appropriateness of emotion experience and/or expression; this method could utilize both self and partner ratings of appropriateness.

The latter two approaches were combined in a method developed by Aune, Buller, and Aune (1996). The theoretical framework underlying their research stems from Berscheid's (1987) theory of closeness and Buck's (1989) theory of emotional communication in personal relationships. Aune et al. (1996) investigated the process of display rule development using a laboratory study design. Their laboratory studies examined the influence of level of relationship development, sex, and valence of emotion on the experience, expression, and perceived appropriateness of emotions. Their method of measuring display rules was also modified for use in two self-report studies. This chapter details the laboratory methodology used and its modification in the self-report studies.

Assessment of Display Rules

In the two studies discussed in Aune et al. (1996), display rules were measured in two ways. A first measure was obtained by assessing the perceived appropriateness of emotion expression. A second measure of display rules was obtained by calculating the difference between measures of the intensity of the experience and intensity of the expression of emotion. The approach taken in the development of this methodology is macroanalytic: a cultural-informants approach (see also, Keeley, this volume). Recording participants' perceptions of the gestalt of emotions felt and expressed reflects naturally occurring processes (see Gottman, 1993).

LABORATORY RESEARCH DESIGN

Participants' Assessment of Emotions

To measure the type and degree of emotions experienced by each partner, couples were separated after a problem-focused 10–15 minute discussion. Five 1-minute segments of interaction were reviewed independently by both partners. The minute beginning *after* the problem discussion began was selected, and every other minute from that point on was included, for a total of 5 minutes. During the review session, individuals were asked to pause the videotape the instant that they recalled an emotion experience during the original discussion. Participants labeled their emotion experience using a list of 17 emotion categories (10 negative, 7 positive).

The list was derived from Gottman's (1983) coding system, with additions from Fletcher and Fitness' (1990) taxonomy and other literature (Izard, 1977; Sprecher, 1987; Tomkins, 1962, 1963; White & Mullen, 1989). Negative emotions included anger, disgust, frustration, sadness, anxiety/fear, guilt, jealousy, embarrassment, regret/sorrow, and negative surprise. Positive emotions included love/affection, pride, happiness, relief/thanks, interest/curiosity, positive surprise, and humor. For each reported instance, the time, category of emotion, intensity of experience, perceived degree of expression, and perceived appropriateness of emotion expression were recorded. The latter three variables were each assessed with two 7-point Likert-type items. The mean number of emotions recorded for participants was 8.8 (range = 0 to 22). The number of negative emotions reportedly experienced by respondents ranged from 0 to 16 ($M = 5.08$). An average of 3.75 positive emotions were experienced by respondents (range = 0 to 14).

The two items assessing intensity of experience were "Indicate how intense the emotion experience was during the original discussion" and "Indicate how strongly you felt the emotion." These items were averaged to form an *intensity of experience* measure. Coefficient *alpha* was computed separately for each of the emotion instances experienced. Mean coefficient *alpha* was .91 (range = .80 to 1.00). The perceived degree of expression was assessed with the following two questions: "Indicate the intensity of the expression of the emotion" and "Indicate the degree to which you expressed the emotion you felt." Mean coefficient *alpha* was .93 (range = .84 to 1.00), so the items were averaged to form an *intensity of expression* measure for each instance. Discrepancy scores were created by subtracting the averaged degree of emotion expression from the averaged degree of emotion experience. For example, a wife may have felt anger to a degree of 7, but expressed it to a degree of 5. The discrepancy between the experience and expression of emotion would be 2. The greater the discrepancy scores, the more the relationship partner managed her/ his emotions, and presumably, the greater evidence of a display rule system governing the affect display.

Finally, the perceived appropriateness of the expression of the emotion was measured by the following: on 1–7 scales, "Indicate how appropriate you feel it is to express the emotion you felt" and "Indicate the degree to which you feel it is right to express this emotion." Mean coefficient *alpha* was .94 (range = .71 to 1.00). The items were averaged to form an *appropriateness of expression* measure. Participants were asked to continue reviewing the selected 1-minute segments and to pause the videotape whenever any change occurred in the type or intensity of the emotion experience. Only those emotions that they actually experienced during the discussion were to be identified (see appendixes for the instruction and recording sheets).

Partners' Assessments of Appropriateness of Emotion Experiences and Expressions

Each participant was also asked to assess his or her partner's emotions. Approximately 15 seconds of the videotape around each instance of emotion experience marked by the participant during the initial review session were shown to the partner. The participant's perception of the appropriateness of the partner's emotion experience and expression was recorded for each instance (with slightly modified items used by participants). For the two items assessing partners' perceptions of the appropriateness of males' emotion experience, coefficient *alpha* was .97 for negative emotions and .99 for positive emotions. Coefficient *alpha* for partners' perceptions of the appropriateness of females' emotion experience was .95 for negative emotions and .91 for positive emotions. Coefficient *alpha* for the two items assessing partners' perceptions of the appropriateness of males' expression was .99 for both negative and positive emotions. Finally, coefficient *alpha* for partners' perceptions of the appropriateness of females' emotion expression was .98 for negative emotions and .95 for positive emotions.

Procedure

In Aune et al. (1996), couples were greeted at the communication laboratory. They were told that they would be interacting with their partners regarding their feelings in their relationship and were seated side-by-side in swivel chairs in front of a one-way mirror. A video camera was positioned behind the one-way mirror, and couples were videotaped with their full bodies visible in order to allow for observation of the largest number of nonverbal cues. Each partner independently listed three salient problems or issues they were currently experiencing in the relationship. Partners also identified the intensity of each issue on a 1 to 10 scale. To exclude highly intense issues and, conversely, insignificant issues, a researcher reviewed each partner's list and selected a common problem that was listed by both partners within the intensity range of 3 and 8. This was done to facilitate consistent discussions between couples that were emotion-filled but not so intense and arousing as to elicit uncontrollable emotions. If there was no exact match on the problem lists, a common theme was identified by the researcher. The vast majority of respondents listed similar or identical issues.

Couples first had a 2–3 minute discussion regarding something of mutual interest to make them feel more at ease (following the procedure outlined by Fletcher & Fitness, 1990; see also Newton & Burgoon, 1990). Then, the mutually selected problem was discussed for about 12 minutes. The couples were left alone during the interaction to encourage spontaneous and natural conversation. They were instructed to act as they would if they were having the discussion at home and not to worry if they became emotional. Couples were instructed to move on to another problem that they listed if the first issue was resolved prior to the experimenter stopping the discussion. After about 15 minutes (2 minutes of open discussion and 13 minutes of topic-centered discussion), the partners were separated. Each person completed assessments of her or his or the partner's emotions. Finally, both participants completed an assessment of the typicality of the discussion. Participants were then debriefed.

Results

The results of the two studies utilizing this methodology of display rule assessment (reported in Aune et al., 1996) revealed that level of relationship development, valence, and biological sex influenced emotions. In the first study using the perceived appropriateness of emotion expression index, early daters' negative emotions were considered least appropriate, followed by marrieds'/cohabitators' negative emotions and positive emotions in both relationship categories. The discrepancy index revealed that partners in more developed relationships managed positive emotions less than negative emotions and less than early daters managed either negative or positive emotions. Males' positive emotions and females' negative emotions were managed the most.

In Aune et al.'s (1996) second study, using partners across all stages of relationship development, evidence was found for a curvilinear pattern for relationship length on discrepancy scores. Partners reported more management of negative emotions in early and later stages of relationship development. Perceived appropriateness of emotion expression was found to increase with relationship development. Sex differences were found for appropriateness of emotion expression, with females' expressions considered least appropriate in early-stage relationships. Overall, the results provide evidence of the evolution of display rule as relationships develop.

SELF-REPORT RESEARCH DESIGN

This methodology was modified for use in two self-report studies of emotions. Aune, Aune, and Buller (1994) examined display rules across three levels of relationship development as measured by relationship length. The survey instrument asked participants to "think about the relationship you have with your partner and the feelings or emotions you feel (or experience) and show (express or display) in your relationship." Respondents were asked to identify, in two or three words, an incident surrounding a negative and a positive emotion experience they had within the past week. The respondents were provided the same list of emotions that was used in the laboratory methodology. The same two-item measures were used wherein respondents identified the intensity of emotion experience, the intensity of emotion expression, and the perceived appropriateness of emotion expression. *Alpha* reliabilities obtained in this study ranged from .78 to .96. The results showed that negative emotions were reportedly experienced and expressed more intensely among couples in the middle stages of relationship development, relative to couples in early and late stages of relationship development.

Aune and Aune (1996) explored cultural differences in the self-reported experience and expression of emotions. Utilizing the same survey instrument already described, *alpha* reliabilities obtained in this study ranged from .82 to .94. The results showed that positive, but not negative emotions differed across three ethnic groups. Filipino-Americans reported the highest level of experience, expression, and perceived appropriateness of positive emotions. Japanese-Americans were lowest on degree of perceived experience and perceived expression of positive emotions. Interestingly, Euro-Americans failed to conform to the predictions and fell in between, or lower than, the other two ethnic groups on emotion experience, expression, and perceived appropriateness.

DISCUSSION

Aune et al. (1996) developed an assessment tool to measure nonverbal and verbal display rules via the intensity of experienced, expressed, and perceived appropriateness of emotions. The methodology has been used in two laboratory studies and provided evidence of the evolution of display rules with relationship development. Aune and Aune (1994, 1996) modified this methodology for use in a self-report instrument. Aune and Aune (1994) found a curvilinear pattern for the experience and expression of negative, but not for positive emotions, across relationship stages, whereas Aune, Aune, and Buller (1996) explored cultural differences in display rules and found evidence for cultural variation in the display rules for positive, but not negative, emotions.

The methodology discussed in this chapter to assess verbal and nonverbal display rule development provides both qualitative and quantitative data regarding the emotional communication of dyads. The methodology utilizes a cross-sectional, laboratory, or self-report study design. Several pertinent issues surround this methodology. For example, a cross-section of partners in relationships at different stages of development offers relative convenience and efficiency. In the first study in Aune et al. (1996), partners in very early stages of relationship development (less than 3 months duration), and partners who were married or living together for over 1 year were recruited. In study two, three levels of relationship development were examined based on length of relationship. Length of relationship, used in both Aune et al. (1996) as well as Aune, Aune, and Buller (1994), while an objective indicator of relationship development, is not necessarily iso-morphic with other relationship qualities such as closeness or intimacy. This de-sign could also be applied to a cross-section of couples using other criteria to determine level of relationship development. One such criterion could be com-mitment, utilizing Rusbult, Martz, and Agnew's (1998) measure. The investment model scale measures four constructs, such as commitment level, and three bases of dependence: satisfaction, quality of alternatives, and investment size.

Another ambitious application of this methodology would be to track couples longitudinally. Specifically, partners in early dating relationships could be asked to repeat their participation in the aforementioned laboratory study approximately every 8 weeks or until the relationship ends. The development and evolution of the display rules governing the relationship could therefore be assessed. The self-report design could be a less arduous way of assessing display rules over time.

Partners in the studies reported here were not experimentally manipulated. Rather, natural conversation was encouraged in the laboratory studies, and actual incidents were assessed in the self-report studies. Obviously, all couples were sub-jected to the relatively artificial conditions/constraints inherent in having a video-taped conversation in a research facility. Nevertheless, the preliminary discussion helped ease couples into the process, and the length of conversation (10–15 min-utes) appeared to facilitate relatively normal and comfortable conversations on the part of the couples. The conversation length allowed partners enough time to expe-rience several emotional instances, yet was short enough to prevent fatigue. Fur-thermore, partners seemed to have no difficulty in recalling the emotions they had experienced during the video playback session. An experimental induction could also be incorporated into this research.

Much more remains to be investigated regarding the process by which partners negotiate and coordinate their feeling and display rules. Examining the perceptions and expectations of partners regarding emotions experienced and expressed—in-cluding what cues (especially nonverbal behaviors) were pertinent to their judg-ments, the verbal and nonverbal feedback provided by individuals in response to emotion displays, and the subsequent adjustment or reaction by each partner—would provide further understanding of display rule negotiation. Given the central-ity of emotions in our interpersonal lives, pursuing this endeavor would be very worthwhile.

REFERENCES

Aune, K. S., & Aune, R. K. (1996). Cultural differences in the self-reported experience and expression of emotions in relationships. *Journal of Cross-Cultural Psychology, 27,* 67–81.

Aune, K. S., Aune, R. K., & Buller, D. B. (1994). The experience, expression, and perceived appropriate-ness of emotions across relationship stages. The *Journal of Social Psychology, 134,* 141–150.

Aune, K. S., Buller, D. B., & Aune, R. K. (1996). Display rule development in romantic relationships: emotion management and perceived appropriateness of emotions across relationship stages. *Hu-man Communication Research, 23,* 115–145.

Aune, R. K., & Aune, K. S. (1994). Cultural differences in appearance management. *Journal of Cross-Cultural Psychology, 25,* 257–271.

Berscheid, E. (1987). Emotion and interpersonal communication. In M. E. Roloff & G. R. Miller (Eds.), *Interpersonal processes: New directions in communication research* (pp. 77–88). Beverly Hills, CA: Sage.

Buck, R. (1989). Emotional communication in personal relationships: A developmental-interactionist view. In C. Hendrick (Ed.), *Close relationships* (pp. 144–163). Newbury Park, CA: Sage.

Clark, M. S., Pataki, S. P., & Carver, V. H. (1996). Some thoughts and findings on self-presentation of emotions in relationships. In G. J. O. Fletcher & J. Fitness (Eds.), *Knowledge structures in close relationships: A social psychological approach* (pp. 247–274). Mahwah, NJ: Lawrence Erlbaum Associates.

Ekman, P., & Friesen, W. V. (1975). *Unmasking the face.* Englewood Cliffs, NJ: Prentice-Hall.

Fitness, J., & Strongman, K. (1991). Affect in close relationships. In G. J. O. Fletcher & F. D. Fincham (Eds.), *Cognition in close relationships* (pp. 175–202). Hillsdale, NJ: Lawrence Erlbaum Associates.

Fletcher, G. J. O., & Fitness, J. (1990). Occurrent social cognition in close relationship interaction: The role of proximal and distal variables. *Journal of Personality and Social Psychology, 59,* 464–474.

Gottman, J. M. (1983). *Rapid coding of specific affects.* Unpublished manuscript, University of Illinois, Urbana-Champaign, IL.

Gottman, J. M. (1993). Studying emotion in social interaction. In M. L. Lewis & J. M. Haviland (Eds.), *Handbook of emotions* (pp. 475–487). New York: Guilford.

Gottman, J. M., & Levenson, R. W. (1986). Assessing the role of emotion in marriage. *Behavioral Assessment, 8,* 31–48.

Guthrie, D. M., & Noller, P. (1988). Spouses' perceptions of one another in emotional situations. In P. Noller & M. A. Fitzpatrick (Eds.), *Perspectives on marital interaction* (pp. 153–181). Philadelphia: Multilingual Matters.

Hochschild, A. R. (1979). Emotion work, feeling rules, and social structure. *American Journal of Sociology, 85,* 551–575.

Izard, C. E. (1977). *Human emotions.* New York: Plenum.

Kemper, T. D. (1993). Sociological models in the explanation of emotions. In M. Lewis & J. M. Haviland (Eds.), *Handbook of emotions* (pp. 41–51). New York: Guilford.

Lewis, M., & Michalson, L. (1983). *Children's emotions and moods: Developmental theory and measurement.* New York: Plenum Press.

Lewis, M. L., & Haviland, J. M. (1993). *Handbook of emotions.* New York: Guilford.

Metts, S. M., & Bowers, J. W. (1994). Emotion and interpersonal communication. In M. L. Knapp & G. R. Miller (Eds.), *Handbook of interpersonal communication* (pp. 508–541). Thousand Oaks, CA: Sage.

Miller, G. R., & Steinberg, M. (1975). *Between people: A new analysis of interpersonal communication.* Chicago: Science Research.

Newton, D., & Burgoon, J. (1990, June). *Nonverbal conflict behaviors: Functions, strategies, and tactics.* Paper presented at the annual meeting of the International Communication Association, Dublin.

Notarius, C. I., & Johnson, J. S. (1982). Emotional expression in husbands and wives. *Journal of Marriage and the Family, 44,* 483–490.

Perlman, D., & Fehr, B. (1987). The development of intimate relationships. In D. Perlman & S. Duck (Eds.), *Intimate relationships: Development, dynamics, and deterioration* (pp. 13–42). Beverly Hills, CA: Sage.

Rusbult, C. E., Martz, J. M., & Agnew, C. R. (1998). The investment model scale: Measuring commitment level, satisfaction level, quality of alternatives, and investment size. *Personal Relationships, 5,* 357–391.

Shimanoff, S. B. (1985a). Rules governing the verbal expression of emotions between married couples. *Western Journal of Speech Communication, 49,* 147–165.

Shimanoff, S. B. (1985b). Expressing emotions in words: Verbal patterns of interaction. *Journal of Communication, 35,* 16–31.

Sprecher, S. (1987, May). *The experience and expression of emotions in the close, heterosexual relationship.* Paper presented at the Iowa Conference on Personal Relationships, Iowa City.

Stearns, P. N. (1993). History of emotions: The issue of change. In M. L. Lewis & J. M. Haviland (Eds.), *Handbook of emotions* (pp. 17–28). New York: Guilford.

Tomkins, S. S. (1962). *Affect, imagery, and consciousness: Vol. 1. The positive affects.* New York: Springer-Verlag.

Tomkins, S. S. (1963). *Affect, imagery, and consciousness: Vol. 2. The negative affects.* New York: Springer-Verlag.

White, G. L., & Mullen, P. E. (1989). *Jealousy: Theory, research, and clinical strategies.* New York: Guilford.

Zivin, G. (1985). *The development of expressive behavior: Biology-environment interactions.* Orlando: Academic Press.

APPENDIX A

Instruction Sheet

1. In the rating sheet, indicate the *specific emotion* that you/your partner experienced during the time period.

   1. Anger/Mad/Furious
   2. Disgust/Contempt/Hatred
   3. Frustration/Whining
   4. Sadness/Hurt/Unhappiness
   5. Anxiety/Fear/Worry
   6. Guilt
   7. Jealousy
   8. Embarrassment
   9. Regret/Sorrow/Apologetic
   10. Humor/Joking
   11. Love/Affection/Caring
   12. Pride/Admiration
   13. Happiness/Enjoyment/Joy
   14. Relief/Thanks/Grateful
   15. Interest/Curiosity
   16. Surprise
   0. Neutral

2. Indicate the intensity of your/your partner's *experience* of emotion.

   Not at all intense   1 2 3 4 5 6 7   Extremely intense

3. Indicate the degree to which you/your partner *experienced* the emotion.

   Not at all   1 2 3 4 5 6 7   A great deal

4. Indicate the intensity of your/your partner's *expression* of emotion.

   Not at all intense   1 2 3 4 5 6 7   Extremely intense

5. Indicate the degree to which you/your partner *expressed* the emotion.

   Not at all   1 2 3 4 5 6 7   A great deal

6. Indicate whether you/your partner tried to show a different emotion to your partner than you felt inside.

   1 = minimize (show less than you feel inside)
   2 = enhance (show more than you feel inside)
   3 = replace (show a different emotion than you feel inside); please specify emotion you tried to display
   0 = did not show a different emotion

7. Indicate how appropriate it was for you/your partner to *express* the emotion.

   Not at all   1 2 3 4 5 6 7   Extremely Appropriate

8. Indicate the degree to which it was right for you/your partner to *express* the emotion.

   Not at all   1 2 3 4 5 6 7   Very right

APPENDIX B

Recording Sheet

Dyad Number_____

Gender: M F

	Emotion	Intense (of Emotion Experience)	Degree	Intense	Degree	Control (of Emotion Expression)	Approp	Right
P1 (time: ___)								
P2 (time: ___)								
P3 (time: ___)								
P4 (time: ___)								
P5 (time: ___)								
P6 (time: ___)								
P7 (time: ___)								
P8 (time: ___)								
P9 (time: ___)								
P10 (time: ___)								
P11 (time: ___)								
P12 (time: ___)								
P13 (time: ___)								
P14 (time: ___)								
P15 (time: ___)								
P16 (time: ___)								
P17 (time: ___)								
P18 (time: ___)								
P19 (time: ___)								
P20 (time: ___)								

161

Specific Affect Coding System

Stephanie Jones
Sybil Carrère
John M. Gottman
University of Washington

INTRODUCTION

The Specific Affect Coding System (SPAFF) was designed to describe the emotional nature of conversation in both nonverbal and verbal channels (Gottman, 1994a; Gottman, McCoy, Coan, & Collier, 1996; Gottman, Woodin, & Coan, in press). It covers the spectrum of positive (e.g., validation, affection, and humor), negative (e.g., stonewalling, belligerence, and contempt), and neutral communicative events. SPAFF has been used primarily to predict divorce and marital quality (e.g., Carrère & Gottman, 1999; Gottman, 1994; Gottman, Coan, Carrère, & Swanson, 1998). In this chapter, we review the development of the SPAFF Coding System, provide a brief overview of the coding system, and discuss the psychometric properties of the scale. We then describe some of the studies that have used the SPAFF Coding System and explore cultural applicability for the system as well as how researchers might utilize it in the future.

Development and Brief Overview of the SPAFF Coding System

The SPAFF Coding System was developed to evaluate the emotional content of couples' problem-solving interactions (Gottman, 1996). Gottman used the Rapid Couples Interaction Scoring System (Gottman, Kahen, & Goldstein, 1996; Krokoff, Gottman, & Haas, 1989) in his studies of couples to assess the quality of their problem-solving skills but found that this coding system was not sensitive enough in identifying precise positive, negative, and neutral affect. Because of the limitations of previous coding systems, Gottman developed the SPAFF Coding System to index just the affect expressed by couples during their marital interactions.

163

The SPAFF Coding System is a gestalt system of observation that integrates non-verbal and physical cues, voice tone, and speech content to identify specific affects. The coding system incorporates the physical muscle movements in the face: elements of Ekman and Friesen's (1978) Facial Action Coding System (FACS; a recently up-dated version can be purchased from http://dataface.nirc.com/Expression/FACS/New_Version/new_version.html or from www.paulekman.com). FACS is a very detailed system that requires coders to scan and assess every muscle movement in the face (called *action units*). Many of these facial muscle movements are associated with emotions (cf. Ekman & Friesen, 1975). For example, sadness or distress is associated with the central portion of the brow being raised (action unit 1) and furrowed (action unit 2), and the two brows drawn together (action unit 4). This creates what is called Darwin's grief muscle, inverted-U shaped wrinkles in the brow (Gottman, 1994). SPAFF coders learn the combinations of facial action units that are associated with different emotions and use this information to help identify the affect being expressed during behavioral interactions.

The SPAFF Coding System also requires observers to listen to the words that are being said (speech content). The goal is to focus on the choice of words, with the understanding that an individual has numerous ways that she or he can express messages (Gottman, Katz, & Hooven, 1996). For example, when someone includes the phrase "yes, but…," as in "yes, but I do housework too," the content of the phrase may best be seen as defensive. In contrast, making a statement like "I need you to recognize that I share equally in the housework" puts across an assertive point rather than a defensive one. Both statements describe the individual's involvement in housework, but the content expresses dissimilar affective messages. The SPAFF Coding System evaluates the emotional content of the words spoken in a conversation to help arrive at an overall index of emotional communication.

The SPAFF Coding System also assesses the lyrical or musical quality of the voice. There is much to be detected about the emotional quality of communication that can be derived from listening to the music of the voice. Many physical qualities of the voice, such as pitch contours, pauses, amplitude, word emphasis, and tempo, can be evaluated (Gottman et al., 1996; see also Tusing, this volume).

Gottman (1994) utilized a "cultural informant" approach to assessing the voice. This approach assumes that members of a culture are experts at detecting the emotional meaning of the voice that goes beyond the more strict physical qualities of speech. The cultural informant approach utilizes both the content and the sound of the words to form a judgment about emotions being conveyed by the speaker. For example, an observer could just listen to the lyrical quality of a speech and miss the nuances of the emotional meaning if he or she does not include the content of the words being spoken. The statement "I don't want to go to the movies with them" can have very different meanings depending on whether the word "I" or the word "them" is emphasized. Solely hearing the quality of the voice without the content of the speech would not capture the emotional meaning of the words accurately. Like-wise, merely reading a transcript of the words would not capture the affect contained in the speech. Thus, both the physical aspects of the voice and the content of what is said must be integrated to evaluate the vocal quality of emotional communication patterns. The SPAFF Coding System integrates these three aspects of communication—physical cues, speech content, and the vocal quality of speech—in arriving at a gestalt coding of affect. The emotions captured by the SPAFF Coding System allow researchers to see the range and sequencing of affect the couples use during their conversations and problem-solving interactions.

The SPAFF Coding System started out as a 10-code system (disgust, anger, whining, sadness, tension, neutral, affection, interest, humor, joy; Gottman et al., 1996). The 10-code system was a microanalytic system that permitted coders to look at the detailed cues to arrive at a final single code or blended code (i.e., the two most dominant emotions displayed). The coding system has been revised twice and turned into a "real time" coding system.[2] In the first revision, the SPAFF codes were expanded to a 16-code system. Blended codes were eliminated because the real-time coding methodology necessitated a simplified set of coding rules. The 16-code system added 5 negative codes (i.e., contempt, belligerence, domineering, defensiveness, and stonewalling) and one positive code (i.e., validation). The negative codes were added to address toxic behaviors that were observed in abusive relationships as well as behaviors that were present in couples who were on a trajectory toward divorce (Gottman, 1994, 1996; Gottman et al., 1995).

The most recent revision consists of 20 codes (Gottman, Woodin, & Coan, in press). The additions to the coding system divided humor into tense humor (short, nervous laughter or humor that has an anxious quality to it) and pure humor devoid of tension. The 20-code SPAFF Coding System includes the additional code of criticism (formerly a part of defensiveness) and incorporates two intensity levels for domineering (low vs. high) and validation (low vs. high). The complete set of 20 codes includes positive codes: interest, low and high validation, affection, humor, tense humor, and joy; negative codes: stonewalling, belligerence, criticism, contempt, disgust, defensiveness, low and high domineering, sadness, whining, and anger; and neutral codes: neutral and tension.

Psychometrics of the SPAFF

The marital research of Gottman and his colleagues (e.g., Carrère & Gottman 1999; Gottman, 1993, 1994a; Gottman et al., 1998) established the validity of the SPAFF Coding System for predicting both marital quality and stability. Carrère and Gottman (1999) found that SPAFF codes discriminated successfully between couples who stayed married and couples who divorced. Gottman and his associates (Gottman et al., 1998) reported that contempt, belligerence, and defensiveness displayed by both the husbands and wives predicted divorce. They also

---

[2]Real time coding refers to coding behaviors as they take place in the "real time" of the videotape playing. There is no stopping the tape, replaying segments, or slowing the tape down for closer examination.

discovered that divorces were more likely to take place in marriages when wives started problem-solving discussions using negative affective patterns and when spouses responded to each other's negative affect with subsequent negative affect (i.e., negative affect reciprocity). In contrast, the amount of positive affect used in conflict discussions not only predicted which couples stayed married (i.e., those who displayed a higher ratio of positive to negative affect), but also which couples were happiest in their marriages 6 years after the initial marital assessment.

Reliability is applied rigorously in Gottman and Carrère's research laboratories at the University of Washington. Every videotape is coded in its entirety by two independent observers using a computer-assisted software program that automates the collection of timing information; each coder notes only the onsets of each code. The coder starts the coding session using the "neutral" code and then indicates the onset of each subsequent emotion as it occurs. The computer program maintains a record of the time that has elapsed from the beginning of the interaction being coded, thus allowing for a second-by-second record of the emotions displayed. In their study of newlyweds, Gottman and Carrère (Carrère & Gottman, 1999; Gottman et al., 1998) used time-locked confusion matrices for each couple's conflict discussion data (data coded using 16-code SPAFF System). Each matrix was computed using a one second window for determining agreement of each code in 1-observer's coding against all of the other observers' coding (Bakeman & Gottman, 1997). The diagonal versus the diagonal-plus-off-diagonal entries in these matrices were then entered into a repeated measures analysis of variance using the method specified by Wiggins (1977).

Behaviors were coded on a second-by-second basis using a computer-automated system that synchronizes observational coding with the original interaction. The Cronbach's *alpha* generalizability coefficients (e.g., Bakeman & Gottman, 1997) were computed for the following SPAFF codes: humor (.96); affection (.86); interest (.75); validation (.96); surprise (.56); anger (.86); tension (.95); domineering (.84); sadness (.72); whining (.81); disgust (.37); belligerence (.91); contempt (.67); defensiveness (.97); and stonewalling (.75). Reliability levels are low for disgust and surprise due in part to the infrequent occurrence of these affects.

In a more recent study (Carrère et al., 2002), two independent observers coded each interaction, and Free Marginals *kappas* were computed for each spouse's set of affects (Dunn, 1989; Swanson, 1998). Only those interactions with .61 or higher *kappa* statistic were used for analyses. Landis and Koch (1977) suggest that a *kappa* level of .61 to .80 represents a substantial strength of agreement between coders. Requiring each couple's SPAFF codes to meet this standard ensures a more stringent level of reliability.

Applications

Gottman and his colleagues have used SPAFF in a number of research studies focusing on marital quality and stability. We provide a brief overview of each of these studies and how SPAFF was utilized. We describe only those studies using real-time versions of the SPAFF coding system.

Longitudinal Study of Married Couples (1983–1987).

Gottman (1993) created a typology of three groups of stable marriages and two categories of dysfunctional, unstable marriages using observational data from Time-1 and Time-2 contacts with a 1983 cohort of married couples. He classified the couples into stable and unstable groups by considering the balance between positive and negative behaviors. The stable couples, who were volatile, validating, or conflict avoiding, had very different mixes of behaviors, but in all cases had more positive behaviors than negative. In contrast, couples who later divorced had communication patterns that were categorized as either hostile or hostile/detached.

Meta-Emotion Structure of Families.

Research by Gottman and his associates (Gottman et al., 1996, 1997; Hooven, Gottman, & Katz, 1995; Katz, 1997; Katz & Gottman, 1991) established the important impact of the family's meta-emotion structure on children's developmental outcomes (see chapter on the Meta-Emotion Interview in this volume). *Meta-emotion* refers to the parents' feelings about both their own emotions and the emotions of their children, as well as their style of communicating about emotions. Gottman et al. (1997) found that spouses who had problematic displays of affective behavior during their marital interactions, as coded using the SPAFF Coding System, also reported difficulties with the emotions of sadness and anger in other aspects of their lives. Thus, people who have difficulty regulating their emotions in one domain of their life experience a spillover of difficulty in managing their emotions in other areas of their life.

Newlywed Marriages.

Carrère, Gottman, and their research team (Carrère & Gottmann, 1999; Gottman, et al., 1998) conducted a longitudinal study of 124 newlywed couples from the greater Seattle area. The 16-code SPAFF Coding System was used to assess the couples' problem-solving communication skills. They found that the affective patterns of communication displayed during the first 3 minutes of the marital interaction were significantly different for couples who remained married and those who later divorced (Carrère & Gottman, 1999). Couples who later divorced showed much greater amounts of negative affect even during the first minutes of a marital conflict. Gottman et al. (1998) found a higher rate of divorce among newlywed couples in which the wives used a greater level of negativity in starting the conflict discussions with their husbands. They also reported that, in couples who remained happily married, husbands were unlikely to escalate the negativity of the marital interaction even when their wives displayed low levels of negative emotions.

Abusive Marriages.

Gottman, Jacobson, and their colleagues (e.g., Coan, Gottman, Babcock, & Jacobson, 1997; Gottman, Jacobson et al., 1995; Jacobson et al., 1994) conducted research examining the physiological effects of marital conflict, violence, and aggressive behavior. Sixty-one married couples from the greater Seattle area completed questionnaires and interviews assessing violence. Three groups of couples participated in this research: married couples with a violent husband, nonviolent couples with low marital satisfaction, and happily married couples. Both battering husbands and their wives tended to be angrier during nonviolent conflict discussion than their nonviolent, but unhappy counterparts (Jacobson et al., 1994). One group of violent husbands, whose heart rates decelerated during marital conflict, were significantly more likely to escalate the negativity of the problem discussion in response to their wives efforts to influence the course of the discussion (Coan et al., 1997). The investigators speculated that this group of violent husbands rejected influence from their wives as a way of maintaining control within the relationship.

Seattle 1998 Study of Marriages.   A study of 128 married couples in Seattle used SPAFF (20-code) to evaluate the association between emotional communication patterns, physiological arousal, and spousal perceptions about the marriage. Although the data from this study are still being analyzed, a number of findings have been reported. For example, Hairston (2001) examined possible cultural differences in emotional communication patterns between 13 Black couples and 13 White couples matched on marital quality. Couples were asked to complete an Oral History Interview (see chapter on the Oral History Interview in this volume) and problem-solving discussion. He found no significant differences between Black and White couples in their affective patterns associated with marital satisfaction.

His research, however, raised important questions about the cultural context of the expression of emotions in marriage, including the necessity of determining cultural differences in affective meaning for specific interaction behaviors (see the Future Work section of this chapter for a fuller discussion of the cultural context issue). Carrère et al. (2002) found that spouses who reported difficulties regulating their anger in work and social situations (i.e., those who displayed anger dysregulation) showed greater levels of anger during marital conflict discussions. In wives, but not husbands, anger dysregulation was associated with an inability to calm themselves physiologically during the marital conflict interactions.

Other Applications

In an interesting extension of the SPAFF Coding System, Waldinger, Schulz, Hauser, Allen, and Crowell (in press) evaluated whether naïve coders could code the emotions of couples accurately. Romantic partners completed two 10-minute conflict discussions. The researchers asked naïve coders to rate the emotional expressions of the couples using a four-category coding system (hostility, distress, empathy, and affection). Waldinger et al.'s coding system was compared to the 20-code SPAFF Coding System to measure how well the two coding systems corresponded with each other. The findings revealed a low correlation between the SPAFF and naïve coding when comparisons were made between the coding of 30-second segments of behavioral interactions. However, Waldinger et al. (in press) found high correlation between the two coding systems when comparisons were made between the coding for the overall discussion. This suggests that less training may be necessary to teach individuals how to assess emotional communication patterns if only global assessments of the affective behavior are required.

Future Work

There are many studies that have utilized the SPAFF Coding System for understanding and predicting marital quality, stability, and discord. The SPAFF Coding System could be applied to other relationship contexts such as cohabiting couples (e.g., heterosexual, gay, and lesbian) and couples contemplating marriage. It could also be adapted for use by therapists in developing clinical interventions. One implication of Waldinger et al.'s (in press) research is that couples can be trained quickly and accurately to develop behavioral observation sensitivity and skills in order to understand the critical moments that can strengthen or damage their relationship. Therapists who learn to use the SPAFF Coding System could develop greater sensitivity and insight in identifying healthy and harmful patterns of communication that affect the couple's emotional connectedness. This would be instrumental in developing clinical interventions that improve the quality of the relationship.

There has been debate over whether facial expression of emotion is universal or culture specific (e.g., Ekman, 1972; Scherer, 1994). In an exploratory examination of marriage among African-American couples, Hairston (2001) asserts that in order to code facial expressions across diverse cultures accurately, coders must have a baseline understanding of the cultures that they are observing and consider acculturation effects. Diverse cultures may attribute different meanings to both the negative and positive affects of the SPAFF Coding System based on their unique cultural experiences. Because the majority of scientific research has been based on U.S. White samples, it is problematic to ascribe these findings to other racial and cultural groups.

An example of this dilemma happened a few years ago when SPAFF coders in Gottman's laboratory were coding a Native American couple. The couple talked about an area of conflict in their relationship. What stood out about this couple was that the husband's nonverbal cues appeared to be what the SPAFF Coding System labels "stonewalling," which is the active shutting out of one's partner. The husband hung his head down with very little eye contact and showed minimal response to his wife's statements. The stonewalling code is considered to be one of the most toxic codes in a couple's interaction and is predictive of marital distress and eventual divorce (e.g., Carrère & Gottman, 1999; Gottman, 1993, 1994; Gottman et al., 1998). Although the husband appeared to be stonewalling his wife, the coders had difficulty in reaching inter-coder reliability due to a lack of consensus about what the behaviors were. The coding team consulted with a Native American therapist who gave insight into a cultural norm held by many indigenous tribes: When the listener is looking down and away and not interrupting the speaker, this conveys the greatest respect for the speaker. As a result of this experience, the coding team realized that there are important cultural factors to consider and understand when making positive or negative judgments about the couples' interaction.

CONCLUSION

It is important for behavioral observers to consider and comprehend the cultural practices and norms of the people they are making analytical judgments about. What may be perceived as damaging in one culture may have different effects in other cultures. More research needs to be conducted to determine the applicability of various coding systems across different cultural groups. More specifically, it will be important to test whether the SPAFF Coding System has the same measurement and predictive power for couples of diverse racial and ethnic heritage.

The SPAFF coding manual and training tapes are available from NCAST-AVENUW Publishications at www.NCAST.org.

REFERENCES

Bakeman, R., & Gottman, J. M. (1997). *Observing interaction: An introduction to sequential analysis.* New York: Cambridge University Press.

Carrère, S., & Gottman, J. M. (1999). Predicting divorce among newlyweds from the first three minutes of a marital conflict discussion. *Family Processes, 38,* 293–301.

Carrère, S., Yoshimoto, D., Schwab, J., Mittman, A., Woodin, E., Tabares, A., Ryan, K., Hawkins, M., Prince, S., & Gottman, J. M. (2002, October). *Anger dysregulation in married couples.* Paper presented at the meeting of the Society for Psychophysiological Research, Washington, DC.

Coan, J., Gottman, J. M., Babcock, J., & Jacobson, N. (1997). Battering and the male rejection of influence from women. *Aggressive Behavior, 23,* 375–388.

Dunn, G. (1989). *Design and analysis of reliability studies: The statistical evaluation of measurement error.* New York: John Wiley & Sons.

Ekman, P. (1972). Universals and cultural differences in facial expressions of emotion. In J. Cole (Ed.), *Nebraska symposium on motivation, 1971* (pp. 207–283). Lincoln, NE: University of Nebraska Press.

Ekman, P., & Friesen, W. V. (1975). *Unmasking the face.* Englewood Cliffs, NJ: Prentice-Hall.

Ekman, P., & Friesen, W. V. (1978). *Facial Action Coding System.* Palo Alto, CA: Consulting Psychologists Press.

Gottman, J. M. (1993). The roles of conflict engagement, escalation, and avoidance in marital interaction: A longitudinal view of five types of couples. *Journal of Consulting and Clinical Psychology, 61,* 6–15.

Gottman, J. M. (1994). *What predicts divorce?: The relationship between marital processes and marital outcomes.* Hillsdale, NJ: Lawrence Erlbaum Associates.

Gottman, J. M. (1996). Overview: A guide to the measures. In J. M. Gottman (Ed.), *What predicts divorce?: The measures.* Mahwah, NJ: Lawrence Erlbaum Associates.

Gottman, J. M., Coan, J., Carrère, S., & Swanson, C. (1998). Predicting marital happiness and stability from newlywed interactions. *Journal of Marriage and the Family, 60,* 5–22.

Gottman, J. M., Jacobson, N. S., Rushe, R. H., Shortt, J., Babcock, J., La Taillade, J., & Waltz, J. (1995). The relationship between heart rate reactivity, emotionally aggressive behavior, and general violence in batterers. *Journal of Family Psychology, 9,* 227–248.

Gottman, J. M., Kahen, V., & Goldstein, D. (1996). Rapid couples interaction scoring system: A manual for coders. In J. M. Gottman (Ed.), *What predicts divorce?: The measures.* Mahwah, NJ: Lawrence Erlbaum Associates.

Gottman, J. M., Katz, L. F., & Hooven, C. (1996). Parental meta-emotion philosophy and the emotional life of families: Theoretical models and preliminary data. *Journal of Family Psychology, 10*, 243–268.

Gottman, J. M., Katz, L. F., & Hooven, C. (1997). *Meta-emotion: How families communicate emotionally.* Mahwah, NJ: Lawrence Erlbaum Associates.

Gottman, J. M., McCoy, K., Coan, J., & Collier, H. (1996). The specific affect coding system for observing emotional communication in marital and family interaction. In J. M. Gottman (Ed.), *What predicts divorce?: The measures.* Mahwah, NJ: Lawrence Erlbaum Associates.

Gottman J. M., & Notarius, C. I. (2000). Decade review: Observing marital interaction. *Journal of Marriage and Family, 62*, 927–947.

Gottman, J. M., Coan, J., & Woodin, E. (in press). *Specific Affect Coding System manual, 20-code version (4.0).* Seattle, WA: NCAST-AVENUW Publications.

Hairston, R. E. (2001). Predicting marital satisfaction among African American couples. *Dissertation-Abstracts-International, 61*, 10-B.

Hooven C., Gottman, J. M., & Katz, L. F. (1995). Parental marital emotion structure predicts family and child outcomes. In J. Dunn (Ed.), *Connections between emotion and understanding development.* Hillsdale, NJ: Lawrence Erlbaum Associates.

Jacobson, N. S., Gottman, J. M., Waltz, J., Rushe, R., Babcock, J., & Holtzworth-Munroe, A. (1994). Affect, verbal content, and psychophysiology in the arguments of couples with a violent husband. *Journal of Consulting and Clinical Psychology 62*, 982–988.

Katz, L. F. (1997, April). *Towards an emotional intelligence theory of adolescent depression.* Paper presented at the biennial meeting of the Society of Research in Child Development, Washington, DC.

Katz, L. F., & Gottman, J. M. (1991). Marital discord and child outcomes: A social psychophysiological approach. In J. Garber & K. A. Dodge (Eds.), *The development of emotion regulation and dysregulation* (pp. 129–155). New York: Cambridge University Press.

Landis, J. R., & Koch, G. G. (1977). The measurement of observer agreement for categorical data. *Biometrics, 33*, 159–174.

Krokoff, L. J., Gottman, J. M., & Hass, S. D. (1989). Validation of a global rapid couples interaction scoring system. *Behavioral Assessment, 11*, 65–79.

Scherer, K. R. (1994). Toward a concept of "model emotions." In P. Ekman & R. J. Davidson (Eds.), *The nature of emotion: Fundamental questions* (pp. 25–31). New York: Oxford Press.

Swanson, C. (1998). *Inter-rater reliability for SPAFF coding.* Unpublished manuscript, University of Washington.

Waldinger, R. J., Schulz, M. S., Hauser, S. T., Allen, J. P., & Crowell, J. A. (in press). Reading others' emotions: The role intuitive judgments in predicting marital satisfaction, quality and stability. *Journal of Family Psychology.*

Wiggins, J. (1977). *Personality and prediction.* New York: Addison-Wesley.

Measuring Conversational Facial Displays

Nicole Chovil
Research Consultant, Burnaby BC Canada

INTRODUCTION

The importance of visible nonverbal acts in face-to-face dialogue is well recognized in the study of communication (for a review see Bavelas & Chovil, 2000). Nonverbal acts, such as facial displays, contribute meaning and serve other important functions that contribute to the dialogue in progress. Facial displays provide an efficient, specialized means of conveying information that is not easily encoded through words. Information conveyed through facial displays may supplement or add more specific meaning to the information delivered through words and phrases. Understanding how and what facial displays contribute is a step toward understanding the multifaceted nature of face-to-face communication.

This chapter presents a relatively new but reliable method to analyze the symbolic and other linguistic functions served by facial displays. To do so, I first present the theoretical basis underlying this measure, along with related findings by other nonverbal researchers. Following this, I outline a system with which to analyze conversational displays and provide evidence for its reliability. Next, I delineate the types of displays discovered initially using this system. In the final section, I discuss the importance of understanding conversational displays with respect to the growing field of computer simulated "talking faces" (or embodied conversational agents), and the need for further exploration of conversational facial displays is outlined.

THE IMPORTANCE OF FACIAL DISPLAYS

One of the most striking aspects of the face in our dialogues with others is the rapidity and precision of movement and change (Bavelas & Chovil, 1997). "In conversation, a speaker can shift quickly from raising a single, quizzical eyebrow over a

173

wry smile to flashing both brows for emphasis on a particular word or phrase, to furrowing the brows and pursing the lips in disbelief or suspicion" (p. 335). When people speak, their faces are rarely still. These facial displays change continuously as the person engages in talk with another, and many of these displays are synchronized to the spoken discourse. People not only talk, but they raise their eyebrows, widen their eyes, smile, and grimace in synchrony with the words they speak.

For example, in Chovil (1991/1992), two participants in a research study were asked to plan a dinner party using only foods they disliked. One participant suggests squid as one food they could include. His conversational partner's remarks were as follows:

Speaker: Yeah that sounds pretty vile.

(eyebrows lowered, and pulled together, eyes squinted)

The speaker's verbal response indicates agreement with the suggested food as one he and his conversational partner could add to the list. At the same time, the speaker conveys his personal reaction to the suggestion facially, indicating dislike of the food choice.

Listeners can contribute effectively to the ongoing talk through their facial displays without interrupting the speaker (Manusov & Trees, 2002). According to Krauss (1987):

> In a normal conversation, the person who at a particular moment occupies the role of receiver is anything but a passive recipient of information. A careful observer will see that facial expressions change, the receiver's head bobs up and down or moves from side to side, and from time to time he or she will interject brief utterances. (p. 85)

Bavelas and Chovil (1997) proposed that facial actions in dialogue are symbolic acts: They depict information that is relevant to the overall dialogue. The theoretical basis for the measurement outlined in this chapter is the Integrated Message Model (Bavelas & Chovil, 2000). This model attempts to map out how verbal and nonverbal acts work in concert with each other to create face-to-face communication. It is important to note that the model is restricted to a subset of nonverbal behaviors that play a role in language (i.e., "visible acts of meaning"). These are a subset of visible behaviors that occur in face-to-face communicative settings.[3] These visible acts of meaning include facial displays made during speech (e.g., eyebrow raises to emphasize a word or phrase; Ekman, 1979) or facial displays conveying reactions such as puzzlement or surprise (Chovil, 1991/1992).[4] Nonverbal acts that are barely perceptible or acts used to accomplish another purpose (e.g., scratching an itch) are not included in this group.

---

[3]For a more detailed description of the model, see Bavelas and Chovil (2000).
[4]The model also includes gestures and other actions that contribute to the overall meaning being conveyed.

The information conveyed by facial displays is highly integrated with the words and other meaningful acts produced in the dialogue, such as gestures. A particular facial action or display can serve multiple functions or contribute to more than one meaning (e.g., eyebrow raises). The particular meaning conveyed by the display is only apparent when it is viewed in its context (i.e., the overall message or ongoing dialogue). Information conveyed by the display may add new information, that was not said verbally, to the overall message or convey a visual picture of the words they accompany (e.g., facial shrug accompanying the words "I guess so").

Researchers have long recognized the "linguistic" functions of facials displays. Fridlund (1991), and Fridlund and Gilbert (1985), for example, proposed that fa- cial displays serve linguistic or paralinguistic functions, and Grant (1969) and Ekman (1979, 1982) observed syntactic functions of facial displays, although their work was limited to eyebrow actions. Scherer (1980) likewise proposed, in general terms, that nonverbal behaviors can be differentiated on the basis of whether they serve syntactic, semantic, pragmatic, or dialogic functions. Rosenfeld's (1987) and Brunner's (1979) research on listener responses also demonstrated that important backchannel or listener responses can be conveyed via facial displays. Ekman and Friesen (1969) and Scherer (1980) distinguished between nonverbal behaviors that convey meaning independently of the words and nonverbal behaviors that illus- trate the verbal content. Finally, Ekman (1977) and Ekman and Friesen (1969) identified displays that have no inherent informational value; that is, they are be- haviors performed in the service of some bodily need or habit.

Although there has been long-standing acknowledgement that facial displays can function in a variety of different ways, research has been limited by the absence of a systematic means with which to code linguistic functions. As I argue elsewhere (Bavelas & Chovil, 2000), it is only by examining these displays in their conversa- tional context that we can begin to understand the meanings and roles they play.

A SYSTEM BASED ON LINGUISTIC FUNCTIONS

A *facial display* is defined as movement or change in one or more areas of the face (i.e., brows, eyes, nose, mouth) as a person engages in dialogue. These facial dis- plays often consist of actions such as eyebrow raising or lowering, eyes widening or squinting, nose wrinkling, upper lip raises, and mouth corners pulled back or down. Displays can be symmetrical or asymmetrical. For example, both eyebrows or a single eyebrow may be raised. Facial shrugs are an example of an assymetrical display in that only one corner of the mouth is often pulled back.

As noted, not all facial actions serve linguistic functions: Some facial movements serve some other function or biological need, for example, actions involved in blinking or swallowing. Referred to as *adaptors*, they are facial actions that do not appear to be connected in a meaningful way to the ongoing dialogue. The action may occur to reduce physiological discomfort or may be a result of another action, for example, scratching an itch. Smiles, however, were not included in the develop-

ment of this measurement because of their high frequency of occurrence in the dialogues. They could, however, be incorporated into the measurement. There has
already been considerable research demonstrating that smiles can serve a number
of different functions and that they convey different kinds of information (e.g.,
Brunner, 1979; Ekman, 1985; Ekman & Friesen, 1982; Rosenfeld, 1972).

Data on facial displays are gathered by videotaping participants while they engage in a dialogue. In Chovil (1991/1992), both participants were videotaped, close
up, in split screen, on high quality color video. The videotapes were analyzed using a
large monitor and industrial quality VCR with stable freeze frame and slow motion.
The sound remained on when played in slow motion, enabling the researcher to
hear what was said when the facial action occurred. A time signal accurate to tenths
of seconds was used to locate the individual displays.

When a facial display of interest occurs, the facial display is coded in terms:

- Who made the display (speaker or listener)[5]
- What the display looked like (that is, the actions or movements involved a
  general configuration of the face)
- The context of the display, that is, what was happening in the conversation
  when it occurred (e.g., did it occur during a silent period or when the partici-
  pants were interacting)
- What was being said at the time of the display's occurrence
- A *verbal* translation of the display (e.g., as if saying, "I don't know")

he scoring system is designed to enable researchers to identify when a display
occurred, the *general* function, and the *specific* function of the facial display. These
three decisions are to some extent interdependent; that is, the decision about the
specific function is not independent of the decision that a display occurred and the
decision about the general function. This issue is addressed next.

Reliability

In Chovil (1989,[6] 1991/1992), reliability of the scoring system was assessed by a second scorer who received training to code the facial displays (see appendix for coding instructions). The training was conducted in the three phases of increasing
difficulty. The first phase consisted of learning to identify facial displays of interest.
When the second scorer reached 90% agreement with the primary scorer on the
occurrence of a facial display, further training was given for judging general and
specific functions.

---

[5]Both participants in a dialogue share the roles of speaker and listener. For the purposes of this article, speaker is defined as the participant who was doing the majority or all of the talking at the time. The
listener was, by definition, the participant who did little or no talking.
[6]Reliability for this scoring system is also reported in Chovil (1991/1992).

First, the scorer was given written definitions and transcripts consisting of examples of the general and specific functions that had been found by the author (see appendix for examples). Second, the scorer watched a videotaped conversation while the author identified different types of facial displays. The scorer was then given two practice trials that involved identifying the general and specific functions of various facial displays without the help of the author (questions were allowed). Reliability was assessed using 20% of the data. For the reliability trial, the scorer was given a list of the times that a display had occurred and the list of all general and specific functions that might occur, and was told to identify the general and specific functions for each display. The second scorer also had to provide some justification for his or her decisions. Justification involved transcribing the verbal content surrounding the display or providing a verbal translation of what the facial display appeared to mean.

The interdependence among the three decisions affected the percentage of agreement between two scorers; the percentage of agreement about the specific function included error due to the preceding decisions. In order to identify specific sources of error that occurred in the scoring process, reliability was assessed in three steps: (a) agreement that a facial display occurred, (b) agreement about the general function, and (c) agreement about the specific function.

Reliability for each decision stage was established by examining the percentage of agreement between the two scorers. The percentage of agreement that a facial display occurred was 90%. Percentage of agreement on the general categories was 96% overall (female–female dyad, 96%; male–female dyad, 94%; male–male dyad, 99%). Percentage of agreement on specific categories was 87% overall (female–female, 81%; male–female dyad, 87%; male–male dyad, 95%). Percentage of agreement for specific categories when there was agreement on the general category was 91% overall (female–female, 84%; male–female, 94%; male–male, 98%). In total, then, there were 5 general categories scored and 24 specific categories scored. The probability of agreement by chance for the general categories is .20, and the probability of agreement by chance for the specific categories is .04.

PREVIOUS AND FUTURE APPLICATIONS

Chovil (1991/1992) used this measure to identify general and specific functions served by facial displays. Twelve conversational dyads were given three topics designed to elicit a range of conversations.[7] Table 12 provides the percentage of facial displays for the general linguistic categories, nonlinguistic facial actions, and those not assigned a category.

Chovil (1991/1992) identified four general functional categories of facial displays. They were syntactic displays, speaker comments, speaker illustrators, and listener comments. *Syntactic displays* were connected with intonation or the

---

[7]More information on the specific topics can be found in Chovil (1991/1992) or Bavelas and Chovil (1997).

TABLE 12

Distribution of Facial Displays Across General Linguistic Categories

General Linguistic Categories	% of Displays
Syntactic	27%
Speaker Comment	14%
Speaker Illustrator	21%
Listener Comment	14%
Nonlinguistic Displays (Adaptors)	25%
Displays Not Assigned a Category	1%

syntactical aspect of the utterance. They can be recognized by their placement in the utterance and by the fact that they do not appear to add any meaningful content to what is being said. *Speaker comments* add information that is not redundant with the verbal content. The display usually accompanies verbal content; however, occasionally they can occur without any accompanying words. In contrast to speaker comments, *speaker illustrators* reflect something that is also being conveyed verbally. The information conveyed by the display is at least partly redundant with the information given verbally by the speaker. Speaker illustrators provide a visual picture of what the speaker is saying, similar to the way gestures often help illustrate a concept or idea the speaker is conveying. *Listener comments* typically indicate that the listener is listening to what the other person is saying; whether the listener understands what is being said; personal reactions to what is being said; or that the listener appreciates the situation being described by the speaker (e.g., indicates sympathy with the person). Table 13 provides the specific types of linguistic functions Chovil (1991/1992) identified. The facial actions that were observed typically are provided, along with an example of the display with the accompanying words or a description of the interactional context. Percentages of how often the facial display occurred are given in the final column.

In total, 82% of the displays (excluding adaptors and displays not categorized) were associated with speaking. A wide variety of both grammatical and semantic functions were discovered, and it is likely there are other meanings and ways in which facial actions help to convey the speaker's thoughts or listener's feedback. Facial displays that accompany spoken words are efficient and precise ways to communicate particular concepts to others. They can help to accentuate the ongoing dialogue and, like hand gestures, they often provide a visual image to the listener.

Chovil's study identified an initial set of functions served by facial displays. Further research is needed to identify other functions as well as to validate these findings. For example, Flecha-Garcia (2001) presented some preliminary evidence that eyebrow movements serve linguistic functions. In that study, eyebrow movements were distributed unequally across conversational move types. Eyebrow raises tended to be associated with conversational moves such as *instruct* or *explain*. Another area for future research would be to explore the effect of including the display versus not including the display in terms of the effect this has on understanding by the listener.

Conversational facial displays have attracted the attention of computer animators in developing more effective human–computer interactions. As computer animators become increasingly sophisticated, the realism that can be created becomes more apparent. However, in order to develop facial animation systems, understanding nonverbal communication and nonverbal behavior is an important priority. Integrating nonverbal behavior such as facial displays, accompanied by speech increases the realism of the Talking Head animation (Pelachaud, Badler, & Steedman, 1996). In an early study, Takeuchi and Nagao (1992) designed a multimodel interface in which facial actions were added. In an experiment analyzing the conversations between users and the speech dialogue system, facial displays ap-

TABLE 13

Specific Types of Linguistic Displays

Syntactic Displays	Facial Actions	Example*	% of Total Displays
Emphasizer	Eyebrows raise	This is **really** silly.	50%
Underliner	Eyebrows raise	The only minor conflicts are with my roommate **and they're darn childish.**	18%
Question mark	Eyebrow raise or lowering	**You don't wear your seatbelt?**	14%
Offer	Eyebrows raise	We could have **tofu as an appetizer**	4%
Sentence Change	Eyebrow raise	… We **leave** the choice up to the guests	3%
End of Utterance	Eyebrow raise (one or both)	Definitely nutritious, I'm sure _____	2%
Story Announcement	Eyebrow action	Um, **my dad**, conflict with my dad	2%
Story Continuation	Eyebrow action	… but that was the latest. Scary one.	6%

Other types of syntactic functions were found but are not included in this table because of their low frequency. These included: Comma (<1%), Topic Change (<1%), Pronunciation Correction (<1%), and Self-Correction (<1%).

(continued on next page)

TABLE 13   *(continued)*

Speaker Illustrators (Redundant)	Facial Actions	Example	% of Total Displays
Personal Reaction	One or more facial actions depending on what reaction was being illustrated	**That was stupid.**	36%
Portrayal	Eyebrow raise	And I said **Is there any need to talk to me like that?**	34%
Thinking/ Remembering	Eyebrow raise or lowering, eyes close or look off to one side or mouth actions such as pulling one side back or twisting mouth to one side	You have little images from your ah, **childhood.**	8%
Facial Shrug	Sudden raising and lowering of eyebrows, downward turning of mouth, or pulling back of one mouth corner	**I don't know,** well I don't like snails, no.	7%
Yes/No	Eyebrow actions	**Yeah,** that's true.	8%
Not (Verbal Negation)	Eyebrow actions or closing of eyes	**I don't have minor conflict**s with people.	3%
But	Eyebrow actions	Oh I do **but** that could be your contribution.	2%

Other speaker illustrators that occurred but with low frequency included: Qualifier (1%), Clarification (<1%), and Explanation (<1%).

Speaker Comment (Nonredundant)	Facial Actions	Example	% of Total Displays
Personal Reaction	Facial actions vary depending on reaction being conveyed	It's too **salty. It's it** I don't know.	45%
Thinking/ Remembering	Eyebrow raise or lowering, mouth twisted to one side, one corner of mouth pulled back	**Well,** no, that's true.	27%
Facial Shrug	Eyebrow flash, mouth corners pulled back, corners of mouth pulled down into horseshoe shape	Soups. I like almost every <u>soup</u>	19%
Interactive	Eyebrow raise	I was going to say spinach salad because **you know** how everyone	4%
Metacommunicative e.g., Sarcasm	Eyebrow raise and slight raise of upper lip	Last January, **it was** a great <u>month.</u>	2%

Other speaker comments included: Qualifier (<1%), Yes (<1%), and Unclassified (1%).

* Placement of display is indicated by the underlined bolded words.

peared to be helpful, especially on initial contact with the system. The study was limited in that the systems had a limited vocabulary and there was no lip synchronization. Nonetheless, it provided a demonstration of the usefulness of incorporating facial displays into human–computer interaction. Work is also currently being undertaken by researchers to better understand how to design embodied conversational agents in order to make them more life-like using natural speech and nonverbal acts that accompany language (e.g., Bente, Kramer, Trogemann, Piesk, & Fischer, 2000). This promises to be an exciting future for human-technology interactions. By building on the work already done, we can enhance our understanding of face-to-face communication and the new forms communication can take with the growing field of technology.

REFERENCES

Bavelas, J. B., & Chovil, N. (1997). Faces in dialogue. In J. A. Russel & J. M. Fernandez-Dols (Eds.), *The psychology of facial expression* (pp. 334–346). New York: Cambridge University Press

Bavelas, J. B., & Chovil, N. (2000). Visible acts of meaning: An integrated message model of language in face-to-face dialogue. *Journal of Language and Social Psychology, 19,* 163–194.

Bente, F., Kramer, N., Trogemann, G., Piesk, J., & Fischer, O. (2000). *Conversing with electronic devices: An integrated approach towards the generation and evaluation of nonverbal behavior in face-to-face like interface agents.* Available: http://citesseer.nj.nec.com/bente00conversing.html

Brunner, L. J. (1979). Smiles can be back channels. *Journal of Personality and Social Psychology, 37,* 728–734.

Chovil, N. (1989). Communicative functions of facial displays in conversation. *Dissertation Abstracts International, 51*–04B, 211.

Chovil, N. (1991/1992). Discourse-oriented facial displays in conversation. *Research on Language and Social Interaction, 25,* 163–164.

Ekman, P. (1972). Universals and cultural differences in facial expressions of emotion. In J. Cole (Ed.), *Nebraska Symposium on Motivation, 1971* (pp. 207–283). Lincoln, NE: University of Nebraska Press.

Ekman, P. (1976). Movements with precise meanings. *Journal of Communication, 26,* 14–26.

Ekman, P. (1977). Biological and cultural contributions to body and facial movement. In J. Blacking (Ed.), *The anthropology of the body* (pp. 39–84). London: Academic.

Ekman, P. (1979). About brows: Emotional and conversational signals. In J. Aschoof, M. von Cranach, K. Foppa, W. Lepenies, & D. Ploog (Eds.), *Human ethology* (pp. 169–202). Cambridge: Cambridge University Press.

Ekman, P. (1982). Methods for measuring facial action. In K. R. Scherer & P. Ekman (Eds.), *Handbook of methods in nonverbal behavior research* (pp. 45–90). Cambridge: Cambridge University Press.

Ekman, P. (1985). *Telling lies.* New York: Berkeley Books.

Ekman, P., & Friesen, W. V. (1969). The repertoire of nonverbal behavior: Categories, origins, usage, and coding. *Semiotica, 1,* 49–98.

Ekman, P., & Friesen, W. V. (1982). Felt, false, and miserable smiles. *Journal of Nonverbal Behavior, 6,* 238–252.

Flecha-Garcia, M. (2001). *Facial gestures and communication: What induces raising eyebrow movements in Map Task dialogues.* Paper presented at Post Graduate Conference 2001, University of Edinburgh, UK.

Fridlund, A. J. (1991). Evolution and Facial action in reflex, social motive, and paralanaguage. *Biological Psychology, 32,* 3–100.

Fridlund, A. J., & Gilbert, A. N. (1985). Emotions and facial expressions. *Science, 230,* 607–608.

Grant, E. C. (1969). Human facial expression. *Man, 4,* 525–536.

Krauss, R. M. (1987). The role of the listener: Addressee influences on message formulation. *Journal of Language and Social Psychology, 6,* 81–98.

Manusov, V., & Trees, A. R. (2002). "Are you kidding me?" The role of nonverbal cues in the verbal accounting process. *Journal of Communication, 52,* 640–656.

Pelachaud, C., Badler, N., & Steedman, M. (1996). Generating facial expressions for speech. *Cognitive Science, 20,* 1–46.

Rosenfeld, H. M. (1972). The experimental analysis of interpersonal influence process. *Journal of Communication, 22,* 424–442.

Rosenfeld, H. M. (1987). Conversational control functions of nonverbal behavior. In A. W. Siegman & S. Feldstein (Eds.), *Nonverbal behavior and communication* (2nd ed., pp. 563–601). Hillsdale, NJ: Lawrence Erlbaum Associates.

Scherer, K. R. (1980). The functions of nonverbal signs in conversation. In R. N. St. Clair & H. Giles (Eds.), *The social and psychological contexts of language* (pp. 225–244). Hillsdale, NJ: Lawrence Erlbaum Associates.

Takeuchi, A., & Nagao, K. (1993). *Communicative facial displays as a new conversational modality.* SCSL-TR-92-019. Sony Computer Science Laboratory Inc. Computing Systems INTECHI'93 Conference Proceedings ACM.

APPENDIX

Training Instructions for Scoring Function of Facial Displays

You will be scoring the general category the facial display belongs in and the specific category the facial display belongs in, as well as providing some justification for your choice of each. You will need to write down a summary statement or enough information that describes why you placed the display into the categories (general and specific) you chose. You must be able to defend or justify your decision. You can paraphrase what was said, or summarize the context it occurred in, or give a transcription indicating where the display occurred. Examples of what you could write down are as follows: display is portraying "I'm cool "; person is acknowledging what was said; speaker talked about getting hit by car; eyebrow adds emphasis in utterance; "She said that was okay"; talking about raw fish; telling about something said in the past. For adaptors, you only need to write down what the action was, for example, lip bite, scratches eyebrow, etc.

General Categories

There are five general categories: Syntactic, Speaker Comments, Speaker Illustrators, Listener Comments, and Adaptors. Within each category are a number of specific categories. You must first make a decision about which general category the facial display belongs in. Then you have to decide what specific category the facial display belongs in. To do this, you have to decide what kind of information is being conveyed by the display. It is important to stay very close to what is being said verbally and also use the rest of the context as well.

Syntactic Displays

Syntactic displays are facial displays that serve syntactic functions; that is, they are usually connected with intonation or the syntactical aspect of the utterance. Syntactic displays can be recognized by their placement in the utterance and by the fact that they do not appear to add any meaningful content to what is being said.

Word emphasis/stress and question markers are the most common Syntactic displays. *Word emphasis* displays can be recognized by the fact that the facial actions (usually eyebrow movements) co-occur with one word that is stressed, usually with intonation as well. *Underliners* are displays that emphasize a clause or part of an utterance. Again, usually the person also uses intonation as well. *Question marker* displays help to indicate that the utterance is a question or is to be taken as a question. The facial action may occur with one word or may be held for the entire question. *Comma/pauses* displays are facial actions that occur where there is a pause or where a comma would be placed in the utterance. *Sentence change* displays are displays that occur when the person changes what he or she was going to say. The person begins his or her statement but then stops midway through and begins a new state-ment. The facial display usually occurs when the person begins the new statement. *Pronunciation correction* displays occur when the person mispronounces a word. The facial display occurs when the person repeats the word using the correct pronounciation.

Story announcement, continuation, and ending displays are facial displays that mark the organization of the topic. Story announcement displays occur with the introduction of a story. Story continuation displays occur with conjunctions such as so, but, then, so anyways, etc. They appear to indicate that the speaker is mov-ing on to another point or idea. Story or topic ending displays mark the comple-tion of the topic.

Speaker Comments

Speaker Comments are facial displays that add information that is *not* redundant with the verbal content. The display usually accompanies verbal content; however, occasionally a Speaker Comment can occur without words; for example, neither person is speaking and one person raises his or eyebrows as if to say "Well, now what do we do?" Be careful not to confuse these with Listener Comments (see Lis-tener Comments section below). When Speaker Comments accompany verbal ut-terances the information given by the display is different from the verbal content. The main point to remember is that Speaker Comments *do not* illustrate or repeat what is being said. Speaker Comments are nonverbal ways of expressing an idea or thought. They are nonverbal equivalents of spoken utterances.

Speaker Comments can be *personal reactions* to something that is happening at the time of interaction. For example the person could make a disgust display while talking about eating raw fish or could frown to indicate uncertainty while discuss-ing what foods he or she dislikes. Other personal reactions can be evaluations about what is being said (e.g.. disagreement, uncertainty). When the display is an emotion display, it must be connected to something that is occurring at the time, that is, it is not a reenactment of a past emotion display (i.e., one that occurred in the past such as a reenactment is a Speaker Illustrator).

Another type of Speaker Comment is the *facial shrug.* These are displays that indicate comments such as "What can I say?"; "Too bad."; "I don't know." etc. Of-ten these displays consist of eyebrow flashes. *Thinking/remembering* displays are those that indicate that speaker is recalling something from memory or is think-ing about what he or she will say next. *Interactive* displays are displays that attempt to include the listener in the interaction, for example "You know?" or "Well, what now?" *Metacommunicative* displays are displays that tell the listener how to take a message, for example, the person is being sarcastic or that the person is only kid-ding. *Analogic "no/yes"* displays are displays that indicate a "no" comment by the speaker, it is the equivalent of the speaker saying "No/Yes" or "Not really."

Speaker Illustrators

Speaker Illustrators are facial displays that illustrate something that is also being conveyed verbally. The information being given by the display is at least partly redundant with the information given by the verbal content. A Speaker Illustrator forms a visual picture of what the speaker is saying. For example, a person could be saying "That's disgusting" while at the same time, displaying a disgust face. The verbal content may also provide information that forms the context for how the display should be interpreted. For example, it may be obvious from the verbal content that the speaker is reenacting a past conversation and so the facial display is an illustration of this conversation. Another example is when the speaker hesitates and says "Um, ah, I'm not sure" and lowers his or her eyebrows at the same time.

Specific categories include *personal reactions, thinking/remembering, metacommunicative,* and *analogic "not."* In addition, there are *portrayal* displays. These are displays that are reenactments of someone not present or something that occurred in the past (portrayal of something the speaker did or said in the past is also included in the category). The display may indicate that the speaker is taking the role of another person and his or her speech; it is as if the speaker was putting quotation marks around the utterance. The display can also be a reenactment of behaviors or an emotion display that occurred in the past.

Listener Comments

Listener Comments are facial displays made by the person who is not talking at the time. They are responses to something said by the speaker. The person is considered to be a listener when he or she says either nothing at all or gives a comment that has no substantial meaning to it, for example, "Oh really," "That's interesting." If the person comments for any longer, he or she should be considered a speaker. Listener Comments will sometimes be *backchannel* displays, which are displays that indicate that the listener is following/listening. Sometimes the backchannel display will accompany a verbal backchannel (e.g., um, yeah, mhmm). You will have to decide whether the listener is conveying any information by what he or she says or if the verbal content is just a backchannel comment (for example, when the listener says "yeah"). In order to make this decision, you should check such things as whether the speaker has tried to elicit a response from the listener or if the speaker treats what the listener has said as a response. If the speaker makes no reaction to what the listener said, but rather just continues on as if it did not occur, then the listener's verbal content is probably just a backchannel response. Also listen closely to the intonation, it often provides clues as to whether the person is responding to the speaker's utterance or just acknowledging that something was said (for example, how enthusiastic does the person sound?).

Listener Comments can also serve as *personal reactions* to what is being said, including whether or not the listener understands. These displays can either stylized displays or may just mark the comment. Verbal reactions to a speaker's utterance can be distinguished from back channels by how enthusiastically the listener responded. This will help you to decide whether the display marks a backchannel or personal reaction. *Motor mimicry* displays are displays that are appropriate to the situation being described by the speaker; it is as if the situation were happening to the listener. Wincing while listening to a story involving someone being hurt is an example of a motor mimicry display. *Understanding* displays are displays that indicate the listener understands and appreciates the situation being described by the speaker; these displays may indicate sympathy or "I know what you mean."

Adaptors

Adaptors are facial actions that do not appear to be connected to anything in the interaction. They have no meaning value. The action may occur to reduce physiological discomfort or may be a result of another action, for example, scratching. The most common are lip wipes and biting the lip. They often occur after the person has finished speaking or while the other person is talking. If they occur in the middle of an utterance, they may also function as a comma. If so, note both.

Miscellaneous Category

If it is not possible to code a display in these categories; that is, if the display does not seem to fit into any of these categories, you should leave the category sections blank but write in the "Comments" section anything that might help to understand its function (e.g., where the display occurred; always at the end of the speaker's utterance). It is your idea of what the display seems to convey or do.

Examples of Scoring Facial Displays

(Display's occurrence is indicated by the underlining)

DYAD NUMBER: 7
SEX OF PARTICIPANTS: M/M
TIME DISPLAY OCCURRED: 3:00
TOPIC: Getting Acquainted
GENERAL CATEGORY: Speaker Illustrator
SPECIFIC CATEGORY: "How do I say this?"
FACIAL ACTIONS: Brows lowered
SPEAKER: B
FACIAL DISPLAYER: B
CONTEXT: B: ... get in without it, it's not mmm it's not

behaviorism or anything like that.

COMMENTS:

DY: 7
SX: M/M
TI: 10:07
TOP: Getting Acquainted
CAT: Syntactic
SPC: Question Marker
FA: Brows raised
SP: B
DIS: B
CNT: B: Not any type of fish?

COM:

DY: 7
SX: M/M
TI: 7:14
TOP: Dinner Planning
CAT: Speaker Comment
SPC: "I can't think of one."
FA: Right side of mouth pulled back (twitch) then eyebrows
   Raised
SP: Neither
DIS: B
CNT: B's trying to think of a soup he dislikes, makes display
   then B: I can't think of anything for soup, I I...

—

COM:

DY: 7
SX: M/M
TI: 22:11
TOP: Close Call
CAT: Listener Comment
SPC: Motor mimicry
FA: Mouth forms O shape, eyebrows lowered slightly
SP: B
DIS: A
CNT: B: ... falling on the street and then having this car
    car go over top. A: Wow.
    ——————-

COM:

The Nature and Functions of Tie-signs

Walid A. Afifi
The Pennsylvania State University

Michelle L. Johnson
The College of Wooster

INTRODUCTION

The actions that people perform (or do not perform) with one another give observers a great deal of information regarding the nature of their relationship. Certain actions signal formality, others signal turmoil, and yet others signal discomfort. Actions that provide evidence of a personal relationship have been called *tie-signs* (Goffman, 1971; Morris, 1977), and tie-signs can take a number of forms. For example, body-proximity, facial expressions, and verbal exchanges can all serve as tie-signs. The purpose of this chapter is to describe a method of observing and coding *touch* tie-signs as they occur in the field, incorporating both the types and the functions of touch-based tie-signs. As part of that discussion, we describe the tie-sign coding sheet used by Afifi and Johnson (1999) and suggest methodological revisions that may improve the utility of future applications of the measure.

Touch and Tie-Signs

Touch has long been recognized as one of the most powerful methods for conveying messages (see Henley, 1973; Andersen, this volume). Specifically, there is strong empirical evidence that individuals have a physiological and psychological need for touch throughout their lives (for review, see Montagu, 1978). Evidence also exists that touch behavior may send a range of meanings in interactions. For example, in one of the most comprehensive examinations of the meanings of touch across contexts, Jones and Yarbrough (1985) observed twelve "distinct and relatively unambiguous" (p. 50) interpretations of touch. The category of positive affect touches, when combined with the subcategory of playful affection, accounted for the greatest number of touch meanings.

Indeed, one of the most widely studied functions of touch is the transmission of affection. Thayer (1986) specified that interpersonal touch "directly and immediately escalates the balance of intimacy" in a relationship (p. 8). Considerable research has supported that claim (see chapter by Jones, this volume, for a review). For example, Johnson and Edwards (1991) reported that the type of touch between people is perceived to be reflective of their relational stage. In a similar vein, Burgoon, Buller, and Woodall (1989) summarized the literature on touch by noting that "the likelihood of touch increases as the familiarity of relationship increases" (p. 105).

As we noted, touch tie-signs are a set of haptic behaviors characterized by their communication of intimacy. Goffman (1971) defined tie-signs in this way:

> When persons theretofore unacquainted come into each other's immediate presence, the fact that their relationship is anonymous, or at best has just begun not to be, is made evident for them and others by means of many signs. Similarly, when those with an anchored relation come into unobstructed range for effecting social contact, the fact that theirs is not an anonymous relation is made evident. All such evidence about relationships … I shall call "tie signs." (p. 194)

Goffman also labeled these behaviors as "with markers," noting that they typically serve as relational indicators to the dyad using the behaviors and to their audience. Evidence that a personal relationship has been formed includes such indirect tie-signs as wedding rings, sharing a glass when drinking, or a tattoo (Morris, 1977). Direct tie-sign evidence is seen in actions such as guiding another through a door, taking another's hand, patting another on the back, standing in very close proximity to another, whispering in another's ear, and the use of similar facial expressions or gestures.

Morris' (1971) work on nonverbal action that "indicates the existence of a personal relationship" (p. 86) contributes in important ways to our knowledge of tie-signs and provides specific form to Goffman's (1971) observations. Morris' (1971) ethnographic observations led to the cataloging of 457 tie-signs, which he pared down to 14 major categories that varied in their relative intimacy and represented common, social body-contact behaviors (as opposed to private or professional body-contact behaviors). This categorization scheme remains the most exhaustive effort to capture the types of tie-signs in which individual engage. Morris' (1971, 1977) and Goffman's (1971) observations, together with empirical work establishing the use of affection displays in intimate relationships (cf., Guerrero & Andersen, 1991; Johnson & Edwards, 1991), served as the foundation for the categories we chose to examine in our investigation of tie-sign use (Afifi & Johnson, 1999).

Functions of Tie-signs

Researchers studying tie-signs and other affection displays generally overlay an ideology of intimacy onto the enactment of these behaviors. Goffman (1971) conceptualized tie-signs primarily as ways in which we communicate our relationship status to others, and Morris (1971) noted their intimacy-expression function. However, an examination of the literature on nonverbal functions, close inspection of their treatment by Goffman (1971) and Morris (1971), and attention to Jones and Yarbrough's (1985) work, shows other purposes that tie-signs may serve. Patterson (1988), in a summary of nonverbal functions, identifies seven purposes underlying behavior that are relevant to this extension: information-giving, interaction regulation, intimacy expression, social control, presentation, affect management, and service–task.

The *intimacy expression* function is the one most commonly associated with tie-signs: An individual may express his or her liking to the other by holding that person's hand. Tie-signs used for *social control* are those that involve efforts to influence another person. An individual who holds his or her partner's hand in an effort to influence what the other says or how he or she acts is applying the social control function of nonverbal behavior. *Information-giving*, on the other hand, reflects behavior enacted to provide a target with information about the actor or the environment. For example, an individual may grab his or her partner's hand in a way that communicates sudden anxiety. The interaction regulation function applies in cases where individuals use tie-signs to affect the flow of an interaction. For example, an individual may help include his or her partner into a group interaction through the use of a shoulder embrace.

Patterson (1988) divides the *presentational function* into relationship presentation (i.e., presenting an image of the relationship to an audience) and self-presentation (i.e., presenting an image of the self to an audience). The relationship-presentation function reflects Goffman's (1971) notion of "with markers." Specifically, individuals may initiate tie-signs to reap identity benefits that come with being relationally connected to their partner or friend. The *affect management* function, when applied to tie-signs, reflects cases where individuals use these behaviors to express a particular emotion (separate from intimacy, that would be captured by the intimacy expression function). For instance, an individual may express joy to a friend or partner by hugging him or her. Finally, the *service–task* function applies when an individual initiates a nonverbal action primarily to fulfill a service or task purpose. Individuals may place an arm around their partner as a way to offer physical assistance.

The Tie-sign Coding Sheet

As part of our interest in studying the communication of relationship status in cross-sex friendships, we examined the public enactment of tie-signs more closely to look for the ways in which such signs may work to represent the multiple communicative functions just reviewed. Although considerable work has been conducted on the measurement of touch (see Jones, this volume; Andersen & Guerrero, this volume), we were unable to find measures that coded tie-signs. As a result, we developed the tie-sign coding sheet. The measure is intended as an observational coding form and, in its original version, is limited to dyadic interaction. It allows coders to capture the frequency with which individuals initiate each of the 14 tie-signs we delineated.

Given difficulties in the valid recall of nonverbal behavior (see Scherer & Ekman, 1982, for a more complete discussion of this concern), it was important to have coders assess the initiation of tie-signs as they occurred. Moreover, because of features of laboratories that might limit the range of naturally initiated tie-signs, it was important to investigate the phenomenon in public settings where, in our case, *North American cultural display rules sanction the use of tie-signs.* College bars were chosen for this reason and also because they are a setting in which relational properties are likely salient. To buffer the possible effects of alcohol, we rated behavior that occurred relatively early in the evening and avoided observing dyads who where drinking rapidly or were visibly intoxicated.

Coders went to the targeted bars in pairs and sat at a table that allowed maximum viewing of the bar area. In addition, to maintain some level of anonymity, they ordered nonalcoholic drinks that could be mistaken in color for alcoholic ones, ordered bar snacks, and used small coding sheets (approximately 4 in. × 5 in.). They were instructed to observe the activity of currently interacting dyads for 15 minutes. Coders were trained to recognize the features of each of the 14 tie-signs (see Table 14) and, using the coding sheet (see appendix), mark each instance of tie-signs initiation. "Credit" for initiation was given the individual who was first seen extending the arm, face, or body toward the other person. For example, even though hand-holding involves activity by both members of a dyad, the person coded as the initiator was the one who first extended his or her hand toward the other's. Data on five dyads were used to assess coder reliability. Across all tie-signs, coder agreement reached 95%. When separated by tie-signs, reliability remained high, ranging from 85% for shoulder embraces and pats to 100% for hand-holding, arm links, hand-to-head, head-to-head, body guides, body supports, mock attacks, and kisses.

Given our interest in comparing cross-sex friendships and romantic relationships at the relationship level—and males and females at the individual level—the coding sheets also allowed coders to note the initiator's sex and the relationship's status. Status information was gathered after observation, at which time the coder approached the dyad, informed them of the study and the coding, requested their consent to use the data, and asked whether they were friends or romantic partners. All 70 dyads gave consent, but 5 were eliminated because they did not fit either relationship status option (four were on their first date, and one pair were siblings).

Summary of Results.   Our results reveal several important patterns associated with the use of tie-signs in college bars. First, we found a wide variance in the frequency with which the various tie-signs are used (see Table 14). Second, a comparison of relationship types showed that daters and cross-sex friends differ in their use of only 5 of the 14 tie-signs. Specifically, daters are more likely to initiate shoulder embrace, waist embrace, body support, kisses on the cheek, and kisses on the lips than cross-sex friends. The use of the remaining nine tie-signs did not differ significantly across relationship type. On the whole, then, we found daters and cross-

TABLE 14
Tie-Sign Typology (and Reported Frequency)

Hand shake:	This appears where a personal bond is absent or weak. ($n = 8$)
Body guide:	A dominance move that is often characterized by one partner moving the other in a particular way. For example, one partner may put his or her hands on the shoulders of the other from behind and "steer" the other to a particular destination. ($n = 14$)
Pat/rub:	The pat is a kind of miniature embrace. Only the hand is used; it does not involve entire body contact. Greeting pats, congratulatory pats, comforting pats, loving pats, and friendly pats are examples. Caressing another's arm, leg, or back is also coded in this category (i.e., rubs). ($n = 151$)
Arm link:	The most obvious and publicly displayed of all tie-signs. As a tie-sign, it could almost be described as a signal of mutual ownership. ($n = 7$)
Shoulder embrace:	This behavior is characterized by a half embrace. It is often done among friends as a greeting behavior and during conversations. A minor version of it, the hand-on-shoulder, is sometimes preferred. ($n = 59$)
Full embrace:	A full body hug. It is often done during greeting or parting. ($n = 29$)
Hand in hand:	This is signified by actual hand-holding and is different from the hand shake in both hand positioning and length of hold. ($n = 56$)
Waist embrace:	Partners are usually positioned side by side and have an arm resting around the other's waist. ($n = 31$)
Kiss:	Kisses can be divided into kisses on the lips ($n = 34$) and kisses on the cheek. ($n = 30$)
Hand-to-head:	This is characterized as only occurring among intimates because the head is a very sensitive area and the hand is the most damaging. Behaviors indicative of this include caressing another's hair or face. ($n = 19$)
Head-to-head:	This behavior denotes exclusivity because it incapacitates the couple with regard to other activities. ($n = 18$)
Body support:	Behaviors indicative of this include leaning one's head on another's shoulder, supporting one's body against the other's, or helping someone up from a chair. ($n = 21$)
Mock attack:	Mock attacks signify that the mock attacker is so bonded to the "victim" that he or she can indulge in these pseudohostile actions without the slightest fear that the sender will be misinterpreted. ($n = 7$)

Note: From Afifi & Johnson (1999).

sex friends to be more similar than different in their use of tie-signs in college bars. Finally, our analysis of sex differences produced two significant patterns: Males initiated waist embraces more often than did their female counterparts, whereas females more often initiated pats/rubs than did males. These differences seem to reflect differential control and intimacy functions and are worth further investigating. Again, though, the results suggest far more similarities than differences.

Suggested Revisions. The tie-sign measure worked very well to capture the frequency of tie-signs. As such, it served its purpose. Nevertheless, future users of the measure may consider making revisions to allow for more precise coding of the intensity of certain tie-signs. Intensity may vary along several dimensions, including the location, duration, and force of the touch. For example, a 1-second kiss on the mouth is significantly less intense and intimate than a 20-second one. The coding system we used did not allow for that distinction. In addition, a full embrace that involves full body contact and one that involves minimum body contact may not differ in terms of duration, but in terms of "force." That dimension also leads to qualitatively different experiences of tie-signs. Intense tie-signs are likely to carry significantly more "weight" than shorter, less forceful ones of similar type. As such, future coding of tie-signs should incorporate an intensity assessment. Our recommendation is that the measurement of tie-sign intensity be operationalized as a subjectively coded rating of intensity, varying from 1 ("not at all intense") to 7 ("extremely intense"). Coders/raters would be trained to recognize consistently features that place particular behaviors along specific locations of the continuum.

There are several reasons to recommend a subjective rating as opposed to discrete assessments of time or force. First, accurate assessment of time during live field observations may be extremely challenging, given the difficulty in knowing when to precisely begin the timing of the touch. Second, many tie-signs involve milliseconds of touch, again making accurate coding difficult. Finally, discrete assessments of force are almost impossible in field settings. As a result, global subjective coder ratings may offer the best method of capturing intensity.

As well as suggesting an addition that captures duration and force (i.e., intensity), a revised measure should also allow more complete coding of touch location. Although the location of the touch is captured in many of the tie-sign categories, it is absent for body guide (individuals could guide the body from the upper region of the body or the lower region, with different intimacy implications) and pats/rubs (which, again, should be divided according to location—lower and upper body). Obviously, the location of these touches would play an important role in their perceived intimacy. The revised measure is included in the appendix.

Tie-Signs Functions Measure

Our goal was to understand not only the types of tie-signs initiated in college bars by friends and romantic partners but also their function(s). Although much of the research attention has been devoted to the intimacy-expressive function of tie-signs, it seemed important to more fully examine variance in their possible functionality. Hand-holding may be used to for relationship presentation, self-presentation, and intimacy expression simultaneously, for example.

To accomplish our goal, we asked participants (a sample separate from the one we observed) to rate the likelihood that they would use a specified set of tie-sign types (grouped conceptually) in a college bar with a friend or romantic partner (depending on condition). Both samples/studies are reported in Afifi and Johnson (1999). The functions were adapted from Patterson's (1988) typology and operationalized with single items that captured specific components of each function (see appendix). The operationalization focused on function subtypes that were particularly relevant in the context of college bars. For instance, the specific information provision goal used in this investigation was that of communicating an interest in physical affection. In addition, based on the results of pilot study data, self- and relationship-presentation were separated as distinct functions (although used as one function by Patterson, 1988), and the service–task function was not included. Finally, participants were allowed to note other functions that tie-signs may serve. Across two samples, only 6.5% of participants indicated the presence of a purpose other than those captured by the measure, thus lending some support to its completeness as an assessment of tie-sign functions.

Summary of Results.   Although there were a few complex interactions among relationship type, sex of initiator, and type of tie-sign, the results generally revealed that cross-sex friends were more likely to use tie-signs to achieve self-presentation goals than were daters. Conversely, daters were more likely to use tie-signs to show physical affection than cross-sex friends. When combined with the frequency data from the first study, these results offer particularly intriguing insight into the motivations underlying some public behavior in cross-sex friendships. In terms of comparison of males to females, the results showed that males were more likely than females to engage in tie-signs for the purposes of relationship presentation and self-presentation. Women, on the other hand, were more likely than males to initiate tie-signs for the purposes of inclusion and affection. Yet, perhaps the most noteworthy set of results was related to perceptual accuracy between senders and receivers. Our data suggested that individuals overestimate the similarity between their intentions for initiating tie-signs and their relational partners' intentions for initiating the same behavior. This perception seems to exist in the face of significant differences between men and women in their intentions for these behaviors.

Suggested Revisions.   Although the one-item measure of functions served our purposes in this investigation, the inclusion of additional items would undoubtedly strengthen the measure and allow for reporting of psychometric properties not possible with single-item assessments. By so doing, the information provision function could be able to assess more than simply the desire to express physical affection, the interaction regulation assessments could be able to capture more than simply inclusion, and all functions would be represented more completely. In addition, we hesitate to recommend our measure of tie-sign functions without evidence of its stability and exhaustiveness across contexts. Finally, future work using revised versions of this measure should consider including the service–task function as part of the possible functions served by tie-signs. By so doing, the percentage of participants noting functions other than those listed in the measure may be even less than the 6.5% we reported (Afifi & Johnson, 1999).

SUMMARY

In sum, tie-signs are behaviors rich in relational meaning. Unfortunately, relatively few studies have examined these behaviors and their relational implications. There is much still to be learned about how tie-signs operate in the development of close relationships. In Afifi and Johnson (1999), we offered preliminary measures that allowed for the public coding of these behaviors and for the assessment of their functions. Although these measures served our purposes adequately, future researchers should consider extending these assessment tools in the ways described in this chapter.

REFERENCES

Afifi, W. A., & Johnson, M. L. (1999). The use and interpretation of tie signs in a public setting: Relationships and sex differences. *Journal of Social and Personal Relationships, 16,* 9–38.

Burgoon, J. K., Buller, D. B., & Woodall, W. G. (1989). *Nonverbal communication: The unspoken dialogue (1st ed.).* New York: McGraw-Hill.

Goffman, E. (1971). *Relations in public.* New York: Basic Books.

Guerrero, L. K., & Andersen, P. A. (1991). The waxing and waning of relational intimacy: Touch as a function of relational stage, gender and touch avoidance. *Journal of Social and Personal Relationships, 8,* 146–165.

Henley, N. M. (1973). Status and sex: Some touching observations. *Bulletin of the Psychonomic Society, 2,* 91–93.

Jones, S. E., & Yarbrough, A. E. (1985). A naturalistic study of the meanings of touch. *Communication Monographs, 52,* 19–56.

Johnson, K. L., & Edwards, R. (1991). The effects of gender and type of romantic touch on perceptions of relational commitment. *Journal of Nonverbal Behavior, 15,* 43–55.

Montagu, M. F. A. (1978). *Touching: The human significance of the skin (2nd ed.).* New York: Harper & Row.

Morris, D. (1971). *Intimate behavior.* New York: Random House.

Morris, D. (1977). *Manwatching: A field guide to human behavior.* New York: Harry N. Abrams.

Patterson, M. L. (1988). Functions of nonverbal behavior in close relationships. In S. Duck (Ed.), *Handbook of personal relationships: Theory, research, and interventions* (pp. 41–56). Chichester, England: John Wiley and Sons.

Scherer, K. S., & Ekman, P. (1982). Methodological issues in studying nonverbal behavior. In K. R. Scherer & P. Ekman (Eds.), *Handbook of methods in nonverbal behavior research* (pp. 1–44). Cambridge, MA: Cambridge University Press.

Thayer, S. (1986). Touch: Frontier of intimacy. *Journal of Nonverbal Behavior, 10,* 7–11.

APPENDIX

Afifi and Johnson's (1999) Tie-signs Coding Sheet

Observation Start Time: _____   Observation End Time:_____
Relationship status: _____

Coding Method: Place a checkmark in the appropriate "cell" for each instance of
   an initiated tie-sign.

Tie-Signs	Male Initiated	Female Initiated
Hand Shake		
Pat/Rub		
Arm Link		
Shoulder Embrace		
Full Embrace		
Waist Embrace		
Hand-in-Hand		
Hand-to-Head		
Head-to-Head		
Body Support		
Body Guide		
Mock Attack		
Kiss on Cheek		
Kiss on Lips		

Tie-sign Coding Sheet with Suggested Revisions

Observation Start Time: _____   Observation End Time:_____
Relationship status: _____

Coding Method: For each instance of an initiated tie-sign, rate the intensity of
   the touch from 1 = not at all intense to 7 = extremely intense in the
   appropriate "cell." Each rating represents an initiated tie-sign
   (total ratings = total tie-signs).

Tie-Signs	Male Initiated	Female Initiated
Hand Shake		
Pat/Rub—Upper Body		
Pat/Rub—Lower Body		
Arm Link		
Shoulder Embrace		
Full Embrace		

Waist Embrace
Hand-in-Hand
Hand-to-Head
Head-to-Head
Body Support
Body Guide—Upper Body
Body Guide—Lower Body
Mock Attack
Kiss on Cheek
Kiss on Lips

Items for tie-sign functions (Afifi & Johnson, 1999)

Function	Item
Information management	To show this person a desire for physical affection.
Interaction regulation	To include this person in an interaction.
Expressing intimacy	To show this person that you care about him/her.
Social control	To influence/control this person.
Relationship presentation	To suggest to other people in the bar that this person is "taken."
Self presentation	To enhance the image that people other than this person have of you.
Affect management	To express your current mood to this person (i.e. happiness, sadness, boredom, anger).

Note: The instructions accompanying these items asked participants to "Please rate the likelihood that the following reasons would typically explain your use of this set of behaviors." The accompanying scale ranged from (1) "Very unlikely" to (7) "Very likely."

A Procedure to Measure Interactional Synchrony in the Context of Satisfied and Dissatisfied Couples' Communication

Danielle Julien
University of Québec at Montreal

INTRODUCTION

Most theories of communication suggest that communicating involves interdependence between partners' behaviors in interaction (Burgoon, Stern, & Dillman, 1995; see Cappella, this volume). In the specific area of marital communication, research has shown that partners' reciprocation of negative affect is a particularly important communication pattern that discriminates satisfied from dissatisfied couples and is one of the most robust findings in clinical research with couples (e.g., Gottman, 1994). The *negative reciprocity framework,* designed to discuss patterns of behaviors, entails that negative behaviors of one partner are responded to in kind by the other partner (e.g., attack elicits counterattack, yelling elicits crying). Over time, these patterns can have a harmful influence on the partners' relationship.

In previous research, negative reciprocity (also called *negative escalation* or *negative affect cycle*) has been measured with sequential dependencies between the two partners' negative behaviors (e.g., Miller & Bradbury, 1995). More recently, however, researchers have raised concerns on whether some positive communication processes discriminate satisfied from dissatisfied couples and whether such processes contribute unique variance in the development and maintenance of marital satisfaction (e.g., Gottman, Coan, Carrère, & Swanson, 1998; Julien, Chartrand, Simard, Bouthillier, & Bégin, in press). There is some empirical evidence that rates of positive communication behaviors are somewhat higher in satisfied couples than in dissatisfied couples (e.g., Gottman & Levenson, 1992; Gottman et al., 1998). However, few studies have focused on whether positive behaviors of satisfied

199

spouses are more likely to elicit positive responses from their partner (for an exception, see Manusov, 1995).

The limited research on positive reciprocity raises questions regarding the ways positive dimensions of marital communication should be measured to yield communication processes that discriminate satisfied from dissatisfied couples. This chapter presents a procedure for examining *interactional synchrony* as a process that discriminates between satisfied and dissatisfied couples' communication. This procedure comprises a first step in rating couples' levels of immediacy behavior, followed by transformation of the ratings into categories of changes in partners' immediacy levels, and finally by analytical strategies for testing synchrony between partners' changes in immediacy levels. Before presenting the procedure, however, I examine why the behavior reciprocity framework in clinical studies of marriage has been limited for understanding positive communication in marriage.

It is possible that a positive behavior reciprocity framework entails too many constraints on the nature of the behaviors to be associated. Indeed, a wife can respond in kind to her husband's touch, laugh, or smile, but, conceptually and practically, it is difficult to imagine that satisfied couples would engage in unending chains of these contingent positive behaviors: The cycle cannot develop indefinitely. A different analytical framework is therefore needed to understand positive communication processes in marriage. The theoretical and empirical literature on behavior synchrony may help redefine the question.

THE BEHAVIORAL SYNCHRONY FRAMEWORK

Synchrony takes place when there is coincidence between two or more partners' respective timing of changes in behaviors, regardless of similarities of behaviors or directions of behavior changes (Bernieri & Rosenthal, 1991; Trees, this volume). By comparison with behavior reciprocity, in which behaviors elicit behaviors in kind, synchrony uses the timeframe of behavior change as the unit of interest for analyzing contingency between partners' behaviors (see Cappella, this volume). For example, when the body movements of two partners in an interaction have similar temporal patterns, the partners are considered to be "in sync" with each other, even though they do not use exactly the same behaviors. Because synchrony does not take into account the nature of the partners' behaviors or the direction of behavior changes, it contains fewer constraints on the behaviors to be enacted and permits flexible contingencies between the two partners' behaviors.

Theoretically, interactional synchrony has been conceptualized as a general proclivity enabling humans to form secure bonds, facilitating communication, and regulating partners' involvement, interest, and solidarity (e.g., Cappella, 1991, 1997). It has been shown in infant–caretaker and adult dyads (e.g., Feldman, Greenbaum, & Yirmiya, 1999; Hatfield, Cacioppo, & Rapson, 1994) that higher levels of synchronous interactions between infants and adults are associated with higher levels of self-control and lower levels of negative emotional states in infants, suggesting the emotional function of interactional synchrony (Bernieri, Reznick, & Rosenthal, 1988). Similarly, in adult interactions, synchrony between adults has been associated with participants' and observers' reports of positive rapport between participants in the interactions (e.g., Cappella, 1997).

A synchrony framework is also consistent with clinical literature on marriage. Because satisfied spouses, relative to dissatisfied, are better listeners, better observers, and better supporters of their partners (e.g., Julien et al., in press), they should be more attuned to their partners' behaviors, more perceptive of changes in their partners' behaviors during communication, and more likely to adjust contingently to those changes. The lower levels of listening skills in dissatisfied spouses would make them more likely to ignore their partners' changes during communication. Yet, few studies have examined interactional synchrony in satisfied and dissatisfied couples' relationships.

NONVERBAL BEHAVIORS IN THE CONTEXT OF DISTRESSED AND NONDISTRESSED RELATIONSHIPS

Clinical studies of marital communication have usually examined partners' nonverbal behaviors in their emotion-expression function (e.g., expressions of anger, sadness, and contempt). According to Patterson (1991), other nonverbal behaviors such as gazing, body openness, distance, touching, and body position express degrees of union during interaction (see, also, Guerrero, this volume). Called *immediacy behaviors*, these behaviors serve the function of regulating nonverbal intimacy between partners during conversations. For example, in engaging in various levels of gazing, touching, or body openness, partners in an interaction determine various degrees of openness to one another (for a review, see Burgoon et al., 1995).

Marital studies have included some immediacy behaviors in their observation systems, but these behaviors have generally been aggregated into larger neutral or positive affect codes (e.g., Coding Interaction Scoring System [CISS], Gottman, Markman, & Notarius, 1977; Katerogoriensystem Für Partnerschaftliche Interaktion, KPI, Hahlweg et al., 1984). Thus, the function of immediacy behaviors in regulating intimacy has rarely been studied in the context of marital interactions. The proposed procedure uses immediacy behaviors to rate partners' levels of union during communication. Then, changes in immediacy behaviors and partners' synchronization of their changes in immediacy behaviors could be analyzed. Satisfied partners, relative to the dissatisfied, should show stronger synchrony of changes in immediacy behaviors.

THE PROCEDURE FOR EXAMINING INTERACTIONAL SYNCHRONY

Step 1: Rating Immediacy Behaviors

The first step in examining interactional synchrony entails collecting a database of partners' levels of immediacy behaviors. The development of the Immediacy Behaviors Rating System (SOCNIC; Système d'observation des comportements non-verbaux d'intimité chez les couples, Brault, Julien, & Turcotte, 1991) was based on a functional approach to nonverbal exchange (Patterson, 1991). It includes five nonverbal behaviors: gaze direction, touching, body openness, body position, and body orientation. A 30-second interval is used as the main observation unit. The five nonverbal behaviors are rated for each successive 30-second interval composing an interaction, yielding three time series for each partner. The ratings use a 5-point Likert scale from Low immediacy (0), to Moderate immediacy (2), to High immediacy (4). See the appendix for a description of the behaviors. The rating decisions are based on the rules described next.

Rating Rules and Observers' Agreement on Immediacy Ratings.   The scoring decisions for rating immediacy levels for each behavior during a given 30-second interval take account of the frequency, duration, and, when it applied, intensity of the cues for that behavior during the 30-second interval. For example, body openness is rated 4 for a given 30-second interval when the arms are moving in the space continuously throughout the 30-second interval. However, when the arms are moving in the space for only 10 seconds, and then were crossed over the chest during the remaining 20 seconds, the 30-second interval is rated 1 for body openness.

It takes approximately 10 days to train raters to use the system reliably. The videotapes should be observed with the sound turned off, and wives' and husbands' respective behaviors should be rated by different observers. Observers watch the first 30-second interval, then rate the five behaviors. Then the next interval is watched and the five behaviors rated, and so on until the end of the rating session. Julien et al. (in press) recommend estimating observers' agreement on 25% of the interactions, using the Spearman-Brown-corrected correlations among the scores of the raters.

Step 2: Coding of Changes in Immediacy Levels

The second step of our procedure involves transforming the ratings into "units of contingency" that will be used for tests of synchrony between the two partners' changes in immediacy levels. Units of contingency are defined as the change (1) or no change (0) between two consecutive ratings for a partner's specific behavior. For a given partner, all possible pairs of consecutive ratings for one immediacy behavior created a time series of contingency units (e.g., for a husband's gaze, 1, 1, 0, 1, 0, 1, 1, 0…). Thus, each couple has 10 time series (2 partners × 5 immediacy behaviors).

Figure 2 illustrates the reduction of the ratings into units of contingency: For a specific behavior, the first 4 minutes of a conversation yielded eight 30-second intervals, thus 8 ratings for husbands, 8 ratings for wives, 7 units of contingency for husbands, and 7 for wives. At this level of data transformation, the proportion of changes (1) can provide a measure of the dynamic of the interactions. It is calculated using the number of changes (1) relative to the sum of changes (1) and no changes (0). Also, for a given partner, the within-subject correlations between the time series relative to the five specific behaviors can also be computed to estimate the degrees with which changes in immediacy levels tend to occur in the same timeframe.

Step 3: Testing Synchrony Between Two Partners' Changes in Immediacy Levels

The third step of our procedure consists in testing whether changes in immediacy levels in one partner are associated with changes in immediacy levels in the other partner more often than chance would suggest (synchrony), and whether marital satisfaction (or any other dyadic outcome variable) is associated with the two partners' contingent changes (synchrony) more often than chance would suggest. Two types of synchrony could be examined: *simultaneous synchrony* in which the two partners change their respective levels of immediacy within the same timeframe, and *concatenous synchrony*, in which the two partners change their respective levels of immediacy in two adjacent timeframes (Burgoon & Saine, 1978). Figure 2 illustrates a case of concatenous synchrony. For simultaneous synchrony, the contingency table should cross-classify the group (satisfied, dissatisfied) by husbands' units (change, no change) and by wives' units (change, no change). For concatenous synchrony, contingency tables could be formed similarly, using husbands' initiated sequences and wives' initiated sequences, respectively.

If the number of contingency units (1,0) in the time series of each couple is large enough (depending on the durations of interactions), then transition proba-

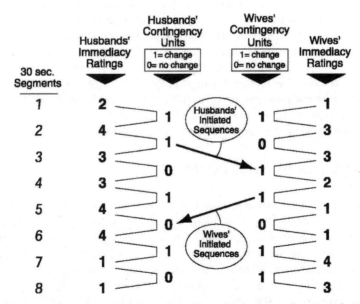

FIG. 2.   Immediacy ratings, changes in partners' immediacy ratings, and sequences between the two partners' respective changes in immediacy ratings.

bility scores can be computed between the two partners' contingency units (corrected z scores; Allison & Liker, 1982). Z scores reflect the strength of the relationship between husbands' and wives' contingency units. The associations can be examined for all the combinations between the behaviors (e.g., partner 1's change in body openness → partner 2's no change in body openness, partner 1's change in body openness → partner 2's change in body position, partner 1's no change in openness → partner 2's change in gaze). Z scores higher than 1.96 indicate that changes in immediacy levels in one partner are associated with changes in immediacy levels in the other partner more often than chance would suggest (synchrony, Gottman & Roy, 1990). The higher the z scores, the stronger the associations between the contingency units. The z scores for the various combinations can then be used as the dependent variables in a MANOVA in which group and sex are between-subjects factors.

If the number of contingency units $(1, 0)$ in the time series of each couple is too small for defining z-scores for each couple (as it is often the case for short laboratory interactions), Julien et al. (in press) recommend using Bakeman and Gottman's (1986) suggestion to pool the time series across couples. Synchrony can then be tested using chi-square analyzes, and the associations between marital satisfaction, husbands' units, and wives' units can be analyzed using loglinear techniques. For each combination, a loglinear model can be fitted to a 2 (satisfied vs. dissatisfied) × 2 (partner 1 change vs. no change) × 2 (partner 2 change vs. no change) contingency table. Two-way significant associations between contingency units in one partner and contingency units in the other partner indicate whether changes in immediacy levels in one partner are associated with changes in immediacy levels in the other partner more often than chance would suggest (synchrony). Three-way significant associations would indicate whether synchrony is stronger in one group of couples as compared to the other group. To verify that one partner's changes in immediacy elicit the other partner's changes in immediacy, the χ^2 for the associations between husbands' units and wives' units has to be significant. To verify whether there is stronger synchrony in the satisfied group relative to the dissatisfied group, the χ^2 associated with the three-way contingency has to be significant.

RESEARCH USING THE PROCEDURE

One study tested the procedure described in this chapter with a sample of 10 satisfied and 10 dissatisfied couples, as measured by the Marital Adjustment Test (Locke & Wallace, 1959). A 15-minute videotaped problem-solving interaction in a laboratory setting was rated using the SOCNIC and analyzed for interactional synchrony (for a complete report, see Julien, Brault, Chartrand, & Bégin, 2000). A number of significant issues can be noted.

First, regarding the SOCNIC ratings, touching produced insufficient variance across couples (i.e., the partners rarely touched each other in our laboratory). Also, the two-dimensional image of the screen did not enable observers to assess body orientation accurately. Therefore, touching and body orientation were not included in the analyses. Correlations for the raters' agreement for openness, body position, and gaze varied between .75 and .85. Second, the coding of the SOCNIC data into behavior changes yielded good variance in the proportions of changes. There were also very low intrasubject correlations between the three time series for husbands and wives, which suggested that changes in the levels of immediacy for the three behaviors did not occur within the same timeframe.

Third, the small number of changes in the time series constrained the pooling of the behavior changes database across couples, and loglinear techniques were used to test whether behavior changes in the two partners were synchronous and whether synchrony discriminated between the satisfied and dissatisfied couples. The findings indicated no group differences for simultaneous synchrony. For concatenous synchrony, husbands' initiated sequences were analyzed separately from wives' initiated sequences. As compared to dissatisfied partners, satisfied husbands' changes in body openness were more strongly associated with their wives' changes in gaze engagement and body openness during the next interval. Likewise, relative to dissatisfied partners, satisfied wives' changes in body openness were more strongly associated with their husbands' changes in body position and in body openness during the next interval. Thus, spouses' synchronous changes in immediacy levels during conversation discriminated satisfied from dissatisfied couples. In using adjacent temporal frames for alternating changes, satisfied husbands and wives achieved an ongoing process of attuned mutual engagement within the task at hand. By contrast, dissatisfied spouses' behavior changes were more likely to stay unacknowledged, showing the two partners were independent actors in the discussion.

Overall, the study suggests that interactional synchrony is a useful framework for understanding the organization of positive nonverbal behaviors during marital communication and to identify processes of positive communication that discriminate between satisfied and dissatisfied couples. With regard to the organization of positive behaviors in marital interaction, our study suggested that when the analytical framework relaxes the constraints on the nature of the behaviors to be associated and the direction of changes, there is likely some interdependence between partners' behaviors.

Suggestions for Future Work Using the Procedure

This procedure is in its early stages of development; thus, there are a number of suggestions for its future use. First, it is important to test the procedure with variable numbers of transitions between contingency units. For example, it is possible that larger numbers of transitions between contingency units would have yielded significant findings for gaze and body positions. Second, the size of our measurement unit (30-second interval) might have increased error variance by failing to detect dynamic changes within those intervals (e.g., gaze shifts) or dynamic changes using larger interval units (e.g., body position). Appropriate measurement units for the behaviors observed and for the size of the timeframe defining causation between behaviors are empirical questions that should be pursued. Third, the use of aggregated data across couples for sequential analyses permitted some couples to contribute more sequences than others. Therefore, it would be important to test the procedure using the couples as the units of analyses.

Fourth, the large number of statistical analyses for the various combinations of behaviors raises the probability of experiment-wise error. A solution might be to reduce the number of behaviors empirically by examining whether some behaviors are better suited to analyzing behavior synchrony. For instance, the organizational picture that emerged from the findings in the first study using the procedure shows that *body openness* entrained changes in the other partner's behaviors. Thus, arm and hand gestures, which were important cues for rating openness levels in this study, may be especially efficient in influencing partners' nonverbal involvement, as has been suggested by the theory of interactive gestures (Bavelas, Chovil, Coates, & Roe, 1995). Because people usually speak when using arm and hand gestures, and because satisfied spouses usually are good listeners of each other's speech, we might have been measuring smooth and regular speech turns in satisfied couples and a lack of regular speech turns in dissatisfied couples. The synchrony findings convey the impression that positive marital interactions function similar to a gear system in which a cogwheel transmits its movement smoothly to another cogwheel.

Finally, from a clinical point of view, and because there is substantial evidence in studies that dissatisfied partners escalate negative affect, we need to examine whether interactional synchrony contributes unique variance in marital satisfaction beyond that accounted for by negative affect reciprocity. We also need to test the procedure with other types of dyads such as same-sex couples and friends. As well, our procedure is based on nonverbal behaviors emitted in the context of verbal exchanges. Whether nonverbal synchrony facilitates cognitive processing and enables couples to carry on problem solving are also questions that deserve further investigation.

REFERENCES

Allison, P. D., & Liker, J. K. (1982). Analyzing sequential categorical data on dyadic interaction: A comment on Gottman. *Psychological Bulletin, 91,* 393–403.
Bakeman, R., & Gottman, J. M. (1986). *Observing interaction: An introduction to sequential analyses.* Cambridge: Cambridge University.
Bavelas, J. B., Chovil, N., Coates, L., & Roe, L. (1995). Gestures specialized for dialogue. *Personality and Social Psychology Bulletin, 21,* 394–405.
Bernieri, F. J., Reznick, J. S., I & Rosenthal, R. (1988). Synchrony, pseudosynchrony, and dissynchrony: Measuring the entrainment process in mother-infant interactions. *Journal of Personality and Social Psychology, 54,* 243–253.
Bernieri, F. J., & Rosenthal, R. (1991). Interpersonal coordination: Behavioral matching and interactional synchrony. In R. S. Feldman & B. Rimé (Eds.), *Fundamentals of nonverbal behavior* (pp. 401–432). Cambridge: Cambridge University Press.

Brault, M., Julien, D., & Turcotte, M. J. (1991). *Système d'Observation des Comportements Nonverbaux d'Intimité chez les Couples* [Intimacy nonverbal behavior coding system]. Unpublished manuscript, Université du Québec à Montréal, Montréal, Québec.

Burgoon, J. K., & Saine, T. (1978). *The unspoken dialogue: An introduction to nonverbal communication.* Boston: Houghton-Mifflin.

Burgoon, J. K., Stern, L. A., & Dillman, L. (1995). *Interpersonal adaptation.* Cambridge: Cambridge University.

Cappella, J. N. (1991). The biological origins of automated patterns of human interaction. *Communication Theory, 1,* 4–35.

Cappella, J. N. (1997). Behavioral and judged coordination in adult informal social interactions: Vocal and kinesic indicators. *Journal of Personality and Social Psychology, 72,* 119–131.

Feldman, R., Greenbaum, C. W., & Yirmiya, N. (1999). Mother–infant affect synchrony as an antecedent of the emergence of self-control. *Developmental Psychology, 35,* 223–231.

Gottman, J. M. (1994). *What predicts divorce?* Hillsdale, NJ: Lawrence Erlbaum Associates.

Gottman, J. M., Coan, J., Carrère, S., & Swanson, C. (1998). Predicting marital happiness and stability from newlywed interactions. *Journal of Marriage and the Family, 60,* 5–22.

Gottman, J. M., & Levenson, R. W. (1992). Marital processes predictive of later dissolution: Behavior, physiology, and health. *Journal of Personality & Social Psychology, 63,* 221–233.

Gottman, J. M., Markman, H. J., & Notarius, C. I. (1977). The topography of marital conflict: A sequential analysis of verbal and nonverbal behaviors. *Journal of Marriage and the Family, 39,* 466–477.

Gottman, J. M., & Roy, A. K. (1990). *Sequential analysis: A guide for behavioural researchers.* New York: Cambridge University Press.

Hahlweg, K., Reisner, L., Kohli, G., Vollmer, M., Schindler, L., & Revenstorf, D. (1984). Development and validity of a new system to analyze interpersonal communication: Kategoriensystem für partnershaftliche Interaktion [Dyadic Interaction Coding System]. In K. Hahlweg & N. S. Jacobson (Eds.), *Marital interaction: Analysis and modification* (pp. 182–198). New York: Guilford.

Hatfield, E., Cacioppo, J. T., & Rapson, R. (1994). *Emotional contagion.* Cambridge: Cambridge University.

Julien, D., Brault, M., Chartrand, E., & Bégin, J. (2000). Immediacy behaviors and synchrony in satisfied and dissatisfied couples. *Canadian Journal of Behavioral Sciences, 32,* 84–90.

Julien, D., Chartrand, E., Simard, M. C., Bouthillier, D., & Bégin, J. (2003). Conflict, social support, and relationship quality in heterosexual, gay, and lesbian couples' communication. *Journal of Family Psychology, 17,* 419–428.

Locke, H. J., & Wallace, K. M. (1959). Short Marital Adjustment and Prediction Tests: Their reliability and validity. *Marriage and Family Living, 21,* 251–255.

Manusov, V. (1995). Reacting to changes in nonverbal behaviors: Relational satisfaction and adaptation patterns in romantic dyads. *Human Communication Research, 21,* 456–477.

Miller, G. E., & Bradbury, T. N. (1995). Refining the association between attributions and behaviors in marital interaction. *Journal of Family Psychology, 9,* 196–208.

Patterson, M. L. (1991). A functional approach to nonverbal exchange. In R. Feldman & B. Rimé (Eds.), *Fundamentals of nonverbal behavior* (pp. 458–498). Cambridge: Cambridge University.

APPENDIX

Behaviors Coded/Rated in the Procedure for Examining Interactional Synchrony

Gaze direction. Score 0: Gaze directed at video camera or other targets (e.g., table, own clothes). Score 1: Gaze directed at other targets with short looks at partner (1 s or 2 s). Score 2: Sustained face orientation toward partner's body, avoiding partner's face. Score 3: Sustained face orientation toward partner's body, alternating gaze directed at face and gaze directed at body. Score 4: Sustained face orientation toward partner's face, sustained eye contact. While speaking, the observee was expected to alternate gazing at partner and gazing away (e.g., during filled pause). While listening, the observee was expected to sustain gaze at partner. Discrepancies from these expected patterns were also used in rating decisions.

Touching. Touching was defined as any physical contact initiated by one partner. Score 0: No physical contact. Score 1: Touching partner with one or two feet. Score 2: Touching partner with leg or knee. Score 3: Touching partner with hand, patting partner, pull part of partner's clothes. Score 4: Touching partner with hand and foot or hand and leg, caress partner, holding partner's hand, kissing partner.

Body openness. Body openness was defined using arm and hand positions in terms of levels of obstruction between the observee and the other partner (i.e., less obstruction, more openness). Leg position was not coded because of wives' and husbands' different clothes constraints. Cues were the following: Score 0: Arms folded on chest or on abdomen. Score 1: Both forearms rested on lower abdomen, crossed; one forearm crossing chest or resting on abdomen, other forearm vertical supporting chin or head; both forearms up with crossed hands supporting or close to chin, arms not resting on chest. Score 2: One forearm crossing lower abdomen, other arm bodyside, or forearm raised or moving; both forearms or both hands resting on thighs or indirect contact (holding a cup of coffee); both forearms or both hands resting or crossed on knee or thigh. Score 3: Part of lower face covered by hand, other arm bodyside; one forearm raised with hand supporting chin, other arm bodyside. Score 4: Arms opened, not touching trunk, or arms bodyside; forearms on armrests; hands in the pockets; hands in hair; moving arms; one arm on armrest, other arm bodyside; elbow on armrest, forearm raised, other arm bodyside; both hands resting behind back of the neck.

Body position. Body position was defined using the observee's trunk position relative to the chair. Score 0: Trunk leaning backward (more than 90°), back of shoulders resting on back of chair. Score 1: Upper trunk slightly leaning forward (e.g., 80°) lower trunk touching back of chair but shoulders not touching back of chair; one or both shoulders leaning forward. Score 2: Trunk 90°, not touching back of chair; whole trunk slightly leaning forward. Score 3: Trunk 90° or slightly leaning forward, body sitting on front half of chair. Score 4: Trunk 90°, body sitting on front of chair; trunk leaning strongly forward (e.g., 45°).

Body orientation. Body orientation was defined by the angle between the two partners' body and trunk. Score 0: Trunk turned away from partner, trunk oriented toward camera, or angle between partners' trunks is larger than 90°. Score 1: Body and trunk forms an angle of 90° relative to partner's body. Score 2: Angle is 66°. Score 3: Angle is 33°. Score 4: Body and trunk face partner's body and trunk.

The Oral History Coding System: A Measure of Marital Cognition

Kim Buehlman
Sybil Carrère
Chelsea Siler
University of Washington

INTRODUCTION

Nearly one third of all marriages fail within the first 5 years (National Center for Health Statistics, 1991), and between one half and two thirds eventually end in divorce (Cherlin, 1992; Martin & Bumpass, 1989). An area of marital research that may help to explain these statistics is *marital cognition*. Fincham, Bradbury, and Scott (1990) suggest that it is important to understand the role cognition plays in driving emotional expression, behavioral interactions, and satisfaction in marriage. Indeed, a number of researchers (e.g., Fincham et al., 1990; Gottman, 1994; Notarius, Benson, Sloane, Vanzetti, & Hornyak, 1989; Weiss, 1980) have found that the manner in which individuals organize information about their partner or the marriage is crucial to the health of the marriage.

Fincham et al. (1990) argued specifically that information is organized and structured in memory on the basis of what is cognitively salient. Bradbury and Fincham (1987) linked memory and affect and suggested that individuals are most likely to retrieve units of memory that are congruent with the current mood they are experiencing. Thus, distressed couples are more likely to remember negative events than positive ones. Fincham and his colleagues (1990) theorized that unhappy couples use negative events from the past to make sense of present marital interactions and to shape future behaviors. Weiss (1980) used a similar theoretical construct, *sentiment override*, to explain the tendency of unhappy spouses to overlook the positive behaviors of their partners. Weiss suggested that unhappy marital partners tend to view each other through perceptual filters that selectively focus on the unpleasant things their spouses do. These unhappy couples, Weiss argues, also view positive or neutral behaviors by their spouses in a negative light.

Our research (i.e., Buehlman, Gottman, & Katz, 1992; Carrère, Buehlman, Gottman, Coan, & Ruckstuhl, 2000) indicates that perceptual biases and a spouse's tendency to attend selectively to only certain characteristics of his or her partner's behavior may predict a couple's trajectory toward divorce. Buehlman and her colleagues (1992) used the Oral History Interview (OHI) to predict with 94% accuracy which couples would remain married 2 years later, and Carrère and her associates (2000) found that the Oral History Interview was able to predict a trajectory toward divorce among newlywed couples with 87% accuracy.

The *Oral History Interview* and its coding system evaluate the marital cognitions and perceptual biases that spouses hold about each other and their relationship. The semistructured interview invites couples to tell the story of their relationships and to share their philosophy of marriage. It indexes a variety of behaviors of couples (e.g., how couples talk about each other and how they interact with each other during the interview) and what they attend to selectively in the past history of the relationship. These subjective and biased perceptions of historical marital events related by a couple provide valuable insights about the health of their relationship. In this chapter, we review the development and psychometrics of the Oral History Coding System and include brief descriptions of the eight dimensions that are coded. We then describe some of the major datasets that have used the Oral History Coding System. Finally, we discuss the coding system in the context of nonverbal communication.

Description of Interview

The Oral History Interview is modeled after the interview methods of sociologist/reporter Studs Terkel. It is a semistructured interview in which the interviewer asks a set of open-ended questions with both the husband and wife present. Krokoff (1984) developed the Oral History Interview, which queries couples about the history of their relationship, their philosophy of marriage, and how their relationship has changed over time. Questions about the history of the relationship focus on the couple's courtship, their wedding, and the good and difficult times of their marriage. When the spouses discuss the philosophy of marriage, they are asked to think of a good marriage and a bad marriage and compare these marriages to their own.

The goal of the interview is to get a clear picture of the marital cognitions each spouse has of his or her partner and their marriage. The focus is on the tenor of how they tell their story over the course of the interview, and thus nonverbal cues help provide information about the couple's marital cognitions. In their assessment of the meanings embedded in the OHI, coders evaluate nonverbal behaviors such as the tone each spouse uses to answer questions, how they look at each other, what interactive mannerisms they have, whether they move toward each other or away as they answer each of the questions, demonstrations of physical affection, and the nonverbal emotions they express toward each other.

Description of Coding System

The Oral History Coding System measures spouses' global perceptions about the marriage and about each other (Buehlman, Siler, & Gottman, in press[8]). The thesis of the coding system is consistent with Fincham et al.'s (1990) proposal that individuals are most likely to retrieve units of memory that are congruent with their present perceptions about their marriage. It also taps into sentiment override (Weiss, 1980), which is defined as the tendency to assess one's spouse's behavior as either positive or negative on the basis of more globally held perceptions about the partner rather than on the objective nature of the partner's immediate behavior. That is to say, if one partner has negative perceptual biases about his or her spouse, he or she will see the other's behavior as negative, whereas an objective coder would not. The Oral History Coding System assesses how each spouse sees his or her partner and the marriage, based on marital cognitions.

Rather than coding the content of the interview (e.g., how long the couple dated before becoming engaged, whether the couple has children, and whether the couple has a good relationship with in-laws), the coding system indexes how the couple tells the story of their relationship. More specifically, it focuses on the positive or negative nature of the events the spouses choose to recall from the history of their relationship. For example, some couples minimize negative aspects and emphasize the romance or naturalness of the relationship. Other couples can only remember how hard it was to get together and what a struggle their marriage has been.

The coding system also measures how each spouse describes and talks about his or her partner in the telling of the story. Again, the focus is on the tenor of the description over the course of the interview, an important issue for many nonverbal researchers. For example, when they are asked to describe what first attracted them to their partner, do spouses seem unsure or do flattering descriptions of their partner's personality or appearance readily come to mind for them? In a similar fashion, the coding system takes into account how the spouses interact as they tell the story of their relationship. For example, do they tease each other? Do they finish each other's sentences and validate what the other person has said? Alternatively, do they snipe at each other, argue about the history of events, or describe their spouse or history of the marriage in cynical or disillusioned tones? Overall, however, the coding system consists of eight dimensions or variables (Buehlman, Siler, Carrère, & Gottman, in press; see Table 15).

---

[8]For a complete manual of the coding system, including detailed guidelines of the coding rules used for each subscale of the system, and videotaped examples of the dimensions, please see NCAST-AVENUW Publications at www.NCAST.org.

TABLE 15
Dimensions of the Oral History Coding System

(1) Fondness/Affection Toward Spouse: This dimension rates spouses according to how much they seem to be in love or fond of each other. This includes compliments, reminiscing about romantic, special times, and positive affect (individual codes for each spouse);

(2) Negativity Toward Spouse: This dimension assesses the extent to which spouses are vague or general about what attracted them to their spouse and the degree to which they display negative affect during the interview (individual codes are given to each spouse);

(3) We-ness Versus Separateness: This dimension codes how much a spouse identifies himself or herself as part of a couple versus emphasizing his or her individuality or independence (individual codes are given for each spouse);

(4) Expansiveness Versus Withdrawal: This dimension categorizes each spouse according to how expressive he or she is. It separates individuals who give expressive and expansive answers from those who are withdrawn (individual codes are given to each spouse);

(5) Gender Role Stereotypy: This dimension assesses how traditional a couple's beliefs and values are. Couples are also coded on how gender stereotyped they are in emotional expression, responsiveness, and traditional male/female roles (one code is given for the couple);

(6) Chaotic Relationships: This dimension rates how much control couples perceive they have over their own lives. Couples may have had unexpected problems and hardships within their relationship that they were not prepared to deal with (one code is provided for the couple);

(7) Glorifying the Struggle: This dimension is for couples who have had hard times in their marriage but have gotten through them and are proud of the fact. The difficult times have helped them grow stronger and closer together (one code for the couple);

(8) Marital Disappointment and Disillusionment: This dimension assesses the extent to which spouses have given up on their marriage. Spouses who feel defeated or depressed about their marriage score high on this dimension (individual codes for each spouse).

Validity and Reliability of the Oral History Coding System

The construct validity of the Oral History Coding System has been examined with two different populations. Buehlman, Gottman, and Katz (1992) tested the psychometric properties of the instrument in their study of 52 married couples with young children and found the Oral History Coding System to have good internal construct validity. Using a principal components analysis of the variables, Buehlman and her colleagues found that nine of the subscales had a greater than .70 loading on one principal component. Notably, the subscales for wives' fondness, negativity, and expansiveness did not have strong loading values. A discriminant function analysis using the nine variables loading on the oral history principal component had 94% accuracy in predicting which of the married couples in the study would still be married 3 years later. Nine variables from the Oral History Coding System were used as predictors of divorce: husband fondness, husband negativity toward spouse, husband we-ness, wife we-ness, husband expansiveness, husband disappointment, wife disappointment, chaos, and glorifying the struggle.

Carrère et al. (2000) repeated the validation test of the Oral History Coding System with a cohort of newlywed couples. Ninety-five newlywed couples completed the Oral History Interview as well as yearly follow-up phone interviews to determine the couples' marital status. Carrère et al. found a similar loading of the subscales on the one principal component (.71 or greater: husband fondness, wife fondness, husband expansiveness, wife expansiveness, husband we-ness, wife we-ness, husband negativity, wife negativity, husband disappointment, wife disappointment, and chaotic relationship), that the authors called *marital bond*. The more positive the perceptions were that the spouses held about each other, the greater the marital bond score. Results indicated that marital bond scores could predict the participants' marital status with 87% accuracy after 4 to 6 years of marriage, and 81% accuracy after 7 to 9 years of marriage.

In the 2000 data, wives' fondness, negativity, and expansiveness subscales all had loadings equal to or greater than .71. However, the *Glorifying the Struggle* relationships subscale had a loading value of .53 and was not included in subsequent validity analyses for this newlywed cohort. The authors concluded that, given the relatively short experience these couples had in their marriages, it was understandable that a variable measuring the extent to which they had struggled through hard times would not be as helpful as other variables in predicting the health of their marriage. Discriminant construct validity analyses with the 2000 data, however, further established the construct validity of the measure: (a) There was only a moderate correlation with the related but not identical construct of marital satisfaction (Locke & Wallace, 1959); and (b) there was no correlation with the Marlowe-Crowne Social Desirability scale, a construct that should have no theoretical overlap but which offers a competing explanation for spousal behavior during the interview (Crowne & Marlowe, 1960).

Interrater reliability for the Oral History Coding System has been reasonably good. Buehlman et al. (1992) had an overall intraclass correlation of .75 for the Oral History Coding System, with intraclass correlations ranging between .71 and .91 on the subscales. In the study of newlyweds (Carrère et al., 2000), the intraclass correlation for the perceived marital bond scale in the Oral History Interview coding was .75, while intraclass correlations for the subscales ranged between .81 (husband's negativity) and .35 (gender stereotypy).

Additional Applications

Hawkins, Carrère, and Gottman, 2002. The investigators in this study used the marital bond score from the Oral History Interview to determine whether newlywed couples applied sentiment override in evaluating their partners' behaviors during a marital conflict interaction. High marital bond scores on the Oral History Interview indicated more positive perceptions about one's spouse and the marriage. Sentiment override, either positive or negative, was defined as a discrepancy between the objective coding of a spouse's affect during a marital conflict interaction, and the partner's rating of the same behavior. Results showed that wives with high marital bond scores demonstrated positive sentiment override when rating their husband's displays of anger and humor. These happy wives rated their husbands' displays of anger and humor more positively than did wives who had low marital bond scores. Husbands did not exhibit sentiment override in rating their wives affective behavior. The results of this study extend prior research suggesting that marital cognitions are associated with sentiment override among wives, but not among husbands (Notarius, et al., 1989). The results provide further evidence for the mechanisms by which the marital bond, at least in wives, may protect couples when disagreements arise through the operation of positive sentiment override.

Shapiro, Gottman, and Carrère, 2000.   This study sought to identify factors in a marriage that would predict the decline, increase, or stability in couples' marital satisfaction after the birth of their first child. Eighty-two couples—43 who became parents and 39 who remained childless—were followed for 6 years, beginning with the first year of their marriage. All couples participated in the Oral History Interview during the first year of the study. Husbands' fondness, as well as both the husbands' and wives' expansiveness about their marriage, predicted stable or increasing marital satisfaction for the wives. The husband's disappointment with his marriage, his negativity toward his wife, and the couple's descriptions of their lives as chaotic were predictive of the wives' decline in marital satisfaction after the birth of the child.

Boesch, 2001.   This study examined 53 cohabiting gay male couples who participated in the Oral History Interview and completed questionnaires to determine marital satisfaction. Results showed that the Oral History Coding System variables of we-ness and fondness correlated positively with current relationship satisfaction, whereas negativity, disappointment, and chaos correlated negatively with relationship satisfaction.

Hairston, 2001.   This study sought to determine whether marital communication research on Caucasian couples could also be applied to African-American couples. Thirteen African American couples and 13 Caucasian couples were used for analyses. Couples took part in research consisting of the Oral History Interview, a marital conflict interaction, and questionnaires about the couples' marital satisfaction (MAT; Locke & Wallace, 1959) to determine marital satisfaction. Although the strength of the correlations between the marital variables were similar for the African American and the Caucasian couples (i.e., Oral History codes, affective behavior during the marital conflict interaction, and marital satisfaction), the re-search raised significant questions about the cultural sensitivity of these marital measures. Hairston called for future work to evaluate the psychometric properties of these marital measures with African-American married couples.

DISCUSSION

The Oral History Coding System is a tool for assessing marital cognition and per-mits researchers to evaluate the impact of perceptual biases and selective attention on the stability of marriage. Specifically, spouses' cognitions about how they per-ceive their partner and their relationship may influence marital interactions in the present and subsequently result in trajectories toward marital stability or dissolu-tion. The ways in which couples interact with each other, talk about each other, and describe the history of the marriage are strongly interrelated. This association supports Fincham et al.'s (1990) thesis that how spouses remember the past corre-sponds with how they behave toward one another in the present.

The predictive strength of the Oral History Coding System comes from indexing both what spouses report about the marriage and how they interact with each other during the Oral History Interview. This may be the advantage of using a "narrative" interview in which the spouses tell their story rather than using either a question-naire or interview with explicit questions about marriage. Veroff, Sutherland, Chadiha, and Ortega (1993) suggested that direct, specific questioning may reflect a person's social self-presentation, in contrast to narratives, which are less inhibiting and more consistent with how people organize their experiences. Veroff and his as-sociates also suggested that the meaning that spouses give to their relationship in the telling of their story could be diagnostic of how they will function as a couple. The Oral History Coding System supports this perspective. It permits observations of how the couple operates as a unit and provides insights about how their percep-tions and behaviors are indicative of what will take place in the marriage over time.

Nonverbal Applications

The current Oral History Coding System incorporates, but it does not quantify ex-plicitly, nonverbal behaviors associated with the marital bond. Coding rules ask behavioral observers to look for comments and behaviors that support their cod-ing decisions on the different dimensions. The Oral History Interview does offer several avenues to explore nonverbal affect and communication between couples. For this reason, the Oral History Interview is now videotaped, rather than audio-taped. Couples are asked to sit together on a couch for the length of the interview so that their physical interactions can be observed including playful or warm touches, holding hands, physical referencing of each other, and synchrony of movement. These observations can then be coded in the fondness, we-ness, and expansiveness dimensions of the coding system.

Other nonverbal information is also observed between couples throughout the interview. Eye contact between partners is noted, as are the backchannels (paralinguistic cues that demonstrate that one is listening) that an individual offers when listening to his or her partner speak. These types of nonverbal behaviors can be coded in the we-ness dimension. Other cues are each individual's facial expressions throughout the interview (both directed at the partner as well as the interviewer), including smiles, eye-rolls, and grimaces, among others, again coded using the fondness, expansiveness, and negativity subscales.

Finally, the positive and negative nonverbal affect that the couple directs at each other throughout the interview provides valuable information. Examples of these affective behaviors include affection, humor, positive energy, criticism, contempt and sadness that can be assessed through the fondness, negativity, and marital disappointment dimensions. The Specific Affect Coding System (SPAFF; Gottman, Woodin, & Coan, in press) provides useful facial expression codes to index nonverbal emotions, and can be used in observations of the Oral History Interview (please refer to the chapter in this volume on SPAFF coding by Jones, Carrère, & Gottman for further information).

The Oral History Coding System offers a robust measure of couples' marital cognitions using a synergistic combination of verbal and nonverbal behaviors. It is a powerful tool for evaluating the health and stability of intimate relationships.

REFERENCES

Boesch, R. P. (2001). *External validation of oral history correlates of relationship satisfaction.* Unpublished doctoral dissertation, The Catholic University of America, Washington, DC.

Bradbury, T. N., & Fincham, F. D. (1987). Affect and cognition in close relationships: Toward an integrative model. *Cognition and Emotion, 1,* 59–87.

Buehlman, K. T., Gottman, J. M., & Katz, L. F. (1992). How a couple views their past predicts their future: Predicting divorce from an oral history interview. *Journal of Family Psychology, 5,* 295–318.

Buehlman, K. T., Siler, C., Carrère, S. C., & Gottman, J. M. (in press). *The oral history coding system, 2nd edition.* Seattle: NCAST-AVENUW Publications.

Carrère, S., Buehlman, K. T., Gottman, J. M., Coan, J. A., & Ruckstuhl, L. (2000). Predicting marital stability and divorce in newlywed couples. *Journal of Family Psychology, 14,* 42–58.

Cherlin, A. (1992). *Marriage, divorce, and remarriage.* Cambridge, MA: Harvard University Press.

Crowne, D. P., & Marlowe, D. (1960). A new scale of social desirability independent of psychopathology. *Journal of Consulting Psychology, 24,* 349–354.

Fincham, F. D., Bradbury, T. N., & Scott, C. K. (1990). Cognition in marriage. In F. D. Fincham & T. N. Bradbury (Eds.), *The psychology of marriage* (pp. 118–149). New York: Guilford.

Gottman, J. M. (1994). *What predicts divorce?: The relationship between marital processes and marital outcomes.* Hillsdale, NJ: Lawrence Erlbaum Associates.

Gottman, J. M., Woodin, E., & Coan, J. (in press). The Specific Affect Coding System, Version 4.0: Real time coding with the affect wheel. Seattle, WA. NCAST-AVENUW Publications.

Hairston, R. E. (2001). *Predicting marital satisfaction among African American couples.* Unpublished doctoral dissertation. Seattle Pacific University.

Hawkins, M. W., Carrère, S., & Gottman, J. M. (2002). Marital sentiment override: Does it influence couples' perceptions? *Journal of Marriage and the Family, 64,* 193–200.

Krokoff, L. J. (1984). *The anatomy of blue-collar marriages.* Unpublished doctoral dissertation, University of Illinois at Urbana-Champaign.

Locke, H. J., & Wallace, K. M. (1959). Short marital adjustment and prediction tests: Their reliability and validity. *Marriage and Family Living, 21,* 251–255.

Martin, T. C., & Bumpass, L. L. (1989). Recent trends in marital disruption. *Demography, 26,* 37–51.

National Center for Health Statistics (1991). Advance report of final marriage statistics, 1988. *Monthly Vital Statistics Report, 39* (Vol. 12, Suppl. 2). Hyattsville, MD: Public Health Service.

Notarius, C. I., Benson, P. R., Sloane, D., Vanzetti, N. A., & Hornyak, L. M. (1989). Exploring the interface between perception and behavior: An analysis of marital interaction in distressed and nondistressed couples. *Behavioral Assessment, 11,* 39–64.

Shapiro, A. F., Gottman, J. M., & Carrère, S. (2000). The baby and the marriage: Identifying factors that buffer against decline in marital satisfaction after the baby arrives. *Journal of Family Psychology, 14,* 59–70.

Veroff, J., Sutherland, L., Chadiha, L., & Ortega, R. (1993). Newlyweds tell their stories: A narrative method for assessing marital experiences. *Journal of Social and Personal Relationships, 10,* 437–457.

Weiss, R. L. (1980). Strategic behavioral marital therapy: Toward a model for assessment and intervention. In J. P. Vincent (Ed.), *Advances in family intervention, assessment and theory* (Vol I, pp. 229–271). Greenwich, CT: JAI Press.

APPENDIX

The Oral History Interview

Part 1: History of the Relationship

Q1: (**Meeting Each Other**) Why don't we start from the beginning … tell me how the two of you met and got together? Do you remember the time you met for the first time? Tell me about it … Was there anything about (spouse's name) that made him/her stand out? What were your first impressions of each other?

Q2: (**Dating**) When you think back to the time you were dating, before you got married, what do you remember? What stands out? How long did you know each other before you got married? What do you remember of this period? What were some of the highlights? What were some of the tensions? What types of things did you do together?

Q3: (**Decision**) Tell me about how you decided to get married. Of all the people in the world, what led you to decide this was the person you wanted to marry? Was it an easy or difficult decision?

Q4: (**Wedding and Honeymoon**) Do you remember the wedding: Tell me about your wedding. Did you have a honeymoon? What do you remember about it?

Q5: (**First Year of Marriage Adjustments**) When you think back to the first year you were married, what do you remember? Were there any adjustments to being married? What compromises have you had to make since you got married? What adjustments have you had to make to your partner's personality and habits? (If the couple has children) What was the transition to being parents? Tell me about this period in your marriage. What was it like for the two of you?

Q6: (**Division of Work**) One of the important issues that couples face is the division of work inside the home and work outside the home (i.e., career). (Process) How do you decide on the "who does what" in your marriage? (Actual workload) How do you actually divide these different responsibilities (examples: housework, meal preparation, child care, bills, house/yard maintenance, laundry, etc.) in your relationship? How do the two of you feel about the arrangements? (Are you satisfied?) Would you like to see any changes?

Q7: (**Making Decisions**) We talked about the process you went through to divide work responsibilities. On a more general note, how do the two of you make important decisions in this marriage–what is the process? Who has the major say in important decisions in this relationship? When you have competing "wants" (my way versus your way), how do you resolve it? (examples of important decisions: job decisions, deciding to have children, major purchases, styles of managing money).

Q8: (**Good Times in Marriage**) Looking back over the times you have been married, what moments stand out as the really good times in your marriage? What were the really happy times? (Get a feel for what a good time is like for this couple)

Q9: (**Path of Marriage**) Many of the couples we've talked to say that their relationship goes through periods of ups and downs. Would you say this is true of your marriage? How would you characterize the path your marriage has taken (examples: wild mountain road with lots of curves, comfortable rolling path of small rises and dips, straight level path).

Q10: (**Hard Times in Marriage**) Looking back over the time you have been married, what moments stand out as the really hard times in your marriage? Why do you think you stayed together? How did you get through these difficult times?

Q11: (**What Do You Know Now About Marriage**) How would you say your marriage is different from when you first got married? What do you know now that you didn't know back then?

Part 2: The Philosophy of Marriage

Q12: (**Good and Bad Marriages**) We are interested in ideas about what makes a marriage work. Why do you think some marriages work while other don't? Think of a couple you know that has a particularly good marriage and one that you know who has a particularly bad marriage. (Let them decide together who these marriages are). What is different about these two marriages? How would you compare your own marriage to each of these couples?

Q13: (**Parents' Marriages**) Tell me about your parents' marriages. (Ask each spouse) What were their marriages like? Would you say they are very similar or different from your own marriage? How so?

Q14: (**Things They Want to Add**) What would you like to say about your marriage or marriage in general that we haven't touched on? Do you have any advice for young couples who are thinking about getting married?

PROMPT: I think we are just about done now, but let me go check with my colleague to make sure. I will be right back. (Check to see if the oral history coder has been able to code all the items. If not, go back and ask the question/s that need to be asked to help complete the coding).

Observer Ratings of Nonverbal Involvement and Immediacy

Laura K. Guerrero
Arizona State University

INTRODUCTION

Behaviors such as gaze, touch, vocal animation, and smiling can give life to an otherwise dull interaction. These types of behaviors, termed *involvement* or *immediacy* cues, reflect the degree to which a person is actively involved in a conversation. In this chapter, the constructs of nonverbal involvement and immediacy are conceptualized and then operationalized via a coding scheme that researchers can use to record specific behaviors related to involvement and immediacy.

CONCEPTUALIZING IMMEDIACY AND INVOLVEMENT

Although some scholars use the terms immediacy and involvement interchangeably, others have conceptualized these constructs differently. Immediacy is sometimes defined as a set of behaviors that send messages of approachability and positive affect or liking simultaneously (e.g., J. Andersen, P. Andersen, & Jensen, 1979; P. Andersen, 1985; Mehrabian, 1981). Other scholars, however, have conceptualized immediacy as one of several dimensions that fall under the broader construct of involvement (e.g., Burgoon & Newton, 1991; Cappella, 1983; Dillard, Solomon, & Palmer, 1999).

Immediacy as Approach Behavior Reflecting Positive Affect

Mehrabian (1967) was the first to use the term immediacy to describe a set of behaviors that reflect the "directness and intensity of interaction" between two people (p. 325). Later, he expanded this definition to include behaviors that signal attentiveness, heighten sensory stimulation, and show liking and rapport

(Mehrabian, 1981). Mehrabian argued that the immediacy construct is an apt metaphor for general approach and avoidance tendencies, with approach tendencies associated with liking and avoidant tendencies associated with disliking. Similarly, P. Andersen (1985) described four characteristics of immediacy behaviors: They increase physical and psychological closeness, increase sensory stimulation, signal availability for interaction, and communicate positive affect.

From this perspective, immediacy is conceptualized as a set of "approach" behaviors that reflect liking and positive regard. Behaviors such as close proxemic distancing, positive forms of touch, smiling, and vocal warmth are a sampling of a longer list of immediacy behaviors that can signal both liking and a willingness to communicate simultaneously (J. Andersen et al., 1979; P. Andersen, 1999). In the majority of work conducted in instructional contexts, for example, researchers have conceptualized teacher immediacy as a set of approach behaviors that communicate positive affect. For example, early work by J. Andersen (1979; J. Andersen et al., 1979) defined teacher immediacy in terms of warm, direct, and expressive behaviors, such as smiling, eye contact, and gesturing. J. Andersen argued that these types of behavior foster positive affect within the classroom, which leads to a positive environment that is conducive to learning.

Immediacy as a Subset of Involvement Behavior

Other scholars have conceptualized immediacy as a subset of involvement behaviors (e.g., Burgoon & Newton, 1991; Cappella, 1983; Coker & Burgoon, 1987; Prager, 1995). Under this view, immediacy behaviors are related most closely to the degree of directness, intensity, and physical closeness present in an interaction, independent of whether or not these behaviors send messages of positive affect. From this perspective, immediacy refers to a specific class of approach behaviors that signal physical and temporal closeness. Involvement, in contrast, is a broader construct that reflects how actively engaged a person is in a given conversation (Cappella, 1983; Cegala, 1981; Coker & Burgoon, 1987). Thus, the degree of conversational involvement can be thought of as falling somewhere on an engagement–detachment continuum.

In contrast to scholars who conceptualize immediacy as encompassing messages related to both approach tendencies and positive affect, scholars taking the view that immediacy is a subset of involvement behaviors argue that positive affect is independent from immediacy. According to the latter perspective, immediacy reflects approach behavior but not necessarily liking or positive affect. For example, Burgoon (1994) described positive versus negative affect as a separate dimension that is relevant but not essential to conversational involvement. She argued that involvement behaviors such as forward lean, direct body orientation, and vocal/kinesic expressiveness may be present in conversations that are characterized by negative affect (e.g., a heated argument) or positive affect (e.g., making up after the argument). Similarly, Dillard et al. (1999) argued that involvement is related to the intensity of interaction, and that involvement cues can be present in interactions characterized by either dominance or affiliation (see Cappella, 1983; Prager, 1995, for similar claims).

SPECIFIC BEHAVIORS RELATED TO IMMEDIACY AND INVOLVEMENT

Despite differences in the ways scholars define immediacy and involvement, the behaviors that are relevant to these conceptualizations are much more similar than different. P. Andersen (1985, 1999; P. Andersen & Guerrero, 1998) advanced one of the most comprehensive lists of immediacy behaviors that can reflect simultaneously both approach tendencies and positive emotion. He organized this list in terms of the subcodes of nonverbal communication. Proxemic and haptic cues such as close conversational distances, forward lean, direct body orientation, positive forms of touch, and communication on the same physical plane (e.g., sitting at eye level rather than one person standing and the other sitting) can all communicate immediacy. The most important kinesic behaviors related to immediacy include high levels of gaze, mutual eye contact, smiling, affirmative head nods, gestural animation, postural congruence, lack of random movement, and open, relaxed body positions. Vocalic immediacy behaviors include vocal variety in terms of pitch, amplitude, duration, and tempo; greater vocal fluency, warmth, and expressiveness; clearer articulation, reinforcing vocalizations such as "uh-huh;" and smooth turn-taking. Finally, chronemic immediacy cues include spending time with people, focusing only on the conversation (rather than on multiple tasks), and being punctual (P. Andersen, 1985, 1999; P. Andersen & Guerrero, 1998).

Scholars focusing on nonverbal involvement have investigated similar behaviors. Coker and Burgoon (1987), for example, identified five categories of nonverbal involvement behaviors: immediacy, expressiveness, altercentrism, smooth interaction management, and composure. Within Coker and Burgoon's system, touch, close proximity, direct body/face orientation, gaze, and forward lean were classified as *immediacy* behaviors, similar to earlier work by Mehrabian (1969) and Patterson (1983). Each of these cues contributes to an overall picture of the "distance" between two individuals. *Expressiveness* refers to the degree of animation and dynamism displayed by a communicator. Behaviors such as vocal variety (in terms of varied pitch, tempo, and volume), facial animation, and gesturing (especially illustrators, emblems, and expansive gestures) have been linked to overall perceptions of expressiveness (Burgoon & Newton, 1991; Coker & Burgoon, 1987; Spitzberg & Hecht, 1984). *Interaction management* has been defined as "the degree to which participants in conversation engage in smooth-flowing conversation" (Coker & Burgoon, 1987, p. 473). Coker and Burgoon mentioned shorter response latencies, fewer silences, overall fluency, and overall coordination in body movements as indicators of smooth interaction management.

GUERRERO

224

Altercentrism, or other-orientation, refers to the degree to which a person focuses on the partner during an interaction. Research suggests that still posture, eye contact (especially when listening), serious vocal tone, nodding, vocal backchanneling (e.g., saying "uh-hum"), and spending time with someone are all indicative of altercentrism (Coker & Burgoon, 1987; Spitzberg & Hecht, 1984). *Composure* can be defined as the degree to which an individual displays confidence and assertiveness rather than tension and nervousness (Spitzberg & Hurt, 1987). Behaviors such as a relaxed and/or confident voice, postural relaxation, minimal fidgeting, and a lack of random movement have been associated with composure (Coker & Burgoon, 1987). Finally, Burgoon (1994; Burgoon & Newton, 1991) recommended that researchers rate *affect* in addition to involvement, so that a more complete picture of the type of interaction (e.g., involved but hostile or involved and intimate) would emerge. *Positive affect* is generally communicated through smiling, general facial pleasantness, vocal warmth, and relaxed laughter (Burgoon & Newton, 1991; Guerrero, 1997).

A CODING SCHEME FOR MEASURING NONVERBAL INVOLVEMENT AND IMMEDIACY

Although there are excellent questionnaires available for reporting perceptions of immediacy (e.g., J. Andersen et al., 1979; Kearney, 1994; Richmond, Gorham, & McCroskey, 1987), less research has focused on measuring specific immediacy and/or involvement cues through direct observation. This led Guerrero (1996, 1997) to develop a system for coding nonverbal behaviors relevant to involvement and immediacy. Using items from Coker and Burgoon (1987) as a guide, Guerrero (1996, 1997) created scales to measure specific involvement/immediacy behaviors that could be rated by coders. These scales are designed to tap into the six dimensions relevant to nonverbal involvement: immediacy, expressiveness, altercentrism, smooth interaction management, composure, and positive affect.

Although the coding scheme can be used in its entirety, particular scales could also be chosen based on the focus of one's research. For example, researchers interested in studying teacher immediacy during classroom lectures may focus on expressiveness, positive affect, and certain immediacy cues, while opting not to code factors (e.g., touch, smooth interaction management, and altercentrism) that are less relevant when one person is addressing a large audience. In the following section, the most up-to-date version of these rating scales is presented along with guidelines for training coders to use these rating scales. Reliabilities from past studies are reported. In all cases, Cronbach's *alpha* statistic was used to estimate interitem reliability, and Ebel's intraclass correlation was used to estimate interrater reliability. A sample coding sheet is included (see Appendix A) as are examples of the various scales as they have been grouped in past research (see Appendix B).

Immediacy

Touch. The five immediacy behaviors identified by Mehrabian (1969), Patterson (1983), and Coker and Burgoon (1987) are touch, close proxemic distancing, forward lean, body orientation, and gaze. Within this coding system, touch is measured using both tally counts and a percentage that allows researchers to estimate both touch frequency and touch duration. Specifically, coders put a tally mark on the coding sheet each time a discrete touch occurs. Coders also use stopwatches to measure the total time that the dyad spends touching (by starting and stopping the stopwatch throughout the interaction). The latter measure is converted into a percentage by dividing the total time spent touching by the length of the coding segment. So, for example, if a dyad touches holds hands for 30 seconds out of a 60-second segment, they would have a score of 1 in terms of frequency and a score of .50 in terms of duration. Because frequency counts and percentage measures often lead to skewed distributions, before entering them into statistical analyses they should be converted to interval measures using square root transformations and arc sign transformations, respectively (see Snedecor & Cochran, 1969). Past research (e.g., Guerrero, 1994, 1997) suggests that the touch measures are best utilized as separate scales. Using Ebel's intraclass correlation, interrater reliabilities for the frequency measures have been excellent for both the touch frequency measure (.87 and .96) and the duration measure (.82 and .91) in Guerrero's (1994, 1997) studies.

Proxemic Distancing. Proxemic distancing is measured by having coders rate how close versus far the distance is between the interactants' faces and bodies. This method provides a good estimate of conversational distancing given that it is possible for two people to sit with their legs or knees touching but their faces farther apart. Generally, however, these two types of distancing are correlated, with inter-item reliabilities ranging from .76 to .92 in Guerrero's (1996, 1997) studies. In these studies, partners were seated next to one another on a sofa. Coders were trained so that they would rate the distance between their bodies as "far" if they were sitting at opposite ends of the sofa with maximum space between them. By contrast, if their arms or the trunks of their bodies are touching coders would rate distancing as "close." For distance between faces, a "close" distance was defined as six inches or less, whereas a "far" distance was defined as having both interactants' faces near the opposite side arms of the sofa.

Forward Lean. Forward lean has also been accessed with two items (with inter-item reliabilities ranging from .91 to .96), with one item focusing on how much a person leans forward versus backward, and the other focusing on whether a person was generally positioned as leaning toward or away from the partner. For the former item, coders were trained to focus on whether the person is in a forward position (bent at the waist) versus a backward position (leaning against the sofa). For the latter item, coders also focused on the direction of the lean in relation to the partner. Interrater reliabilities were above .90 in Guerrero's (1996, 1997) studies.

Body Orientation.   Coders rated body orientation by determining the extent to which a person faced toward or away from the partner, as well as the face-to-face versus side-by-side positioning of the interactants. As such, the first of these items focuses on an individual's behavior, whereas the second item focuses on the dyad's positioning. In both cases, coders were trained to think of body orientation in terms of the angle of the body. In Guerrero's (1997) study, both interitem (.73) and inter-rater (.97) reliabilities were acceptable. However, in Guerrero's (1996) study, these two items were not sufficiently correlated (interitem reliability was .38). Thus, this subscale may need further refinement.

Gaze.   Eye behavior has been assessed using three items. First, coders accessed the extent to which one person looked at the other (never vs. always), with the end-points conceptualized as zero gaze and 100% gaze during the interaction. Gaze was defined in terms of looking at the partner's face. Second, coders accessed how steady versus unsteady gaze was. In this case, coders were trained to determine whether people tended to gaze at the partner's face for relatively long segments of time or whether they tended to look at the partner's face and then look at something else. Finally, coders rated the extent to which a person engaged in eye contact, with eye contact defined as both people looking into one another's faces. This measure of gaze has yielded interitem reliabilities above .90 in two studies (Guerrero, 1996, 1997), with interrater reliabilities of .64 and .87. It is also noteworthy that gaze was rated in real time rather than via videotape in Guerrero's studies. Because pilot test-ing showed that coders had difficulty making accurate ratings of eye behavior via videotapes, Guerrero had coders evaluate gaze from behind a one-way mirror as the actual interaction took place. The main downfall to this method, however, is that coders have to make their ratings relatively quickly so they do not miss part of the interaction. Using an additional camera that provides a close-up view of faces is a good alternative to coding gaze as it occurs.

Expressiveness

Kinesic Animation.   The body and the voice are the two channels that are pri-marily responsible for creating impressions of dynamism and animation. Thus, ex-pressiveness has been measured in terms of kinesic and vocalic animation. Kinesic animation is measured with three items (with interitem reliabilities ranging from .87 to .98): the degree of facial expression, the frequency of gesturing, and the over-all level of expressive kinesic movement. For facial expression, coders are trained to look for expression of both positive and/or negative emotion. The more emotion they see, the higher they rate the level of facial expression. For gesturing, coders are trained to look for emblems, illustrators, and other expansive gestures. Overall ki-nesic animation is defined in terms of the degree of body movement, including ges-tures and facial expression, but excluding nervous and random movements. Interrater item reliability has ranged from .87 to .98 for kinesic animation in Guerrero's (1996, 1997) studies.

Vocal Animation. For vocal animation, coders are trained to listen to video-tapes with a piece of paper covering the upper part of the screen so only the timer is showing. Vocal animation is measured with three items. The first focuses on how much vocal variety is present. Coders are trained to listen for variety in terms of tempo, volume, and pitch, with "no variation" operationalized as a monotone voice. The second item focuses on how inexpressive versus animated the voice sounded overall. Coders are instructed to judge how well the person's voice conveys the person's mood and/or emotions, with voices that project mood and/or emotion rated as the most expressive. Finally, coders rate the degree to which a person's voice sounds "dull" versus "full of life." Coders are asked to think about how generally animated and full of life they imagine the person is, based on her or his voice. Interitem reliability has been good for these or similar measures across studies, ranging from .88 to .98 (Coker & Burgoon, 1987; Guerrero, 1996, 1997), and interrater reliability has ranged from .76 to .83 (Guerrero, 1996, 1997).

Altercentrism

General Attentiveness and Interest. Altercentrism can be measured in terms of global impressions of attentiveness and interest (Coker & Burgoon, 1987; Guerrero, 1996, 1997). To measure attentiveness, Guerrero had coders focus on the totality of a person's nonverbal behavior to rate how inattentive/attentive, distracted/focused, unalert/alert, bored/interested, and detached/involved a person appears. Interitem reliabilities for these or similar scales have been above .90 across studies by Coker and Burgoon (1987) and Guerrero (1996, 1997). Interrater reliabilities have ranged from .57 to .81 (Guerrero, 1996, 1997).

Nods. Head nods may also reflect an altercentric orientation, particularly when they are used as a backchanneling cue that encourages the partner to continue speaking and/or signals agreement or understanding. Guerrero (1996) had coders count the number of times a person nodded during a particular time segment. A nod was defined as a discrete up-and-down movement of the head, so that if someone moved her or his head up and down three times in a row, three nods would be recorded. As for touch frequency, nods were transformed via square root transformations before entering them in the analysis. Using this system, Guerrero (1996) obtained a very high interrater reliability of .99 using Ebel's intraclass correlation.

Smooth Interaction Management

Speech Fluency and Response Latencies. Smooth interaction management entails fluency at the individual level as well as coordination between conversational partners. At the individual level, smooth interaction management has been accessed in terms of fluency and response latencies. Fluency has been measured using two scales, with the first scale focusing on the extent to which a person's speech is characterized by nonfluencies (operationalized as vocalized pauses and within-speaking-turn silences) versus fluency (lack of vocalized pauses and within-speaking-turn silences). The second scale focuses on how choppy or smooth a person's speech is, with hesitancies, stammering, unclear or nervous vocalizations, awkward pauses, and slurred speech described as contributing to "choppiness." These two items, which create a scale measuring speech fluency, were significantly correlated (with interitem reliabilities of .89 and .97) in Guerrero's (1996, 1997) study. Interrater reliability ranged from .47 to .61 in these studies. Response latencies have been measured using a one-item scale that gauges how long versus short the target's response latencies are, with response latencies defined as the length of time between the end of the partner's speaking turn and the beginning of the target individual's speaking turn. Interrater reliability for this item has ranged from .48 to .66 (Guerrero, 1996, 1997).

Interactional Fluency.   Smooth interaction management is also related to how "in sync" two individuals are. Conversations marked by frequent interruptions, long and awkward silences, and uncoordinated turn-taking are far from smooth. Thus, these three components comprise a measure of conversational fluency. Coders judge interruptions via a frequency-based measure. Prior to training coders, a sample of the videotapes can be reviewed by the researchers to ascertain what constitutes a high number of interruptions within a given type of interaction. This estimate can then be used to anchor the "a lot" side of the interruptions scale. Similarly, coders should be given guidelines on what constitutes a lot of silence within a given type of interaction, based on the researcher's review of the videotapes. Finally, coders can judge the level of coordination within a given interaction based on the smooth exchange of turns. When turn-taking is marked by interruptions, talk-overs, long response latencies, awkward silence, and/or hesitancies, it is less coordinated. These three items have worked together as a composite scale in pilot tests, and have also been used separately (see Coker & Burgoon, 1987; Guerrero, 1994; Guerrero & Jones, 2000). When used a composite, interitem reliability has ranged from .73 to .81. Interrater reliabilities have ranged from .68 to .78 for the composite measure, and .41 to .87 for single measures (Guerrero, 1996, 1997).

Composure

Vocal and Bodily Relaxation.   Composure is communicated by vocal and bodily relaxation and the absence of nervous behaviors. Vocal relaxation has been measured using two items: tense/relaxed and anxious/calm. So that coders relied only on vocalics, Guerrero (1996, 1997) instructed them to cover the television screen with paper (so that just the timer was showing) when making these ratings. A tense voice was defined as sounding tight and slightly high-pitched; an anxious voice was defined as sounding shaky or nervous. In Guerrero's (1996, 1997) studies, interitem reliability ranged from .87 to .96, and interrater reliability ranged from

.56 to .82. Bodily relaxation was measured using three items: tense/relaxed, closed/open, and rigid/loose. Coders were told that signs of a tense body include sitting in a stiff, erect position and having clenched limbs. A closed body position was defined in terms of a defensive stance, with arms and/or legs stiffly crossed and the body taking up little space. Finally, a rigid body position was defined by stiffness and lack of expressive movement. In Guerrero's (1996, 1997) studies, this measure yielded interitem reliabilities of .87 and .93, and interrater reliabilities of .68 to .70. A similar scale by Coker and Burgoon (1987) yielded an interitem reliability of .75 and an average interrater reliability of .69.

Lack of Random Movement. Three items have been used to measure lack of random movement. First, coders determine the extent to which a target exhibited nervous movement such as self- and object-adaptors (e.g., twisting a strand of hair, licking one's lips). Second, coders look for rocking or twisting behaviors, such as rocking from side to side, twisting one's hands in one's lap, twisting one's angle, or rocking one's foot back and forth. Third, coders look for the overall degree of trunk and limb movement, which includes those behaviors as well as shaking, tapping fingers, and other forms of fidgeting. This 3-item scale has yielded interitem reliabilities above .90 and interrater reliabilities around .75 (Guerrero, 1996, 1997).

Positive Affect

Smiling. Positive affect behaviors reflecting warmth and affiliation include smiling, general facial pleasantness, and vocal warmth. As with gaze, smiling has been measured on-line from behind a one-way mirror. Two simple measures of smiling have been utilized: always smiling versus never smiling, and smiled a little versus smiled a lot. Coders are taught to make a subtle distinction when utilizing these items. When using the always versus never rating, they are instructed to think about the percentage of time that a target smiled, with "never" equaling zero and "always" equaling 100%. For the "a little" versus "a lot" measure, coders are instructed to think about how many times a person smiled. Coders are also told to focus on smiling that reflected friendliness, affirmation, or positive affect and to discard smiling that seems to be sarcastic or inappropriate. In Guerrero's (1994, 1997) work, this 2-item measure of smiling has been reliable in terms of both internal consistency (.95 to .96) and coder ratings (.82 to .89).

Facial Pleasantness. Although smiling is the primary way people express positive affect, a person's overall facial expression can also communicate positive emotion. For example, a person's face might look relaxed while he or she is smiling slightly, whereas another person might smile more broadly but then furrow his or her brow. In Guerrero's (1996, 1997) studies, coders rated overall facial pleasantness with two general measures: the degree to which the target's face was facially pleasant versus unpleasant and the degree to which the target's face communicated negative versus positive affect. Coders were instructed to rate pleasantness based on the overall level of warmth and relaxation present in the face, whereas affect was judged by the frequency with which the target showed positive versus negative emotion. For the former scale, a neutral rating of 4 indicated that the face was neutral in terms of pleasantness; for the latter scale, a neutral rating indicated that the face communicated equal levels of positive and negative emotion, or no emotion at all. In Guerrero's (1996, 1997) studies, this measure of facial pleasantness has yielded inter-item reliability above .90 and interrater reliability around .75 when coded on-line.

Vocal Pleasantness.   As with most of the other vocal measures, vocal pleasantness is rated via videotapes with paper covering the screen. Guerrero (1996, 1997) used three straightforward items measuring how cold/warm, unpleasant/pleasant, and unfriendly/friendly a person's voice sounded. Coders were asked to rate warmth in terms of the overall tone of the voice, including softness. Pleasant voices were described as those that are clear, expressive, and warm. For friendliness, coders were asked about whether the person they were listening to sounded likeable. These items have shown high interitem reliability above .90 across different studies, with interrater reliability ranging from .74 to .81 (Coker & Burgoon, 1987; Guerrero, 1996, 1997).

Additional Recommendations

A few additional recommendations may be helpful when using this system. First, during training it is essential that coders are provided with good examples of what constitutes behavior at the high and low ends of each scale within the particular situation under observation. For instance, the amount of space that constitutes "far" proxemic distancing is affected by factors such as the type and position of furniture within a room. Second, after an initial training session or two, coders should practice their ratings using sample tapes. After these ratings are completed, reliabilities can be checked and the coders can get together with the researcher to discuss any discrepant ratings. Third, if coders are viewing a relatively long interaction (over 3 minutes), it is advisable to have them make their ratings in smaller time intervals, such as every minute, every 2 minutes, or every 3 minutes (see Appendix A). This procedure keeps coders focused and increases accuracy. Coder ratings can then be averaged across these time segments.

Fourth, coders should only concentrate on two or three different behaviors at a time, and if possible the behaviors should be related. For instance, in the examples provided (see Appendix B), behaviors are grouped so that coders can focus on related cues—such as overall impressions of behavior, the voice, or behaviors related to body positioning—at the same time. Fifth, coders should be instructed to stop and review the tape whenever they are unsure of their ratings. Sixth, for statistical reasons, it is best that the same two coders rate all the behaviors falling under a given dimension. Finally, because nonverbal involvement behaviors are often perceived as a gestalt (P. Andersen, 1985, 1999), it may also be helpful to measure involvement at a global level. For example, Guerrero (1996) had raters access a target individual's overall level of involvement (in terms of a general impression) as well as specific involvement behaviors (such as gaze, response latencies, and vocal warmth). This allows researchers to obtain a measure of observers' general impressions of immediacy or involvement. Moreover, researchers can then test to see which specific nonverbal behaviors are related to global impressions of immediacy or involvement.

CONCLUSION

Coding nonverbal behaviors is a challenging enterprise that demands considerable time and effort. The system presented in this chapter is intended as a guide for researchers who wish to take up this challenge by measuring some of the many specific behaviors that have been identified as part of the involvement/immediacy construct. Yet the system presented in this chapter is not comprehensive. Some involvement behaviors, such as spending time together, cannot be captured adequately in experimental or observational settings. Thus, to understand how nonverbal involvement functions in communicative exchanges, scholars should use multiple methodologies, including laboratory observations, experiments, natural observations, diary studies, and questionnaire studies. The coding system presented in this chapter may be particularly helpful for researchers using the former two methods to try to understand the complexities and subtleties of actual communicative behavior.

REFERENCES

Andersen, J. F. (1979). Teacher immediacy as a predicator of teaching effectiveness. In D. Nimmo (Ed.), *Communication Yearbook 3* (pp. 545–559). New Brunswick, NJ: Transaction Books.

Andersen, J. F., Andersen, P. A., & Jensen, A. D. (1979). The measurement of nonverbal immediacy. *Journal of Applied Communication Research, 7,* 153–180.

Andersen, P. A. (1985). Nonverbal immediacy in interpersonal communication. In A. W. Siegman & S. Feldstein (Eds.), *Multichannel integrations of nonverbal behavior* (pp. 1–36). Hillsdale, NJ: Lawrence Erlbaum Associates.

Andersen, P. A. (1999). *Nonverbal communication: Forms and functions.* Mountain View, CA: Mayfield Publishing.

Andersen, P. A., & Guerrero, L. K. (1998). The bright side of relational communication: Interpersonal warmth as a social emotion. In P. A. Andersen & L. K. Guerrero (Eds.), *Handbook of communication and emotion: Research, theory, applications, and contexts* (pp. 303–329). San Diego, CA: Academic Press.

Burgoon, J. K. (1994). Nonverbal signals. In M. L. Knapp & G. R. Miller (Eds.), *Handbook of interpersonal communication* (2nd ed., pp. 229–285). Thousand Oaks, CA: Sage.

Burgoon, J. K., & Newton, D. A. (1991). Applying a social meaning model to relational messages of conversational involvement: Comparing participant and observer perspectives. *Southern Communication Journal, 56,* 96–113.

Cappella, J. N. (1983). Conversational involvement: Approaching and avoiding others. In J. M. Wiemann & R. P. Harrison (Eds.), *Nonverbal interaction* (pp. 113–148). Beverly Hills, CA: Sage.

Cegala, D. J. (1981). Interaction involvement: A cognitive dimension of communicative competence. *Communication Education, 30,* 109–121.

Coker, D. A., & Burgoon, J. K. (1987). The nature of conversational involvement and nonverbal encoding patterns. *Human Communication Research, 13,* 463–494.

Dillard, J. P., Solomon, D. H., & Palmer, M. T. (1999). Structuring the concept of relational communication. *Communication Monographs, 66,* 49–65.

Guerrero, L. K. (1994). *An application of attachment theory to relational messages and nonverbal involvement behaviors in romantic dyads.* Unpublished doctoral dissertation, University of Arizona, Tucson.

Guerrero, L. K. (1996). Attachment-style differences in intimacy and involvement: A test of the four-category model. *Communication Monographs, 63,* 269–292.

Guerrero, L. K. (1997). Nonverbal involvement across interactions with same-sex friends, opposite-sex friends, and romantic partners: Consistency or change? *Journal of Social and Personal Relationships, 14,* 31–58.

Guerrero, L. K., & Jones, S. M. (2000, June). *Attachment-style differences in social skills.* Paper presented to the annual conference of the International Communication Associations, Acapulco, Mexico.

Kearney, P. (1994). Nonverbal immediacy behaviors instrument. In R. B. Rubin, P. Palmgreen, & H. E. Sypher (Eds.), *Communication research measures: A sourcebook* (pp. 238–241). New York: Guilford Press.

Mehrabian, A. (1967). Attitudes inferred from nonimmediacy of verbal communication. *Journal of Verbal Learning and Verbal Behavior, 6,* 294–295.

Mehrabian, A. (1969). Some referents and measures of nonverbal behavior. *Behavioral Research Methods and Instruments, 1,* 213–217.

Mehrabian, A. (1981). *Silent messages: Implicit communication of emotions and attitudes* (2nd ed.). Belmont, CA: Wadsworth.

Patterson, M. L. (1983). *Nonverbal behavior: A functional perspective.* New York: Springer-Verlag.

Prager, K. J. (1995). *The psychology of intimacy.* New York: Guilford.

Richmond, V., Gorham, J., & McCroskey, J. (1987). The relationship between selected immediacy behaviors and cognitive learning. In M. McLaughlin (Ed.), *Communication yearbook, 10* (pp. 574–590). Beverly Hills, CA: Sage.

Snedecor, G. W., & Cochran, W. G. (1969). *Statistical methods* (6th ed.). Ames: Iowa State University Press.

Spitzberg, B. H., & Hecht, M. L. (1984). A component model of relational competence. *Human Communication Research, 4,* 575–599.

Spitzberg, B. H., & Hurt, H. T. (1987). The measurement of interpersonal skills in instructional contexts. *Communication Education, 36,* 28–45.

APPENDIX A:

Coding Sheet for Eye Behavior

Coder: _____   Dyad: _____

Time Segment :00–1:00

The target:

never looked at the partner	1	2	3	4	5	6	7	always looked at the partner
exhibited unsteady gaze	1	2	3	4	5	6	7	exhibited steady gaze
gave no eye contact	1	2	3	4	5	6	7	gave constant eye contact

Time Segment 1:01–2:00

The target:

never looked at the partner	1	2	3	4	5	6	7	always looked at the partner
exhibited unsteady gaze	1	2	3	4	5	6	7	exhibited steady gaze
gave no eye contact	1	2	3	4	5	6	7	gave constant eye contact

Time Segment 2:01–3:00

The target:

never looked at the partner	1	2	3	4	5	6	7	always looked at the partner
exhibited unsteady gaze	1	2	3	4	5	6	7	exhibited steady gaze
gave no eye contact	1	2	3	4	5	6	7	gave constant eye contact

Time Segment 3:01–4:00

The target:

never looked at the partner	1	2	3	4	5	6	7	always looked at the partner
exhibited unsteady gaze	1	2	3	4	5	6	7	exhibited steady gaze
gave no eye contact	1	2	3	4	5	6	7	gave constant eye contact

APPENDIX B:

Examples of Immediacy/Involvement Scales

Based on your observation of the target's face, the target:

never smiled	1 2 3 4 5 6 7	always smiled
was facially pleasant	1 2 3 4 5 6 7	was facially unpleasant
smiled a little	1 2 3 4 5 6 7	smiled a lot
conveyed negative affect	1 2 3 4 5 6 7	conveyed positive affect

The target:

leaned away from the partner	1 2 3 4 5 6 7	leaned toward to the partner
faced away from the partner	1 2 3 4 5 6 7	faced toward the partner
sat in a side-by-side position	1 2 3 4 5 6 7	sat in a face-to-face position
leaned back a lot	1 2 3 4 5 6 7	leaned forward a lot

The distance between bodies *was:*	*far*	1 2 3 4 5 6 7	*close*
The distance between faces *was:*	*far*	1 2 3 4 5 6 7	*close*

Touch and Nods

Record the # of times (using tally marks) the target nodded her/his head: _____
Record the # of times (using tally marks) that touch occurred: _____
What was the total time that the dyad spent touching? (recorded typically in seconds/minutes; can then be converted to a percentage): _____

The target's voice:

was monotone	1 2 3 4 5 6 7	contained vocal variety
sounded tense	1 2 3 4 5 6 7	sounded relaxed
sounded cold	1 2 3 4 5 6 7	sounded warm
sounded anxious	1 2 3 4 5 6 7	sounded calm
was inexpressive	1 2 3 4 5 6 7	was animated
sounded unpleasant	1 2 3 4 5 6 7	sounded pleasant
was unfriendly	1 2 3 4 5 6 7	was friendly
was dull	1 2 3 4 5 6 7	was full of life

The target showed:

very little facial expression	1 2 3 4 5 6 7	a lot of facial expression
lots of nervous movement	1 2 3 4 5 6 7	very little nervous movement
frequent rocking or twisting	1 2 3 4 5 6 7	infrequent rocking or twisting
little gesturing	1 2 3 4 5 6 7	a lot of gesturing
little kinesic expression	1 2 3 4 5 6 7	a lot of kinesic expression
a lot of trunk/limb movement	1 2 3 4 5 6 7	very little trunk/limb movement

Based on her/his nonverbal behavior, the target seemed:

anxious	1 2 3 4 5 6 7	calm
inattentive	1 2 3 4 5 6 7	attentive
distracted	1 2 3 4 5 6 7	focused
unalert	1 2 3 4 5 6 7	alert
restless	1 2 3 4 5 6 7	still
flustered	1 2 3 4 5 6 7	composed
bored	1 2 3 4 5 6 7	interested
detached	1 2 3 4 5 6 7	involved

The target's speech was:

filled with nonfluencies	1 2 3 4 5 6 7	very fluent
very choppy	1 2 3 4 5 6 7	very smooth
marked by long response latencies	1 2 3 4 5 6 7	marked by short response latencies

The conversation was characterized by:

a lot of interruptions	1 2 3 4 5 6 7	no interruptions
a lot of awkward silence	1 2 3 4 5 6 7	very little awkward silence
uncoordinated turn-taking	1 2 3 4 5 6 7	coordinated turn-taking

Overall, the target's body position was:

tense	1 2 3 4 5 6 7	relaxed
closed	1 2 3 4 5 6 7	open
rigid	1 2 3 4 5 6 7	loose

Measuring Nonverbal Indicators of Deceit

Judee K. Burgoon
University of Arizona

INTRODUCTION

The very foundation of social organization is the ability of humans to work together to develop a system of social signals that makes cooperation possible. In turn, the exchange of social signals is grounded in the presumption of truthfulness (Grice, 1989; Habermas, 1979). Ironically, however, it is that very trust that humans and other social species exploit to their advantage through deceit. Deceit, in fact, whether it takes the form of hyperbole, evasion, concealment, distortion, camouflage, masquerade, or outright lies, may be a fundamental social skill that contributes to survival of the fittest (Riggio & Friedman, 1983). In light of its central significance in human discourse, deception—messages and actions intended to create false impressions or conclusions by their targets—and its nonverbal manifestations are a natural object of social research.

Historical Overview of Deception Measurement

The task of identifying and measuring reliable indicators (cues) of deceit has attracted attention from scholars in a range of disciplines. Despite decades of research and hundreds of published investigations, however, few nonverbal and verbal behaviors have emerged as ones that distinguish truthful from deceptive communication accurately and consistently. Too often the behaviors that people associate with deception stereotypically are, in fact, *not* diagnostic; in other words, they do not actually reflect how deceivers behave.

Although several meta-analyses (e.g., DePaulo et al., 2003; Zuckerman, DePaulo, & Rosenthal, 1981; Zuckerman & Driver, 1985) and other recent summaries (e.g., Vrij, 2000; Vrij & Mann, in press) have identified some cues that are associated systematically with lying or truth-telling, those same meta-analyses have identified a variety of moderator variables that not only alter which nonverbal cues are likely to be present under a given circumstance but also their directionality. For example, under one condition, deceivers might gesture more than will truth tellers, whereas under another condition they might gesture less (Vrij, Akehurst, & Morris, 1997). High-stakes lies may produce markedly different displays than low-stakes lies (Frank & Ekman, 1997). Moreover, seldom is a single cue likely to be an effective discriminator: Usually multiple cues are needed to declare a given behavioral display as deceptive or truthful. Adding to the complexity of measuring indicators of deceit is the fact that deception cues are highly transitory and changeable over time so that overt manifestations at the beginning of a deceptive interchange may differ substantially from those at its conclusion (Buller & Burgoon, 1996; Burgoon, Buller, White, Afifi, & Buslig, 1999; White & Burgoon, 2001).

All these caveats notwithstanding, it is possible to identify some prospective indicators of deceit and to even specify the conditions under which their occurrence is most probable. Toward that end, I present a typology that includes five, non-exhaustive classes of cues and then discuss how they have been measured in prior research. This classification scheme was developed in the context of analyzing verbal as well as nonverbal cues and should be useful in research decisions regarding the most relevant cues to observe depending on the nature of deception investigated.

CLASSIFICATION OF NONVERBAL DECEPTION INDICATORS

Over the last half century, many of the empirical efforts to uncover reliable nonverbal cues were guided by Ekman and Friesen's (1969) seminal work on the *leakage hypothesis* and by the four-factor theory, both of which proposed that deception instigates a number of involuntary telltale signs that unconsciously "leak" from deceivers. Because deception is thought to be arousing and fraught with such negative emotions as guilt and fear of detection, two of the four factors underlying possible deception cues are arousal and negative affect. Additionally, deception was thought to be a more difficult communication task than telling the truth and therefore should entail more mental effort. Finally, it was argued that deceivers would attempt to suppress any overt indications of their deceit. Thus, some cues would be related to attempted behavioral control.

These four factors—arousal, negative affect, cognitive effort, and attempted control—are captured in the first, second, fourth, and fifth categories identified in this chapter. As postulated in interpersonal deception theory (Buller & Burgoon, 1996, 1997), however, profiles of deception indicators must include strategic (purposive, controllable, and goal-directed) as well as nonstrategic (unintentional, involuntary) acts. Because humans are quite facile at "running off" deceptive routines, strategic activity should not be construed as requiring a high degree of cognitive awareness or mindfulness. Indeed, the general communicative strategies and associated specific behavioral tactics that are directed toward deception are the same strategies that may be employed in service of other, nondeceptive purposes and therefore constitute overlearned and highly refined communicative routines, a factor that partially accounts for receivers' abysmal success in detecting them.

The most comprehensive meta-analysis to date, by De Paulo et al. (2003), includes the bulk of cues to be discussed here (see Hall, this volume, for additional discussion of meta-analysis as a tool for nonverbal researchers). However, DePaulo et al.'s meta-analysis failed to include several communication experiments, especially ones in which actors and targets (judges of an utterance's or message's truthfulness) interacted with one another and for an extended period of time (e.g., Buller, Burgoon, White, & Ebesu, 1994), well as several recently completed investigations (see e.g., Burgoon & Buller, in press, for a summary). Therefore, I created Table 16, which groups cues according to a five-category classification. Those that are more speculative in nature (i.e., have received little systematic empirical attention or support yet) are denoted with an asterisk. It is important to note that those five categories and their constituent cues are not mutually exclusive. Long response latencies, for example, may arise from memory processes being activated, excessive cognitive load, or intentional efforts to appear uncertain and submissive.

Arousal-Related Cues

Traditionally, deception has been associated with indicators of arousal, based on the assumption that telling lies, especially high-stakes ones, creates involuntary anxiety and arousal that becomes unintentionally manifest through one's nonverbal behaviors. Thus the body can betray the liar. Behaviors that have been associated reliably with lying include vocal nonfluencies such as stuttering, garbled sounds, and word repetitions (but not other types of "vocalized pauses" such as "um," "er," and "ah"); higher pitch or fundamental frequency in the voice; more vocal tension; dilated pupils; more lip presses; more fidgeting; more general nervousness; and higher bodily tension under conditions of high motivation (such as being offered monetary incentives to lie) (see Burgoon, Buller, & Woodall, 1996; Rockwell et al., 1997a, b; Vrij & Mann, in press). However, contrary to what one might expect, deceit is more often associated with less, not more, finger, hand, and lower limb movement.

There are several problems with designating these body cues as the most valid indicators of deceit, problems that are equally applicable to many of the other behaviors to be discussed. First, most of the research has focused specifically on lying, not other forms of deceit such as equivocation, evasion, exaggeration, or concealment. Thus, some forms of deceit, such as omitting truthful details or being ambiguous, may not be (as) physiologically arousing and result in the same nonverbal displays. Second, it is unclear whether lying and other forms of deceit are in fact highly arousing. Certainly the kinds of mundane white lies, polite evasions, well-selected omissions, and other low-stakes lies that populate daily discourse and that may roll off the tongue without hesitation are unlikely to generate a lot of physiological changes.

TABLE 16

Behavior Indicators of Deceit

Behavioral Class	Definition	Indicators of Deceit
I. Arousal		
Nervousness/negative arousal	psychological activation in the autonomic nervous system, central nervous system, and/or limbic systems	overall high arousal
		fidgeting/random trunk & limb movement
		rocking & twisting
		self-adaptors (self-touches such as hair twisting, scratching)
		object adaptors (manipulation of objects such as tapping a pen)*
		pupil dilation
		increased blinking
		less facial segmentation (fewer facial movements)
		more bodily segmentation (more body movements)
		lip pursing/biting*
		pitch (fundamental frequency) rise
Tension		postural rigidity or stiffness
		kinesic tension (still, tensed arms, legs, head, and torso)
		high vocal tension
		absence of relaxed laughter*
II. Emotional States	innate overt reactions that signal discrete and transitory psychological feeling states and associated arousal	overall negative affect/less "cooperative" demeanor
		fewer authentic smiles/more feigned smiles
		less facial pleasantness
		micro facial expressions of fear or guilt*
		less vocal pleasantness
		above-mentioned arousal indicators

240

III. Memory Processes	accessing real versus fabricated or imagined memories of people and events	
Quantity of content/details		reduced verbosity/talk time
Access to specific and diverse details		more non-ah nonfluencies—stutters, restarts, incompletions, incoherent sounds, repetitions, etc.—longer response latencies
Semantic segmentation		parakinesic (punctuating) head movements vocal juncture and stress
Uncertainty/ambiguity		more shoulder shrugs
IV. Message Production	converting thoughts to verbal and nonverbal messages	
Processes		
Cognitive effort/difficulty		gaze aversion long response latency cessation of gesturing reduction in overall movement more pauses more noninfluencies/more "ah" nonfluencies—ums, ers, ahs, other vocalized pauses more "ah" nonfluencies—ums, ers, ahs, other vocalized pauses
Expectancy violations		more unusual behaviors more channel discrepancies
V. Communicator Strategies & Tactics	intentional actions designed to create a credible message, preserve a positive image, and evade detection	
Behavioral control		greater postural stillness increasing postural relaxation over time
Involvement		increasing kinesic and vocalic involvement

(continued on next page)

TABLE 16 (*continued*)

Behavioral Class	Definition	Indicators of Deceit
Nonimmediacy		initial nonimmediacy; increasing immediacy over time
		physical distancing*
		touch avoidance*
		indirect body orientation
		lean away/less forward lean*
		initial gaze aversion; increasing eye contact over time
Expressiveness		increasing overall expressiveness over time
		increasing facial animation over time
		increasing illustrator gestures over time
		more head nodding over time
		increasing vocal variety (pitch, tempo) over time
Conversation management		reduced response latencies & smoother turn-switches over time
		few pauses, hesitations
Valence/Pleasantness		increasing overall pleasantness
		increasing facial pleasantness
		increasing vocal pleasantness
		smiling
Dominance		high dominance under persuasive conditions and when planning, editing or rehearsal is available
		nondominance with spontaneous responding and factual narratives
		loud voice (dominant); soft voice (nondominant)
Formality		overall high formality*

*These are speculative

This leads to the third problem: that previous findings related to arousal may be primarily associated with high-stakes lies, ones for which there are either serious adverse consequences if discovered or for which there are substantial incentives for succeeding. If this is true, it may also be the case that some reliable arousal-based indicators may have failed to receive empirical verification because researchers have been unable (sometimes due to valid Institutional Research Board prohibitions) to create truly high-stakes deceit. Fourth, the vast majority of experiments on deception have created deceptive and truthful behavioral samples that may be as brief as a single utterance or may last no more than 30 seconds. Such research cannot answer the question of whether arousal may dissipate with time, in which case the associated behavioral indicators should also lessen or disappear.

Fifth, until the emergence of interaction-based research, in which deceivers carry on extended conversations with their intended targets, there was no consideration given to the possibility that deception indicators may be highly dynamic and responsive not only to behavior of other interlocutors but also the dynamics of conversation itself. Some communication research (e.g., Buller & Aune, 1987; Burgoon & Buller, 1994; Burgoon, Buller, Dillman, & Walther, 1995; Burgoon et al., 1999; White & Burgoon, 2001) has confirmed that nonverbal and verbal deception displays change over time and may eventually approximate truthful displays. The practical import of these findings is that deception indicators are transitory. In the case of arousal-related ones, unless one can assure that arousal remains high, behaviors assumed to be indicators of deception-generated arousal may be inconsistent or absent.

Finally, there is not a one-to-one correspondence between arousal and deception. For example, behaviors such as blushing that sometimes accompany deceit do not occur invariably with lying and when they do occur may instead be due to another emotional state such as embarrassment at being accused of lying. Thus, behaviors indicative of arousal need not signal deceit, yet they are often taken as such. Nervousness at being questioned about a crime may be mistaken as evidence that a person is guilty (leading to what is called the "Othello error," judging truthful behavior as deceptive). Many of the behaviors that are associated stereotypically with deceit but are not actually valid indicators of it are ones that typify arousal and nervousness.

With those caveats in mind, the arousal behaviors most commonly associated with deceit fall into two classes: those indicative of nervousness and those indicative of tension. The former include random trunk and limb movements, rocking, twisting, self-touching, fidgeting, and other bodily movements (sometimes referred to as body segmentation), although it is important to note that many times these behaviors are suppressed by deceivers such that truthtellers may actually show more hand movements than deceivers. Deceivers are also more likely to show impassivity and inactivity in their faces than are truthtellers. More reliable arousal indicators that can be captured by human coders are ones in the voice, such as increases in fundamental frequency (i.e., pitch) and nonfluencies. As for tension indicators, both posture and the voice are reliable sites for signaling tension, whereas other kinesic regions such as the face, arms, and hands may actually connote relaxation and composure by virtue of being still. Two other indicators listed in this category—lip-pursing or biting and relaxed laughter—have yet to be verified, but based on our research group's observations may prove to be useful indicators.

Emotion-Related Cues

Closely associated with arousal indicators are indicators of emotional states. Technically, emotions are discrete, innate reactions to a stimulus that motivates the organism to behave adaptively with respect to the stimulus and are comprised of psychological, physiological, and behavioral components (Buller & Burgoon, 1997). The first two are internal; the latter is external. In the context of deception, the research focus has been on those overt involuntary reactions that result from guilt about lying, fear of detection, or other negative emotions that come with the act of lying (although Ekman & Friesen, 1969, noted that some liars might instead experience delight at duping another). Arousal can occur without specific emotions, but emotions by definition have some degree of arousal associated with them, which makes this category confounded with the previous one.

Moreover, under this heading are found both discrete emotional states and more global degrees of positivity–negativity associated with one's demeanor. Micromomentary facial expressions of negative emotions such as fear or guilt are possible indicators of deceit but have received little systematic investigation. Those displays that have received empirical confirmation include fake rather than felt smiles, less facial pleasantness, and a less cooperative demeanor. In general, this category of cues has failed to yield many reliable indicators, perhaps because deceptive displays can include a mix of positive and negative affects and/or deceivers are adept at rapidly covering negative displays with positive ones.

Memory Processes

This category refers to indicators associated with memory or accessing memory. Recent work on coding verbal content (e.g., Vrij, 2000; Vrij & Mann, in press) is premised on the notion that invented or imagined events are more pallid and short on detail than those derived from actual memory. Therefore, one's verbal content should reliably distinguish between truthful and deceptive narratives.

Although this work has more implications for verbal than nonverbal coding, the predicted reduction in details would seem to correspond to the frequently found pattern of less vocalization or talk time by deceivers. Speculatively, other indicators such as greater expressivity and more semantic segmentation through use of para-kinesics (e.g., punctuating head movements) and prosodic vocal behaviors (e.g., pauses and stress) may also correspond to accessing actual memory; indicators related to uncertainty (e.g., nonimmediacy within-turn pauses) may signal inability to locate definitive memories. As more research zeroes in on the relationship between memory and behavior, other potential nonverbal indicators may surface.

Message Production Processes

This category refers to indicators associated with speech or message production itself, in other words, with the process of translating thoughts into utterances. The most commonly investigated aspect has been cognitive effort. It has long been thought that deception is a more difficult mental task than creating truth, and several investigations have confirmed this experimentally. Many nonverbal indicators of deceit are therefore thought to signal not deceit per se but rather the cognitive taxation or challenge of creating plausible lies and making them consistent with other statements or known facts.

Behaviors that have been found to be indicative of greater cognitive effort include shorter responses or less talk time, slower speaking, longer response latencies under certain conditions, fewer illustrator gestures (the ones that accompany speech), and gaze aversion (although the last indicator may only be associated with cognitive effort and not with deception specifically). Research has also shown that deceivers use fewer filled pauses and "non-ah" nonfluencies under high motivation but more filled pauses and nonfluencies under low motivation. What makes this category problematic is that low-stakes lies and forms of deceit that are half-truths may require little cognitive effort and therefore would not be accompanied by such indicators.

Communicator Strategies and Tactics

The preceding categories have all centered on aspects of behavior that are involuntary, nondeliberate, and/or outside senders' conscious control. This remaining category encompasses a host of what we regard as strategic acts: ones that are voluntary and functionally related to typical communication goals. As posited by interpersonal deception theory (Buller & Burgoon, 1996; Burgoon & Buller, in press), deceivers may manage the information and accompanying behaviors in their messages so as to evade detection by working to approximate a normal communication pattern, convey an honest demeanor, and appear credible more generally (Burgoon, Buller, Floyd, & Grandpre, 1996).

Different circumstances may call for different strategies and may afford deceivers varying opportunities for thoughtful, planned, and rehearsed action. For example, deceivers who must respond to accusations on the spot, with little time for careful forethought, may opt for brevity (what DePaulo et al., 2003, capture under the heading of "being less forthcoming"). They may also adopt a submissive demeanor that creates the impression of nonculpability and that effectively shifts conversational responsibilities to their questioner, who may unwittingly help construct a plausible rendition of the issue in question. Conversely, deceivers who have ample time to plan a lie may take a more assertive, dominant stance to maximize their persuasiveness. As an oversimplification, deceivers' initial responses may tend either toward a "fight" (aggressive, engaging, and approach) or "flight" (submissive, withdrawing, and avoidant) response pattern.

Many initial nonverbal response patterns fit the nondominant, tentative flight pattern: Deceivers exhibit less nonverbal immediacy and involvement, more vocal uncertainty, shorter responses, longer response latencies, and more silent pauses. But over time, consistent with the prediction that given time they modify their behavior and respond to receiver feedback, deceivers increase involvement as conversations progress (Burgoon et al., 1999; White & Burgoon, 2001). Initial rigidity and overcontrol of behavior may give way to increased relaxation and expressivity. Similarly, initial unpleasantness may change to increases in smiling, facial pleasantness, and vocal pleasantness. As well, responses may vary according to motivation type and level. For example, relative to truthtellers, deceivers exhibit less eye contact under identity-relevant motivation, fewer "non-ah" types of nonfluencies under instrumental motivation, and more such speech disturbances when motivation is low.

USING THE CLASSIFICATION

The rating form and instructions in the appendix come from an investigation in which my colleagues and I measured nonverbal involvement and immediacy during interviews of truthful and deceptive senders to test the hypothesis that deceivers initially show reduced involvement and immediacy but increase them over time (Burgoon et al., 1999). Because we regard involvement and immediacy as fairly dynamic, and because it is important to code the behaviors of both interactants in order to investigate interdependencies, separate teams of trained coders were assigned to observe and rate either the interviewer or the interviewee after each interview question. The coding instructions identify the specific behaviors to be observed. In this case, we used live observation through a one-way mirror in hopes of capturing any subtle nuances of behavior that might elude videotaping. However, videotapes of interactions provide a means for repeated review and coding for multiple categories of behavior by different teams of coders. In general, we recommend recording interactions for subsequent coding even if live observation is also used.

SUMMARY

There is an enormous range of nonverbal indicators that could be examined by researchers interested in studying the role of nonverbal cues in deception. Research investigating these behaviors has used four assessment methods: (a) physiological instrumentation (e.g., Galvanic Skin Response, Vocal Stress Analyzer, Polygraph), (b) self-reports of behavior by deceivers and truthtellers, (c) partner or observer reports of behavior, and (d) trained coder ratings. As discussed in Burgoon, Buller, Floyd et al. (1996), sender, receiver, and observer perspectives may differ, and decisions about which reports are the most valid depend on the research question. Those that are more objective and more proximal in time to the deceptive display, however, are to be preferred over those that are more distant and dependent on hazy and potentially self-serving recollections of past events.

Like other forms of nonverbal measurement, measurement of deception can take a variety of forms and include a large constellation of behaviors, many of which are substitutable for one another, can have multiple etiologies, are transitory, and are highly responsive to contextual and relationship factors. Researchers seeking to measure deception nonverbally are therefore advised to take a multimethod, multibehavior, multicode approach, obtaining both subjective and objective measures, and to include multiple behaviors from visual, vocal, proxemic, and verbal codes. It is also recommended that researchers clearly delineate which behavioral displays are expected to be universal versus context-dependent, and in the latter case, to spell out what contextual features are expected to moderate the displays. Finally, it is recommended that measurements be repeated over the course of a deceptive episode to verify the constancy of deception displays.

REFERENCES

Buller, D. B., & Aune, R. K. (1987). Nonverbal cues to deception among intimates, friends, and strangers. *Journal of Nonverbal Behavior, 11*, 269–290.
Buller, D., & Burgoon, J. K. (1996). Interpersonal deception theory. *Communication Theory, 6*, 203–242.
Buller, D. B., & Burgoon, J. K. (1997). Emotional expression in the deception process. In P. A. Andersen & L. K. Guerrero (Eds.), *Communication and emotion* (pp. 381–402). Orlando, FL: Academic Press.
Buller, D. B., Burgoon, J. K., White, C., & Ebesu, A. S. (1994). Interpersonal deception: VII. Behavioral profiles of falsification, equivocation, and concealment. *Journal of Language and Social Psychology, 13*, 366–396.
Burgoon, J. K., & Buller, D. B. (1994). Interpersonal deception: III. Effects of deceit on perceived communication and nonverbal behavior dynamics. *Journal of Nonverbal Behavior, 18*, 155–184.
Burgoon, J. K., & Buller, D. B. (in press). Interpersonal deception theory. In J. Seiter & R. Gass (Eds.), *Readings in persuasion, social influence and compliance-gaining.* New York: Allyn & Bacon.
Burgoon, J. K., Buller, D. B., Dillman, L., & Walther, J. B. (1995). Interpersonal deception: IV. Effects of suspicion on perceived communication and nonverbal behavior dynamics. *Human Communication Research, 22*, 163–196.
Burgoon, J. K., Buller, D. B., Floyd, K., & Grandpre, J. (1996). Deceptive realities: Sender, receiver, and observer perspectives in deceptive conversations. *Communication Research, 23*, 724–748.
Burgoon, J., Buller, D., White, C., Afifi, W., & Buslig, A. (1999). The role of conversational involvement in deceptive interpersonal interactions. *Personality and Social Psychology Bulletin, 25*, 669–685.
Burgoon, J. K., Buller, D. B., & Woodall, W. G. (1996). *Nonverbal communication: The unspoken dialogue.* New York: McGraw-Hill.
DePaulo, B., Lindsay, J., Malone, B., Muhlenbruck, L., Charlton, K., & Cooper, H. (2003). Cues to deception. *Psychological Bulletin, 129*, 74–118.
Ekman, P., & Friesen, W. V. (1969). Nonverbal leakage and clues to deception. *Psychiatry, 32*, 88–105.
Frank, M. G., & Ekman, P. (1997). The ability to detect generalizes across different types of high stake lies. *Journal of Personality and Social Psychology, 72*, 1429–1439.
Galasinski, D. (2000). *The language of deception: A discourse analytical study.* Thousand Oaks, CA: Sage.
Graumann, C. F. (1995). Commonality, mutuality, reciprocity: A conceptual introduction. In C. G. I. Marková & K. Foppa (Ed.), *Mutualities in dialogue* (pp. 1–24). Cambridge: Cambridge University Press.

Grice, H. P. (1989). *Studies in the way of words*. Cambridge, MA: Harvard University Press.
Habermas, J. (1979). *Communication and the evolution of society*. London: Heinemann.
Riggio, R. E., & Friedman, H. S. (1983). Individual differences and cues to deception. *Journal of Personality & Social Psychology, 45*, 899–915.
Rockwell, P., Buller, D. B., & Burgoon, J. K. (1997a). The voice of deceit: Refining and expanding vocal cues to deception. *Communication Research Reports, 14*, 451–459.
Rockwell, P., Buller, D. B., & Burgoon, J. K. (1997b). Measurement of deceptive voices: Comparing acoustic and perceptual data. *Applied Psycholinguistics, 18*, 471–484.
Vrij, A. (2000). *Detecting lies and deceit: The psychology of lying and the implications for professional practice*. Chichester: Wiley and Sons.
Vrij, A., Akehurst, L., & Morris, P. (1997). Individual differences in hand movements during deception. *Journal of Nonverbal Behavior, 21*, 87–103.
Vrij, A., & Mann, S. (in press). Detecting deception: The benefit of looking at a combination of behavioral, auditory and speech content related cues in a systematic manner. *Group Decision and Negotiation.*
White, C., & Burgoon, J. K. (2001). Adaptation and communicative design: Patterns of interaction in truthful and deceptive conversations. *Human Communication Research, 27*, 9–37.
Zuckerman, M., DePaulo, B., & Rosenthal, R. (1981). Verbal and nonverbal communication of deception. In L. Berkowitz (Ed.), *Advances in experimental social psychology* (Vol. 14, pp. 1–59). New York: Academic Press.
Zuckerman, M., & Driver, R. (1985). Telling lies: Verbal and nonverbal correlates of deception. In A. W. Siegman & S. Feldstein (Eds.), *Nonverbal communication: An integrated perspective* (pp. 129–147). Hillsdale, NJ: Lawrence Erlbaum Associates.

APPENDIX

Observer Instructions

Your task is to observe and rate the communication of the *Interviewer/Interviewee*. *After each question*, make your ratings on the attached forms. For each question, you will make six judgments, using a 1–9 rating scale. Circle a 1, 2, 3, 4, 5, 6, 7, 8, or 9, depending upon where on the scale you think the person's behavior fit. Work quickly, recording your first impression, so that you are prepared to observe the beginning of the next question. Here are the following categories you will be rating and a guide to how each term should be interpreted:

1. *Involvement* concerns the degree to which the individual seems to be cognitively, emotionally, and behaviorally engaged in the interview. People who are involved in an interaction should appear to be interested, attentive, alert, and responsive to the other individual. Those who are uninvolved should appear disinterested, apathetic, distracted, withdrawn, and detached. A person's level of involvement or detachment may be evident through verbal language, voice, and "body language."
You will make general judgments on the following two scales:

    a. *involved*—reflecting the degree to which you think the person is not at all (1) to very involved (9).

    b. *detached*—reflecting the degree to which you think the person is not at all (1) to very detached (9).

    Make your judgments based upon a comparison to how you think normal people would behave in an interview, where a normal or average level of involvement would be a 5 on the 9-point scale.

2. *Nonverbal Immediacy* includes a cluster of behaviors signaling the degree to which people communicate a sense of closeness and approach or distance and avoidance through their actions (rather than their words). Higher scores represent greater immediacy in all cases. The four behaviors you will be rating are the following:

    a. *Physical closeness*: This rating represents the actual distance between the two people. You will rate the person on a scale from very far to very close. Consider a rating of 5 to be an average distance of about 4 feet between the torsos (at midchest) of the two people. Give a rating of 1 if the person you are rating adopts a very far distance (6 feet or more). Give a rating of 9 if they adopt a very close distance (2 feet or less). Use ratings of 2–4 and 6–8 for degrees in-between.

    b. *Lean*: This rating represents the degree to which a person's upper trunk is tilted toward or away from the other person. You will rate the person on a scale from all-backward lean (1) to all-forward lean (9). Give a 9 if the person is leaning as far forward as you think would be possible and still be natural; give a 1 if you think they are leaning as far back as you think would be possible in the chairs and still be natural. Consider a 5 to be a straight up (perpendicular) posture. Use ratings of 2–4 and 6–8 for degrees of forward and backward lean. If a person's lean changes during the interaction, give a rating that reflects what you think was the average lean during the interaction. For example, if the lean was a 2 for most of the time and a 6 for part of the time, you might give a rating of 3.

    c. *Gaze and facing*: This represents the degree to which the person appears to be looking at the other person. If you can actually see that the person you are rating is gazing toward the other, rely on actual gaze to make your rating. Sometimes it is difficult to actually see the eyes. When this happens, use the degree of facing—how directly one person's face is oriented toward the other's face—to infer that gaze is occurring. Give a rating of 5 if you think the amount of gaze is normal or average. Give a rating for 1 if the person seems to be completely avoiding eye contact with the other person and give a rating of 9 if the person seems to be gazing and facing constantly. Very brief glances away or toward the other need not be counted. If a person's gaze changes during the interaction, give a rating that reflects what you think was the average gaze during the interaction.

d. *Body orientation:* This represents the degree to which the torso of the person is rotated toward or away from the other person. You will rate the body orientation from very indirect (1) to very direct (9). Give a 1 if you think the person is turned at a 90-degree angle or greater away from the other person. This would be a position facing the mirror directly rather than the other person. Give a 5 if you think the person is oriented at a 45-degree angle. Give a 9 if the person's torso is directly facing the other person. Give ratings of 2–4 and 6–8 for degrees in-between. If a person's body orientation changes during the interaction, give a rating that reflects what you think was the average body orientation during the interaction.

Interactional Sensitivity: Rating Social Support, Attachment, and Interaction in Adult Relationships

April R. Trees
University of Colorado, Boulder

INTRODUCTION

Attachment theory directs attention toward both the development of attachment
bonds (significant personal relationships that we turn to in times of distress and
that shape our sense of well-being; Ross & Spinner, 2001) and the impact of attachment bonds in our relational lives. Although much of the research developed from
Bowlby's (1969, 1973, 1977) attachment theory focuses on attachment styles and
their link to various outcome variables, attachment theory also directs attention
toward a set of interaction behaviors that likely constitute an important dimension
of bonding in adult attachment relationships. Interactional sensitivity, the active
involvement in a conversation with a relational partner in which a person responds
appropriately to his or her partner's needs in a smooth, synchronized manner, incorporates both verbal and nonverbal features of conversation.[9] In addition to
contributing to our understanding of the development of attachment patterns,
interactional sensitivity provides a framework for thinking about supportive interaction in conversations about distressing events.

This chapter draws on existing rating schemes for involvement (Coker &
Burgoon, 1987; see Guerrero, this volume) and synchrony (Bernieri & Rosenthal,

---

[9]The term *sensitivity* appears in the social skills literature as interpersonal sensitivity (Bernieri, 2001)
and emotional and social sensitivity (Riggio, 1986). These conceptions of sensitivity focus typically on
individual differences in decoding ability rather than specific behavior in interaction. Additionally,
Goldsmith, McDermott, and Alexander (2000) use the term *sensitivity* to refer to attentiveness toward
and acknowledgement of others' emotions during problem talk conversations. Although there is some
conceptual overlap with each of these uses of the term sensitivity, Bowlby's (1973) conceptualization refers to specific behaviors in interaction that demonstrate more than responsiveness to emotional needs.

1991; see Bernieri, this volume) to develop a system for assessing interactional sensitivity in conversations between adults in attachment relationships. After reviewing theory and research on attachment and interactional sensitivity, I outline a method for measuring interactional sensitivity that combines interaction rating and a stimulated recall procedure. A brief report of a study using this assessment of interactional sensitivity to demonstrate its connection to conversational supportiveness (Trees, 2000) follows the description of the measure.

THEORY AND RESEARCH ON INTERACTIONAL SENSITIVITY

Attachment Theory

Attachment theory (Bowlby, 1969, 1973, 1977) seeks to explain children's tendency to develop strong affectional bonds with an attachment figure and to exhibit attachment behavior (i.e., crying) when distressed by separation from the attachment figure. Through interaction with the attachment figure, children develop "working models," or internal pictures of themselves in relation to others (Bowlby, 1973). These models or attachment patterns develop from ongoing transactions that create expectations concerning the availability and responsiveness of the attachment figure (Bretherton, 1985). The two major elements of the working model—conception of self and conception of the attachment figure—are interdependent and reflect judgments regarding whether the attachment figure is someone who will respond to calls for support and whether the self is the sort of person someone will respond to in a helpful way (Bowlby, 1973). Based on infants' reactions in a strange situation, Ainsworth, Blehar, Waters, and Wall (1978) classified attachment patterns into three categories: secure, avoidant, and anxious.[10]

Interactional sensitivity, or the way a mother or other primary caregiver responds to an infant's attachment behaviors, plays a key role in the creation of children's working models of self and other. Bowlby (1973) described sensitive mothers as "tuned in" to receive signals and as likely to interpret them correctly and respond promptly and appropriately. Ainsworth et al. (1978) concluded likewise that it is the mother's sensitive responsiveness to the infant that differentiates securely attached babies from the other two styles. Later research supports the link between attachment patterns and interactional sensitivity. For example, mothers of securely attached infants are more likely to provide appropriate responses than mothers of anxious-avoidant infants or anxious-resistant infants (Smith & Pederson, 1988), and sensitively responsive care-giving and low levels of rejection are linked to secure attachment relationships (Isabella, 1993).

---

[10]Drawing on possible combinations of positive and negative views of self and other, Bartholomew and Horowitz (1991) divided avoidant styles into either dismissive-avoidant or fearful-avoidant, depending on whether or not the individual has a negative or positive self model in combination with a negative other model.

Interactional Sensitivity and Adult Relationships

Although it originated as a theory concerning parent–infant relating, other researchers extended attachment theory to *adult* relationships (e.g., Hazan & Shaver, 1987). This body of work focuses on attachment patterns as cognitive schemata that influence various dependent variables such as communication behaviors (e.g., Guerrero & Burgoon, 1996;) or relational qualities (e.g., Collins & Read, 1990). Bowlby (1988), however, emphasized the importance of interactional behaviors, concluding "that it is just as necessary for analysts to study the way a child is really treated by his parents as it is to study the internal representations he has of them" (p. 44). Close relational partners' interactional sensitivity, particularly in distressing situations, may continue to be influential in adult relationships.

Variation in relationship-specific attachment orientations supports the continued importance of interactional sensitivity in understanding bonding in adult attachment relationships. Fraley and Davis (1997), for example, argued that factors such as trust and dependency, which facilitate infant attachment formation, also influence adult attachment formation. Consistently attentive and responsive interactions (or inattentive and unresponsive interactions) over time may help to understand relationship-specific variations in attachment patterns in adulthood.

Interactional sensitivity not only potentially helps to explain the development of relationship-specific attachment patterns, it also directs attention to an important quality of conversation for supportive interaction as individuals talk about distressing situations or experiences with relational partners. Internal working models reflect a generalized sense of support (Sarason, Pierce, & Sarason, 1990), and attachment relationships are affectional bonds with individuals to whom one would turn (or want to turn) in times of distress (Ross & Spinner, 2001; Trinke & Bartholomew, 1997). Part of the influence of interactional sensitivity, then, lies in its supportive nature as a response to relational partners' needs in particular conversations. Attentive and responsive interaction behaviors when individuals are talking about problems or difficulties likely contribute to distressed individuals' perception of the supportiveness of a specific interaction.

Conceptualizing Sensitivity

Interactional sensitivity, as conceptualized by Bowlby (1969, 1973) and Ainsworth et al. (1978), points toward nonverbal cues as well as verbal features of interaction that may make a relational partner feel supported. In Bowlby's (1969, 1973) work, three major aspects of sensitivity reflect the importance of availability and responsiveness: being "tuned in" to receive the baby's signals, being likely to interpret them correctly, and responding to the signals promptly and appropriately. His conceptualization of sensitivity includes both a cognitive awareness of the child's needs and a behavioral response to those needs. Similarly, Ainsworth et al. (1978) describe maternal sensitivity to the baby's signals in terms of being able to see things from the baby's point of view, being alert to perceive signals, interpreting them accurately, and responding promptly and appropriately. Others confirmed the importance of responsiveness, appropriateness, and timing or coordination to sensitive communication between mothers and babies in later research (e.g., Isabella & Belsky, 1991; Smith & Pederson, 1988).

MEASURING INTERACTIONAL SENSITIVITY

In adult interaction, the dimensions of sensitivity identified by Bowlby (1969, 1973) and Ainsworth et al. (1978) can be combined into a definition of sensitivity with three important components. *Conversational involvement* (being "tuned in," alert to perceived signals), *responding appropriately* to the partner's needs (the ability to take the partner's viewpoint and understand his or her needs reflected in appropriate responses), and *synchronized response* (meshing with the conversational patterns of the partner) constitute interactional sensitivity behaviors. This section describes a set of measures to tap into each of these dimensions.

Conversational Involvement

The first of the three major components of interactional sensitivity, conversational involvement, refers to attentiveness to a conversation. Coker and Burgoon (1987) explain conversational involvement as "the degree to which participants are enmeshed in the topic, interpersonal relationship, and situation" (p. 463). Behaviors reflecting conversational involvement demonstrate physical and psychological engagement in an interaction, indicating activity, arousal, and interest in the conversation at hand. These behaviors reflect an *approach* orientation (Guerrero & Burgoon, 1996; Mehrabian, 1981).

Coker and Burgoon (1987) laid out a set of behavioral indicators of involvement. Rating these behaviors requires a combination of midlevel cue and global percept judgments across time increments in a conversation. Each specific behavior or global judgment is rated separately (see Appendix A for rating instructions) and then grouped conceptually into related cue composites. One composite, orientation/gaze, includes gaze, body orientation, postural openness, and facial orientation. The second cue grouping, facial animation, incorporates smiling, facial animation, facial pleasantness, and facial concern. Vocal expressiveness, the third set of cues, includes volume, pitch, rate, and vocal expressiveness. The fourth composite, kinesic/proxemic attentiveness, includes kinesic/proxemic involvement, gestural animation, kinesic/proxemic attentiveness, and kinesic/proxemic interest.[11] Vocal warmth/interest, the fifth set of cues, included vocal pleasantness, interest, and warmth as well as vocal attentiveness measures. Kinesic/proxemic compo-

---

[11]Although Coker and Burgoon (1987) did not include gestural animation within this composite, it fit with the emphasis in this grouping on judgments made from kinesic/proxemic animation.

sure, the sixth factor, contained both kinesic/proxemic calm and kinesic/proxemic composure items. In addition to vocal warmth/interest, Coker and Burgoon (1987) identified three more sets of vocal cues. Vocal fluency includes smoothness and fluency ratings, latencies and silences constitute a grouping, and vocal relaxation involves judgments of vocal rhythm and clarity. Four cues—body lean, self-adaptors, random movement, and nodding—contribute to involvement individually rather than as a composite set.[12]

Following Coker and Burgoon (1987), Trees (2000) investigated the degree to which mothers' interactional sensitivity predicted young adult children's perceptions of mothers' supportiveness in conversations about children's relational problems with someone outside the relationship. Raters were assigned a set of four or five cues in a particular region (i.e., vocal cues) for assessment. Training involved a discussion of the conceptual and operational definitions for each cue and joint rating and discussion of behaviors in unrelated videotaped conversations. Raters judged 16 interactions jointly and discussed any discrepancies and then rated the remaining 63 interactions separately for the *alpha* reliability assessment. The reliabilities of these ratings of conversational involvement cues ranged from .11 to .96, and the reliabilities of the cue composites using only reliably rated involvement cues ranged from .62 to .94.[13] The vocal fluency, latency/silence, and vocal relaxation cue composites were left out of the analyses in this study due to low composite reliabilities. Findings indicated support for the relationship between conversational involvement and perceived supportiveness. Specifically, the two sets of involvement cues reflecting nonverbal altercentrism behaviors—vocal warmth/ interest and kinesic/proxemic attentiveness—were the strongest predictors of various support dimensions.

Appropriate Responses

The second component of interactional sensitivity, appropriateness of response, incorporates participants' judgments of verbal as well as nonverbal communication. Appropriateness is a difficult concept to define. Canary and Spitzberg (1987) use the terms *appropriateness* and *effectiveness* as two fundamental properties of communication competence. Appropriate communication, according to their view, is that which avoids violating the situational or relational rules governing the communicative context.

---

[12]In Coker and Burgoon's (1987) set of composites, nodding and smiling are grouped under the category of *positive reinforcers*. However, given that smiling is also a part of facial animation, it was not combined with nodding as well in the Trees (2000) study. Additionally, whereas three different ratings of random movement are provided by Coker and Burgoon (1987), an overall judgment combining the different types of random movement (head and trunk) was used in Trees (2000).

[13]Three vocal cues (relaxation, calmness, and focus) were left out of the analyses due to interrater reliabilities below .6. The poor reliabilities for these vocal cues in this study reflects, in part, a rater who was unable to make distinctions in vocal variations, but it also seems that vocal qualities are more difficult to rate reliably than other dimensions of nonverbal behavior.

The appropriateness of interactants' conversational contributions, particularly in responses to distressed individuals, can vary along three different dimensions (content, intensity, and valence). First, the correspondence in content between what individuals perceive as their need in an interaction and what their relational partner does most likely contributes to judgments of appropriateness. For example, in support research, tangible aid has the potential to be helpful, but unwanted practical assistance is not helpful (Dakof & Taylor, 1990). Bowlby's use of the term *appropriate* applies to this idea of correspondence, referring to understanding the infant's need and responding in a way that matches that need. As a major component of appropriateness, then, the content of potentially supportive messages must fit the requirements of the particular support episode.

Second, the intensity or degree of concern in the conversational partner's responses may be more or less appropriate. Attachment research suggests mothers can exhibit emotional overinvolvement, which is associated with less secure attachment styles (Isabella & Belsky, 1991). Similarly, in support research, emotional overinvolvement can be a negative aspect of support-intended behavior (i.e., Gottlieb & Wagner, 1991). An apathetic response may, likewise, not be in line with situational and relational demands. A lack of concern about a problem in a relationship that is considered a source of help in times of trouble may be seen as a violation of relational rules. Thus, more (or less) is not necessarily better; appropriateness refers in part to the right level of intensity of a relational partner's reaction.

Finally, the valence of relational partners' behaviors, both negative and positive, may also influence judgments of appropriateness. Too much positivity, particularly in conversations about distressing events, may be seen as a minimization of feelings or concerns. At the same time, negative behaviors when positive behaviors are expected also would violate situational or relational rules. Valence, then, may also constitute an important dimension of an appropriate response.

To assess appropriateness, Trees (2000) used a retrospective recall procedure, showing children two different 2-minute segments of the 10-minute conversation and asking them to evaluate appropriateness using six 6-point semantic differential items (see Appendix B). These scales include two items regarding appropriate content (*alpha* = .84), two items assessing appropriate intensity (*alpha* = .66), and two items specific to valence (*alpha* = .89) appropriateness. For the intensity and valence items, children chose between overly involved or uninvolved and overly positive and overly negative dimensions before responding to the items. Findings indicated that children's judgments of content appropriateness (i.e., telling the child what she or he needed to hear) were related to their perceptions of various support dimensions.

Synchrony

The final component of interactional sensitivity, synchrony, takes two different forms: behavior matching or movement synchrony (Bernieri & Rosenthal, 1991).

Behavior matching refers to postural mirroring or mimicry, focusing on the similarity of movements at a particular point in time (Bernieri, 1988). Postural similarity is a type of behavior matching (LaFrance, 1979). *Movement synchrony* describes the coordination and timing of movements and includes simultaneous movement, tempo similarity, and coordination or smoothness (Bernieri, Reznick, & Rosenthal, 1988).

Judgment studies indicate that raters can differentiate synchronous behavior patterns, including simultaneous movement (beginning and ending at same moment), tempo similarity (similar beats), and coordination or smoothness (meshing smoothly), beyond that due simply to chance (Bernieri & Rosenthal, 1991).[14] Postural similarity is assessed by rating the degree to which interactants' kinesic cues match (see Appendix C for rating instructions). In Trees' (2000) study, interrater *alpha* reliabilities for the synchrony cues ranged from .46 (simultaneous movement) to .91 (postural similarity). Results for this dimension of interactional sensitivity indicated that greater movement coordination predicted greater perceived supportiveness across dimensions of support. Thus, elements of all three dimensions of interactional sensitivity were associated with children's evaluations of mothers' supportiveness in conversations about problems.

CONCLUSIONS

The measure of interactional sensitivity in adult interactions outlined in this chapter could contribute to both research on attachment in adult relationships and social support research for a number of reasons. First, attachment theory allowed prediction of conversational patterns that affect young adult children's perceptions of mothers' supportiveness. A consistent pattern of interactional sensitivity (or lack thereof) in adult relationships may affect adult proximity-seeking and relationship-specific attachment styles. Given this possibility, research on adult attachment relationships might attend to how individual attachment styles in conjunction with partners' interactional sensitivity may influence the development of attachment bonds in adult relationships. Second, from a support communication perspective, interactional sensitivity provides a global assessment of interaction quality. This directs attention toward interaction behaviors that avoid the oversimplification of coding schemes that dichotomize behaviors into emotion- or problem-focused support.

REFERENCES

Ainsworth, M. D. S., Blehar, M. C., Waters, E., & Wall, S. (1978). *Patterns of attachment: A psychological study of the strange situation.* Hillsdale, NJ: Lawrence Erlbaum Associates.

---

[14]Due to difficulty in creating a clear operationalization of tempo similarity, however, this item was dropped, and raters judged the remaining two items in movement synchrony. Use of physiological measures may be one way to capture tempo similarity (see Kinney, this volume and Tusing, this volume).

Andersen, P. A. (1999). *Nonverbal communication: Forms and functions.* Mountain View, CA: Mayfield Publishing Company.

Arkowitz, H., Lichtenstein, E., McGovern, K., & Hines, P. (1975). The behavioral assessment of social competence in males. *Behavior Therapy, 6,* 3–13.

Bartholomew, K., & Horowitz, L. M. (1991). Attachment styles among young adults: A test of a four-category model. *Journal of Personality and Social Psychology, 61,* 226–244.

Bayes, M. A. (1972). Behavioral cues of interpersonal warmth. *Journal of Consulting and Clinical Psychology, 39,* 333–339.

Bell, R. A. (1985). Conversational involvement and loneliness. *Communication Monographs, 52,* 218–235.

Bernieri, F. J. (1988). Coordinated movement and synchrony in teacher–student interactions. *Journal of Nonverbal Behavior, 12,* 120–138.

Bernieri, F. J. (2001). Toward a taxonomy of interpersonal sensitivity. In J. A. Hall & F. J. Bernieri (Eds.), *Interpersonal sensitivity: Theory and measurement* (pp. 3–20). Mahwah, NJ: Lawrence Erlbaum Associates.

Bernieri, F. J., & Rosenthal, R. (1991). Interpersonal coordination: Behavior matching and interactional synchrony. In R. Feldman & R. Rime (Eds.), *Fundamentals of nonverbal behavior* (pp. 401–432). Cambridge: Cambridge University Press.

Bernieri, F. J., Reznick, S., & Rosenthal, R. (1988). Synchrony, pseudosynchrony, and dissynchrony: Measuring the entrainment process in mother–infant interactions. *Journal of Personality and Social Psychology, 54,* 243–253.

Bowlby, J. (1969). *Attachment and loss: Vol. 1 Attachment.* New York: Basic Books.

Bowlby, J. (1973). *Attachment and loss: Vol. 2 Separation: Anxiety and anger.* New York: Basic Books.

Bowlby, J. (1977). The making and breaking of affectional bonds. *British Journal of Psychiatry, 1130,* 201–210.

Bowlby, J. (1988). *A secure base: Parent–child attachment and healthy human development.* New York: Basic Books.

Brandt, B. R. (1979). On linking social performance with social competence: Some relations between communicative style and attributions of interpersonal attractiveness and effectiveness. *Human Communication Research, 5,* 223–237

Bretherton, I. (1985). Attachment theory: Retrospect and prospect. In I. Bretherton & E. Waters (Eds.), *Growing points of attachment theory and research* (pp. 3–35). *Monographs of the Society for Research in Child Development, 50.*

Buller, D. B., & Burgoon, J. K. (1986). The effects of vocalics and nonverbal sensitivity on compliance: A replication and extension. *Human Communication Research, 13,* 126–144.

Burgoon, J. K., & Aho, L. (1982). Three field experiments on the effects of violations of conversational distance. *Communication Monographs, 49,* 71–88.

Canary, D. J., & Spitzberg, B. H. (1987). Appropriateness and effectiveness perceptions of conflict strategies. *Human Communication Research, 14,* 93–118.

Coker, D. A., & Burgoon, J. K. (1987). The nature of conversational involvement and nonverbal encoding patterns. *Human Communication Research, 13,* 463–494.

Collins, N. L., & Read, S. J. (1990). Attachment, working models, and relationship quality in dating couples. *Journal of Personality and Social Psychology, 58,* 644–663.

Dakof, G. A., & Taylor, S. E. (1990). Victims' perceptions of social support: What is helpful to whom? *Journal of Personality and Social Psychology, 58,* 80–89.

Fraley, R. C., & Davis, K. E. (1997). Attachment formation and transfer in young adults' close friendships and romantic relationships. *Personal Relationships, 4,* 131–144.

Goldsmith, D. J., McDermott, V. M., & Alexander, S. C. (2001). Helpful, sensitive, and supportive: Measuring the evaluation of enacted support in personal relationships. *Journal of Social and Personal Relationships, 17,* 369–391.

Gottlieb, B. H., & Wagner, F. (1991). Stress and support processes in close relationships. In J. Eckenrode (Ed.), *The social context of coping* (pp. 165–188). New York: Plenum.

Guerrero, L. K., & Burgoon, J. K. (1996). Attachment styles and reactions to nonverbal involvement change in romantic dyads: Patterns of reciprocity and compensation. *Human Communication Research, 22,* 335–370.

Hazan, C., & Shaver, P. (1987). Romantic love conceptualized as an attachment process. *Journal of Personality and Social Psychology, 52,* 511–524.

Isabella, R. A. (1993). Origins of attachment: Maternal interactive behavior across the first year. *Child Development, 64,* 605–621.

Isabella, R. A., & Belsky, J. (1991). Interactional synchrony and the origins of infant–mother attachment: A replication study. *Child Development, 62,* 373–384.

Kraut, R. E., & Johnston, R. E. (1979). Social and emotional messages of smiling: An ethological approach. *Journal of Personality and Social Psychology, 37,* 1539–1553.

LaFrance, M. (1979). Nonverbal synchrony and rapport: Analysis by the cross-lag panel technique. *Social Psychology Quarterly, 42,* 66–70.

Mehrabian, A. (1969). Methods and design: Some referents and measures of nonverbal behavior. *Behavior Research Methods and Instruments, 1,* 203–207.

Mehrabian, A. (1981). *Silent messages: Implicit communication of emotions and attitudes* (2nd ed.). Belmont, CA: Wadsworth Publishing.

Riggio, R. E. (1986). Assessment of basic social skills. *Journal of Personality and Social Psychology, 51,* 649–660.

Ross, L. R., & Spinner, B. (2001). General and specific attachment representations in adulthood. *Journal of Social and Personal Relationships, 18,* 747–766.

Sarason, B. R., Pierce, G. R., & Sarason, I. G. (1990). Social support: The sense of acceptance and role of relationships. In B. R. Sarason, I. G. Sarason, & G. R. Pierce (Eds.), *Social support: An interactional view* (pp. 97–128). New York: John Wiley and Sons.

Scherer, K. R. (1982). Methods of research on vocal communication: Paradigms and parameters. In K. R. Scherer & P. Ekman (Eds.), *Handbook of methods in nonverbal behavior research* (pp. 136–189). New York: Cambridge University Press.

Smith, P. B., & Pederson, D. R. (1988). Maternal sensitivity and patterns of infant-mother attachment. *Child Development, 59,* 1097–1101.

Trees, A. R. (2000). Nonverbal communication and the support process: Interactional sensitivity in interactions between mothers and young adult children. *Communication Monographs, 67,* 239–261.

Trinke, S. J., & Bartholomew, K. (1997). Hierarchies of attachment relationships in young adulthood. *Journal of Social and Personal Relationships, 14,* 603–625.

APPENDIX A

Conversational Involvement Rating

Orientation/Gaze Cue Composite

Gaze: Proportion of the segment in which the interactant is looking directly at the conversational partner (not identical to eye contact) (Arkowitz, Lichtenstein, McGovern, & Hines, 1975; Mehrabian, 1969).

　　　None　　　　　　1 2 3 4 5 6 7　　　　　Constant

Facial Orientation: The number of degrees the participant's face is turned away from the median plane of the addressee. Could be down or up as well as sideways.

　　　Indirect　　　　　1 2 3 4 5 6 7　　　　　Direct

Body Orientation: The degree to which a plane perpendicular to the plane of the communicator's shoulders is turned away from the median plane of the addressee (Mehrabian, 1969). Note that this is distinct from facial orientation, which refers to the position of the head in relationship to the other person.

　　　Indirect　　　　　1 2 3 4 5 6 7　　　　　Direct

Postural Openness: The degree to which the participant's torso area is open to the other person (i.e., arms are not crossed and legs are not crossed or pulled in toward body).

　　　Very closed　　　　1 2 3 4 5 6 7　　　　　Very open

Facial Animation Cue Composite

Smiling: Either closed (corners of mouth turned up, lips together, teeth together) or open (corners of mouth turned up, lips parted to show teeth) (Kraut & Johnston, 1979).

　　　None　　　　　　1 2 3 4 5 6 7　　　　　Frequent

Facial Pleasantness: Degree of positive (such as smiling) compared to negative (such as frowns or sneers) affect expressions during the interaction. Primarily indicated by the brow and mouth area (lowered brow, wrinkled forehead, and downturned mouth is usually more unpleasant; raised brow, smooth forehead, and upturned mouth is more pleasant) (Mehrabian, 1981).

　　　Unpleasant　　　　1 2 3 4 5 6 7　　　　　Pleasant

Facial Animation: Any movement of the face to a non-neutral position (either positive or negative); frequency and variety of facial expressions (Brandt, 1979; Mehrabian, 1969).

　　　Impassive　　　　1 2 3 4 5 6 7　　　　　Animated

Facial Concern: The degree to which the participant facially appears to be worried or concerned and care about the topic of conversation (generally reflected in a wrinkled forehead and serious face, attentive gaze).

      Indifferent   1 2 3 4 5 6 7   Concerned

Vocal Expressiveness Cue Composite

Volume: The loudness of the talk; function of amplitude or intensity of speech waves (Scherer, 1982).

      Loud   1 2 3 4 5 6 7   Soft

Rate: Number of words per minute; speed of talk and whether or not it is fast and hurried (Mehrabian, 1969; Scherer, 1982).

      Slow   1 2 3 4 5 6 7   Fast

Pitch: Amount of intonation or variation in pitch (Mehrabian, 1969).

      Monotone   1 2 3 4 5 6 7   Varied

Vocal Expressiveness: Degree to which voice incorporates affective or attitudinal expression; can involve variation in pitch, volume, and rate.

      Inexpressive   1 2 3 4 5 6 7   Expressive

Kinesic/Proxemic Attentiveness Cue Composite

Gestural Animation: Movements of hand or of fingers in interaction, excluding self-adaptors. Includes side-to-side, forward–back, and up-and-down movements (Bell, 1985; Mehrabian, 1969). For measuring animation, need to include not only a consideration of frequency of gestures, but also size (small to large) and activity level (slow movement to energetic and/or quick).

      Impassive   1 2 3 4 5 6 7   Animated

Kinesic/Proxemic Involvement: Degree to which the person's kinesic and proxemic cues suggest he or she is engaged in and focused on the interaction (indicated in part by more facial and gestural expressiveness, forward lean, direct eye gaze).

      Uninvolved   1 2 3 4 5 6 7   Involved

Kinesic/Proxemic Interest: Degree to which the participant's kinesic and proxemic cues indicate that he or she is interested in the conversation as opposed to finding the conversation dull and/or tedious (reflected in more animated kinesics, perhaps forward lean, more direct eye gaze, fewer yawns, and engaged look on face).

      Bored   1 2 3 4 5 6 7   Interested

Kinesic/Proxemic Attentiveness: Degree to which the participant appears to be attentive to or focusing on the other person and what he or she has to say, with the participant's kinesic and proxemic cues reflecting alter-centered (other-centered) attentiveness (probably reflected in part by still posture, direct eye gaze, and absence of adaptor behaviors).

Inattentive   1 2 3 4 5 6 7   Attentive

Vocal Warmth/Interest Cue Composite

Vocal Attentiveness: Degree to which the participant appears to be attentive to or focusing on the other person and what he or she has to say, with the participant's vocal cues reflecting alter-centered (other-centered) attentiveness reflected in part through vocalic behaviors such as backchanneling (e.g., uh huhs, hmms) and smoother, less disjointed flow of speech.

Inattentive   1 2 3 4 5 6 7   Attentive

Pleasantness: Degree of positive affect in the participant's vocal tone communicating pleasure (vs. displeasure). A more pleasant voice has a happier, agreeable, more positive vocal expression, whereas a more unpleasant voice has an unhappy, disgusted, or angry vocal expression. A more pleasant voice has more tone variation, slightly higher than average overall pitch, and is slightly slower than a moderate rate, whereas a more unpleasant voice is more tense, has lower overall pitch, and is faster with more precise enunciation (Buller & Burgoon, 1986; Mehrabian, 1981; Scherer, 1982).

Unpleasant   1 2 3 4 5 6 7   Pleasant

Vocal Interest: Degree to which the participant's vocal cues suggest he or she is interested in the conversation as opposed to finding the conversation dull and/or tedious (more interested vocal cues are probably reflected in a more varied voice [both in terms of pitch, volume, and rate] as well as shorter response latencies).

Bored   1 2 3 4 5 6 7   Interested

Vocal Warmth: Degree to which the speaker indicates positive affect with his or her voice, communicating affection, liking, and/or concern (Bayes, 1972) reflected in part by a mellow, soothing voice (not strident or terse) (Scherer, 1982).

Cold   1 2 3 4 5 6 7   Warm

Kinesic/Proxemic Composure Cue Composite

Kinesic/Proxemic Calm: Degree to which person's kinesic and proxemic cues suggest he or she is on an emotionally even keel (rather than nervous), serene (probably reflected in fewer self adaptors and random movement, still relaxed posture).

Anxious   1 2 3 4 5 6 7   Calm

Kinesic/Proxemic Composure: Degree to which participant appears at ease, poised, and in control of his or her responses in the interaction (probably reflected in smoother proxemic/kinesic cues, direct eye gaze, and less fidgeting).

Uncomposed   1 2 3 4 5 6 7   Composed

Vocal Relaxation Cue Composite

Clarity: Degree to which voice is clear and easily understood; crisp enunciation.

Unclear   1 2 3 4 5 6 7   Clear

Rhythm: the degree to which the voice has a smoothly flowing pattern.

Jerky   1 2 3 4 5 6 7   Rhythmic

Vocal Fluency Cue Composite

Smooth: Degree to which the participant's speaking flows evenly and smoothly, not disjointed (reflected in smooth rather than sudden and jerky shifts in vocal qualities such as rate, pitch, and volume as well as a lack of awkward pauses).

Choppy   1 2 3 4 5 6 7   Smooth

Fluency: The smoothness or fluidity of the talk, not choppy or disjointed.

Nonfluent   1 2 3 4 5 6 7   Fluent

Silences/Latencies Cue Composite

Silences: Noticeable points in the conversation when no one is saying anything. You have to make judgments about which interactant is responsible for the silence.

None   1 2 3 4 5 6 7   Frequent

Response Latencies: Response latency refers to the degree of pause that occurs before an interactant responds when he or she has been given the conversational turn.

Very inappropriate 1 2 3 4 5 6 7 Very appropriate

Independent Cues

Body Lean: The number of degrees that a plane defined from a communicator's shoulders to his or her hips is away from the vertical plane (Mehrabian, 1969).

Backward   1 2 3 4 5 6 7   Forward

Head Nodding: The amount of cyclical up and down (vertical) movements of the head made while listening (Arkowitz, Lichtenstein, McGovern, & Hines, 1975; Bell, 1981; Mehrabian, 1969).

None   1 2 3 4 5 6 7   Frequent

Random Movement: The amount of purposeless movement of legs, feet, torso, or arms and hands (i.e., swinging feet, shaking legs, tapping hand against side of chair; excludes hand and arm movements that are a part of self adaptors—self-touching or manipulation—or illustrator gestures) (Burgoon & Aho, 1982; Mehrabian, 1969).

    None   1 2 3 4 5 6 7   Frequent

Self-Adaptors: Self-touching behaviors; self-manipulation or motion of a part of the body in contact with another (i.e., playing with hair, scratching arm, fiddling thumbs, rubbing legs) (Andersen, 1999; Mehrabian, 1969).

    None   1 2 3 4 5 6 7   Frequent

APPENDIX B

Appropriateness Scale

INSTRUCTIONS: While watching the following segment of your conversation, please think about your needs during this part of the conversation and then please *evaluate the appropriateness of your conversational partner's response* on the following dimensions. Note that the first four items have two different scale choices separated by an OR for each question. Choose the option that is most relevant to your evaluation of your conversational partner's responses and respond to that scale. To what degree where his/her responses:

1. Too intense   1   2   3   4   5   6   An appropriate level of intensity

                                    OR

   Too apathetic   1   2   3   4   5   6   An appropriate level of intensity

2. Excessively positive   1   2   3   4   5   6   Appropriately positive or negative

                                    OR

   Excessively negative   1   2   3   4   5   6   Appropriately positive or negative

3. Overinvolved   1   2   3   4   5   6   Appropriately involved

                                    OR

   Inadequately involved   1   2   3   4   5   6   Appropriately involved

4. Too pleasant   1   2   3   4   5   6   Appropriately pleasant

                                    OR

   Too unpleasant   1   2   3   4   5   6   Appropriately pleasant

5. Completely irrelevant to your needs   1   2   3   4   5   6   Completely relevant to your needs

6. Not at all what you needed to hear   1   2   3   4   5   6   Exactly what you needed to hear

APPENDIX C

Synchrony Ratings

Interactional synchrony refers the extent to which people interacting with one another appear to become one or to form a unit. It involves the distinction between two people acting independently of one another versus acting with one another (for example, you might think about the image of couples ice skating or dancing).

Behavior Matching: Extent to which the two interactants are adopting the same posture, holding their body in the same way; the amount of similarity between the positions of interactants' hands, legs, and torso. Look for how often the interactants adopt similar postures. For example, ask yourself, are they both sitting upright, crossing their legs, leaning forward or backward, holding their hands in their lap, etc.

    Not at all similar   1 2 3 4 5 6 7   Almost identical

Coordination or Smoothness of Behaviors: Gestalt-like perception of the degree of behavior unity or "smoothness" achieved by the interactants; the extent to which the behaviors of the two fit together evenly. To what extent do their behaviors mesh or combine evenly and smoothly (Bernieri, 1988). Look for the degree of movement that appears connected with one another. Ask yourself, how smoothly do they coordinate their motions with each other, are there any false starts or hesitations.

    Not coordinated   1 2 3 4 5 6 7   Completely coordinated

Simultaneous Movement: Changes in movement that start, stop, change speed, or change direction in the same instant (as if were occurring on the down beat of a measure in a musical score). Key criterion is the *timing* of the movements (Bernieri, 1988).

    None   1 2 3 4 5 6 7   Frequent

The Affect Measures of the Couple Communication Scales

Nigel Roberts
Patricia Noller
University of Queensland

INTRODUCTION

Two major approaches to the study of human emotion have dominated the literature: a dimensional approach and a discrete emotions approach. The *dimensional* approach holds that emotion is best understood in terms of a small number of underlying dimensions, particularly valence and arousal (Levenson, 1988; Reisenszein, 1994; Russell, 1980), and more specific emotions are defined as being located within the affective space defined by the these two bipolar, continuous orthogonal dimensions. According to the *discrete* emotions approach, on the other hand, there are a fixed number of or basic (Ekman, 1994) or fundamental (Izard, 1991) emotions, although there is some disagreement about which emotions should be considered basic or fundamental (see Ekman, 1989, 1994).

In this chapter, we describe work on a set of scales developed for rating the affect of couples discussing a conflict issue. A discrete emotions approach (Ekman & Friesen, 1984) was taken in developing the scales. These affect scales are part of the Couple Conflict Scales (CCS), which also include content scales for rating the verbal behavior of couples (Roberts, 1998). The content scales are not discussed here, but for researchers who wish to have it, information can be obtained from the authors. Because our main focus was on conflict in couples—and more particularly in violent couples—we chose five specific negative emotions to form the CCS Affect Scales: fear/anxiety, anger, contempt/disgust, shame, and sadness. This choice was based in work on primary emotions (Ekman & Friesen, 1984; Izard, 1991) and research on emotions useful for discriminating happy and unhappy couples and assessing violence in relationships (Gottman, 1994; Retzinger, 1991).

The expression of emotion is an essential component of couple interaction (Jacob & Tennenbaum, 1988; Schaap, Buunk, & Kerkstra, 1988). Negative, more often than positive, affect has been shown to be the main differentiator between distressed and nondistressed couples (Gottman, 1979, 1994; Gottman & Levenson, 1986; Julien, Markman, & Lindahl, 1989) and between couples in violent and nonviolent relationships (Lloyd, 1988). It is important to acknowledge, however, that negative emotions may be seen as the primary differentiator between happy and unhappy couples because so much work has been concentrated on understanding couple interaction during conflict (Gottman, 1994; Noller, Feeney, Bonnell, & Callan, 1994; Schaap et al., 1988; see Roberts & Greenberg, 2002 for a discussion of this issue).

THE COUPLE COMMUNICATION SCALES

Rationale

As noted earlier, the Couple Communication Scales (CCS) were developed for a study of conflict interaction in violent and nonviolent couples (Noller & Roberts, 2002; Roberts, 1998). This study involved time-series analysis, physiological measures (skin-conductance and heart-rate), self-reports of emotional experience (anxiety), and outsider coding of content and affect in several conflict interactions. Although the CCS Affect Scales are similar in basic design to Roberts and Krokoff's (1990) Marital Interaction Rating System (MIRS), a specific attempt has been made in developing the CCS to separate content and affective processes, so that the nonverbal expression of emotion could be the main focus. In this way, we wanted to differentiate the scales from other scales such as the Specific Affect Coding System (SPAFF, Gottman, 1994; Gottman, McCoy, Coan, & Collier, 1996; Jones, Carrére, & Gottman, this volume) where there is a greater focus on behaviors associated with emotion, such as whining, defensiveness, domineering, belligerence, and stonewalling.

Guidelines for Coding

Like the MIRS, the CCS uses a cultural informants approach, which involves coders making "interpretations of the social meaning of the interactants' behavior," and "requires an integration of all available cues" (Roberts & Krokoff, 1990, p. 98). Gottman and Levenson (1986) distinguished between a cultural informants approach and a physical features approach where the emphasis is on describing the communication by recording observable behavior. In the development of the CCS, basic guidelines were provided for coders (see Tables 17 through 21), but it was assumed that raters would use their own knowledge of the culture in making their judgments.

TABLE 17

Guidelines for Coding Anxiety/Fear Using the CCS Affect Scales

Definitions	*Anxiety:* pain or uneasiness of mind in respect to some event, future or uncertain (Lexicon Webster Dictionary, p. 46). *Fear:* A painful emotion caused by an expectation of evil or impending danger (Lexicon Webster Dictionary, p. 357).
Synonyms	Scared, worried, apprehensive, stressed, uneasy, tense, apprehensive, shaky, jittery, terrified, afraid.
Verbal references	Fear is indicated by references to the anticipation of harm, physical or psychological (Ekman & Friesen, 1984). References to threats to security such as references to self-esteem, failure, as well as threats to physical safety suggest anxiety/fear. Feelings of danger, being in trouble, or overpowered also lead to anxiety/fear (Izard, 1991).
Facial cues	Eyebrows raised and drawn together, giving impression of being straightened, and creating wrinkles in the forehead. Eyes opened wider, with lower lid tensed and upper lid raised. Lips are tensed and stretched backwards (Ekman & Friesen, 1984).
Paralinguistic cues	Paralinguistic cues for fear include pitch contour up, fast tempo, many harmonics, high pitch level, round envelope, small pitch variation (Scherer, 1986). Anxiety can also be indicated by the presence of stuttering and other speech disturbances. Nervous laughter can also indicate fear or anxiety.
Additional cues	Fear/anxiety may also be reflected in "nervous" behavior such as leg jiggling, finger and hand wringing, fidgeting, or quick, jerky nervous gestures (Carlson & Hatfield, 1992).

TABLE 18

Guidelines for Coding Anger Using the CCS Affect Scales

Definition	*Anger:* a violent, revengeful passion or emotion, excited by a real or supposed injury to oneself or other (Lexicon Webster Dictionary, 1979, p. 39).
Synonyms	Wrath, rage, frustration, annoyance, vengefulness, fury, aggravation.
Verbal references	References to aggravation or annoyance, criticism, blame and dislike can all reflect feelings of anger (Retzinger, 1991).
	References to being misled, betrayed, treated unjustly, used or hurt by others may indicate anger, as do expressions of hatred, destruction, or revenge (Izard, 1991).
Facial cues	Anger is expressed in the face by the brows being lowered and drawn together, with vertical lines appearing between them; the eyelids are narrowed and tense in a hard fixed stare and may have a bulging appearance; the mouth can be closed with lips pressed together; the corners of the mouth can be straight or down, and the mouth can be open but tense and square (Retzinger, 1991).
	In anger, the lower eyelids are tensed and may be raised; the upper lids are also tensed and the lowering of the brow may lead to the upper lid also being lowered; the nostrils may also be flared or dilated (Ekman & Friesen, 1984).
Paralinguistic cues	Anger is signaled by staccato speech (distinct breaks between successive tones); loud, heavy stress on certain words; sing-song pattern (ridicule); and strident harsh voice (Retzinger, 1991).
	The voice of anger includes many harmonics, fast tempo, high pitch level, small pitch variation, pitch contours up (Scherer, 1986).
Additional cues	Anger can also be indicated by the interactant leaning forward toward the other in a challenging stance; clenched fists, waved fists, and hitting motions also signal anger (Retzinger, 1991).

TABLE 19

Guidelines for Coding Contempt/Disgust Using the CCS Affect Scales

Definition	*Contempt*: the feelings or actions with which one regards anything considered mean, vile, or worthless (Lexicon Webster Dictionary, 1979, p. 219). *Disgust*: Distaste, nausea, aversion excited by something offensive in the manners, conduct, language, or opinions of others (Lexicon Webster Dictionary, 1979, p. 286).
Synonyms	For contempt, include disdain, scorn, derision; for disgust, include distaste, nausea, loathing, repugnance, abhorrence.
Verbal references	References to being superior, or to something being wrong, stupid, and foolish (Izard, 1991); disgust involves getting-rid-of and getting-away-from responses; references to being nauseated, revolted, or disapproving may signal disgust.
Facial cues	Standing tall and tilting or cocking the head upward at an angle so as to look down on the object or person of contempt; a face full of contempt may involve a lifted brow, a lifted corner of the upper lip, or tightened mouth corners (Izard, 1991). The sneer, a variation of the unilateral lip curl in which the upper lip is raised exposing the teeth is also a clear indication of contempt (Ekman & Friesen, 1984). Disgust is displayed in the face first by the brows being drawn down and together in a frown; second, the nose is commonly screwed up, giving it a wrinkled appearance; in addition, the mouth can have a rectangular shape as the upper lip is pulled up, and the lower lip is pulled downward (Izard, 1991).
Paralinguistic cues	Disgust is expressed in the voice through many harmonics, small pitch variation, round envelope, and a slow tempo (Scherer, 1986); contempt can be conveyed through a sing-song voice, a patronizing tone, sarcasm, or a mocking, condescending laugh.

TABLE 20

Guidelines for Coding Shame Using the CCS Affect Scales

Definition	The painful feeling arising from the consciousness of something dishonorable, improper, ridiculous, or the like, done by oneself or another, or of being in a situation offensive to decency, self-respect, or pride (Lexicon Webster Dictionary, 1979, p. 886).
Synonyms	Ignominy, disgrace, dishonor, and feelings of embarrassment, humiliation, foolishness, ridicule, and sheepishness.
Verbal references	Shame is indicated by verbal references to being ridiculed, inadequate, ashamed, embarrassed, exposed, or deficient; reference to oneself in relation to another with a negative evaluation placed on self; negative ideation about one's appearance in relation to another, or obsessive ideation of what one might have said or done (Retzinger, 1991).
	References to being inept or disappointed in self, or of being stupid or legally or morally wrong, all indicate shame (Izard, 1991).
Facial cues	Shame is indicated by lip biting, a parting of the lips, a lowering of the upper eyelids, and a lowering of the head (Burgoon, Buller, & Woodall, 1989).
	Shame is expressed by a lowering or turning of the head, an aversion of gaze, and blushing (Izard, 1991).
	Shame is also indicated by a turning in, biting, or licking of the lips, and biting of the tongue. False or embarrassed smiles also indicate shame (Retzinger, 1991).
Paralinguistic cues	Oversoft speech, irregular rhythm, hesitation, self-interruption, self-censorhip, pauses and filled pauses, stammering/stuttering, fragmented speech, rapid condensed speech, and laughed words are all cues to the emotion of shame (Izard, 1991; Retzinger, 1991).
Additional cues	Shame can also be indicated by hiding behavior such as the use of the hand to cover all or parts of the face, and face touching in general; gaze aversion and a lowering of the eyes can be included as hiding behaviors (Retzinger, 1991).

TABLE 21

Guidelines for Coding Sadness Using the CCS Affect Scales

Definition	Affected with grief, expressing sorrow (Lexicon Webster Dictionary, 1979, p. 845).
Synonyms	Sorrowful, mournful, downhearted, grief-stricken, doleful, dejected, dispirited.
Verbal references	References to loss, suffering, hopelessness, or disappointment may indicate sadness (Ekman & Friesen, 1984)
Facial cues	The inner corners of the brows are drawn obliquely upward and together, while the eyes are slightly narrowed and the corners of the mouth are pulled downward; the chin can be pushed upward and may quiver; the face seems to lack muscle tone and gains a drooping appearance, and the eyes may not seem as bright as usual (Izard, 1991). The corners of the lips are drawn down and the lips may appear to tremble, particularly at great intensities of sadness (Ekman & Friesen, 1984).
Paralinguistic cues	Crying or sobbing, slower speech, and less frequent speech may all indicate sadness (Izard, 1991). Sadness is shown in the voice by slow tempo, low pitch level, few harmonics, round envelope, pitch contour down (Scherer, 1986).
Additional cues	Sadness is accompanied by a slowing of both mental and bodily functioning (Izard, 1991); crying can be a key feature of sadness (Averill, 1968).

The basic guidelines for the coders include dictionary definitions, synonyms, verbal references and subjective thoughts likely to indicate the particular emotion, facial cues, paralinguistic cues, and some additional cues that did not fit clearly in other categories. In describing the facial and paralinguistic cues, in particular, we relied heavily on the work of Ekman and Friesen (1984), Retzinger (1991), and Scherer (1986). Synonyms are provided, and these reflect the vastly different intensities at which an emotion can be experienced (Ekman & Friesen, 1984; Reisenzein, 1994).

The CCS also involve bipolar rating scales, rather than categorical coding, in order to provide the continuous streams of data needed for time-series analysis. In addition, the rating system described here uses a fixed-time interval of 10 seconds. Using this fixed-time interval also allows the matching of physiological data with specific behavioral and affective events, and the data can then be analyzed using bivariate time-series analysis (Williams & Gottman, 1981).

The Affect Scales of the CCS

The five affect scales of the CCS are all negative, and it is important to emphasize that these scales are not meant to represent an exhaustive range of emotions that could be displayed during couple interaction, but rather those that are most likely to be displayed in the context of conflict. In fact, one advantage of the CCS is that observers only have to consider a limited number of discrete emotions of interest and focus on a limited number of behaviors.

Two of the scales of the CCS affect scales, fear/anxiety and contempt/disgust, require special attention because they combine two emotions that are seen by some theorists as distinct. Although some scholars distinguish carefully between anxiety and fear (e.g., Izard, 1991), many do not, using the terms anxiety and fear interchangeably (Burgoon & Saine, 1978; Carlson & Hatfield, 1992). In addition, these two emotions are combined in the SPAFF (Gottman et al., 1996; Jacob & Tennenbaum, 1988). Even Izard (1991) acknowledges that fear is the emotion underlying all forms of anxiety. Thus, although distinctions can be made between fear and anxiety, these two emotions do tend to overlap and are generally treated as synonyms by researchers.

Contempt and disgust are also closely related, although some distinctions can be made. For example, disgust is an aversive response to something distasteful or repulsive, whereas contempt is a reaction to people or the actions of people. Unlike disgust, contempt involves a sense of superiority (Ekman & Friesen, 1984; Izard, 1991). In terms of couple interaction, however, we suggest that these emotions are likely to be evoked by similar stimuli, and their expression is likely to convey similar messages.

Empirical Findings

At this stage, the CCS scales have been used in only one study and reported in two papers. The study involved 48 couples (Noller & Roberts, 2002; Roberts, 1998).

Of these 48 couples, 33 were married, and 15 were cohabiting. Females' ages ranged from 18 to 51 years, and males' ages ranged from 19 to 67 years. Participants had been together for an average of 7 years. Couples engaged in four interactions: a serious conflict nominated by the wife, a serious conflict, nominated by the husband, a trivial conflict, and a discussion of a disappointment or sadness not involving the partner. The interactions were coded by outsiders using ratings made on each scale of the CCS affect scales at 10-second intervals. During the interactions, physiological measures (skin conductance and heart-rate) were also recorded.

Reliability of the Affect Scales of the CCS. Because of the relatively low interrater reliabilities for the anger and sadness scales, and because the raters seemed to be blurring the distinction between contempt/disgust and anger, and between sadness and shame, we collapsed the anger and contempt/disgust scales into a summary scale labeled "hostility" and the sadness and shame scales into a summary scale labeled "despair." Using this strategy resulted in higher reliability coefficients and three affect scales: fear/anxiety (.64), hostility (.54), and despair (.56). These three scales were included in all further analyses.

Links Between Affect During Conflict, Satisfaction, and Violence. We first examined the association between expression of affect during conflict, relationship satisfaction, and violence. For ratings of fear/anxiety, happy couples showed more signs of fear/anxiety than unhappy couples. This finding was somewhat surprising given that self-report and physiological measures of couples' experience of anxiety suggested that happy couples experienced less anxiety than unhappy couples. It seems likely that happy couples were more apt to feel free to express their fear/anxiety than were unhappy couples.

With regard to the ratings of hostility, participants expressed less hostility during discussion of the sad issue, relative to the three conflict issues, lending support to the validity of the hostility scale of the CCS in differentiating between these contexts. Further validation comes from the finding that, as would be expected, unhappy couples displayed more hostility than happy couples during the critical issues of disagreement. In addition, participants generally expressed more despair during the critical issues of disagreement than during the trivial issue of disagreement, and during the sad issue than during the three conflict issues, $F(1,43) = 61.92$, $p < .001$. These findings regarding the despair scale tend to support the validity of that scale.

Linking Partners' Affect and Behavior

Because we were using time-series analysis in this study (see Noller & Roberts, 2002), the dependent variables were the degrees of temporal linkage between various streams of data. Although we explored other links, our focus here is on the links involving the affect scales. We explore the association (a) between one individual's expression of affect and the partner's expression of affect, and (b) between one individual's behavior and the partner's expression of affect. Only significant findings are be reported here, and those interested in more detailed findings should consult the authors.

In creating each dependent variable, the measures of temporal linkage (that is, occurring in the following 30 seconds) were averaged across the male and female conflict issues. Bivariate time-series analysis was used to quantify, in terms of a z-score, the extent to which one time-series was able to account for the other time-series after controlling for the second time-series' own past (Williams & Gottman, 1981). Analysis of variance was then used, with these z-scores as the dependent variables, to determine whether the degree of linkage differed for couples in violent versus nonviolent and happy versus unhappy relationships during discussion of a current conflict.

Linking One Partner's Affective Display and the Other's Affective Display.[15]
For the linkage between partners' expressions of fear/anxiety, the analysis revealed an interaction between violence and satisfaction, indicating that the link between one partner's expression of fear/anxiety and the other partner's expression of fear/anxiety was greater for those in violent unhappy relationships than for those in nonviolent unhappy relationships. Analysis on the despair–hostility linkage revealed an interaction of violence, satisfaction, and gender. The expression of hostility by males in happy violent relationships was more predictable from the partner's expression of despair than was true for men in nonviolent happy relationships. In other words, males in violent happy relationships were more likely to become hostile if their partner expressed despair.

Linking One Partner's Affect and the Other Partner's Behavior.   For the hostility–withdrawal linkage, there was an interaction of violence and gender. This finding showed that the withdrawal of females in violent relationships was more predictable from the hostility of the partner than was true for females in nonviolent relationships. In addition, an analysis on the invalidation–hostility link revealed a main effect for satisfaction. Those in unhappy marriages were more likely to respond to the partner's use of invalidation with hostility. The findings from this study point to differences between happy and unhappy couples and between violent and nonviolent couples in their emotional reactivity and in the extent to which their reactions to their partner's behavior can be predicted. These findings also support the claim by Lloyd (1990) that couples in violent relation-

---

[15]It is important to note that only the magnitude and not the direction of the temporal associations are provided by the Gottman-Ringland procedure for conducting bivariate time-series analysis. We have taken the liberty of interpreting the data in accordance with what we know about these behaviors, but it should be kept in mind that either an increase or a decrease in the predicted behavior is possible. This issue is relevant for the next series of analyses presented as well.

ships are more reactive to one another's negativity. The findings also support the validity of the CCS Affect Scales.

DISCUSSION

Although the validity of the CCS Affect Scales was supported by a number of the reported findings from the work presented here, the reliability of the scales was of some concern. Reliability improved when the anger and contempt/disgust scales were combined into a summary scale labeled "hostility" and the sadness and shame scales were combined into a summary scale labeled "despair." There may, however, be times when a researcher is interested in discriminating between anger and contempt/disgust, and between sadness and shame, so combining the measures may not always work. It may be that greater reliability would be obtained by training coders to recognize the nonverbal behaviors outlined in this chapter and to discriminate more clearly between different expressions of emotion.

Despite the fact that the descriptions of the various emotions and their concomitants seem to differentiate the various emotions clearly, it is possible that these descriptions could be made more specific. It is also possible that the more similar emotions are distinguished more clearly when the verbal channel is also available. It is always important to remember that most communication is a synthesis of the verbal and nonverbal components, and both channels are often needed to decode the message accurately. More research using these scales is needed, and we encourage future research involving the use of the five scales. It would also be interesting to see the scales used in the context of other relationships, such as parent–child relationships or sibling relationships where conflict patterns are likely to be learned (e.g., Noller, Feeney, Peterson, & Sheehan, 1995).

CONCLUSIONS

We have tested the validity of the CCS Affect scales in two ways: first by comparing the frequency of the expression of these affects among the different types of couple relationships, and second, by exploring the temporal linkage of these affects to one another and to verbal behavior. The data presented here support the validity of the CCS Affect Scales, with these scales differentiating between relationships high and low in satisfaction (fear/anxiety and hostility), and between topics (hostility and despair). There were no differences between violent and nonviolent couples in terms of the frequency with which the various affects were expressed.

There were differences between violent and nonviolent couples, however, in terms of when these affects were expressed. For example, one partner was more likely to express fear/anxiety when the other had expressed fear/anxiety if they were in a violent unhappy relationship than if they were in a nonviolent unhappy relationship. In addition, females in violent relationships were more likely to withdraw when the partner expressed hostility than was true for females in nonviolent relationships. There was also evidence for different patterns being related to satisfaction, with those unhappy in their relationships more likely to respond to invalidation with hostility than was true for those who were happy with their relationships. These patterns provide further evidence for the validity of these scales.

REFERENCES

Averill, J. R. (1968). Grief: Its nature and significance. *Psychological Bulletin, 70,* 721–748.
Burgoon, J. K., Buller, D. B., & Woodall, W. G. (1989). *Nonverbal communication: The unspoken dialogue.* New York: Harper & Row.
Burgoon, J. K., & Saine, T. (1978). *The unspoken dialogue: An introduction to nonverbal communication.* Boston: Houghton Mifflin.
Carlson, J. G., & Hatfield, E. (1992). *Psychology of emotion.* Fort Worth, TX: Harcourt Brace Jovanovich.
Ekman, P. (1989). The argument and evidence about universals in facial expressions of emotion. In H. Wagner & A. Manstead (Eds.), *Handbook of psychophysiology* (pp. 143–164). Chichester, England: Wiley.
Ekman, P. (1994). All emotions are basic. In P. Ekman & R. Davidson (Eds.), *The nature of emotion: Fundamental questions* (pp. 15–19). New York: Oxford University Press.
Ekman, P., & Friesen, W. V. (1984). *Unmasking the face: A guide to recognizing emotions from facial expressions.* Palo Alto, CA: Consulting Psychologists Press.
Gottman, J. M. (1979). *Marital interaction: Empirical investigations.* New York: Academic Press.
Gottman, J. M. (1994). *What predicts divorce? The relationship between marital processes and marital outcomes.* Hillsdale, NJ: Lawrence Erlbaum Associates.
Gottman, J. M., & Levenson, R. W. (1986). Assessing the role of emotion in marriage. *Behavioral Assessment, 8,* 31–48.
Gottman, J. M., McCoy, K., Coan, J., & Collier, H. (1996). The specific affect coding system (SPAFF) for observing emotional communication in marital and family interaction. In J. M. Gottman (Ed.), *What predicts divorce? The measures.* Mahwah, NJ: Lawrence Erlbaum Associates.
Izard, C. E. (1991). *The psychology of emotions.* New York: Plenum Press.
Jacob, T., & Tennenbaum, D. L. (1988). *Family assessment: Rationale, methods and future directions.* New York: Plenum Press.
Julien, D., Markman, H. J., & Lindahl, K. M. (1989). A comparison of a global and microanalytic coding system: Implications for future trends in studying interactions. *Behavioral Assessment, 11,* 81–100.
Levenson, R. W. (1988). Emotion and the autonomic nervous system: A prospectus for research on autonomic specificity. In H. Wagner (Ed.), *Social psychophysiology and emotion: Theory and applications* (pp. 17–42). London: Wiley.
Lexicon Webster Dictionary. (Encyclopaedic edition). (1979). Lexicon.
Lloyd, S. (1988, November). *Physical aggression and stress in marriage: The role of everyday marital interaction.* Paper presented at the National Council on Family Relations Annual Conference, Philadelphia.
Lloyd, S. (1990). Conflict types and strategies in violent relationships. *Journal of Family Violence, 5,* 269–284.
Noller, P., Feeney, J. A., Bonnell, D., & Callan, V. J. (1994). A longitudinal study of conflict in early marriage. *Journal of Social and Personal Relationships, 11,* 233–251.
Noller, P., & Roberts, N. D. (2002). The communication of couples in violent and nonviolent relationships: Temporal associations with own and partner's anxiety/arousal and behavior. In P. Noller & J. A. Feeney (Eds.) *Understanding marriage: Developments in the study of couple interaction* (pp. 348–378). New York: Cambridge University Press.
Noller, P., Feeney, J. A., Peterson, C., & Sheehan, G. (1995). Learning conflict patterns in the family: Links between marital, parental and sibling relationships. In T. Socha & G. Stamp (Eds.), *Parents, children and communication: Frontiers of theory and research* (pp. 273–298). Hillsdale, NJ: Lawrence Erlbaum Associates.
Reisenzein, R. (1994). Pleasure arousal theory and the intensity of emotions. *Journal of Personality and Social Psychology, 67,* 525–539.

Retzinger, S. (1991). *Shame and rage in marital quarrels.* Newbury Park, CA: Sage.

Roberts, L. J., & Krokoff, L. (1990). A time-series analysis of withdrawal, hostility, and displeasure in satisfied and dissatisfied marriages. *Journal of Marriage and the Family, 52,* 95–105.

Roberts, L. J., & Greenberg, D. R. (2002). Observational "windows" to intimacy processes in marriage. In P. Noller & J. A. Feeney (Eds.) *Understanding marriage: Developments in the study of couple interaction* (pp. 118–149). New York: Cambridge University Press.

Roberts, N. D. (1998). *Communication in violent relationships: The role of attachment and arousal.* Unpublished doctoral thesis, University of Queensland, Australia.

Russell, J. A. (1980). A circumplex model of affect. *Journal of Personality and Social Psychology, 39,* 1161–1178.

Schaap, C., Buunk, B., & Kerkstra, A. (1988). Marital conflict resolution. In P. Noller & M. A. Fitzpatrick (Eds.), *Perspectives on marital interaction* (pp. 203–244). Clevedon, UK: Multilingual Matters.

Scherer, K. R. (1986). Vocal affect expression: A review and model for future research. *Psychological Bulletin, 99,* 143–165.

Williams, E. A., & Gottman, J. M. (1981). *A user's guide to the Gottman-Williams time-series analysis computer programs for social scientists.* New York: Cambridge University Press.

Rating Interactional Sense-Making in the Process of Joint Storytelling

Jody Koenig Kellas
University of Nebraska, Lincoln

April R. Trees
University of Colorado, Boulder

INTRODUCTION

Telling stories helps people make sense of their experiences and develop a sense of control and understanding (Bochner, Ellis, & Tillmann-Healy, 1997; Harvey, 1996). Research portrays storytelling as integral to human understanding (e.g., Bruner, 1990; Fisher, 1989), personal relationships (e.g., Duck, 1994), individual and family identity (e.g., Linde, 1993; Stone, 1988), and ways of interacting (e.g., Mandelbaum, 1987, 1989; Miller, Mintz, Hoogstra, Fung, & Pottset, 1992). Although stories may be thought of as told individually, it is with, and most often for, others that we tell stories. People often collaborate on telling stories, and this joint telling serves as one of the ways in which relational partners and family members construct and make sense of their relationships as well as their life experiences (Duck, 1994). As a prevalent mode of sense-making that occurs in our interactions with others, stories deserve more attention as communicative or behavioral processes that people do together.

The shift in conversational activities from an individual to a joint process, however, requires a change in methods for rating narrative behavior. This chapter thus offers a system for rating interactive (verbal and nonverbal) behaviors during joint storytelling. We focus on the development of a rating scheme that assesses family behavior and collaborative sense-making. Although it is in its initial stages of development, the system provides a means for rating a set of global percepts involving communication behavior in joint storytelling. We first present a brief grounding in theory and research on storytelling and sense-making, then describe the rating system and the rating process, and finally discuss the analysis of two different sets of stories using this system.

DEVELOPMENT OF THE RATING SYSTEM

Current Theory and Research on Sense-Making and Storytelling

Researchers have identified a number of characteristics of individual storytelling that likely explain how telling stories helps to make sense of experiences in life. These characteristics include labeling experiences and emotions and placing them in a logical organizational structure (Clark, 1993; Harber & Pennebaker, 1992; Labov & Waletsky, 1967). Additionally, telling a story necessitates a consideration of multiple perspectives, which provides an opportunity for personal insight and requires creating a coherent story that hangs together (Clark, 1993; Koenig Kellas & Manusov, 2003; Neimeyer & Levitt, 2000). Each of these features constitutes an important activity in the sense-making process achieved through telling stories.

The current literature on storytelling in personal relationships contains three primary coding or rating schemes for assessing marital storytelling behaviors. The first, from the Early Years of Marriage study (Veroff, Sutherland, Chadiha, & Ortega, 1993a, 1993b; Veroff, Chadiha, Leber, & Sutherland, 1993), is used in research investigating the process through which newlyweds jointly presented the story of how they met, fell in love, and got married. The second rating assessment, from the Family Narrative Consortium (i.e., Fiese & Sameroff, 1999, Fiese et al., 2001), involves a system of global judgments assessing the processes associated with narrative style, coordination, and husband/wife disconfirmation and confirmation in collaborative storytelling. Finally, Buehlman, Gottman, and their colleagues developed the Oral History Interview (OHI) to assess the history of a couple's relationship and their philosophy on marriage (Buehlman & Gottman, 1996; Carrère, Buehlman, Gottman, Coan, & Ruckstuhl, 2000, see also Buehlman, Carrère, & Siler, this volume).

Each of these coding/rating systems contains a collaboration dimension for analyzing couples' stories and, in combination with research on sense-making, points toward some important process dimensions for storytelling. They all, however, have limitations for studying collaborative interactional sense-making in jointly told family stories. First, family systems theory suggests that families are made up of interdependent members whose behaviors mutually influence one another, providing a theoretical rationale for attending to gestalt, macrolevel assessments of family-level interaction patterns in storytelling (Kerig, 2001). The turn-by-turn analysis of Veroff et al.'s (1993a) system does not provide a global rating of behaviors across the interaction. Second, in the context of jointly told family stories, concepts like coherence, central to sense-making and storytelling literature, become joint accomplishments. Fiese et al.'s (2001) and Buehlman and Gottman's (1996) rating systems, although extremely useful for other types of analysis, contain global judgments about narrative behavior but treat concepts like coherence and the communication of we-ness as individual rather than shared behaviors.

Finally, these research protocols inform an understanding of how couples negotiate the process of constructing narratives jointly. Because families do not necessarily identify with one another in the same way that romantic couples do, and because the addition of even one family member to a communicative context complicates and changes the dynamics of the interaction, other aspects of process may assume significance. For example, with three people rather than two, the issue of how involved each family member acts, who has room to talk, and how the family takes turns may shift in important ways for measurement. Previous story-coding schemes can, however, be used as a place to start in the development of coding in jointly told family stories.

Interactional Sense-Making

Given our interest in stories as sense-making activities, Koenig and Trees (2000) drew from the literature on sense-making and storytelling and began to develop a new rating system for collaborative sense-making in jointly told stories involving multiple family members. We used an initial set of 12 stories about stressful family experiences jointly told by three family members and conducted a qualitative analysis of the emergent sense-making processes in these stories. With Fiese and Sameroff's (1999), Veroff et al.'s (1993a), and Buehlman and Gottman's (1996) coding schemes as guides for examining process in the jointly told stories, we used a combination of deductive and inductive analyses to uncover the elements of process that seemed most relevant to families' sense-making in joint storytelling.

We identified sets of stories in which family members seemed to share similar conclusions about the meaning of stories for difficult family experiences and sets of stories where they seemed to have either different meanings or where the narrative failed to reflect any expressed sense-making concerning the meaning of the story. In looking at interaction patterns among these different stories, engagement, turn-taking, perspective-taking, and coherence emerged as relevant dimensions of joint process. Both verbal and nonverbal behaviors contribute to overall judgments concerning each of these process qualities within joint family storytelling in multiple contexts and for many story topics. Level of engagement, degree of perspective-taking, fluidity of turn-taking, and story coherence, then, reflect characteristics of the storytelling process and content that appear to contribute centrally to the "jointness" of a shared family story (Koenig & Trees, 2000). Each of these interaction characteristics can be judged globally at the level of the family story, attending to how the family, as a whole, interacts.

DESCRIPTION OF THE RATING SYSTEM

This section describes the elements of the interactional sense-making rating system. Each element is measured along two dimensions on five-point, Likert-type scales. These ratings involve judgments of the joint storytelling process as a whole, rather than as separate assessments of individual contributions to the process. In addition to the rating system, this section also provides information on the process of training raters and rating stories. In general, the ratings for joint storytelling processes take the story as the unit of analysis and involve gestalt perceptions of each dimension.

Engagement

Engagement is measured according to the degree of involvement and the degree of warmth present in the story. *Involvement* refers to liveliness of the storytelling or the degree to which the family as a whole participates verbally in telling the story and expresses interest and engagement nonverbally while both speaking and listening. Behavioral indicators of involvement include kinesic/proxemic animation (use of gestures, facial expressiveness), vocal animation, eye contact, back channels (head nods, uh huhs), touch, and forward lean, as well as verbal contributions to the story being told (see also, Guerrero, this volume). These verbal indicators include active participation and adding on to one another's comments. *Warmth* refers to the degree to which the family's interaction (both verbal and nonverbal) is characterized by warmth, affection, and positive affect versus coldness, distance, and dissociation from each other and/or negative affect. Behavioral indicators of warmth include nonverbal behaviors such as pleasant facial expressions, smiles, forward lean, touch, vocal warmth, and eye contact. Verbal behaviors include statements of encouragement, affection, positive humor, and/or approval, as well as attentiveness and expressions of positive feelings/affect about each other and the story. The combination of verbal and nonverbal behaviors influences judgments of warmth (i.e., family members may engage in conflict, but if the vocal tone and facial expressions are positive, it can still be warm).

Turn-Taking

The second feature of joint storytelling processes, turn-taking, involves assessments of the degree to which turn-taking in stories is dynamic and evenly distributed. The *dynamic* feature of turn-taking refers to the degree to which families' turn-taking or shifts in speech are segmented and compartmentalized versus mixed, free-flowing, and dynamic. Behavioral indicators of more dynamic turn-taking include interruptions, additions to what others are saying, interjections, and elaborations. Indicators of more structured turn-taking are distinct, separate turns and explicit turn-taking behaviors such as, "And what would you like to add?" *Distribution of turns* measures the degree to which each family member both takes and is allowed to take turns at telling the story. This dimension focuses on the balance of talking across the telling of the story. The primary behavioral indicator of turn distribution is talk time.

Perspective-Taking

The third element of the rating system involves assessments of perspective-taking behavior, or the extent to which families attend to and confirm one another's perspectives during the joint telling. *Attentiveness to others' perspectives* is operationalized as the degree to which family members, as they tell the story together, acknowledge each other's views and perspectives and combine and integrate them to create the story. Behavioral indicators of attentiveness to others' perspectives include asking others about their perspectives explicitly, statements that indicate an understanding that others may have seen things differently, acknowledging perspectives others have contributed to the story, and including others' perspectives in one's own contribution to the story. Nonverbal cues such as gestures and eye contact toward others may accompany these verbal perspective-taking moves.

Confirmation of perspectives refers to the degree to which family members are confirming of the experience/perspective of other members of the family and respond positively to their contributions to the story. This variable focuses specifically on how family members respond to others' contributions to the story through statements affirming the validity of others' experiences (e.g., "That's a good point.") or agreement. Agreement does not necessarily indicate agreement with the point, but with the description of people's own experiences (e.g., "I can see where you would feel that way."). Nonverbal behaviors indicating agreement or disagreement also contribute to this process (e.g., head nodding or shaking, disbelieving/believing or disapproving/approving facial or vocal expressions).

Coherence

Structural characteristics of the story related to sense-making include organization and integration. *Organization* is the degree to which the overall story told is logically organized and clearly sequential. Behavioral indicators of organization include a clear beginning, middle, and end as well as minimal jumping around from one part of the story to the other. *Integration* involves rating the degree to which family members tell a single, intertwined, integrated story that hangs together and makes sense. Neimeyer and Levitt (2000) point out that stories may be chaotic and completely lacking in coherence, or they can be conflictual, with individually coherent stories that are competing. As a judgment of the joint construction of a story overall, stories that contain somewhat coherent individual contributions but fail to hang together as a whole receive a low rating, despite individual coherence.

RATING AND TRAINING PROCESS

To assess stories, raters must be trained to make gestalt judgments based on the overall interaction of multiple family members at once. In our research developing this rating system (Koenig & Trees, 2000), we also developed a procedure for training raters to use the scheme.

We started by discussing each dimension with raters, covering the conceptual definitions of each element as well as the behavioral indicators and decision rules for differentiating stories along the rating scale (a more detailed description of the decision rules that raters were given is in the appendix). Rater training also included practice rating of set of 11 stories. This process is most effective if stories scoring relatively high and relatively low on each scale are included as examples to give raters a sense of the end points of the rating scheme. In both the training and the actual story rating, the raters viewed the story through once before rating, independently, the components they were assessing. Each element of the narrative was rated separately to ensure that raters did not have to focus on too many dimensions of conversation at one time. Raters were given a note-taking sheet to document behavioral markers relevant to the dimension being rated.

USING THE INTERACTIONAL SENSE-MAKING RATING SYSTEM: TWO TYPES OF STORIES

Thus far, we have used the interactional sense-making rating system to assess the features of joint storytelling process in two types of family stories. In a study involving 58 family triads (two parents and one child or two children and one parent), we asked families to select and tell together, first, a story that best represents the family (Koenig, 2002) and that the family often tells, and, second, a story of a stressful family experience (Trees & Koenig, 2003). In addition to providing an opportunity to test the reliability of the rating system, these stories also allowed us to assess the relationship between joint narrative behavior and family qualities and outcomes.

Rating and Reliability

Because family stories have been described as one of the primary ways in which people learn the norms, values, and behaviors expected of family members (e.g., Norrick, 1997; Stone, 1988), and because these stories may be consequential to relational beliefs, affect, and the formation of individual identities (Sherman, 1990), we first asked families to tell an often-told story that they feel best represents the family. Trained raters followed the procedures we have described to rate the stories for the degree of engagement, turn-taking, perspective-taking, and organization. Based on a subset of 12 stories rated by two different raters, Cronbach's *alpha* revealed good interrater reliability for involvement (*alpha* = .92), warmth (*alpha* = .78), dynamic turn-taking (*alpha* = .74), distribution of turns (*alpha* = .87)[16] and confirmation of others' perspectives (*alpha* = .92). Attentiveness to others' per-

---

[16]This dimension was unreliable initially (*alpha* = .44), however, after all 58 stories were re-rated for reliability, the alpha was acceptable.

spectives, organization, and integration were not rated reliably and, therefore, were not used for this set of stories.

Research on sense-making and stress (e.g., Harber & Pennebaker, 1992) focuses on the link between disclosure about stressful events and positive outcomes for tellers. Because family members often turn to one another to discuss stressful situations and tell stories about them, the second type of story families told was about a difficult family experience (Koenig & Trees, 2000). Given that our initial use of the interactional sense-making rating system elicited low interrater reliability for one of the perspective-taking variables and both coherence variables, we revised the rating and training system to ensure both the validity and reliability of the rating scheme as applied to the stories of stressful family experiences. This involved developing a more detailed description of the ways in which to think about integration, organization, and attentiveness to perspectives at the level of the story rather than the individual (included in the appendix). Reliability calculations were based on a subset of 12 stories rated by two different raters. These were adequate for all eight dimensions of interactional sense-making (engagement, *alpha* = .85; warmth, *alpha* = .79; dynamic, *alpha*, = .79; distribution, *alpha* = .92; attentiveness, *alpha* = .86; confirmation, *alpha* = .91; organization, *alpha* = .72; integration, *alpha* = .73).

For both types of stories, we assessed correlations among joint storytelling processes and family satisfaction and functioning. For the often-told family identity story, we found that family satisfaction (measured using a scale from Vangelisti, 1992) correlated positively with the degree to which family members confirmed one another's perspectives, the degree of warmth, and the even distribution of turns during the telling (Koenig, 2002). Adaptability, cohesion, and overall family functioning (measured using FACES II from Olson, 2000) correlated positively with all five features of joint storytelling process: involvement, warmth, confirmation of perspectives, dynamism of turn-taking, and distribution of turns[17] (Koenig, 2002).

For the difficult family experience story, we found that family satisfaction correlated positively with warmth, attentiveness to other perspectives, and confirmation of other perspectives. Similarly, family cohesion related to warmth, as well as attentiveness to other perspectives and confirmation of other perspectives. Additionally, correlations were identified between adaptability and coherence, as well as with attentiveness to others' perspectives, and storytelling warmth. We also found significant relationships between overall family functioning and warmth, attentiveness to others' perspectives, confirmation of others' perspectives, and overall story coherence.

---

[17]All five features of joint process correlated significantly with family cohesion, family adaptability, and overall family functioning, except involvement with family adaptability or dynamism of turns with family adaptability or overall family functioning. These exceptions, however, did reflect hypothesis-confirming trends toward positive relationships (see Koenig, 2002)

CONCLUSION

Our goal in developing this rating system was to extend previous research on couples and offer a means for globally assessing the features of joint storytelling behavior in families. Our research (Koenig, 2002; Koenig & Trees, 2000; Trees & Koenig, 2003) indicates that engagement, perspective-taking, turn-taking, and coherence are important verbal and nonverbal features of interaction relating to sense-making and family satisfaction and functioning.

In our future work, we plan to examine multiple story types in order to tease out the notion that the behaviors associated with joint storytelling and sense-making shift according to the nature of the narrative. These further assessments will also assist us in confirming the validity and improving the reliability of the rating system. We also hope to better understand how joint storytelling differs across cultures and in more naturalistic settings. The ways in which family members interact verbally and nonverbally have implications for family satisfaction and functioning (Buehlman & Gottman, 1996; Koenig, 2002; Trees & Koenig, 2003). Given that family stories are avenues for affecting and reflecting family identity and culture, further use of this rating system in families across different topics and contexts may provide insight into how to maintain satisfying and productive family relationships.

REFERENCES

Bochner, A. P., Ellis, C., & Tillmann-Healy, L. M. (1997). Relationships as stories. In S. W. Duck (Ed.), *Handbook of personal relationships: Theory, research, and interventions* (2nd ed., pp. 107–124). Chichester: Wiley.

Bruner, J. (1990). *Acts of meaning*. Cambridge, MA: Harvard University Press.

Buehlman, K. T., & Gottman, J. M. (1996). The Oral History Interview and the Oral History Coding System. In J. M. Gottman (Ed.), *What predicts divorce? The measures*. Mahwah, NJ: Lawrence Erlbaum Associates.

Carrere, S., Buehlman, K. T., Gottman, J. M., Coan, J. A., & Ruckstuhl, L. (2000). Predicting marital stability and divorce in newlywed couples. *Journal of Family Psychology, 14*, 42–58.

Clark, L. F. (1993). Stress and the cognitive-conversational benefits of social interaction. *Journal of Social and Clinical Psychology, 12*, 25–55.

Duck, S. W. (1994). *Meaningful relationships: Talking, sense, and relating*. Thousand Oaks, CA: Sage.

Fiese, B. H., & Sameroff, A. J. (1999). The family narrative consortium: A multidimensional approach to narratives. *Monographs for the Society for Research in Child Development, 64*, 1–36.

Fiese, B. H., Sameroff, A. J., Grotevant, H. D., Wamboldt, F. S., Dickstein, S., & Fravel, D. L. (2001). Observing families through the stories they tell: A multidimensional approach. In P. K. Kerig & K. M. Lindahl (Eds.), *Family observational coding systems* (pp. 259–271). Mahwah, NJ: Lawrence Erlbaum Associates.

Fisher, W. R. (1989). *Human communication as narration: Toward a philosophy of reason, value, and action*. Columbia, SC: University of South Carolina Press.

Harber, K. D., & Pennebaker, J. W. (1992). Overcoming traumatic memories. In S. Christianson (Ed.), *The handbook of emotion and memory: Research and theory* (pp. 359–387). Hillsdale, NJ: Lawrence Erlbaum Associates.

Harvey, J. H. (1996). *Embracing their memory: Loss and the social psychology of storytelling*. Needham Heights, MA: Allyn and Bacon.

Kerig, P. K. (2001). Introduction and overview: Conceptual issues in family observational research. In P. K. Kerig & K. M. Lindahl (Eds.), *Family observational coding systems: Resources for systemic research* (pp. 1–22). Mahwah, NJ: Lawrence Erlbaum.

Koenig, J. (2002). *Family ties: Identity, process, and relational qualities in joint family storytelling.* Unpublished doctoral dissertation, University of Washington, Seattle.

Koenig, J., & Trees, A. R. (2000, June). *Finding meaning in difficult family experiences: Sense-making and interaction processes during joint family storytelling.* Paper presented to the International Network on Personal Relationships, Prescott, AZ.

Koenig Kellas, J., & Manusov, V. (2003). What's in a story? The relationship between narrative completeness and adjustment to relationship dissolution. *Journal of Social and Personal Relationships, 20,* 285–307.

Labov, W., & Waletsky, J. (1967). Narrative analysis: Oral versions of personal experience. In J. Helm (Ed.), *Essays on the verbal and visual arts: Proceedings of the 1966 annual spring meeting of the American Ethnological Society* (pp. 12–44). Seattle: University of Washington Press.

Linde, C. (1993). *Life stories: The creation of coherence.* New York: Oxford University Press.

Mandelbaum, J. (1987). Couples sharing stories. *Communication Quarterly, 35,* 144–170.

Mandelbaum, J. (1989). Interpersonal activities in conversational storytelling. *Western Journal of Speech Communication, 53,* 114–126.

Miller, P. J., Mintz, J., Hoogstra, L., Fung, H., & Potts, R. (1992). The narrated self: Young children's construction of self in relation to others in conversational stories of personal experience. *Merill-Palmer Quarterly, 38,* 45–65.

Neimeyer, R. A., & Levitt, H. M. (2000). What's narrative got to do with it? Construction and coherence in accounts of loss. In J. H. Harvey & E. D. Miller (Eds.), *Loss and trauma: General and close relationship perspectives* (pp. 401–412). Philadelphia: Brunner-Routledge.

Norrick, N. R. (1997). Twice-told tales: Collaborative narration of familiar stories. *Language in Society, 26,* 199–220.

Olson, D. H. (2000). Circumplex model of marital and family systems. *Journal of Family Therapy, 22,* 144–167.

Sherman, M. H., (1990). Family narratives: Internal representations of family relationships and affective themes. *Infant Mental Health Journal, 11,* 253–258.

Stone, E. (1988). *Black sheep and kissing cousins: How our family stories shape us.* New York: Times Books.

Trees, A. R., & Koenig, J. (2003, February). *Telling tales: Enacting family relationships in joint storytelling about difficult family experiences.* Paper presented at the Western States Communication Association Convention, Salt Lake City, UT.

Vangelisti, A. L. (1992). Older adolescents' perceptions of communication problems with their parents. *Journal of Adolescent Research, 7,* 382–402.

Veroff, J., Sutherland, L., Chadiha, L., & Ortega, R. M. (1993a). Newlyweds tell their stories: A narrative method for assessing marital experiences. *Journal of Social and Personal Relationships, 10,* 437–457.

Veroff, J., Sutherland, L., Chadiha, L., & Ortega, R. M. (1993b). Newlyweds tell their stories: Predicting marital quality from narrative assessments. *Journal of Marriage and the Family, 55,* 317–329.

Veroff, J., Chadiha, L., Leber, D., & Sutherland, L. (1993). Affects and interactions in newlyweds' narratives: Black and white couples compared. *Journal of Narrative and Life History, 3,* 361–390.

APPENDIX

Interactional Sense-making Ratings

ENGAGEMENT

Involvement

    Uninvolved   1 2 3 4 5   Involved

5: All three family members are both verbally and nonverbally engaged in the telling of the story. Each person shows interest in both telling and listening to the story. Family members are consistently animated, interested, and engaged verbally and nonverbally and are involved throughout the telling.

4: All family members are animated and engaged for most of the telling, with infrequent occurrences of family members "tuning out" at certain points in the story. Or, two members are highly involved throughout and one member is involved through part of the story and not involved at other times.

3: There is either a balance between involvement and uninvolvement or moderate involvement throughout. Family members are at times verbally and nonverbally engaged in the telling and at times seem to "tune out" from involvement in telling or listening. Or, one member is highly involved in the telling and listening of the story and the other two members are sometimes involved and sometimes uninvolved. Alternatively, family members may be moderately involved, somewhat lively but not highly animated.

2: Family members are less animated and interested in the telling. They less frequently engage in involvement behaviors while telling or listening to the story. One family member might be involved, but others appear uninterested or two people are moderately involved and one is quite uninvolved in the story telling.

1: Family members do not seem interested in telling the story (e.g., seem bored and uninvolved) or in listening to other members (e.g., no eye contact or back-channeling). There is little to no liveliness; telling the story seems like a chore.

Warmth

    Cold   1 2 3 4 5   Warm

5: Family interaction is characterized by warm interaction including laughter, smiles, verbal attentiveness and encouragement and affection both verbally and nonverbally.

4: The family interaction is mostly warm with some instances of family members disassociating themselves from the interaction and/or the story is often, but not always characterized by warmth and affection. If they in conflict, they do so with positive nonverbal cues.

3: The storytelling interaction is balanced between warm attentiveness and distance or is neither warm nor cold, but relatively neutral.

2: Family members are more distant than they are warm. There may be one or two instances of laughter, attentiveness, or affection, but, in general, the family is distant and does not express warm attentiveness. Expressions of negative affect are also possible.

1: Family members appear distant and cold. There is very little or no warmth and affection. Family members do not appear associated with one another. May express negativity and engage in negatively valenced conflict.

TURN-TAKING

Dynamic

Structured   1 2 3 4 5   Fluid

5: Family members interact in a fluid, dynamic, and free manner. The interaction is marked by interruptions, overlaps, and energy. Little attention is paid to structured/polite turn-taking. Family members add without asking.

4: The interaction is fluid and flowing, but somewhat more reserved. Family members may still interrupt and build off one another freely, but they ask more frequently (e.g., "I just have to add something here").

3: Family members occasionally interrupt each other and build dynamically upon each other's comments, but they tend to also listen politely and wait their turn to talk. Or part of the story may be one family member telling the story and then the other half is marked by interruptions, overlaps, and energy.

2: Family members rarely jump in to add to another's comments. Aside from a few additions or interruptions, family members wait their turn to talk.

1: Turn-taking is extremely structured. The telling is characterized by one person talking/telling their version of the story, followed by the next person, followed by the next person. Each person has a turn and they rarely deviate from that format.

Distribution of Turns

Uneven Distribution   1 2 3 4 5   Even Distribution
    of Turns   of Turns

5: Each family member contributes equally to the telling of the story. There is an even distribution of who gets to talk; how many turns each person takes.

4: The telling is fairly evenly distributed across the family. One or two family members may dominate the telling, but the other(s) contributes a fair/almost equal amount.

3: Every family member gets a turn, but there is a sense that one or two family members take more turns than others. There is some uneven distribution.

2: At least one or two family members have more room to tell the story than others. Turns are more unevenly than they are evenly distributed.

1: One person dominates the telling of the story, with the others' taking very few to no turns.

PERSPECTIVE-TAKING

Attentiveness to Others' Perspectives

Ignored   1   2   3   4   5   Integrated

5: During the telling of the story, family members demonstrate an understanding that others may have a different perspective, listen to others' views, and incorporate others' perspectives into the telling (e.g., acknowledge others' comment and make it part of their subsequent comments).

4: Family members sometimes acknowledge each other's perspectives and include them in their subsequent comments and/or one or two family members are particularly attentive to others' perspectives throughout the storytelling.

3: Family members sometimes acknowledge each other's perspectives and sometimes ignore them (e.g., do not acknowledge the other person had a different experience/something to add and do not incorporate this perspective into their subsequent comments). There is a balance in perspective taking. It may be that one person consistently acknowledges others' perspectives, but the other two family members do so minimally. Family members acknowledge others' perspectives, but do not integrate them into their own comments.

2: Family members rarely take each other's perspectives into account. Family members may occasionally verbally or nonverbally acknowledge the other person(s)' comments, but generally do not integrate these comments into their own and do not explicitly seek out others' perspectives. May be that two family members engage in moderate perspective-taking behavior and one ignores others' perspectives.

1: Family members seem to ignore the perspectives of others in the family. There is a sense that the stories are separate and distinct for each family member and members only recognize their own experience of the story.

Confirmation of Perspectives

Disconfirming   1   2   3   4   5   Confirming

5: Others' perspectives are always or almost always acknowledged and confirmed (e.g., "Oh that's a good point;" "Yes, I can see where you would feel that way"; nodding, smiling at another's perspective.)

4: Family members confirm each other's perspectives some of the time and do not engage in any disconfirming behaviors.

3: Family members sometimes confirm and sometimes disconfirm (e.g., "that's not what happened;" "no, you're wrong, I was there") each other's perspectives or they are neither particularly confirming nor particularly disconfirming, but relatively neutral.

2: Family members tend to disagree with each other's tellings more than agree. There is more of a disconfirming tone in response to others' contributions than confirming comments. More disagreement.

1: Family members consistently disconfirm each other's experience of the story. They continually disagree with the other person(s)' comments. Disagreements are frequently and potentially negative.

COHERENCE

Organization

Disorganized   1 2 3 4 5   Organized

5: Very Well-Organized: The story follows a logical sequence throughout with a clear beginning, middle and end. Very little to no backing up and jumping around.

4: Relatively Well-Organized: The story has an overall structure that generally gets followed with only some places where the telling gets messy and disorganized.

3: Moderately between the two: Parts of the story are well organized and parts are quite disorganized or it is moderately organized throughout with a moderately discernable underlying structure guiding plot development.

2: Relatively Disorganized: Much of the story does not follow a logical sequential development of the plot very well but there is some minimal discernable underlying structure.

1: Very Disorganized: The story doesn't have a discernable overall structure and lacks sequential development.

Integration

Parallel   1 2 3 4 5   Collaborative

5: Family members consistently add on to each other's comments to build the story. There is one overall story being told and the various contributions "hang together"; A high degree of "jointness" to the story.

4: Family members often build on each other's comments, integrating their stories, although occasionally one or two members tell portions of the story without much collaboration from other members. Generally, with some exceptions, the parts of the overall story being told fit together.

3: Family members balance between adding to each other's stories and telling more separate individual versions. Family members sometimes collaborate and sometimes provide parallel comments. Overall, moderately coherent story with parts that fit together well and other parts that don't.

2: Family members generally tell separate versions of the story, with rare additions from other members. Family members occasionally add onto one anothers' comments, but it is rare.

1: Family members tell parallel stories, with little to no integration. They seem to be separate stories that don't hang together well at all.

Measuring Conversational Equality at the Relational Level

Leanne K. Knobloch
University of Illinois

Denise Haunani Solomon
The Pennsylvania State University

INTRODUCTION

Achieving equality between partners is often a formidable task for participants in close relationships: It requires them to wield equal status, attend to each other equivalently, accommodate each other at similar levels, and seek the well-being of both partners (Knudson-Martin & Mahoney, 1996). Maintaining equality also involves ongoing negotiation and compromise between individuals (Rosenbluth, Steil, & Whitcomb, 1998; Steil, 1997). Despite the effort involved in obtaining and maintaining equality, the benefits appear to be substantial. Indeed, equality corresponds with greater relationship satisfaction (Medvene, Teal, & Slavich, 2000; Sprecher & Schwartz, 1994) and better mental health for both partners (Steil, 1997). Given the benefits that equality may provide, it is not surprising that participants in close relationships generally embrace the ideal of achieving equality between partners (Harris, 1997; Knudson-Martin & Mahoney, 1998; Rosenbluth et al., 1998).[18]

Whereas most scholarship on equality within close relationships emphasizes its psychological and sociological qualities (for reviews, see Sprecher & Schwartz, 1994; Steil, 1997), we believe that the conversational component of equality is also important to understand (see also Burgoon & Hale, 1984; Wish, Deutsch, & Kaplan, 1976). Conversation not only offers a venue for people to reveal, negotiate,

---

[18]The ideal of achieving equality between partners may be most prominent in Western cultures that emphasize individualism. Equality between partners may be less relevant to societies that accentuate collectivist patterns of social relations (e.g., Hoppe, Snell, & Cocroft, 1996).

and reinforce equality between them (Burgoon & Hale, 1984; Rogers & Millar, 1988), but it also represents a channel through which psychological and sociological aspects of equality influence how individuals relate to one another (e.g., Knudson-Martin & Mahoney, 1998). For these reasons, we see merit in understanding communicative manifestations of equality, which we refer to as *conversational equality*. Our twin goals in this chapter are to explicate conversational equality and to describe an observational rating scheme we created to operationalize it.

EXPLICATING CONVERSATIONAL EQUALITY

Whereas equality, in general, refers to the degree to which partners receive similar resources within a relationship (e.g., Cate, Lloyd, & Henton, 1985; Martin, 1986; Steil, 1997), we define *conversational* equality as those messages that display equivalent amounts of influence, authority, and control between partners. Messages conveying unequal status suggest that one person possesses the capacity to dictate activity within the relationship (Rogers & Millar, 1988). Conversely, messages communicating equal status imply that individuals wield equivalent degrees of control within the dyad (Burgoon & Hale, 1984).

Like all kinds of messages, conversational equality can be manifest on two different levels within an interpersonal exchange (e.g., Bateson, 1972; Watzlawick, Beavin, & Jackson, 1967). Conversational equality is negotiated on a content level when it constitutes the denotative referent of the conversation (e.g., when interactants talk specifically about equality within their relationship). In contrast, conversational equality is conveyed on a relational level when utterances signal information about the nature of the relationship between communicators (e.g., when interactants communicate about a different topic but their exchange provides insight into the equality within their relationship). Those subtle and ubiquitous relational level messages exert a powerful effect on interaction (e.g., Burgoon & Hale, 1984; Dillard, Solomon, & Samp, 1996), particularly because they provide an ongoing venue for negotiating status (Rogers & Millar, 1988). Hence, like other scholars before us (Burgoon & Hale, 1984, 1987; Martin, 1986), we focus our attention on conceptualizing and operationalizing conversational equality at the relational level of messages.

Conversational equality, considered as an aspect of relational messages, transpires through a diverse array of behaviors within interaction. For example, it is evident when partners engage in approximately equal amounts of giving and taking instructions, offering and receiving evaluative comments, asserting opinions, changing topics, and interrupting (e.g., Palmer, 1989; Rogers & Farace, 1975; Sluzki & Beavin, 1965). Conversational equality also arises when partners assert similar levels of status through nonverbal cues such as eye contact, voice inflection, body proximity, and touch (e.g., Burgoon, 1991; Burgoon, Buller, Hale, & deTurck, 1984; Tusing & Dillard, 2000). Thus, conversational equality is not encapsulated in a limited number of communication behaviors. Rather, it is negotiated mutually across the whole spectrum of cues that comprise interaction (Sluzki & Beavin, 1965; Watzlawick et al., 1967) and emerges from the combined behavior of both partners (Millar & Rogers, 1976). It entails a comparison between partners' behaviors rather than judgments about the absolute amounts of status displayed by interactants. Accordingly, conversational equality is not a feature of speaking turns enacted by individuals. Instead, it is defined by partners' negotiation of status within conversation (Millar & Rogers, 1976; Rogers & Farace, 1975).

At first glance, conversational equality appears to closely resemble the relational message theme of dominance–submissiveness (Burgoon & Hale, 1987; Walther & Burgoon, 1992; see also Dillard & Solomon, this volume; Hall, this volume), but we posit that conversational equality is not merely the absence of dominance. Messages conveying dominance reveal the distribution of control between partners (Burgoon & Dunbar, 2000; Burgoon, Johnson, & Koch, 1998; Dunbar & Burgoon, this volume; Millar & Rogers, 1976; Walther & Burgoon, 1992). The cooperation, mutual respect, and coordination implied by conversational equality, however, appear to evoke judgments of affiliation rather than dominance (Burgoon & Hale, 1987; Dillard, Solomon, & Palmer, 1999; Walther & Burgoon, 1992). Consistent with this logic, several empirical examinations of relational messages have recovered separate factors representing equality and dominance (Dillard et al., 1999; Kelley & Burgoon, 1991; Walther & Burgoon, 1992).

Thus far, we have argued that conversational equality is pervasive at the relational level of messages, is conveyed by a host of behaviors, is a component of conversation between partners, and is distinct from the relational message theme of dominance. This conceptual explication lays the foundation for our efforts to develop a measure of conversational equality that is tailored specifically to the nuances of interaction. In the following section, we describe an empirical investigation designed to operationalize conversational equality in a manner consistent with our theoretical assumptions.

MEASURING CONVERSATIONAL EQUALITY

Guided by our conceptual explication of conversational equality, we conducted an empirical study to address two goals. Our primary objective was to create a reliable and valid measure of conversational equality that focuses on the relational level of messages, attends to the broad range of behaviors (including nonverbal cues) that signal equality, employs the conversation as the unit of analysis, and emphasizes equality rather than the absence of dominance. Our secondary objective, which stemmed from our desire to understand how people experience conversational equality within close relationships, was to evaluate the association between conversational equality and emotion. At the outset of this chapter, we noted that equality tends to correspond with heightened relationship satisfaction (Medvene et al., 2000; Sprecher & Schwartz, 1994), and people typically champion equality as the ideal way of regulating power, control, and authority within close relationships (Knudson-Martin & Mahoney, 1998; Rosenbluth et al., 1998). Conversations signaling equality, then, should be a pleasurable experience for participants in intimate associations. Based on this logic, we expect that conversational equality should correspond with diminished feelings of negatively valenced emotions like anger, sadness, fear, and jealousy within close relationships. Conversely, we anticipate that conversational equality should coincide with heightened feelings of positively valenced emotions such as happiness within intimate associations.

Sample and Procedures

Although conversational equality is relevant to interaction within all relationship contexts (e.g., Dillard et al., 1996), we examined interaction within courtship in this first study because equality furnishes considerable consequences for romantic relationships (Medvene et al., 2000). The sample, recruited from a college student population, contained 120 heterosexual couples in which at least one individual indicated romantic interest in his or her partner (see Knobloch & Solomon, 2003a, for a complete description of the study's method, sample, and procedures). Participants reported being romantically interested in their partner for an average of 11 months (*range* = 1 week to 6 years, *SD* = 12.29 months, *median* = 7 months).

Data collection ensued in four phases. First, partners individually completed questionnaire items measuring perceptions of their relationship. Then, couples engaged in a 5-minute warm-up conversation about an informal topic (see Table 22); this warm-up conversation served as an introduction to the microphone and videotape procedures. Next, partners were randomly assigned to one of three conversation topics for the main interaction and engaged in a 10-minute videotaped conversation on their topic. Finally, participants individually completed self-report measures of the emotions they experienced during the main conversation.

Measures

Emotions. We measured participants' experience of various emotions using an operationalization developed in previous research (Dillard, Kinney, & Cruz, 1996; Knobloch & Solomon, 2003b). Participants indicated how much they felt particular emotions during the interaction (1 = not at all, 6 = a lot). We used confirmatory factor analysis to identify unidimensional sets of items; then, we averaged responses to the individual items to create composite scales. *Anger* contained four descriptors: (a) angry, (b) mad, (c) frustrated, and (d) irritated (*M* = 1.76, *SD* = 1.15, α = .89); *sadness* included three items: (a) sad, (b) gloomy, and (c) depressed (*M* = 1.61, *SD* = 1.09, α = .88); *fear* was comprised of three items: (a) afraid, (b) scared, and (c) frightened (*M* = 1.49, *SD* = 1.05, α = .92); *jealousy* incorporated three items: (a) jealous, (b) insecure,

TABLE 22

Conversation Topics

Informal Talk

At this time, we would like you and your partner to have an informal conversation about anything you like. You might spend this time gossiping, joking around, catching up, recapping the day's events, or getting to know each other better. Your goal is simply to have an informal conversation.

Positive Talk

We would like you and your partner to have a conversation that is positive in tone. You may focus on any relatively unimportant topic that you like. You may want to reminisce about a shared activity, make up after a disagreement, express affection, or talk about the nature of your relationship. Your goal is to discuss a pleasant topic of conversation.

Negative Talk

We would like you and your partner to have a conversation that addresses a negative topic. You might want to spend this time talking about an area of conflict, engaging in an in-depth conversation about a serious issue, talking about a problem, breaking bad news, or complaining. Your goal is simply to engage in conversation about some negative issue.

Surprising Event Talk

At this time, we would like you and your partner to talk about a recent and unexpected event that caused you to be more or less certain about some aspect of your relationship. You may want to talk about a surprising event that caused you to be more sure about the nature of your relationship. Perhaps you want to talk about an unexpected behavior that made you question some aspect of your relationship. The recent event that you discuss may be either positive or negative in nature, but it should have changed the level of certainty you had about your relationship.

Note. Conversation topics were selected in a pretest to the study (see Knobloch & Solomon, 2003a, for details).

and (c) threatened ($M = 1.50$, $SD = 0.90$, $\alpha = .77$); and *happiness* contained three items: (a) happy, (b) excited, and (c) glad ($M = 3.87$, $SD = 1.33$, $\alpha = .84$).

Conversational Equality. To measure this construct at the relational level of messages, we trained three independent judges to rate conversational equality within each 1-minute interval of interaction (the appendix contains the rating manual for the judgment). Judges used a 5-point Likert scale (1 = disagree strongly, 5 = agree strongly) to indicate their response to the following item: "Participants had equal status within this interval." Judges first attended a training session in which they rated sample intervals excerpted from the warm-up conversations. Next, judges independently rated a set of 15 conversations, met to recalibrate their decision rules, and repeated the process by rating another set of 15 conversations. Because judges were unable to achieve an acceptable level of reliability within the first 30 conversations they evaluated, we replaced the 5-point rating scale with a 3-point rating scale (1 = disagree strongly, 3 = agree strongly).

Despite completing substantial training and adopting the 3-point rating scale, judges earned an *alpha* reliability level of only .65 during their first pass through the data. When we computed a reliability score for each conversation individually, we discovered that most of the 40 conversations (33% of the sample) with the greatest variance in ratings had been rated very early in the cycle. Thus, we implemented a second round of rating to resolve discrepancies in the scores for those conversations. Reliability levels from the second wave of rating indicated that judges achieved less variance in their judgments for 90% of the rerated conversations. Hence, we employed judges' revised ratings as a basis for computing conversational equality. We calculated a single score for each conversation by averaging judges' ratings across the 10 time intervals ($M = 2.52$, $SD = 0.31$, revised $\alpha = .72$).

Results

We conducted a set of hierarchical regression analyses to evaluate our expectation that conversational equality would be negatively associated with people's experience of negatively valenced emotions, but would be positively associated with their experience of positively valenced emotions. To address the statistical dependence present in our data set because both partners reported the emotions they felt (e.g., Kenny & Cook, 1999), we examined the couple as the unit of analysis ($N = 120$ couples). We first regressed couples' averaged emotion score onto two variables that were dummy-coded to represent the three conversation topics; this step covaried the variance due to conversation assignment. Then, on the second step, we entered the conversational equality score for the couples' interaction.

Results of these tests, which are included in Table 23, were consistent with our predictions. In particular, conversational equality was negatively associated with anger, sadness, fear, and jealousy over and above the variance due to conversation topic. Conversely, conversational equality was positively associated with happiness after conversation topic was covaried.[19]

---

[19]We also evaluated the extent to which the associations between conversational equality and the emotions varied as a function of conversation topic. Specifically, on the third step of the regression analyses, we included two interaction terms computed as the product of conversational equality and each of the dummy codes representing conversation topic. Findings indicated that the set of interaction terms explained a statistically significant portion of additional variance in both anger and sadness. The nature of this effect was similar for both dependent variables: Conversational equality was unrelated to anger and sadness for positive talk (anger $B = .28$, ns; sadness $B = -.10$, ns), but it was negatively associated with anger and sadness for negative talk (anger $B = -1.03$, $p < .05$; sadness $B = -1.95$, $p < .05$) and surprising event talk (anger $B = -1.42$, $p < .01$; sadness $B = -1.10$, $p < .05$). We interpret these results as preliminary evidence that the link between conversational equality and negatively valenced emotion may depend on the topic of people's conversation.

TABLE 23
The Regression of Emotions Onto Conversational Equality

	Anger	Sadness	Fear	Jealousy	Happiness
R^2 Δ Set of Covariates	.10 **	.09 **	.04	.03	.11**
Dummy Code 1 β	−.25*	−.24*	−.21	−.18	.25*
Dummy Code 2 β	.10	.09	.00	−.02	−.13
R^2 Δ Equality	.05*	.11***	.06**	.05*	.06**
Equality β	−.23*	−.35***	−.26**	−.23*	.26**

Note. $N = 120$. Dummy Code 1 was coded such that positive talk = 1, negative talk = 0, and surprising event talk = 0. Dummy Code 2 was coded such that positive talk = 0, negative talk = 1, and surprising event talk = 0. * $p < .05$; ** $p < .01$; *** $p < .001$.

We find these results notable for two reasons. First, our findings offer initial evidence in favor of the construct validity of our measure of conversational equality. Second, our results support the idea that conversational equality contributes to the emotions people experience in interaction with close relationship partners.

RECOMMENDATIONS FOR USE OF THE MEASURE AND DIRECTIONS FOR FUTURE RESEARCH

The lessons we learned from our study suggest both insights about how to use our measure and ideas for subsequent research. A first recommendation for using our measure originates from the relatively low level of reliability we achieved in this first study. To address that problem, we suggest scholars employ a larger number of judges to rate interactions. Conversational equality is a difficult construct to evaluate because it can stem from so many different cues, and the three judges we utilized were only enough to achieve a marginal degree of reliability. Thus, we encourage scholars to incorporate a generous number of judges within the rating task.

A second suggestion for employing our measure concerns the metric of the scale used to rate conversational equality. Difficulty in evaluating equality on a 5-point rating scale is not unique to this study; for example, Martin (1986) also substituted a 3-point rating scale for a 5-point rating scale when her judges were examining equality within written narratives that described a close relationship. On one hand, the similarity of the problem that emerged in both studies suggests to us that conversational equality may not be conceptually distinguishable at the level of detail required by a 5-point rating scale. On the other hand, we are unwilling to conclude definitely on the basis of two studies that the construct does not exist in five degrees of specificity. We appreciate the increased opportunity for variation that corresponds with a 5-point rating scale rather than a 3-point rating scale; thus, we recommend that researchers begin the rating process using a 5-point rating scale in an effort to obtain both adequate reliability and maximum variability. If the team of judges is not able to achieve satisfactory reliability, then we advocate adopting the 3-point rating scale as a reasonable next strategy. Once a corpus of studies has operationalized conversational equality, we will be better equipped to determine if the construct can be discriminated at more than three levels.

A complementary strategy for generating more precise evaluations of conversational equality is to elaborate our operationalization. Although we devoted our initial effort to developing a global judgment, we are well aware that a variety of behaviors give rise to conversational equality (cf. Burgoon, 1991; Palmer, 1989; Rogers & Farace, 1975). Accordingly, a next step is to craft a variegated measure containing judgments of specific behaviors. For example, such a measure might evaluate if people's messages display equivalent degrees of (a) control over the course of the conversation, (b) attention to topics broached by both interactants, (c) respect for each other's speaking turns, (d) sensitivity to the opinions of both interactants (see Trees, this volume), and/or (e) involvement in the conversation (see Guerrero, this volume). We are confident that a detailed measure would prove useful for addressing questions about nuanced facets of conversational equality.

CONCLUSION

Recognizing that recent scholarship on equality has tended to neglect its communicative aspects, we proposed a conceptualization of conversational equality grounded in the nuances of interaction. In particular, we defined conversational equality as those messages that display equivalent amounts of control between partners. Our explication characterized conversational equality as a theme of relational messages, as a product of a number of cues within interaction, as an element of conversation rather than of individual speaking turns, and as divergent from the absence of dominance. We then described an observational rating scheme we developed in a study of conversations between couples within romantic relationships. We are optimistic that both our conceptualization and our measure will prove useful to scholars who seek to understand the antecedents and consequences of conversational equality within interaction.

REFERENCES

Bateson, G. (1972). *Steps to an ecology of mind.* New York: Ballantine.

Burgoon, J. K. (1991). Relational message interpretations of touch, conversational distance, and posture. *Journal of Nonverbal Behavior, 15,* 233–259.

Burgoon, J. K., Buller, D. B., Hale, J. L., & deTurck, M. A. (1984). Relational messages associated with nonverbal behaviors. *Human Communication Research, 10,* 351–378.

Burgoon, J. K., & Dunbar, N. E. (2000). An interactionist perspective on dominance–submission: Interpersonal dominance as a dynamic, situationally contingent skill. *Communication Monographs, 67,* 96–121.

Burgoon, J. K., & Hale, J. L. (1984). The fundamental topoi of relational communication. *Communication Monographs, 51,* 193–214.

Burgoon, J. K., & Hale, J. L. (1987). Validation and measurement of the fundamental themes of relational communication. *Communication Monographs, 54,* 19–41.

Burgoon, J. K., Johnson, M. L., & Koch, P. T. (1998). The nature and measurement of interpersonal dominance. *Communication Monographs, 65,* 308–335.

Cate, R., Lloyd, S., & Henton, J. (1985). The effect of equity, equality, and reward level on the stability of students' premarital relationships. *Journal of Social Psychology, 125,* 715–721.

Dillard, J. P., Kinney, T. A., & Cruz, M. G. (1996). Influence, appraisals, and emotions in close relationships. *Communication Monographs, 63,* 105–130.

Dillard, J. P., Solomon, D. H., & Palmer, M. T. (1999). Structuring the concept of relational communication. *Communication Monographs, 66,* 49–65.

Dillard, J. P., Solomon, D. H., & Samp, J. A. (1996). Framing social reality: The relevance of relational judgments. *Communication Research, 23,* 703–723.

Harris, S. R. (1997). Status inequality and close relationships: An integrative typology of bond-saving strategies. *Symbolic Interaction, 20,* 1–20.

Hoppe, A. K., Snell, L., & Cocroft, B. (1996). Elementary structures of social interaction. In W. B. Gudykunst & S. Ting-Toomey (Eds.), *Communication in personal relationships across cultures* (pp. 57–78). Thousand Oaks, CA: Sage.

Kelley, D., & Burgoon, J. K. (1991). Understanding marital satisfaction and couple types as functions of relational expectations. *Human Communication Research, 18,* 40–69.

Kenny, D. A., & Cook, W. (1999). Partner effects in relationship research: Conceptual issues, analytic difficulties, and illustrations. *Personal Relationships, 6,* 433–448.

Knobloch, L. K., & Solomon, D. H. (2003a). Manifestations of relationship conceptualizations in conversation. *Human Communication Research, 29,* 482–515.

Knobloch, L. K., & Solomon, D. H. (2003b). Responses to changes in relational uncertainty in dating relationships: Emotions and communication strategies. *Communication Studies, 54,* 282–305.

Knudson-Martin, C., & Mahoney, A. R. (1996). Gender dilemma and myth in the construction of marital bargains: Issue for marital therapy. *Family Process, 35,* 137–153.

Knudson-Martin, C., & Mahoney, A. R. (1998). Language and processes in the construction of equality in new marriages. *Family Relations, 47,* 81–91.

Martin, J. N. (1986). Patterns of communication in three types of re-entry relationships: An exploratory study. *Western Journal of Speech Communication, 50,* 183–199.

Medvene, L. J., Teal, C. R., & Slavich, S. (2000). Including the other in the self: Implications for judgments of equity and satisfaction in close relationships. *Journal of Social and Clinical Psychology, 19,* 396–419.

Millar, F. E., & Rogers, L. E. (1976). A relational approach to interpersonal communication. In G. R. Miller (Ed.), *Explorations in interpersonal communication* (pp. 87–103). Beverly Hills, CA: Sage.

Palmer, M. T. (1989). Controlling conversations: Turns, topics and interpersonal control. *Communication Monographs, 56,* 1–18.

Rogers, L. E., & Farace, R. V. (1975). Analysis of relational communication in dyads: New measurement procedures. *Human Communication Research, 1,* 222–239.

Rogers, L. E., & Millar, F. E. (1988). Relational communication. In S. Duck (Ed.), *Handbook of personal relationships* (pp. 289–306). New York: Wiley.

Rosenbluth, S. C., Steil, J. M., & Whitcomb, J. H. (1998). Marital equality: What does it mean? *Journal of Family Issues, 19,* 227–244.

Sluzki, C. E., & Beavin, J. (1965). Symmetry and complementarity: An operational definition and typology of dyads. *Acta Psiquiatrica y Psicologica de America Latina, 11,* 321–330.

Sprecher, S., & Schwartz, P. (1994). Equity and balance in the exchange of contributions in close relationships. In M J. Lerner & G. Mikula (Eds.), *Entitlement and the affectional bond: Justice in close relationships* (pp. 11–41). New York: Plenum.

Steil, J. M. (1997). *Marital equality: Its relationship to the well-being of husbands and wives.* Thousand Oaks, CA: Sage.

Tusing, K. J., & Dillard, J. P. (2000). The sounds of dominance: Vocal precursors of perceived dominance during interpersonal influence. *Human Communication Research, 26,* 148–171.

Walther, J. B., & Burgoon, J. J. (1992). Relational communication in computer-mediated interaction. *Human Communication Research, 19,* 50–88.

Watzlawick, P., Beavin, J. H., & Jackson, D. D. (1967). *Pragmatics of human communication.* New York: Norton.
Wish, M., Deutsch, M., & Kaplan, S. (1976). Perceived dimensions of interpersonal relations. *Journal of Personality and Social Psychology, 33,* 409–420.

ACKNOWLEDGMENTS

The authors are grateful to Carolynne Bernard, Katy Carpenter-Theune, Patricia Costello, Amanda Dobervich, Stephanie Lundberg, Yoonsoo Nam, Jamie Olson, Annie Richert, and Sarah Wang for their assistance with library research, data collection, and coding.

APPENDIX

Conversational Equality

(Begin each rating session by reviewing the information presented in this handout.)

Your goal in this task is to rate the degree of *conversational equality* between partners. Please follow these directions to code effectively.

- Code during times when you know you will be able to view the videotapes without distractions. Be prepared to concentrate on the rating task. This task is very complex, and you will be able to do your best when you are not interrupted.
- Make sure you have the following materials on hand: videotapes of the conversation, copies of the rating sheets, and this rating manual.
- Begin by recording the dyad's identification number on the rating sheet.
- This task requires a judgment for each 1-minute time interval. So, you should watch the conversation and make an evaluation for *each* 1-minute interval during the conversation.

Record a score for the degree to which participants speak in ways that show equal degrees of status, power, and control between them.

The rating is about the extent to which partners communicate in ways that convey an equivalent distribution of power within the relationship. The rating requires you to make a decision about the degree to which people's communication patterns show similar levels of status, control, and influence. In short, you should consider the level of equality within the conversation.

PLEASE NOTE: This judgment is more concerned with people's speaking behavior at the moment rather than what the content of their talk says about their relationship. Do your best to consider the negotiation of status within the speaking patterns rather than the history of the relationship that may be conveyed in the conversation.

Use a rating of "5" for intervals that display equal status between partners.

These conversations show equal amounts of control between participants. Participants in these intervals relate to each other as peers, collaborators, and colleagues. Their conversation behaviors show a "level playing field"—for example, partners may give and/or receive advice, evaluation, and direction equally within conversation. They may share the responsibility of choosing topics, distribute "talk time" equally, interrupt at the same rate, and show equality in joking, teasing, and telling stories.

Nonverbally, these conversations show balanced degrees of control, influence, and power between participants. These intervals are marked by equivalent degrees of dominance granted and received by participants' eye contact, tone of voice, volume and rate of speaking, body language, gestures, and posture.

Use this rating if participants have similar amounts of control within the interval.

Use a rating of "1" for intervals that contain unbalanced degrees of status between partners.

These conversations show mismatched levels of power and influence between partners. These intervals are marked by one partner behaving aggressively, and the other partner behaving passively or obediently. These conversations involve one partner being clearly more "in control" than the other. For example, these intervals may depict one partner providing feedback, orders, and assertions more frequently than the other. One partner may receive more power to choose topics, interrupt, joke, tease, tell stories, and talk for longer periods of time. In short, these intervals convey that participants don't "call the shots" equally within the interaction.

Nonverbally, these intervals show mismatched degrees of control, influence, and power between partners. For example, their nonverbal cues such as eye contact, tone of voice, volume and rate of speaking, body language, gestures, and posture may suggest inequality between them.

Use this rating if participants have an unequal distribution of power within the interval.

CONVERSATIONAL EQUALITY

Dyad's Identification Number _____

Conversation Topic _____

"Participants had equal status within this interval"

1	2	3	4	5
Strongly Disagree	Somewhat Disagree	Neither Agree Nor Disagree	Somewhat Agree	Strongly Agree

TIME INTERVAL	CONVERSATIONAL EQUALITY JUDGMENT
0:00 to 0:59	
1:00 to 1:59	
2:00 to 2:59	
3:00 to 3:59	
4:00 to 4:59	
5:00 to 5:59	
6:00 to 6:59	
7:00 to 7:59	
8:00 to 8:59	
9:00 to 10:00	
_____ number of seconds beyond 10:00	

Measures of Judged Adaptation

Joseph N. Cappella
University of Pennsylvania

INTRODUCTION

A substantial body of research indicates that social interactions involving adults, children, and even infants are marked by processes of adaptation of automatic and deliberate, often nonverbal, behaviors (Cappella, 1981, 1991, 1994, see chapter on adaptation, this volume). Adaptation is the process of interactants adjusting to and/or mutually influencing one another (Burgoon, Stern, & Dillman, 1995). There are a variety of forms that adaptation may take including synchrony, matching, and entrainment (see Bernieri, this volume), and the varied processes are linked with a number of important outcomes (e.g., Bernieri, 1988; Chartrand & Bargh, 1999; Street, 1982; Tickle-Degnen & Rosenthal, 1987; Welkowitz & Kuc, 1973). Measuring adaptation is, therefore, an important research tool, and this chapter discusses one useful way to assess it: the use of judgment scales.

ADAPTATION PROCESSES AND OUTCOMES

In adult interactions, mutual adaptation has been observed for various nonverbal speech behaviors including speech rate (Street, 1984; Webb, 1972), pauses (Cappella & Planalp, 1981; Feldstein & Welkowitz, 1978), latency to respond (Cappella & Planalp, 1981), vocal intensity (Natale, 1975), fundamental vocal frequency (Buder, 1991), and turn durations (Matarazzo & Wiens, 1972). A range of kinesic behaviors exhibit adaptive patterns as well, including postural and gestural behaviors (LaFrance, 1982; Maurer & Tindall, 1983), movement synchrony (Bernieri, Reznick, & Rosenthal, 1988), gaze (Klienke, Staneski, & Berger, 1975; Noller, 1984), head nods and facial affect (Hale & Burgoon, 1984), facial displays of emotion (Krause, Steimer, Sanger-Alt, & Wagner, 1989), and more generalized hostile affect (Gottman, 1979; Pike & Sillars, 1985). Movement coordination has been observed to occur cross-culturally (Grammer, Honda, Juette, & Schmitt,

309

1999) and in response to staged specific gestures (see Chartrand & Bargh, 1999). Emotional coordination among co-workers and dormitory mates has been reported as well (Bakker & Schaufeli, 2001).

Infants and children, who do not yet have well-developed language capacity, have been found to exhibit adaptation with adult partners in noncontent speech behaviors (Street & Cappella, 1989). Jasnow and Feldstein (1987), for example, noted matching in latency of response for mothers and their 9-month-old infants. Bernieri et al. (1988) observed greater synchrony in body movements between mothers and their 14–18-month-old infants than between mothers and a different infant. Adaptation of the infant to the mother has also been observed even earlier with 3- and 4-month olds (Cohn & Tronick, 1987; Symons & Moran; 1987). Berghout-Austin and Peery (1983) found a statistically reliable movement synchrony between neonates 30–56 hours old and an experimenter.

The ability to coordinate interaction is important in that its effective use is tied to a range of positive outcomes. In particular, higher social evaluations are often associated with certain types of coordination in interaction. Welkowitz and Kuc (1973) found that partners who were rated higher on warmth also exhibited greater similarity on speech latency. Street (1982) constructed audio tapes in which an interviewee's speech rate, latency, and duration converged, partially converged, or diverged with respect to that of an interviewer, finding that the divergent speech was evaluated more negatively. Bernieri (1988, see chapter in this volume) observed that judges' ratings of movement synchrony were positively associated with self-reports of rapport, a conclusion espoused by Tickle-Degnen and Rosenthal (1987) on the basis of their literature review. Even ratings of movement synchrony between infants and their mothers are positively associated with independent ratings of the child's positivity (Bernieri et al., 1988). Gesture matching has also been shown to be associated with rapport in stringent experimental tests (Chartrand & Bargh, 1999). Similar patterns of covariation exist in the interactions between infants and their primary caretakers. Isabella, Belsky, and van Eye (1989), for example, tested the coordination-attachment between mothers and their infants at 1, 3, and 9 months of age. Pairs that were coordinated at ages 1 month and 3 months tended to be securely attached at 1 year. These data are important indications of the potential significance of adaptation to the development of the human organism.

DEVELOPMENT OF A JUDGMENT-BASED MEASURE

The majority of studies on adaptation just reviewed use behavioral observations. Although the measure of behavioral adaptation provides an informative indicator of nonverbal responsiveness in social interaction, it is an expensive measure to obtain and calculate. Bernieri (1988) suggested that untrained raters are capable of producing reliable, aggregate judgments of the degree of behavioral coordination that partners exhibit in social interaction and that these are related to important relational outcomes such as rapport and empathy (see Tickle-Degnen & Rosenthal, 1987, White & Sargent, this volume.).

In response to this, my colleagues and I conducted a series of three studies to assess whether judges' ratings of adaptation were related to behavioral adaptation measures (Cappella, 1997). For these studies, we used several tapes of interactions from our archive: four high and four low in nonverbal adaptation were selected. Two 1-minute segments from each were randomly selected and edited out for showing to subjects. The sixteen 1-minute segments included eight male–male and eight female–female interactions. It is important to keep clear that when a randomly selected segment comes from a high (or low) adaptation interaction, the segment itself may or may not be well coordinated behaviorally. The segments were not chosen to be high or low in adaptation; the *interactions* from which the segments come were.

Participants viewed the 16 segments in two random, but fixed, orders. Three studies were conducted on these 16 segments. In studies 1 and 2, the voices of the participants were audible. The content of what they were saying was not discernible, however, because the voices were filtered through throat microphones that have the effect of cutting off high and low pitch sounds, effectively garbling the content. In study 3, vocal cues were eliminated by turning off the volume. As well, in study 3, not only were vocal cues eliminated, but the facial cues were also reduced. The video channel was altered using the quantized mosaic technique pioneered by Berry (Berry, Kean, Misovich, & Baron, 1991; Berry, Misovich, Kean, & Baron, 1992) and used in coordination studies by Bernieri, Davis, Rosenthal, and Knee (1994). This procedure hides many of the details of facial action but does allow the audience to see movement in the mouth, eye, and brow regions of the face. Cues to specific facial emotions are removed, but facial animation resulting from vocalization and facial activity is visible.

At the end of each 1-minute segment, raters evaluated the segment on questions measuring coordination. In study 1, four measures of judged coordination were used. These were taken from Bernieri et al. (1988) and were posed in the form of nine-point (very strongly agree to very strongly disagree) scales. The statements are listed in Table 24.

TABLE 24
List of Items to Measure Adaption Derived From Bernieri, Reznick, & Rosenthal

The partners engaged in simultaneous movement.

The partners had similar tempos of activity.

The partners' interaction was coordinated and smooth.

The partners matched one another's behaviors.

The internal reliability of the four items was estimated for each of the 16 segments separately. The standardized alphas ranged from .62 to .79 with a mean of .72 and a standard deviation of 0.05. The four items were averaged to create an index labeled *judged coordination.*

In studies 2 and 3, observers rated each of the segments on three aspects of coordination on a nine-point (very strongly agree to very strongly disagree) scale. The rating scales were basically the same as the first three items used in study 1, with the fourth item (i.e., "partners' matched")—a more static measure—dropped. The three items were averaged to create a judged coordination scale comparable to that of study 1.

SUMMARY OF STUDIES' RESULTS

These studies were undertaken to understand how to best measure coordination in human interaction via judgments of naïve raters or through behavioral coding. The findings can be summarized as follows. Judges were reliable, and they were able to distinguish high from low adaptation interactions on the basis of 1-minute slices for male, but not female, dyads. Segments judged to be coordinated had partners smiling in synchrony but with complementary patterns of gazing and gesturing. Both measures correlated with conversational satisfaction, but only behavioral coordination predicted attraction (Cappella, 1996).

CAN UNTRAINED PEOPLE MAKE JUDGMENTS OF COORDINATION?

In all three studies, judges were consistent with one another. The internal reliability of the larger and smaller samples of judges, those with full information and partial information, was quite good. This finding provides additional support for Bernieri's previous work (Bernieri, 1988, this volume; Bernieri, Davis, Rosenthal, & Knee, 1994; Bernieri, Gillis, Davis, & Grahe, 1996; Bernieri, Reznick, & Rosenthal, 1988) and suggests that untrained judges can generate sound measures of the synchrony between partners in brief segments of conversation.

Not only are people able to make these judgments consistently, but the rank ordering of segments on mean judged coordination was also quite consistent from one group to the next. The three studies conducted differed in the kinds of questions used to rate coordination and in the amount of information available to the judges. No voice or cues to facial emotion were available in the third study. Despite these differences, correlations among mean ratings for segments was quite strong.

WHOLES AND SLICES

The eight interactions chosen for study were originally 30 minutes long. They were evaluated as high or low in coordination on a time series index of behavioral activity (including gaze, gesture [2 types], smiles, and vocalization). The index used all 30 minutes of interaction. One very stringent test of the utility of the judged coordination measure, however, is whether judged coordination of segments of an interaction can replace measures of behavioral coordination for the entire interaction. If judged coordination of a segment of interaction is a good predictor of behavioral coordination in the entire interaction, then considerable efficiencies arise.

Our data show that judged coordination of segments of interaction from male–male dyads is associated with the overall behavioral coordination of those dyads. But the same claim cannot be made of female–female dyads. One explanation for the difference between the two is found in the fact that the female segments differed from the male interactions in the level of coordinated smiling. The segments of male–male interactions that were chosen from the high coordination conversations also had elevated levels of coordinated smiling. The correlation between overall coordination score and the level of coordinated smiling of the segment was $r(8) = .61$ for the male dyads. For the female dyads, the correlation was actually negative, $r(8) = -.26$. Some of the high coordination female–female segments actually had low levels of coordinated smiling and vice versa.

In addition, judged coordination averaged across the three studies correlated, $r = .56$, with smile coordination. For female–female dyads, judged coordination was predicted by smile coordination very strongly, $r = .85$; for male–male dyads, the correlation was significant but lower, $r = .36$. Judges were evaluating the partners' coordination (particularly that of females) in terms of whether they smiled in synchrony or not. Thus, judged coordination appears to be dependent on cues associated with mutual smiling. This finding is consistent with previous research that suggests that people appear to be sensitive to this form of behavioral contagion during interaction (Hatfield, Cacioppo, & Rapson, 1994) and are capable of recognizing it and treating it and its absence—even from brief slices of interaction—as evidence of overall coordination.

WHICH BEHAVIORS YIELD JUDGED COORDINATION?

In order to determine just what the bases of judged coordination were in behavioral terms, our analysis moved to the level of the segments. When rating interactions for coordination, judges are looking for signs of simultaneity of affect (e.g., as manifested by simultaneous facial emotion and perhaps more generally by simultaneous facial animation; Cappella, 1996). Judges also seem to use behavioral signs of speaker and hearer role in their ratings of coordination. Specifically, when face-directed gaze or illustrative gestures are complementary, judged coordination is higher. Partners' behaviors are judged to be "meshed" in the sense that neither is trespassing on the conversational space of the partner.

Our data support but extend Bernieri's (1988; Bernieri et al., 1988; Bernieri et al., 1996) findings that judgments of coordination are reliable. Accepted measures of behavioral adaptation covary with judged coordination and, moreover, do so in a way that implies that judged coordination is based on synchronous affect and complementary signs of speaker–hearer role.

OUTCOMES INCLUDING ATTRACTION AND SATISFACTION

Both judged and behavioral coordination also successfully predicted participants' evaluations of one another and their evaluations of the interaction. Although the partners' self-reports were based on full information (including verbal discourse) and on 30 minutes of conversation, the judges' ratings and the behavioral coordination scores were based on single minutes of interaction from the whole. The presence of any correlation between interaction pattern (judged or coded) and outcome is significant testimony to the importance of coordination to attraction and conversational satisfaction.

Synchronous smiling was implicated as a key predictor. The stronger the synchronous smiling, the more positive are partners' attitudes toward one another. A similar result holds for satisfaction with the quality of the conversation. Not only do judges of interactions rely on mutual smiling, but participants in the interactions themselves may as well. The direction of causality is not clear, however. Positive attitudes about the partner and the conversation may produce more coordinated smiling.

CONCLUSION

The data from the studies reported in this chapter hold out real hope that coordination in social interaction can be studied using judgment methods and slices of interaction rather than behavioral coding of lengthy interactions. Before interaction researchers allow granting agencies to use the line item veto for their coding budgets, several lines of further study should be explored. Over half of the variance between coding and judgment measures is still not explained. Our analyses used only a few behaviors, none of them verbal ones, and ignored potentially important aspects of bodily movement and vocal affect. Despite these remaining questions, one can entertain seriously the possibility that judged coordination is a surrogate for behavioral adaptation.

REFERENCES

Bakker, A. B., & Schaufeli, W. B. (2001). Burnout contagion processes among teachers. *Journal of Applied Social Psychology, 30,* 2289–2308.
Berghout-Austin, A. M., & Peery, J. C. (1983). Analysis of adult–neonate synchrony during speech and nonspeech. *Perceptual and Motor Skills, 57,* 455–459.
Bernieri, F. J. (1988). Coordinated movement and rapport in teacher-student interactions. *Journal of Nonverbal Behavior, 12,* 120–138.

Bernieri, F. J., Davis, J. M., Rosenthal, R., & Knee, C. R. (1994). International synchrony and rapport: Measuring synchrony in displays devoid of sound and facial affect. *Personality and Social Psychology Bulletin, 20,* 303–311.

Bernieri, F. J., Gillis, J. S., Davis, J. M., & Grahe, J. E. (1996). Dyad rapport and the accuracy of its judgment across situations: A lens model analysis. *Journal of Personality & Social Psychology, 71,* 110–129.

Bernieri, F. J., Reznick, J. S., & Rosenthal, R. (1988). Synchrony, pseudosynchrony, and dissynchrony: Measuring the entrainment process in mother–infant interactions. *Journal of Personality and Social Psychology, 54,* 243–253.

Berry, D. S., Kean, K. J., Misovich, S. J., & Baron, R. M. (1991). Quantized displays of human movement: A methodological alternative to the point–light display. *Journal of Nonverbal Behavior, 15,* 81–97.

Berry, D. S., Misovich, S. J., Kean, K. J., & Baron, R. M. (1992). Effects of disruption of structure and motion on perceptions of social causality. *Personality and Social Psychology Bulletin, 18,* 237–244.

Buder, E. (1991). *Vocal synchrony in conversations: Spectral analysis of fundamental voice freuqency.* Unpublished doctoral dissertation, Department of Communication Arts, University of Wisconsin, Madison, WI.

Burgoon, J., Stern, L. A., & Dillman, L. (1995). *Interpersonal adaption: Dyadic interaction patterns.* New York: Cambridge University Press.

Cappella, J. N. (1981). Mutual influence in expressive behavior: Adult–adult and infant–adult dyadic interaction. *Psychological Bulletin, 89,* 101–132.

Cappella, J. N. (1991). The biological origins of automated patterns of human interaction. *Communication Theory, 1,* 4–35.

Cappella, J. N. (1994). The management of conversational interaction in adults and infants. In M. L. Knapp & G. R. Miller (Eds.), *Handbook of interpersonal communication* (2nd ed., pp. 380–419). Newbury Hills, CA: Sage.

Cappella, J. N. (1996). Dynamic coordination of vocal and kinesic behavior. In J. Watt & C. A. van Lear (Eds.), *Dynamic patterns in communication processes* (pp. 353–386). Thousand Oaks, CA: Sage.

Cappella, J. N. (1997). Behavioral and judged coordination in adult informal social interactions: Vocal and kinesic indicators. *Journal of Personality and Social Psychology, 72,* 119–131.

Cappella, J. N., & Planalp, S. (1981). Talk and silence sequences in informal conversations III. Interspeaker influence. *Human Communication Research, 7,* 117–132.

Chartrand, T. L., & Bargh, J. A. (1999). The chameleon effect: The perception–behavior link and social interaction. *Journal of Personality and Social Psychology, 76,* 893–910.

Cohn, J. F., & Tronick, E. Z. (1987). Mother–infant face-to-face interaction: The sequence of dyadic states at 3, 6, and 9 months. *Developmental Psychology, 23,* 68–77.

Feldstein, S., & Welkowitz, J. (1978). A chronography of conversation: In defence of an objective approach. In A. W. Siegman & S. Feldstein (Eds.), *Nonverbal behavior and communication* (pp. 329–378). Hillsdale, NJ: Lawrence Erlbaum Associates.

Gottman, J. M. (1979). Detecting cyclicity in social interaction. *Psychological Bulletin, 86,* 338–348.

Grammer, K., Honda, M., Juette, A., & Schmitt, A. (1999). Fuzziness of nonverbal courtship communication unblurred by motion energy detection. *Journal of Personality and Social Psychology, 77,* 487–508.

Hale, J. L., & Burgoon, J. K. (1984). Models of reactions to changes in nonverbal immediacy. *Journal of Nonverbal Behavior, 8,* 287–314.

Hatfield, E., Cacioppo, J. T., & Rapson, R. L. (1994). *Emotion contagion.* New York: Cambridge University Press.

Isabella, R. A., Belsky, J., & van Eye, A. (1989). Origins of mother–infant attachment: An examination of interactional synchrony during the infant's first year. *Developmental Psychology, 25,* 12–21.

Jasnow, M., & Feldstain, S. (1987). Adult-like temporal characteristics of mother–infant vocal interactions. *Child Development, 57,* 754–761.

Kleinke, C. L., Staneski, R. A., & Berger, D. E. (1975). Evaluation of an interviewer as a function of interviewer gaze, reinforcement of subject gaze, and interviewer attractiveness. *Journal of Personality and Social Psychology, 31,* 115–122.

Krause, R., Steimer, E., Sanger-Alt, C., & Wagner, G. (1989). Facial expression of schizophrenic patients and their interaction partners. *Psychiatry, 52,* 1–12.

LaFrance, M. (1982). Posture mirroring and rapport. In M. Davis (Ed.), *Interaction rhythms: Periodicity in communicative behavior* (pp. 279–298). New York: Human Sciences Press.

Matarazzo, J. D., & Wiens, A. N. (1972). *The interview: Research on its anatomy and structure.* Chicago: Aldine.

Maurer, R. E., & Tindall, J. H. (1983). Effects of postural congruence on clients' perception of counselor empathy. *Journal of Counseling Psychology, 30,* 158–163.

Natale, M. (1975). Convergence of mean vocal intensity in dyadic communication as a function of social desirability. *Journal of Personality and Social Psychology, 32,* 790–804.

Noller, P. (1984). *Nonverbal communication and marital interaction.* Oxford: Pergamon Press.

Pike, G. R., & Sillars, A. L. (1985). Reciprocity and marital communication. *Journal of Personal and Social Relationships, 2,* 303–324.

Street, R. L., Jr. (1982). Evaluation of noncontent speech accommodation. *Language and Communication, 2,* 13–31.

Street, R. L., Jr. (1984). Speech convergence and speech evaluation in fact-finding interviews. *Human Communication Research, 11,* 139–169.

Symons, D. K., & Moran, G. (1987). The behavioral dynamics of mutual responsiveness in early face-to-face mother–infant interactions. *Child Development, 58,* 1488–1495.

Tickle-Degnen, L., & Rosenthal, R. (1987). Group rapport and nonverbal behavior. *Review of Personality and Social Psychology, 9,* 113–136.

Webb, J. T. (1972). Interview synchrony: An investigation of two speech rate measures. In A. W. Siegman & B. Pope (Eds.), *Studies in dyadic communication* (pp. 115–133). New York: Pergamon.

Welkowitz, J., & Kuc, M. (1973). Interrelationships among warmth, genuineness, empathy, and temporal speech patterns in interpersonal interaction. *Journal of Consulting and Clinical Psychology, 41,* 472–473.

Methods for Measuring Speech Rate

David B. Buller
Cooper Institute, Denver

INTRODUCTION

Speech rate or tempo is a fundamental feature of the human voice (Burgoon, Buller, & Woodall, 1996). It has been classified variously as a voice quality (Poyatos, 1991, 1993; Trager, 1958, 1961;), prosodic feature (Crystal, 1969), and paralanguage (Street, 1990). It is also linked closely to speech, being present whenever someone talks. Speech rate, however, can also be seen as is part of the larger set of nonsegmental features associated with time (Burgoon et al., 1996; Harris & Rubenstein, 1975): duration of talk (message length), number and duration of silent portions (fluency and pausing), and speaking turn. Perceptually, listeners associate it as well with vocal frequency and intensity (Bond, Feldstein, & Simpson, 1988).

Speech rate has been implicated in several communication functions. It is especially important in emotional expression, relational communication, and social influence (Burgoon et al., 1996). For instance, faster rates are associated with more pleasant emotions and emotions linked to high arousal (e.g., anger, fear), whereas slower rates are present in unpleasant emotions and emotions associated with more placid states (e.g., disgust, sadness; Scherer & Oshinski, 1977). Moderately fast tempo typically conveys higher status and dominance (Burgoon et al., 1996).

The tie to relational communication and social influence, however, is most notable in the patterns of vocal cues that occur *between* people. Indeed, speakers often alter their vocal style intentionally to either match or depart from the vocal style of their conversational partners. This process has been witnessed in how people shift their speech rate (Buller & Aune, 1988, 1992; Buller, Le Poire, Aune, & Eloy, 1992; Putnam & Street, 1984; Smith, Brown, Strong, & Rencher, 1975; Street & Brady, 1982), as well as accent patterns (Giles & Powesland, 1975; Thakerar, Giles, & Cheshire, 1982), utterance duration (Street & Giles, 1982), response latency (Street, 1982), pause duration (Jaffe & Feldstein, 1970), and interaction length (Stang,

1973) within and across interactions. According to communication accommodation theory, matching of vocal style signals approach, attachment, or inclusion to the other, whereas maintenance of one's own style or departure from the style of the conversational partner distances or excludes the other (Giles & Smith, 1979; Street & Giles, 1982; Thakerar et al., 1982).

This chapter describes several methods for measuring speech rate that I used in previous research and reviews some of the results stemming from these measures to illustrate the utility of the assessments. The first of these methods is an assessment of rate as measured in *syllables-per-minute*. As is shown, a reliable assessment can be obtained with trained observers or mechanical devices. A second set of measures assesses *perceptions* of speech rate: perceived similarity of the speaker's speech rate to the listener's and perceived speaker speech rate. Importantly, perceptions of speech rate do not correspond well to observations of speech rate (Rockwell, 1994) and may be influenced by the intensity of speech as signaled by pitch and loudness (Bond et al., 1988). Perceptions of speech rate *are* associated consistently with certain interpretations of speakers' communication, however, and in those circumstances, the perceptions, regardless of their accuracy, play an important role in the outcomes of speech.

SYLLABLES-PER-MINUTE MEASURE OF SPEECH RATE

Speakers can and do manipulate their speech rate actively, and the degree to which the speaker's rate is similar to the listener's speech affects perceptions of the speaker and the relationship between speaker and listener. I first measured speech rate in a series of studies investigating the role of vocal behavior in gaining compliance with simple requests (Buller & Aune, 1988, 1992; Buller & Burgoon, 1986; Buller et al., 1992). In these investigations, my colleagues and I alternately measured speech rate by estimating the syllables per minute spoken by the sender or by perceptual assessments of the similarity tempo from the interactants themselves. In one study on deception (Buller & Aune, 1987), we measured tempo as judged by observers. I describe each of these measurement methods in turn and reference the utility of these measures by providing a sample of some of the outcomes of the studies in which the measures were employed.

To assess predictions that speech rate explained changes in listeners' compliance with simple requests, my colleagues and I conducted three studies (Buller & Aune, 1988, 1992; Buller et al., 1992) in which we used a measurement method first developed by Street and Brady (1982). Individuals were recorded while engaging in natural speech. This sample of tapes was obtained while the speakers were either completing the task of describing a friend (Buller & Aune, 1988), persuading a friend to lend them money for a date (Buller et al., 1992), or reading a 250-syllable paragraph in a conversational style (Buller & Aune, 1992).

In Buller and Aune (1988) and Buller et al. (1992), 1-minute segments of speech were recorded using a studio-quality microphone and tape recorder.

From each segment, we selected the middle 30 seconds of speech: from the 15-second mark to the 45-second mark on the tape recording. Following the recordings, a trained coder listened to each segment and counted the number of syllables spoken. This count was doubled to estimate the speech rate in syllables-per-minute. The middle 30-second segment was selected because it provided time for the speaker to settle into a normal speech pattern and allowed us to easily double the observed number of syllables to obtain the syllable-per-minute estimate. The reliability of these counts was estimated through a second coder following the same procedure on a random subset of 30-second speech segments. The intraclass correlation between the coders was very high, $r = .99$ (Buller et al., 1992).

In the third study (Buller & Aune, 1992), we modified the measurement method slightly to eliminate the need for a coder to count syllables. Instead, we simply reviewed the tape recording of each subject speaking the 250-syllable paragraph, measured the amount of time that it took for her or him to complete it, and converted this assessment into a syllable-per-minute estimate. Speech rate in syllables-per-minute can also be estimated mechanically using acoustic analysis of the digitized recording of a speaker's voice, as shown by Rockwell (1994). The estimates of speech rate in syllables-per-minute were used to distinguish people who naturally spoke faster or slower by "splitting" the speakers' scores at the median speech rate. In Buller and Aune (1988), the median was 204 syllables/min. Fast speakers spoke at an average rate of 239 syllables/min. and slow speakers, at 166 syllables/min.

Another group of participants then listened to a compliance message, requesting that they volunteer for another research project, recorded by a speaker at fast (352 syllables/min.) and slow (154 syllables/min.) speech rates. As predicted, participants who also scored higher on the Profile of Nonverbal Sensitivity (PONS; Rosenthal, Hall, DiMatteo, Rogers, & Archer, 1979), a test of nonverbal decoding ability, had faster speaking rates and evaluated the speaker as more intimate and less nonimmediate (see Guerrero, this volume) when the compliance message was spoken faster. By contrast, those who scored lower on the PONS spoke slower and rated the speaker as more intimate and nonimmediate when the compliance message was spoken slower.

In Buller et al. (1992), we measured the *similarity* of subjects' speech rate as estimated using the syllable-per-minute method with the speaker's speech rate when recording the compliance message at very slow (155), slow (215), moderate (275), and fast (335) rates. This was the absolute difference between the subject and speaker rates. As predicted, this measure of actual speech rate similarity was associated with higher intimacy ($r = -.30, p < .05$) and sociability/character ($r = .18, p < .05$) evaluations of the speaker by the listener. Greater sociability/character evaluations were in turn associated with higher compliance when the speaker benefited more from listener compliance than when he did not, R^2 change = .01, $F(1,255) = 3.18, p < .05$.

PERCEPTIONS OF SPEECH RATE SIMILARITY

Perceived Speech Rate Similarity

In Buller et al. (1992) and Buller and Aune (1992), we measured the degree to which participants perceived that the speech rate of the speaker–prerecorded at various tempos–was similar to their own speech rate and preferred by them. Perceived similarity in both experiments was measured with an item worded as, "Compared to the way I talk, the speaker spoke slower than me (–4) /faster than me (+4)." The scale was transformed such that the midpoint ("0") represented the greatest similarity, and –4 (spoke slower) and +4 (spoke faster) both became "4" and reflected the greatest dissimilarity in speech rate. The final scale ranged from 0 (very dissimilar) to 4 (very similar). In both experiments, an item using the same –4 to +4 rating scale assessing perceived similarity in the rate of pauses by the speaker was included as a foil.

In Buller et al. (1992), perceived speech rate was correlated more broadly with evaluations of the speaker than was actual speech rate similarity (measured as described previously). For example, the measure of perceived speech rate similarity was positively correlated with interpretations of the speaker's intimacy ($r = .27$, $p < .05$), immediacy ($r = .30$, $p < .05$), sociability/character ($r = .31$, $p < .05$), dominance ($r = .24$, $p < .05$), and competence ($r = .20$, $p < .05$). Likewise, perceived speech rate similarity was correlated with intimacy ($r = .19$, $p < .05$), immediacy ($r = .19$, $p < .05$), and sociability/character ($r = .26$, $p < .05$), but tests on actual speech rate similarity did not show any significant effects on evaluations of the speaker in Buller and Aune (1992).

Speech Rate Preferences

In Buller and Aune (1992), we also devised a speech rate preference test based on the "return potential curve" (i.e., a distribution mapping the changes in preferences from unfavorable to favorable as behavior moved into a listener's perceived norm and back to unfavorable as it shifted beyond this norm; Jackson, 1960; Strom, 1963). We presented participants with recordings of a speaker encoding a 250-syllable message at nine speech rates ranging from 93 syllables/min. to 581 syllables/min. The initial 63-syllables from each of the nine recordings were presented in a random order. After listening to each recording, participants rated the recording on two items (I approve of this voice, and I prefer this voice), using response categories ranging from –4 to +4. The responses to the two items were summed to provide the preference measure. It was expected that a curvilinear pattern of preference ratings would emerge, with positive ratings occurring in the latitude of preferred rates, and negative ratings outside of this latitude.

Analyses of the preference measure showed that rates between 252 syllables/min. and 382 syllables/min. defined the latitude of preferred speech rates (received positive ratings of 2.95 to 4.95), whereas rates slower and faster than this range were outside of this latitude (received negative ratings of −1.56 to −6.80). These differences among the speech rates were statistically significant, $F(1, 236) = 2019.42$, $p < .05$. Moreover, subjects' ratings of the perceived similarity of the speech rates with their own speech rates were strongly correlated with ratings of speech rate preference ($r = .73$, $p < .05$), but actual similarity in speech rates was not related to the preference measure. However, slow-speaking listeners perceived slower rates and fast-speaking listeners felt faster rates were more similar to their own speech rates, $F(1, 247) = 7.08$, $p < .05$.

Perceived Speech Rate

Finally, my colleague and I assessed speech rate by having coders observe people in conversation and evaluate their overall rate of speaking. In Buller and Aune (1987), coders rated speakers' voices from slow (1) to fast (7). Using factor analysis, this item clustered with measures of vocal clarity, loudness, pitch variety, pleasantness, and fluency to describe the speakers' level of vocal activity (*alpha* reliability = .18 for single item on speech rate; .86 for entire factor). Other investigators have shown higher item reliability with observers' perceptions of speech rate (e.g., *alpha* = .69, .94; Burgoon & Baesler, 1991). In our study, senders who were in an intimate relationship with the conversational partner displayed more vocal activity during deception than senders who were strangers or friends of the partner. This suggested that intimates experienced more arousal when deceiving an intimate as opposed to a friend or stranger, perhaps because discovery by the intimate carried more serious negative consequences for the relationship than discover by a friend or stranger.

One of the potential limitations of perceptual measures of speech rate is that observers' judgments may not be based solely on the rate at which vocal units are spoken. Bond and his colleagues (Bond & Feldstein, 1982; Bond et al., 1988; Feldstein & Bond, 1981) showed that vocal frequency and intensity, as indicated by pitch, loudness, and duration of speech, affect perceptions of speech rate. Receivers judged speech rate to be faster when speakers used higher pitch, spoke louder, and had longer utterances. This may be in part due to the fact that speaking tempo is part of global evaluations of vocal activity or expressivity.

Burgoon and her colleagues have included perceptions by coders of speech rate as a component of vocal expressiveness (see e.g., Burgoon, Kelley, Newton, & Keeley-Dyreson, 1989; Burgoon, Le Poire, Beutler, Bergan, & Engle, 1992; Coker & Burgoon, 1987). It may be difficult for people to separate speech rate completely from other vocal cues when asked to determine how fast someone is talking. Researchers should exercise care, then, when using perceptions of speech rate and when treating it as an accurate measure of tempo, separately from other vocal cues.

SUMMARY

When the goal is to measure speech rate, the most precise measure is obtained by observing the number of syllables spoken in a defined period of time, usually expressed as syllables/min. This can be done with trained coders or by mechanical acoustic analysis. However, our research suggests that when it comes to the communicative function of speech rate, perceptions of speech rate may matter more than actual speech rate. In particular, the similarity of speech rate, and its role in signaling vocal activity or expressivity, plays a powerful role in determining the interpretations people make of speech. Measuring tempo for individual communicators may not capture the entire communication function of this important feature of speech. Some interpretations depend on the relative similarity or dissimilarity of the speech rates of conversational partners and, again, measures of perceptions of rate similarity appear to be more instrumental than assessments of actual similarity.

REFERENCES

Bond, R. N., & Feldstein, S. (1982). Acoustical correlates of the perceptions of speech rate: A experimental investigation. *Journal of Psycholinguistic Research, 11,* 539–557.
Bond, R. N., Feldstein, S., & Simpson, S. (1988). Relative and absolute judgments of speech rate from masked and content-standard stimuli: The influence of vocal frequency and intensity. *Human Communication Research, 14,* 548–568.
Buller, D. B., & Aune, R. K. (1987). Nonverbal cues to deception among intimates, friends, and strangers. *Journal of Nonverbal Behavior, 11,* 269–290.
Buller, D. B., & Aune, R. K. (1988). The effects of vocalics and nonverbal sensitivity on compliance: A speech accommodation theory explanation. *Human Communication Research, 14,* 301–332.
Buller, D. B., & Aune, R. K. (1992). The effects of speech rate similarity on compliance: Application of communication accommodation theory. *Western Journal of Communication, 56,* 37–53.
Buller, D. B., & Burgoon, J. K. (1986). The effects of vocalics and nonverbal sensitivity on compliance: A replication and extension. *Human Communication Research, 13,* 126–144.
Buller, D. B., Le Poire, B. A., Aune, R. K., & Eloy, S. V. (1992). Social perceptions as mediators of the effect of speech rate similarity on compliance. *Human Communication Research, 19,* 286–311.
Burgoon, J. K., & Baesler, E. J. (1991). Choosing between micro and macro nonverbal measurement: Application to selected vocalic and kinesic indices. *Journal of Nonverbal Behavior, 15,* 57–78.
Burgoon, J. K., Buller, D. B., & Woodall, W. G. (1996). *Nonverbal communication: The unspoken dialogue* (2nd ed.) New York: McGraw-Hill.
Burgoon, J. K., Kelley, D. L., Newton, D. A., & Keeley-Dyreson, M. P. (1989). The nature of arousal and nonverbal indices. *Human Communication Research, 16,* 217–255.
Burgoon, J. K., Le Poire, B. A., Beutler, L. E., Bergan, J., & Engle, D. (1992). Nonverbal behaviors as indices of arousal: Extension to the psychotherapy context. *Journal of Nonverbal Behavior, 16,* 159–178.
Coker, D. A., & Burgoon, J. K. (1987). The nature of conversational involvement and nonverbal encoding patterns. *Human Communication Research, 13,* 463–494.
Crystal, D. (1969). *Prosodic systems and intonation in English.* Cambridge: Cambridge University Press.
Feldstein, S., & Bond, R. N. (1981). Perceptions of speech rate as a function of vocal intensity and frequency. *Language and Speech, 24,* 385–392.
Giles, H., & Powesland, P. F. (1975). *Speech style and social evaluation.* London: Academic.
Giles, H., & Smith, P. M. (1979). Accommodation theory: Optimal levels of convergence. In H. Giles & R. St. Clair (Eds.), *Language and social psychology* (pp. 45–65). Baltimore: University Park Press.

Harris, R. M., & Rubenstein, D. (1975). Paralanguage, communication, and cognition. In A. Kendon, R. M. Harris, & M. R. Key (Eds.), *Organization of behavior in face-to-face interaction* (pp. 251–276). Chicago: Aldine.

Jackson, J. M. (1960). Structural characteristics of norms. In National Society for the Study of Education, *The dynamics of instructional groups.* Washington, DC: Author.

Jaffe, J., & Feldstein, S. (1970). *Rhythms of dialogue.* New York: Academic.

Poyatos, F. (1991). Paralingustic qualifiers: Our many voices. *Language and Communication, 11,* 181–195.

Poyatos, F. (1993). *Paralanguage: A linguistics and interdisciplinary approach to interactive speech and sounds.* Amsterdam: Johns Benjamins.

Putnam, W. B., & Street, R. L., Jr. (1984). The conception and perception of noncontent speech performance: Implications for speech-accommodation theory. *International Journal of the Sociology of Language, 46,* 97–114.

Rockwell, P. A. (1994). *The voice of deceit: Comparing acoustic and perceptional data.* Unpublished dissertation, University of Arizona, Tucson.

Rosenthal, R., Hall, J. A., DiMatteo, M. R., Rogers, P. L., & Archer, D. (1979). *Sensitivity to nonverbal communication: The PONS test.* Baltimore: Johns Hopkins University Press.

Scherer, K. R., & Oshinsky, J. S. (1977). Cue utilization in emotion attribution from auditory stimuli. *Motivation and Emotion, 1,* 331–346.

Smith, B. L., Brown, B. L., Strong, W. J., & Rencher, A. C. (1975). Effects of speech rate on personality perception. *Language and Speech, 18,* 145–152.

Stang, D. J. (1973). Effect of interaction rate on ratings of leadership and liking. *Journal of Personality and Social Psychology, 27,* 405–408.

Street, R. L., Jr. (1982). Evaluation of noncontent speech accommodation. *Language and Communication, 2,* 13–31.

Street, R. L., Jr. (1990). The communicative functions of paralanguage and prosody. In H. Giles & W. P. Robinson (Eds.), *Handbook of language and social psychology* (pp. 121–140). Chichester: Wiley.

Street, R. L., Jr., & Brady, R. M. (1982). Speech rate acceptance ranges as a function of evaluative domain, listener speech rate and communication context. *Communication Monographs, 49,* 290–308.

Street, R. L., Jr., & Giles, H. (1982). Speech accommodation theory: A social cognitive approach to language and speech behavior. In M. Roloff & C. Berger (Eds.), *Social cognition and communication* (pp. 193–226). Beverly Hills, CA: Sage.

Strom, R. D. (1963). Comparison of adolescent and adult behavioral norm properties. *Journal of Educational Psychology, 54,* 322–330.

Thakerar, J. N., Giles, H., & Cheshire, J. (1982). Psychological and linguistic parameters of speech accommodation theory. In C. Fraser & K. R. Scherer (Eds.), *Advances in the social psychology of language* (pp. 205–255). Cambridge: Cambridge University Press.

Trager, G. L. (1958). Paralanguage: A first approximation. *Studies in Linguistics, 13,* 1–12.

Trager, G. L. (1961). The typology of paralanguage. *Anthropological Linguistics, 3,* 17–21.

Measuring the Relevance of Relational Frames: A Relational Framing Theory Perspective

James Price Dillard
Denise Haunani Solomon
The Pennsylvania State University

INTRODUCTION

A starting point for many interaction scholars is the assumption that relationships are created, revealed, and modified by interpersonal exchange (Watzlawick, Beavin, & Jackson, 1967), and that relational messages are often conveyed through noncontent and nonverbal aspects of behavior (Burgoon, 1991; Burgoon, Buller, Hale, & deTurck, 1984). Although much attention has been given to clarifying the nuances of the relational messages that people extract from nonverbal cues (e.g., Burgoon & Hale, 1984), less consensus exists concerning the processes by which people draw these relational inferences.

Recently, however, we advanced *relational framing theory* to explain the ways in which relational judgments are framed by fundamental dimensions of social reality (see Dillard, Solomon, & Palmer, 1999; Dillard, Solomon, & Samp, 1996). The logic of relational framing theory specifies that distinct frames provide lenses for making sense of communication behaviors, particularly ambiguous nonverbal cues. A critical component of testing relational framing theory, then, is the measurement of the relevance of relational frames to interaction episodes. This chapter describes how we measure the relevance of relational frames in the program of research evaluating relational framing theory. To provide a foundation for that discussion, we first present an overview of relational framing theory.

RELATIONAL FRAMING THEORY

Relational framing theory exists as a set of assumptions about both the substance of relational judgments and the process by which relational information is extracted from verbal and nonverbal behavior. As a basic assumption, relational framing theory specifies dominance–submission and affiliation–disaffiliation as the primary dimensions underlying all relational judgments, including those based on nonverbal cues. *Dominance–submission* reflects the degree to which one actor attempts to control the behavior of another, either directly or by establishing status over the other. *Affiliation–disaffiliation* is the appreciation or esteem one person has for another. Both are conceptualized as bipolar dimensions that range, respectively, from highly dominant to highly submissive and from extremely positive affiliation to extremely negative affiliation, and both are assumed to correspond with verbal and nonverbal messages. Our thinking aligns with a substantial body of research supporting a two-dimensional conceptualization of interpersonal behavior (e.g., Bochner, 1984; Kemper, 1973; White, 1980; Wiggins, 1982, but see Hale, Burgoon, and Householder, this volume).

Beyond identifying the substance of relational messages, social interactants are also attentive to the extremity of the messages. Differences between positive regard and unmitigated devotion, mild dislike and outright hatred, respect and obeisance, and authority and subjugation are nontrivial distinctions defining relational status. According to relational framing theory, the intensity of the relational message is conveyed partially by verbal and nonverbal involvement cues. In contrast to dominance–submission and affiliation–disaffiliation, involvement has no substance or experiential content (cf., Cappella, 1983). Rather, it reflects the degree to which partners are engaged with one another or enmeshed in the conversation (Cegala, Savage, Brunner, & Conrad, 1982; Coker & Burgoon, 1987; see Guerrero, this volume).

Our focus on dominance–submission and affiliation–disaffiliation as the substance of relational messages echoes prior research; however, relational framing theory departs from previous traditions by suggesting that these dimensions also function as frames that guide the processing of verbal and nonverbal involvement cues. *Relational frames*, defined as mental structures consisting of organized knowledge about social relationships, simplify the problem of interpreting social reality by directing attention to particular behaviors, resolving ambiguities, and guiding inferences. We suggest that relational frames structure the perception of otherwise ambiguous nonverbal and verbal involvement behaviors (cf. Planalp, 1985; Smith, 1995), akin to the top-down processes involved in comprehending letters, words, or speech (cf. Anderson, 1985; van Dijk & Kintsch, 1983). Because dominance– submission and affiliation–disaffiliation are the dimensions underlying relational judgments, they also likely define the frames used to make sense of interaction (Dillard et al., 1999).

For a variety of reasons, we argue that the dominance–submission and affiliation–disaffiliation frames are differentially salient within interaction; in other words, either one or the other tends to define the communication episode (Dillard et al., 1996; Solomon, Dillard, & Anderson, 2002; but see Lannutti & Monahan, 2002). In addition, relational framing theory proposes that the salient frame organizes the stream of verbal and nonverbal behavior so that communicators can deduce both the nature and the intensity of relational messages (i.e., the level of involvement). And importantly, the relational judgment associated with the salient relational frame informs inferences of relationship status on the alternative dimension (Dillard, Palmer, & Kinney, 1995). In these ways, relational frame relevance shapes fundamentally the meaning that individuals attach to verbal and nonverbal involvement cues.

The centrality of the relational frame concept to relational framing theory necessitated the development of a measure to assess the relevance of relational frames within interaction. In developing this measure, we were guided by the assumption that people can consciously access the concepts that are applicable to comprehending and evaluating particular events. For example, one might understand a meal in terms of taste, presentation, and nutritional balance; other concepts such as height, patriotism, and page length seem considerably less relevant. We exploited this simple observation as a means of assessing relational frame activation. Thus, in the investigations conducted thus far, we operationalized the relevance of relational frames by asking study participants to evaluate the applicability of concepts instantiating dominance–submission and affiliation–disaffiliation to hypothetical interaction scenarios.

PROCEDURES FOR MEASURING THE RELEVANCE OF RELATIONAL FRAMES

Our general procedures require participants to consider a variety of interaction scenarios and to rate the relevance of concepts associated with dominance–submission and affiliation–disaffiliation to making sense of those episodes. Although we expected that people could report the concepts that apply to various situations, we were concerned that reporting intensity judgments would be a more familiar and natural task than would relevance judgements. Thus, our procedures commenced with an extended example on the nature of relevance judgments. The example we employed was built around the findings of a study designed to uncover the subjective dimensionality of tactile surface perceptions (Hollins, Faldowski, Rao, & Young, 1993). That study showed that individuals naturally organize their tactile perceptions in terms of two dimensions: hard/soft and rough/smooth. Our intention in using these findings was to enhance the validity of the relevance judgments. Modeled on the procedures used by Hollins et al. (1993), the instructions are in Table 25.

After working through the example and addressing questions, participants are instructed to rate the relevance of each of a series of word pairs to interaction scenarios. In the first use of this measure (Dillard et al., 1996), the items intended to as-

TABLE 25
Procedures Based on Hollins et al. (1993)

Imagine that you have been given several different kinds of materials: wax paper, sand paper, velvet, a rubber eraser, and a brick, and asked to feel the surface of each of the different materials. Your task is judge the relevance of each word pair to making a judgment about the materials.

Rough/Smooth...........................1 2 3 4 5

Loud/Quiet................................1 2 3 4 5

Hard/Soft..................................1 2 3 4 5

High-Pitched/Low-Pitched.........1 2 3 4 5

Most people would say that the Rough/Smooth and Hard/Soft dimensions were relevant to the task and that the Loud/Quiet and High-Pitched/Low-Pitched dimensions were irrelevant. *Note*: you are NOT evaluating how rough, smooth, loud, quiet, hard, soft, high-pitched, or low-pitched the surfaces are. Instead, you are indicating whether the dimension defined by the word pair is relevant to evaluating those surfaces. Of course, your judgments might be reversed if the task were to judge sounds rather than the surfaces in this example. In that case, the Rough/Smooth and Hard/Soft dimensions would less relevant, and you would probably rate the Loud/Quiet and High-Pitched/Low-Pitched as more relevant.

sess dominance–submissiveness were dominance/submission, persuade/concede, influence/comply, and controlling/yielding. The affiliation–disaffiliation scales were affection/disaffection, liking/disliking, attraction/aversion, and positive regard/negative regard. Finally, the involvement scales were engaged/withdrawn, involved/uninvolved, interested/disinterested, and active/inactive. In every case, judgments were made on a 5-point scale where 1 = completely irrelevant, and 5 = completely relevant. Next, we discuss the measurement properties of this scale as indicated across three empirical studies.

DIMENSIONALITY AND RELIABILITY
OF THE RELATIONAL RELEVANCE SCALES

Dillard et al. (1996) conducted a principal axis factor analysis followed by an oblique rotation on data gathered from 146 participants, each of whom provided judgment data for 12 scenarios. This yielded an effective N of 1752 (before missing cases). As expected, the analysis produced a three-factor solution (see Table 26). Each of the items intended to measure dominance–submissiveness, affiliation–disaffiliation, and involvement showed their highest loading on the intended factor. After establishing the structure of the data, individual items were assigned to

TABLE 26

Rotated Factor Matrix Adapted from Dillard et al. (1996)

Items	Involvement	Dominance	Affiliation
involved/uninvolved	.69	.09	.21
interested/disinterested	.59	−.03	.34
active/inactive	.54	.20	.17
engaged/withdrawn	.53	.10	.23
persuade/concede	.07	.76	−.10
influence/comply	.08	.72	−.11
controlling/yielding	.09	.64	.08
dominance/submission	.17	.55	.05
liking/disliking	.42	−.08	.67
attraction/aversion	.15	.11	.59
affection/disaffection	.29	−.20	.56
positive regard/negative regard	.39	−.00	.42
Variance accounted for:	19%	16%	6%

Note: Highest factor loadings are indicated in italics.

one of three scales, which produced the following coefficient *alpha* reliability estimates: .76 for dominance–submissiveness, .66 for affiliation–disaffiliation, and .77 for involvement.

In a second use of this measure, Solomon et al. (2002) had participants make relational relevance judgments with regard to the same hypothetical scenarios employed in the previous study (*N* of subjects = 196, *N* of observations = 2443). Due to concern that the interested/disinterested word pair on the involvement dimension had connotations of affiliation–disaffiliation, it was eliminated and "fast/slow" substituted; however, this item performed poorly and was ultimately eliminated. As Table 27 makes plain, the results of a principal axis factor analysis followed by varimax rotation on the remaining items showed the expected three-dimensional structure. Cronbach's *alpha* coefficients were .75 for the dominance–submissiveness scale, .76 for the affiliation–disaffiliation scale, and .69 for the involvement scale.

In a third study employing these procedures, Tusing (2001) created four vignettes that depicted interactions high in dominance, submissiveness, affiliation, or disaffiliation. One hundred ninety six participants made relevance judgments for each of the scenarios (*N* of observations = 784). To buttress the involvement scale, one additional item was added: connected/disconnected. Principal axis factor analysis followed by varimax rotation again produced the expected three-factor solution (see Table 28). Reliabilities for the corresponding scales were .76 for dominance–submissiveness, .87 for affiliation–disaffiliation, and .72 for involvement.

TABLE 27
Rotated Factor Matrix from Solomon et al. (2002)

Items	Dominance	Affiliation	Involvement
persuade/concede	*.77*	−.13	.00
influence/comply	*.77*	−.14	.00
controlling/yielding	*.60*	.00	.00
dominance/submission	*.51*	.00	.00
liking/disliking	.00	*.81*	.00
affection/disaffection	−.18	*.61*	.12
attraction/aversion	.00	*.60*	.13
positive regard/negative regard	.00	*.55*	.17
involved/uninvolved	.00	.11	*.78*
engaged/withdrawn	.00	.13	*.57*
active/inactive	.15	.13	*.55*
Variance accounted for:	17%	16%	12%

Note. Highest factor loadings are indicated in italics.

TABLE 28
Rotated Factor Matrix from Tusing (2001)

Items	Affiliation	Dominance	Involvement
liking/disliking	*.91*	−.19	.01
affection/disaffection	*.77*	−.21	.04
attraction/aversion	*.70*	−.17	.15
positive regard/negative regard	*.69*	−.15	−.01
controlling/yielding	−.12	*.76*	−.13
dominance/submission	−.19	*.70*	−.24
influence/comply	−.21	*.64*	.11
persuade/concede	−.15	*.50*	.17
involved/uninvolved	−.02	.05	*.72*
engaged/withdrawn	.03	−.09	*.62*
active/inactive	−.02	.13	*.60*
connected/disconnected	.23	−.14	*.57*
Variance accounted for:	28%	14%	10%

Note. Highest factor loadings are indicated in italics.

In sum, three separate studies provide favorable evidence of the dimensionality and reliability of the items used to measure relational frame activation. Although the values for coefficient *alpha* were not always as high as might be desired, the scales were sufficiently reliable to show the effects predicted by the theory. Lannutti and Monahan (2002) added several items to the dominance–submissiveness and affiliation–disaffiliation scales, which had the desirable effect of increasing reliability. These items were as follows. For affiliation, the scale end points were caring/indifference, fondness/lack of fondness, and friendly/unfriendly. For dominance, the additional terms were convincing/being convinced, coaxing/giving in, and demanding/relenting. Because their small sample ($N = 51$) precluded a meaningful factor analysis, further measurement work is needed to assess the validity of their additions.

RELEVANCE VERSUS INTENSITY JUDGMENTS

Our procedures for measuring the relevance of relational frames were developed as a necessary part of testing relational framing theory. Accordingly, the effectiveness of this measure depends on its ability to capture the concepts people use to make sense of relational information, independent of the content judgments they ultimately reach. Many previous studies of relational communication asked participants to judge the degree to which some feature of sociality is present or absent in the communicative exchange (Burgoon & Hale, 1984, 1987; Dillard et al., 1999). Importantly, relational framing theory assumes that those intensity judgments are conceptually distinct from relevance judgments. But, do they really provide a different form of information in practice?

Tusing's (2001) study was conducted to address this question. In that project, four scenarios were constructed that were intended to represent each end of the two relational framing dimensions: dominance, submissiveness, affiliation, and disaffiliation. For example, in the dominance vignette, an authoritative boss forcefully instructed a subordinate to solicit applications from customers. In the affiliation scenario, a friend and peer suggested going to a movie. In addition to the relevance judgments, participants also provided data on the extent to which they thought that the interactions expressed particular relational qualities. These intensity judgments were made using unipolar scales that consisted of the same words used in the relevance word pairs. Like the relevance judgments, intensity judgments were made on 5-point scales; in this case, 1 = absent and 5 = present. As expected, factor analysis of the intensity data yielded a four-factor solution: dominance, submissiveness, affiliation, and disaffiliation.

The results of the study highlighted how the relevance and intensity of relational judgments varied as a function of the hypothetical scenario. Each row in Table 29 presents data from one scenario; each row also contains mean ratings of two intensity judgments and one relevance judgment. In the first row are intensity values that

TABLE 29

Intensity and Relevance Judgments by Scenarios From Tusing (2001)

Scenario	Intensity		Relevance
	Dominance	Submissiveness	Dominance
Dominance	4.28$_a$	2.28$_b$	4.35$_a$
Submissiveness	2.48$_a$	3.20$_b$	3.62$_c$
	Affiliation	Disaffiliation	Affiliation
Affiliation	4.24$_a$	1.42$_b$	4.41$_c$
Disaffiliation	1.25$_a$	4.30$_b$	4.50$_c$

Note.   The range of the intensity scale is 1 = absent to 5 = present; the range of the relevance scale is 1 = irrelevant to 5 = relevant. Means in the same row that do not share subscripts differ at $p < .05$ in paired-sample t-tests (df for the comparisons range from 192–195).

suggest that individuals viewed the dominant scenario as high in dominance and low in submissiveness. In addition, people reported that the dominance–submissiveness frame was highly relevant to understanding the interaction. In the second row, which shows the submissiveness scenario, the intensity means are reversed, but the relevance mean is still (fairly) high. The last two rows show a similar, but even cleaner, pattern for the affiliation–disaffiliation judgments.

Overall, Tusing's (2001) results show that relevance judgments are sensitive to displays of either dominance or submissiveness intensity and either affiliation or disaffiliation intensity. This result accords well with relational framing theory's conception of dominance–submissiveness and affiliation–disaffiliation as bipolar variables and signals that the procedures show good correspondence with the concepts that are central to the theory. Moreover, the pattern of means clearly indicates that intensity and relevance judgments are not one and the same. Each provides unique information about individual perceptions of social interaction. Hence, these data provide evidence of the construct validity of the relevance procedures.

SUMMARY

Empirically drawn conclusions concerning the nature and functioning of relational communication are only as valid as the tools used to measure the phenomena under study. In this chapter, we described the procedures we employed to assess the activation of relational frames as lenses for making sense of interpersonal situations. Data collected thus far on the measures' properties with respect to dimensionality and internal reliability are promising. Furthermore, we have evidence that the measure of relational frame relevance captures a phenomenon distinct from the intensity of relational messages. Thus, the data reviewed in this chapter provide uniformly favorable evidence of the psychometric soundness of the relevance methodology.

Although our methodology was developed using messages presented in a written form, the logic of relational framing theory applies to the full range of interaction cues. In fact, we have suggested that, because nonverbal messages are particularly relevant to conveying involvement, their meanings may be especially influenced by the salient relational frame (Dillard et al., 1996). Thus, we are encouraged that the procedures detailed in this chapter can be adapted easily and fruitfully to the task of measuring relational frame salience within interactions that are textured by nonverbal messages.

REFERENCES

Anderson, J. R. (1985). *Cognitive psychology and its implications* (2nd ed.). New York: W. H. Freeman.

Bochner, A. P. (1984). The function of human communication in interpersonal bonding. In C. Arnold & J. W. Bowers (Eds.), *Handbook of rhetorical and communication theory* (pp. 544–621). Boston: Allyn & Bacon.

Burgoon, J. K. (1991). Relational message interpretations of touch, conversational distance, and posture. *Journal of Nonverbal Behavior, 15,* 233–259.

Burgoon, J. K., Buller, D. B., Hale, J. L., & deTurck, M. A. (1984). Relational messages associated with nonverbal behaviors. *Human Communication Research, 10,* 351–378.

Burgoon, J. K., & Hale, J. L. (1984). The fundamental topoi of relational communication. *Communication Monographs, 51,* 193–214.

Burgoon, J. K., & Hale, J. L. (1987). Validation and measurement of the fundamental themes of relational communication. *Communication Monographs, 54,* 19–41.

Cappella, J. N. (1983). Conversational involvement: Approaching and avoiding others. In J. M. Wiemann & R. P. Harrison (Eds.), *Nonverbal interaction* (pp. 113–148). Newbury Park, CA: Sage.

Cegala, D. J., Savage, G. T., Brunner, C. C., & Conrad, A. B. (1982). An elaboration of the meaning of interaction involvement: Toward the development of a theoretical concept. *Communication Monographs, 49,* 229–248.

Coker, D. A., & Burgoon, J. K. (1987). The nature of conversational involvement and nonverbal encoding patterns. *Human Communication Research, 13,* 463–494.

Dillard, J. P., Palmer, M. T., & Kinney, T. A. (1995). Relational judgments in an influence context. *Human Communication Research, 21,* 331–353.

Dillard, J. P., Solomon, D. H., & Palmer, M. T. (1999). Structuring the concept of relational communication. *Communication Monographs, 66,* 49–65.

Dillard, J. P., Solomon, D. H., & Samp, J. A. (1996). Framing social reality: The relevance of relational judgments. *Communication Research, 23,* 703–723.

Hollins, M., Faldowski, R., Rao, S., & Young, F. (1993). Perceptual dimensions of tactile surface texture: A multidimensional scaling analysis. *Perception & Psychophysics, 54,* 697–705.

Kemper, T. D. (1973). The fundamental dimensions of social relationships: A theoretical statement. *Acta Sociologica, 16,* 41–58.

Lannutti, P. J., & Monahan, J. L. (2002). When the frame paints the picture: Alcohol consumption, relational framing, and sexual communication. *Communication Research, 29,* 390–421.

Planalp, S. (1985). Relational schemata: A test of alternative forms of relational knowledge as guides to communication. *Human Communication Research, 12,* 3–30.

Smith, S. W. (1995). Perceptual processing of nonverbal-relational messages. In D. Hewes (Ed.), *The cognitive bases of interpersonal communication* (pp. 87–112). Hillsdale, NJ: Lawrence Erlbaum Associates.

Solomon, D. H., Dillard, J. P., & Anderson, J. W. (2002). Episode type, attachment orientation, and frame salience: Evidence for a theory of relational framing. *Human Communication Research, 28,* 136–152.

Tusing, K. J. (2001, November). *Intensity and relevance of relational judgments: Same or different concepts?* Paper presented at the annual meeting of the National Communication Association, Seattle, WA.

van Dijk, T. A., & Kintsch, W. (1983). *Strategies of discourse comprehension.* Orlando, FL: Academic Press.

Watzlawick, P., Beavin, J. H., & Jackson, D. D. (1967). *Pragmatics of human communication.* New York: W. W. Norton.

White, G. M. (1980). Conceptual universals in language. *American Anthropologist, 82,* 759–781.

Wiggins, J. S. (1982). Circumplex models of interpersonal behavior in clinical psychology. In P. C. Kendall & J. N. Butcher (Eds.), *Handbook of research methods in clinical psychology* (pp. 183–221). New York: Wiley.

Assessing Attributions Given to Nonverbal Cues

Valerie Manusov
University of Washington

INTRODUCTION

One of the ubiquitous characteristics of nonverbal cues is their capacity to take on multiple meanings. That is, given the context, the schema of the communicators, the cultural environment in which the behaviors occur, and other framing characteristics, most nonverbal cues can be interpreted in more than one way. The potential for nonverbal cues to take on—or be given—multiple meanings opens the possibility for researchers to explore the choices involved in applying meaning to nonverbal cues. One way to explore meaning choices is using *attribution theories* (Manusov, 1990, 1995, 2002). This chapter presents some background on attribution research, discusses particular applications to the study of nonverbal cues, and uses this background to develop attribution measures that can assess the meaning of nonverbal (and other) cues.

ATTRIBUTION THEORIES

In 1958, Heider observed that people, in their attempts to make sense of or give order to their social worlds, act as "naïve scientists" by providing causes for the events in which they, and others, engage. Providing causes is a cognitive process and, for Heider, concerns *causal loci* primarily (e.g., whether a cause lay internal or external to a person). Researchers have since added to the number of dimensions involved in making attributions; these include globality, stability, intentionality, and controllability (e.g., Harvey & Weary, 1981; Jones & Davis, 1965; Weiner, 1985, 1986), The former—locus, globality, and stability—are often called *causal attributions*; the latter—intentionality and controllability, along with the sometimes-

335

used dimension of personal responsibility—are typically said to be *responsibility attributions* (Fincham & Bradbury, 1992).

Additional research has focused on attributions within certain contexts or relationships. Interaction behaviors that occur between spouses or dating partners have been a particularly important relational context in which to study attribution making (see, for example, Bradbury & Fincham, 1992; Fletcher, Fincham, Cramer, & Heron, 1987; Holtzworth-Munroe & Jacobson, 1985, 1988). As Fletcher et al. (1987) note, "[l]ove and intimate relationships are of central importance in people's lives. Hence it is hardly surprising that on occasions we invest considerable cognitive activity" (p. 481). Within this large body of research, the primary finding has been that more satisfied relational partners are likely to make "relationship enhancing" attributions (i.e., where the partner is more likely the cause of and responsible for positive actions but not for negative behavior) and that distressed couples tend to make "distress-maintaining" or "maladaptive" attributions (i.e., where the partner is more likely the cause of and responsible for negative actions but not for positive behavior; Holtzworth-Munroe & Jacobson, 1985, 1988; Karney, Bradbury, Fincham, & Sullivan, 1994).

APPLICATIONS TO NONVERBAL BEHAVIOR

Although considerable research has been done on attributions for a range of behaviors that couples may enact, and a number of researchers have applied attributional perspectives to other communication behavior (e.g., Canary & Spitzberg, 1990; Derlega & Winstead, 2001; Sillars, 1980; Vangelisti, 2001; Wilson & Whipple, 2001), my colleagues and I have conducted the majority of studies applying attribution theories to nonverbal communication thus far. Following McMahan (1976), I have argued that people can and do make attributions for the nonverbal behaviors in which they, and others, engage (see Manusov, 1990, 1995, 2002), and that such attributions are involved in "giving" meaning to nonverbal cues. Indeed, for scholars interested in the messages communicated by nonverbal behaviors, an attributional perspective provides a particularly useful framework for tapping into the diversity of interpretations for any given nonverbal cue and for finding possible links between attributions and other relational variables. The following studies provide data to support this claim and are used to suggest some means of measuring attributions for nonverbal behavior.

PREVIOUS STUDIES

Manusov (1990)

In the first of my investigations, 63 couples, who were married or living together, engaged in playing a game of *Trivial Pursuit*. Unbeknownst to one partner, the other had become a confederate in the study and altered his or her behaviors (after practice with research assistants) to act particularly positive and particularly negative nonverbally at two points in their interaction (the game context, with written questions and specific answers, allowed for less involvement of verbal behavior and to have the timing for behavioral change marked on the cards). Following their game, the nonconfederate partners watched a copy of the videotaped interaction and were asked to stop it at any point where they recalled thinking about their partners' behaviors. At those points, the participants wrote down the behaviors they noticed and the meanings that they gave to the behaviors. Research assistants rated the videotapes following data collection to assure that the confederates used significantly different—and correctly valenced—behaviors in each condition.

Research assistants also coded participants' open-ended answers for five attributional dimensions: locus, globality, stability, control, and intentionality. Specifically, after assessing whether there was at least one attribution made (unitizing reliability = .82; Guetzkow, 1950; responses could contain more than one attribution for the same behavior/set of behaviors), the coders then determined *for each attribution* whether it was (a) internal or external, (b) intentional or unintentional, (c) a global or specific cause, (d) stable or unstable, and (e) controllable or not controllable. Cohen's *kappa*, as a measure of intercoder reliability, ranged from .96 for intentionality to .60 for controllability. The codes were then transformed into ratio-level data by determining—across all attributions made for positive and, separately, for negative behavior—what percent was internal, intentional, global, stable, and controllable. So, if a participant wrote down that her spouse's facial expression was likely due to his nervousness about being at the study and his general bad disposition, both attributions (the study and the disposition) were coded. Where both codings were consistent (i.e., they would both have internal loci in this example), the percentage given to the dimension was the full score (i.e., 100% internal). Where they were inconsistent (e.g., the nervousness is specific and the disposition is global), the entry was given a partial score (i.e., 50% was global in this case). This procedure was chosen specifically to allow for weighting where multiple attributions were made for the behaviors, although some participants included only one statement that was coded as an attribution.

Pearson correlations were run between the percentages for the 10 attribution dimensions (five for positive and five for negative) and the participants' satisfaction scores (as measured by Spanier's, 1976, Dyadic Adjustment Scale). All of the dimensions were related significantly to satisfaction for at least one set of behaviors. Satisfaction correlated with stability, control, and intent for negative behaviors and with locus, globality, and stability for positive behaviors. That is, as satisfaction increased, the meanings given to the negative behaviors were rated by observers (who were blind to the DAS scores of the participants) as more unstable, less controllable, and less intentional; for positive cues, the attributions were more likely to be rated as more internal, global, and stable. These results were encouraging for studying the attributions embedded in the meanings of nonverbal cues.

Manusov (1995)

In a second, and very different, study, both members of 23 couples took home diaries that they completed over a 2-week period. In the diaries, the couple members were asked to record the times that they "found themselves *thinking about why ...* their partner may have used a [nonverbal] behavior or set of behaviors" (p. 347). They wrote down the behavior(s) noted, and the participants also rated the behaviors in each entry on two scales: (a) the valence of the behavior as they saw it, and (b) the intentionality that they judged was behind the nonverbal behavior(s). On the scales, 0 represented a very negative or spontaneous (unintentional) attribution, and 100 stood for a very positive or highly intentional attribution. Following the diary keeping, two research assistants checked the entries to make sure that they were acceptable (i.e., that the entry referenced nonverbal cues; percent of agreement was .96). Only those that were acceptable were kept in the analyses. The coders also determined the proportion of positive (those cues with scores given by the participants that were greater than 50), negative (less than 50), and neutral (50). These proportion scores, and the overall means for the intentionality ratings given to the positive and negative cues as determined this way, were assessed for their correlation with satisfaction (in this study, the measure was Norton's, 1983, Quality Marital Index).

Consistent with previous research (e.g., Bradbury & Fincham, 1990, 1992; Fincham & Bradbury, 1992; Gottman, 1980), the proportion of negative valence attributions given to the cues correlated with satisfaction in these diary entries such that as dissatisfaction increased, the likelihood of giving negative attributions to a partner's nonverbal cues also increased. In this study, there was no straightforward relationship between intentionality attributions and satisfaction. I did find, however, that different nonverbal cues were judged to be more or less intentional. Specifically, proxemic behaviors were rated as most intentional, followed by haptics, vocalics, kinesics, silence, eye behavior, and, finally, facial expressions. Satisfaction was linked significantly with the tendency to view facial expressions as more intentional. Although not as comprehensive as Manusov (1990), this study provided additional application of attributional coding for nonverbal cues.

Manusov, Floyd, and Kerssen-Griep (1997)

The next study brought 60 couples to the laboratory to investigate six attributions: three causal judgments (locus, stability, and globality), and three responsibility judgments (controllability, intentionality, and personal responsibility). In this study, my colleagues and I were interested in comparing attributions that people made for their own *and* their partners' behaviors. Again, one couple member was asked to become a confederate, and he or she practiced and then changed his or her behavior according to cards held up by the camera operator (located behind the other participant). This set of behaviors occurred as the couple discussed upcoming travel or party plans. As in Manusov (1990), the nonconfederates watched the videotapes after the interaction ostensibly because "[w]e are concerned that we get videotapes of behaviors that are pretty 'natural' or typical of the types of behaviors that people use when they are together in daily life" (Manusov et al., 1997, pp. 243–244). They were asked if there were any behaviors that they noticed during the interactions—their own or their partners—that stood out to them. After assessing the type and timing of the behaviors, the participants were asked these questions: What did the behaviors mean to you/what was communicated? Referring to the same behaviors, what do you think could explain the behaviors?

The open-ended questions were then coded and rated by the two junior authors. As before, they first went through the questions to assess whether they were referencing nonverbal cues (*kappa* = .87) and whether the meaning given to the behavior(s) was positive or negative (*kappa* = .91). They then used 7-point bipolar scales (see appendix) to judge the degree to which the attributions were internal/external (causal locus), stable/unstable, global/specific, in the person's control/not in the person's control, intentional/unintentional, and personally responsible/not responsible for the behavior. Cronbach's *alpha* as a gauge of interrater consistency ranged from .61 for personal responsibility to .87 for locus.

As noted, the primary aim of this study was to look for possible differences in attributions given to one's own nonverbal behaviors and those given by (or given to) one's partner. We were also interested in possible correlations between differences and satisfaction (rated on the QMI; Norton, 1983). We found the following. For *locus*, there were two significant findings: (a) as satisfaction decreased, the tendency to view their partner's behaviors as more internal than they viewed their own increased, and (b) people in general viewed their own negative behaviors as more external than their partner viewed the behaviors. For intentionality, there were three significant results: (a) with males, as satisfaction decreased, the tendency to view their partner's nonverbal behaviors as more intentional than they viewed their own increased, (b) males and females both viewed their own negative behaviors as less intentional than the partner viewed the behaviors, and (c) dissatisfied males were more likely than satisfied males to view their own negative behaviors as less intentional than their partner viewed them. For controllability, there was one finding: participants viewed their own negative behaviors as less controllable than the partner viewed the partners' behaviors. There was also one finding for personal responsibility: people viewed their own negative behaviors as less personally responsible than the partner viewed the partners' behaviors. Although not all of the attributions related significantly with satisfaction, five of the six dimensions emerged as important differentiators.

Manusov and Koenig (2001)

This next study also involved analyzing the open-ended responses given by couples for their partners' nonverbal cues. The responses were drawn from data collected by Manusov, Trees, Liotta, Koenig, and Cochran (1999), when 51 married couples interacted while talking about neutral, positive, and negative topics. As in previous investigations, one couple member became a confederate; this time he or she was asked to "show the affect you feel for the topic nonverbally" as he or she engaged with the partner. As in the other studies, the confederates' behaviors were checked for differences across valenced topics.

Our goal in this investigation was to go beyond the six attributional dimensions investigated in much of the previous work on attributions in personal relationships. Specifically, we wanted to assess whether the meanings that couple members gave for their partners' behaviors could be assessed on additional dimensions. In particular, we conducted a qualitative analysis to check for the occurrence of two additional dimensions noted in the literature: relational attributions (see Vangelisti, Corbin, Lucchetti, & Sprague, 1999, where an aspect of the relationship is identified as the cause of a behavior), and interpersonal attributions (Fletcher et al., 1987; Newman, 1981; Vangelisti et al., 1999; where "interaction between partners is the focus" of the attribution, Manusov & Koenig, 2001, p. 142). Although not tested in Manusov and Koenig (2001), Fletcher et al. (1987) argued "that relationship happiness and love will tend to be at their highest when the cognitive focus of the participants is on the relationship itself and the dynamic interplay between partners" (p. 482).

In our (Manusov & Koenig, 2001) analyses, we found evidence of both types of "new" attributions. Although relatively uncommon, our participants did occasionally reference their relationship as an explanation for the cause of or meaning behind a nonverbal cue or set of cues. We found more evidence of interpersonal attributions, where the attributor was implicated in (i.e., perceived to be the cause of) the other's behavior. More notably, and in an additional extension, we found that attributions mentioning specifics of communication (what can be called *communicational* attributions) occurred frequently. That is, a common type of attribution included mention of something specific to the talk that explained the behavior (e.g., one wife referenced her husband's gestures and said that their "cause" was his emphasis of something he was saying in the interaction; a husband attributed his wife's forward lean and lack of movement to her desire to interject into the conversation). Our argument was that, for nonverbal behaviors at least, these communicational attributions may be particularly important, as nonverbal cues are often used to help manage—and to make sense of—other interactional behaviors (especially language). Manusov and Doohan (2003) found similar results in a recent diary study.

Manusov (2002)

In the final published study I did on attributions for nonverbal behavior, the same videotapes used in Manusov and Koenig (2001) were analyzed further for the nonverbal behaviors the attributors used following their partners' behaviors for which they had made judgments. In Manusov et al. (1999), the participants also rated their partners' behaviors in addition to providing the open-ended data analyzed for Manusov and Koenig (2001). Those interactants who reported that they noticed the behaviors—and after they described the behaviors and provided assessments of what they meant to them—were also asked to rate the nonverbal cues on five dimensions, using 7 point scales. These scales were locus, control, stability, intent, and valence. The attributional ratings were then analyzed for the participants' own behaviors that the attributions appeared to have elicited, and several significant relationships were found for both positive behaviors and negative behaviors (see Table 30). Together, these results indicate that not only do people make differential attributions for nonverbal behavior; the attributions may have an effect on how the attributors themselves act, nonverbally, in return (see, also, Fincham & Bradbury, 1993).

TABLE 30
Attribution Dimensions Useful in Predicting Nonverbal Cues (from Manusov, 2002)

Dimension	Nonverbal Cues
Causal locus	Vocal animation
	Volume
	Vocal pleasantness
	Facial animation
	Facial pleasantness
	Gaze
	Fluency
	Posture
Stability	Fluency
	Physical animation
	Lean
Controllability	Facial pleasantness
	Gaze
	Posture
	Fluency
	Lean
Intentionality	Facial animation
	Gaze
	Shifting
	Touch
	Fluency
	Lean
Valence	Adaptors
	Vocal pleasantness
	Lean
	Nodding

DISCUSSION

The review presented here is designed to argue for the relevance of attributional judgments to help understand people's interpretations of—and reactions to—others' nonverbal cues. It was also designed to show some possible procedures for measuring those attributions in research. Attributions for nonverbal behaviors can be assessed through logs or diaries studies (see Manusov, 2001; Manusov & Doohan, 2003) and in laboratories. Although only assessed minimally thus far in natural settings (see Manusov & Rodriguez, 1989), they are likely to be useful in observational studies as well. In addition, attributions can be coded or rated and done so by observers/researchers and/or by the participants themselves.

Additional applications of attributions for nonverbal behavior are also possible. For example, researchers studying relationships are often concerned with the accuracy of judgments (e.g., Noller, 1992, this volume). Studies where both participants provide the attributions for the same behavior provide an opportunity to look for the degree to which partners are seeing the same causes behind the behavior. Additional work should also focus more on making attributional judgment scales that include more than one item per dimension so that the reliability of the assessments can be determined; this should also increase the scales' validity, as multiple terms can be provided for vague constructs (such as stability). This increase in the measure's reliability is especially important when participants are asked to use the scales themselves.

REFERENCES

Bradbury, T. N., & Fincham, F. D. (1990). Attributions in marriage: Review and critique. *Psychological Bulletin, 107,* 3–33.

Bradbury, T. N., & Fincham, F. D. (1992). Attributions and behavior in marital interaction. *Journal of Personality and Social Psychology, 63,* 613–628.

Canary, D. J., & Spitzberg, B. H. (1990). Attribution biases and associations between conflict strategies and competence outcomes. *Communication Monographs, 57,* 139–151.

Derlega, V. J., & Winstead, B. A. (2001). HIV-infected person's attributions for the disclosure and non-disclosure of the seropositive diagnosis to significant others. In V. Manusov & J. H. Harvey (Eds.), *Attribution, communication behavior, and close relationships* (pp. 266–284). Cambridge, UK: Cambridge University Press.

Fincham, F. D., & Bradbury, T. N. (1992). Assessing attributions in marriage: The Relationship Attribution Measure. *Journal of Personality and Social Psychology, 62,* 457–468.

Fincham, F. D., & Bradbury, T. N. (1993). Marital satisfaction, depression, and attributions: A longitudinal analysis. *Journal of Personality and Social Psychology, 64,* 442–452.

Fletcher, G. J. O., Fincham, F. D., Cramer, L., & Heron, N. (1987). The role of attributions in the development of dating relationships. *Journal of Personality and Social Psychology, 53,* 481–489.

Gottman, J. M. (1980). Consistency of nonverbal affect and affect reciprocity in marital interaction. *Journal of Consulting and Clinical Psychology, 48,* 711–717.

Guetzkow, H. (1950). Unitizing and categorizing qualitative data. *Journal of Clinical Psychology, 6,* 47–58.

Harvey, J. H., & Weary, G. (1981). *Perspectives on attributional processes.* Dubuque, IA: William C. Brown.

Heider, F. (1958). *The psychology of interpersonal relations.* New York: Wiley.

Holtzworth-Munroe, A., & Jacobson, N. S. (1985). Causal attributions of married couples: When do they search for causes? What do they find when they do? *Journal Personality and Social Psychology, 48,* 696–703.

Holtzworth-Munroe, A., & Jacobson, N. S. (1988). Toward a methodology for coding spontaneous causal attributions: Preliminary results with married couples. *Journal of Social and Clinical Psychology, 7,* 101–112.

Jones, E. E., & Davis, K. (1965). From acts to dispositions: The attribution process in person perception. In L. Berkowitz (Ed.), *Advances in experimental social psychology* (Vol. 2, pp. 219–267). New York: Academic Press.

Karney, B. R., Bradbury, T. N., Fincham, F. D., & Sullivan, K. T. (1994). The role of negative affectivity in the association between attributions and marital satisfaction. *Journal of Personality and Social Psychology, 66,* 413–424.

Manusov, V. (1990). An application of attribution principles to nonverbal messages in romantic dyads. *Communication Monographs, 57,* 104–118.

Manusov, V. (1995). Intentionality attributions for naturally-occurring nonverbal behaviors in intimate relationships. In J. E. Aitken & L. J. Shedletsky (Eds.), *Intrapersonal communication processes* (pp. 343–353). Plymouth, MI: Midnight Oil Multimedia.

Manusov, V. (2001, June). *Discerning couples' meaning for nonverbal behavior: A diary to access the degree of symbolism in the perception of nonverbal messages.* Paper presented to the International Network on Personal Relationships, Prescott, AZ.

Manusov, V. (2002). Thought and action: Connecting attributions to behaviors in married couples' interactions. In P. Noller & J. A. Feeney (Eds.), *Understanding marriage: Developments in the study of couple interaction* (pp. 14–31). Cambridge, UK: Cambridge University Press.

Manusov, V., & Doohan, E. M. (2003, November). *"My facial expression showed her that the woman could talk forever!": Meanings assigned to nonverbal cues used in relationships.* Paper presented to the National Communication Association, Miami.

Manusov, V., Floyd, K., & Kerssen-Griep, J. (1997). Yours, mine, and ours: Mutual attributions for nonverbal behaviors in couples' interactions. *Communication Research, 24,* 234–260.

Manusov, V., & Koenig, J. (2001). The content of attributions in couples' communication. In V. Manusov & J. H. Harvey (Eds.), *Attribution, communication behavior, and close relationships* (pp. 134–152). Cambridge, UK: Cambridge University Press.

Manusov, V., & Rodriguez, J. S. (1989). Intentionality behind nonverbal messages: A perceiver's perspective. *Journal of Nonverbal Behavior, 13,* 15–24.

Manusov, V., Trees, A. R., Liotta, A., Koenig, J., & Cochran, A. T. (1999, May). *I think therefore I act: Interaction expectations and nonverbal adaptation in couples' conversations.* Paper presented to the International Communication Association, San Francisco.

McMahan, E. M. (1976). Nonverbal communication as a function of attribution in impression formation. *Communication Monographs, 43,* 287–294.

Newman, H. (1981). Communication within ongoing intimate relationships: An attributional perspective. *Personality and Social Psychology Bulletin, 7,* 59–70.

Noller, P. (1992). Nonverbal communication in marriage. In R. S. Feldman (Ed.), *Applications of nonverbal behavioural theories and research* (pp. 31–59). Hillsdale, NJ: Lawrence Erlbaum Associates.

Norton, R. (1983). Measuring marital quality: A critical look at the dependent variable. *Journal of Marriage and the Family, 45,* 141–152.

Sillars, A. L. (1980). Attributions and communication in roommate conflicts. *Communication Monographs, 47,* 180–200.

Spanier, G. B. (1976). Measuring dyadic adjustment: New scales for assessing the quality of marriage and similar dyads. *Journal of Marriage and the Family, 38,* 15–28.

Vangelisti, A. L. (2001). Making sense of hurtful interactions in close relationships: When hurt feelings create distance. In V. Manusov & J. H. Harvey (Eds.), *Attribution, communication behavior, and close relationships* (pp. 38–58). Cambridge, UK: Cambridge University Press.

Vangelisti, A. L., Corbin, S. D., Lucchetti, A. E., & Sprague, R. J. (1999). Couples' concurrent cognitions: The influence of relational satisfaction on the thoughts couples have as they converse. *Human Communication Research, 25,* 370–398.

Weiner, B. (1985). "Spontaneous" causal thinking. *Psychological Bulletin, 97,* 74–84.

Weiner, B. (1986). *An attributional theory of motivation and emotion.* New York: Springer-Verlag.

Wilson, S. R., & Whipple, E. E. (2001). Attributions and regulative communication by parents participating in a community-based child physical abuse prevention program. In V. Manusov & J. H. Harvey (Eds.), *Attribution, communication behavior, and close relationships* (pp. 227–247). Cambridge, UK: Cambridge University Press.

APPENDIX

Descriptions and Possible Coding/Scales for Attribution
Categories/Dimensions

Descriptions

Causal Dimensions:

Locus (the more that the behavior is due to a personal, dispositional, the more internal; the more the behavior is due to environmental or situational circumstances or events, the more external: Manusov et al., 1997; these other terms in the description may be useful for making a multi-item measure for locus, and the same can be applied below).

Stability (the more that a nonverbal cue is seen as caused by something that is unchanging, fluctuates, or that would occur in the future, the more stable is the attribution; the more it is seen as caused by something that is infrequent, temporary, or unlikely to reoccur, the more it is judged as unstable; Fincham & Bradbury, 1992; Weiner, 1985).

Globality (the more a behavior is seen caused by something that influences many other things [i.e., aspects of a relationship], the more global it is; the more that the cause is tied to a particular situation, the more specific it is; Fincham & Bradbury, 1992).

Responsibility Dimensions:

Intentionality (the more a behavior is viewed as spontaneous, the more unintentional it is perceived; the more it is seen as purposeful, the more intentional it is rated; Fincham & Bradbury, 1992; Manusov, 1995).

Controllability (the more that the cause of a behavior is seen to be under the volition of the other and subject to effort, the more it is seen as controllable; the less volition (i.e., cannot be willed to change, the more it is attributed to uncontrollable causes; Weiner, 1985).

Personal Responsibility (the more a person is seen to be accountable or liable for the behavior, the more personal responsibility that is attributed; the less accountable, the more the other is seen as not personally responsible; Fincham & Bradbury, 1993).

Interactional/Relational Dimensions:

Interpersonal (a behavior is seen as more interpersonal when it focuses on the inter-action between a couple or some other pairing/group; it is not interpersonal or external when a cause does not reference the interaction; Fletcher et al. [1987] argue that this category should be used instead of causal locus for attributions as made in relationships).

Relational (a behavior is seen as more relational when the relationship is seen as the cause [i.e., the couple is the unit of analysis]; it is not about the relationship or ex-ternal when it does not; Fletcher et al., 1987; Fincham & Bradbury, 1993, also note that it may be important to assess the degree to which one partner is seen to be the cause, responsible, and/or blameworthy, whereas the other is not).

Communicational (attributions for nonverbal cues are more about the communi-cation or metacommunicative if they reference the conversation or its context explicitly; they are noncommunicational or not metacommunicative if they do not reference the communication that is occurring; Manusov & Doohan, 2003; Manusov & Koenig, 2001).

Use of Measures

These scales can be used by coders/raters and/or the participants themselves. They can also take a number of forms including but not limited to the following:
They can be *dichotomous* categories:
   This behavior was (these behaviors were):
      internal [1] or external [2]
      stable [1] or unstable [2] etc.   OR
      intentional; yes [1] no [0], unintentional; yes [1] no [0]
Placed on bipolar scales:
   "This behavior was caused by something:"
   Global   1 2 3 4 5 6 7   Specific
Used as a Likert-type measure:
   To what extent do you agree with the following statement:
      "My nonverbal cues were in my control"
   strongly disagree   1 2 3 4 5 6 7   strongly agree

Notes: Other possible "responsibility" dimensions include *blameworthy* and *self-ishly motivated* (Karney et al., 1994, although Fincham & Bradbury, 1992, argue that there may also be a category of attributions of *blame*). These have not been used as yet to assess nonverbal cues but may well be useful dimensions. Karney et al. (1994) also created composite scores for causal and responsibility attributions by summing the scores within the dimensions (after assessing their consistency. In their study, Cronbach's *alpha* for the causal dimensions averaged .80 and, for the responsibility dimension, the average *alpha* was .85).

The rating scales do not have to be 7-point, and indeed when using raters, a 5-point scale may lead to higher reliability. They can also be more detailed, as in this 6-point scale that purposefully has no midpoint (e.g., 1 = strongly disagree, 2 = disagree 3 = somewhat disagree, 4 = agree somewhat, 5 = agree, 6 = strongly agree; see Fincham & Bradbury, 1992).

The Expression of Rapport

Frank J. Bernieri
Oregon State University

INTRODUCTION

People sometimes use particular terminology to describe interpersonal interactions that go exceedingly well. For example, statements, such as "We hit it off," "We really clicked," and "We had chemistry between us," suggest a synergistic relationship, a sense that the interaction was more than the sum of its partners. All are also understood as indicating high *rapport* interactions. This chapter focuses on how rapport between interactants can be assessed.

DEFINING RAPPORT

The very first issue in measuring rapport is to define it. The dictionary meaning of rapport describes it as quality in the relation or connection between interactants, especially relations marked by harmony, conformity, accord, and affinity (The Concise Oxford English Dictionary, 2002). In this regard, rapport is distinct from many of the constructs examined in this volume because it applies to relationships, not individuals. Rapport exists between people, not within them. It is not a private internal state to which both (or all) are privy but rather a condition characterizing the relation between them. Likewise, it is more than an emotional state, attitude, or orientation. Rapport is a social construct that must be assessed at the group or dyad level.

For the purpose of this chapter, the three defining features of the construct of rapport are as follows: (a) rapport is defined at the dyad or group level; it refers to a quality of the relation or connection between individuals, (b) rapport is evaluatively positive for interactants, and (c) a critical aspect of rapport involves the gestalt principle of unity, a feature that finds expression in such terms as harmony, coordination, and accord (Bernieri & Gillis, 2001; Tickle-Degnen & Rosenthal, 1987, 1990).

347

MEASURING RAPPORT

The challenge for rapport researchers involves the operationalization of relational components that may transcend the individuals contributing to them. Tickle-Degen and Rosenthal (1987, 1990) reviewed the relevant literature and identified three operationally definable components that, taken together, constitute interactant rapport: (a) positive affect, (b) mutual focus of attention, and (c) interpersonal coordination. They defined rapport as a composite construct made up of three subconstructs that are distinct and conceptually orthogonal, yet are likely to correlate naturally across the varying ecology (Bernieri & Gillis, 2001). For example, two members of a surgical team who do not particularly like each other may experience a great deal of coordination and mutual focus while performing the surgery. They may not have as much rapport as they would if they also *enjoyed* working together, but they would be experiencing more rapport than two other team members who disliked each other *and* who failed to coordinate their surgical activities.

Verbal Reports of Rapport

Self-report scales based on this conceptualization of rapport appeared first in studies that validated the importance of interpersonal coordination to the construct of rapport (Bernieri, 1988a, 1988b; Bernieri, Davis, Rosenthal, & Knee, 1994). Specifically, an 18-item rapport questionnaire (see Appendix A) was developed that asks each participant to assess an interaction on items pertaining to emotional tone, mutual focus, and physical coordination/harmony. This contrasts with self-reports that typically ask participants to assess themselves or even their partner (e.g., DePaulo, Kenny, Hoover, Webb, & Oliver, 1987; Snodgrass, 2001). Factor analysis of the scale reported in Appendix A revealed a strong first unrotated principle component with high internal consistency and three correlated factors that represent the hypothesized constituents of rapport (for full reports of validity and scale reliability see Bernieri, 1988a; Bernieri et al., 1994).

Interestingly, intradyad agreement of rapport has not been impressively high ($r < .40$), raising a reliability issue for the measure (Bernieri & Gillis, 2001). The construct's definition itself may, however, help resolve the issue. The qualities of harmony, agreement, and accord work to define rapport, and they are manifest in the observed reliability of interactants' dyad reports. In other words, high states of rapport involve higher levels of agreement, whereas lower levels of agreement, by definition, may be diagnostic of lower states of rapport. Obviously, a dyad where both interactants report high positivity, high focus, and high levels of coordination is achieving a higher state of rapport than a dyad where there is less agreement.

Thus, the interrater reliability within dyads and groups, by definition, holds a direct and causal relationship to the level of rapport achieved. The internal consistency of reports from interacting partners does, however, tend to increase over time and acquaintanceship (Bernieri, Gillis, Davis, & Grahe, 1996; Colvin & Funder, 1991). Agreement is not meant to be synonymous with rapport, however. Two people who agree on the lack of rapport between them are not paradoxically enjoying high rapport. The point argued here is simply that two people who agree that there is high rapport between them are, by definition, experiencing higher rapport than two people who do not agree on this assessment.

Nonverbal Expression of Rapport

The next step in my colleagues' and my approach to measuring rapport was to document how rapport is encoded within the behavioral stream. For example, in one study (Bernieri et al., 1996), we examined an initial archive of 50 dyadic interactions involving newly acquainted participants that spanned across two interaction contexts. Although the interactions themselves ranged from 20 to 50 minutes in length, only two "thin slices" (see Ambady, Bernieri, & Richeson, 2000; Ambady, La Plante, & Johnson, 2001), approximately 50s in length were coded for nonverbal expression. More than 70 different nonverbal, verbal, and paralinguistic features were coded. Features considered ranged from those objectively definable and showing near-perfect reliability between coders (e.g., leg crossed or not, asks question, holds/grabs item) to those features assessed more subjectively, showing less internal consistency among raters, and thus requiring more coders to assess reliably (e.g., expressivity, behavior mimicry). Many features were measured in terms of both frequency and duration (e.g., smiles) and others were time sampled (e.g., interpersonal distance).

Analyses revealed that many of the measures taken were correlated. On the basis of zero order correlations, principal components analysis, and content validity involving the behavior or feature being assessed, the initial set of over 70 features was reduced to a smaller set of composite variables. For example, proximity was a composite variable formed from the distance between interactants' noses, their chairs, and their two closest body parts, sampled every 10 seconds throughout the interaction. An example of a smaller set of composite variables is summarized in Appendix B and presented as a fairly comprehensive set of nonverbal and expressive features that can be extracted from recorded interactions.

The goal of the initial project (Bernieri et al., 1996) was to map the nonverbal behavioral ecology of rapport, employing the 18-item self-report measure, discussed previously, as the criterion. Issues involving the validity of employing subjective reports over behavioral expression and other more objectively assessed criteria have never been resolved decidedly within the assessment of affect (e.g., Camras, Malatesta, & Izard, 1991) and attitude (e.g., Breckler, 1984; McGuire, 1985; Rosenberg & Hovland, 1960). Therefore, there is little reason to expect that the assessment of rapport would be immune to this issue as well. The goal of our program of research, however, was to cross-validate and converge on a more robust and valid measurement method by carefully operationalizing and measuring rapport via these two distinct information sources (Bernieri & Gillis, 2001; Gillis & Bernieri, 2001). We attained a number of interesting results.

Rapport Within Context. Participants who volunteered for a study on "social interaction" came to the lab and were told that they would be videotaped interacting with an opposite-sex partner. They were shown to their seats (armless swivel typing chairs on castors), positioned 3 feet apart in front of a small, low-lying coffee table on which lay a folded map of the world. They were given a few minutes to introduce themselves and to chat. They were then instructed to imagine being given $20,000 to go on a trip around the world together. They were asked to plan the trip using the map in front of them and the $20,000 dollars in play money that was sitting on it. Their only guidelines were that they must plan to travel together (i.e., arrive and leave the same city at the same time, taking the same means of transportation) and that they must be able to make it back to their point of departure using no more money than their allotted funds.

In nearly all cases the inevitable question was asked, "Okay, where do you want to go?" However, the variations in the interaction behavior following this were extreme. Some dyads spent more than 30 minutes squeezing in as many far-off locations as they could, demonstrating their prowess for traveling on a shoestring budget. These interactions often became frenetic, slipping into the absurd: "We can catch a fishing boat in Calcutta and hitch a ride to Bangladesh for free! I heard you can do that." Those interactions appeared animated, energetic, and involving.

Trips planned by other dyads had a decidedly different tone. For instance, a woman in one dyad grabbed all of the remaining play money after only 4 minutes and plunked it down over Europe declaring, "There! That'll do it. We go to Paris where we'll spend the rest. We're done" leaving her male traveling companion gawking silently down at the map. Similar observations were made within another interaction context where interactants were asked to first select a topic about which they could disagree and debate and then debate the issue over a period of 10 minutes. Variations in interaction tone, energy, and behavior were not subtle here, either.

The next step was to determine more precisely which of the nonverbal composite features we coded were actually predictive of self-reports. The full report containing coding reliabilities and intercorrelations of coded variables can be found in Bernieri et al. (1996). Analyses revealed that, in general, interactant self-reports of their positive affect, mutual attention, and coordination were predicted by (a) how animated (expressive) the interactants appeared, (b) how close they moved in toward each other, and (c) how much interactional synchrony/behavior coordination they demonstrated (for the correlations, see Table 31).

Not surprisingly, the three features that correlated robustly with self-reports also appear to be associated with emotional positivity, mutual attention, and coordination, the three components of rapport theorized by Tickle-Degnen and Rosenthal (1987, 1990). Interactional synchrony, for example, is an explicit mea-

TABLE 31

The Nonverbal Expression of Rapport in Two Different Contexts

Composite nonverbal variable	Raw Pearson r with mean dyad self-report in 50 dyads	
	Adversarial context	Cooperative context
Adaptors	−.08	.00
Attractiveness (dyad mean)	.05	.10
Attractiveness discrepancy	−.15	−.21
Backchannel responses	**.42**	**.06**
Expressivity	.17	.26
Eye contact	**.33**	**.06**
Forward Lean	**−.28**	**−.06**
Gestures (female)	.44	.22
Gestures (male)	.17	.08
Mutual silence	**−.36**	**−.02**
Nervous behavior	−.26	−.19
Orientation	−.09	−.11
Posture shifts	−.38	−.23
Proximity	.27	.32
Racial similarity	−.20	−.25
Smiling	−.03	.13
Synchrony	.31	.40

Note: Nonverbal behaviors most likely to have been influenced by the situational constraints imposed by the specific social context appear bolded. All behaviors were coded within a 50-s thin slice.

sure of interpersonal coordination (Bernieri & Rosenthal, 1991; see, also, Trees, this volume). Interpersonal distance, on the other hand, can be argued to be a diagnostic indicator of both attentional focus (i.e., people approach things that attract their attention) and positive affect (i.e., people approach desired objects).

Smiling, a quintessential cue reflecting a positive affective state, however, was unrelated to self-reports. This may seem surprising at first, but it illustrates an extremely important coding issue that nonverbal behavior researchers must face chronically. Smiling in the aforementioned studies was coded by relatively untrained coders who were not asked to differentiate between sincere joyful smiles and any other type of smile, of which there are many (Ekman, 1982; Ekman & Friesen, 1978; Ekman & O'Sullivan, 1991). Coding schemes do exist that allow one to code precisely, for example, the various muscle groups involved in a typical facial expression, making it possible to discriminate among different kinds of smiles (e.g., Facial Affect Coding System [FACS]; Ekman & Friesen, 1978).

If such a coding scheme was employed in these rapport studies, we would predict that the sincere joyful smile, referred to as the Duchenne smile (e.g., Ekman &

Friesen, 1978; Ekman & O'Sullivan, 1991), would be correlated with self-reports. It is more than likely, however, that only a minority of the smiles measured in these studies were of this type. The evaluation apprehension that goes with participation in an experiment and meeting someone for the first time, combined with the self-consciousness stemming from being video taped, undoubtedly resulted in a large number of smiles that might be called polite smiles and nervous smiles. Unless the coding scheme employed can discriminate between them, the interpretation of smiling in reported studies will remain equivocal.

Other Findings. Interactant rapport, as assessed with the 18-item self-report, is also related to how quickly two people can arrive at a consensus. For example, unpublished data from the Bernieri et al. (1996) study revealed that the length of time it took for interactants to agree on a topic about which they could disagree and debate was correlated negatively with their reported rapport ($r = -.32, p < .05$). Several studies have now shown that posture mimicry and interactional synchrony correlate with the 18-item rapport scale (Bernieri, 1988b; Bernieri et al., 1994; Gada, 1999; Gillis, Bernieri, & Wooten, 1995). Add to this the fact that interpersonal distance and mutual silence are also correlated with rapport (see Table 31), and it becomes clear that rapport is very much an interpersonal or group phenomenon, not an individual phenomenon.

Rapport does have an impact on the individual, however. Gestures and posture shifts, which are assessed at the level of the individual, appear diagnostic of rapport (see Table 31 and Bernieri et al., 1994). Finally, but perhaps less interestingly, self-reports of rapport in cooperative contexts (e.g., planning a trip) are higher than in adversarial contexts, such as debating or discussing a controversial topic (Bernieri et al., 1996). Thus, rapport must be considered a function of the interactants *and* the situation.

The predictive relationship between the nonverbal expression of rapport and its self-report is now known to differ across contexts. The variables showing the largest change in predictive validity across situations have been bolded in Table 31 and are worth discussing. Eye contact and backchannel responses (e.g., head nods) are not as relevant when two people focus their attention on a common object (e.g., a map of the world) as when they are face-to-face debating one another. Therefore, these two cues only reflect rapport when the primary interaction activity is face-to-face communication. Likewise, two highly engaged interactants mutually working on a joint activity may slip into a silent and efficient teamwork unit, anticipating and accommodating each other's needs and actions. Therefore, mutual silence may not mean anything at all in some contexts. If the primary interaction activity is a face-to-face discussion or conversation, however, then a 3-second pause in the conversation can take on more meaning.

Another coded feature, forward lean, has long been associated with expressions of interest and caring (e.g., Scheflen, 1964). The fact that it was associated with low rapport, not high rapport, may appear surprising. This negative relationship with rap-

THE EXPRESSION OF RAPPORT

port occurred only when the interactants were discussing a topic on which they disagreed. This may be because, in an adversarial situation, forward lean can communicate aggression and competitiveness. Eye-contact works in a similar way. Eye-contact is well understood as a behavior that can be diagnostic of interest and liking (see Guerrero, this volume) but in some contexts can be diagnostic of aggression and intimidation (e.g., Ellsworth & Carlsmith, 1968; Exline, 1972; Grumet, 1983).

Thus, researchers interested in assessing rapport are advised that they will find no definitive "rapport movement" that provides an unbiased objective assessment within any particular setting. Instead, researchers will have to consider the interaction context that they are observing and will be obliged to knowledgably select a subset of potential rapport features associated with rapport within that context. The behaviors or features that will be most promising will be those that have the potential to reveal at least one of the three subcomponents of rapport: positivity, mutual attention, and interpersonal coordination.

Other Measurement Issues and Caveats

How Much Behavior Do You Need? Recent reviews examining the relationship between the length of behavior being analyzed and the predictive validity of the summarized measurements have come to a most unexpected, yet convenient, conclusion (Ambady et al., 2000; Ambady et al., 2001; Ambady & Rosenthal, 1992). There is little evidence to suggest that increasing the amount of behavior coded from 1 minute to 5 minutes to 5 hours increases the predictive validity or functional utility of any nonverbal assessment. Published studies based on analyses of 4 to 5 minutes of behavior were no better in predicting interaction outcome criteria than studies analyzing less than a minute's worth (Ambady et al., 2000; Ambady & Rosenthal, 1992). Furthermore, studies analyzing and measuring thin slices (5 minutes of recorded behavior and less) were found to be just as good at predicting various clinical and professional achievement outcomes as studies employing more labor-intensive instruments such as structured interviews, Rorschach protocols, and personality inventories (Ambady & Rosenthal, 1992).

When assessing expressive behavior diagnostic of rapport, more behavior is not necessarily more informative. In fact, all of the relevant empirical research to date suggests that researchers will do fine to analyze intensively only a couple of thin slices (30s) within any interaction (Ambady et al., 2000). Whatever information expressive behavior is diagnostic of, it must be of a nature that is chronically embedded within the behavioral stream. Therefore, it may not matter much from where it is sampled or how much is assessed. Measuring much more of the behavioral stream will certainly give a researcher more information, but it may not provide him or her with demonstrable increases in predictive validity.

Rapport Versus Relationship. Much of the development of the rapport scale and its behavioral correlates has involved the analysis of relatively unacquainted people interacting for the first time over the course of 5 to 50 minutes. The measures were created to assess interactions and not relationships. When interactants are unacquainted, their relationship is practically defined by the level of rapport within their interaction. There is little risk of a reporting bias stemming from expectations based on their preexisting knowledge of the relationship.

As the relationship progresses, however, it becomes possible for an unstable and temporary state of rapport to diverge from the more stable and chronic tone of the underlying relationship. For example, imagine a person who suddenly gets a job at a local retail store and discovers that his or her best friend of many years is now the supervisor. Any assessment of interaction should be distinct, at least primarily, from the status of their ongoing relationship that spans many years. It is possible that the 18-item rapport scale in Appendix A might fail to discriminate sufficiently between the relationship and interaction under these circumstances. The movement from relying on self-reports to other, more behavioral measures as acquaintanceship lengthens may be the way to resolve this relationship expectancy bias in self-reports.

DISCUSSION

Rapport is best conceptualized as an interpersonal construct defined at the dyad or group level. It can be thought of as being a composite of positivity, mutual attention, and interpersonal coordination. It is a construct that applies more directly to the nature of interactions than to interpersonal relationships, but this distinction may be lost as acquaintanceship approaches zero. The work reported here is better suited to studying the rapport between relatively unacquainted individuals because it is believed that as people become acquainted with one another, their assessments of their interactions will become increasingly biased by their evaluations of their relationship and the expectations this creates.

I presented a set of nonverbal interaction features that attempts to assess comprehensively the relevant information that might be extractable from recorded interactions. Such measures can be operationalized objectively and thus are not subject to any reporting biases. Empirical work employing these behaviors has found that (a) there is a strong relationship between reports of interactant rapport and their expressive behavior, (b) less than a minute of a recorded interaction may be sufficient to extract diagnostic information with sufficient predictive validity, and (c) the diagnosticity of a given nonverbal feature may vary according to the situation context and interaction activity being considered.

Researchers have to be ever mindful of the situational constraints placed on participants. Their best strategy will be to employ a construct of rapport, such as the one used here (see, also, Tickle-Degnen & Rosenthal, 1987, 1990), that will allow them to derive theoretically relevant features and behaviors to measure. Nonverbal features such as interpersonal distance, interactional synchrony, and general expressivity levels have shown the most robust relationships to rapport, whereas other features such as mutual eye-contact and talkativeness have been shown as having situationally dependent diagnosticity. What is clear from the work presented here is that there is no single "rapport movement" or muscle that always, and by itself, serves a valid indicator of, or proxy for, rapport. Researchers are thus obliged to tailor measures carefully and precisely to the particulars of the physical and interpersonal environments within which they are operating.

REFERENCES

Ambady, N., Bernieri, F. J., & Richeson, J. A. (2000). Toward a histology of social behavior: Judgmental accuracy from thin slices of the behavioral stream. *Advances in Experimental Social Psychology, 32,* 201–271.
Ambady, N., LaPlante, D., & Johnson, E. (2001). Thin slice judgments as a measure of interpersonal sensitivity. In J. A. Hall & F. J. Bernieri (Eds.), *Interpersonal sensitivity* (pp. 89–102). Mahwah, NJ: Lawrence Erlbaum Associates.
Ambady, N., & Rosenthal, R. (1992). Thin slices of expressive behavior as predictors of interpersonal consequences: A meta-analysis. *Psychological Bulletin, 111,* 256–274.
Bernieri, F. (1988a). *Coordinated movement in human interaction: Synchrony, posture similarity, and rapport.* Doctoral dissertation, Harvard University, Cambridge, MA.
Bernieri, F. (1988b). Coordinated movement and rapport in teacher–student interactions. *Journal of Nonverbal Behavior, 12,* 120–138.
Bernieri, F. J., Davis, J. M., Rosenthal, R., & Knee, C. (1994). Interactional synchrony and rapport: Measuring synchrony in displays devoid of sound and facial affect. *Personality and Social Psychology Bulletin, 20,* 303–311.
Bernieri, F. J., & Gillis, J. S. (2001). Judging rapport: Employing Brunswik's lens model to study interpersonal sensitivity. In J. A. Hall & F. J. Bernieri (Eds.), *Interpersonal sensitivity* (pp. 67–88). Mahwah, NJ: Lawrence Erlbaum Associates.
Bernieri, F. J., Gillis, J. S., Davis, J. M., & Grahe, J. E. (1996). Dyad rapport and the accuracy of its judgment across situations: A lens model analysis. *Journal of Personality and Social Psychology, 71,* 110–129.
Bernieri, F. J., Reznick, J. S., & Rosenthal, R. (1988). Synchrony, pseudosynchrony, and dissynchrony: Measuring the entrainment process in mother–infant interactions. *Journal of Personality and Social Psychology, 54,* 243–253.
Bernieri, F. J., & Rosenthal, R. (1991). Coordinated movement in human interaction. In R. S. Feldman & B. Rime (Eds.), *Fundamentals of nonverbal behavior* (pp. 401–432). Cambridge: Cambridge University Press.
Breckler, S. (1984). Empirical validation of affect, behavior, and cognition as distinct components of attitude. *Journal of Personality and Social Psychology, 47,* 1191–1205.
Camras, L. A., Malatesta, C., & Izard, C. E. (1991). The development of facial expression in infancy. In R. S. Feldman & B. Rime (Eds.) *Fundamentals of nonverbal behavior* (pp. 73–105). Cambridge: Cambridge University Press.
Colvin, C. R., & Funder, D. C. (1991). Predicting personality and behavior: A boundary on the acquaintanceship effect. *Journal of Personality and Social Psychology, 60,* 1152–1162.
DePaulo, B., Kenny, D. A., Hoover, C., Webb, W., & Oliver, P. V. (1987). Accuracy of person perception: Do people know what kind of impressions they convey? *Journal of Personality and Social Psychology, 52,* 303–315.
Ellsworth, P. C., & Carlsmith, J. M. (1968). Effects of eye-contact and verbal content on affective response to a dyadic interaction. *Journal of Personality and Social Psychology, 10,* 15–20.
Ekman, P. (1982). Methods for measuring facial action. In K. Scherer & P. Ekman (Eds.), *Handbook of methods in nonverbal behavior research* (pp. 45–90). Cambridge: Cambridge University Press.
Ekman, P., & Friesen, W. V. (1978). *Facial Action Coding System.* Palo Alto, CA: Consulting Psychologists Press.

356BERNIERI

Ekman, P., & O'Sullivan, M. (1991). Facial expression: Methods, means, and moues. In R. S. Feldman & B. Rime (Eds.), *Fundamentals of nonverbal behavior* (pp. 163–199). Cambridge: Cambridge University Press

Exline, R. (1972). Visual interaction: The glances of power and preference. In J. Cole (Ed.), *Nebraska symposium on motivation, 1971* (pp. 163–206). Lincoln: University of Nebraska Press.

Gada, N. (1999). *Beyond the handshake: Intentional synchrony effects on job interview evaluation.* Unpublished masters thesis, University of Toledo, Toledo, OH.

Grumet, G. W. (1983). Eye contact: The core of interpersonal relatedness. *Psychiatry, 48,* 172–188.

Gillis, J. S., & Bernieri, F. J. (2001). The perception and judgment of rapport. In K. Hammond & T. R. Stewart (Eds.), *The essential Brunswik: Beginnings, explications, applications* (pp. 380–384). Oxford: Oxford University Press.

Gillis, J. S., Bernieri, F. J., & Wooten, E. (1995). The effects of stimulus medium and feedback on the judgment of rapport. *Organizational Behavior and Human Decision Processes, 63,* 33–45.

McGuire, W. J. (1985). Attitudes and attitude change. In G. Lindzey & E. Aronson (Eds.), *The handbook of social psychology* (Vol. II, pp. 233–345). New York: Random House.

Persall, J. (Ed.). (2002). *The concise Oxford English dictionary* (10th ed.). Oxford: Oxford University Press.

Rosenberg, M. J., & Hovland, C. I. (1960). Cognitive, affective, and behavioral components of attitude. In M. J. Rosenberg, C. I. Hovland, W. J. McGuire, R. P. Abelson, & J. W. Brehm (Eds.), *Attitude organization and change: An analysis of consistency among attitude components* (pp. 1–14). New Haven, CT: Yale University Press.

Scheflen, A. E. (1964). The significance of posture in communication systems. *Psychiatry, 27,* 316–331.

Snodgrass, S. E. (2001). Correlational method for assessing interpersonal sensitivity within dyadic interaction. In J. A. Hall & F. J. Bernieri (Eds.), *Interpersonal sensitivity* (pp. 201–218). Mahwah, NJ: Lawrence Erlbaum Associates.

Tickle-Degnen, L., & Rosenthal, R. (1987). Group rapport and nonverbal behavior. *Review of Personality and Social Psychology, 9,* 113–136.

Tickle-Degnen, L., & Rosenthal, R. (1990). Group rapport and its nonverbal correlates. *Psychological Inquiry, 1,* 285–293.

APPENDIX A

18-item Rapport Questionnaire
(Bernieri, Davis, Rosenthal, & Knee, 1994)

Please rate the *interaction* you just experienced between you and your partner on each of the characteristics listed.

The interaction was:	not at all								extremely
1. Well-coordinated	0	1	2	3	4	5	6	7	8
2. Boring	0	1	2	3	4	5	6	7	8
3. Cooperative	0	1	2	3	4	5	6	7	8
4. Harmonious	0	1	2	3	4	5	6	7	8
5. Satisfying	0	1	2	3	4	5	6	7	8
6. Comfortably paced	0	1	2	3	4	5	6	7	8
7. Cold	0	1	2	3	4	5	6	7	8
8. Awkward	0	1	2	3	4	5	6	7	8
9. Engrossing	0	1	2	3	4	5	6	7	8
10. Focused	0	1	2	3	4	5	6	7	8
11. Involving	0	1	2	3	4	5	6	7	8
12. Intense	0	1	2	3	4	5	6	7	8
13. Friendly	0	1	2	3	4	5	6	7	8
14. Active	0	1	2	3	4	5	6	7	8
15. Positive	0	1	2	3	4	5	6	7	8
16. Dull	0	1	2	3	4	5	6	7	8
17. Worthwhile	0	1	2	3	4	5	6	7	8
18. Slow	0	1	2	3	4	5	6	7	8

APPENDIX B

Description of Composite Features Coded in Dyadic Interactions

Detailed tables reporting reliabilities and intercorrelations between these composite variables in different social contexts can be found in Bernieri, Gillis, Davis, and Grahe (1996).

1. *Adaptors* refer to manipulations of one's own body such as rubbing, scratching, preening, and, where relevant, swiveling/rocking a chair back and forth. These behaviors are believed to be indicators of anxiety; however, in cases of extreme anxiety, they may cease entirely as a result of behavioral "freezing" (Ekman & Freisen, 1972).

2. *Gestures* (male or female) refer to nonverbal acts that have direct verbal translations (e.g., the "OK" sign) or are used to illustrate or punctuate speech (e.g., pointing and fist pounding).

3. *Mutual Eye-Contact* refers to the amount of time the interactants were gazing into each other's eyes.

4. *Forward Lean* refers to the total time spent by interactants maintaining a postural configuration in which their head was forward of the upright, vertical position relative to their hips.

5. *Mutual Silence* refers to the total time spent in which interactants were simultaneously silent for periods longer than 1.5 seconds.

6. *Orientation* refers to the degree to which an individual's trunk was oriented directly toward his or her partner. Values for orientation increase as interactants adapt a face-to-face orientation.

7. *Posture Shifts* refers to the frequency with which the interactants changed their posture or appeared to shift their weight in the chair.

8. *Proximity* represents the average distance separating the interactants' noses, chairs, and closest knees sampled at different time intervals.

9. *Racial/Ethnic Similarity* refers to the apparent similarity of the racial composition of the interaction dyads measured on a simple three-point scale.

10. *Smiling* refers to the total time spent by both interactants smiling and laughing.

11. *BackChannel Responses* refer to head nods and "uh hmms" while listening to a speaker but not when used to communicate an explicit affirmative response to a direct question.

12. *Attractiveness* refers to the physical attractiveness of each interactant as rated by a sample ($N > 10$) of independent naïve judges.

13. *Attractiveness Discrepancy* refers to the absolute difference between physical attractiveness ratings of each member within the dyad after standardizing within sex.

14. *Expressivity* is consensus rating from a sample ($N > 16$) of independent naïve judges on the extent to which an individual's total behavior was active, animated, and exaggerated. People who are expressive show their emotions quite readily, whereas those who are not expressive tend to have "poker faces" and move very little.

15. *Nervous Behaviors* is a consensus rating from a sample ($N > 20$) of independent judges on the extent to which a person's movements could be described as reflecting fear, anxiety, nervousness, or discomfort. Specifically, the extent to which a person was fidgeting, shaking, knocking his or her knees, quivering in his or her voice, swallowing, or totally "freezing."

16. *Synchrony* refers to the extent to which the behaviors and the behavioral stream of each interactant were similar to and coordinated with (i.e., synchronized) each other (see Bernieri & Rosenthal, 1991). Manifestations of synchrony may take the form of posture mimicry, simultaneous movement, and synchronized or coordinated movement. Synchrony is essentially a consensus rating by a sample of independent judges who need to be given some training. Explicit instructions can be found in Bernieri, 1988; Bernieri, Davis, Rosenthal, & Knee, 1994; Bernieri, Reznick, & Rosenthal, 1988.

Measuring Nonverbal Dominance

Norah E. Dunbar
California State University, Long Beach

Judee K. Burgoon
University of Arizona

INTRODUCTION

Dominance–submission is a fundamental construct that defines the very nature of interpersonal relationships: Humans try to influence one another and position themselves favorably within the context of social organizations by asserting their own powerfulness or status and eliciting deference or submission from others. Historically, dominance has attracted multidisciplinary interest from fields as diverse as ethology, biology, anthropology, sociology, psychology, psychiatry, communication, and personal relationships. Perhaps the most significant contributions to the scientific study of nonverbal behavior and dominance, however, can be traced to writings by Charles Darwin on *The Expressions of Emotions in Man and Animals* in 1872, Freud's psychoanalytic treatises, several works by personality and social psychologists in the early 1900s, anthropological works by Ray Birdwhistell on *Kinesics and Context,* and by Edward Hall on *The Silent Language* and *The Hidden Dimension* in the mid-1900s (see Ellyson & Dovidio, 1985).

The research tributaries flowing into the study of nonverbal dominance following this grounding work have been richly diverse. They include naturalistic observation of human and nonhuman species, correlational studies of personality and developmental differences in dominance and aggressiveness, psychoanalytic case studies, linguistic analysis of the structure of nonverbal behavior, and experimental studies of dominance as either the independent or the dependent variable. Although one might expect that the confluence of this impressive amount of attention to nonverbal dominance would bring great clarity and understanding to how nonverbal dominance is enacted and measured, such consensus is lacking, partly due to the conceptual conflating of the constructs of dominance, power, influence, and status, an issue to which we next turn our attention. This chapter attempts to provide greater cohesion for measuring nonverbal dominance.

Distinguishing Dominance From Related Constructs

Over the past several decades of interaction research, many scholars debated how to define what dominance is and how to distinguish it from related constructs such as power, status, authority, and domineeringness. These related constructs have been defined in numerous, often synonymous, ways by a variety of theorists and researchers (e.g., Ellyson & Dovidio, 1985; Harper, 1985; Maple & Mitchell, 1985, see Hall, this volume). We, like others, have argued for some time, however, that these constructs are theoretically and operationally distinct (Burgoon & Dillman, 1995; Burgoon & Dunbar, 2000; Burgoon, Dunbar, & Segrin 2002; Burgoon, Johnson, & Koch, 1998; Dunbar, 2000; Dunbar & Burgoon, in press). To achieve conceptual clarity and to eliminate confusion, these concepts should therefore be differentiated.

Scholars from diverse fields converge on the definition of *power* generally as the capacity to produce intended effects (cf. Berger, 1994; Dunbar, 2000), and in particular, the ability to influence the behavior of another person. On the other hand, *status* generally refers to one's position in a social hierarchy (Ellyson & Dovidio, 1985). In contrast to power and status, which may be latent, *dominance* is necessarily manifest. It refers to context- and relationship-dependent interactional patterns in which one actor's assertion of control is met by acquiescence from another (Burgoon et al., 1998; Mack, 1974; Rogers-Millar & Millar, 1979).

Although dominance elsewhere may be viewed as a personality trait (see Hall, this volume), in the context of communication it is a dynamic state that reflects a combination of individual temperament and situational features that demand, release, or encourage dominant behavior (Aries, Gold, & Weigel, 1983; Burgoon & Dunbar, 2000). Unlike *domineeringness*, which refers to individual attempts to control the interaction, dominance refers to the acceptance of the control attempts by the interactional partner (i.e., it is defined by the sequence of "one-up" and "one-down" acts between two parties; Rogers-Millar & Millar, 1979). Dominance is thus both behavioral and relational. Burgoon et al. (1998) further defined interpersonal dominance as a dyadic and interactional construct, specifically describing it as expressive, relationally-based strategies and as one set of communicative acts by which power is exerted and influence achieved.

Measurement Issues With Nonverbal Dominance

The particular acts a researcher examines depends on the research question being asked. There are several key issues pertaining to the measurement of nonverbal dominance that should be examined before selecting which form of measurement is appropriate for the question at hand (Baesler & Burgoon, 1987; Burgoon &

Baesler, 1991; Scherer & Ekman, 1982). These include (a) whether objective or subjective measures are used, (b) how macroscopic or microscopic the unit of analysis is, (c) whether individually based behaviors or relationally based behaviors are examined, and (d) whether the observation takes place in a naturalistic or laboratory setting.

The first issue has to do with whether or not the measurement involves objective physical behaviors or some holistic interpretation of whether a particular actor appears dominant. The *objective* approach often uses equipment or a notational system to record dominance behavior precisely (see Tusing, this volume, for a physiological measure of dominance). For example, Ellyson, Dovidio, and colleagues examined gaze patterns to establish a visual dominance ratio in which more dominant individuals have a higher ratio of looking-while-speaking to looking-while-listening than those who are submissive (Dovidio & Ellyson, 1985; Ellyson, Dovidio, Corson, & Vinicur, 1980; Exline, Ellyson, & Long, 1975). In this method, a stopwatch is used by trained coders to count the frequency and duration of gaze while both speaking and listening during an interaction. Kimble and Musgrove (1988) used a similar method to record visual dominance and also used recording equipment to measure the amplitude (loudness) of participants' voices. By contrast, the subjective approach requires observers to make inferences about the intention and purpose of the behaviors of others. Often, this involves training coders to rate an individual's overall dominance on Likert-type scales (e.g. Burgoon, Birk, & Pfau, 1990; Snodgrass & Rosenthal, 1984) but can also be used by untrained, naive observers (Burgoon & Dunbar, 2000).

The second measurement issue, concerning the unit of analysis, has to do with whether macroscopic or microscopic behaviors are measured. *Macroscopic* measures identify large-scale, molar phenomena, whereas, *microscopic* measures identify precise, fine-grained behavior (Baesler & Burgoon, 1987). Moscowitz (1988, 1990) used both methods conjunctively in his research. He asked raters to judge "how much the person tried to dominate the partner" (1988, p. 833) as an overall, aggregate measure; he also trained coders to make counts of certain behaviors such as smiling or making jokes. Behaviors coded at the microscopic level are often examined in precise detail by coders who have undergone long, intensive training sessions. Friedlander and Heatherington (1989), using a variation of Rogers and Farace's (1975) Relational Communication Control Coding System (RCCCS), obtained adequate intercoder reliability only after 30 to 40 hours of training. Gottman and his colleagues (Gottman, 1993; Gottman & Krokoff, 1989; Gottman, McCoy, Coan, & Collier, 1995) also created coding systems for microanalysis of nonverbal behavior. In the Specific Affect Coding System (SPAFF; this volume) and the Rapid Couples Interaction Scoring System (RCISS), coders use verbatim transcripts and videotapes of couples' interactions to classify each speaking turn according to the minute facial, vocal, and bodily actions performed by the speakers. These systems, based on the microscopic facial movements of Ekman and Friesen's (1978) Facial Action Coding System (FACS), are not designed to measure dominance per se, but are indicators of a host of positive and negative emotions in which dominance plays a role.

The third measurement issue concerns whether the behaviors being rated are individually based or relationally based. Most studies of nonverbal dominance examine a particular individual's dominance behavior such as talking time, eye gaze, speech loudness (Kimble & Musgrove, 1988; Burgoon, Buller, Hale, & deTurck, 1984; Lamb 1981), posture, elevation (Schwartz, Tesser, & Powell, 1982), body lean, smiling, proximity, and touch (Burgoon et al., 1984). Aries, Gold, and Weigel (1983) examined a number of cues in one study of dominance displays during group discussions. For each individual in the group, the researchers measured the amount of talking time, arm and leg positions, and body lean. By contrast, relationally based measurement examines dominance at the dyadic level, as dominance by one partner is often met with submissiveness on the part of the other partner.

Gonzales and Griffin (1997) suggest a "pairwise method" for examining psychological processes at both the dyadic level and the individual level simultaneously that could be applied to coded or rated dominance measures. Rogers and Farace's (1975) RCCCS has also been extended to nonverbal relational control by Siegel, Friedlander, and Heatherington (1992). In the original coding scheme, certain types of verbal comments (e.g., answer, instruction, order, topic change) made by interactants are coded for their content and then a "one-up" or "one-down" code is applied to designate it as dominant or submissive. These codes are not examined in isolation, however; they are considered part of a "transaction" with the code that immediately precedes or follows it. Similarly, Siegel et al. (1992) examined nonverbal behaviors associated with the verbal comments of the RCCCS (such as "puts head on shoulder," "moves to sit as instructed," "nods head 'yes'," "sticks tongue out") as part of a transactive process in family therapy interactions.

The fourth measurement issue is whether the dominance behavior is measured in its natural environment or is observed in a laboratory or some other setting created by the researcher. Virtually all of the studies mentioned previously in which dominance behavior was measured, coded, or observed have taken place in a laboratory, including many of our own studies (e.g., Aries et al., 1983; Burgoon & Dunbar, 2000; Burgoon et al., 1998; Dovidio & Ellyson, 1985; Moscowitz, 1988; Rogers & Farace, 1975; Siegel et al., 1992). Some researchers have extolled the virtues of observing dominance behavior in naturalistic settings for reasons of ecological validity, because people can be observed over a large number of occasions and because the "strangeness" of the laboratory setting may invoke atypical responses (Small, Zeldin, & Savin-Williams, 1983). However, in a laboratory the researcher has control over the environment, and the setting makes it far easier to record the behavior for future analyses. These advantages often outweigh the desire for ecological validity.

Research Exemplars

In our studies of interpersonal dominance, we measured dominance in three ways: as a self-report measure of an individual's own dominance, as a measure of partner or observer perceptions of another person's dominance, and using trained coders who observe interactions while looking for particular markers of dominance. These observations often take place in a laboratory, use both objective and subjective measures, examine both macroscopic and microscopic levels of analyses, and involve both individually based and relationally based behaviors. This review examines the way dominance has been measured in six distinct areas of inquiry and suggests ways that other scholars could implement our measures into their own programs of research.

For over two decades, Burgoon and her colleagues have been studying dominance in association with other relationally based messages in interpersonal interactions. The work began with investigations validating the fundamental themes of relational communication, of which dominance is a major part (Burgoon et al., 1984; Burgoon & Hale, 1984; Hale, Burgoon, & Householder, this volume). Early measurement work on the Likert-format Relational Communication Scale (RCS; Burgoon & Hale, 1987) showed that the proposed 12 nonorthogonal themes could be combined into four composite measures: intimacy, immediacy, emotional arousal, and dominance. Reliability for the 5-item dominance measure, however, was inadequate (coefficient alpha reliability of .60) and prompted continued work to improve measurement. Whereas the RCS utilized a Likert format that has proven useful for participant and untrained observer reports, later studies investigating interactional dominance expanded the measurement repertoire to include a semantic differential approach utilizing 10 different adjective pairs (see Appendix A). Studies using various versions of the semantic differential measure have found the scale to be reliable with individuals, their partners, and trained coders, with reliabilities ranging from .66 to .92 (Burgoon et al., 1999; Burgoon et al., 2002; Dunbar, 2000; Dunbar, Ramirez, & Burgoon, 2003). Such approaches rely on subjective judgments rather than focusing on specific, objectively measured behaviors.

In an attempt to improve both the conceptualization and measurement of interactional dominance, Burgoon, Johnson, and Koch (1998) launched a second line of inquiry to develop and test two separate dominance measures to identify the characteristics and behaviors associated with dominant and submissive individuals and to clarify the sometimes muddy distinction between dominance and other constructs: an attribute-based instrument (see Appendix B) and a behavior-based instrument (see Appendix C). The results for the attribute checklist indicated that there are at least 31 different attributes consistently associated with dominance and 13 attributes associated with submission. This instrument offers a means of assessing dominance or submissiveness through the use of impressionistic qualities and is suitable for more global or subjective judgments in social encounters.

The factor analysis for the behavior-based instrument identified five different dimensions of dominance: influence, conversational control, focus and poise, panache, and self-assurance, with *alphas* ranging from .73 to .88. The first three dimensions are implicitly more relationally based, as they concern the extent to which actors are persuasive, take control of the conversational floor, and show poise in the context of the interaction. The latter two dimensions are more related to individual actors' communication style. The behavior-based instrument can thus be used to assess more precisely what dominant and submissive individuals do during actual interaction. Moreover, the instrument can be used as a multidimensional scale or can be used unidimensionally and still attain high reliability (ranging from .78 to .90; Burgoon et al., 1998; Burgoon & Dunbar, 2000).

In contrast to the subjective and gestalt nature of dominance–submission measurement in the preceding investigations, other work has combined subjective judgments with more objective ones. A third line of inquiry by Burgoon, Birk, and Pfau (1990) used a Brunswickian lens model to research nonverbal contributors to persuasion and credibility. According to the posited model, distal cues (i.e., those that can be objectively measured), such as a speaker's vocal amplitude or frequency of illustrator gestures, should generate proximal percepts (i.e., gestalt perceptions) such as "warmth," "pleasantness," or "dominance" that represent subjective judgments abstracted from the objective cues. It is the proximal percepts that should most directly impact perceptions of credibility and persuasion. In that investigation, Burgoon et al. (1990) measured dominance with trained coders using the semantic differential scales (reliability = .81), similar to that found in Appendix A. Correlational analysis showed that the nonverbally dominant communicator was kinesically and vocally dynamic (using more gestures, greater eye gaze, more vocal animation, and greater amounts of talk), yet relaxed and confident. Kinesic dominance cues (including distal cues like facial expressiveness and the number of illustrator gestures) were especially important for generating perceptions of competence, composure, character, and sociability and also affected the speaker's persuasiveness.

A fourth line of inquiry investigated what specific nonverbal behaviors are associated with relational messages of dominance, intimacy, immediacy, and composure. Burgoon and Le Poire (1999) trained coders to rate a wide range of microlevel and macrolevel nonverbal behaviors, then correlated the nonverbal measures with general ratings of dominance supplied by participants (Ps) and by third-party observers (Os). Results showed that for both Ps and Os, greater dominance was associated with (a) greater involvement on global vocalic and kinesic measures, (b) greater pleasantness on global vocalic and kinesic measures, (c) greater immediacy on all proxemic and kinesic indicators, (d) greater expressivity on all vocal and kinesic indicators (with a curvilinear but also increasing pattern on intensity), (e) greater positivity (e.g., smiling), (f) among Ps, greater relaxation in the form of a relaxed voice and body with few object manipulations, and (g) among Os, more fluent speech but also less smooth turn-switching (indicative of more interruptions).

Combined with the preceding results, these patterns indicate that dominance is indicated by higher involvement, immediacy, expressivity and demonstrativeness, relaxation and composure, synchronous and fluent speech, influence attempts, conversational control, and pleasantness, whereas submissiveness is associated with low levels of these nonverbal patterns.

A fifth area of inquiry examined dominance as a means to gain control of a social encounter (Dunbar, 2000; Dunbar, in press, Dunbar & Burgoon, in press). Following from Dunbar's investigations testing dyadic power theory, global impressions of dominance (from both participants and observers) are compared with individual verbal and nonverbal indicators using both micro- and macrolevel coding. These investigations have revealed that overall impressions of dominance are associated with greater vocal control, more verbosity, more illustrator gestures, fewer dysfluencies, greater facial expressiveness, and a higher visual dominance ratio—as defined by Dovidio and Ellyson (1985) and already described. The measurement of global dominance in these and the Burgoon and Le Poire (1999) studies used the scales found in Appendixes A and C (with *alphas* ranging from .78 to .92) along with the ratings of coders trained to examine individual verbal and nonverbal behaviors. The description of coder training and practices is beyond the scope of this chapter but is described in detail elsewhere (e.g., Burgoon & Le Poire, 1999; Dunbar & Burgoon, in press).

The preceding results underscore the importance of conceptualizing and measuring dominance as a pattern or profile of behavior, rather than being communicated by single indicators. Burgoon and a graduate class at Michigan State University initiated a final line of work to attempt just such a multicue approach to dominance by developing an observational coding scheme for relational communication. One objective was to merge dominance strategies and tactics (Burgoon & Hoobler, 2002) with the Specific Affect (SPAFF) coding scheme developed by Gottman et al. (1995), but to do so in a manner that (a) included only relational messages, not individual affective states, and (b) expanded the observational window beyond the face to include the voice and body. A further objective was to produce an unbiased measure, one that was not fraught with the stereotypic view that dominance is necessarily negatively valenced. As our previous research had demonstrated, dominance can be expressed in conjunction with either negative or positive affect, just as submissiveness can also be positively or negatively toned.

The SPAFF identifies discrete behaviors that may be indicative of particular emotions. Although we disagree with labeling dominance as an emotion, it is one of the 16 affects represented in their system. Thus, our objective was to identify specific behaviors that might be associated with four different quadrants produced by crossing dominance–submission with positivity–negativity (see Appendix D). Although the original intent of the quadrant approach was for purposes of conceptualization, we found that judges could, after watching a videotaped segment of an interaction, place the actor's behavior into one of the four quadrants of behavior, thus rendering gestalt judgments based on sets of interrelated cues (Kam, Burgoon, & Bacue, 2001).

DISCUSSION

These six distinct lines of inquiry emphasize the importance of dominance as a nonverbal relational message. Dominance should not be seen as the only nonverbal cue that influences communication outcomes in interaction, but as one part of the communication process. The overall, gestalt judgments that individuals make when interacting with others are certainly influenced by dominance but also by other salient cues such as involvement, intimacy, friendliness, credibility, and emotional arousal. In addition, the combination of verbal and nonverbal cues, as well as the inclusion of multiple indicators of dominance, is crucial to fully appreciate the complexity and the richness of interpersonal dominance. These cues, when taken together, present us with an opportunity to better understand the way that individuals define and understand their relationships with one another.

REFERENCES

Aries, E. J., Gold, C., & Weigel, R. H. (1983). Dispositional and situational influences on dominance behavior in small groups. *Journal of Personality and Social Psychology, 44,* 779–786.

Baesler, E. J., & Burgoon, J. K. (1987). Measurement and reliability of nonverbal behavior and percepts. *Journal of Nonverbal Behavior, 11,* 205–233.

Berger, C. R. (1994). Power, dominance, and social interaction. In M. L. Knapp & G. R. Miller (Eds.), *Handbook of interpersonal communication* (2nd ed., pp. 450–507). Thousand Oaks, CA: Sage.

Burgoon, J. K., & Baesler, E. J. (1991). Choosing between micro and macro nonverbal measurement: Application to selected vocalic and kinesic indices. *Journal of Nonverbal Behavior, 15,* 57–78.

Burgoon, J. K., Birk, T., & Pfau, M. (1990). Nonverbal behaviors, persuasion, and credibility. *Human Communication Research, 17,* 140–169.

Burgoon, J. K., Bonito, J., Bengtsson, B., Ramirez, A., Jr., Dunbar, N. E., & Miczo, N. (1999). Testing the interactivity model: Communication processes, partner assessments, and the quality of collaborative work. *Journal of Management Information Systems, 16,* 35–58.

Burgoon, J. K., Bonito, J. A., Ramirez, A., Jr., Dunbar, N. E., Kam, K., & Fischer, J. (2002). Testing the interactivity principle: Effects of mediation, verbal and nonverbal modalities, and propinquity in decision-making interactions. *Journal of Communication, 52,* 657–677.

Burgoon, J. K., Buller, D. B., Hale, J. L., & deTurck, M. (1984). Relational messages associated with nonverbal behaviors. *Human Communication Research, 10,* 351–378.

Burgoon, J. K., & Dillman, L. (1995). Gender, immediacy and nonverbal communication. In P. J. Kalbfleisch & M. J. Cody (Eds.), *Gender, power, and communication in human relationships* (pp. 63–81). Hillsdale, NJ: Lawrence Erlbaum Associates.

Burgoon, J. K., & Dunbar, N. (2000). An interactionist perspective on dominance–submission: Interpersonal dominance as a dynamically, situationally contingent social skill. *Communication Monographs, 67,* 96–121.

Burgoon, J. K., Dunbar, N. E., & Segrin, C. (2002). Nonverbal communication and social influence. In J. P. Dillard & M. Pfau (Eds.), *Persuasion: Developments in theory and practice* (pp. 445–473). Thousand Oaks, CA: Sage.

Burgoon, J. K., & Hale, J. L. (1984). The fundamental topoi of relational communication. *Communication Monographs, 51,* 193–214.

Burgoon, J. K., & Hale, J. L. (1987). Validation and measurement of the fundamental themes of relational communication. *Communication Monographs, 54,* 19–41.

Burgoon, J. K., & Hoobler, G. (2002). Nonverbal signals. In M. L. Knapp & J. Daly (Eds.), *Handbook of interpersonal communication* (pp. 240–299). Thousand Oaks, CA: Sage.

Burgoon, J. K., Johnson, M. L., & Koch, P. T. (1998). The nature and measurement of interpersonal dominance. *Communication Monographs, 65,* 309–335.

Burgoon, J. K., & Le Poire, B. A. (1999). Nonverbal cues and interpersonal judgments: Participant and observer perceptions of intimacy, dominance, composure, and formality. *Communication Monographs, 66,* 105–124.

Dovidio, J. F., & Ellyson, S. L. (1985). Patterns of visual dominance behavior in humans. In S. L. Ellyson & J. F. Dovidio (Eds.), *Power, dominance, and nonverbal behavior* (pp. 129–150). New York: Springer-Verlag.

Dunbar, N. E. (2000). *Explication and initial test of dyadic power theory.* Unpublished doctoral dissertation, University of Arizona, Tucson, AZ.

Dunbar, N. E. (in press). Dyadic power theory: Constructing a communication-based theory of relational power. *Journal of Family Communication.* Paper presented to the National Communication Association Annual Convention, Miami Beach, FL.

Dunbar, N. E., & Burgoon, J. K. (2002, November). *Perceptions of power and dominance in interpersonal encounters.* Paper presented at the National Communication Association Convention, New Orleans, LA.

Dunbar, N. E., Ramirez, A., Jr., & Burgoon, J. K. (2003). The effects of participation on the ability to judge deceit. *Communication Reports, 16,* 23–33.

Ekman, P., & Friesen, W. V. (1978). *Facial Action Coding System: A technique for the measurement of facial movement.* Palo Alto, CA: Consulting Psychologists Press.

Ellyson, S. L., & Dovidio, J. F. (1985). Power, dominance, and nonverbal behavior: Basic concepts and issues. In S. L. Ellyson & J. F. Dovidio (Eds.) *Power, dominance, and nonverbal behavior* (pp. 1–28). New York: Springer-Verlag.

Ellyson, S. L., Dovidio, J. F., Corson, R. L., & Vinicur, D. L. (1980). Visual dominance behaviors in female dyads: Situational and personality factors. *Social Psychology Quarterly, 43,* 328–336.

Exline, R. V., Ellyson, S. L., & Long, B. (1975). Visual behavior as an aspect of power role relationships. In P. Pliner, L. Krames, & T. Alloway (Eds.), *Advances in the study of communication and affect* (Vol. 2, pp. 21–52). New York: Plenum Press.

Friedlander, M. L., & Heatherington, L. (1989). Analyzing relational control in family therapy interviews. *Journal of Counseling Psychology, 36,* 139–148.

Gonzalez, R., & Griffin, D. (1997). On the statistics of interdependence: Treating dyadic data with respect. In S. Duck (Ed.), *Handbook of personal relationships* (pp. 271–302). Chichester: Wiley.

Gottman, J. M. (1993). Studying emotion in social interaction. In M. Lewis & J. M. Haviland (Eds.), *Handbook of emotion* (pp. 475–487). New York: Guilford.

Gottman, J. M., & Krokoff, L. J. (1989). The relationship between marital interaction and marital satisfaction: A longitudinal view. *Journal of Consulting and Clinical Psychology, 57,* 47–52.

Gottman, J. M., McCoy, K., Coan, J., & Collier, H. (1995). *The specific affect coding system (SPAFF) for observing emotional communication in marital and family interaction.* Mahwah, NJ: Lawrence Erlbaum Associates.

Harper, R. G. (1985). Power, dominance, and nonverbal behavior: An overview. In S. L. Ellyson & J. F. Dovidio (Eds.), *Power, dominance, and nonverbal behavior* (pp. 29–48). New York: Springer-Verlag.

Kam, K. Y., Burgoon, J. K., & Bacue, A. E. (2001, June). *A comprehensive approach to the observational coding of relational messages.* Paper presented at the annual meeting of the International Network on Personal Relationships, Prescott, AZ.

Kimble, C. E., & Musgrove, J. I. (1988). Dominance in arguing mixed-sex dyads: Visual dominance patterns, talking time, and speech loudness. *Journal of Research in Personality, 22,* 1–16.

Lamb, T. A. (1981). Nonverbal and paraverbal control in dyads and triads: Sex or power differences? *Social Psychology Quarterly, 44,* 49–53.

Mack, D. E. (1974). The power relationship in black families and white families. *Journal of Personality and Social Psychology, 30,* 409–413.

Mitchell, G., & Maple, T. L. (1985). Dominance in nonhuman primates. In S. L. Ellyson & J. F. Dovidio (Eds.), *Power, dominance, and nonverbal* behavior (pp. 49–66). New York: Springer-Verlag.

Moskowitz, D. S. (1988). Cross-situational generality in the laboratory: Dominance and friendliness. *Journal of Personality and Social Psychology, 54,* 829–839.

Moskowitz, D. S. (1990). Convergence of self-report and independent observers: Dominance and friendliness. *Journal of Personality and Social Psychology, 58,* 1096–1106.

Rogers, L. E., & Farace, R. V. (1975). Analysis of relational communication in dyads: New measurement procedures. *Human Communication Research, 1,* 222–239.

Rogers-Millar, L. E., & Millar, F. E. (1979). Domineeringness and dominance: A transactional view. *Human Communication Research, 5,* 238–246.

Scherer, K. R., & Ekman, P. (1982). Methodological issues in studying nonverbal behavior. In P. Ekman & K. Scherer (Eds.), *Handbook of nonverbal communication research* (pp. 1–44). New York: Cambridge University Press.

Schwartz, B., Tesser, A., & Powell, E. (1982). Dominance cues in nonverbal behavior. *Social Psychology Quarterly, 45*, 114–120.

Siegel, S. M., Friedlander, M. L., & Heatherington, L. (1992). Nonverbal relational control in family communication. *Journal of Nonverbal Behavior, 16*, 117–139.

Small, S. A., Zeldin, S., & Savin-Williams, R. (1983). In search of personality traits: A multimethod analysis of naturally occurring prosocial and dominance behavior. *Journal of Personality, 51*, 1–16.

Snodgrass, S. E., & Rosenthal, R. (1984). Females in charge: Effects of sex of subordinate and romantic attachment status upon self-ratings of dominance. *Journal of Personality, 52*, 355–371.

APPENDIX A

Semantic-Differential Rating Scales
(Reproduced from Dunbar, 2000)

Directions: Answer the following questions about how your partner behaved during your interaction. Look at the adjective pairs below. Each is on a scale from 1 to 7, with 1 representing a high degree of the adjective on the left and 7 representing a high degree of the adjective on the right. For example, 1 = very dominant and 7 = very submissive. Circle the number that reflects your general impression of YOUR PARTNER'S DISCUSSION OF THE TOPIC. You may circle 1, 2, 3, 4, 5, 6, or 7. If you are neutral or unsure, circle a 4. Work quickly, indicating your first response.

Very dominant	1 2 3 4 5 6 7	Very submissive
Very confident	1 2 3 4 5 6 7	Very unconfident
Very low status	1 2 3 4 5 6 7	Very high status
Very sluggish	1 2 3 4 5 6 7	Very energetic
Very hesitant	1 2 3 4 5 6 7	Very decisive
Very aggressive	1 2 3 4 5 6 7	Very meek
Very outgoing	1 2 3 4 5 6 7	Very withdrawn
Very silent	1 2 3 4 5 6 7	Very talkative
Very dynamic	1 2 3 4 5 6 7	Very passive
Very awkward	1 2 3 4 5 6 7	Very poised

NOTE: Items 1, 2, 6, 7, and 9 should be reverse-coded.

APPENDIX B

Dominance Checklist
(Reproduced from Burgoon, Johnson, & Koch, 1998)

INSTRUCTIONS: Think of the person in your circle of friends you consider to be the *most dominant/least dominant* in interactions. Identify the person who is usually the most/least dominant rather than someone who is dominant/lacks dominance only in specific or limited situations. Put a check by all of the adjectives that you believe best describe this friend's style of interaction. Leave blank those adjectives that do not describe this friend's interaction style.

Please put the initials of the person you consider the most/least dominant here: ____.

What is the gender of this person? ____ Male ____ Female?

____ accommodating	____ diplomatic	____ impulsive
____ adventurous	____ dissatisfied	____ insincere
____ aggressive	____ docile	____ indecisive
____ ambitious	____ dynamic	____ independent
____ argumentative	____ easily led	____ influential
____ assertive	____ efficient	____ inhibited
____ authoritative	____ energetic	____ takes initiative
____ awkward	____ enterprising	____ intelligent
____ boastful	____ ethical	____ intimidating
____ bossy	____ expressive	____ introverted
____ cautious	____ extroverted	____ jolly
____ commanding	____ feminine	____ kind
____ compliant	____ flexible	____ lazy
____ confident	____ fluent	____ loud
____ conforming	____ forceful	____ masculine
____ competitive	____ friendly	____ mature
____ considerate	____ generous	____ mischievous
____ contented	____ gentle	____ meek
____ controlling	____ headstrong	____ methodical
____ conventional	____ hesitant	____ meticulous
____ curious	____ high-strung	____ mild
____ decisive	____ hostile	____ modest
____ demanding	____ humble	____ obedient
____ dependent	____ impatient	____ opinionated
____ determined	____ impression-leaving	____ opportunistic

_____ optimistic   _____ rebellious   _____ stubborn
_____ outspoken   _____ relaxed   _____ subdued
_____ overbearing   _____ reserved   _____ submissive
_____ passive   _____ resourceful   _____ successful
_____ patient   _____ retiring   _____ talkative
_____ persevering   _____ sad   _____ temperamental
_____ persuasive   _____ satisfied   _____ timid
_____ playful   _____ self-centered   _____ tolerant
_____ pleasant   _____ self-confident   _____ trusting
_____ poised   _____ serious   _____ unassuming
_____ possessive   _____ shrewd   _____ unconventional
_____ powerful   _____ shy   _____ unresourceful
_____ prestigious   _____ sincere   _____ weak
_____ quiet   _____ stern   _____ withdrawn
_____ realistic   _____ strong   _____ zany

APPENDIX C

Interpersonal Dominance Rating Scale

Please rate the degree to which you agree or disagree with the following statements as they relate to the person you identified above. Using the following scale, please circle the number that best corresponds with your opinion: 1 = Strongly Disagree, 2 = Disagree, 3 = Somewhat Disagree 4 = Neutral, 5 = Somewhat Agree, 6 = Agree, and 7 = Strongly Agree

	Strongly Disagree						Strongly Agree
1. This person usually takes charge of conversations.	1	2	3	4	5	6	7
2. People often turn to this person when decisions have to be made.	1	2	3	4	5	6	7
3. This person rarely influences others.	1	2	3	4	5	6	7
4. This person is often responsible for keeping the conversation going when we talk.	1	2	3	4	5	6	7
5. This person usually does more talking than listening.	1	2	3	4	5	6	7
6. This person has very little skill in managing conversations.	1	2	3	4	5	6	7
7. This person never finds out what others think before taking a stand on an issue.	1	2	3	4	5	6	7
8. This person often stops to think about what to say in conversations.	1	2	3	4	5	6	7
9. It seems as if this person finds it hard to keep his/her mind on the conversation.	1	2	3	4	5	6	7
10. I am often influenced by this person.	1	2	3	4	5	6	7
11. This person often insists on discussing something even when others don't want to.	1	2	3	4	5	6	7
12. This person often makes his/her presence felt.	1	2	3	4	5	6	7
13. This person often wins any arguments that occur in our conversations.	1	2	3	4	5	6	7
14. This person is completely self-confident when interacting with others.	1	2	3	4	5	6	7
15. This person often acts nervous in conversations.	1	2	3	4	5	6	7
16. This person is often concerned with others' impressions of him/her.	1	2	3	4	5	6	7
17. This person has a natural talent for winning over others.	1	2	3	4	5	6	7
18. This person seems to have trouble concentrating on the topic of conversation.	1	2	3	4	5	6	7
19. This person is very expressive during conversations.	1	2	3	4	5	6	7
20. This person is often the center of attention.	1	2	3	4	5	6	7
21. This person has a dramatic way of interacting.	1	2	3	4	5	6	7
22. This person is usually relaxed and at ease in conversations.	1	2	3	4	5	6	7
23. This person often avoids saying things in conversations because he/she might regret it later.	1	2	3	4	5	6	7
24. This person is more of a follower than a leader.	1	2	3	4	5	6	7
25. This person often has trouble thinking of things to talk about.	1	2	3	4	5	6	7
26. This person has a way of interacting that draws others to him/her.	1	2	3	4	5	6	7
27. This person remains task oriented during conversations.	1	2	3	4	5	6	7
28. This person shows a lot of poise during interactions.	1	2	3	4	5	6	7
29. This person is not very smooth verbally.	1	2	3	4	5	6	7
30. This person often acts impatient during conversations.	1	2	3	4	5	6	7
31. This person is usually successful in persuading others to act.	1	2	3	4	5	6	7
32. This person has a memorable way of interacting.	1	2	3	4	5	6	7

(Reproduced from Burgoon, Johnson, & Koch, 1998)

APPENDIX D

Quadrant Coding

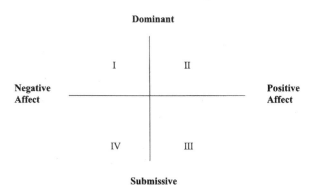

Quadrant I: dominant, negative affect
A person's behavior in this quadrant may be belligerent, patronizing, contemptuous, and taunting—using these communication styles to be domineering/dominant, create power distances, make others their victims, and/or cause them to be submissive. This may include expressions of disgust, sarcasm, "eye rolls," and aversion or stonewalling.

Quadrant II: dominant, positive affect
A person's behavior in this quadrant can be characterized as persuasive, confident, and charismatic. Behaviors combine being expressive and pleasant while also maintaining the center of attention and attempting to influence the partner. Behavioral displays may include holding the conversational floor (i.e., longer utterances and talk time), expansive gestures and postures, taking up lots of physical space, joking, laughter, and humor.

Quadrant III: submissive, positive affect
A person's behavior in this quadrant would include expressions of happiness, empathy, yielding the floor to partner, summarizing, agreeing, etc., where he or she is not showing power over others. This person may backchannel or otherwise show respect, deference, or submissiveness toward the partner. Other behaviors that characterize this quadrant include taking up less physical space, mirroring, trying to synchronize with the partner's behavior, and encouraging the partner to take the floor by asking probing questions or encouraging more disclosure.

Quadrant IV: submissive, negative affect
A person's behavior in this quadrant may be characterized as playing the "victim" role by whining and/or being defensive. Individuals here will show negative emotions and act submissively. They may display sadness, pout, constrain their anger with the "lip press" or tense facial muscles, and engage in "yes—but" statements.

Analysis of Coded Nonverbal Behavior

Roger Bakeman
Georgia State University

INTRODUCTION

A phrase such as "observational methods" admits to a variety of meanings, but two stand out. More broadly, observational methods might include procedures by which informed observers produce narrative reports, and so could include qualitative methods generally (see LeBaron, this volume). Such reports have greatly enriched our understanding of all kinds of human phenomena but require talent and wisdom on the part of the observer that often comes with time and is not taught easily (the works of Irving Goffman stand as paradigmatic examples). More narrowly, observational methods are often understood to reference procedures that result in quantification of the behavior observed, and that is the sense in which I use the term here.

Thus procedures that permit students of nonverbal behavior to reduce observed behavior to scores that can be analyzed are the focus of this chapter. If data are understood as generally quantitative, then data collection means measurement, which can be defined as procedures that, when applied to things or events, produce scores. What then makes observational methods different from other measurement approaches? For what circumstances are they recommended? What kinds of researchers have found them useful? In this chapter, in an attempt to address the first question, I consider five topics in turn and explain their relevance for observational methods. These topics concern coding schemes, coding and recording, representing, reliability, and reducing. Then, at the end of the chapter, I return to the second and third questions.

Coding Schemes

Coding schemes, which can be thought of as measuring instruments just like rulers and thermometers, are central to observational methods. They consist of sets of pre-

375

defined behavioral categories representing the distinctions that a researcher finds conceptually meaningful and wishes to study further. One example involves the study of marital interaction. A researcher might define such codes as complain, emote, approve, empathize, and negative (to name a few) and then apply them to the talk of marital partners. Examples of other coding schemes can be found in Bakeman and Gottman (1997) and in the coding section of this volume, but most share this in common: They consist of a single set of mutually exclusive and exhaustive codes, as in the example of marital interaction codes given here, or of several such sets, each set coding a different dimension of interest. In the simplest case, a set could consist of just two codes, presence or absence; thus if observers were asked to note occurrences of five different behaviors, any of which could co-occur, this could be regarded as five sets, with each set containing two codes: yes or no.

It is sometimes objected that coding schemes are too restrictive and that predefined codes may allow potentially interesting behavior to escape unremarked. Earlier, I termed observing without the structure of a coding scheme observation in a broad sense, and I assume that such qualitative, unfettered observation occurs while coding schemes are being developed. Once defined, coding schemes have the merits of replicability and greater objectivity shared with other quantitative methods; even so, coders should remain open to the unexpected and make qualitative notes as circumstances suggest. Further refinement of the measuring instruments is always possible.

Coding and Recording

Armed with coding schemes and presented with samples of behavior, observers are expected to categorize (i.e., code), quickly and efficiently, various aspects of the behavior passing before their eyes. One basic question concerns the thing coded. Is it a neatly bounded episode such as a marital partner's turn of talk or successive n-second intervals, as is often encountered in the literature? Or is it an event of some sort? For example, observers might be asked to identify episodes of struggles over objects between preschoolers and then code various dimensions of those struggles or, as often happens, they might be asked to segment the stream of behavior into sequences of events or states, coding the type of the event and its onset and offset times.

A second basic question concerns the type of measurement. Probably most coding schemes ask observers to make categorical (or nominal) judgments; such judgments are also called qualitative, although the counts and sequences that result from categorical measurement can be subjected to quantitative analysis in a way that qualitative narrative reports cannot (unless they were subsequently coded). Some coding schemes, however, ask observers to make ordinal judgments, for example, rating the emotional tone of each n-second interval on a 1 to 7 scale. Thus the rating scales discussed earlier in this volume can regarded as observational data, especially when successive intervals of time are rated (see Cappella's chapter on coding adaptation, this volume).

Typically, coding schemes used in research on nonverbal behavior require human judgment and cannot be automated as, for example, the position of an animal in an enclosure or a person's physiological responses might be (see the physiological measures chapter in this section). Thus observers need to record their judgments in some way. It is possible to observe behavior live, in real time, recording the judgments made with simple pencil and paper or some sort of handheld electronic device or specially programmed lap-top computer. More likely, the behavior of interest recorded for later coding.

Video recordings have the merit of being subject to multiple viewings, in both real time and slow motion, and they permit reflection (and, literally, re-view) in a way live observation does not. With current video technology, time will usually be recorded as a matter of course, but it has not always been so. Especially in older literature, *interval recording*, which is often called zero-one or partial-interval or simply time sampling (Altmann, 1974), is encountered. Typically, rows on a paper recording form represented successive intervals (often quite short, e.g., 15 seconds), columns represented particular behaviors, and observers noted with a tick mark the behaviors that occurred within each interval. The intent of the method was to provide approximate estimates of both frequency and duration of behaviors in an era before readily available recording devices automatically preserved time, but the method was a compromise with desire, reflecting the technology of the time, and no longer seems recommended.

Representing

Occasionally investigators may refer to video recordings as data, but making a video recording is not the same as recording data. Thus the question remains, given video recordings, how should the results of coding be recorded? More generally, how should any data be represented (literally, re-presented) for subsequent processing? If a no-tech approach to coding relies only on pencil and paper and the naked eye, and if a high-tech approach connects computers and video recordings, then a relatively low-tech approach to coding video material might assume video recording but rely on a visual time code and would require observers to record not just codes but also the time they occurred. Almost always, data will be processed ultimately by computer so observers viewing video could use pencil and paper for their initial records and then enter the data in computer files later, or key their observations directly into a computer as they worked, whichever they find easier. Such a system retains all the advantages that accrue to coding previously recorded material and is attractive when budgets are constrained.

When feasible, a more high-tech approach has advantages, and a number of systems are available (e.g., Long, 1996). Such systems combine video recordings and computers in ways that serve to automate coding. Perhaps the best known is *The Observer* (Noldus, Trienes, Henriksen, Jansen, & Jansen, 2000; for current information see http://www.noldus.com). In general, computer-based coding systems permit researchers to define the codes they use, and record the codes' attributes. Coders can then view previously recorded information, in real time or slow motion, as they decide how the material should be coded. Computer programs then organize codes and their associated times into computer files. Such systems tend to the clerical tasks, freeing coders to focus on their primary task, which is making decisions as to how behavior should be coded.

No matter how coding judgments are captured initially, they can be reformatted using standard conventions for sequential data (SDIS or Sequential Data Interchange Standard; Bakeman & Quera, 1995). Such data files can then be analyzed with GSEQ (Generalized Sequential Querier; for current information, see http://www.gsu.edu/~psyrab/sg.htm or http://www.ub.es/comporta/sg.htm), a program for sequential observational data that has considerable capability and flexibility (see Bakeman & Quera, 1995, for examples).

Reliability

The accuracy of any measuring device needs to be established before weight can be given to the data collected with the particular device. For the sort of observational systems I am describing, the measuring device consists of trained human observers applying a coding scheme or schemes to streams of behavior, often video recorded. Thus the careful training of observers, and establishing their reliability, is an important part of the enterprise. As noted previously, usually observers are asked to make categorical distinctions, thus the most common statistic used to establish inter-observer reliability is Cohen's *kappa* (Cohen, 1960), a coefficient of agreement for categorical (i.e., nominal) scales. Cohen's *kappa* corrects for chance agreement and thus is much preferred to the percentage agreement statistics sometimes seen, especially in older literature. Moreover, the agreement matrix, required for its computation, is useful when training observers due to the graphic way it portrays specific sources of disagreement.

When judgments are made sequentially in time (e.g., when two observers code a couple as making joint eye contact, person A looking at B only, person B looking at A only, neither looking at the other), each observer's coding of the interaction could be displayed along a time line and disagreements noted. The GSEQ program (Bakeman & Quera, 1995), in fact, can produce such plots, and examination of them also often proves useful when training observers.

Reducing and Analyzing

In contrast with both self-report or questionnaire methods, and more similar with automatic collection of physiological data (see Tusing's & Kinney's chapters, this volume), observational methods often result in voluminous data. Thus data reduction is often a necessary prelude to analysis. A useful strategy is to collect slightly more detailed data than one intends to examine; thus initial data reduction may consist of "lumping" some codes. Other data reduction techniques may involve computation of conceptually targeted indices (e.g., an index of the extent to which mothers are responsive to their infants' gaze), which then serve as scores for multiple regression or other kinds of statistical analyses. Several examples of this useful and productive strategy for observational data are given in Bakeman and Gottman (1997) and Bakeman, Deckner, and Quera (in press), and a specific example is presented in the following paragraphs.

Earlier I noted that sequences of events might be coded without recording their onset or offset time. Such *event sequences* are amenable to Sackett's (1979) lag-sequential analysis. However, when events are coded along with their onset and offset times—and the digital revolution makes timing information ever easier to record—such *timed sequences* afford analytic options not available with event sequences (Bakeman & Quera, 1995). Timed sequences can consist of any number of mutually exclusive or co-occurring behaviors, and the time unit, not the event, can be used as the tallying unit when constructing contingency tables. This can be very useful. Often researchers want to know whether one behavior occurred within a specified time relative to another, and they are not particularly concerned with its lag position, that is, with whether or not other behaviors intervened.

For example, Deckner (2003) wanted to know whether mothers and their toddlers matched each other's rhythmic vocalizations and so coded onset and offset times for mothers' and toddlers' rhythmic vocalizations. Her time unit was a second, and Table 32 shows results for one dyad. For the rows, each second of the observed interaction was classified as within (or not within) a 5-second time window; the window began the second the mother began a rhythmic vocalization and extended for the next 4 seconds. For the columns, seconds were classified as a second the toddler began a rhythmic vocalization, or not.

A useful way to summarize this 2 × 2 table is to note that the odds the toddler began a rhythmic vocalization within 5 seconds of her mother beginning one were

TABLE 32

Toddler's Onsets of Rhythmic Vocalizations Cross-Classified by Whether or Not They Occurred Within Five Seconds of the Mother Beginning a Rhythmic Vocalization

Within 5s after mother's onset	Toddler Onset		
	Yes	No	Totals
Yes	11	189	200
No	29	971	1,000
Totals	40	1,160	1,200

Note. This mother-toddler dyad was observed for 1,200 seconds or 20 minutes; the tallying unit is the second. For these data the odds ratio is 1.95, indicating that a toddler is almost twice as likely to begin a rhythmic vocalization shortly after the mother has than at other times.

0.0582 to 1 (i.e., 11 ÷ 189), whereas the corresponding odds otherwise were 0.0299 to 1 (i.e., 29 ÷ 971). Thus the odds ratio—a statistic probably more used in epidemiology than in other social science fields—is 1.95 (i.e., 0.0582 ÷ 0.0299).

The odds ratio deserves to be better known and used more by students of nonverbal behavior and other behavioral researchers. It is useful on two counts: First, it is useful descriptively to say how much greater the odds are that a behavior will occur in the presence as opposed to the absence of another behavior (here, that the toddler will start a rhythmic vocalization shortly after the mother does as opposed to other times). Second, the natural logarithm of the odds ratio, which varies from minus to plus infinity with zero indicting no effect, is an excellent score for standard statistical analyses (the odds ratio itself, which varies from zero to plus infinity with 1 representing no effect, is not). Thus Deckner (2003) could report that 24-month-old females were more likely to match their mother's rhythmic vocalization than 24-month-old males or either male or female 18-month-old toddlers.

In sum, Deckner's study provides an excellent example of how analysis of observational data can proceed with timed sequences. Onset and offset times for events are recoded, then a computer program (GSEQ; Bakeman & Quera, 1995) tallies seconds and computes indices of sequential process (here, an odds ratio) for individual cases, and finally a standard statistical technique (here, mixed model analysis of variance) is applied to the sequential scores (here, the natural logarithm of the odds ratio). Deckner was interested specifically in whether mothers and toddlers matched each other's rhythmic vocalizations, but the same technique could apply to other sets of partners and other behaviors. It could be used easily to study interpersonal synchrony generally, and as such could add to the other measures that study interactional synchrony described in this volume.

SUMMARY

Historically, observational methods have proven useful when process aspects of behavior are more important than behavioral products or for studying any behavior that unfolds over time. They have been used widely for studying nonverbal organisms (e.g., infants) and nonverbal behavior generally, especially social behavior. The study of social interaction generally and interactional synchrony in particular are two areas in which observational methods have been used widely. Observational methods seem to have a kind of "naturalness" not always shared with other measurement strategies. Observers are not always passive or hidden, and situations are often contrived, and yet the behavior captured by observational methods seems freer to unfold, reflecting more the target's volition, than seems the case with, for example, self-report questionnaires. Self-reflection is not captured, but aspects of behavior outside immediate articulate awareness often are.

With recent advances in technology, observational methods have become dramatically easier and less effortful. Handheld devices can capture digital images and sound, computers permit playback and coding while automating clerical functions, and computer programs permit flexible data reduction and analysis. Whether or not future investigators of nonverbal behavior select observational methods will depend more on whether the method fits the behavior and far less on some of the technical obstacles of the past. Here, as elsewhere, computer technology has dramatically expanded our choices and made easy what only a few years ago seemed impossibly difficult. Increasingly, it is our imagination and little else that limits us.

REFERENCES

Altmann, J. (1974). Observational study of behaviour: Sampling methods. *Behaviour, 49*, 227–267.
Bakeman, R., Deckner, D. F., & Quera, V. (in press). Analysis of behavioral streams chapter. In D. M. Teti, (Ed.), *Handbook of research methods in developmental psychology*. Oxford, UK: Blackwell.
Bakeman, R., & Gottman, J. M. (1997). *Observing interaction: An introduction to sequential analysis* (2nd ed.). New York: Cambridge University Press.
Bakeman, R., & Quera, V. (1995). *Analyzing interaction: Sequential analysis with SDIS and GSEQ*. New York: Cambridge University Press.
Cohen, J. A. (1960). A coefficient of agreement for nominal scales. *Educational and Psychological Measurement, 20*, 37–46.
Deckner, D. F., Adamson, L. B., & Bakerman, R. (2003). Rhythm in mother-infant interactions. *Infancy, 4*, 201–217.
Long, J. (1996). *Video coding system reference guide*. Caroga Lake, NY: James Long Company.
Noldus, L. P. J. J., Trienes, R. J. H., Henriksen, A. H. M., Jansen, H., & Jansen, R. G. (2000). The Observer Video-Pro: New software for the collection, management, and presentation of time-structured data from videotapes and digital media files. *Behavior Research Methods, Instruments, and Computers, 32*, 197–206.
Sackett, G. P. (1979). The lag sequential analysis of contingency and cyclicity in behavioral interaction research. In J. D. Osofsky (Ed.), *Handbook of infant development* (1st ed., pp. 623–649). New York: Wiley.

Coding Mutual Adaptation in Dyadic Nonverbal Interaction

Joseph N. Cappella
University of Pennsylvania

INTRODUCTION

Coordination is arguably the essential characteristic of every interpersonal inter-action. If person A's behaviors do not affect those of B, then one partner cannot be said to be sensitive to alterations in the other's actions in any observable way (see Cappella, 1987). Without such contingent responsiveness, it would be difficult to distinguish two monologists disengaged from their partners from two partners sensitive to and engaged with one another. Interpersonal communication *requires* the coordination of behavior.

Coordination (Bernieri & Rosenthal, 1991; Tickle-Degnen & Rosenthal, 1987) includes interpersonal responsiveness captured in two ways: in more static form, by the term *mutual influence,* and more dynamically by *mutual adaptation.* Mutual in-fluence[20] usually refers to the similarity (or reciprocity) and difference (or compen-sation) in aggregate behaviors exhibited by partners. This core concept is at the root of Ashby's (1963) discussion of communication between systems, Hinde's (1979) characterization of interpersonal relations, Davis' (1982) concept of responsive-ness, and Cappella's (1987) definition of interpersonal communication. Evidence for the presence of mutual influence is usually, but not always, static measures of sameness or difference. The phrase *mutual adaptation,* however, refers to the dy-namic process by which partners respond to changes in one another's behavior dur-ing interaction. Measuring adaptation thus involves tapping into the changing,

---

[20]Various researchers have used different names in place of mutual influence to denote what is at es-sence the same process: the effect of the behavior of person A on the behavioral response by partner B over and above expectation. Jaffe and Feldstein (1970) call it *congruence* or sometimes *interspeaker influ-ence,* Condon and Ogston (1967) call it *synchrony,* Chapple (1971) calls it *entrainment,* Giles, Mulac, Bradac, and Johnson, (1987) call it *convergence* and *divergence.*

over time, and/or sequential nature of interaction. This chapter discusses some of the key issues involved when designing a study to measure nonverbal behaviors as they occur dynamically.

REPRESENTING SEQUENCES OF NONVERBAL BEHAVIOR

Observation and Time

In order to study the temporal patterns of nonverbal behavior between persons in social interaction, one must (a) observe behaviors of participants, and (b) represent those observations in some systematic way. Two aspects of interactional processes are implicated. First, observation implies that features of social interaction must be selected and given a systematic representation. Second, the features must be observed as they evolve over time; thus, the conception of time employed must be made explicit.

Choices that researchers make at the outset of their work on these two issues—what to observe and when to observe it—determine how patterns can be analyzed later. In between observation and analysis is *representation*. Representation refers to the transformation of raw observations into a form more suitable for analysis. Three crucial decisions thus face the researcher in conducting an interaction study: what to observe (coding), how to represent observations (data representations), and when and how frequently to make the observations (time).

Coding and Data Representation

Coding is a procedure of representing the behavior stream as an abstract set of symbols that maps selected subsets of the behavior stream into a set of symbols (see chapters by Bakeman and White, & Sargent, this volume). In deciding what to observe in social interaction, the researcher must make some choices. It is impossible to describe comprehensively and exhaustively what is occurring in even a few seconds of social interaction. Rather, the researcher must choose to observe certain features because they bear some relationship to the underlying questions and problems that are being posed. Specifically, three basic distinctions need to be made: categorical versus continuous codes, codes versus variables, and degree of inference in coding.

Continuous Versus Categorical States. The most basic distinction that can be drawn among coding systems is whether the states are categorical or continuous. Categorical state descriptions mark the presence or absence of a certain feature of the interaction. It is presumed that the feature is not present in degrees but rather simply exists or does not. For example, in coding gestures, an illustrator by the right hand at a given point in time either occurs or does not. Continuous behavioral codes are based on the assumption that the feature of the behavior being observed falls along some metric. For example, one might code various quantitative features of the voice such as hostility (Gottman, 1979a, 1979b), loudness (Natale, 1975a, 1975b), or speech rate (Street & Cappella, 1985, 1989). Other coding procedures include rating systems (e.g., the judged rate of gesturing per 30-second interval) and interpretational codes (e.g., the degree of speaker animation per 30-second interval). These codes provide a representation of the interaction, although rating and interpretational codes are further removed from the behavior than are some categorical and continuous systems.

Coding Versus Variables.   The coding of interaction must be distinguished from the variable values that are constructed from the codes. Coding concerns data acquisition, whereas variables constructed from codes concern conceptual and data analysis. To a certain extent, coding determines what variables are possible, but the range of possible variables from codes is much greater than might at first be assumed. For example, in the case of two persons in conversation, one coding of this conversation might map all the audible sounds made by a person into a state called "1" and all inaudible sounds into a state called "0." Every one-half second, for instance, each person is coded as being in the state 1 (audible sound) or 0 (no sound). The first two rows of Table 33 represent a sample of 10 seconds (20 time units) of interaction for two persons, A and B, coded in a 0–1 system.

Variable construction either preserves the complexity of the coded information or reduces it by some kind of summary procedure. One summary procedure removes all temporal information, indicating that A spoke for 4 seconds and B for 6.5 seconds. A summary that preserves some temporal information and uses 2-second intervals as an example is represented in the bottom rows of Table 33. The number of different variables that can be constructed from a microscopic coding process is only limited by the researcher's imagination. The transformation from coding to variable may, however, preserve complexity, or it may reduce it. The finer and more comprehensive the coding process, the more different variables and the greater the number of questions that can be posed about the interaction. As the fineness and

TABLE 33

Coding Vocalizations in 10 Seconds of Two-Person Interaction:
Two Summary Time Intervals

Time Units (0.5 sec)	1–4	5–8	9–12	13–16	17–20	Total Vocal (in secs)
Person A	0 0 0 0	0 1 1 1	1 1 1 1	1 0 0 0	0 0 0 0	4 secs
Person B	1 1 1 1	1 1 0 0	1 1 0 0	0 0 0 1	1 1 1 1	6.5 secs
Time Units (2.0 sec)	1	2	3	4	5	
Person A	0	3	4	1	0	4 secs
Person B	4	2	2	1	4	6.5 secs

exhaustiveness of the coding system increases, so does the energy, time, effort, and money required to complete the coding process and the analysis, however. Consequently, the researcher must decide between flexibility of analysis and resources in determining how exhaustive and how microscopic coding should be for the research question posed.

Degree of Inference.   The previous discussion includes examples where coders (or machines) record the occurrence of behavior. Judgment studies, on the other hand, are based on rating scales and interpretational codes. In these cases, coders are faced often with complex and difficult judgments or inferences. The consequence is that reliability of judgment may be a significant problem. Reliability of complex judgments can be improved, however, with a simple procedural change. If a researcher were building a scale to measure, say, attraction, that person would not begin by building a single item scale. Rather, several items would be generated, tested for consistency, and a final scale built from the sum (or average) of the items that tap consistently into the underlying construct. This procedure is based on classical test theory (Nunnally, 1978), which assumes that each item acting as an indicator of the underlying construct is subject to random measurement error. The scale constructed from the summed items is less susceptible to the random perturbations of individual items.

When coding judgments are complex and subject to a large amount of random variation, the researcher should consider using more than one judge and basing coding decisions on the mean of the judges' scores (under the assumption that the scores are positively correlated). In this case the judges are like the items serving as indicators of the underlying construct. This is the procedure that Rosenthal (1987) and his colleagues followed in their studies of nonverbal behavior (see also the chapter on judged adaptation by Cappella, this volume). Rather than carrying out the more costly procedure of objective coding or building an explicit interpretational code, many judges are used to render their impressions on rating or judgment scales of particular segments of interaction. Using the Spearman-Brown prophecy formula, Rosenthal showed that with relatively low levels of interjudge correlation, a sufficient number of judges can yield acceptable levels of effective reliability. For example, with a mean inter-judge reliability of .30 across a group of 10 judges, an effective reliability of .81 is obtained (Rosenthal, 1987, p. 11). Of course, the minimum requirement is that the judges' average inter-correlation be positive.

Time

In addition to coding, the second set of choices that the interaction researcher faces concerns when and how frequently to observe/code the events under study. When temporal sequences are the focus of study, then the timing of observations is crucial.

Basic Conceptions of Time.   Four conceptions of time are appropriate to the study of social interactions: continuous or "clock" time, "event" time, "embedded" time, and phenomenological or "experienced" time. *Clock time* is also called real or objective time. Descriptions of a phenomenon along a clock time base array the phenomena along a time line that is an interval or ratio scale fixed by a standard clock. For example, Jaffe and Feldstein (1970) adopted a clock time measuring unit assessing the presence and absence of vocalization every 300 milliseconds. The crucial feature of this case is that the time units are chosen *a priori* (sometimes for theoretical and sometimes for only practical reasons) and dictated by the standard clock.

Event time marks the time scale as ordinal rather than as interval. Time is marked by the occurrence of an event as defined operationally within the coding rules adopted by the researcher. In this case, coding and time of observation are intertwined inextricably. Once coding rules are established defining what constitutes an event, then time is necessarily marked by the event regardless of its relation to the ticks of a clock. For example, suppose a coding scheme focuses on who carries out deictic gestures in a three-person group (A, B, C). In Table 34, the sequence of events is represented in column 1, and the time of origination of the gesture in column 3. Event time only notes the sequence of events and their origination times. What is ignored in this representation is the clock time duration of the events (although it can be readily inferred in this case because the end time is included).

Much research, particularly research involving categorical coding schemes, adopts an event conception of time implicitly. For example, coding particular types of gestures such as deictic gestures are readily conceptualized as events. It is possible to have continuous coding systems associated with event time, but the conditions would be unusual. For example, the machine analysis of fundamental frequency of voice (Scherer, 1986) is a continuous measure defined in the presence of speech by a person. In the absence of speech, the frequency is not zero: It simply does not exist. In this case, it might be necessary to code fundamental frequency as a continuous code but defined only at those time points at which speech by the focal person is occurring.

Embedded time is a combination of clock and event time. In this case, time is established by the clock, but events are identified in their own right. They do not exist simply as "points" followed by other point events at some indeterminate time later. Rather they exist as events with a duration (time from initiation to termination) and latency (time from completion of the event to the beginning of the next event). The hypothetical data of Table 34 represent data in embedded time when one includes the times of column 4 in their description. Not only do we know that A initiated with deictic gesture, which was followed by one by B, but we also know that A's gesture took 5.0 seconds, and that no other gestures ensued until 23.0 seconds had elapsed.

Phenomenological time concerns the temporal evolution of the interaction as experienced by the participants or observers of the interaction. The basis for considering phenomenological units of time involves the argument that participants could not possibly process all that is occurring in an interaction while it is developing, so

TABLE 34

Representing Gestures as Events for a Group of Three:
Event Time Begins With Onset of an Event

Event	Person	Start Time (tenths of sec)	End Time
Gesture A1	A	000	050
Gesture B1	B	230	260
Gesture C1	C	285	345
Gesture A2	A	1080	1120
Gesture C2	C	1235	1285
Gesture B2	B	1300	1350
Gesture A3	A	1560	1575
Gesture C3	C	1635	1690

their units of decoding may shrink or expand as a function of various external conditions. For example, during periods of high conflict, decoding units may be finer than during periods of initial ritualized acquaintance making. From the encoding side, participants may produce their verbal and kinesic output in temporal units that are psychologically meaningful but have little clear relationship to clock time or researcher-defined coding events. The search for phenomenological units of time is the search for units of decoding and encoding that are meaningful to the participants in the interaction because they represent psychologically real units of reception and production respectively.

Terminology

Discussion of temporal coding can quickly become a confusing morass unless some clear definitions are set forward at the outset. Most of the definitions presented are pertinent to clock time rather than event time. "Observational time unit" means the smallest unit of time employed in coding. In some circumstances, particularly involving the machine coding of behavior (talk and silence patterns, loudness levels, etc.), a distinction between observational time unit and *observational window* is necessary. The observational window is the duration per observational time unit during which data acquisition actually occurs. For example, even though the observational time unit in the machine coding of talk and silence patterns may be 300 milliseconds, the sampling (i.e., the observational window) may be much shorter than that. In such a case, some kind of smoothing may be necessary so that results obtained during the window of observation are, in fact, representative of what is occurring during the entire observational time unit. These are technical questions that differ by behavior, acquisition device, and computer software.

A *sample* normally refers to a segment of the population selected according to some rule, usually in the hopes that the sample's characteristics are representative of the characteristics of the population as a whole. With regard to interaction there are two features of a sample to consider. The first is the sample of dyads or groups from the population selected for study. The second is the sample of interaction from the population of interactions that have or could occur. The sample of dyads or groups is not of special interest here because sampling considerations are no different from sampling of other individual cases from a population. The interaction sample is of special interest. "Interaction sample" is the proportion of the observed or recorded interaction selected for coding and analysis along with the rule for selection. For example, dyads might be brought into the laboratory for a series of eight 1-hour interactions over the course of a semester. This is the *population* of observed interactions. The researcher may select out, randomly, ten 20-turn sequences from each of the eight sessions for intensive coding and analysis. The ten 20-turn sequences from each of the eight sessions would be the sample, and the sampling rule would be random selection from the set of 20-turn sequences selected without replacement.

The third important basic term is *statistical time unit*. The observational unit does not need to be the time unit of statistical analysis. For example, Jaffe and Feldstein (1970) used a 300-millisecond observational unit but a 2-minute unit for statistical analysis of the sequential structure of talk–silence sequences. Clearly, the statistical unit will be equal to or larger than the observational unit in as much as the observational unit captures the maximal information available from the data.

Choosing an Observational Unit

Each observation unit has its own set of characteristics that may make it desirable (or not) for nonverbal researchers. The fundamental issue in clock time is deciding how frequently to carry out the process of observation. This question is independent of a coding system. If one codes too infrequently, real changes in behavior may be missed. If one codes too frequently, not only is the coding effort inefficient (and therefore costly), but too many codes without any actual behavioral change are obtained. When the observational unit is too coarse, transitions can be missed. When observational units are too fine, the frequency of a code following itself $f(1|1)$ and $f(0|0)$ becomes increasingly numerous and distorts the real within-state transitions.

What can be done? The researcher would like to be able to observe frequently enough to pick up all real changes but not so frequently as to distort the frequency of codes following themselves. Arundale (1978, 1980, 1996) addressed this problem in a series of papers. When the codes are categorical, then in order to resolve completely all of the real transitions between states, the smallest observational unit must be less than the shortest interval that a variable can remain in one of its states. When the codes are continuous, cycles or periods are possible in the trajectory of the data, and these cycles or periods must be resolved. The conclusion is that the smallest observation unit must be at least one half the period of fastest cycle.

Arundale (1978) points out that when precise temporal timing is crucial to one's research questions, then preliminary studies should be undertaken with a variety of observational time units, which decrease in size. Two outcomes should be obtained for the different observational time units: between-state transitions and sojourn times. As the observational time unit approaches the optimal unit, the *between-state* transitions should stop changing in frequency. This asymptote would indicate that all real state changes are being detected. *Sojourn times* are the duration that the system is in a particular state. For example, the average sojourn times for dyads remaining in a state of mutual silence has been reported as 0.413 seconds with standard deviations of 0.055. The mean minus two standard deviations gives a good idea of the shortest state durations within this set of codes. Thus, the observational time unit of 0.300 appears to be a good choice for the observational time unit for these data. Cappella and Streibel (1979) applied these techniques to assessing the observational time unit for talk–silence analyses.

A wholly different approach to the time unit problem is to remove it from the objective domain and place it into the *perceptual* domain. This is exactly what Walker and Trimboli (1982) did with the pause unit in human speech. If people cannot detect pauses smaller than some minimum value and if one research's questions are dependent on this detection (as they are in most applications of talk–silence research), then perhaps that perceptual minimum should constitute the observational time unit for study. Walker and Trimboli (1982) found that 42% of the 100-millisecond pauses were accurately detected, 52% of the 200-millisecond pauses, 69% of the 300-millisecond pauses, 77% of the 400-millisecond pauses, and so on. Researchers must keep their research domains clearly in mind when considering issues related to temporal measurement. Some studies require careful attention to the observational time unit and some pretesting to determine optimal values. Such studies are concerned with precision timing of behavior relative to other behaviors or between persons.

Likewise, there are two ways to capture events, one based on objective definitions, and the other based on social definitions of events. Only the latter is appropriate for event time formulations. An objective definition of an event would be based on the presence of a sequence of identical codes for a particular categorical code in clock time. For example, consider the following talk and silence strings at 300-millisecond intervals for two persons, A and B:

A: SSSSSTTTTTTTTTTSSSSSSSSSTTSSSSSSSSSSSSSTTTTTTTT

B: SSTTTSSSSSSSSSSSSSTTTTTTTTTTTTTTTTTTTSSSSSSSSSSS

On the basis of an objective definition, there are three talk events for A and two for B. The events are defined by the sequence of T codes bounded at either end by S codes. These sequences can be identified as events in clock time, not in event time. Event time assumes that the time domain is divided in terms of occurrences of certain sorts. For example, an event could be a word, a phrase unit, an utterance, a proposition, a turn at talk, a gestural initiation and termination, and so on. Codes are then made on the units that define event time.

One fundamental issue that is rarely addressed in studies of social interaction concerns how people are capable of processing all the stimulation present. Are they simply very powerful absorbers of information? Or, more realistically, are they only differentially monitoring what is happening in social interactions? If the latter, then it is important to know when more careful monitoring is occurring. These periods of careful and more superficial monitoring suggest that time is not spread evenly across the interactional stream, but, rather, it is experienced as more and less dense as a function of factors relevant to the process of the interaction itself (i.e., phenomenal time).

Whereas no direct research has studied whether participants or observers monitor interactions more or less carefully, research by Newtson (1976) has shown that subjects *can* identify break points in behavioral streams with some consistency, that there are individual differences in how finely people monitor action sequences, and that the information density is greater within the vicinity of identified breakpoints than it is at nonbreakpoints. In interaction contexts, we might speculate that the breakpoints would accumulate when more careful monitoring occurs. The implication for interaction analysis is that more precise and complete analysis would be directed at these temporally denser time periods than at others.

SUMMARY

This chapter discussed the general issues of data coding and temporal display of nonverbal behavior. Analysis of sequences both within-person and between-person depends in large measure on the quality and amount of data to which the researcher has access. The quality of data depends on the coding of variables and the conceptions of time implicit in the coding and selected explicitly by the researcher.

REFERENCES

Arundale, R. B. (1978). Sampling across time for communication research: A simulation. In P. M. Hirsch, P. V. Miller, & F. G. Kline (Eds.), *Strategies for communication research* (pp. 257–285). Beverly Hills, CA: Sage.

Arundale, R. B. (1980). Studying change over time: Criteria for sampling continuous variables. *Communication Research, 7*, 227–263.

Arundale, R. B. (1996). Indexing pattern over time: Criteria for studying communication as a dynamic process. In J. Watt & C. A. van Lear (Eds.), *Dynamic patterns in communication processes* (pp. 95–118). Thousand Oaks, CA: Sage.

Ashby, W. R. (1963). *An introduction to cybernetics.* New York: Science editions.

Bernieri, F. J., & Rosenthal, R. (1991). Interpersonal coordination: Behavior matching and interactional synchrony. In R. S. Feldman & B. Rime (Eds.), *Fundamentals of nonverbal behavior* (pp. 401–432). Cambridge: Cambridge University Press.

Cappella, J. N. (1987). Interpersonal communication: Definitions and questions. In C. R. Berger & S. Chaffee (Eds.), *The handbook of communication science* (pp. 184–238). Beverly Hills, CA: Sage.

Cappella, J. N., & Streibel, M. J. (1979). Computer analysis of talk–silence sequences: The FIASSCO system. *Behavior Research Methods and Instrumentation, 11*, 384–392.

Davis, D. (1982). Determinants of responsiveness in dyadic interaction. In W. I. Ickes & E. S. Knowles (Eds.), *Personality, roles, and social behaviors* (pp. 85–139). New York: Springer-Verlag.

Gottman, J. M. (1979a). *Marital interaction.* New York: Academic Press.

Gottman, J. M. (1979b). Detecting cyclicity in social interaction. *Psychological Bulletin, 86*, 338–348.

Hinde, R. A. (1979). *Towards understanding relationships.* London: Academic Press.

Jaffe, J., & Feldstein, S. (1970). *Rhythms of dialogue.* New York: Academic Press.

Natale, M. (1975a). Convergence of mean vocal intensity in dyadic communication as a function of social desirability. *Journal of Personality and Social Psychology, 32*, 790–804.

Natale, M. (1975b). Social desirability as related to convergence of temporal speech patterns. *Perceptual and Motor Skills, 40*, 827–830.

Newtson, D., & Engquist, G. (1976). The perceptual organization of on9going behavior. *Journal of Experimental Social Psychology. 12*, 436–450.

Nunnally, J. C. (1978). *Psychometric theory* (2nd ed.). New York: McGraw-Hill.

Rosenthal, R. (1987). *Judgment studies: Design, analysis and meta-analysis.* Cambridge: Cambridge University Press.

Scherer, K. R. (1986). Vocal affect expression: A review and a model for future research. *Psychological Bulletin, 99*, 143–165.

Street, R. L., & Cappella, J. N. (Eds.). (1985). *Sequence and pattern communication behavior.* London: Edward Arnold.

Street, R. L., & Cappella, J. N. (1989). Social and linguistic factors influencing adaptation in children's speech. *Journal of Psycholinguistic Research, 18*, 497–519.

Tickle-Degnen, L., & Rosenthal, R. (1987). Group rapport and nonverbal behavior. *Review of Personality and Social Psychology, 9*, 113–136.

Walker, M. B., & Trimboli, C. (1982). Smooth transitions in conversational interactions. *The Journal of Social Psychology, 117*, 305–306.

Objective Measurement of Vocal Signals

Kyle James Tusing
University of Arizona

INTRODUCTION

Speech was the first form of human communication, predating the alphabet (Kent & Read, 2002). Even in the current technology-laden world, speech continues to be a fundamental part of the human communication experience. One's speech, and by extension, one's voice, is linked inextricably with the meaning behind one's words and with one's unique identity. As such, the study of the human voice is of interest to those who study human behavior, particularly those who study human communication. The study of the human voice is also sometimes known as *the study of nonverbal features of speech*: vocal cues, prosodic cues, acoustic analysis, psychoacoustics, or vocalics.

One way to distinguish different research approaches to studying the voice is to focus on the measurement strategy adopted, namely, whether subjective or objective methods are used to measure the voice. *Subjective voice measurement* refers to observer judgments about a vocal signal (e.g., Berry, 1992; Burgoon, Birk, & Pfau, 1990). For example, participants or coders might be asked to rate the pitch of an actor's voice on a 1–7 scale where 1 = low and 7 = high. In such cases, the voice is regarded as a perceptual construct. On the other hand, *objective voice measurement* refers to physical measures of voice that are not subject to judgment (e.g., Ohala, 1982, 1983, 1984; Scherer, 1974; Scherer & Oshinsky, 1977). For example, the fundamental frequency (F_0) of an actor's voice, which generally corresponds to perceived pitch, can be determined with the appropriate equipment. Here, the voice is studied as a physical construct.

This chapter discusses an objective measurement strategy for the voice. Although subjective measurement strategies are easier to employ and do not require mastery of any complex equipment or software, the data produced by subjective

393

measurement strategies are qualitatively different from objectively derived voice data. That is not to say that one measurement technique or type of data is better than the other; they are just different. Objectively derived voice data tend to "cost" more due to time, equipment, and labor investments, but once the initial investment is made, the payoff can be rewarding in terms of the types of research questions one can investigate and the conclusions that may emerge (Scherer, 1986). A brief history about the development of objective vocal measurement is discussed first, followed by a review of how it has been applied in recent communication research. Then, how the measure can be used is explained. Finally, the chapter concludes with potential applications of the objective vocal measurement technique.

A BRIEF HISTORY OF OBJECTIVE VOCAL MEASUREMENT

Development

There is a long history of objective measurement of the human voice. The voice has been and continues to be studied objectively in a wide variety of disciplines including communication, communication disorders, linguistics, physics, and psychology. The initial difficulty in studying the voice and its physical properties was that the voice is, and continues to be, fleeting. However, the invention of devices that could record, store, and analyze the human voice allowed research that had not previously been possible. Despite the invention of these devices, significant investment in labor, materials, and costs were incurred. The digital revolution that has seen computer equipment become affordable to the average researcher has made objective measurement of the voice an option for social scientists of all types. As with many other tasks, such as word processing and accounting, modern methods of speech analysis have been fully integrated with the digital computer (Kent & Read, 2002). Similarly, an abundance of affordable and, in some cases, free computer software is now available for researchers' use. No longer does cost-prohibitive hardware or software serve as a barrier to objective measurement of the voice (see Table 35 for a range of software choices).

Definitions

According to Frick (1985), prosodic features of the voice refer to any nonverbal feature, such as pitch, loudness, or rate. Speech can be described in any of three different ways. First, it can be described by referencing its auditory features, which refers to how speech is perceived. Auditory features correspond to subjective voice measurement strategies. Second, speech can be described by its articulatory elements, which corresponds to the production of speech. Third, speech can be described by its acoustic characteristics, which refers to properties of sound independent of perception as measured mechanically. Thus, the acoustic features of the voice correspond to objective measurement strategies. Auditory terms for

TABLE 35
Software Resources for Objective Vocal Measurement

1) Audio Spectrum Analysis; Spectrogram Version 6. Cost: register for shareware ($25).
http://www.visualizationsoftware.com/gram.html
2) Cool Edit Pro. Cost: $399; can be downloaded for 30-minute sessions to try it out.
http://www.syntrillium.com/cep/
3) PRAAT. Cost: free; request program from author.
http://www.fon.hum.uva.nl/praat/
4) Speech Analyzer. Cost: free.
http://www.sil.org/computing/catalog/speechanalyzer.html
5) Speech Filing System. Cost: free.
http://www.phon.ucl.ac.uk/resource/sfs/
6) TF32. Cost: varies for different versions.
http://userpages.chorus.net/cspeech/
7) Wavesurfer. Cost: free.
http://www.speech.kth.se/wavesurfer/

vocal characteristics are pitch and loudness, which are subjective judgments. Acoustic terms that correspond to pitch and loudness are F_0 and intensity, respectively, which are objective features of the voice. When a person speaks, an objective vocal signal with defined properties is perceived by an observer, rendering the signal subjective. As such, the names for the objective and subjective parts of the message are different.

Pittam (1994) distinguishes three parameters that are basic to physical measures of vocal cues: measures underlying loudness, pitch, and time. Whereas *loudness* is a perceptual phenomenon influenced by a number of physical correlates of which amplitude is one, *amplitude* refers to the amount of sound energy expended to produce a vocalization. The perception of loudness increases as amplitude increases, although other factors such as frequency also moderate loudness judgments. Two amplitude measures are *mean amplitude* (i.e., average) and *amplitude variation* (i.e., the extent to which a vocalization varies around its mean amplitude value).

Similarly, whereas *pitch* is a perceptual phenomenon commonly represented by a physical measurement of F_0, F_0 is the number of vibrations per second made by the vocal folds to produce a vocalization. Perceived pitch increases as F_0 increases, although the relationship is not perfectly linear. As with amplitude, two measures of F_0 are *mean F_0* (i.e., average) and *F_0 variation* (i.e., the extent to which a vocalization varies around its mean F_0 value).

Variables associated with *time* are not vocal measures per se; rather, they co-occur with, or accompany, vocalizations. *Speech rate* is one such commonly studied variable; it refers to the number of words or syllables uttered in a given period of time, either a second or a minute (see Buller, this volume). However, it too can be measured objectively by taking word counts and measurements of time, rather than having observers make judgments of a speaker's rate.

Purpose and Validation of Objective Measurement

The purpose of objective measurement of vocal cues is to provide a physical, rather than perceptual, description of the human voice. A physical description of the voice is useful because it is not subject to human error. In addition, some theoretical questions require physical measures of the voice, rather than judgments. Ultimately, objective measurement of the voice provides a fundamentally different type of data from subjective judgments made about the voice.

There are two important validity concerns when considering objective measurement of the voice. First, care must be taken with the vocal signal at all times. There are multiple steps in the recording, conversion, storing, and analyzing process where the vocal signal could become corrupted. Because any conclusions are only as valid as the vocal signal that is measured is genuine, it is important to make sure the vocal signal corresponds to the same phenomenon that the researcher is investigating. Second, the ease of analyzing vocal cues with computer software requires caution, as results that lack meaning can easily be produced. The problem is similar to that of using computerized statistical programs. That is, one can fairly easily load a data set and then perform statistical operations such as factor analysis by using pull-down menus. However, if the user is not aware of the many decision points that can change the outcome of a factor analysis, or if the user interprets the results of the factor analysis incorrectly, then in effect the results that are produced are not useful.

APPLICATIONS OF OBJECTIVE VOCAL MEASUREMENT

A recent project that employed objective methods to measure the human voice is Tusing and Dillard's (2000) investigation of the impact of the voice on the relational variable of dominance. This study is used as an exemplar to illustrate how objective measures can be paired with research questions to produce unique conclusions that would not be possible with subjective measures of the voice. Tusing and Dillard observed that larger organisms generally are able to dominate smaller organisms. As a result, low frequency, high amplitude sounds became associated with intimidation and hostility, the sounds made by large animals, whereas high frequency, low amplitude sounds became associated with submissiveness and a lack of aggression, or the sounds made by small animals. So, mean levels of fundamental frequency and amplitude were argued to communicate dominance directly, whereas speech rate and measures of central tendency with respect to fundamental frequency and amplitude were argued to convey dominance indirectly by virtue of their indication of involvement. This set of predictions was best tested using objective measures of the human voice.

Tusing and Dlard had multiple groups of participants listen to 320 brief messages delivered b videotaped actors. Participants rated how dominant the messages were perceived to be. However, instead of having participants also provide subjective ratings of acoustic properties of the messages such as pitch and loudness, fundamental freqency and amplitude properties of each videotaped message were measured with cmputer software designed for that task. This measurement strategy allowed the relational judgment of dominance to be compared to the various objective acoustic variables. The hypothesis tests and conclusions that emerged from the study would not have been possible without the objective methodology employed.

EQUIPMENT NEEDED FOR OBJECTIVE VOCAL MEASUREMENT

Three areas to consider when objectively measuring the human voice are recording, hardware, and software. At each step, the decisions that are made can greatly influence the final research product. Each of these three areas is reviewed in turn.

Recording

When recording voices, achieving a usable vocal signal is important. To achieve a usable vocal signal, it is necessary to be aware of the quality of one's recording equipment. The quality of the vocal signal one has to analyze is dependent on the recording equipment one uses as well as the recording technique used to archive voice recordings. Audio technicians should be consulted on microphone selection and placement prior to recording. Once such decisions are made, the recording specifications should be kept consistent so that variation is provided only by the different characteristics of each voice that is recorded. Laboratory environments offer a great advantage in terms of eliminating noise in the signal. However, researchers should also consider field recordings for their authenticity. Last, archived vocal signals are often convenient, but they do not provide control over recording of the signal. When information about how the vocal signal was recorded is available, it should be specified.

Hardware

In addition to recording, there are hardware decisions to be made. Hardware considerations revolve around the computing power one has available to store and analyze vocal signals. Computers represent sound waves as numbers (Ladefoged, 1996), and those numbers require memory and processing speed to be stored and analyzed. A simple dictum is that the more memory and processing speed one's computer has, the better. That being said, many research labs and offices have the necessary computer speed and memory for large scale analysis of vocal signals. Hard-drive space is especially useful for storage and quick retriev of vocal signals. External storage is also an option, but it tends to slow down the analysis.

One piece of additional equipment necessary for acoustic anlysis is a sound-card. This is a device that allows a computer to perform a number of basic acoustic functions, including playing back vocal signals. Often included in soundcard is an analog-to-digital (A/D) converter, which transforms sound waves o digital format, allowing analysis to take place. A/D converters can also be acquire separately from a soundcard.

Software

A last issue to consider is software. This is a matter of personal choce and software performance. As with most software programs, there is a fair amount of labor that must be invested before one is adept at using it. Thus, ease of use or documentation may be the most important criterion when selecting a program to analyze speech. For other researchers, cost may be the most important variable. Many of the popular software programs perform similar analytic functions, but car should always be taken that one can perform the desired task with a given program. Table 35 provides a list of popular software programs along with information about the cost, as well as web sites to consult for additional information.

ANALYZING THE SIGNAL

Once a researcher has a signal to analyze and the proper equipment assembled, three steps are necessary for digitally analyzing a speech signal. They are digitization, filtering, and analysis. These three steps are described in the order in which they should be carried out.

Digitizing the Signal

Digitizing an analog speech signal consists of two parts: sampling and quantization. *Sampling* is the process of converting an analog signal to a series of samples. After this conversion process is complete, the samples can be stored digitally in a computer. For example, at a rate of 22 kilohertz (kHz), a speech signal is sampled 22,000 times per second. Using a sampling rate of 22 kHz captures all the sounds of interest associated with the human voice (Ladefoged, 1996). Once a speech signal has been sampled, it is converted from continuous time to discrete time. However, the amplitude or energy level of each sample also must be converted to digital form for digitization to be complete. *Quantization* is the process where the continuous amplitude variations of an analog signal are converted to discrete amplitude increments. A *quantum* is an increment of energy. Thus, as the number of quantization levels increases, the quantized digital signal bears a stronger resemblance to the continuous analog signal. Kent and Read (2002) suggest 12-bit conversion (where 4096 quantization levels are used) as the minimum for analyzing speech, and note that 16-and 32-bit conversions are becoming readily available with the rapid advancement of computer technology.

Filtering the Signal

Serious sampling errors, termed *aliasing*, can result if frequencies at greater than half the sampling frequency are analyzed (Kent & Read, 2002). Aliasing is the term given to a speech signal that is undersampled because it is a false representation, or an alias, of an original speech signal. Filters, which can be external hardware components or digital soundcard components, allow researchers the ability to manipulate the frequency of a speech signal that is sampled. Consequently, when a filter is used in concert with a known sampling rate, researchers have the ability to avoid aliasing errors. For this reason, it is critical to filter a speech signal any time speech is digitally analyzed. Nyquist's sampling theorem (see Kent & Read, 2002; Ladefoged, 1996 for applications) states that the sampling rate must be at least twice the highest frequency of interest to prevent aliasing errors from occurring.

Analyzing the Signal

Once an analog signal is digitized and filtered, software programs allow measurement operations to be performed on a digitized speech signal to derive objective information about acoustic properties of an original speech signal. Utterances can be selected so that one can analyze single words or entire sentences. After the vocal signal is selected, any number of analyses can be performed on the chosen speech unit. Typical operations would be an analysis of the F_0 and amplitude properties of the vocal signal. More sophisticated analyses are also possible given one's research agenda and methodological competence.

POTENTIAL USES OF OBJECTIVE VOCAL MEASUREMENT

There are a number of theoretical and applied questions that objective voice data can be used to study. For example, Tusing and Dillard (2000) investigated vocal signals and dominance and used an evolutionary perspective to develop their hypotheses, focusing on the adaptive advantage offered by communicating dominance with nonverbal features of the voice. Similarly, inferences about other relational judgments such as affiliation, formality, and trust can be derived from the causal association between the voice that produces such messages and the effect that those messages have on receivers. In a similar fashion, message judgments such as source expertise and credibility can be investigated based on objective properties of the voice that produced those messages.

Other nonverbal communication behaviors such as gestures, gaze, proximity, and touching behavior can be investigated in conjunction with objective indices of nonverbal characteristics of the voice. Nonverbal behaviors other than the voice are frequently measured objectively (see Kinney's chapter in this volume), but due to previous methodological constraints, the voice has relied on subjective participant judgments. Some studies have compared objective and subjective vocal data (Rockwell, Buller, & Burgoon, 1997) and have found that the two methods do not always produce similar results, particularly with respect to loudness or intensity. Past studies using participant ratings of the voice could be reconceived to determine if the conclusions hold up.

Another potential area for applying objective vocal measurement is investigating the link between the human voice and one's self-concept and personality (Louth, Williamson, Alpert, Pouget, & Hare, 1998). The voice is part of one's identity, and as such represents and reflects one's personality and sense of self. Much like the way smiling can have a positive impact on the smiler's mood (Strack, Martin, & Stepper, 1988), the sound of one's voice may be linked to conceptions of self and how the self is presented to others. Finally, researchers have spent considerable time investigating communication in the context of deception (Burgoon, Buller, Ebesu, & Rockwell, 1994). Gains could be made by analyzing objective characteristics of the voice as indicators of deceptive social actors, just as other objective nonverbal indicators such as smiling have been linked to deception (Ekman, Friesen, & O'Sullivan, 1988).

REFERENCES

Berry, D. S. (1992). Vocal types and stereotypes: Joint effects of vocal attractiveness and vocal maturity on person perception. *Journal of Nonverbal Behavior, 16,* 41–54.

Burgoon, J. K., Birk, T., & Pfau, M. (1990). Nonverbal behaviors, persuasion, and credibility. *Human Communication Research, 17,* 140–169.

Burgoon, J. K., Buller, D. B., Ebesu, A. S., & Rockwell, P. (1994). Interpersonal deception: V. Accuracy in deception detection. *Communication Monographs, 61,* 303–325.

Ekman, P., Friesen, W. V., & O'Sullivan, M. (1988). Smiles when lying. *Journal of Personality and Social Psychology, 54,* 414–420.

Frick, R. W. (1985). Communicating emotion: The role of prosodic features. *Psychological Bulletin, 97,* 412–429.

Kent, R. D., & Read, C. (2002). *The acoustic analysis of speech* (2nd ed.). Albany, NY: Singular/Thomson Learning.

Ladefoged, P. (1996). *Elements of acoustic phonetics* (2nd ed.). Chicago, IL: University of Chicago Press.

Louth, S. M., Williamson, S., Alpert, M., Pouget, E. R., & Hare, R. D. (1998). Acoustic distinctions in the speech of male psychopaths. *Psycholinguistic Research, 27,* 375–384.

Ohala, J. J. (1982). The voice of dominance. *Journal of the Acoustical Society of America, 72,* S66.

Ohala, J. J. (1983). Cross-language use of pitch: An ethological view. *Phonetica, 40,* 1–18.

Ohala, J. J. (1984). An ethological perspective on common cross-language utilization of F_0 of voice. *Phonetica, 41,* 1–16.

Pittam, J. (1994). *Voice in social interaction: An interdisciplinary approach.* Thousand Oaks, CA: Sage.

Rockwell, P., Buller, D. B., & Burgoon, J. K. (1997). Measurement of deceptive voices: Comparing acoustic and perceptual data. *Applied Psycholinguistics, 18,* 471–484.

Scherer, K. R. (1974). Acoustic concomitants of emotional dimensions: Judging affect from synthesized tone sequences. In S. Weitz (Ed.), *Nonverbal communication* (pp. 105–111). New York, NY: Oxford University Press.

Scherer, K. R. (1986). Vocal affect expression: A review and a model for future research. *Psychological Bulletin, 99*, 143–165.

Scherer, K. R., & Oshinsky, J. S. (1977). Cue utilization in emotion attribution from auditory stimuli. *Motivation and Emotion, 1*, 331–346.

Strack, F., Martin, L. L., & Stepper, S. (1988). Inhibiting and facilitating conditions of the human smile: A nonobtrusive test of the facial feedback hypothesis. *Journal of Personality and Social Psychology, 54*, 768–777.

Tusing, K. J., & Dillard, J. P. (2000). The sounds of dominance: Vocal precursors of perceived dominance during interpersonal influence. *Human Communication Research, 26*, 148–171.

The Role of Physiological Measures in Understanding Social Support Communication

Terry A. Kinney
University of Minnesota

INTRODUCTION

With the current emphasis within the social and psychological sciences that is placed on the relationship between emotions and well-being (e.g., Diener, Lucas, & Oishi, 2002; Snyder & Lopez, 2002) and its manifestation within communication (e.g., Andersen & Guerrero, 1998), nonverbal behavior is experiencing a resurgence of theoretical interest and perceived functional importance (Andersen, 1999). This resurgence is especially prominent for an area that can be captured by the label "social support." The communication of social support can take a number of forms, involving both verbal (Applegate, 1980; Burleson, 1982, 1994a) and nonverbal expressions (Andersen, 1999; Barbee, Rowatt, & Cunningham, 1998; Jones & Guerrero, 2001; Trees, 2000, this volume). Thus, examining its complexities and the processes that link it to social and psychological outcomes is essential to understand how social support works.

One of the important factors that underlie the communication of social support is the ability to express affective and emotional states that serve both social and emotional functions. Often, attempts to be supportive are driven by a desire to connect in a meaningful and significant way to one's partner to foster acceptance, affiliation, comfort, concern, and interest (Bippus, 2001; Burleson, 1994a; Cutrona, 1996). Successful installation of relational, psychological, and affective outcomes suggests that social support is strategic (cf. Bippus, 2001; Burleson, 1994b). This acknowledgment makes understanding the specific mechanisms that underlie the effectiveness of social support messages of particular importance.

Scholars who focus on the communication of social support are able to position nonverbal behavior as an essential component of supportive interactions (e.g., Barbee & Cunningham, 1995; Jones & Guerrero, 2001; Trees, 2000). The focus on nonverbal cues has effectively moved this class of behaviors from a supporting role into one that functions to drive the nature of the interaction and its outcomes (e.g., Jones & Guerrero, 2001) and to convey meaning (e.g., Manusov & Trees, 2002; Trees, 2000). This focus also points up the need to expand our set of conceptual and operational measures to assess how aspects of nonverbal behaviors relate to social support processes and their outcomes.

One important aspect of nonverbal behavior that has not been examined systematically by social support researchers is physiology and its relationship to the effectiveness of social support messages. Understanding how physiological processes relate to aspects of social support communication reveals how the processes of affect and arousal link to the effectiveness of social support messages for both the source and the target. This chapter discusses a select, but representative, set of conceptual and methodological issues surrounding the use of *physiological measures* in social science research. The goal of this discussion is to demonstrate that the use of physiological measures is as important as cognitive and behavioral indices when one is examining what makes social support communication effective.

Due to space constraints, however, this chapter is not designed to be a technical primer for how to conduct studies using physiological measures or how to use the technology of physiological measurement. Several excellent sources exist for this information (e.g., Blascovich, 2000; Cacioppo & Petty, 1983; Cacioppo, Petty, & Andersen, 1988; Cacioppo & Tassinary, 1990; Cacioppo, Tassinary, & Berntson, 2000; Coles, Donchin, & Porges, 1986; Martin & Venables, 1980; Obrist, Black, Brener, & DiCara, 1974; Stern, Ray, & Davis, 1980), and technical manuals are readily available from specific equipment vendors (see appendix).

JUSTIFICATION

As noted, researchers who study the communication of social support have embraced a set of cognitive and behavioral measures to assess the nature and intensity of affective, psychological, and relational outcomes related to receiving social support messages. Furthermore, these methodologies have been very successful in providing an understanding of what makes social support communication effective, especially in terms of its nature (e.g., Bippus, 2001; Burleson, 1994a, 1994b; Jones & Guerrero, 2001). However, in general, scholars who examine the process of social support have been less willing (or able) to include assessments of physiological events and processes in their research designs—even though these measures are related theoretically to affective and social outcomes (Blascovich, 2000; Cacioppo, Petty, & Tassinary, 1989; Diamond, 2001, 2003; Gottman & Levenson, 1988; Wagner, 1988; Wagner & Manstead, 1989) and potentially lend themselves to less subjectivity and perceptual bias than self-reports or behavioral coding techniques (see Tusing, this volume).

Incorporation of physiological measures into research that examines social support processes may add significantly to our understanding of the effectiveness of social support behavior. Inclusion of a wider array of measures that assess various aspects of social support communication is particularly important when one considers the prominence that physiological (i.e., autonomic, central nervous system, and hormonal) processes play in the activation and expression of emotional states (Ekman & Davidson, 1994; Ekman, Levenson, & Friesen, 1983). Theoretically, emotional states can be defined and discriminated along cognitive, physiological, and behavioral indices (see Ekman & Davidson, 1994). This delineation suggests that researchers should consider including measures of physiological processes when examining aspects of emotional communication to ensure that the essential components of emotions are included into their research designs.

Another way that the importance of physiological measures is demonstrated is through the theoretical and methodological sophistication that can be employed by their use. Often, the measurement of physiological processes allows for assessments of emotional intensity, type, or effects within overtime or "online" (i.e., real time) designs. Questions of mutual influence, reactivity, or adaptation during social interaction are quite easily assessed using physiological measurements. In some cases, the use of physiological measurements is more precise and sensitive than either self-report technologies or third-party coding of videotaped interaction sequences. This is especially true when one needs to assess subtle and fleeting aspects of social interaction or when one desires to assess interaction tendencies that may be masked due to social desirability pressures. For example, work that has examined the effect of receiving hostility (i.e., lack of social support) shows that the affective and physiological reactions of those exposed to hostility can be used to explain decreased relational satisfaction, relational violence, and emotional abuse (Gottman, Coan, Carrère, & Swanson, 1998; Gottman, Jacobson, Rushe, & Shortt, 1995; Gottman & Levenson, 1992; Gottman & Notarius, 2000; Jacobson et al., 1994; Levenson & Gottman, 1985).

Conversely, work that has examined the effect of receiving social support shows that social support relates to increased liking (Burleson & Samter, 1985), increased relational quality (Carrère, Buehlman, Gottman, Coan, & Ruckstuhl, 2000; Cutrona, 1996; Cutrona & Suhr, 1994; Gurung, Sarason, & Sarason, 1997), reduced stress (Cutrona & Russell, 1990; Cutrona & Suhr, 1992), and positive mood states (Bippus, 2001), indicating that the affective and physiological states experienced during the process of social support play an important role in increasing the effectiveness of social support messages (cf. Shortt & Gottman, 1997). These studies suggest that affective and physiological states activated in response to types of (non)supportive communication exert influence on perceptions of relational quality, highlighting the role that physiology plays during interaction. In fact, recently, Diamond (2001, 2003) argued for the use of physiological measures to examine the processes underlying affective bonding among adults, which is arguably an important outcome of the social support process.

This is not to say that physiological measures are without their problems. From a measurement perspective, however, taking into account the physiological aspects of social support communication allows more complete exploration of support processes, especially in terms of its functions and effects. Based on the belief that physiological measures are important and maybe of particular use to nonverbal researchers, the discussion turns to the conceptual and technical issues surrounding the measurement of physiological events.

What Do Physiological Measures Measure?

Physiological measures, which range from simple assessments of autonomic activation (sweating, temperature, blood pressure, and heart rate) to sophisticated assessments of central nervous system and brain activation, are generally assumed to be indicators of information processing, cognitive loads, or the activation of affective states and behavioral scripts (see Blascovich, 2000; Cacioppo & Tassinary, 1990; Coles, Donchin, & Porges, 1986). Thus, physiological measurements can inform us on the nature and intensity of cognitive activities and their relationship to affective, behavioral, and social outcomes.

Why Are Physiological Measures of Value to Nonverbal Researchers?

The fact that aspects of physiology are activated under a wide array of conditions is testament to the centrality of the link between environment, thoughts, emotions, and response/action tendencies (Clore, 1994; Ellsworth, 1994; Frijda, 1994; Izard, 1994). For example, frowns and smiles can be discriminated using physiological measures even when the person under study is not consciously aware he or she has activated a frown or a smile response. The implication for nonverbal researchers is that even if the facial display is not manifest with sufficient intensity to be detected by another interactant, or by coders, the activation of the behavioral script may influence how an individual interacts by altering his or her reactions and thoughts; these thoughts may then be displayed in very subtle ways. Detection and discrimination of these subtle displays (and other physiological events such as heart rate changes or changes in sweating) and their relationship to the effectiveness of social support communication is of fundamental importance for many scholars, including nonverbal researchers.

Physiological measures add to our measurement toolbox the ability to "see" how cognitive loads, effort, and affective activation link to the process of social support and its outcomes. As Gottman and colleagues' body of work (e.g., Gottman et al., 1998; Gottman et al., 1995; Gottman & Notarius, 2000) illustrates regarding interpersonal hostility, inclusion of physiological measures adds explanatory power not only to detect reactions that are meaningful, but also to advance predictions regarding the effectiveness of communication to bring about psychological and social change. One of the important and consistent findings that surfaced from

Gottman's work with married couples is that their physiological responses to interpersonal interactions are able to predict relational quality and success.

Clearly, the implication for nonverbal research is that a deeper understanding of how social support communication works may be gleaned by using physiological measures that link messages and behavioral displays of the person who is producing the supportive communication to the affective reactions of the recipient. As a result, the ability of verbal and nonverbal behavioral sequences to produce affective states in recipients can be linked to psychological and social outcomes such as closeness, affection, comfort, concern, and caring. Thus, understanding the physiological markers that may form the foundation for these psychological and social outcomes will advance our understanding of the process of social support and will contribute to our understanding of its effectiveness

It is likely that the intensity and nature of one's physiological and affective reactions during an interaction influence the extent to which one perceives warmth, caring, concern, and connectedness. It remains to be seen if the outcomes traditionally associated with social support are distinct physiologically so that they can be discerned and attributed to specific outcomes. However, theoretical developments in social psychophysiology (Blascovich, 2000; Cacioppo, Petty, & Andersen, 1988; Cacioppo, Petty, & Tassinary, 1989; Gottman & Levenson, 1988), adult attachment (Diamond, 2001), affective bonding (Diamond, 2003; Gottman, 1998), and the psychobiology of stress (Gunnar & Davis, 2003) suggest that physiological systems may operate distinctly enough to discern unique patterns regarding social behavior and social outcomes. These developments are exciting and significant because they provide researchers with the conceptual tools to advance predictions regarding the significance of physiology to the process and outcomes of social support.

An additional value of physiological measures for nonverbal researchers is found in the fact that these measures allow researchers to link internal states to specific nonverbal behaviors or to sets and sequences of nonverbal displays. The methodological sophistication surrounding physiological measures, coupled with the use of videotape or digital technologies, allows nonverbal researchers to link internal states with behavioral displays at a very precise level in both the source and target. This ability enables researchers to test the assumption that specific behaviors or sequences of displays are manifestations of internal cognitive, emotional, or behavioral states, and to form explanations regarding the effectiveness of messages and message features to induce affective states in recipients. Thus, nonverbal researchers are able to examine the extent to which physiological processes contributed to the nature and effectiveness of nonverbal displays during interaction.

The technology that acquires physiological measures provides real-time records that are distinctly different from videotaped or audiotaped records, allowing for the monitoring of multiple systems during experimental tasks and conditions to assess the interaction between tasks, conditions, and each research participant's internal state. In addition, advances in acquisition technology have made the interface between subject and data collection equipment largely unobtrusive, or sufficiently unobtrusive enough to be easily ignored or forgotten. Furthermore, the data can be acquired at astonishingly high frequencies to allow precise parsing of the sequence of events that allow second-by-second discriminations of responses evoked by subjects. In addition, these measures can be acquired over extended time periods to examine long-term changes to subjects across conditions or within conditions.

What Are the Costs and Benefits?

Costs.   Depending on the type of measure that is desired or warranted by the questions of interest, physiological data can be costly to acquire. In many cases, researchers need lab space, specialized equipment, and trained staff to conduct studies using physiological measures. These requirements can be resource intensive. Once acquired, the data can be difficult to process, especially if "art scoring" (i.e., the process of manually inspecting and editing the data stream) is required to reduce data artifacts due to muscle movements, environmental "noise," and equipment failures. Even data generated from simple autonomic measures such as sweating and heart rate must be examined to edit out artifacts within the data stream. To edit out artifacts present in the data, specialized software must be purchased or written.

The technical and hardware aspects of some physiological measurement systems can be overwhelming to researchers or staff who have no formal training. Depending on vendor, system hardware setup can be difficult and cumbersome. However, recent advances in technologies are making the use of simple autonomic measures user friendly. The ease of use usually comes at the price of nonflexibility of use and/or the inability to edit the raw data stream for artifacts. Finally, data analyses are usually repeated measures, and therefore studies must be designed carefully, taking into account the potential pitfalls of repeated measures designs such as learning/adaptation and nonindependence of conditions/trials. Often, data-specific analysis software is required and must be mastered.

Benefits.   Certainly, one benefit of using physiological measures is that large amounts of data can be acquired quickly. This ability allows researchers to examine very precise aspects of the process of social interaction. In fact, as with video and audio recordings, second-by-second progressions are easily analyzable. Depending on the system that one develops or purchases, data analysis can be streamlined, making the collection, art-scoring, and analysis of physiological data efficient and fast.

A second benefit is found in the flexibility of the measures to be incorporated into a large array of experimental manipulations. Questions at the level of specific behaviors to long sequences of behaviors can be posed and assessed, often within the same data collection effort. Given that the measures are collected at high frequencies across time, examination of time-linked processes are possible as they unfold during an interaction. Another aspect of physiological measures that adds to their flexibility is that often the researcher sets the data acquisition rate. Thus, varying the precision with which the data are gathered may be of great value if a researcher is using a multichannel system that collects several different types of signals simultaneously. Along these same lines, many systems allow researchers to change the type of physiological signal that is acquired during data collection. That is, if a lab possesses a general system (e.g., Grass amps and different interface modules), researchers can configure (and reconfigure) the system to collect autonomic measures for one study and EEG measures for another study run in the same facility.

CONCLUSION

In this chapter I argued that inclusion of physiological measures into one's measurement "toolbox" is essential if one desires to assess the full array of conceptual components that comprise social support communication and its relationship to nonverbal behaviors and other social processes. The technology surrounding physiological measurements has advanced to such a state that training our graduate students in the basics of physiological measurement systems is feasible. Familiarity with these measures is as essential as training in survey design, attitude scales, and behavioral coding techniques. Inclusion of physiological measures opens a window into the internal states of research participants that is not readily available when researchers employ self-report or video recordings only. Many aspects of nonverbal communication are subtle and fleeting and may occur at levels undetected by the camera or the subject. However, these subtle and fleeting processes may influence the nature and direction of the interaction in important ways. Using physiological measures to reveal the internal states of interactants and how those internal states manifest in relation to the process of social support and nonverbal communication is an exciting opportunity to be exploited.

REFERENCES

Applegate, J. L. (1980). Person-centered and position-centered teacher communication in a day care setting. *Studies in Symbolic Interactionism, 3,* 59–96.

Andersen, P. A. (1999). *Nonverbal communication: Forms and functions.* Mountain View, CA: Mayfield.

Andersen, P. A., & Guerrero, L. K. (Eds.). (1998). *Handbook of communication and emotion: Research, theory, applications, and contexts.* New York: Academic Press.

Barbee, A. P., & Cunningham, M. R. (1995). An experimental approach to social support communications: Interactive coping in close relationships. *Communication Yearbook, 18,* 381–413.

Barbee, A. P., Rowatt, T. L., & Cunningham, M. R. (1998). When a friend is in need: Feelings about seeking, giving, and receiving social support. In P. A. Andersen & L. K. Guerrero (Eds.), *Handbook of communication and emotion: Research, theory, applications, and contexts* (pp. 281–301). New York: Academic Press.

Bippus, A. M. (2001). Recipients' criteria for evaluating the skillfulness of comforting communication and the outcomes of comforting interactions. *Communication Monographs, 68,* 301–313.

Blascovich, J. (2000). Using physiological indexes of psychological processes in social psychological research. In H. Reis & C. M. Judd (Eds.), *Handbook of research methods in social and personality psychology* (pp. 117–137). New York: Cambridge University Press.

Burleson, B. R. (1982). The development of comforting communication skills in childhood and adolescence. *Child Development, 53,* 1578–1588.

Burleson, B. R. (1994a). Comforting messages: Significance, approaches, and effects. In B. R. Burleson, T. L. Albrecht, & I. G. Sarason (Eds.), *Communication of social support: Messages, interactions, relationships, and community* (pp. 3–29). Thousand Oaks, CA: Sage.

Burleson, B. R. (1994b). Comforting messages: Features, functions and outcomes. In J. A. Daly & J. W. Wiemann (Eds.), *Strategic interpersonal communication* (pp. 135–161). Hillsdale, NJ: Lawrence Erlbaum Associates.

Burleson, B. R., & Samter, W. (1985). Individual differences in the perception of comforting messages: An exploratory investigation. *Central States Speech Journal, 36,* 39–50.

Cacioppo, J. T., & Petty, R. E. (1983). *Social psychophysiology: A sourcebook.* New York: Guilford.

Cacioppo, J. T., Petty, R. E., & Andersen, B. L. (1988). Social psychophysiology as a paradigm. In H. Wagner (Ed.), *Social psychophysiology and emotion: Theory and clinical applications* (pp. 273–294). Chichester, NY: Wiley.

Cacioppo, J. T., Petty, R. E., & Tassinary, L. G. (1989). Social psychophysiology: A new look. In L. Berkowitz (Ed.), *Advances in experimental social psychology* (Vol. 22, pp. 39–91). San Diego, CA: Academic Press.

Cacioppo, J. T., & Tassinary, L. G. (1990). *Principles of psychophysiology: Physical, social, and inferential elements.* New York: Cambridge University Press.

Cacioppo, J. T., Tassinary, L. G., & Berntson, G. G. (Eds.). (2000). *Handbook of psychophysiology,* (2nd ed.). New York: Cambridge University Press.

Carrère, S., Buehlman, K. T., Gottman, J. M., Coan, J. A., & Ruckstuhl, L. (2000). Predicting marital stability and divorce in newlywed couples. *Journal of Family Psychology, 14,* 42–58.

Clore, G. L. (1994). Why emotions require cognition. In P. Ekman & R. J. Davidson (Eds.), *The nature of emotion: Fundamental questions* (pp. 181–191). New York: Oxford University Press.

Coles, M. G. H., Donchin, E., & Porges, S. W. (1986). *Psychophysiology: Systems, processes, and applications.* New York: Guilford.

Cutrona, C. E. (1996). Social support as a determinant of marital quality: The interplay of negative and supportive behaviors. In G. R. Pierce, B. R. Sarason, & I. G. Sarason (Eds.), *Handbook of social support and the family* (pp. 173–194). New York: Plenum Press.

Cutrona, S. E., & Russell, D. (1990). Types of social support and specific stress: Toward a theory of optimal matching. In B. R. Sarason, I. G. Sarason, & G. R. Pierce (Eds.), *Social support: An interactional view* (pp. 319–366). New York: Wiley.

Cutrona, S. E., & Suhr, J. A. (1992). Controllability of stressful events and satisfaction with spouse support behaviors. *Communication Research, 19,* 154–174.

Cutrona, S. E., & Suhr, J. A. (1994). Social support communication in the context of marriage: An analysis of couples' supportive interactions. In B. R. Burleson, T. L. Albrecht, & I. G. Sarason (Eds.), *Communication of social support: Messages, interactions, relationships, and community* (pp. 113–135). Thousand Oaks, CA: Sage.

Diamond, L. M. (2001). Contributions of psychophysiology to research on adult attachment: Review and recommendations. *Personality and Social Psychology Review, 5,* 276–295.

Diamond, L. M. (2003). What does sexual orientation orient? A biobehavioral model distinguishing romantic love and sexual desire. *Psychological Review, 110,* 173–192.

Diener, E., Lucas, R. E., & Oishi, S. (2002). Subjective well-being: The science of happiness and life satisfaction. In C. R. Snyder & S. J. Lopez (Eds.), *Handbook of positive psychology* (pp. 63–73). New York: Oxford University Press.

Ekman, P., & Davidson, R. J. (Eds.). (1994). *The nature of emotion: Fundamental questions.* New York: Oxford University press.

Ekman, P., Levenson, R. W., & Friesen, W. V. (1983). Autonomic nervous system activity distinguishes between emotions. *Science, 221,* 1208–1210.

Ellsworth, P. C. (1994). Levels of thought and levels of emotion. In P. Ekman & R. J. Davidson (Eds.), *The nature of emotion: Fundamental questions* (pp. 192–196). New York: Oxford University Press.

Fridja, N. H. (1994). Emotions require cognitions, even if simple ones. In P. Ekman & R. J. Davidson (Eds.), *The nature of emotion: Fundamental questions* (pp. 197–202). New York: Oxford University Press.

Gottman, J. M. (1998). Toward a process model of men in marriages. In A. Booth & A. C. Crouter (Eds.), *Men in families: When do they get involved? What difference does it make?* (pp. 149–192). Mahwah, NJ: Lawrence Erlbaum Associates.

Gottman, J. M., Coan, J., Carrère, S., & Swanson, C. (1998). Predicting marital happiness and stability from newlywed interactions. *Journal of Marriage & the Family, 60,* 5–22.

Gottman, J. M., Jacobson, N. S., Rushe, R. H., & Shortt, J. W. (1995). The relationship between heart rate reactivity, emotionally aggressive behavior, and general violence in batterers. *Journal of Family Psychology, 9,* 227–248.

Gottman, J. M., & Levenson, R. W. (1988). The social psychophysiology of marriage. In P. Noller & M. A. Fitzpatrick (Eds.), *Perspectives on marital interaction* (pp. 182–200). Philadelphia, PA: Multilingual Matters.

Gottman, J. M., & Levenson, R. W. (1992). Marital processes predictive of later dissolution: Behavior, physiology, and health. *Journal of Personality and Social Psychology, 63,* 221–233.

Gottman, J. M., & Notarius, C. L. (2000). Decade review: Observing marital interaction. *Journal of Marriage & the Family, 62,* 927–947.

Gunnar, M. R., & Davis, E. P. (2003). The developmental psychobiology of stress and emotion in early childhood. In I. B. Weiner (Series Ed.), & R. M. Lerner, M. A. Easterbrooks, & J. Mistry (Vol. Eds.), *Handbook of Psychology: Vol. 6, Developmental Psychology* (pp. 113–143). New York: Wiley.

Gurung, R. A. R., Sarason, B. R., & Sarason, I. G. (1997). Personal characteristics, relationship quality, and social support perceptions and behavior in young adult romantic relationships. *Personal Relationships, 4,* 319–400.

Izard, C. E. (1994). Cognition is one of four types of emotion activating systems. In P. Ekman & R. J. Davidson (Eds.), *The nature of emotion: Fundamental questions* (pp. 203–207). New York: Oxford University Press.

Jacobson, N. S., Gottman, J. M., Waltz, J., Rushe, R., Babcock, J., & Holtzworth-Munroe, A. (1994). Affect, verbal content, and psychophysiology in the arguments of couples with a violent husband. *Journal of Consulting and Clinical Psychology, 62,* 982–988.

Jones, S. M., & Guerrero, L. K. (2001). The effects of nonverbal immediacy and verbal person centeredness in the emotional support process. *Human Communication Research, 27,* 567–596.

Levenson, R. W., & Gottman, J. M. (1985). Physiological and affective predictors of change in relationship satisfaction. *Journal of Personality and Social Psychology, 49,* 85–94.

Martin, I., & Venables, P. H. (1980). *Techniques in psychophysiology.* Chichester, NY: Wiley.

Manusov, V., & Trees, A. R. (2002). "Are you kidding me?": The role of nonverbal cues in the verbal accounting process. *Journal of Communication, 52,* 640–656.

Obrist, P. A., Black, A. H., Brener, J., & DiCara, L. V. (1974). *Cardiovascular psychophysiology: Current issues in response mechanisms, biofeedback, and methodology.* Chicago, IL: Aldine Publishing Co.

Shortt, J. W., & Gottman, J. M. (1997). Closeness in young adult sibling relationships: Affective and physiological processes. *Social Development, 6,* 142–164.

Snyder, C. R., & Lopez, S. J. (2002). *Handbook of positive psychology.* New York: Oxford University Press.

Stern, R. M., Ray, W. J., & Davis, C. M. (1980). *Psycho-physiological recording.* New York: Oxford University Press.

Trees, A. (2000). Nonverbal communication and the support process: Interactional sensitivity in the interactions between mothers and young adult children. *Communication Monographs, 67,* 239–261.

Wagner, H. (1988). The theory and application of social psychophysiology. In H. L. Wagner (Ed.), *Social psychophysiology and emotion: Theory and clinical applications* (pp. 1–15). Chichester, NY: Wiley.

Wagner, H., & Manstead, A. (Eds.). (1989). *Handbook of social psychology.* Chichester, NY: Wiley.

APPENDIX

Following are links to websites that provide additional conceptual and technical information regarding physiological measures, measurement techniques, and equipment:

Association for Applied Psychophysiology and Biofeedback:
  http://www.aapb.org/

Department of Psychology, psychophysiology:
  http://www.hull.ac.uk/psychophysiology/

Equipment Links:
  http://gsr.psyc.ncat.edu/robinson/resequ.htm

Equipment vendor:
  http://www.jameslong.net/

International Organization of Psychophysiology:
  http://www.iop-world.org/

Journal of Psychophysiology:
  http://www.hhpub.com/journals/jop/

Laboratory of Learning and Cognitive Psychophysiology:
  http://www.psy.uq.edu.au/~landcp/

Laboratory of Personality and Cognition–Emotions:
  www.grc.nia.nih.gov/branches/lpc/eqpu.htm

Neuroscience and psychophysiology resources:
  http://www.socialpsychology.org/neuro.htm

Nonverbal Behavior Research Centers:
  www3.usal.es/~nonverbal/researchcenters.htm

Oberlin College Psychophysiology Laboratory:
  www.oberlin.edu/~psych/labs/physiolab/default.html

Positive Emotions Psychophysiology Laboratory:
  http://www.umich.edu/~psycdept/emotions/

Psychology 305: Human Psychophysiology Home Page:
http://www.oberlin.edu/~psych/p305/de

Psychophysiology Around the World:
http://rcf.usc.edu/~vanman/psyphy.html

Psychophysiology Lab–UOW:
http://www.psyc.uow.edu.au/psychophys/

Psychophysiology Laboratory at Washington University in St. Louis:
http://www.artsci.wustl.edu/~psycphys/

Questia (online library) @ WWW.questia.com and search for "psychophysio-logical measurement" to view specific online texts regarding theoretical and practical issues surrounding physiological measures

Social Psychology Network:
http://socialpsychology.org

Social Psychophysiology Laboratory:
http://www.er.uqam.ca/nobel/r24700/en

Society for Psychophysiological Research:
http://liberty.uc.wlu.edu/~spr

Stanford Psychophysiology Laboratory:
http://sucia.stanford.edu/~psyphy/

St. Olaf College Psychophysiology:
http://www.stolaf.edu/depts/psych/psy

The Berkeley Psychophysiology Laboratory:
http://ist-socrates.berkeley.edu/~ucb

USM Psychophysiology Research Laboratory:
http://ocean.otr.usm.edu/~gejones/psy

Wisconsin Emotive Lab:
http://psych.wisc.edu/harmonjones/hom

III. PARADIGMS AND PRACTICES

Standard Content Methodology: Controlling the Verbal Channel

Patricia Noller
University of Queensland

INTRODUCTION

Although nonverbal behavior is often considered to occur separately from words (e.g., a smile, a wave, a look, a gesture, a silence), many nonverbal behaviors actually accompany words and can change the meaning of those words. A major issue in studying accuracy in decoding nonverbal behavior, therefore, involves separating the words from the nonverbal component of a message. Using this strategy does not involve denying the fact that "verbal and nonverbal messages ... (are) co-occurring and interrelated phenomena" (Jones & LeBaron, 2002, p. 499), but rather it enables the researcher to explore the ways in which the nonverbal behavior modifies the verbal behavior. Separating the verbal and nonverbal channels allows the researcher to explore the separate contributions of the verbal and nonverbal channels to the way that a message is interpreted. This issue is particularly important, given the dubious claims sometimes made about the superiority of the nonverbal channel (Argyle, 1975; Mehrabian, 1972), claims that are unlikely to be true in all contexts.

The standard content methodology was developed as a way to achieve this goal of focusing on the nonverbal behavior and assessing the extent to which individuals are able to discriminate nonverbal behavior of different affective/emotional tone (Kahn, 1970; Noller, 1984). Because the words used in this research paradigm are ambiguous and can have different meanings depending on the nonverbal behavior (both visual and vocal) accompanying those words, senders and receivers have to rely on encoding or decoding the appropriate nonverbal behavior. Central to the method is the assumption that, if words are held constant, changes in the meaning of the message must be the result of changes in the nonverbal behavior (Noller, 1984). This chapter presents the history of this method for separating the verbal and

417

nonverbal channels for research purposes, discusses its application to married couples, describes past research using the method, and includes the strengths and limitations of this method.

The History of the Method

A number of different strategies have been used in the development of the standard content methodology. Some of the early methods involved using forms of communication that were totally unrelated to typical conversation, but, as we shall see, useful developments were made over time, including the use of ambiguous messages.

Early strategies.   Some of the earliest researchers used meaningless content, such as reciting the alphabet or counting, in order to control the verbal channel. For example, Davitz and Davitz (1959) asked participants to recite the alphabet while expressing different emotions such as anger, sadness, and happiness. Argyle, Salter, Nicholson, Williams, and Burgess (1970) had participants express superior, inferior, or neutral status to another person while counting. These can be fun activities for helping individuals recognize the importance of tone of voice to communication, but they do not really relate to everyday interactions.

Ambiguous Messages.   More realistic and somewhat easier tasks were developed with the introduction of ambiguous messages that could have different meanings depending on the nonverbal behavior accompanying the message. Mehrabian and Ferris (1967) used the single words "really" and "maybe" and asked participants to use different affective tone when using these words. For example, "really" could be said in ways that meant "That's interesting" (a neutral tone), "That's great but I can hardly believe it!" (positive tone), or "Oh dear, that's terrible!" (negative tone). Duckworth (1975) had participants in his study ask the question, "What are you doing?" which can also involve a positive, neutral, or negative tone.

Applications to Married Couples.   At the next stage of progress in this methodology, Kahn (1970) developed a set of ambiguous messages suitable for use with married couples. He created two separate sets of eight messages, one appropriate for husbands to send to wives, and one fitting for wives to send to husbands. Examples of husband messages and wife messages are presented in Table 36. Kahn had each partner take the role of encoder (sender) and decoder (receiver). The encoder's task was to send messages to the partner, using words set by the experimenter but encoding one of three possible messages that could be conveyed by those words. The decoder's task was to choose, between the three alternative possibilities, which of the three meanings was intended. (See Tables 37 and 38).

Noller (1980) added the question used by Duckworth (1975), "What are you doing?" to both sets of messages because this question is, in many ways, a prototypical

TABLE 36
Examples of Husband and Wife Items as Used Noller (1980, 1984)

Gender of encoder	Message	Alterative meanings
Husband	Didn't we have chicken for dinner a few nights ago?	a. You are irritated with her for preparing the same meal again and are warning her that she had better not make the same mistake in the future of a closely repeated meal. b. You do not mind but are curious to see if your memory for meals is correct. c. You are elated because chicken is one of your favorites and you're not accustomed to her serving it so often for you.
Wife	You really surprised me this time.	a. You are quite satisfied with the gift, although you really would have preferred what you were expecting. b. You are very disappointed and annoyed that he didn't get you what you had expected. c. You are pleasantly surprised by the unexpected gift.

TABLE 37
Example of an Encoding Card

Section	Content
Situation	Your wife tells you about a wonderful vacation that one of her friends just took with her husband. She tells you that she wishes that you and she could also take a trip to the same place.
Intention	You feel that a trip to that place is unappealing and would hardly be worthwhile.
Statement	Do you know what a trip like that costs?

TABLE 38
Example of a Decoding Card

Situation	Your wife tells you about a wonderful vacation that one of her friends just took with her husband. She tells you that she wishes that you and she could also take a trip to the same place.
Alternative meanings	a. You feel that a trip to that place is unappealing and would hardly be worthwhile. b. You are pleased that she would want to go with you on such a trip and would like to make serious enquiries about it. c. You are interested in finding out if she knows the approximate cost of their trip before committing yourself one way or the other.

ambiguous message. This question is in common use and is appropriate to many contexts, suitable for both wives and husbands; in addition, the meaning can be changed readily by using different nonverbal behavior.

When Kahn (1970) carried out his study of nonverbal accuracy, he made no attempt to separate male and female contributions, assuming that each partner contributed equally to the final score. He also did not separate encoding and decoding processes, presumably assuming that he was basically studying a decoding process. Later researchers have sought to build on his methodology, predominantly by focusing on the encoding process as well as the decoding process.

Gottman and Porterfield (1981).   These researchers also used the standard content method to assess the communicative competence of married couples, "assessing nonverbal competence independent of verbal competence" (p. 817). They used a modified version of Kahn's (1970) Marital Communication Scale (MCS). Because the items were also to be shown to strangers for decoding, the items were recorded, and spouses decoded from the video rather than live as the behaviors occurred. Each spouse received a decoding score, based on the number of items (out of eight) where the encoder's intention matched the decoder's choice. Thus, if on five of the eight messages the husband chose the alternative (positive, neutral, or negative) that the wife indicated that she sent, he would receive a score of five. Gottman and Porterfield correlated the sender's marital satisfaction score with the partner's decoding score. Wives' marital satisfaction was strongly correlated with husbands' decoding scores, but there was no relation between husbands' marital satisfaction and wives' decoding scores.

Gottman and Porterfield (1981) then went on to ask whether the husbands' scores on the MCS were a function of the husbands' decoding or the wives' encoding. To answer this question, they used the data from the strangers who had also decoded the messages of the opposite-sex spouse. They found a nonsignificant correlation between the marital satisfaction of the original group of wives and the decoding scores of the stranger husbands, suggesting that when the scores of husbands in distressed marriages are compared with those of the male stranger who decoded their wives' messages, there is evidence that husbands in distressed marriages have a "receiver deficit," or problems in decoding the nonverbal aspects of their wives' messages. Thus the researchers were able to locate the deficit in the decoding of males, but this methodology did not allow them to explore sex and message-type differences as well as did the methodology used by Noller in her 1980 study.

Noller (1980).   Noller also used Kahn's (1970) MCS, adding the extra item as described earlier. A message was scored as correct if the decoder identified the intent of the message sent by the encoder. (Of course, it should be kept in mind that the encoder's intent was actually set by the experimenter.) Noller (1980), however, used a different method for separating the encoder and decoder effects, and for separating the contributions of wives and husbands.

In this study, as well as being decoded by their own partner, the videotaped items of each spouse were also decoded by groups of students whose task was the same as that of the spouse: that is, to decide whether the message was positive, neutral, or negative. Each message received a score representing the proportion of those decoders who correctly identified the intent of the message. The way that these scores were used is described in more detail later in this chapter after the administration of the MCS has been presented. In the next section, I describe, in detail, the administration of the Marital Communication Scale, including the creation of the stimulus materials (cards), the administration of the experimental task, and the calculation of encoding and decoding scores by sex and message-type. A complete set of contexts, statements, and alternative intentions is presented in Table 39 for husbands' messages, and in Table 40 for wives' messages.

ADMINISTERING THE MARITAL COMMUNICATION SCALE WITHIN THE STANDARD CONTENT PARADIGM

Creating and Using the Cards

In order to administer the Marital Communication Scale, two sets of cards are needed: an encoding set of 27 cards, and a decoding set of nine cards. An example of an encoding card can be seen in Table 37, and there is one encoding card for each alternative message. Each encoding card includes the context in which the message is to be sent, the alternative intention to be conveyed, and the words to be used. An example of a decoding card is presented in Table 38. Each of these cards should have the number of the message (1 to 9) on the back so that the decoder knows which decoding card to select. Each decoding card includes the context and the three alternative intentions from which the decoder must choose the alternative that he or she believes the partner wanted to convey. Encoding cards should be shuffled to ensure that they are presented in random order. The encoder is asked to record the order in which the messages were sent (e.g., 4a, 6b, 9a, 7c) on a form provided, and the decoder is asked to record the number of the item and the alternative (a, b, or c) that he or she thinks applies. It is important that neither spouse can see the other's form.

The encoder and decoder are generally positioned opposite each other so that they have full view of each other's faces. If the messages are to be videotaped, the camera should be positioned to record the upper body of the encoder, including the number on the back of the card. The encoder's list is assumed to reflect the order in which the messages were sent, and the scoring is carried out by comparing the decoder's list with the encoder's list. Responses that match the encoder's list are assumed to be correct. At this point, each spouse is given a score, out of 27, that represents the number of items that he or she decoded correctly. In the next section, I will demonstrate how we were able to score each message in terms of whether it

TABLE 39

Context, Statement, and Alternative Intentions for Husbands' Messages

Message No.	Context	Statement	Alternative Intentions
1	You come to the dinner table as your wife begins to serve chicken, a main course you recall having had four days ago for dinner too.	Didn't we have chicken for dinner a few nights ago?	a. You are irritated with her for preparing the same meal again and are warning her that she had better not make the same mistake in the future of a closely repeated meal. b. You do not mind but are curious to see if your memory for meals is accurate. c. You are elated because chicken is your one of your favorites and she doesn't usually serve it so often.
2	Your wife is modeling a new outfit for you that she just bought. She asks you how you like it.	That's really something. Where did you get the money to buy an outfit like that?	a. You are curious to know how she managed to save the money to buy such an outfit. b. You think that the outfit looks good, are pleased with the purchase, and are pleasantly surprised that she could afford such an expensive looking outfit. c. You think that the outfit is totally unbecoming on her and therefore not worth the money.
3	Your wife tells you about the wonderful vacation that one of her friends just took with her husband. She wishes that you and she could also take a trip to the same place.	Do you know what a trip like that costs?	a. You think that a trip to that place is unappealing and would hardly be worthwhile. b. You are pleased that she would want to go with you on such a trip and would like to make serious inquiries about it. c. You are interested in finding out whether she knows the approximate cost of the trip before committing yourself one way or the other.
4	You and your wife are discussing a life insurance policy that you recently purchased.	I'm not sure you'll need this insurance, because if I die you'll probably remarry.	a. You hope that your wife would remarry so that her happiness and welfare would be maintained. b. You want your wife to say that she would never consider remarrying, and would never love another man. c. You wonder what her attitude to remarriage is, as you've not talked about it before.

422

Message No.	Context	Statement	Alternative Intentions
5	You and your wife are both ready for bed at night. It is a night when sexual relations are a possibility.	Do you really want to have sex tonight?	a. You are not interested in having sexual relations that night. b. You are interested in having sexual relations and want to let her know, but you are afraid she might be unwilling. You hope that your eagerness will convince her to agree. c. You would like to make love only if she would like to, and are interested in her attitude.
6	A neighbor phones and invites you and your wife to visit him at a get-together at his home on the following Saturday evening. You and your wife had previous plans to go out alone that evening. You tell your neighbor to hold on while you confer with your wife.	Would you prefer us to go on our own as we planned?	a. You would much prefer to go out with your wife. b. You are not really keen to go out with your wife and would rather go to your neighbor's house. c. You have no preference at the moment and will accept whatever alternative your wife selects.
7	Your wife tells you to clean up a mess you made in the apartment.	I was going to clean it up, fusspot.	a. You are annoyed and will not clean up the mess because she nagged you. b. You intended to clean up the mess, and are just letting her know that. c. You are quite happy to clean up the mess, but you enjoy affectionately teasing your wife about her housekeeping.
8	As you walk into the bathroom unbuttoning your shirt, you find your wife partly undressed and turning on the shower. You were on your way to have a shower yourself.	I didn't know you were thinking of a shower, I'm planning to take one myself.	a. You are glad to find her going into the shower so that you can take one together and enjoy the sex play. b. You are annoyed and expect her to wait until you take your shower first. c. You are just surprised at the coincidence.
9	You walk into the room and unexpectedly come across your wife. You ask her what she is doing.	What are you doing?	a. You are just curious to know what she is doing. b. She is obviously doing something you have asked her not to do and you are angry. c. You have caught her doing something to surprise you.

TABLE 40

Message No.	Context	Statement	Alternative Intentions
1	It is approximately the time when you and your husband usually go to bed together but he seems engrossed in a TV show.	Do you really want to watch the rest of that?	a. You hope that he will turn off the TV and come to bed with you so that you can make love. b. You are tired and will not mind if he continues to watch his show while you fall asleep. c. You are annoyed because he knows this is not the kind of show you enjoy, and you want him to turn to another channel.
2	At a social gathering, an attractive single girl wearing a dress with a plunging neckline is introduced to you and your husband. She acts very flirtatiously towards your husband and then leaves your company.	She was really something, wasn't she?	a. You think that she was vulgar and you are angry at your husband for the attention he paid her. b. You just wonder what he thought of her. c. You thought this woman was attractive, and you feel flattered that she has taken notice of your husband.
3	Your husband just presented you with your birthday present. You had been expecting a completely different gift.	You really surprised me this time.	a. You are quite satisfied with the gift, although you really would have preferred what you were expecting. b. You are very disappointed and annoyed that he didn't get you what you expected. c. You are pleasantly surprised by the unexpected gift.
4	You and your husband are sitting alone in your living room on a winter evening. You feel cold.	I'm cold, aren't you?	a. You wonder if he also is cold, or it is only you who are cold. b. You want him to warm you with physical affection. c. You're feeling that he is being inconsiderate in not having turned up the heat by now, and you want him to turn it up right away.
5	You come home to find the washing you had left in the washing machine hanging on the line.	Did you do that?	a. You are angry because some of the clothes are hung in a way that would spoil their shape and you wish it had been left for you. b. You are curious about whether it was your husband or one of the children who hung it out. c. You are pleased that he has done such a thing to help you.

Message No.	Context	Statement	Alternative Intentions
6	It's time for you and your husband to get dressed for a special event you were planning to go to that evening. You have a headache and feel uncomfortable.	I've got a headache and I'm not sure whether to go.	a. You want to find out how much he wants to go before making up your mind. b. You are angry with him about something that happened earlier and don't think you'd enjoy going out with him. c. You want him to encourage you to go and enjoy the performance despite the headache, because you are keen to go out with him.
7	You and your husband have begun talking about the purchase of new bedroom furniture. Assume that you currently own a set with a double bed. You point out a twin bed set in a shop window.	Look at that twin bed set. Why don't we get it?	a. You know that you both want another double bed because you cherish the closeness it fosters, but you sometimes tease about twin beds. b. You are serious in bringing up the possibility of twin beds because they would give you some escape from his sexual advances, which you don't enjoy. You want your husband to realize this. c. You have never really talked about the issue of twin versus double beds, and you are interested in knowing his attitude.
8	You have just come out of the bathroom. It is a few days past when your menstrual period usually begins, but you have seen no sign of it starting. You tell your husband about the current situation.	You know, I'm a few days late on my period this month.	a. If you are pregnant you regard it as his fault for not taking better precautions and you will be extremely angry at him. b. You are delighted that you might be pregnant and want to share the good news with him c. You just want him to know, although you don't really care one way or the other.
9	You walk into a room and unexpectedly come across your husband. You ask him what he is doing.	What are you doing?	a. You are just curious to know what he is doing. b. He is obviously doing something you have asked him not to do and you are angry. c. You have caught him doing something to surprise you.

425

was a good communication or a bad communication, and each error in terms of whether it occurred because of poor encoding or poor decoding.

Scoring the Marital Communication Scale

To score the communication in terms of whether they were good or bad communications, we used as our criterion the proportion of the students who were able to decode each communication. (This procedure is outlined in an earlier section). "Good communications" were those identified correctly by two thirds or more of the external decoders, and "bad communications" were those identified correctly by fewer than two thirds of the decoders. The communications were then further divided into encoding errors, decoding errors, and idiosyncratic messages.

Encoding errors were defined as "bad communications" decoded incorrectly by the spouse; in other words, these were messages not sent clearly, so that neither the spouse nor the external coders were able to decode them correctly. Decoding errors were defined as good or clearly sent communications able to be decoded by the external coders, but decoded incorrectly by the spouse. Idiosyncratic communications were "bad communications" decoded correctly by the spouse. That is, although these communications were not sent clearly (that is, the external coders had trouble decoding them), they were decoded correctly by the spouse. Spouses' ability to decode these messages may be based on some kind of private message system.

Message-type. Because three different types of message were always included (that is, positive, negative, and neutral), separate scores could be obtained for each message-type. In other words, participants could obtain scores for positive, neutral, and negative "good communications," "bad communications," encoding errors, decoding errors, and idiosyncratic communications. In some analyses, these message-type differences were quite important; for example, the differences between husbands and wives in "good communications" and encoding errors were particularly strong for positive messages, with wives tending to send positive messages more clearly than husbands (Noller, 1980).

Effects of Sex and Encoding Versus Decoding. The importance of being able to separate the contributions of encoders and decoders, and of wives and husbands, is confirmed by the findings of analyses involving both of these variables (that is, encoding versus decoding, and husbands versus wives). Wives had significantly more of their messages rated as "good communications" than did husbands, and they made significantly fewer encoding errors. In addition, those with low marital adjustment sent significantly fewer "good communications" than did those high in marital adjustment, and this was particularly true for husbands. Those in the low marital adjustment group made a greater percentage of decoding errors than those in the high marital adjustment group, and this difference was largely due to the differences between the males in these two groups (Noller, 1980).

Alternative Scoring

Because three different types of messages were used in the Noller (1980) study, it was also possible to calculate a "bias score," representing the tendency for individuals to decode with a negative or a positive bias. If participants decoded a negative message incorrectly as neutral, they were given a score of +1, if they incorrectly decoded a negative message as positive they were given a score of +2. Similarly, if they decoded a positive message incorrectly as neutral, they were given a score of –1, and if they decoded a positive message incorrectly as negative, they were given a score of –2. Thus these scores reflect both the direction and the magnitude of a participant's bias. Analyses of these bias scores showed that wives tended to make errors in a positive direction, whereas husbands tended to make errors in a negative direction.

Other Ways of Using These Messages

Particularly when the standard content messages have been videotaped, there are other ways that they can be used. For example, Noller (1980) had the spouses in her study decode the messages using only the visual channel (picture with sound turned down) or only the vocal channel (sound, with picture turned down) and was then able to explore such questions as which channel contributed the most to accuracy. When husbands were decoding wives, there was a significant relationship between both vocal and visual accuracy scores and total scores. In addition, there was greater accuracy when only the vocal channel was used.

Another study (Noller & Venardos, 1986) explored the level of participants' awareness of their own encoding and decoding. This issue is an important one in terms of resolving misunderstandings. Encoders were asked to rate the clarity with which they believed they sent the message and to predict whether the partner would correctly decode the message. Decoders, on the other hand, were asked to rate their confidence in their own decoding. If a spouse thinks that he or she is a very clear message sender, then the partner is likely to get the blame for any misunderstandings that occur, whether the problem was actually in the encoding or the decoding. Our study showed that spouses low in marital adjustment tended to be equally confident about their decoding, irrespective of whether they were correct or incorrect, whereas those higher in marital adjustment were more confident when they were correct than when they were incorrect. The well-adjusted spouses were also better at predicting whether their spouses would interpret their messages correctly.

Noller and Gallois (1986) microanalyzed the standard content messages in order to explore the question of why the messages of husbands seemed to be more difficult to decode than those of wives. Each message was coded for the presence of 16 specific nonverbal behaviors, including head nods, forward lean, head down, and open gestures. Because the same words are used for all three types of communications (positive, neutral, or negative), these messages are matched for length (that is, number of words) and thus are ideal for this type of coding. If the messages were of different lengths, scores on the different behaviors would need to be corrected for the number of words in the message.

When analyses were conducted to look at the differences between the three message types, we found that negative messages were characterized by frowns and eyebrow furrows, and positive messages were characterized by smiling, eyebrow raises, and forward lean. Neutral messages seemed to be characterized by the absence of distinctive nonverbal behaviors. Analyses of gender effects indicated that females tended to smile on positive messages and frown on negative messages, differentiating clearly between their positive and negative messages and using the behaviors most characteristic of the particular type of message they were sending. Males, on the other hand, tended to raise their eyebrows on both positive and negative messages, and did not seem to differentiate adequately between them.

Another study (Noller & Feeney, 1994), related accuracy scores to the attachment dimensions of anxiety over abandonment and comfort with closeness. We found that couples where the husband was anxious over abandonment were less accurate than other couples for all three types of messages, and couples where the wife was uncomfortable with closeness were less accurate than other couples for neutral and negative messages. Thus the nonverbal accuracy being tested using this methodology may be related to a range of cognitive and affective processes. We are currently planning a study to explore the links between nonverbal accuracy and rejection sensitivity (Downey, Feldman, & Ayduk, 2000) and the overattribution bias (Schweinle & Ickes, 2002) in a sample of couples where violence has occurred (Robillard, 2001).

Strengths and Limitations of the Standard Content Method

As was shown, the standard content method is a useful way of separating the verbal and nonverbal aspects of a message by controlling the verbal channel through the use of messages that can have different meanings, depending on the accompanying nonverbal behavior. The method is easy to administer and assesses communication in a dyadic context; if it is used in the way developed by Noller (1980), encoding effects and decoding effects can be looked at separately, and gender effects can also be explored. It can be important for those working with couples who report frequent misunderstandings to assess whether the problems are likely to be related to the encoding or decoding processes, and to explore the relative contributions of each member of the dyad. The fact that the test is *dyadic* is important, given the finding that husbands in distressed relationships often have difficulty decoding their wives' messages but not the messages of female strangers (Noller, 1981). This finding suggests that a test involving the decoding of strangers would not be useful in assessing the decoding within a particular close dyadic relationship.

One problem with using standard content messages concerns the external validity of the method. For example, participants may be asked to imagine themselves in situations that they are unlikely to encounter in their everyday lives. They may also be asked to use words that they would not normally use. Participants in Noller's (1980) study claimed, for example, that they differentiated clearly between the different types of messages by using positive, negative, or neutral words as appropriate. Noller (1982), however, showed that most messages sent in a laboratory interaction were neutral in the verbal channel, with many of these communications being changed into positive and negative messages through the visual and/or vocal channels.

In addition, the use of two entirely different sets of messages for husbands and wives may be problematic, and it may be important to develop a single set of messages that can be used by both husbands and wives. For example, if the messages are not of equal difficulty, or the alternatives are not equally good exemplars of that message-type, spurious differences between the sexes could be obtained. Although these problems would probably be minimized across 10 messages, such issues do need to be considered.

CONCLUSION

Although there are some remaining problems related to the use of standard content messages (Noller, 2001), it is nevertheless a useful way of controlling the verbal channel and enabling researchers to focus on accuracy in the nonverbal channel. The more recent methods offer great improvements over earlier methods, although early researchers provided the basis for the development of newer ways of exploring these issues. Given the importance of misunderstandings in close relationships like marriage, learning more about the processes involved should bring benefits for researchers, counselors, and couples alike.

REFERENCES

Argyle, M. (1975). *Bodily communication.* London: Methuen.

Argyle, M., Salter, V., Nicholson, H. M., Williams, M., & Burgess, P. (1970). The communication of inferior and superior attitudes by verbal and nonverbal signals. *British Journal of Social Psychology, 9,* 222–231.

Davitz, J. R., & Davitz, L. J. (1959). Correlates of accuracy in the communication of feelings. *Journal of Communication, 9,* 110–117.

Downey, G., Feldman, S. I., & Ayduk, O. (2000). Rejection sensitivity and male violence in romantic relationships. *Personal Relationships, 7,* 45–61.

Duckworth, D. (1975). Personality, emotional state and perceptions of nonverbal communication. *Perceptual and Motor Skills, 40,* 325–326.

Gottman, J. M., & Porterfield, A. L. (1981). Communicative competence in the nonverbal behavior of married couples. *Journal of Marriage and the Family, 39,* 817–824.

Jones, S. E., & LeBaron, C. D. (2002). Research on the relationship between verbal and nonverbal communication: Emerging interactions. *Journal of Communication, 52,* 499–521.

Kahn, M. (1970). Nonverbal communication and marital satisfaction. *Family Process, 9,* 449–456.

Mehrabian, A. (1972). *Nonverbal communication.* Chicago: Aldine-Atherton.

Mehrabian, A., & Ferris, S. R. (1967). Inferences of studies from nonverbal communication in two channels. *Journal of Consulting Psychology, 31,* 248–252.

Noller. P. (1984). *Nonverbal communication and marital interaction.* Oxford: Oxford University Press.

Noller, P. (1980). Misunderstandings in marital communication: A study of couples' nonverbal communication. *Journal of Personality and Social Psychology, 39,* 1135–1148.

Noller, P. (1981). Gender and marital adjustment level differences in decoding messages from spouses and strangers. *Journal of Personality and Social Psychology, 41,* 272–278.

Noller, P. (1982). Channel consistency and inconsistency in the communications of married couples. *Journal of Personality and Social Psychology, 43,* 732–741.

Noller, P. (2001). Using standard content methodology to assess nonverbal sensitivity in dyads. In J. A. Hall & F. Bernieri (Eds.), *Interpersonal sensitivity: Theory, measurement and applications.* Mahwah, NJ: Lawrence Erlbaum Associates.

Noller, P., & Feeney, J. A. (1994). Relationship satisfaction, attachment and nonverbal accuracy in early marriage. *Journal of Nonverbal Behavior, 18,* 199–221.

Noller, P., & Gallois, C. (1986). Sending emotional messages in marriage: Nonverbal behavior, sex and communication clarity. *British Journal of Social Psychology, 25,* 287–297.

Noller, P., & Venardos, C. (1986). Communication awareness in married couples. *Journal of Social and Personal Relationships, 3,* 31–42.

Robillard, L. M. (2001). *Rejection sensitivity, information-processing deficits and attachment style in violent relationships.* Unpublished document, University of Queensland.

Schweinle, W. E., & Ickes, W. (2002). On empathic accuracy and husbands' abusiveness: The "over-attribution bias." In P. Noller & J. A. Feeney (Eds.), *Understanding marriage: Developments in the study of marital interaction* (pp. 222–250). New York: Cambridge University Press.

The Passing Encounters Paradigm: Monitoring Microinteractions Between Pedestrians

Miles L. Patterson
University of Missouri-St. Louis

INTRODUCTION

It is common to think of interactions as simply occasions for conversation. There are, however, a variety of situations where we interact with others in the absence of spoken words. As we stand in line at the grocery store, share an elevator ride, or choose a seat in a crowded waiting room, we make subtle behavioral adjustments to the close presence of others. Goffman (1963, p. 24) used the term *unfocused interactions* to describe these situations in which people simply are mutually present, and he contrasted them with *focused interactions* in which people share a common focus of attention around a conversation. Unfocused interactions, however, are particularly interesting for nonverbal researchers, because individuals necessarily negotiate their position and relationship to one another largely through their nonverbal behaviors. These nonverbal adjustments regulate limited contact with others and, in the process, make these situations more comfortable and predictable.

One ubiquitous circumstance for unfocused interactions occurs when walking past other people, whether it is on sidewalks, in stores, or in other public spaces. Goffman (1963) suggested that the primary way in which people negotiate these passing encounters with strangers is through "civil inattention." Presumably, civil inattention occurs when people approaching one another recognize the presence of the other person with a brief glance and then look away to show that they (a) are not concerned about the other person, and (b) want to respect the other's privacy. According to Goffman (1963), pedestrians can initiate the recognition glance up to a distance of approximately 8 feet in order to determine just where the other person is walking. Inside of 8 feet, however, people typically look down, a reaction similar to dimming the lights for an approaching car.

431

In a series of four studies on pedestrian passings, however, Cary (1978) found little evidence for civil inattention. Specifically, pedestrians did not consistently avoid looking at the approaching person inside of 8 feet. Although Cary's research did not permit an analysis of the more subtle behavioral adjustments that pedestrians make as they approach and pass one another, it does highlight the issue of just what kinds of subtle adjustments pedestrians do make in these unfocused interactions. For example, what circumstances affect the frequency of looking in these passing encounters? When is a person likely to do more than simply glance at the approaching person, that is, also smile, nod, or initiate a greeting? Are the patterns of recognition and avoidance dependent on the sex composition of the pedestrian pair? On the practical side, how can we examine these microinteractions in the field while maintaining a high level of experimental control?

These are a few of the questions that directed the development of the *passing encounters paradigm*. In the rest of this chapter I describe this paradigm, then discuss briefly some of the results from initial studies my colleagues and I have conducted, and finally consider the application of this methodology to other important issues.

THE PASSING ENCOUNTERS PARADIGM

Overview

About 10 years ago, I decided to examine in more detail just how pedestrians behave in these passing encounters. With the help of a few undergraduate students, we initiated and observed a large number of confederate/pedestrian passings in order to estimate the distance at which people were likely to glance at one another. Observations were limited to those involving a solitary approaching pedestrian. From these informal observations, it appeared that many glances occurred between the 8-foot outer limit of Goffman's civil inattention zone and about 10 or 12 feet.[21] Consequently, we defined the critical "passing zone" as approximately 12 feet and closer as participants passed by the confederate. Of course, the issue of determining when an approaching confederate was at approximately 12 feet was not a simple one, because a typical walking pace (at least for college age students) was in the range of 4 to 5 feet per second (Patterson, Kelly, & Douglas, 1977). In other words, two approaching pedestrians closed approximately 8 to 10 feet per second. In preliminary work, we found that, after several practice trials, confederates could reliably (i.e., +/- 2 ft) estimate a 12-foot distance between themselves and an approaching pedestrian. Specifically, a stop or freeze technique was used as two approaching assistants walked toward one another and then the distance between them was measured.

---

[21]To the extent that these glances occurred at distances greater than 8 feet, such a finding supports the range suggested by Goffman. Our concern was not, however, determining specific distance limits, but determining the factors affecting recognition patterns as pedestrians were about to pass one another.

Next, it was important that the confederate was not the only person monitoring the reactions of the approaching pedestrian. There were two primary reasons for engaging a second assistant in the role of an observer. First, interrater reliabilities had to be computed in order to have confidence in the measures that were taken. This meant that the confederate and an observer would have to judge the same encounters. Second, an observer walking behind the confederate provided an opportunity for collecting additional demographic information on the pedestrians. That is, it was easier for an observer to monitor and record the additional information because the confederate had the critical responsibility of estimating the start of the passing zone and initiating the appropriate condition. The observers had to be close enough to monitor gaze changes of oncoming pedestrians in the passing zone but not so close that the pedestrians were likely to start looking at the observers before they passed the confederates. In other words, we had to limit the possibility that pedestrians might be distracted by a closely following observer and not be responsive to the confederate. Through trial and error, we settled on a following distance of 30 to 40 ft.

Because the observers had to know when to start monitoring the oncoming pedestrians, the confederates provided a signal: specifically, clenching the left fist (i.e., the side closer to the approaching pedestrian). This was complicated, however, by the fact that the separation between the confederate and the oncoming pedestrian was decreasing at approximately 8 to 10 feet per second. That is, the closing speed was fast enough that we had to build in a reaction time adjustment for the observer. This corrected for the time from which the confederate gave the signal until the observers changed their attention from the confederate's left hand to the approaching pedestrian. After some experimentation, we found that adding approximately 4 feet to the 12 feet critical distance provided enough time for the observers to redirect their attention and for the confederates to start the appropriate condition. Confederates practiced approaching and passing one another until they could reliably (i.e., +/− 2 ft) give the clenched fist signal at approximately 16 feet.

Settings

Because the passing encounters paradigm is employed in field settings, there is a wide range of locations that can be used. Most of our work has been done in and around college campuses, but data have also been collected in downtown areas. In any given location, several different sidewalks are used so that the confederate and observer pairs do not become conspicuous in walking back and forth on the same sidewalk. The selected sidewalks were relatively flat, straight, or only slightly curving and allowed unobstructed vision to identify approaching participants. Sidewalks where there was considerable traffic in and out of buildings were avoided so that people exiting the buildings did not interfere with the trials. When the trials were run on a campus, times immediately around class changes were avoided, because pedestrian traffic levels were too high. For practical reasons, trials were not run on very cold days and when there was inclement weather.

Procedure

In order to make sure that each participant had a comparable opportunity to notice and react to the confederate, a number of restrictions were placed on the potential participants. These restrictions included the following circumstances: (a) the sidewalk had to be uncrowded with no more than a few people in the oncoming traffic; (b) the participant had to be walking alone on the right side of the sidewalk; (c) there had to be a gap of at least 30 to 40 feet between the participant and the person walking in front of him/her (i.e., in order for the participant to have a clear view of the approaching confederate); (d) the participant could not have just turned the corner on to the sidewalk; (e) participants could not be involved in other activities while walking (talking on cell phones, wearing headphones, smoking, reading, eating, carrying heavy or awkward objects); (f) participants could not be running or obviously disabled (which might slow their pace and require more attention to where they were walking); and (g) participants could not be wearing sunglasses, as it was too difficult to monitor their gaze direction. In addition, participants could not be someone the confederate knew or someone who had been observed previously. Confederates were encouraged to be candid about procedural errors and rerun the condition when there was a problem.

We employed an experimental design so that we could control one side of the encounters and examine the participants' behavioral reactions to the confederate. The basic format required the confederates to initiate different levels of recognition in the passing zone. These included a Look, a Look & Smile, or simply avoiding the oncoming pedestrian (Avoid condition, i.e., look straight ahead). The Look and the Look & Smile conditions, initiated at approximately 12 feet, lasted less than 1 second. They also involved a slight head turn toward the participant that was easily discernible.

Each confederate ran the three conditions in a block-randomized order. Observers were blind to the conditions. After completing one or two blocks of conditions, the confederate and observer switched roles. Confederates and observers were dressed causally, typical of the students on campus, and carried a book and a notebook. The confederate positioned him/herself at one end of a sidewalk, a location where he or she could identify a potential participant. The observer was behind and separated physically from the confederate. No attempt was made to select participants by gender or race. That is, the first person meeting the requirements described earlier was approached. When the confederate started to move down the sidewalk, the observer followed at approximately 30 to 40 feet behind the confederate. After the confederate and observer passed the participant and reached the end of the sidewalk, they stopped in separate locations and recorded their observations.

It is important to make explicit an assumption underlying these behavioral adjustments in pedestrian passings: in particular, it is assumed that most people engage in some degree of monitoring as they approach and pass a stranger and, consequently, they are able to react to what the other person (or confederate) does.

There is the possibility, however, that very brief glances might be so quick that the approaching pedestrian does not notice the other or that some people clearly avoid others by looking down or away and will not be affected by what the confederate does. Nevertheless, the results of Cary's (1978) studies suggest that such occurrences are infrequent. Furthermore, the findings of our two studies (Patterson & Tubbs, 2003; Patterson, Webb, & Schwartz, 2002) show clear condition effects indicating that, in some way, most approaching pedestrians pay some attention to the confederates.

Response Measures

The observer's data sheet (see appendix) contains items on the time of day, location, temperature, weather, race and sex of participant, and the approximate age of participant (18–30, 31–40, 41–50, 51–60, and over 61 year old). The participant's reactions toward the confederate in the passing zone (12 ft to 0 ft) were recorded on the following dimensions: (a) glance, (b) nod, (c) smile, and (d) a verbal greeting. On each of the measures, reactions were scored as present, absent, or uncertain. For the Look and Look & Smile conditions, confederates independently made the same judgments as the observers on glance, nod, smile, and verbal greeting. Confederates did not attempt any ratings in the Avoid condition, because they were not looking in the direction of the oncoming pedestrians.

Interrater reliabilities have been computed on the judgments of the confederates and observers in Look and Look & Smile conditions. In our first study, employing nine different assistants (Patterson, Webb, & Schwartz, 2002), Cohen's *kappas* (Cohen, 1960), which correct for chance agreement, were adequate, but not high, for glances (.60), nods (.57), smiles (.60), and greetings (.59). Cohen's *kappas* in a second study (Patterson & Tubbs, 2003), with a smaller set of more experienced assistants, were much higher for glances (.76), nods (.90), smiles (.95), and greetings (1.00).

Analyses

Because the effects of multiple categorical variables (Condition, Sex of Participant, and Sex of Confederate) were examined, we have employed log-linear analyses. According to Howell (1997, p. 628), "sparse matrices" should be collapsed across variables to increase expected cell frequencies. For example, in our first study, nods and greetings occurred with less than 5% of the participants, and, though over 600 passings were observed, there were too few occurrences to test anything beyond the main effects of our variables on nods and greetings (Patterson et al., 2002). Specific comparisons in log-linear analysis are usually made in term of odds ratios, that is, the ratios of two conditional probabilities (the odds) for a dichotomous outcome. Because odds ratios can assume any value between 0 and infinity and are not affected by the marginal frequencies, they are particularly useful measures of effect size (Fleiss, 1994). A significant partial Chi-square indicates that the odds ratios are significantly different from 1.0

Initial Results

In our first study (Patterson et al., 2002), we examined the main and interaction effects of the degree of attention from the confederate (Avoid, Look, Look & Smile), Sex of Participant, and Sex of Confederate. Significant condition effects were found for *glances back* at the confederates, with approaching pedestrians displaying much higher levels of glancing in the Look & Smile condition than in the Avoid and Look conditions. Second, female confederates received more glances than male confederates. But these main effects on glances were qualified by a Condition × Sex of Confederate interaction. In the Look condition, female confederates received glances almost four times as often as male confederates.

One explanation for this difference is that, because a look alone is ambiguous (i.e., typically other cues are needed to choose what type of meaning is behind a "look"), there is less concern with a simple look from a female stranger than from a male stranger. That is, a look alone from a female stranger may have been seen as less threatening than a comparable look from a male stranger. Consequently, it could be more comfortable to return the look from the female confederate than from the male confederate. Among those who did glance at the confederate, approximately 25% smiled, and slightly less than 10% nodded and/or initiated a verbal greeting. In general, the condition effect for smiles, nods, and greetings was similar to that for glances. That is, smiles, nods, and greetings were much more frequent in the Look & Smile condition than in both the Avoid and Look conditions. Apparently, compared to a confederate displaying only a look, the addition of a smile provides a more clear, friendly signal that increases the likelihood of not only glancing back, but also of reciprocating with a smile, nod, and/or greeting.

In our second study (Patterson & Tubbs, 2003), we examined the effects of Condition (Avoid, Look, and Look & Smile), Sex of Confederate, and Sunglasses on passing pedestrians. A log-linear analysis of the results replicated the significant Condition effect in the first study, with more glances and smiles in the Look & Smile condition than in the Avoid and Look conditions. Furthermore, the magnitude of the Condition effect was virtually identical to the same effect in the first study. The hypotheses, that confederates who wore sunglasses would receive fewer glances than those who did not and that this effect would be greater for the male confederate, were not supported.

There was, however, a significant Sunglasses × Sex of Confederate effect on smiles, with pedestrians smiling more at the male confederate when he wore sunglasses than when he did not and smiling less at the female confederate when she wore sunglasses than when she did not. The contrasting effect of sunglasses for the male and female confederate may reflect the different functions of a smile in pedestrian encounters. Specifically, if the male confederate is viewed as more dominant, then he is likely to precipitate appeasement smiles (LaFrance & Hecht, 1999). In contrast, if the female confederate is viewed as more friendly, then she is likely to precipitate more spontaneously friendly smiles. Because the wearing of sunglasses can increase the power of an individual relative to a partner (Argyle, Lalljee, Cook, 1968), then the net result is that the male is seen as even more dominant and the female is seen as less friendly. Thus, appeasement smiles toward the male confederate increased and friendly smiles toward the female confederate decreased in the sunglasses condition.

Broader Applications

The passing encounters paradigm provides a structured, experimental approach for examining microinteractions between pedestrians. The results of our first two experiments point to some interesting patterns in the way that pedestrians manage these encounters, but these studies are just a start. There is much more that merits attention. For example, it is important to sample more settings with a broader range of confederates and participants. Because cultural differences affect a wide range of behaviors, including gaze, distance, facial expressions, gestures, and touch (see Burgoon, Buller, & Woodall, 1996, pp. 217–231), the subtle adjustments that people make in these microinteractions may well vary across culture. Along these lines, we have a study in progress comparing passing encounters between pedestrians on our U.S. Midwest, urban campus and those on campuses in Japan (Patterson, Iizuka, Tubbs, Ansel, & Anson, 2003).

It seems likely that there are regularities in the way that these microinteractions evolve, at least within a given culture. But the main and interaction effects of the sex of the confederate that we found in our two studies suggest that individual differences in the characteristics of pedestrians also influence their behavior. Because these passing encounters are ubiquitous, and because they are nonreactive in nature, they provide a particularly fertile ground for examining the effects of confederate appearance and participants' attitudes on patterns of recognition and avoidance.

If the general methodology described here is supplemented by the laboratory (or natural, follow-up) assessment of attitudes or personality, then it is possible to go beyond simply studying the influence of demographic factors (sex, race, age) to examining the effect of individual differences on these microinteractions. Specifically, attitude and personality measures may be taken in a controlled setting and then participants' reactions can be observed in a subsequent passing encounter. Furthermore, because the anonymity of individual participants can be guaranteed, it is more likely that they will be candid in responding to the relevant scales. The format simply requires that participants arrive individually (perhaps every 15 minutes) at the laboratory to take a small number of attitude or personality measures. No names are required on the answer sheets and participants are simply identified the order of their appearance (1-N).

The setting requires that there be only one exit route out of the building from the laboratory room. At the end of the hallway, a confederate will be waiting to walk toward the participant and monitor his/her reactions. This would necessarily involve some variant of a look by the confederates so that they can observe the participant's reactions in the passing zone. For example, if one were interested in examining the effect of racial attitudes on reactions to Black, White, and Asian confederates, then those confederates would take turns walking past the participants as they left the laboratory room. The confederates would necessarily be blind to the attitude scores of the participants and, consequently, this would not bias confederate behavior in the passing encounters. Later, the attitude score and behavioral observations of the participant could be linked in a data file. Studies of this kind are already in the planning stage.

Ethics for the Passing Encounters Paradigm

It is important to say something about the ethical issues in observing and recording the behavior of individuals in public settings. In laboratory studies, participants are necessarily identified, at least temporarily, so that they can be compensated or can receive extra credit points later for participating in the study. Later, names are replaced with arbitrary codes to maintain the anonymity of the participants. In the passing encounters paradigm, pedestrians remain anonymous from the start. In fact, if the confederate does know the approaching pedestrian, the individual is excluded from the study. From the very beginning of an observation, participants are identified by a trial number. Thus, the privacy of the participants' reactions is ensured.

But what about informed consent? In the materials provided for the institutional review board (IRB) in our studies, the case was simple and direct. These passing encounters are ever-present occurrences that we all experience, typically many times a day. The manipulations in these studies, that is, avoiding, looking, and smiling for a fraction of a second, are the common reactions of people who pass by us in malls, hallways, or on sidewalks. Because participants are not stressed and are not at risk, informed consent is unnecessary. For researchers and IRBs that are concerned with doing any research that involves observation without consent, participants can be stopped afterward and told about the study. When additional information is sought (e.g., personality variables), the questionnaire and debriefing can be done concurrently.

On the practical side, however, the impediments to seeking consent either before or after a passing encounter are substantial. One could not seek consent prior to an encounter and then expect spontaneous behavior as the participant passed by the confederate a few seconds later. If debriefing were initiated immediately after a passing encounter and consent sought then, as noted above, other problems could arise. Specifically, this would get the attention of other passersby and over a short period of time sensitize pedestrians that something unusual was happening on the sidewalks. Seeking consent either before or after the encounter would also necessitate that participants not to talk to others about their experience. In the case of running several hundred participants in a particular location, it is likely that information about the study would spread and affect later participants. Researchers, however, need to make choices for themselves about what concerns are most important to them and to the nature of their research.

SUMMARY

The passing encounters paradigm is a structured, nonreactive means to examine the brief, subtle interactions that occur as pedestrians walk past one another. This methodology provides an interesting window into the way that social order is reflected in these public and everpresent microinteractions. Perhaps just as important, the passing encounters paradigm also provides a way to study unobtrusively the behavioral correlates of specific attitudes and personality characteristics. At a time when the cognitive underpinnings of interaction and communication receive so much attention in the research literature, it is important to appreciate that our social worlds are maintained by the way that people behave with one another.

REFERENCES

Argyle, M., Lalljee, M., & Cook, M. (1968). The effects of visibility on interaction in a dyad. *Human Relations, 21*, 3–17.

Burgoon, J. K., Buller, D. B., Woodall, W. G. (1996). *Nonverbal communication: The unspoken dialogue* (2nd ed.). New York: McGraw-Hill.

Cary, M. S. (1978). Does civil inattention exist in pedestrian passing? *Journal of Personality and Social Psychology, 36*, 1185–1193.

Cohen, J. (1960). A coefficient of agreement for nominal scales. *Educational and Psychological Measurement, 20*, 37–46.

Fleiss, J. L. (1994). Measures of effect size for categorical data. In H. Cooper & L. V. Hedges (Eds.), *The handbook of research synthesis* (pp. 245–260). New York: Russell Sage Foundation.

Goffman, E. (1963). *Behavior in public places*. New York: Free Press.

Howell, D. C. (1997). *Statistical methods for psychology* (4th ed.). Belmont, CA: Duxbury Press.

LaFrance, M., & Hecht, M. A. (1999) Option or obligation to smile. In P. Philippot, R. S. Feldman, & E. J. Coats (Eds.), *The social context of nonverbal behavior* (pp. 45–70). Cambridge, UK: Cambridge University Press.

Patterson, M. L., Iizuka, Y., Tubbs, M. E., Ansel, J., & Anson, J. (2003). *Effects of culture on the passing encounters of pedestrians: A Japanese-American comparison.* Unpublished data.

Patterson, M. L., Kelly, C. E., & Douglas, E. A. (1977, May). *Walking intrusions: Proximity for a change of pace.* Paper presented at the annual convention of the Rocky Mountain Psychological Association, Albuquerque, NM.

Patterson, M. L., & Tubbs, M. E. (2003). *Through a glass darkly: Effects of visibility on recognition and avoidance in passing encounters.* Manuscript under review.

Patterson, M. L., Webb, A., & Schwartz, W. (2002). Passing encounters: Patterns of recognition and avoidance in pedestrians. *Basic and Applied Social Psychology, 24*, 57–66.

APPENDIX

Examples of Confederate and Observer Response Sheets

Confederate Sheet

Trial #_____ Day_____ Condition_____ Conf ID_____

Condition OK?   Yes   No   (Specify)

Participant (only in look and look & smile conditions)

Glance	Yes	No	?
Nod	Yes	No	?
Smile	Yes	No	?
Greeting	Yes	No	?

Observer Sheet

Observer #

Trial #   Day   Location
Time   9   10   11   12   1   2   3   4   5   6   7   8
Temperature   Wind   Low   Moderate   High
Sunny   Partly Cloudy   Mostly Cloudy   Cloudy
Subject Black   White   Asian   Gender   M   F
Age   18–30   31–40   41–50   61–60   61 and up
Unusual Circumstances
Looking into the sun Yes   No   Somewhat
Glance   Yes   No   ?
Nod   Yes   No   ?
Smile   Yes   No   ?
Greeting   Yes   No   ?

The Meta-Emotion Interview and Coding System

Eve-Anne M. Doohan
University of San Francisco

Sybil Carrère
Marianne G. Taylor
University of Washington

INTRODUCTION

The expression and management of emotion has long been of interest to scholars of nonverbal behavior (e.g., Andersen & Guerrero, 1998; Dillard, 1998; Guerrero, Andersen, & Trost, 1998; Planalp, 1998; Planalp, DeFrancisco, & Rutherford, 1996). Within the field of psychology, an individual's ability to self-regulate his or her emotional response *adaptively* to distressing, arousing stimuli in the environment is a hallmark of developmental health (e.g., Garber & Dodge, 1991; Thompson, 1991; Underwood, 1997; Walden & Smith, 1997). *Problematic* regulation of emotions has been linked to negative outcomes such as increased rates of physical and mental health symptoms, behavior troubles in children, and decreased marital satisfaction in couples (e.g., Achenbach, 1991; Carrère et al., 2002; Eisenberg & Fabes, 1994; Eisenberg, Fabes, & Murphy, 1996; Gottman, Katz, & Hooven, 1997; Hooven, Gottman, & Katz, 1995; Leadbeater, Kuperminc, Hertzog, & Blatt, 1999).

This chapter examines a particular technique used to study emotion: the Meta-Emotion Interview (MEI; see appendix for complete interview). The organization of this chapter is as follows: an explanation of the concept of meta-emotion and a brief description of the interview and coding system; previous applications of the interview; the psychometrics of the MEI; and limitations of this system, future directions, and applications. As discussed throughout this chapter, the MEI is an interview that can be adapted to meet the needs of different research foci. Although the nonverbal component of the MEI may not be as apparent as other measures of nonverbal communication in this volume, this chapter emphasizes the nonverbal

441

aspects of the MEI research paradigm in the hopes that nonverbal researchers may see the potential of the MEI for generating relevant data.

WHAT IS META-EMOTION?

The concept of meta-emotion seeks to tap into an individual's feelings about feelings, or what has come to be called one's meta-emotion structure. A meta-emotion structure is a person's organized set of emotions and cognitions about emotions (Hooven et al., 1995) and can be applied to an individual's understanding of his or her own emotions as well as to an individual's understanding of the emotions of others. The MEI and Coding System stem from the family and marital research of Gottman and his associates and have been used to study parents' coaching of their child's emotions (Hooven et al., 1995) and marital interactions (Carrère et al., 2002). A version of the MEI has also been developed for use with children (Taylor & Carrère, 2002).

Description of Interview

The MEI is a semistructured interview that takes about 1 hour to complete, in which a husband and wife are interviewed separately about their emotions. It can also be adapted for use with same-sex partners, dating relationships, and friends. The MEI's goal is to get as clear a picture as possible of what the experience of a particular emotion is like for each person. The original version of the interview was used with parents of preschool-aged children (Gottman, Katz, & Hooven, 1996, 1997; Hooven et al., 1995; Katz, 1997; Katz & Gottman, 1991) and examined two emotions: sadness and anger. More recent research projects have expanded the interview to include pride and love/affection (Carrère et al., 1998; Carrère & Katz, 2002); however, coding criteria for these two additional emotions are still under development.

The MEI is organized around each coded emotion, such that all of the questions about one emotion are covered before the interviewer moves onto the next emotion. For each emotion, individuals are asked to remember back to when they were growing up in their family of origin and how that emotion was expressed in their family. They are then "moved" to the present time and asked how they experience that emotion now, especially in their relationship with their spouse. Depending on the focus of the research, people are then asked questions about their spouse's experience of the emotion—or their child's experience of the emotion—and how they respond to their spouse and/or child.

The nonverbal expressions of emotion are highlighted at two points during the interview. Individuals are asked a series of questions to get them to describe their nonverbal responses to experiencing each emotion. For example, the interviewer asks the following questions: "What do you look like when you are sad?" "How could I tell if you were sad?" Individuals are also asked to describe the nonverbal behaviors of their spouse and/or their child. Because individuals self-report about their experiences with these different emotions, the narrative data provide information about how individuals perceive their own nonverbal behaviors and the nonverbal behaviors of others.

Description of Coding System

The MEI is videotaped and then reviewed and coded. A brief description of the Coding System is presented here, but copies of the lengthy coding manual can be requested from the second author. The four main dimensions of awareness, acceptance, dysregulation, and coaching are coded for each emotion. *Awareness* has to do with the extent to which individuals recognize and acknowledge that they experience the emotion and whether they can speak as an expert about this emotion. If the coder has a good idea of what the experience of this emotion is like for this individual, then the person would receive a high score on the awareness dimension. The *acceptance* dimension is concerned with whether individuals allow themselves to experience this emotion and if they are comfortable expressing this emotion. An individual with a high level of acceptance feels that expressing emotions is important and generally feels comfortable expressing emotions both verbally and nonverbally. *Dysregulation* refers to individuals' concerns and reported difficulties regulating their expression of the emotion. This code is designed such that extreme scores on this dimension refer to significant problems for individuals in regard to their emotional expression. *Coaching* assesses the degree to which individuals have the ability to identify, accept, and remediate their partner's (and/or child's) emotional experience in a positive and effective manner. An effective coach helps one's partner (or child) through the experience of the emotion.

For both the Marital and Parental MEI, coders examine awareness, acceptance, and dysregulation for the individuals themselves (their self-reports) and for their reports of their partner's (and/or child's) emotions. The Marital MEI also assesses emotion coaching in the individual and the partner (the last dimension just listed), whereas the Parental MEI measures the amount of emotion coaching the parent uses with the child. Each code is accompanied by several statements, which are rated by the coders along a 5-point Likert-type scale ranging from strongly agree to strongly disagree. Each spouse receives a score for each of the four main dimensions that reflects the sum of the ratings from the Likert-type scales. For example, seven statements, such as "experiences this emotion and describes emotion easily," are rated individually and then added together to assess the overall code of *awareness*.

Nonverbal behavior is assessed in two different ways in this coding scheme. One way that it is captured is by what individuals actually report about their experiences of each emotion. For example, one specific statement asks coders to rate how participants express the emotion nonverbally (according to their self-reports). In other words, how aware are individuals about their nonverbal behaviors? How detailed are the descriptions of their nonverbal experience of the emotion? Depending on the emotion being described and the individual's perceived experience of the emotion, this code can assess reported facial expressions, gestures, eye behaviors, and vocalic cues.

The other way that nonverbal behavior is assessed is by looking at how individuals act as they talk about the emotions during the interview. For example, one specific statement asks whether the individual describes the emotion easily. This statement assesses the conversational flow and looks specifically at vocalic indicators of the individual's talk about the emotion, such as whether or not there are speech disfluencies. Another statement asks coders to rate how tense or anxious the individual appears during the interview. Although this code can include verbal acknowledgment of discomfort, it also includes nonverbal indicators of tension such as fidgeting, nervous laughter, self-adaptors (e.g., playing with hair, touching face), and an overall rigid body.

PREVIOUS APPLICATIONS

Parental Meta-Emotion

Research by Gottman and his associates established the important impact of the family's meta-emotion structure on children's developmental outcomes. As noted previously, meta-emotion refers to the parent's feelings about the child's emotions and that parent's style of communicating with the child about emotions (Gottman et al., 1996, 1997; Hooven et al., 1995; Katz, 1997; Katz & Gottman, 1991). This meta-emotion structure is embedded in parent–child interactions and appears to buffer children even from the negative outcomes associated with marital distress and divorce. Gottman et al. (1997) suggest that the meta-emotion of the parents and parenting techniques are instrumental in children's ability to regulate emotions and physiology, children's cognitive abilities, and their social competence. Results from this body of research also indicate a link between parental meta-emotion and behavioral problems associated with externalizing and internalizing disorders. More recently, Windecker-Nelson, Katz, and Haynes (2002) found that spousal symptomatology (depression, anger, anxiety, social withdrawal, and emotional style) predicted scores on the self-report sections of the MEI (e.g., self-reports of awareness, acceptance, and dysregulation).

Marital Meta-Emotion

Carrère et al. (2002) extended the meta-emotion paradigm from child developmental issues to adult emotion dysregulation responses to interpersonal stressors. They examined anger dysregulation and parasympathetic control of the cardiovascular system during marital conflict. The parasympathetic system is responsible for returning the body to homeostasis after a stressor. Married couples ($N = 54$) participated in laboratory procedures that included a marital conflict discussion and the Marital MEI. Greater anger dysregulation in the wives was correlated with reduced parasympathetic control, more displays of anger during the conflict interaction, and lower marital satisfaction. Anger dysregulation in husbands was associated with greater displays of anger during marital conflict and lower marital satisfaction, but not parasympathetic control.

PSYCHOMETRICS OF THE MEI AND CODING SYSTEM

The original Parental MEI was not evaluated comprehensively for its psychometric properties, although its predictive validity for child developmental outcomes was reported (Gottman et al., 1996, 1997; Hooven et al., 1995; Katz, 1997; Katz & Gottman, 1991). The psychometrics for the expanded versions of both the Parental and Marital MEI and Coding Systems (which include the emotions of sadness, anger, pride, happiness, and love/affection) are being developed currently . Reported here are the psychometrics from the Marital MEI Coding System, assessing the emotions of sadness and anger for both the husband and wife (Carrère et al., 2002; Yoshimoto et al., 2000). The sample used for these series of analyses consisted of 62 married couples from the Puget Sound area of Washington State. The mean level of marital satisfaction for the sample was very similar to normative scores on the Marital Adjustment Test (MAT; Locke & Wallace, 1959) for the United States (U.S. mean = 100, SD = 15; sample mean for husbands = 104.9, SD = 22; sample mean for wives = 104.9, SD = 23.7).

Internal Construct Validity

A principal-components factor analysis was conducted to determine the latent variables present in the Marital MEI. The individual, rather than the couple, was used as the unit of analysis because the interview measures individuals' perceptions of their own emotions as well as their perceptions of their partners' emotions. The analysis yielded similar two-component solutions for both husbands and wives (see Table 41). Together, the two components accounted for 67.9% of the variance for husbands and 69.0% of the variance for wives. Following Comrey and Lee's (1992) suggestion, only those subscales with a loading of .71 (absolute value) or higher were used, as they are excellent indicators of the underlying components. In the case of the Marital MEI, all subscales fit into one of these two factors.

The first component in the analysis explained 45.3% of the variance for husbands, and the corresponding component explained 45.7% of the variance for wives. This component, *awareness/acceptance*, included the subscales of anger awareness, anger acceptance, sadness awareness, and sadness acceptance for both the husbands and the wives. The second component accounted for an additional 22.6% of the variance for husbands and 23.3% of the variance for wives. This second component, *dysregulation*, included the subscales of anger dysregulation and sadness dysregulation both for the husbands and the wives.

TABLE 41

Factor Loadings for Husband and Wife Anger and Sadness on Marital MEI

Factor 1: Awareness/Acceptance		Factor 2: Dysregulation	
W Anger Awareness	.842	W Anger Dysregulation	.806
W Anger Acceptance	.815	W Sadness Dysregulation	.764
W Sadness Awareness	.772		
W Sadness Acceptance	.790		
H Anger Awareness	.771	H Anger Dysregulation	.742
H Anger Acceptance	.787	H Sadness Dysregulation	.755
H Sadness Awareness	.737		
H Sadness Acceptance	.787		

Predictive Validity

To assess the predictive validity of the Marital MEI, we hypothesized that individuals' scores on the Marital MEI would be associated with their depression and marital satisfaction. Typically, people who have difficulty regulating anger and sadness are expected to have mental health outcomes that are emotionally laden, such as depression (Achenbach, 1991; Carrère et al., 2002; Leadbeater et al., 1999). Furthermore, if partners were having trouble with emotion regulation, these troubles could interfere with communication in the marriage, which could, in turn, have an impact on marital quality. To test these hypotheses, we conducted linear regression analyses. The scores for awareness/acceptance and dysregulation were entered separately as the independent variables in the regression model. Results of the linear regression analyses are reported in Table 42.

Depression was measured using the Beck Depression Inventory (BDI; Beck, Ward, Mendelson, Mock, & Erbaugh, 1979). Awareness/acceptance significantly predicted depression for both husbands and wives. As awareness and acceptance of emotions decreased, depression increased. Dysregulation also predicted depression significantly. As emotional dysregulation increased, depression also increased for both the husbands and wives. Awareness/acceptance was a stronger predictor of depression for the wives, whereas dysregulation was a stronger predictor of depression for the husbands.

Marital satisfaction was measured using the Locke-Wallace MAT (Locke & Wallace, 1959). Awareness/acceptance of both anger and sadness was predictive of marital satisfaction for the husbands but not the wives. Husbands who expressed higher awareness and acceptance reported higher levels of marital satisfaction. In contrast, dysregulation was predictive of marital satisfaction for the wives but not for the husbands. Wives who were more dysregulated reported lower levels of marital satisfaction. Whereas MEI scores for husbands and wives were predictive of de-

TABLE 42
Predicting Husband and Wife Depression, Hostility, and Marital Satisfaction from the Marital MEI

Predictors	F(df)	Standardized β	Adjusted R²
Depression			
Awareness/Acceptance			
Husbands	5.22* (1,68)	−.267	.058
Wives	9.21*** (1,59)	−.367	.120
Dysregulation			
Husbands	9.82*** (1,68)	.355	.113
Wives	6.35* (1,59)	.312	.082
Marital Satisfaction			
Awareness/Acceptance			
Husbands	7.50** (1,66)	.319	.088
Wives	3.27 (1,58)	.231	.037
Dysregulation			
Husbands	1.60 (1,66)	−.154	.009
Wives	4.24* (1,58)	−.261	.052

Note: * $p < .05$; ** $p < .01$; *** $p < .005$.

pression, contrary to our predictions, there were differences between husbands' and wives' marital satisfaction outcomes. Future research should examine possible explanations for these sex differences in more detail.

Intercoder Reliability of the MEI Coding System

Intercoder reliability was calculated via intraclass coefficients (ICCs) for every dimension of the Coding System. ICCs for the MEI Coding System have been reasonably good, with all but one dimension (wife's awareness of partner's sadness) falling in the range between .60 and .83 (Carrère et al., 2002; Yoshimoto et al., 2000).

LIMITATIONS, FUTURE DIRECTIONS, AND APPLICATIONS

As previously noted, there was very little psychometric work done to evaluate the construct validity of the original Parental MEI Coding System. Whereas the instrument and its subscales are predictive of important childhood outcomes (e.g., academic achievement, health, and social competence), the internal and discriminant construct validities have not yet been assessed. Another limitation of the original Parental MEI Coding System (Hooven, 1994) used in the first studies (e.g., Gottman et al., 1997; Hooven et al., 1995) was that the response sets for the coding categories (i.e., strongly agree, agree, neutral, disagree, and strongly disagree) were not composed of the same number of categories consistently. Some coding categories in the original Parental MEI Coding System had all five Likert-type response choices, whereas others had four (strongly agree, agree, neutral, and disagree), three (agree, neutral, and disagree), or two response choices possible (agree, disagree).

The Parental MEI Coding System also had coding categories for behaviors that were discussed infrequently by the parents being interviewed. For example, one of the coding categories for parent's acceptance of the child's emotion was "Parent wants child to talk to them about the emotion." The parents are not questioned directly about whether they want the child to talk to them about the emotion but, rather, are asked more general questions about how they respond when their child expresses the emotion. The coding categories for infrequently occurring topics meant that there was an unusually large amount of missing data when calculating the scores for the Parental MEI. These missing data raised concerns about how to interpret the scores for the parental interview.

With this in mind, Yoshimoto et al. (2000) revised the self-reports of husbands' and wives' acceptance, awareness, and dysregulation scores as part of developing the Marital MEI Coding System (i.e., response sets are equivalent for all coding categories; categories; are always codable if the interview was completed in full). The psychometrics for the revised self-report of the husbands' and wives' Marital MEI Coding System are reported earlier in this chapter. Mittman and Carrère (2002) have similarly revised the parents' report section of the Parental MEI Coding System (parent's acceptance and awareness of the child's emotion, the degree to which the parent perceives the child to be emotionally dysregulated, and the level of emotion coaching by the parent). The revised Parental MEI Coding System is being used in Carrère, Gottman, and Doohan's current research with families. Reports on the construct validity, predictive validity, and reliability will be reported in future publications.

One application that was developed by Taylor and Carrère (2002) is a child version of the MEI. The Child MEI examines emotional awareness, acceptance, and dysregulation for 7–8-year-olds. By this point in development, children are able to understand, regulate, and display many of the emotions that shape their daily social interactions. Although parental reports, and even teacher or peer reports, provide insight into children's emotional competence and meta-emotion structure, children themselves can share vital information about their own experiences with emotions and may provide corroborating evidence for others' impressions.

Like the Parental MEI and Marital MEI, the Child MEI (Taylor & Carrère, 2002) includes separate sections focusing on each of the emotions of interest. In addition to the central emotions of anger, sadness, pride, and love/affection covered by the Parental MEI and Marital MEI, the positive emotion of happiness and the negative emotion of fear have been added to the Child MEI. To gain social competence, particularly in peer relations, children must learn the appropriate cultural display rules for positive emotions as well as negative ones. For each emotion in the Child MEI, separate sections of the interview address children's recent experiences with that emotion, the people they approach when they experience that emotion, their own self-regulation strategies, and the way that their mothers and fathers interact with them around that emotion.

As with the Parental MEI and the Marital MEI, the Child MEI (Taylor & Carrère, 2002) has the potential to provide researchers with a rich dataset from which to explore children's self-reports of their nonverbal displays of emotion. Moreover, it enables researchers to pursue new lines of research examining children's patterns of language use and nonverbal behaviors for conveying emotional information. It also allows for comparisons of nonverbal behavioral patterns within families or other types of relationships.

CONCLUSION

The MEI is of potential interest to researchers and students who study nonverbal cues because it taps into individuals' perceptions of their own nonverbal behaviors and incorporates nonverbal indicators of emotional awareness and acceptance. One important focus here would be to examine cultural or sex differences or similarities in nonverbal cues as they occur during the MEI. The MEI may also be used to assess emotion regulation and meta-emotion structure in contexts beyond the family. For example, the interview could be used to look at how individuals experience, express, and manage different emotions in their work relationships or friendships. The MEI also provides a rich source of data for researchers who wish to develop new coding systems addressing specific nonverbal processes and behaviors (e.g., the relationship between nonverbal cues and emotional expression and language use).

REFERENCES

Achenbach, T. M. (1991). *Integrative guide for the 1991 CBCL/4–8 YSR, and TRF Profiles.* Burlington: University of Vermont.
Andersen, P. A., & Guerrero, L. K. (1998). Principles of communication and emotion in social interaction. In P. A. Andersen & L. K. Guerrero (Eds.), *Handbook of communication and emotion: Research, theory, applications, and contexts* (pp. 49–96). San Diego, CA: Academic Press.
Beck, A. T., Ward, C. H., Mendelson, M., Mock, J., & Erbaugh, J. (1979). *Beck depression inventory.* Palo Alto, CA: Psychological Corporation.
Carrère, S., Gottman, J. M., McGonigle, M., Prince, S., Yoshimoto, D., Hawkins, M. W., Dearborn, S., & Tabares, A. (1998). *Marital meta-emotion interview.* Unpublished manuscript, University of Washington at Seattle.
Carrère. S., & Katz, L. F. (2002). *The revised parental meta-emotion interview.* Unpublished manuscript, University of Washington at Seattle.
Carrère, S., Yoshimoto, D., Schwab, J., Mittman, A., Woodin, E., Tabares, A., Ryan, K., Hawkins, M., Prince, S., & Gottman, J. M. (2002, October). *Anger dysregulation in married couples.* Paper presented at the meeting of the Society for Psychophysiological Research National Conference, Washington, DC.

450   DOOHAN, CARRÈRE, TAYLOR

Comrey, A. L., & Lee, H. B. (1992). A first course in factor analysis (2nd ed.). Hillsdale, NJ: Lawrence Erlbaum Associates.
Dillard, J. P. (1998). The role of affect in communication, biology, and social relationships. In P. A. Andersen & L. K. Guerrero (Eds.), Handbook of communication and emotion: Research, theory, applications, and contexts (pp. xvii–xxxii). San Diego, CA: Academic Press.
Eisenberg, N., & Fabes, R. A. (1994). Mothers' reactions to children's negative emotions: Relations to children's temperament and anger behavior. Merrill-Palmer Quarterly, 40, 138–156.
Eisenberg, N., Fabes, R. A., & Murphy, B. C. (1996). Parents' reactions to children's negative emotions: Relations to children's social competence and comforting behavior. Child Development, 67, 2227–2247.
Garber, J., & Dodge, K. A. (Eds.). (1991). The development of emotion regulation and dysregulation. New York: Cambridge University Press.
Gottman, J. M., Katz, L. F., & Hooven, C. (1996). Parental meta-emotion philosophy and the emotional life of families: Theoretical models and preliminary data. Journal of Family Psychology, 10, 243–268.
Gottman, J. M., Katz, L. F., & Hooven, C. (1997). Meta-emotion: How families communicate emotionally. Mahwah, NJ: Lawrence Erlbaum Associates.
Guerrero, L. K., Andersen, P. A., & Trost, M. (1998). Communication and emotion: Basic concepts and approaches. In P. A. Andersen & L. K. Guerrero (Eds.), Handbook of communication and emotion: Research, theory, applications, and contexts (pp. 3–28). San Diego, CA: Academic Press.
Hooven, C. (1994). The meta-emotion coding system. Unpublished manuscript, University of Washington at Seattle.
Hooven, C., Gottman, J. M., & Katz, L. F. (1995). Parental meta-emotion structure predicts family and child outcomes. Cognitions and Emotion, 9, 229–264.
Katz, L. F. (1997, April). Towards an emotional intelligence theory of adolescent depression. Paper presented at the biennial meeting of the Society of Research in Child Development, Washington, DC.
Katz, L. F., & Gottman, J. M. (1991). Marital discord and child outcomes: A social psychophysiological approach. In J. Garber & K. A. Dodge (Eds.), The development of emotion regulation and dysregulation (pp. 129–155). New York: Cambridge University Press.
Leadbeater, B. J., Kuperminc, G. P., Hertzog, C., & Blatt, S. J. (1999). A multivariate model of gender differences in adolescents' internalizing and externalizing problems. Developmental Psychology, 35, 1268–1282.
Locke, H. J., & Wallace, K. M. (1959). Short marital-adjustment and prediction tests: Their reliability and validity. Marriage and Family Living, 21, 251–255.
Mittman, A., & Carrère, S. (2002). The revised parental meta-emotion interview coding system. Unpublished manuscript, University of Washington at Seattle.
Planalp, S. (1998). Communicating emotion in everyday life: Cues, channels, and processes. In P. A. Andersen & L. K. Guerrero (Eds.), Handbook of communication and emotion: Research, theory, applications, and contexts (pp. 29–48). San Diego, CA: Academic Press.
Planalp, S., DeFrancisco, V. L., & Rutherford, D. (1996). Varieties of cues to emotion occurring in naturally occurring situations. Cognition and Emotion, 10, 137–153.
Taylor, M. G., & Carrère, S. (2002). The child meta-emotion interview and coding system for 7–8-year-olds. Unpublished manuscript, University of Washington at Seattle.
Thompson, R. A. (1991). Emotion regulation and emotional development. Educational Psychology Review, 3, 269–307.
Underwood, M. K. (1997). Top ten pressing questions about the development of emotion regulation. Motivation and Emotion, 21, 127–146.
Walden, T. A., & Smith, M. C. (1997). Emotion regulation. Motivation and Emotion, 21, 7–25.
Windecker-Nelson, B., Katz, L. F., & Haynes, C. (2002). Parental meta-emotion philosophy: Relations to parental symptomatology and marital quality. Manuscript submitted for publication.
Yoshimoto, D., Mittman, A., Woodin, E., Tabares, A., Carrère, S., Schwab, J., Ryan, K., & Gottman, J. (2000). Marital meta-emotion coding system. Unpublished manuscript, University of Washington at Seattle.

APPENDIX

The Parenting Meta-Emotion Interview

A Modification of the Original Meta-Emotion Interview
Developed by Lynn Katz and Sybil Carrère

Introduction

Interviewer: I am going to ask you some questions about how you feel about your feelings, and we are going to talk about four different emotions in particular. We will start off talking about sadness, then move on to anger, then pride and being proud of something, and then we will finish up with love and affection. For each of these emotions, I am going to start off by asking you, just briefly, what it was like growing up in your family. Then we will move back to the present time and talk about what that emotion is like for you now, especially in your relationship with your spouse. Then we will move on and talk about your child's experience of that emotion. Let me use surprise as an example to get us started. Some people love being surprised. If you threw them a surprise party, they would love it. Surprise is a feeling that they really enjoy and they would like to have more of it in their lives. Now, other people don't like being surprised at all. They don't like to be caught off guard, and they like everything to be planned out and certain. So, the point is that people are just different. There are no right or wrong answers to any of these questions. It is your opinions and feelings. Do you have any questions before we get started?

Part One: The Interviewee's and Child's Sadness

Interviewer: Let's start off by talking about sadness.
1. What was your experience with sadness when you were growing up? How was sadness expressed your family?
2. Can you remember a particular time when you were sad growing up? Can you tell me what happened?
3. How did your parents respond to your sadness?

Interviewer: Let's move to the present.
1. What is it like for you to be sad now?
2. What do you look like when you are sad? How could I tell if you were sad?
3. Can you give me a recent example of when you were sad?
4. Who is approachable to you when you are sad? Who do you talk to or who comforts you when you are sad (i.e., spouse, immediate or extended family members, friends, clergy persons)?
5. How does your partner respond to your sadness in general?

6. How do you feel about your partner's response to your sadness in these situations?
7. How does your partner respond to you when you are sad because of something s/he has done?
8. How do you feel about your partner's response in these situations?
9. In general, what are your thoughts and feelings about sadness? (In general, how do you feel about your sadness?)

Interviewer: Let's talk about your child's sadness.
1. What about _____ (the child)? Can you tell when (s)he's sad? Can you tell the subtle signs? Tell me what that is like.
2. What makes him/her sad?
3. Can you give me a recent or vivid example of one time that ____ (child) was sad? What happened, what did s/he do, and how did you respond? (try to get a play by play account of what happened).
4. What does your child do to get over being sad?
5. How do you respond to ___ (child) sadness? What might you do?
6. What would be your goals in this situation when you are responding to your child's sadness?
7. What do you think you are trying to teach ____ (child) about sadness?
8. How does your child respond to your teaching style?
9. What does your child's sadness bring out in you?
10. In general, what are your reactions, thoughts and feelings about _____ (child's) sadness?

Part Two: The Interviewee's and Child's Anger

Interviewer: Let's talk about feeling angry.
1. What was your experience with anger when you were growing up, how was anger expressed your family?
2. How did your parents respond to your anger?
3. Can you remember a particular time when you were angry growing up? Can you tell me what happened?

Interviewer: Let's move to the present.
1. What is it like for you to be angry now?
2. What do you look like when you are angry? How could I tell if you were angry?
3. Can you give me a recent example of when you were angry?
4. Who is approachable to you when you are angry? Who do you talk to when you are angry (i.e., spouse, immediate or extended family members, friends, clergy persons)?
5. How does your partner respond to your anger in general?

6. How do you feel about your partner's response to your anger in these situations?
7. How does your partner respond to you when you are angry because of something s/he has done?
8. How do you feel about your partner's response in these situations?
9. In general, what are your thoughts and feelings about anger? (In general, how do you feel about your anger?)

Interviewer: Let's talk about your child's anger.
1. What about _____ (the child)? Can you tell when (s)he's angry? Can you tell the subtle signs? Tell me what that is like.
2. What makes him/her angry?
3. Can you give me a recent or vivid example of one time that _____ (child) was angry? What happened, what did s/he do, and how did you respond? (try to get a play by play account of what happened).
4. How does your child get over being angry?
5. How do you respond to _____ (child) anger? What might you do?
6. What would be your goals in this situation when you are responding to your child's anger?
7. What do you think you are trying to teach _____ (child) about anger?
8. How does your child respond to your teaching style?
9. What does your child's anger bring out in you?
10. In general, what are your reactions, thoughts and feelings about _____ (child's) anger?

Part Three: The Interviewee's Pride and Child's Pride

Interviewer: Let's talk about pride and being proud of something.
1. What was your experience with pride growing up? What did your family do when someone in your family was proud of something/someone?
2. How did your parents respond to you when you were proud of something?
3. Can you remember a particular time when you felt proud when you were growing up? Can you tell me what happened?

Interviewer: Let's move to the present.
1. What is it like for you to feel proud of something in your life now?
2. What do you look like when you are proud of something? How could I tell if you were proud?
3. Can you give me a recent example of when you felt proud?
4. Who do you talk to when you are feeling proud (i.e., spouse, immediate or extended family, teachers, clergy persons, friends)?
5. How does your partner respond to you when you are proud of something in general?

6. How do you feel about your partner's response in these situations?
7. How does your partner respond to you when you are proud because of something s/he had done?
8. How do you feel about your partner's response in these situations?
9. In general, what are your thoughts and feelings about pride or being proud?

Interviewer: Let's talk about your child's sense of pride.
1. What about _____ (the child)? Can you tell when (s)he is proud? Can you tell the subtle signs? Tell me what that is like.
2. What makes him/her proud?
3. Can you give me a recent or vivid example of one time that _____ (child) was proud of something? What happened, what did s/he do, and how did you respond? (try to get a play by play account of what happened).
4. How do you respond to _____ (child's) pride? What might you do?
5. What would be your goal in this situation?
6. Are there times when _____ (child) expresses pride in a way that is problematic?
7. How does _____ (child) transition from the problematic behavior to a more appropriate behavior?
8. What are you trying to teach your child about pride?
9. How does your child respond to your teaching style?
10. What does your child's pride bring out in you?
11. In general, what are your reactions, thoughts and feelings about _____ (child's) pride?

Part Four: The Interviewee's and Child's Affection and Love

Interviewer: Let's talk about affection and love.
1. What was your experience with affection and demonstrations of love when you were growing up? What was affection and expression of love like in your family?
2. How did your parents let you know they loved you? Can you think of a time when they let you know they loved you?
3. How did your parents respond to you when you were affectionate?

Interviewer: Let's move to the present.
1. What is it like for you to be affectionate and express your love now?
2. When do you feel affectionate now?
3. What do you do when you are affectionate? How could I tell if you were feeling loving and affectionate?
4. Can you give me a recent example of when you felt affectionate?
5. Who are you affectionate towards, and who is affectionate towards you?

6. How does your partner respond to your affection?
7. How do you feel about your partner's response to your affection?
8. In general, what are your thoughts and feelings about affection?

Interviewer: Let's talk about your child's affection and love.
1. What about _____ (the child)? Can you tell when (s)he's feeling affectionate and loving? Can you tell the subtle signs? Tell me what that is like.
2. What makes him/her feel loving/affectionate?
3. Can you give me a recent or vivid example of one time that ____ (child) was feeling loving and affectionate? What happened, what did s/he do, and how did you respond? (try to get a play by play account of what happened).
4. How do you respond to ___ (child) affection and love? What might you do?
5. What would be your goals in this situation when you are responding to your child's affection and love?
6. Are there times when ____ (child) expresses affection inn a way that is problematic?
7. How does ____ (child) transition from the problematic behavior to a more appropriate behavior?
8. What do you think you are trying to teach ____ (child) about affection and love?
9. How does your child respond to your teaching style?
10. What does your child's affection and loving behavior bring out in you?
11. In general, what are your reactions, thoughts and feelings about ____ (child's) affection and love?

Measuring Emotional Experience, Expression, and Communication: The Slide-Viewing Technique

Ross Buck
University of Connecticut

INTRODUCTION

In the slide-viewing technique (SVT), senders watch a series of emotionally loaded color slides and rate their reaction to each along a variety of emotion scales. The senders' spontaneous facial expressions are filmed by a hidden camera and televised to receivers who attempt to judge (a) what kind of slide the sender viewed on each trial, and (b) the sender's emotional responses. The technique captures the rated emotional *experience* of the sender, the rating of the sender's emotional *expression* by receivers, and *communication* from sender to receiver. Communication is measured as the number of slides that receivers are able to categorize correctly (percent correct measure) and the correlation coefficient between senders' and observers' ratings of the senders' emotional response (emotion correlation measure). This chapter discusses the slide-viewing technique in more detail, beginning with an overview of its purpose and development, its theoretical underpinnings, and an exemplar study that used SVT.

PURPOSE AND DEVELOPMENT

Capturing Dynamic, Spontaneous Emotional Expression

Origin: The Cooperative Conditioning Technique. The SVT was developed based on the cooperative conditioning technique developed by Miller and colleagues to assess the communication of emotion in rhesus monkeys (Miller, Banks, & Ogawa, 1962; Miller, Caul, & Mirsky, 1967). The SVT, however, was created to study the communication of emotion in humans (Buck, Miller, & Caul, 1974; Buck,

457

Savin, Miller, & Caul, 1972). Initial studies determined that color slides, presented on a backlit screen allowing normal room illumination for filming, were effective in eliciting emotional facial expressions. Pilot studies also determined the usefulness of asking participants to verbally describe the emotional feelings evoked by the slides after an initial silent viewing period: That appeared to increase the participants' involvement in the slide-viewing task, and also constituted an additional source of data relating to emotional expression. Accordingly, in the SVT today, the sender views the slide silently for 10 seconds, at which time a light cues the sender to describe his or her emotional response.

The Slides.   Several types of emotionally loaded slides can be used, depending upon the senders involved (see Table 43). *Sexual* slides showing nude and seminude males and females have been used only with healthy adult senders. *Scenic* slides show pleasant landscapes, and *Pleasant People* slides show happy-looking children and adults. *Unpleasant* slides have been chosen based on the senders involved. Healthy adults have been shown strongly unpleasant slides (D1 to D5), preschool children have seen mildly unpleasant slides (D6 to D9), and patient groups have viewed moderately unpleasant slides (D10 to D13). *Unusual* slides show strange photographic effects. *Familiar People* slides show persons familiar to the sender (i.e., the sender himself or herself, friends at school, teachers, ward personnel, the experimental assistant, etc.). The latter can be made by an SLR camera with 50mm lens using high speed film and natural lighting or Polaroid instant slide film with flash.

Unique Features of the SVT.   The genesis of the SVT in animal research is reflected in a number of unique features of the SVT. One of its major features is that the technique involves spontaneous rather than symbolic or posed nonverbal behavior. The sender is told that filming may occur at some point during the experiment, but the camera is hidden.[22] A second feature is that the SVT involves dynamic displays of emotion rather than static images. A third feature is that the SVT can be used with a wide variety of senders: It is not upsetting, and on the contrary has been enjoyed by the great majority of participants from preschool children to hospitalized psychiatric patients. Also, it requires virtually no instructions, allowing the study of senders who are incapable of reacting to complex instructions, including brain-damaged persons.

A fourth feature is that the SVT can assess the experience, expression, and communication of specific emotions (i.e., separate measures of happiness, sadness, fear, anger, surprise, disgust, and pleasantness/unpleasantness can be taken). A fifth feature of the SVT is that it involves a simple judgment task that does not require trained judges, whose training might itself introduce bias. It

---

[22]The senders' reactions, although filmed, are not observed. At the end of the experiment, the presence of the camera is revealed and the sender is asked to sign a reconsent form allowing the use of the filmed records. Thus, the sender is not observed without consent.

TABLE 43
Slides used in the Slide-Viewing Technique

Sexual Slides	Unpleasant Slides.
A1. A woman being photographed by men	D1. Facial burn
A2. A couple kissing in a doorway	D2. Severe facial injury
A3. Embracing couple	D3. Burned infant
A4. Smiling couple facing camera	D4. Burned child
A5. Seated woman	D5. Scene of facial operation
Scenic Slides	D6. Crying woman
B1. New York harbor	D7. Crying infant
B2. Sunset over a lake	D8. Grasshopper close-up
B3. Autumn scene	D9. Grotesque fashion model
B4. Stream scene	D10. Starving child
B5. Sailboat at dock	D11. Wounded infant
Pleasant People Slides	D12. Crying child with crutch
C1. Group of laughing children	D13. Falling people
C2. Woman with a young child	*Unusual Slides*
C3. Young girl	E1. Time exposure: Turnpike
C4. Young child bending down	E2. Time exposure: Merry-go-round
C5. Young child touching flower	E3. Time exposure: Light pattern
C6. Child clowning	E4. Multiple exposure: Airport
C7. Sleeping baby	E5. Multiple exposure: Sunset
C8. Bathing baby	E6. Horizontal light pattern
C9. Smiling young girl	E7. Ice and sun
C10. Children in preschool	
C11. Kissing couple	
C12. Child urinating on tree	

Note: The slides are copyrighted by author or others and are available for research use only. Contact author for details.

takes advantage of the natural abilities of people to judge emotion in others. At the same time, the communication scores from the SVT are not simple subjective ratings. The criterion of communication accuracy is objective and unambiguous. The receiver is clearly either right or wrong in his judgment about the type of slide the sender is viewing or the rating of the sender's emotional experience. Finally, the SVT can be used to assess both sending accuracy (measured across receivers) and receiving ability (measured across senders). In the Communication of Affect Receiving Ability Test (CARAT), video sequences from the SVT were used as "items" (Buck, 1976).

Specific Emotion and Communication Measures From the SVT

The following discussion reflects how different variables are measured using the SVT. Each sender's self-reported emotional response to each slide is computed for each of seven emotions—happiness, sadness, fear, anger, surprise, disgust, and pleasant/unpleasant—for each of the N slides viewed by the sender. Each sender's emotional response to the slides is created by computing the mean of the receivers' ratings of each of the seven emotions across each of the N slides viewed by the sender. Emotion communication accuracy of each sender for each of the seven emotions is the Pearson correlation coefficient computed, across the N slides, of the sender's self-report of each emotion and the mean receivers' rating of that emotion. This yields a communication score for each emotion, for each sender. Finally, category communication accuracy is determined by the percent of slides correctly identified and is computed by assessing the number of receivers accurately identifying the slide viewed by the sender on each slide, averaged by the number of receivers involved, yielding a percent correct figure for each of the slides viewed by the sender. The mean of these scores constituted the percent correct measure for that sender.

Complements to the SVT

The Segmentation Technique. The SVT does not by itself indicate *when* the behaviors important to communication occur, nor does it specify *what* those behaviors are. The segmentation procedure, however, has been used to identify consensually meaningful events in the dynamic stream of expression. It is deceptively simple. Judges are instructed to watch the senders' expressions and to press a button or make a mark whenever "something meaningful" occurs in the stream of expression. The definition of meaningfulness is left to the judges, but studies have demonstrated that observers tend to agree on the location in time of meaningful points, so that consensually meaningful points (CPs), which are defined as 1-second points that receive more than one standard deviation over the mean number of button presses for a given stimulus person, can be determined. These points correspond to high-information points in the stream of expression (Buck, Baron, & Barrette, 1982; Buck, Baron, Goodman, & Shapiro, 1980; Newtson, Engquist, & Bois, 1977). The consensually meaningful points identified by the procedure are not tied to specific behaviors but emerge solely due to their meaningfulness as perceived by naïve raters. The extent of consensus—therefore, presumably, meaningfulness—can be specified mathematically. Segmentation produces an objective representation of the dynamic behavior stream potentially able to detect subtle, complex, and idiosyncratic patterns of response.

The number of button presses to a sender is a measure of expressiveness that complements measures of communication accuracy produced by the SVT. The evidence suggests that expressiveness bears a curvilinear relationship to sending accuracy in that persons who receive either many or few button presses tend to be poor senders. In healthy samples, the relationship between button presses and sending accuracy is positive: Poor senders are not expressive. However, persons in psychiatric groups who are poor senders may show much, even excessive, expression. Easton (1995) found, relative to comparison persons, that a subgroup of schizophrenia patients received more segmentation points, even though they were also poor senders, and Goldman (1994) observed that some behaviorally disordered children respond to pictures of themselves with complex expressions including apparent disgust, that confuse receivers. This suggests that communication accuracy is best in a moderate range of expressiveness.

Behavior Coding Systems. Coding systems such as Ekman and Friesen's (1978) Facial Action Coding System (FACS) and Izard's (1979) Maximally Discriminative Facial Movement Coding System (MAX) can also complement the SVT, and segmentation can make applying such systems highly efficient. Rather than code the entire videotaped sequence, coding may be applied only to those points identified by the segmentation technique as meaningful. Thus, a three-step process in the analysis of emotional expression and communication is suggested. First, the SVT can capture the rated experience of the sender, the nature of the sender's expressions as judged by receivers, and the sender's communication accuracy. Second, the high-information points in the stream of expression can be identified by the segmentation technique. Third, the nature of the behaviors occurring at those points can be specified through behavior coding systems (Buck, 1984, 1990).

THEORETICAL AND RESEARCH BASE

Empirical Research Findings

Individual Differences in Sending Accuracy. The SVT has been used to investigate the complex interplay of emotional responses: physiological, expressive, and experiential. One of the first findings was the substantial gender difference in sending accuracy that characterized adults but not preschool children. Adult women have been found repeatedly to be better senders than men, in that receivers are better able to make correct judgments based on their expressions (Buck et al., 1972, 1974; Wagner, Buck, & Winterbotham, 1993; Sheehan, 2002). Preschool children, however, did not show a significant gender difference in sending accuracy: Although there were substantial individual differences in sending accuracy in children, they did not relate to gender (Buck, 1975, 1977). This finding suggested that adult differences in sending accuracy are based on gender-role-related learning that boys should inhibit emotional expression.

Notably, the children's sending accuracy in the laboratory was significantly related to their teachers' ratings of their behavior in the preschool. Good senders tended to be rated as active, aggressive, friendly, and expressive extraverts, whereas poor senders were seen to be cooperative, responsible, solitary, and shy introverts. The significant relationships with teachers' ratings constituted some of the early evidence of the external validity of the SVT measure of emotional communication.

Another, initially unexpected, early finding supporting external validity was the discovery of externalizing and internalizing response patterns: Good senders had smaller physiological responses to the slides (skin conductance deflections and heart rate accelerations; Buck, 1979). Sheehan (2002) found similar effects recently using blood pressure responses. These results suggest that spontaneous sending accuracy is related to a continuum of emotional inhibition/disinhibition with important implications for physical health (Buck, 1993; Gross & Levenson, 1993). They also relate to the phenomenon of alexithymia—no words for mood—that has been implicated in psychosomatic illness (Nemiah & Sifneos, 1970), and the results suggest that emotional communication is essential developmentally for emotional education and the attainment of emotional competence (Buck, 1983, 1999).

Effects of the Social Environment on Communication.   The SVT was used to address Fridlund's (1991) contention that facial expressions are not emotional displays but rather reflect strategic interaction goals on the part of the sender. This argument implied that facial expressions would not occur when alone, but rather would require an interaction partner. The SVT as applied to healthy persons, of course, involves solitary expression, suggesting that the presence of other is not, in fact, necessary. Moreover, Buck, Losow, Murphy, and Costanzo (1991) demonstrated that the presence of strangers actually had inhibitory effects on expressions to the slides. The presence of a friend, in contrast, had facilitative effects on expressive responses to some slides (i.e., sexual slides) but inhibitory effects on others (i.e., unpleasant slides). This and other evidence has demonstrated that both emotional and learned, strategic factors are important in the control of facial expression (Jakobs, Manstead, & Fischer, 1999).

Dyadic Effects in Communication.   The SVT has also been used to study emotional communication in marital dyads using a round-robin design and allowing the use of the Warner, Kenny, and Stoto (1979) Social Relations Model. Sabatelli, Buck, and Kenny (1986) analyzed the ability of wife and husband to communicate with one another relative to their ability to communicate to other men and women, allowing the investigation of unique dyad-level effects. They found that communication from husband to wife was composed of 22% individual sending accuracy of the husband, 10% individual receiving ability of the wife, and 68% unique dyadic communication with individual sending and receiving accuracies controlled (plus error). The latter figure reflected the wife's unique ability to "read" the husband's expressive behaviors. Similarly, communication from wife to husband was composed of 48% individual sending accuracy of the wife, 1% individual receiving ability of the husband, and 51% unique dyadic communication with individual sending and receiving accuracies controlled, reflecting the husband's unique ability to "read" the wife's expressive behaviors. In all cases, the wife's abilities contributed more to the communication process than those of the husband, and they were, in addition, positively related to marital satisfaction.

Face Verses Slide in Emotion Judgment.   Additionally, the SVT was used to address a long-term controversy in the literature regarding whether facial expression or situational factors contribute more variance in the judgment of emotion. Ekman, Friesen, and Ellsworth (1972) argued that the many studies conducted to deal with this issue were flawed in that they failed to equate the information value, or source clarity, of the facial versus situational cues employed. Nakamura, Buck, and Kenny (1990) used correlation and distance measures to match the source clarity of facial expressions versus the situations (i.e., the slides) that evoked them. The face consistently contributed more than the slides to the judgment of all emotions tested. Effect sizes ranged from .61 to .87.

Psychiatric Symptoms and Communication.   The SVT has been used to assess emotional experience, expression, and communication in behaviorally disordered children and schizophrenia patients (Buck & Duffy, 1980; see also, Buck, Goldman, Easton, & Norelli Smith, 1998; Buck & VanLear, 2002). Patients' rated subjective experience to the slides, and receivers' ratings of patients' displays, were both marginally less appropriate: more positive on negative slides and more negative on positive slides relative to comparison groups. The difference in communication, however, was much stronger than these other differences. Specifically, the average effect size of the difference between schizophrenia and comparison sample males in rated emotional experience was .16, the average effect size of the difference in rated expressive display was .19, and the average effect size of the difference in communication was .34 (Buck, Cartwright-Mills, Sheehan, Ray, & Ross, 2003).

EXAMPLE STUDY

Exact procedure and instructions for the SVT vary somewhat from study to study depending on the senders involved. The following paragraphs detail procedures used in a recent study with schizophrenia patients (Buck et al., 2003). In this study, emotional experience, expression, and spontaneous facial/gestural communication accuracy were assessed in 50 schizophrenia patients and a standardization sample of 68 comparison senders, who were healthy university undergraduates (Sheehan, 2002). Sending accuracy scores were based on the judgments of a total of 288 receivers who were healthy undergraduate students. In the initial contact, patients were informed that a study of emotional communication in hospital patients was being conducted and were asked if they would like to learn more about the details of the study. If they initially consented to have the study explained, the consent form was read to them, and all tests were explained in advance. The consent form revealed they would be video taped at some point during the experiment but gave no specific details. After signing the consent form, interviews and chart reviews were used to determine basic information.

Each participant's photograph was taken using a 35-mm SLR camera with Polaroid instant color slide film. The picture was taken with an automatic flash at a 10-foot distance against a plain background. The film was developed within 5 minutes, and the participant's picture was mounted as a 2" × 2" slide and placed in the slide projector along with other emotionally loaded slides to be shown. The participant was seated beside the experimenter 4 feet in front of a backlighted slide projection screen mounted on a 9" × 11" × 2 3/4" plastic box, in which was concealed a 3/4-inch diameter SVHS color video camera. Also in the box was a solid-state timing device that, upon pressing a button, presented a slide, turned on a light to cue the patient to describe his or her feelings 10 seconds after the slide appeared, and turned off the light and forwarded the slide to a blank after 20 seconds. Thus, each slide was seen for 20 seconds including an initial 10-second "slide period" and a 10-second "talk period." The participant then rated his or her feelings on a rating form attached to a clipboard (See Fig. 3). Happiness, sadness, fear, anger, surprise, and disgust were rated on a scale of 1 = not at all to 7 = very, on a scale illustrated by a neutral face on the left and a drawn face expressing the appropriate emotion on the right. Then participants gave an overall rating of how unpleasant to pleasant they found the slide, where 1 = very unpleasant to 7 = very pleasant: These were illustrated by faces showing a negative emotion blend on the left and a positive blend on the right.

Participants were told the following when they entered the testing room:

> Today, we are going to watch emotionally loaded slides. The slides are designed to make you feel different emotions. You might feel happy, or sad, or angry, or afraid, or surprised, or disgusted, or several of these emotions. There is no right or wrong way to feel about these slides. Everybody feels differently about them based on their individual personality, temperament, and past life experience. All you have to do is watch each slide, and when the light comes on, start talking about how the slide makes you feel. Please keep watching the slide while you talk. After about 20 seconds, the screen will go blank. At that time, I want you to rate your feelings.

Participants viewed eight slides in four categories. Included were two Familiar People slides (the participant him or herself, and the experimenter), two Scenic slides (B2 and B3), two Unpleasant slides (D10 and D11), and two Unusual slides (E1 and E2). Slides were presented in one of two orders, A or B, chosen by randomly selected Latin Squares with the restriction that each order would begin with either a Scenic or an Unusual slide. Orders A and B were alternated so consecutive participants did not view slides in the same order. Order A was E2; participant; B3; D10; B2; D12; experimenter; E1. Order B was B3; participant; D10; E2; D12; B2; E1; experimenter. Participants viewed slides on a Kodak Carousel Ektagraphic 570AF self-contained slide projector and backlit projection screen. Other equipment used

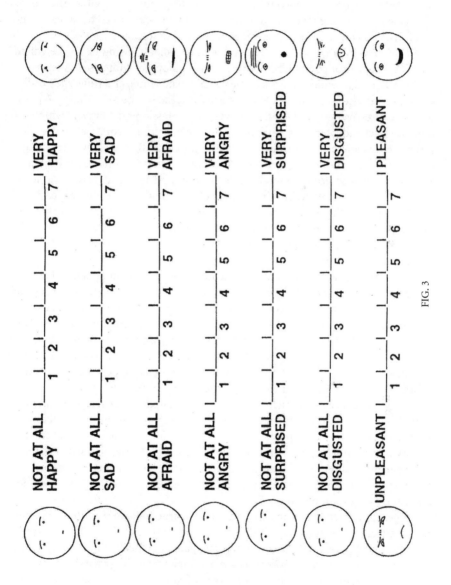

	1	2	3	4	5	6	7	
NOT AT ALL HAPPY								VERY HAPPY
NOT AT ALL SAD								VERY SAD
NOT AT ALL AFRAID								VERY AFRAID
NOT AT ALL ANGRY								VERY ANGRY
NOT AT ALL SURPRISED								VERY SURPRISED
NOT AT ALL DISGUSTED								VERY DISGUSTED
UNPLEASANT								PLEASANT

FIG. 3

465

included a Panasonic AG1960 Proline SVHS videocassette recorder on which participants' expressions and descriptions of their feelings while viewing slides were recorded and a 3/4" Panasonic KS102 SVHS camera and solid-state timing device concealed in the box described previously. After the study, all details of the videotaping procedure were revealed fully, and participants were asked to sign a reconsent form allowing the use of the videotapes in rating sessions.

All original SVHS videotapes taken during the slide-viewing task were edited onto VHS copies for compatibility with the video playback units used in receiving sessions. For each sender, the videotape number, start time, end time, slide order, and slide type were recorded. The editor also rated each expression along a 7-point scale of expressiveness, and characterized each expression qualitatively with brief remarks. Each videotape sequence began approximately 1 second before the slide was presented and ended just after the slide was removed. Each sequence was approximately 22 seconds long, and an 8–10-second period separated each sequence. The eight sequences for each sender lasts 4–5 minutes. The senders were gathered into nine edited videotapes for the purpose of presentation to groups of receivers. The first eight of these "sender videotapes" included nine senders, each showing three repetitions of two participants and a comparison person. Each of these was 35–45 minutes in length. The ninth sender videotape presented five senders and was 25 minutes in length.

Emotion rating and communication scores were based on judgments of undergraduate receivers. The videotaped expressions of senders were rated by groups of judges, and the ratings of all receivers viewing a given sender were averaged to provide stable estimates of judgments. At least 12 receivers viewed a given sender: This number has been found to be more than adequate to provide stable judgments based on reliabilities and effect sizes found in previous research. Receiving sessions were held in an Audience Response Laboratory that was equipped and furnished to afford comfortable television viewing by groups of judges. Nine group judgment sessions were run, each of which included 11 to 15 judges. On arrival, the study was explained briefly, although judges were not told that patient groups were involved. To introduce judges to the procedures of the slide-viewing task in an efficient and consistent way, videotaped instructions were presented. These included pictures of the experiment and examples of the slides viewed by participants, and gave a full and accurate explanation of all procedures. See the appendix for the directions given at this point in the study.

Judges were given sheets on which the same instructions were written verbatim, and questions were encouraged. Each receiving session took 50–60 minutes to complete. Judges assessed the emotion participants were feeling in reaction to the slides by completing a rating form for each participant watching each slide. For each videotape sequence, judges circled what type of slide (familiar person, scenic, unpleasant, or unusual) the participant was viewing. Judges also rated how happy, sad, afraid, angry, surprised, and disgusted the participant felt while watching each slide on a scale of 1 = "not at all" to 7 = "very." Judges also rated how unpleasant or pleasant the participant felt while viewing each slide, where 1 = "very unpleasant" to 7 = "very pleasant." Each emotion-rating scale was illustrated by the facial expression identical to that given to participants for their original ratings, shown in Fig. 3.

ELICITING SPONTANEOUS REACTIONS FROM SENDERS: TRAINING OF EXPERIMENTERS

The slide viewing technique requires that the sender be encouraged to respond to the slides spontaneously. It is too easy for senders to mask their natural expressions to slides if they become self-conscious about being observed or if other affects (i.e., anxiety, boredom) overwhelm the effects of the slides. With adults, standard instructions presented via tape recording are sufficient to generate spontaneous involvement in the slide-viewing task. This is not attempted with children or patient groups, as it was felt that the impersonality, the strangeness, and the lack of structure of such an experimental situation would overwhelm the intended effects of the slides. Instead, these senders viewed the slides in the company of an experimenter.

The experimenter aims to put the sender at ease and encourages him or her to respond spontaneously to the slides without in any way interfering with the sender's spontaneous reactions. Thus, the experimenter is encouraged to passively allow the sender to respond spontaneously, to expect and respect individual differences, and to avoid pressing for a response from an unresponsive sender. To accomplish this, the experimenter sits beside the sender, facing the slides, initiates interaction with the sender in a strictly controlled way, but responds naturally to any interaction initiated by the sender. When the slide comes on in the SVT and the sender initiates interaction (i.e., exclaims, "That's me!"), the experimenter responds briefly in any way that seems appropriate. If the sender does not respond within 10 seconds after the slide appears, the experimenter asks, "What's that," if the slide is of an object or "Who's that," if the slide is of a person. The experimenter then remains silent until the sender responds or the slide is removed. To encourage the sender to attend to the slides, the experimenter looks only at the slide when it is on.

FUTURE DIRECTIONS

New Technologies

The SVT began with black-and-white television and reel-to-reel videotape recorders, and matured with miniature SHVS color cameras and solid state timing devices that were easily portable and allowed one person to run the experiment. New digital video and computer technology will greatly enhance both the sending and receiving aspects of the SVT. The sending aspect can potentially take place without an experimenter's presence, with slides presented on a high-quality computer screen and all timing and recording of video, audio, and self-report responses accomplished by the computer. Digital recordings with small and unobtrusive but nevertheless high quality cameras will make possible much improved picture quality that will not be degraded by repeated copying. Similarly, receiving sessions can be run individually, with senders presented via a website that records and automatically tabulates reviewers' responses.

Functional Magnetic Resonance Imaging

The SVT has been used to study the physiological responding of both senders and receivers, and a natural development of such studies is to investigate directly via functional magnetic resonance imaging (fMRI) the brain processing associated with spontaneous sending and receiving. Slides have been employed as stimuli in fMRI studies of emotion (i.e., Canli, Desmond, Zhao, Glover, & Gabrielli, 1998), but thus far the focus has been on identifying brain areas that show similarities in responding to emotional stimuli across persons. Individual differences in fMRI emotion responding remain to be explored, and to date facial expressions have not been recorded. The design of the SVT—repeated exposure of pictures of comparable emotional content—lends itself to fMRI methodology. On the receiving end, a number of studies have investigated fMRI responses to photographs of posed facial expressions (i.e., Iidaka et al., 2001), but no study has yet appeared on responses to dynamic and spontaneous films of facial expressions such as those obtained by the SVT.

REFERENCES

Buck, R. (1975). Nonverbal communication of affect in children. *Journal of Personality and Social Psychology, 31*, 644–653.
Buck, R. (1976). A test of nonverbal receiving ability: Preliminary studies. *Human Communication Research, 2*, 162–171.
Buck, R. (1977). Nonverbal communication accuracy in preschool children: Relationships with personality and skin conductance. *Journal of Personality and Social Psychology, 33*, 225–236.
Buck, R. (1979). Individual differences in nonverbal sending accuracy and electrodermal responding. In R. Rosenthal (Ed.), *Skill in nonverbal communication: Individual differences* (pp. 140–170). Cambridge, MA: Oelgeschlager, Gunn, & Hain.
Buck, R. (1983). Emotional development and emotional education. In R. Plutchik & H. Kellerman (Eds.), *Emotion in early development* (pp. 259–292). New York: Academic Press.
Buck, R. (1984). *The communication of emotion.* New York: Guilford.
Buck, R. (1990). Using FACS versus communication scores to measure spontaneous facial expression of emotion in brain-damaged patients: A reply to Mammucari et al. (1988). *Cortex, 26*, 275–280.
Buck, R. (1993). Emotional communication, emotional competence, and physical illness: A developmental-interactionist view. In H. Traue & J. W. Pennebaker (Eds.), *Emotional expressiveness, inhibition, and health* (pp. 32–56). Seattle, WA: Hogrefe & Huber.
Buck, R. (1999). The biological affects: A typology. *Psychological Review, 106*, 301–336.
Buck, R., Baron, R., & Barrette, D. (1982). The temporal organization of spontaneous emotional expression: A segmentation analysis. *Journal of Personality and Social Psychology, 42*, 506–517.
Buck, R., Baron, R., Goodman, N., & Shapiro, B. (1980). The unitization of spontaneous nonverbal behavior in the study of emotional communication. *Journal of Personality and Social Psychology, 39*, 522–529.
Buck, R., & Duffy, R. J. (1980). Nonverbal communication of affect in brain-damaged patients. *Cortex, 16*, 351–362.

Buck, R., Cartwright-Mills, J., Sheehan, M., Ray, I., & Ross, E. D. (2003, May). *Expressed emotion and the double-bind: Experience, expression, and communication of specific emotions in schizophrenia and comparison samples.* Paper presented at the meeting of the International Communication Association, San Diego, CA.

Buck, R., Goldman, C. K., Easton, C. J., & Norelli Smith, N. (1998). Social learning and emotional education: Emotional expression and communication in behaviorally disordered children and schizophrenic patients. In W. F. Flack & J. D. Laird (Eds.), *Emotions in psychopathology* (pp. 298–314). New York: Oxford University Press.

Buck, R., Losow, J., Murphy, M., & Costanzo, P. (1991). Social facilitation and inhibition of emotional expression and communication. *Journal of Personality and Social Psychology, 63*, 962–968.

Buck, R., Miller, R. E., & Caul, W. F. (1974). Sex, personality, and physiological variables in the communication of emotion via facial expression. *Journal of Personality and Social Psychology, 30*, 587–596.

Buck, R., Savin, V. J., Miller, R. E., & Caul, W. F. (1972). Nonverbal communication of affect in humans. *Journal of Personality and Social Psychology, 23*, 362–371.

Buck, R., & VanLear, C. A. (2002). Verbal and nonverbal communication: Distinguishing symbolic, spontaneous, and pseudo-spontaneous nonverbal behavior. *Journal of Communication, 52*, 522–541.

Canli, T., Desmond, J. E., Zhao, Z., Glover, G., & Gabrieli, J. D. E (1998). Hemispheric asymmetry for emotional stimuli detected with fMRI. *Neuroreport, 9*, 3233–3239.

Easton, C. (1995). Expression and communication of emotion in schizophrenic patients. (Doctoral dissertation, University of Connecticut, Storrs, 1994). *Dissertation Abstracts International, 55/09*, p. 147.

Ekman, P., & Friesen, W. V. (1978). *Facial Action Coding System (FACS): A technique for the measurement of facial action.* Palo Alto, CA: Consulting Psychologists Press.

Ekman, P., Friesen, W. V., & Ellsworth, P. (1972). *Emotion in the human face.* New York: Pergamon.

Fridlund, A. (1991). Sociality of solitary smiling: Potentiation by an implicit audience. *Journal of Personality and Social Psychology, 60*, 229–240.

Goldman, C. K. (1994). The relationship of emotional communication to social competence: The role of communication accuracy in behaviorally disordered children's social functioning. (Doctoral dissertation, University of Connecticut, Storrs, 1993). *Dissertation Abstracts International-B 55/02*, 611.

Gross, J., & Levenson, R. W. (1993). Emotional suppression: Physiology, self report, and expressive behavior. *Journal of Personality and Social Psychology, 64*, 970–986.

Iidaka, T., Omori, M., Murata, T., Kosaka, H., Yonekura, Y., et al. (2001). Neural interaction of the amygdala with the prefrontal and temporal cortices in the processing of facial expressions as revealed by fMRI. *Journal of Cognitive Neuroscience, 13*, 1035–1047.

Izard, C. E. (1979). *The Maximally Discriminative Facial Movement Coding System (MAX).* Newark: Instructional Resources Center, University of Delaware.

Jakobs, E., Manstead, A. S. R., & Fischer, A. H. (1999). Social motives, emotional feelings, and smiling. *Cognition & Emotion, 13*, 321–345.

Miller, R. E., Banks, J., & Ogawa, N. (1962). Communication of affect in "cooperative conditioning" of rhesus monkeys. *Journal of Abnormal and Social Psychology, 64*, 343–348.

Miller, R. E., Caul, W. F., & Mirsky, I. A. (1967). Communication of affect between feral and socially isolated monkeys. *Journal of Personality and Social Psychology, 7*, 231–239.

Nakamura, M., Buck, R., & Kenny, D. A. (1990). Relative contributions of expressive behavior and contextual information to the judgment of the emotional state of another. *Journal of Personality and Social Psychology, 59*, 1032–1039.

Nemiah, J. C., & Sifneos, P. E. (1970). Psychosomatic illness: Problem in communication. *Psychotherapy and Psychosomatics, 18*, 154–160.

Newtson, D., Engquist, G., & Bois, J. (1977). The objective basis of behavior units. *Journal of Personality and Social Psychology, 35*, 847–862.

Sabatelli, R., Buck, R., & Kenny, D. (1986). Nonverbal communication in married couples: A social relations analysis. *Journal of Personality, 54*, 513–527.

Sheehan, M. (2002). Heart and soul: Thinking modes and nonverbal sending and receiving ability. (Doctoral dissertation, University of Connecticut, Storrs, 2001). *Dissertation Abstracts International, 62*(8-A), 2620.

Wagner, H., Buck, R., & Winterbotham, M. (1993). Communication of specific emotions: Sending accuracy and communication measures. *Journal of Nonverbal Behavior, 17*, 29–53.

Warner, R. M., Kenny, D. A., & Stoto, M. (1979). A new round robin analysis of variance for social interaction data. *Journal of Personality and Social Psychology, 37*, 1742–1757.

APPENDIX

Directions Given to Participants in Buck et al. (2003)

The film you are about to see is a test of your ability to tell how people are feeling. It shows people as they watch a series of emotionally loaded color slides. There are four kinds of slides, including the following examples. Some were familiar people, showing the person him/herself or the experimenter. Some were scenic, showing pleasant landscapes. Other slides were unpleasant, showing starving and wounded children. Other slides were unusual, showing strange photographic effects. We want you to watch the person's facial expressions very carefully. On each trial, guess what kind of slide the person viewed: Familiar, Scenic, Unpleasant, or Unusual. Also, guess how the person felt about the slide: whether they felt happy, sad, afraid, angry, surprised, disgusted, and pleasant or unpleasant. Again, watch the person's facial expressions carefully: Don't take your eyes from the face, for many of the important facial expression occur unexpectedly. Then use your answer sheet to rate what kind of slide was presented, and how the person felt about it. Make your ratings quickly and watch for the next sequence.

Conflict, Real Life, and Videotape: Procedures for Eliciting Naturalistic Couple Interactions

Linda J. Roberts
University of Wisconsin-Madison

INTRODUCTION

As Yogi Berra knew, we can observe a lot just by watching. Systematic observation methods (Bakeman, 2000, this volume; LeBaron, this volume; Sillars, 1991; Weick, 1968) have played a significant role in advancing our understanding of interpersonal processes in marital and other close relationships, particularly because they are able to capture nonverbal and emotional cues. Using observational methods, important interpersonal processes—from conflict and aggression to friendship formation and attachment—can be studied as naturally occurring behavioral transactions that unfold over time.

Unfortunately, scientists have sometimes dismissed the use of observational methods as "just watching." In their classic observational methods chapter, for example, Heyns and Lippitt (1954) recommended that these methods be used only when "other measurement devices are unavailable or inappropriate" (p. 371). Reviewing research in child development, the area of psychology with the strongest observational tradition, Wright (1960) reported that only 8% of empirical studies conducted between 1890 and 1958 utilized observational methods. Observational studies were often disregarded as "dust-bowl" efforts intended to describe rather than explain behavior and therefore not appropriately scientific. Nobel laureate Peter Medawar described the historical reluctance of scientists to embrace observational methodology this way:

> [I]t did not seem ... that there *was* any way of studying behavior "scientifically" except through some kind of experimental intervention—except by confronting the subject of our observations with a "situation" or with a nicely contrived stim-

471

ulus and then recording what the animal did. The situation would then be varied
in some way that seemed appropriate, whereupon the animal's behavior would
also vary. Even poking an animal would surely be better than just looking at it:
that would lead to anecdotalism: that was what the bird watchers did. (quoted in
Chapple, 1970, p. 4)

Although Darwin's (1872/1965) study of the *Expression of the Emotions in Man and
Animals* pioneered the application of observation methods to social (particularly
nonverbal) behavior, it was more than 50 years after its publication before serious
efforts were made to establish observational methods as a reliable approach to the
study of behavior.

The contemporary situation is markedly different. Gottman and Notarius
(2000, p. 927) suggest that observational research is in fact "the main roadway available" for the precise study of interpersonal processes. Observational methods can
contribute to the important task of description, but they are also important for the
development of theory and the specification of precise mechanisms to explain relational phenomena. As Gottman and Notarius argue, the advantage of observational
methods stems in large part from the "power of observational data to reveal a
replicable portrait of complex social interaction that lies beyond the natural awareness of even the most keenly sensitive spouse or partner, and thus lies beyond assessment with self-report instruments" (p. 927). Indeed, observational methods are
uniquely able to take the researcher "beyond words."

To apply observational methods in the study of intimate relationships, an important methodological problem must be addressed. Whereas ethologists are able
to observe aggression, conflict, mating rituals, and other behavioral interactions
in the animal kingdom with relative ease, the interpersonal processes that
uniquely characterize the most intimate human relationships are rarely public.
Yogi Berra's wisdom notwithstanding, "just watching" is not an adequate description of the methodological procedures needed. Instead, the researcher needs
to address how to become privy to processes that usually occur in the privacy of a
couple's home environment, actions that often, if not usually, occur only when no
one else is present.

This chapter provides a discussion of methods for eliciting ordinarily private
dyadic interactions in contexts that are amenable to videotaped observation. Behavioral processes, particularly those involving intimate nonverbal and verbal
processes, cannot be investigated adequately with direct observation methods unless behaviors are elicited in a context that represents an analog to naturally occurring interactions between partners (Weick, 1985). The procedures described here
are designed to optimize, to the greatest degree possible, the naturalness and ecological validity of elicited interactions between intimates. The purpose of these
elicitation procedures is neither to "poke" or provoke, but rather to provide a gen-
tle nudge that creates the opportunity for the researcher to "just watch" (and then
analyze) the natural unfolding of intimate behavioral transactions.

THE CONTEXT OF OBSERVATION: INTERACTION TASK AND SETTING

Given that private interactions among intimates are, by definition, difficult for outsiders to observe, researchers have created opportunities for systematic observation by asking couples or families to engage in a specific interaction task under conditions conducive to observation. Early attempts to apply observation methods to marital and family interaction used highly structured tasks including games, role-playing, and other contrived or improvised tasks (e.g., Straus & Tallman, 1971; Strodtbeck, 1951). However, pioneering work by Gottman (1979) led to the development and widespread adoption of a relatively unstructured *conflict interaction paradigm*.

In this now standard couples interaction task, the researcher helps the couple find an important area of disagreement and asks the couple to discuss and attempt to resolve the issue. The task is structured for the participants, but the topic of discussion is a real-life issue for the couple. Given that the couple has identified the area of disagreement as important, it is assumed that in their everyday life, the couple faces the conversational task the researcher puts before them: to try to resolve their difference on this issue. The conflict task has been highly successful in eliciting naturalistic interactions between partners that include displays of strong negative and contemptuous emotions when partners are maritally distressed. After two decades of observational work with this paradigm, the topography of conflict in marriage is relatively well articulated (for a thorough review of research findings to date using this paradigm, see Heyman, 2001).[23]

Researchers typically have chosen to elicit naturalistic couple interactions in the laboratory where high quality videorecording is possible. The decisions to collect data in couples' homes versus in a laboratory and whether to use live observers or mechanical recording devices necessitate trade-offs among research ideals (see White & Sargent, this volume). Recording interactions is generally desirable when complex coding is to be undertaken or when the researcher wants to examine patterning in the interaction (see Cappella, this volume; Markman & Notarius, 1987).

Review and re-review of videotapes allows for "magnification" of the behavioral phenomena of interest, much like a microscope allows for the magnification of phenomena in the natural world. A laboratory setting designed specifically for high quality recording allows the researcher to maximize tape quality (e.g., record split-screen, full face images) and minimize camera obtrusiveness. Furthermore, the laboratory setting gives the researcher significant control of extraneous environmental variables that may limit the interpretability of data collected in natural settings (e.g., interruptions, phone calls, noises from surrounding areas, etc.).

The external or ecological validity of laboratory interaction tasks is an important and largely unresolved issue (see Jacob, Tennenbaum, & Krahn, 1987). Relatively

---

[23]A noteworthy limitation of the conflict paradigm is that its structure does not allow for an adequate assessment of avoidance and withdrawal issues related to conflict (Roberts, 2000).

few studies have systematically investigated setting and task conditions and their influence on validity. It is clear that elicitation of the tasks by the investigator creates an artificial situation for the couple and that knowledge of the observer creates some degree of reactivity. What is unclear is the degree to which these factors influence the behavioral processes of interest to the investigator.

In early studies of elicited conflict interactions, Gottman (1979) and Gottman and Krokoff (1989) reported little difference between conversations videotaped in the laboratory and conversations audiotaped in the couple's home. Furthermore, couples participating in naturalistic interaction tasks in the lab report that the conversations are comfortable and generally typical of their naturally occurring interactions (Bradbury, 1994; Foster, Caplan, & Howe, 1997; Roberts & Greenberg, 2002). Although not identical to their daily, "on the go" conversations, couples report that their experience in the elicited interaction mirrors conversations they have "when they sit down to talk." Working within the constraints of the laboratory context and a structured interaction task, the investigator can take specific steps to minimize reactivity and artificiality.

GENERAL PROCEDURES FOR ELICITING MAXIMALLY NATURAL INTERACTIONS

Taking care to create a comfortable setting for eliciting interactions is important, but often overlooked. Ideally, the interaction facility should be decorated to resemble a home environment. For example, a couch and chair can be placed in one area of the room and a table for conversing placed in an adjacent area. Any obvious reminders of the institutional, research context (e.g., fluorescent lights, blackboards, file cabinets) should be removed. Similarly, cues that increase the salience of the videorecording process should be eliminated. Remote controlled cameras can be housed unobtrusively in bookshelf units behind smoked glass to minimize participants' awareness of their presence. Microphones can be placed in the ceiling or hidden at the table in a silk plant. The goal is not to deceive the partners—participants should be made aware of the placement of cameras and microphones—but to create a physical environment that does not distract the partners' attention from the conversational task.

There are three task characteristics that are particularly important for increasing the likelihood of natural, nonreactive behavior on the part of the participants: (a) the task that is imposed on the participants should be a natural and familiar one; (b) the structure that is imposed on the interaction and the expectations for behavioral performance communicated by the researcher should create a "demand" for natural behavior; and (c) the task itself should be engaging and emotionally salient for the partners.

The success of the conflict paradigm may be attributed to the optimization of each of these task characteristics. First, the conversational topic—a current unresolved disagreement—is not novel to the couple but is instead familiar ground.

Nearly all couples know how to engage in a discussion of their differences and, in the lab setting, can rely on their habitual response patterns to perform the task. Second, in eliciting the conflict interaction, the researcher counters expectations that certain behaviors or processes are expected or demanded by the situation and instead makes it clear that the goal of this type of research is to understand "everyday talk." Third, the researcher selects the highest rated disagreement from a list provided by the couple. This maximizes the likelihood that the conversation will have strong emotional salience for partners, rendering the artificial laboratory surroundings less salient. Partners are easily primed for the task and engage readily. Once a current, real, unresolved topic is identified, partners are generally clear about what needs to be discussed, and there is ample content to keep them talking.

A RESEARCH PROTOCOL FOR ELICITING CONFLICT INTERACTIONS

The Assessment of Current Disagreements (ACD; see also Leonard & Roberts, 1998) research protocol provides instructions for the elicitation of couple conflict interactions that optimize these three task characteristics. In some previous applications of the conflict paradigm, investigators have asked couples to discuss marital problems or a general area of disagreement. Allowing a couple to choose to focus on an area of disagreement rather than on a *specific* disagreement, however, may compromise the investigator's goal of recording a discussion that is representative of naturally occurring conflict processes for the couple. Similarly, eliciting relationship "problems" from couples may result in discussions of current stresses or difficulties in the marriage about which there is no actual disagreement or conflict. This presents both ethical and representational concerns. Without specific instructions to the contrary, couples may talk generally about household responsibilities instead of focusing on a disagreement about who should do what around the house, or they may discuss a series of financial problems instead of a current real disagreement about what whether they can afford a new car. Couples may also suggest disagreements that have already been resolved or are no longer of concern to one or both partners.

The procedures in this protocol are designed to help the investigator systematically elicit specific, current, and unresolved disagreements between partners, thus optimizing the extent to which lab-based conflict interactions are an analog to naturally occurring interactions. The ACD involves five steps, as described next.

Step 1: Disagreement Listing Procedure

The interviewer's first task is to help the couple generate a list of specific and current disagreements in their relationship. After providing each partner with a response sheet for writing down (and later for rating) the topics that are generated, the interviewer can introduce the task as follows:

Suggested Script: "We're interested in learning more about the kinds of things that couples disagree about in their daily lives. We know that all couples have things that they disagree about from time to time, so right now we want to find out about the things that are currently a source of disagreement between the two of you. What we'll be doing here is making a list of the disagreements you tell me about on this form, and then we'll go back over them and I'll ask you to make some ratings on each one. For example, I'll ask you how long each one has been a disagreement.

The disagreements we list here may be relatively mild and minor, or big, major disagreements, but they must be current and unresolved. The important thing is · that we find disagreements that really are something the two of you don't see eye to eye on, not just things that are problems for you in your relationship. In other words, we aren't interested in general problems you may be experiencing but only in those problems that are causing disagreements between the two of you. For example, not having enough money may be a source of stress and strain for a couple, but it may not involve any disagreement—both partners may be in complete agreement that it is a problem and agree on how it should be handled. However, money problems can also be a source of disagreement between partners. For example, one partner may feel the other is spending too much, one partner may feel they can afford a vacation and the other may not, and so on. Specific disagreements like those are what we want you to list here."

When a partner suggests a topic of disagreement, it is important that the interviewer determine that the topic is, in fact, a disagreement and not simply a problem in the relationship. A disagreement should have two sides or perspectives. Even complaints about one's partner or demands to change (he needs to pick up after himself, she should have a healthy lifestyle, etc.) should not be considered current disagreements if the "accused" partner is in complete agreement that he or she should change. The interviewer should try to delve a little deeper into these issues, however, because it may be that the partners do, in fact, disagree, perhaps about the way in which the change should occur, or when it should occur.

As soon as it is clear that the couple has generated at least one current, unresolved disagreement, the interviewer should ask each partner to write it down in their own words on the rating forms. They should write down exactly what each disagreement is (e.g., "Amy [wife] spends too much money on clothes" rather than "finances" or "money"). If one partner seems to be generating all or most of the topics, the interviewer should focus explicitly on the other partner for a time. Before ending the listing procedure, each partner should be shown the list of areas that often trigger disagreements reproduced in Table 44. The list provides a standard stimulus for couples and is used to make sure that easily forgotten areas of disagreement are not overlooked.

Suggested Script: "It's sometimes difficult to remember certain disagreements when you aren't in the situation, so we've made a list of areas that commonly trigger disagreements between partners that we'd like you each to look at. Let me

TABLE 44
ACD Handout
AREAS THAT OFTEN TRIGGER DISAGREEMENTS

Handling family finances/money	Job or work-related activities
Religion	Demonstrations of affection
Sex	Jealousy
Amount of time spent together	Communication
How to spend time together	Making decisions
Children	Leisure time activities and interests
Parents or in-laws	Values
Relatives	Friends
Household tasks	Correct or proper behavior
Alcohol or other drugs	Daily activities
Personal habits	Living situation/housing

know if, in reading this list, you are reminded of any other important disagreements in your relationship that we should add to your list."

In general, the interviewer should bring out the list when the couple seems to be having difficulty generating more areas of disagreement on their own. For couples that are generating topics readily, the interviewer can stop after the sixth or seventh disagreement and ask, "Would we be missing any other important disagreements if we stopped here?" The interviewer should also offer the list to these couples to see if it triggers recollection of an important disagreement that was missed. Again, the interviewer should make sure any generated topic is an actual disagreement and have the couple write it down, taking care that the partners briefly describe the nature of the disagreement.

Step 2: Ratings of Disagreements

When the partners have completed the listing procedure, the interviewer should ask them a number of specific questions that require them to put a rating next to each topic they have generated. Each partner should work independently.

Suggested Script: "Now we'd like to get some idea of how much disagreement there is between you and your partner on each of these issues. Please indicate how much you and your partner disagree about each issue by placing a number from 1 to 100 in the first column on your rating form. A zero indicates that you do not disagree at all, and a 100 indicates that you disagree very much. In the second column, please write down the number of days, weeks, months, or years that this has been an area of disagreement."

The researcher may request additional ratings from the partners, consistent with his or her research goals.

Step 3: Selection of Topic for Conflict Interaction

After the partners have completed their ratings, the interviewer should eliminate topics that the partners would be unwilling to discuss:

> Suggested Script: "We will be using this list to choose topics for the problem-solving discussion you will have here tonight. So if there are any topics on this list that you feel strongly about not discussing here, please put a check next to the topic."

The interviewer should then select a topic for discussion by first eliminating any topics that either partner indicated an unwillingness to discuss and then choosing the topic that has the highest total when the partners' ratings are combined.

Step 4: Priming the Conflict Interaction

The interviewer should help the couple ease into a discussion of the selected disagreement. To do this, the interviewer should ask the couple questions such as the following:

> Suggested Probes: "What is the basic disagreement here? Who feels what? When was the last time you talked about X? Where were you? What prompted you to talk about it? What did each of you say about this last time? What were the key difficulties for each of you? How did you feel?"

It is important to get out each partner's side of the issue. The interviewer should ask questions only until the couple is engaged in the issue. As soon as the couple seems sufficiently primed and ready to talk, the interviewer should leave and begin the taping. This can be accomplished as follows:

> Suggested Script: "That's fine, why don't we stop here, it seems like you're ready to talk about this one. As soon as I close the door, feel free to start talking, but please remain in your seats while you do so. What I'd like you to do is talk about and try to work out your differences on this issue. Don't feel pressured to do anything in particular in the conversation, just let the conversation flow as it might if you were talking about this topic by yourselves at home. You'll have about 15 minutes, and then I'll come back."

Step 5: Alleviating Any Residual Negative Feelings

After the interaction tasks are completed, the interviewer should engage the couple in a short, semistructured "happy times" interview, focusing on the most positive and meaningful events in their relationship history (e.g., how they fell in love, the birth of their first child, a memorable vacation). The interview is conducted with the purpose of ameliorating any residual negative feelings that may have surfaced in their interaction tasks. The interviewer should conduct the interview in such a way that the couple feels a demand to focus on the positive aspects of their relationship. If the early "falling in love" period is fraught with negative events (e.g., an unwanted premarital pregnancy), the interviewer should move instead to "positive relationship events." If the couple has difficulty generating positive relationship events, they can instead be asked to plan the ideal evening together or the ideal vacation.

In addition to helping each partner remember positive moments or events in the history of the relationship, it is also desirable that this activity lead to positive interactions between the partners in the present. This is particularly important for couples that seem to have had a very conflictual disagreement during the videotaping. The overall goal of the "happy times" interview is to promote positive feelings between the partners.

> Suggested Script: "So far, we've had you focus on problems or disagreements in your relationship, but we realize that this is not a complete picture of your relationship. What we'd like to do now is spend some time talking about the positive aspects of your relationship. Although I have a series of questions, I'd like to encourage you to just talk to me and talk to each other in a free fashion. What I'd like each of you to do first is to take a moment and try to think of the happiest times you've had with each other—maybe while you were first getting to know one another, or perhaps a vacation you took together, or anything that comes to mind."

> Suggested Probes: "How did you meet? What first attracted you to one another? What was/is it that you really love, respect, admire in the other person? What makes your relationship stand out from others you see?"

In general, the interviewer should prompt the couple to continue talking about whatever it is they bring up, as long as it is positive. The length of time spent in this procedure may vary dramatically across couples, depending on the pervasiveness of their negative effect. For many couples, 10 minutes will be sufficient.

BEYOND CONFLICT INTERACTIONS

Although the conflict paradigm is still the most widely used interaction task in couples research, procedures for eliciting naturalistic conversations about topics other than disagreements are gradually being developed. Indeed, if the study of interaction is to move beyond an understanding of conflict processes to the investigation of other interaction processes in intimate relationships in which nonverbal cues are important (e.g., support, caregiving, affection), the development of similarly naturalistic interaction tasks targeting other interpersonal processes is imperative (Roberts & Greenberg, 2002). It is likely that the conflict task maximizes the likelihood of observing negative interaction processes and truncates opportunities for observing positive processes (Cutrona, 1996). Indeed, Melby, Ge, Conger, and Warner (1995) demonstrated that different conversational tasks have a direct effect on the effective elicitation and reliable assessment of positive interaction behavior.

In a significant advance for the field, researchers are beginning to develop procedures to study other naturalistic interactions between intimates, including social support interactions (e.g., Cutrona & Suhr, 1994; Pasch & Bradbury, 1998; Saitzyk, Floyd, & Kroll, 1997; see Trees, 2000, for an application of nonverbal cues to parent–child support), and intimate caregiving interactions (Roberts & Greenberg, 2002). If researchers follow the same formula for eliciting these interactions that has led to success with couple conflict interactions, our understanding of intimate processes in our closest relationships should increase dramatically.

REFERENCES

Bakeman, G. (2000). Behavioral observation and coding. In H. Reis & C. M. Judd (Eds.), *Handbook of research methods in social and personality psychology*. New York: Cambridge University Press.

Bradbury, T. N. (1994). Unintended effects of marital research on marital relationships. *Journal of Family Psychology, 8*, 187–201.

Chapple, E. D. (1970). *Culture and biology: Explorations in behavioral anthropology*. New York: Holt, Rinehart & Winston.

Cutrona, C. E. (1996). Social support as a determinant of marital quality: The interplay of negative and supportive behaviors. In G. R. Pierce, B. R. Sarason, & I. G. Sarason (Eds.), *Handbook of social support and the family* (pp. 173–194). New York, NY: Plenum.

Cutrona, C. E., & Suhr, J. A. (1994). Social support communication in the context of marriage: An analysis of couples' supportive interactions. In B. R. Burleson, T. L. Albrecht, & I. G. Sarason (Eds.), *Communication of social support* (pp. 113–135). Thousand Oaks, CA: Sage.

Darwin, C. (1965). *The expression of emotion in man and animals*. Chicago: The University of Chicago Press. (Original work published 1872)

Foster, D. A., Caplan, R. D., & Howe, G. W. (1997). Representativeness of observed couple interaction: Couples can tell and it does make a difference. *Psychological Assessment, 9*, 285–294.

Gottman, J. M. (1979). *Marital interaction: Empirical investigations*. New York: Academic Press.

Gottman, J. M., & Krokoff, L. J. (1989). Marital interaction and satisfaction: A longitudinal view. *Journal of Consulting and Clinical Psychology, 57*, 47–52.

Gottman, J. M., & Notarius, C. I. (2000). Decade review: Observing marital interaction. *Journal of Marriage and the Family, 62*, 927–948.

Heyman, R. E. (2001). Observation of couple conflicts: Clinical assessment applications, stubborn truths, and shaky foundations. *Psychological Assessment, 13*, 5–35.

Heyns, R. W., & Lippitt, R. (1954). Systematic observation techniques. In G. Lindsey & E. Aronson (Eds.), *Handbook of social psychology* (pp. 370–404). Cambridge, MA: Addison Wesley.

Jacob, T., Tennenbaum, D., & Krahn, G. (1987). Factors influencing the reliability and validity of observation data. In T. Jacob (Ed.), *Family interaction and psychopathology: Theories, methods and findings* (pp. 297–328). New York: Plenum.

Leonard, K. E., & Roberts, L. J. (1998). The effects of alcohol on the marital interactions of aggressive and nonaggressive husbands and their wives. *Journal of Abnormal Psychology, 107*, 602–615.

Markman, H. J., & Notarius, C. I. (1987). Coding marital and family interaction: Current status. In T. Jacob (Ed.), *Family interaction and psychopathology: Theories, methods and findings* (pp. 329–389). New York: Plenum.

Melby, J. N., Ge, X., Conger, R. D., & Warner, T. D. (1995). The importance of task in evaluating positive marital interactions. *Journal of Marriage and the Family, 57*, 981–994.

Pasch, L. A., & Bradbury, T. N. (1998). Social support, conflict, and the development of marital dysfunction. *Journal of Consulting and Clinical Psychology, 66,* 219–230.

Roberts, L. J. (2000). Fire and ice in marital communication: Hostile and distancing behaviors as predictors of marital distress. *Journal of Marriage and the Family, 62,* 693–707.

Roberts, L. J., & Greenberg, D. R. (2002). Observational windows to intimacy processes in marriage. In P. Noller & J. Feeney (Eds.), *Understanding marriage: Developments in the study of couple interaction* (pp. 118–149). New York: Cambridge University Press.

Saitzyk, A. R., Floyd, F. J., & Kroll, A. B. (1997). Sequential analysis of autonomy-interdependence and affiliation-disaffiliation in couples' social support interactions. *Personal Relationships, 4,* 341–360.

Sillars, A. L. (1991). Behavioral observation. In B. M. Montgomery & S. Duck (Eds.), *Studying interpersonal interaction* (pp. 197–218). New York: Guilford.

Straus, M., & Tallman, I. (1971). SIMFAM: A technique for observational measurement and experimental study of families. In J. Aldous, T. Condon, R. Hill, M. Straus, & I. Tallman (Eds.), *Family problem solving* (pp. 379–438). Himsdale, IL: Dryden.

Strodtbeck, F. L. (1951). Husband–wife interaction over revealed differences. *American Psychological Review, 16,* 468–473.

Trees, A. R. (2000). Nonverbal communication and the support process: Interactional sensitivity in interactions between mothers and young adult children. *Communication Monographs, 67,* 239–261.

Weick, K. E. (1968). Systematic observational methods. In G. Lindzey & E. Aronson (Eds.), *Handbook of social psychology, Vol 2* (2nd ed., pp. 357–451). New York: Random House.

Weick, K. E. (1985). Systematic observational methods. In G. Lindzey & E. Aronson (Eds.), *The handbook of social psychology, Vol. 2* (3rd ed., pp. 567–634). New York: Random House.

Wright, H. F. (1960). Observational child study. In P. H. Mussen (Ed.), *Handbook of research methods in child development* (pp. 71–139). New York: Wiley.

Meta-Analysis of Nonverbal Behavior

Judith A. Hall
Northeastern University

INTRODUCTION

Meta-analysis has long been used to address questions about correlates of nonverbal behavior. Topics have included gender differences in accuracy of decoding nonverbal cues (Hall, 1978, 1984; McClure, 2000), gender difference is nonverbal behavior (Hall, 1984; LaFrance, Hecht, & Paluck, 2003), nonverbal cues that mediate interpersonal expectancy effects (Harris & Rosenthal, 1985), nonverbal cues indicative of deception (Zuckerman & Driver, 1985), dominance-status differences in decoding nonverbal cues (Hall, Halberstadt, & O'Brien, 1997), cross-cultural effects in decoding nonverbal cues (Elfenbein & Ambady, 2002), facial feedback effects (Matsumoto, 1987), and facial asymmetry in the expression of emotion (Skinner & Mullen, 1991).

The goal of this chapter is not to identify or summarize all of the available meta-analyses on nonverbal behavior. Nor is it a primer on conducting a meta-analysis because many excellent guides are available at all levels of difficulty (Cooper, 1989; Cooper & Hedges, 1993; Hedges & Olkin, 1985; Lipsey & Wilson, 2001; Rosenthal, 1991). My purpose is to illustrate the application of meta-analysis to the study of nonverbal behavior, drawing on my own experience and, especially, a meta-analysis that I have conducted recently on the relation of dominance-status to nonverbal behavior (Hall, Coats, & Smith LeBeau, 2003).

BACKGROUND

My own involvement in meta-analysis began in the mid-1970s when I participated in the construction of the Profile of Nonverbal Sensitivity (PONS), a standardized audiovisual test of accuracy in understanding the meanings of affective cues conveyed by the face, body, and voice (Rosenthal, Hall, DiMatteo, Rogers, & Archer, 1979). Immediately, it was apparent that there was a gender difference on this instrument, with females scoring higher than males (in elementary school, junior high and high school, college, and older groups, and in many places in the world). This finding stimulated two important questions: (a) Is this difference unique to the PONS test, or does it generalize to other comparable instruments? (The PONS had only one expressor in it—a female—and so it was appropriate to ask whether the effect persisted when expressors were more in number and included males), and (b) If it is generalizable, what is the origin of such a difference?

The first question was answered with a meta-analysis (Hall, 1978), that was later updated (Hall, 1984; Hall, Carter, & Horgan, 2000). It turned out that, rather than being a novel result, the finding that women scored as more accurate in judging the meanings of nonverbal cues had occurred over and over in a literature that went back into the early decades of the last century. Besides demonstrating that the PONS gender differences were remarkably similar to those found with other instruments, the meta-analysis was also able to examine some important potential moderator variables including the gender of the expressors. Across studies, the magnitude of the decoding gender difference was about the same whether males or females were being judged, and this finding was corroborated by studies that provided within-study analyses of the same question (see Hall, 1978 for a list of these studies).

The second question—what is the origin of the gender differences—is not as easy to answer, and indeed it remains unanswered to this day. A short but influential book, *Body politics: Power, sex, and nonverbal communication* (Henley, 1977), provided one theoretical framework, namely that gender differences in nonverbal behavior spring from differences between men and women in dominance and status. Like many seminal theoretical positions, Henley's took the form of a sweeping integration with relatively little empirical support. Indeed, at the time it was written, the available research was limited, and so it remained for other investigators to "fill in the blanks" by providing evidence for two of Henley's crucial claims. One concerned the nature of nonverbal gender differences. The decoding skill meta-analysis already alluded to by Hall (1978), and a monograph that dealt meta-analytically with gender differences for an array of nonverbal behaviors including expression skill, smiling, gazing, vocal behaviors, and body movements (Hall, 1984), helped to document that reliable gender differences do exist.

Henley's (1977) second important claim concerned the relation of dominance and status to nonverbal behavior. Although some research did exist on this question at the time, and researchers continued to do much more of it in the years that followed, no systematic review, and certainly no meta-analytic review, was undertaken other than one dealing with dominance and status in relation to accuracy of decoding nonverbal cues (Hall et al., 1997). Because of the pressing need to test what some were already taking for granted (e.g., Feldman, 1995; Lippa, 1994), my colleagues and I undertook a comprehensive meta-analysis of dominance and status in relation to nonverbal behavior (Hall et al., 2003). Henceforth in this chapter, I use the abbreviation DS to refer to dominance and status (and related concepts such as power, assertiveness, etc.).

DECISIONS

Meta-analysts must make many decisions that are unique to the meta-analyst's research questions and his or her chosen literature, which together shape, and often limit, the analysis and its conclusions. Simply to define "the research question," for example, proves much more complex than one might initially expect. In our case, these decisions included the following.

What Defines the Dominance-Status (DS) Construct?

The DS construct is complex, as many writers have indicated (e.g., Ellyson & Dovidio, 1985; see Dunbar & Burgoon, this volume). Early on, my colleagues and I decided to be fairly inclusive of operational definitions. Specific definitions of DS included personality dominance or assertiveness, assigned roles that differed in DS, achieved DS, and socioeconomic status, each of which had its own code. Certain potentially eligible definitions were excluded: gender, race, age, aggression, competition, and popularity.

We also decided to embrace both actual DS and perceived DS. (In other words, we were interested in both how people of differing degrees of DS behave and also what beliefs people hold about the association of DS to nonverbal behavior). Mostly, researchers examining beliefs did not ask perceivers about their beliefs directly, but rather they asked perceivers to rate the DS of stimulus persons (for example on videotape or in photos) and then correlated those ratings with nonverbal behaviors that had been coded by the investigators. By including both actual DS and beliefs about DS, we could compare actual to perceived effects.

What Nonverbal Behaviors Would Be Included?

We decided to be comprehensive, as no broad review had been done. We included many kinds of facial, postural, proxemic, and kinesic behaviors, gaze-related behaviors, and vocal behaviors; some of these had been studied much more than others, and some had been theorized about much more than others. Another decision was where to draw the line between verbal and nonverbal behavior. We decided to include some behaviors that others might call verbal (e.g., interruptions, speech rate, speech errors, back-channel responses, and pausing behavior).

Because we could not be sure how many studies we would find and therefore what comparisons would ultimately be possible, we maintained a high level of detail in the coding of behavior. For example, we maintained separate codes for rate versus frequency and for various specific kinds of touching (hand to hand, hand to waist, hand to face, etc.). Altogether, we maintained individual codes for over 200 different behaviors. After all studies were coded, we reviewed the list of codes and decided, without reference to the results, how to group them, using face validity as the criterion in conjunction with a pragmatic concern for optimal breadth (defining behavior categories too narrowly would result in too few studies in each behavior category, and a proliferation of analyses). The final list of behavior categories for which there were enough studies to calculate meta-analytic statistics is shown in Table 45.[24]

What About "Leftover" Results?

Many individual nonverbal behaviors were reported too infrequently to permit meta-analytic summary. For example, "nervous facial expression" and "coy look" were each measured only once. In addition, some investigators combined behaviors into unique composites (for example, "immediacy" might be represented by a composite of smiling, leaning forward, and eye contact). In order not to lose these results, we created a separate catalogue of these infrequently occurring results. Table 46 lists most of these behaviors.

What Age of Participants Would Be Included?

We decided to use participants of adolescent age and up, but we included studies of adults interacting with younger children if the person whose behavior was analyzed was old enough to fit our criterion.

What Is a "Study"?

Simple though it sounds, even this is a decision to be made. A study for us was an independent group of participants described in a published source (article or book chapter). A source might contain several studies (e.g., several experiments published in one article or several subgroups whose data were clearly presented within

TABLE 45

Review of Dominance, Status, and Nonverbal Behavior: Behavior Categories
Subjected to Meta-Analytic Summary

Smiling, gazing, raised brows, facial expressiveness, nodding, self-touch, other touch, hand/arm gestures, openness, postural relaxation, body/leg shifting, moving feet, distance, facing orientation, posed encoding skill, vocal variability, loud voice, interruptions, overlaps, pausing/latency to speak, filled pauses, backchannel responses, laughter, speech errors, rate of speech, vocal pitch, vocal relaxation

---

[24]We did not summarize studies that measured the visual dominance ratio, because this phenomenon has clear results that have been well summarized (see Dovidio & Ellyson, 1985; Dovidio, Ellyson, Keating, Heltman, & Brown, 1988). Therefore, we decided that a meta-analysis was not necessary. Research on the visual dominance ratio shows that people who have higher DS (as defined in both state and trait terms), compared to those with lower DS, gaze at an interaction partner a relatively higher percentage of time while speaking than while listening.

TABLE 46

Review of Dominance, Status, and Nonverbal Behavior: Infrequently Reported
Behaviors (Not Subjected to Meta-Analytic Summary)

Animated (smile, talk fast, move head), mouth distortions, facial activity, facial/kinesic
expressiveness, facial nervousness, fearful face, angry face, disgusted face, sad face, facial
emotional contagion, eyebrow flash, head gestures, head shakes, head tilt to side, chin
thrusts, neck relaxed, head tilt up/down, look at other's body, prolonged gaze pattern
(prolonged gaze at end of speaking turn directed to person to designate the next
speaker), breaking initial gaze, break eye contact, coy looks, anxiety (filled pauses,
posture and leg shift, hand to head movements), emblems (nod, shrug, head shake,
making numbers with fingers), object manipulation, relaxed hands, explosive slap of
body preparatory to getting up, sweeping hand movement preparatory to getting up,
victory gestures, points at other, points at other's possessions, reciprocal touch,
handshake, arms akimbo, kinesic animation, arm asymmetry, arm wrap, leg asymmetry,
amount of space claimed by body over table, amount of space claimed by body along
table length, number of departures from spatial invasion, distance adjustments with
chair, walking speed, elevation above other, stand above other, stand versus sit, stand in
front of other, walk around versus stand still, physical intrusions (touch, point at, stand
over, invade space), anxious voice, warm voice, friendly voice, clear voice, thin voice,
nasal voice, throaty voice, orotund voice, bored voice, calm voice, submissive voice,
whiny voice, breathy voice, metallic voice, resonant voice, articulate pronunciation,
vocal attractiveness, persuasive (direct gaze, few speech errors, frequent gestures, no
self-touch, medium voice amplitude), superior (no smile, head raised, loud), immediacy
(hand and arm gestures, facing directly, close proximity), immediacy (eye contact,
relaxed, facing directly, smile, vocal expressiveness, close proximity, touch other, use
gestures), conversational involvement (gaze, close proximity, facing orientation, forward
lean, vocal expressiveness, decreased signs of nervousness)

the context of one experiment). Alternatively, a given study might be presented
piecemeal in more than one source.

What About Unpublished Studies?

We searched for unpublished doctoral dissertations but not other unpublished
works, owing to the difficulty and likely bias in locating them.

How Will We Search?

We conducted PsycINFO and search Dissertation Abstracts International using a
list of nonverbal terms crossed with a list of DS terms (for example, facial expression and dominance, or eye contact and socioeconomic status). We also perused
the bibliographies of articles and consulted our own reprint files.

What Results Information Should We Extract?

We used the Pearson correlation (r) as the indicator of association, and when it was not presented, we calculated it from available ingredients using standard formulas. We extracted (calculated, when necessary) the standard normal deviate Z as the indicator of statistical significance in the original studies, and we also noted the direction of the outcome for each study, even when effect size r or Z could not be obtained. As an example, for perceived DS and smiling, there were 24 studies with known rs (8 positive and 16 negative), and 35 altogether (12 positive, 17 negative, and 6 with unknown direction).

How Do We Summarize Results?

We decided to calculate the mean r, both unweighted and weighted by sample size; the median r; the direction of the effects (by a simple tally, as shown above); statistical significance using a fixed-effects (Stouffer method; Rosenthal, 1991) and a random-effects (single-sample t-test) approach and a homogeneity test. We calculated all of these outcomes (except for the homogeneity test) both for those studies that produced an r, and for all studies with the unknown rs assumed to be zero, thus providing likely upper and lower limits to the overall estimation of outcome. We also calculated the "file drawer N" or number of null results that would have to exist in order to bring a significant combined f into non-significance (Rosenthal, 1991).

How Do We Handle Nonindependence?

Often a study would present results for more than one nonverbal behavior. If these were variants of one behavior category, such as several different kinds of foot movements, the effects were averaged before any further analysis was done in order to maintain statistical independence of the effect sizes entered into the "foot movement" analysis. On the other hand, if a study produced results for two or more behaviors that would not be analyzed together (for example, smiling and interpersonal distance), then both of those results entered their respective analyses. Thus, independence was maintained within an analysis but not necessarily between analyses.

What Study Characteristics Would We to Code?

We developed a detailed coding sheet for both actual and perceived DS studies. Some items were common to both kinds of study, and others were not. To illustrate, for the actual DS studies, the items included study ID, coder ID, title, authors, date and citation, gender of first author, nationality of participants (6 categories), sample size (males, females, total), age of participants (7 categories), setting (lab/field), field setting (5 categories), group size (individual/dyad/group of 3–5/group of 6 or more), gender composition of group (same/opposite/both), recording medium or context (e.g., photo/video only/audio only/audio and video/ confederate/experimenter or interviewer/real person-stranger/real person-acquainted), identity of acquainted person (10 categories, including friend, romantic partner, and co-worker), and DS design (manipulated/measured).

We coded these study attributes for two reasons: first to be able to describe the literature methodologically, and second to analyze potential moderator effects. As examples of the latter, we could theoretically ask whether studies with male first authors found larger effects than studies with female first authors, whether effects have changed over time, and whether effects varied with the particular definition of DS used. Intercoder reliability was established using either percentage agreement between two independent coders or the correlation between the coders, depending on the coding variable.

We were surprised (and disappointed) to discover that in spite of having located a large literature (about 200 studies producing hundreds of individual results), these numbers were deceiving for several reasons. First, many results were nonindependent and had to be averaged together before analysis. Second, we were actually conducting a large number of separate meta-analyses, one for each cell of a matrix formed by crossing type of DS (actual/perceived) by the list of nonverbal behavior categories described earlier. Within each of these cells, the number of independent results was often under 10 and never exceeded 35. Therefore, the search for moderators could not be done in a meaningful statistical manner (too few studies, too many potential moderators, many of which were confounded with each other, and too much capitalizing on chance given these factors and the fact that no formal predictions could be made for which study attributes should moderate the effects and how). Inspection for moderators was done in a *post hoc* fashion, after noting that the distribution of effect sizes was not homogeneous and then examining the studies *post hoc* in light of their methodology.

FINDINGS

The results of this meta-analysis will be surprising to some readers. The analysis of correlations between actual DS and nonverbal behavior showed, for the most part, very little association on average; nonverbal behaviors were not particularly associated with DS defined as personality, assigned or achieved rank or role, or socioeconomic status. Such a conclusion is consistent, however, with the argument I have made elsewhere, that such relations may be negligible overall because the nonverbal behaviors associated with DS are likely to be strongly determined by proximal factors such as a person's emotional state or role-related motives, which are not predictable from DS by itself (e.g., Hall & Friedman, 1999; Hall, Horgan, & Carter, 2002). In other words, if DS can be associated with many different states and motives, then one should not be surprised to find that DS does not predict nonverbal behavior well in general. Without knowing about these proximal states and motives, it will be difficult to predict nonverbal behavior from simply knowing a person's DS.

Indeed, our meta-analysis suggested in two different ways that such moderators might be at work. First, the fact that many studies produced negligible and/or nonsignificant results suggests that, within a study, variation between participants may have negated overall behavior differences as a function of DS. In other words, whereas some people may indeed smile a lot in a low DS role (perhaps because they want to be pleasing), this effect could be canceled by those people who do not smile at all in that role (perhaps because they did not want that role). Second, the heterogeneity tests we performed indicated that, across studies, the results were highly variable, with results not only varying greatly in magnitude but also in direction. This suggests, for example, that having low DS in one study is associated with different emotional or motivational responses than being low DS in another study, but these effects cancel out when averaged across studies. One might hope that inspection of the definitions of DS would help to account for some of this variation; perhaps, for example, studies where DS was defined as personality showed systematically different results from studies in which DS was defined as experimentally defined roles. But these efforts were remarkably unfruitful, and we were often left with little insight into the particular factors moderating the variation across studies.

In contrast, analyses of perceived DS in relation to nonverbal behavior showed rather persistent effects, though these too were highly variable: People thought that higher DS was associated with less smiling, more gazing, more gesturing, less relaxed posture, more vocal variation, and more loudness, among others. When actual DS did have a relation to nonverbal behavior, as was the case for loudness of voice, the corresponding perceived DS result was much stronger.

CONCLUSIONS AND CAUTIONS

After more than 20 years of performing meta-analyses on nonverbal behavior and on other topics, I can say without hesitation that this was by far the most arduous. There are several reasons for this. One, it was not one meta-analysis; it was many. Two, the coding sheet for study attributes was long and complicated: Many iterations were needed to develop it, and much effort went into attaining acceptable intercoder reliability. Furthermore, because it was a long coding sheet, the time required to code each study was great. In hindsight, because we could not do much formal moderator testing, perhaps we did not need to code study attributes in such detail. On the other hand, we did not know this until very late in the game, and a detailed coding sheet at least permits us to describe the literature fully and to identify areas that are particularly in need of more research.

A third reason for the difficulty of this meta-analysis was the sheer number of behavior categories we embraced and, within each, the plethora of specific variables.

The literature was remarkably inconsistent, and often very unclear, in how the nonverbal behaviors were described and measured. Also, studies differed widely in their designs, making the extraction of results a time-consuming and often confusing process. Added to the nearly overwhelming number of specific nonverbal behaviors measured, there was also wide variation in how DS was operationalized. Thus, both of the key constructs in our meta-analysis—nonverbal behavior and DS— were measured complexly and often confusingly.

Aside from the difficulties just enumerated, another challenge with this meta-analysis (like many others) involves causal inference. Although some studies involved experimental manipulation (such as assigning participants to low and high DS roles), which entitles researchers to interpret the results in causal terms, many studies were correlational, meaning that the overall conclusions must be treated as correlations and therefore ambiguous with regard to cause and effect. Furthermore, when comparing subgroups of studies (i.e., looking for moderators), one is still doing a correlational analysis, which again precludes a causal interpretation. Thus one must be careful to draw appropriately judicious inferences at every step.

REFERENCES

Cooper, H. M. (1989). *Integrating research: A guide for literature reviews* (2nd ed.). Newbury Park, CA: Sage.
Cooper, H. M., & Hedges, L. V. (Eds.). (1993). *The handbook of research synthesis.* New York: Russell Sage.
Dovidio, J. F., & Ellyson, S. L. (1985). Patterns of visual dominance behavior in humans. In S. L. Ellyson & J. F. Dovidio (Eds.), *Power, dominance, and nonverbal behavior* (pp. 129–149). New York: Springer-Verlag.
Dovidio, J. F., Ellyson, S. L., Keating, C. F., Heltman, K., & Brown, C. E. (1988). The relationship of social power to visual displays of dominance between men and women. *Journal of Personality and Social Psychology, 54,* 233–242.
Elfenbein, H. A., & Ambady, N. (2002). On the universality and cultural specificity of emotion recognition: A meta-analysis. *Psychological Bulletin, 128,* 203–235.
Ellyson, S. L., & Dovidio, J. F. (Eds.). (1985). *Power, dominance, and nonverbal behavior.* New York: Springer-Verlag.
Feldman, R. S. (1995). *Social psychology.* Englewood Cliffs, NJ: Prentice Hall.
Hall, J. A. (1978). Gender effects in decoding nonverbal cues. *Psychological Bulletin, 85,* 845–857.
Hall, J. A. (1984). *Nonverbal sex differences: Communication accuracy and expressive style.* Baltimore, MD: The Johns Hopkins University Press.
Hall, J. A., Carter, J. D., & Horgan, T. G. (2000). Gender differences in the nonverbal communication of emotion. In A. H. Fischer (Ed.), *Gender and emotion: Social psychological perspectives* (pp. 97–117). Paris: Cambridge University Press.
Hall, J. A., Coats, E. J., & Smith LeBeau, L. (2003). *Dominance, status, and nonverbal behavior: A meta-analysis.* Manuscript in preparation.
Hall, J. A., & Friedman, G. B. (1999). Status, gender, and nonverbal behavior: A study of structured interactions between employees of a company. *Personality and Social Psychology Bulletin, 25,* 1082–1091.
Hall, J. A., Halberstadt, A. G., & O'Brien, C. E. (1997). "Subordination" and nonverbal sensitivity: A study and synthesis of findings based on trait measures. *Sex Roles, 37,* 295–317.
Hall, J. A., Horgan, T. G., & Carter, J. D. (2002). Assigned and felt status in relation to observer-coded and participant-reported smiling. *Journal of Nonverbal Behavior, 26,* 63–81.
Harris, M. J., & Rosenthal, R. (1985). Mediation of interpersonal expectancy effects: 31 meta-analyses. *Psychological Bulletin, 97,* 363–386.

Hedges, L. V., & Olkin, I. (1985). *Statistical methods for meta-analysis*. Orlando, FL: Academic Press.

Henley, N. M. (1977). *Body politics: Power, sex, and nonverbal communication*. Englewood Cliffs, NJ: Prentice-Hall.

LaFrance, M., Hecht, M. A., & Paluck, E. L. (2003). The contingent smile: A meta-analysis of sex differences in smiling. *Psychological Bulletin, 129*, 305–334.

Lippa, R. A. (1994). *Introduction to social psychology* (2nd ed.). Pacific Grove, CA: Brooks/Cole.

Lipsey, M. W., & Wilson, D. B. (2001). *Practical meta-analysis*. Thousand Oaks, CA: Sage.

Matsumoto, D. (1987). The role of facial response in the experience of emotion: More methodological problems and a meta-analysis. *Journal of Personality and Social Psychology, 52*, 769–774.

McClure, E. B. (2000). A meta-analytic review of sex differences in facial expression processing and their development in infants, children, and adolescents. *Psychological Bulletin, 126*, 424–453.

Rosenthal, R. (1991). *Meta-analytic procedures for social research* (rev. ed.). Newbury Park, CA: Sage.

Rosenthal, R., Hall, J. A., DiMatteo, M. R., Rogers, P. L., & Archer, D. (1979). *Sensitivity to nonverbal communication: The PONS test*. Baltimore, MD: The Johns Hopkins University Press.

Skinner, M., & Mullen, B. (1991). Facial asymmetry in emotional expression: A meta-analysis of research. *British Journal of Social Psychology, 30*, 113–124.

Zuckerman, M., & Driver, R. E. (1985). Telling lies: Verbal and nonverbal correlates of deception. In A. W. Siegman & S. Feldstein (Eds.), *Multichannel integrations of nonverbal behavior* (pp. 129–147). Hillsdale, NJ: Lawrence Erlbaum Associates.

Considering the Social and Material Surround: Toward Microethnographic Understandings of Nonverbal Communication

Curtis D. LeBaron
Brigham Young University

INTRODUCTION

Nonverbal communication occurs naturally and necessarily within a social and material environment. When people gesture with their hands, for example, they usually talk to someone at the same time, coordinating their visible and vocal behaviors to be understood altogether (e.g., Schegloff, 1984). Hands (and other nonverbal behaviors) occupy and move within three-dimensional spaces that include physical objects and structures, and our gestures may be largely recognized and understood through their relationship to the material world within reach (e.g., Goodwin, 1997, 2000b; Heath & Hindmarsh, 2000; LeBaron & Streeck, 2000).

Communication is also a process of interaction among participants who jointly create messages and meanings, as when the audience of a gesture helps to co-author that gesture (Streeck, 1994). Additionally, nonverbal behaviors may be embedded within extended processes or activities such that any particular behavior, such as a gesture, is understood through its relationship to the whole activity (e.g., Koschmann, LeBaron, Goodwin, & Feltovich, 2003). Because gestures and other forms of nonverbal behavior occur naturally and are embedded in a larger set of actions and circumstances necessarily, they should, therefore, be analyzed as inseparable from the social and material surround.

Given this argument, this chapter describes and advocates *microethnographic approaches* to the study of nonverbal communication: research methods that examine nonverbal cues through careful consideration of their relationship to other social and material phenomena. Verbal and nonverbal messages have traditionally

493

been studied separately as though they were independent rather than co-occurring and interrelated. A handful of scholars (e.g., Kendon, 1977; Mead, 1975), however, have complained about this artificial separation, insisting that "it makes no sense to speak of 'verbal communication' and 'nonverbal communication'" as though they exist independent of one other" (Kendon, 1972, p. 443). Increasingly, researchers are conducting integrated studies of verbal *and* nonverbal communication (see Jones & LeBaron, 2002; Streeck & Knapp, 1992). To show how this may be done, this chapter provides a brief overview of microethnographic research, including historical origins and research practices, and a sample analysis of naturally occurring interaction, to illustrate briefly how nonverbal behaviors may be examined and understood through their sequential and physical location within an unfolding social scene.

A THUMBNAIL SKETCH
OF MICROETHNOGRAPHIC RESEARCH

Microethnographic research addresses "big" social issues through an examination of "small" communicative behaviors. The approach emerged during the 1960s and 1970s when scholars concerned about the social inequalities of public schools used new technologies (such as videotape) to study the moment-to-moment behaviors whereby social stratification happened within a particular school or classroom (e.g., Erickson & Mohatt, 1977; Mehan, 1979). The researchers' focus was on the interaction rather than the individual. They regarded "microbehaviors," including nonverbal behaviors such as gaze, body posture, and hand movement, as inherently interdependent, as the small means whereby events were jointly accomplished, and as the building blocks of micro-cultures enacted and constituted collectively (Bremme & Erickson, 1977; Erickson, 1971, cited in Streeck, 1983; Erickson & Schultz, 1977; McDermott & Roth, 1978).

Microethnographic research is a convergence of competencies from various disciplines, including anthropology, psychology, sociology, and communication. Early research of this kind was influenced by *context analysis*, a structuralist approach promoted by psychologist Albert Scheflen (e.g., 1963). Context analysts identified contextual frames or coherent units of interaction made visible, for example, by participants' sustained postural configurations (Scheflen, 1976). Once frame boundaries were identified, analysts explicated the participants' moment-by-moment maneuvers whereby the embodied contexts were sustained interactively (Kendon, 1973, 1979). Analysts also identified interaction routines and regularities that exist as cultural forms somewhat independent of (and prior to) the participants who negotiated their particular performance (e.g., Kendon, 1976; Scheflen, 1973).

Through the work of Kendon (1990) and others, context analysis graduated from its heavily structuralist beginnings and is now less concerned with recurring cultural forms and more attentive to the sequential unfolding of human interaction. Specifically, microethnographic work has been influenced more recently by *conversation analysis* (CA), which is a rigorously empirical method for examining naturally occurring talk and the social forms (e.g., greetings, interviews, institutions) that talk embodies. CA was pioneered by sociologist Harvey Sacks and developed in collaboration with Emanuel Schegloff and Gail Jefferson (Sacks, 1992), who envisioned their method as a critique of and a challenge to cultural deterministic approaches such as early context analysis (see Schegloff, 1988). Sacks (1984) insisted that:

> Whatever humans do ... there is order at all points [and] a detailed study of small phenomena may give an enormous understanding of the way humans do things and the kinds of objects they use to construct and order their affairs. (pp. 22–24)

Contemporary microethnographic studies usually include conversation analytic arguments and analysis, but talk is not privileged at the expense of other symbol systems and communicative resources that warrant close examination. Indeed, there is an abiding recognition that "body parts are the first mediating elements in our interaction with the people and objects around us" (Duranti, 1997, p. 322), that "human action is built through the simultaneous deployment of a range of quite different kinds of semiotic resources" (Goodwin, 2000b, p. 2), and that "talk in interaction shares billing with space, with artifacts, with work, and with the visible palpable body" (Moerman, 1990, p. 182).

Although microethnographic research takes various forms, depending on the preferences of the analyst and the nature of the project, certain family resemblances are associated with this method. The 5-step process described in this section is laden with assumptions about the nature of communication and how the social world ought to be examined. These are displayed in Appendix A.

Steps to Take When Conducting a Microethnographic Study

1. Select a Research Site. A site is a location within time and space where people communicate or interact in ways that constitute something recognizably their own. An Internet chat room would be a legitimate research site, but I prefer to examine physical locations where people maneuver their bodies relative to one another in telling ways.

Selecting a site depends on the nature of the research project. Presumably, basic communication research—that is, discovering and documenting features of the interaction order—could be conducted almost anywhere because there is "order at all points" of social life (Sacks, 1984). For example, LeBaron and Jones (2002) examined a beauty salon simply because videotape was available: Among other things, they showed how participants' nonverbal maneuvers in one activity (e.g., hairdressing) may have micro-strategic consequences for their simultaneous involvement in another (e.g., an argument); these features of interaction might occur within a courtroom, a boardroom, and so forth.

Site selection is usually guided by a research agenda. A concern for social stratification within public schools, for example, might guide a researcher to a classroom where children have a variety of socioeconomic backgrounds. As part of a larger research project on deception detection, LeBaron and Streeck (1997) selected a particular police station because it had a reputation for getting confessions from suspects who were later found innocent. Beach and LeBaron (2002) examined one medical consultation between a provider and patient as part of that health care system's long-term efforts to refine medical interviewing techniques. Whether sites are selected for basic research or to pursue a particular research agenda, communicative phenomena are examined as inherently embedded within the local scene.

2. Collect Naturally Occurring Data.   Communication is considered to be "naturally occurring" if it would have occurred whether or not it was observed or recorded by the researcher. Participant observations, field notes, and audio or video recordings of everyday interaction are considered premium data for microethnographic work, but videotape has become a mainstay because it helps analysts avoid an artificial separation of verbal and nonverbal channels, and it captures subtle details of interaction that analysts can review and others can verify.

A variety of cinematic decisions influence the nature of videotaped data. Simply turning a camera on or off is an interpretive act: a decision about what is important or worth recording. I try to turn the camera on before participants arrive and then turn it off after everyone leaves. The camera's scope is often a dilemma: A wide-angle view that includes all participants will not include close-ups of facial expressions and other subtle behaviors; a close-up view of someone's hands may exclude something else. Cameras, however automatic, embody a perspective. Cameras must be placed and pointed, and analysis is always contingent upon the perspective a camera provides. Because cameras cannot record themselves, there must be distance between the camera and the objects of study. Given that cameras cannot point in two directions simultaneously, they should be outside the circle of interaction, not caught between participants at opposite ends. Sometimes two cameras are better than one.

I prefer to set up my camera (in a corner with a wide-angle lens) and then leave the room so that my physical presence and movement do not have consequences for my data. But sometimes, such as when videotaping a large group, it is necessary to remain in the room so that I can work the camera and follow the participants as they move and talk. Cinematic decisions, however, should be a pursuit of naturally occurring data. This microethnographic emphasis on behaviors naturally occurring diverges from other research traditions that rely on imagined communication, surveys, or journals, which depend on people's ability to recollect and account for their behavior and data generated through experimental methods where subjects behave within laboratory conditions, removed from the people and things associated with their everyday lives.

3. Observe Data Carefully and Repeatedly. Soon after recording on video-tape, I watch the tape from beginning to end and create a minute-by-minute log of it. These logs help me to identify (and later locate) specific moments for more careful observation. Moreover, these logs maintain a "big picture" that can be lost during more microanalytic activities such as transcription.

In microethnographic research, careful and repeated observation is the grist-mill for empirical verification. A videotaped moment may "jump out" as obviously noteworthy, but it requires repeated observation to be fully explicated and understood. Through repeated observation, moments may *become* a focus of analysis as the features and patterns of interaction are noticed and appreciated. Throughout this inductive process, analysts' eyes are unavoidably informed by research agendas and literatures. Induction gives way to abduction as researchers look for specific kinds of phenomena related to their emerging claims and conclusions. Sometimes analysts work in groups (called *data sessions*), making rapid progress through synergistic observations and immediate critiques of each other's claims. In the end, research claims must agree with what can be observed in the videotaped data.

4. Digitize and Transcribe Key Moments of Interaction. Emerging technology continues to be an impetus for microethnographic innovation and advance. When I become serious about examining some portion of my videotaped data, I digitize it and then use my computer to microanalyze and transcribe. When computers are used for repeated observation, analysts can get different "views" of an analytic object: Digital video can be manipulated temporally (e.g., slowed down) and spatially (e.g., zoomed in); different interactional moments are easily juxtaposed on the computer screen for comparison. Such technology facilitates new insights by making everyday behavior "strange" and "noticeable" so that analysts can see anew. New technology cannot replace the eyes and ears of a well-trained analyst, but it can support smart and rigorous research. Transcription reduces interaction to a two-dimensional page, which highlights (precisely) structural aspects of talk and its coordination with nonverbal behaviors. One popular transcription system was created by Gail Jefferson to show speech utterances, timing, prosody, and overlap (see Atkinson & Heritage, 1984; Ochs, Schegloff, & Thompson, 1996). Transcription is a process of observing "more exactly."

5. Describe and Report Research Findings. Microethnographic studies describe the details of visible and vocal behaviors that subjects performed for each other and thereby made available for analysis. Claims may appear on the same printed page as transcripts (featuring vocal behaviors) acting as *frame grabs* (showing nonverbal behavior) taken from videotaped data. Empirically grounded claims may be supplemented by ethnographic insights and evidence from participant observations, field notes, interviews, and so forth. Although generalizability is not the sine qua non of microethnographic work, researchers assume and argue that site-specific findings have relevance beyond the site and that particular patterns of behavior resonate with larger social orders.

Recently, published microethnographic reports have been accompanied by CD-ROMs, giving readers access to the raw data that were the basis for research findings (e.g., Koschmann, LeBaron, & MacWhinney, 2002; LeBaron & Barney, 2002). Furthermore, multimedia technology is becoming more than an analytic tool: Microethnographic findings may be presented in the form of minidocumentaries; digitized clips may be looped, slowed, marked up, and in many ways manipulated to bring attention to details of phenomena analyzed.

SAMPLE ANALYSIS OF NATURALLY OCCURRING INTERACTION

This section illustrates briefly how nonverbal communication may be analyzed and understood as socially and materially embedded. I examined approximately 45 seconds of videotaped interaction, focusing specifically on participants' hand gestures: how they were coordinated with talk; how they were located within unfolding sequences of face-to-face interaction; how they related to the social and material environment of which they were a part. This brief illustration does not constitute a microethnographic argument, which would require more extensive analysis and site-specific discussion. Rather, this section demonstrates rigorous attention to the details of interaction, which is a core microethnographic concern.

The videotape shows two sorority sisters (enrolled at a large public university in the midwestern United States) who were sitting at their kitchen table, talking while

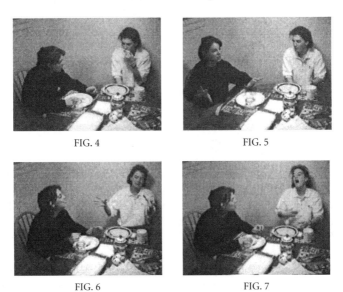

FIG. 4   FIG. 5

FIG. 6   FIG. 7

eating lunch (see Fig. 4). After 20 minutes of conversation, Amy (left) suddenly slapped her knee and told Barb (right) about a broken "condom egg machine." Amy was employed at a reproductive health center that sold condoms (packaged in plastic eggs) out of a vending machine that was located on their university campus. Amy reported that someone broke into the condom machine and stole all the condoms. The moment has been transcribed as follows (consult the transcription key in Appendix B of this chapter):

```
 1   Amy:   ((slap)) (.) Speaking of Jo:rgie someone bro(h)ke our co(h)ndo(h)m e(h)gg
 2          machi(h)ne (0.6) hhu:h ((squeal)) .hhh huh huh .hhhh
 3   Barb:  ┌Where a:t
 4   Amy:   └Jorgie made me think of work and so I thought of my work and
 5          everything but- at (the) UNC: (.) they like (0.2) m-
 6   Barb:  I still don't even know where your condom egg machine is at the UNC
 7              (0.4)
 8   Amy:   It's by the change machine and (.) the stamp machine across from the
 9          vending machines by the bathrooms and The Connection?
10              (0.4)
11   Barb:  I've just n:ever noticed it
12   Amy:   It's kind of hiding.=
13                    ┌((see Fig. 5))
14   Amy:   =It's between the └ trash ca:n and the (1.2) y'know the cha(h)nge machine
15          that's li(h)ke thi(h)s (.) the cha(h)nge machi(h)ne
16              (0.4)
17                       ┌((see Fig. 6))
18   Barb:  .hhh and └ the- (0.2)
19              ┌(see Fig. 7))
20   Barb:  └O:::::h between the (.) trash can and the (0.6) go:t it
```

Slapping her knee, Amy changed the topic of conversation abruptly from "Jorgie" to a "condom egg machine" (line 1), laughing to indicate the newsworthiness of her information (lines 1 and 2). Barb asked immediately where the machine was located (line 3). After accounting for her abrupt topic change (line 4), Amy said that the machine was located in "the UNC" (line 5), which is a building on campus. As Amy began to tell a story about the machine, Barb interjected and announced that she "still" didn't know where the machine was located (line 6). So Amy gave a more detailed description of the machine's location by referring to proximate objects and rooms (lines 8 and 9). Barb withheld recognition (line 10) and insisted that she didn't know the location (line 11). At this point, Amy described the condom machine's location again (lines 14 and 15) by coordinating her talk with hand gestures (see Fig. 5). After watching Amy's gestures, Barb performed the gestures herself (see Fig. 6) while repeating fragments of Amy's talk (line 18). Only then did Barb show recognition of the machine's location (line 20 and see Fig. 7).

My analysis of this brief interaction focuses on the participants' gestures. Amy's three descriptions of the condom machine's location (lines 5, 8–9, 12–15) were increasingly detailed, with only the third incorporating a sequence of gestures. When Amy said, "It's kind of hiding" (line 12), she lifted both hands from the table, making them more obviously visible to Barb. At the same time, Amy shifted her gaze and orientation away from Barb toward a midpoint in the air (see Fig. 5), a behavior that Goffman (1979) described as "mentally drifting from the physical scene" (p. 65). Amy assumed the perspective of someone standing in front of the condom machine that she was describing/imagining. When she said "trash ca:n" (line 14), she gestured with her right hand as though reaching out to touch it; when she said "change machine" (lines 14 and 15), she gestured with her left hand, marking its relative location. In short, Amy performed the experience of being in front of the condom machine, with a trash can on one side and a change machine on the other. Then Amy looked back toward Barb (line 16), indicating a "return" to the present physical scene.

At this point, Barb produced a truncated version of Amy's performance. After a brief silence (line 16), Barb breathed in (line 18) and shifted her gaze and orientation toward a midpoint in the air as though going to the "place" where Amy had just been (see Fig. 6). Barb did not say the words "trash can" and "change machine," but she reproduced the words "and the" (line 18), using the conjunction to denote Amy's two-part list. Moreover, Barb's utterance was coordinated with hand movements that unmistakably imitated Amy's. Barb moved her right hand and then her left, as though touching an invisible change machine (see Fig. 6). Immediately after performing a truncated version of Amy's vocal and visible behaviors, Barb produced a strong display of understanding regarding the condom machine's location. With her hands still suspended within her gesture space, Barb looked back at Amy (see Fig. 7), indicating a "return" to the present physical scene and said loudly "O:::::h" (line 20).

Heritage (1984) observed that the particle "oh" regularly functions as a "change-of-state token," serving to mark the sequential point at which the producer claims to understand:

> The production of "oh" generically proposes that its producer has undergone some kind of change of state. ... While the particle may propose a change of state that is appropriately responsive to a prior turn's informing or repair, its sequential role is essentially backward looking. (p. 324)

Barb's "O:::::h" (line 20) functioned as "change-of-state token" during this moment, marking the sequential point at which she claimed to realize or understand the condom machine's location that Amy had been trying to explain. Barb's next utterance provided additional evidence that she had "come to see" or understand: In her own words, she had "got it" (line 20) at that point in the interaction.

Small moments of naturally occurring interaction, such as this brief exchange between Amy and Barb, are the building blocks of microethnographic arguments.

For instance, my analysis raises questions about gestures, which are basic to the interaction order of social life. Gestures (and other forms of nonverbal behavior) are often regarded as an outward manifestation of internal psychological states. For example, McNeill insisted (e.g., 1985, 1992) that:

> Gestures are the person's memories and thoughts rendered visible. Gestures are like thoughts themselves. They belong, not to the outside world, but to the inside one of memory, thought, and mental images. (McNeill, 1985, p. 12)

Barb's behaviors contrast with this mentalistic view. The origin of her gestures was most obviously Amy, who provided a sequence of gestures that Barb then reproduced. A complete account of Barb's communication must include the social and material surround, from which Barb's gestures were taken. Moreover, notice the sequential location of her change-of-state token: Barb showed recognition or understanding immediately after and only after she reproduced Amy's gestures (line 20). Barb's gestures evidently preceded her understanding of the condom machine's location, not the other way around. Barb's gestures were not simply memories and thoughts rendered visible—they were antecedents to understandings interactively achieved. Careful examination of "small" communicative behaviors may, eventually, build a microethnographic argument that addresses "big" social issues.

CONCLUSION

Microethnographic studies describe and explain nonverbal behaviors by explicating their suspension within "webs of meaning" that the participants themselves have spun (Geertz, 1973). My sample analysis had a strong cognitive bent, which is consistent with recent trends in microethnographic research (see Streeck & Mehus, to appear). That is, my analysis of Amy and Barb's gestures became a discussion of shared understandings accomplished and displayed interactively.

While continuing to emphasize nonverbal communication and embodied cultural practices, microethnographic research has recently found fellowship with a variety of research programs in several disciplines that emphasize the importance of embodied action for the social formation of knowledge, symbols, and concepts. Linguists (e.g., Johnson, 1987; Lakoff, 1987), for example, demonstrate that the conceptual structures of natural languages are rooted in primary bodily experiences. Gardner (1984) argued specifically that people have "multiple intelligences," which include spatial and kinesthetic abilities. Anthropologists have studied the work of artisans and crafts people as "cognitive practice" (Keller & Keller, 1996). Cognitive scientists have argued that human minds extend beyond the skin (e.g., Hutchins, 1991; Lave, 1988; Norman, 1993), that minds incorporate material environments that are themselves mind-made (Lave, Murtaugh, & de la Rocha, 1984), and that knowledge may be "distributed across several individuals whose interactions determine decisions" (Resnick, 1991, p. 3).

Socially situated approaches to cognition are often grounded in work by
Vygotsky (1978), who described individual mental functioning (the psychological
plane) as an aggregate of internalized relations with other people (the social plane).
To understand an individual's psychological processes, he argued, it is necessary to
understand the individual's social interaction, which occurs first and provides
structure for thinking. Such insights across disciplines are remarkable, but they remain incomplete without a full contribution from the field of communication. If
the mind extends beyond the skin (Resnick, 1991), communication researchers can
explicate the basic bodily processes whereby cognition is distributed moment-by-
moment, turn-by-turn, movement-by-movement.

Given these extensions from other research lines, microethnographic studies of
nonverbal communication can be best summarized as involving (a) a specific research site; (b) a detailed analysis of both visible and audible microbehaviors, which
are to be understood as embedded within a particular social and material environment; (c) a recognition that cultural and cognitive phenomena are a product and a
process of naturally occurring communication, experienced by participants who at
the same time make it available for empirical study and interpretation; (d) an abiding awareness of "big" social issues, consistent with the notion that societal "macro"
structures are embodied and sustained through moment-to-moment, face-to-face
interaction; and (e) a noteworthy use of recent technologies, whereby analysts may
look and sometimes see anew the orderly performance of social life.

REFERENCES

Atkinson, J. M., & Heritage, J. (Eds.). (1984). *Structures of social action.* Cambridge, England: Cambridge University Press.
Beach, W., & LeBaron, C. (2002). Body disclosures: Attending to personal problems and reported sexual abuse during a medical encounter. *Journal of Communication, 52,* 3, 617–639.
Bremme, D., & Erickson, F. (1977). Behaving and making sense. *Theory Into Practice, 16,* 153–160.
Button, G. (Ed.). (1993). *Technology in working order: Studies of work, interaction, and technology.* London: Routledge.
Duranti, A. (1997). *Linguistic anthropology.* Cambridge, England: Cambridge University Press.
Ende, J., Pomerantz, A., & Erickson, R. (1995). Preceptors' strategies for correcting residents in an ambulatory care medicine setting: A qualitative analysis. *Academic Medicine, 70,* 224–229.
Erickson, F. (1971). *The cycle of situational frames: A model for microethnography.* Paper presented at the Midwest Anthropology Meeting, Detroit, Michigan.
Erickson, F., & Mohatt, G. (1977). *The social organization of participation structures in two classrooms of Indian students.* Report to the Department of Indian Affairs and Northern Development, Ottawa, Ontario. (ERIC # ED 192 935)
Erickson, F., & Schultz, J. (1977). When is context? Some issues and methods in the analysis of social competence. *The Quarterly Newsletter of the Institute for Comparative Human Development, 1,* 5–10.
Gardner, H. (1984). The development of competence in culturally defined domains: A preliminary framework. In R. A. Shweder & R. A. LeVine (Eds.), *Culture theory: Essays on mind, self, and emotion* (pp. 257–275). Cambridge: UP.
Geertz, C. (1973). *Interpretation of cultures.* New York: Basic Books.
Goffman, E. (1979). *Gender advertisements.* London: Macmillan.
Goodwin, C. (1979). The interactive construction of a sentence in natural conversation. In G. Psathas (Ed.), *Everyday language: Studies in ethnomethodology* (pp. 97–121). New York: Irvington.

Goodwin, C. (1984). Notes on story structure and the organization of participation. In J. M. Atkinson & J. Heritage (Eds.), *Structures of social action* (pp. 225–246). Cambridge, England: Cambridge University Press.

Goodwin, C. (1986). Gestures as a resource for the organization of mutual orientation. *Semiotica, 62,* 29–49.

Goodwin, C. (1987). Forgetfulness as an interactive resource. *Social Psychology Quarterly, 50,* 115–131.

Goodwin, C. (1994). Professional vision. *American Anthropologist, 96,* 606–633.

Goodwin, C. (1995a). Seeing in depth. *Social studies of science, 25,* 237–274.

Goodwin, C. (1995b). Co-constructing meaning in conversations with an aphasic man. *Research on language and social interaction, 28,* 233–260.

Goodwin, C. (1996). Transparent vision. In E. Ochs, E. Schegloff, & S. Thompson (Eds.), *Interaction and grammar* (pp. 370–404). Cambridge, England: Cambridge University Press.

Goodwin, C. (1997). The blackness of black: Color categories as situated practice. In L. B. Resnick, R. Säljö, C. Pontecorvo, & B. Burge (Eds.), *Discourse, tools, and reasoning: Essays on situated cognition* (pp. 112–140). Berlin: Springer-Verlag.

Goodwin, C. (2000a). Practices of color classification. *Mind, Culture, and Activity, 7,* 19–36.

Goodwin, C. (2000b). Action and embodiment within situated human interaction. *Journal of Pragmatics, 32,* 1489–1522.

Goodwin, C. (2003). The semiotic body in its environment. In J. Coupland & R. Gwyn (Eds.), *Discourse, the body and identity.* London: Palgrave/Macmillan.

Goodwin, C. (in press). Pointing as situated practice. In Sotaro Kita (Ed.), *Pointing: Where language, culture, and cognition meet.* Mahwah, NJ: Lawrence Erlbaum Associates.

Goodwin, M. (1990). *He-said-she-said: Talk and social organization among black children.* Indianapolis and Bloomington: Indiana University Press.

Heath, C. (1986). *Body movement and speech in medical interaction.* Cambridge, New York: Cambridge University Press.

Heath, C. (2002). Demonstrative suffering: The gestural (re)embodiment of symptoms. *Journal of Communication, 52,* 499–521.

Heath, C., & Hindmarsh, J. (2000). Configuring action in objects: From mutual space to media space. *Mind, Culture, & Activity, 7,* 81–104.

Heritage, J. (1984). A change-of-state token and aspects of its sequential placement. In J. M. Atkinson & J. Heritage (Eds.), *Structures of social action.* (pp. 299–345). Cambridge, England: Cambridge University Press.

Hindmarsh, J., & Heath, C. (2000). Embodied reference: A study of deixis in workplace interaction. *Journal of Pragmatics, 32,* 1855–1878.

Hutchins, E. (1991). *Cognition in the wild.* Cambridge, MA: MIT Press.

Hutchins, E., & Palen, L. (1997). Constructing meaning from space, gesture, and speech. In L. B. Resnick, R. Säljö, C. Pontecorvo, & B. Burge (Eds.), *Discourse, tools, and reasoning: Essays on situated cognition* (pp. 24–40). Berlin: Springer-Verlag.

Johnson, M. (1987). *The body in the mind: The bodily basis of meaning, imagination, and reason.* Chicago: University Press.

Jones, S., & LeBaron, C. (2002). Research on the relationship between verbal and nonverbal communication: Emerging integrations. *Journal of Communication, 52,* 3, 499–521.

Keller, C., & Keller, J. D. (1996). Imagery in ironwork. In S. Levinson & J. J. Gumperz (Eds.), *Rethinking linguistic relativity* (p. 115). Cambridge: University Press.

Kendon, A. (1972). Review of the book *Kinesics and context* by Ray Birdwhistell. *American Journal of Psychology, 85,* 441–455.

Kendon, A. (1973). The role of visible behavior in the organization of face-to-face interaction. In M. V. Cranach & I. Vine (Eds.), *Social communication and movement: Studies of interaction and expression in man and chimpanzee* (pp. 29–74). New York: Academic Press.

Kendon, A. (1976). Some functions of the face in a kissing round. *Semiotica, 15,* 4.

Kendon, A. (1977). *Studies in the behavior of social interaction.* Bloomington: Indiana University Press.

Kendon, A. (1979). Some emerging features of face-to-face interaction studies. *Sign Language Studies, 22,* 7–22.

Kendon, A. (1990). *Conducting interaction: Patterns of behavior in focused interaction.* Cambridge: Cambridge University Press.

Koschmann, T., & LeBaron, C. (2002). Learner articulation as interactional jointing: Studying gesture conversationally. *Cognition and Instruction, 20,* 249–282.

Koschmann, T., LeBaron, C., Goodwin, C. & Feltovich, P. (2003, May). *Pointing things out: On the reflexivity of objects and unfolding procedure.* Paper presented at the 53rd Annual Conference of the International Communication Association, San Diego, CA.

Koschmann, T., LeBaron, C., & MacWhinney, B. (2002). CD-ROM to accompany the special issue of *Cognition and Instruction, 20,* 2. Mahwah, NJ: Lawrence Erlbaum Associates.

Lakoff, G. (1987). *Women, fire, and dangerous things: What categories reveal about the mind.* Chicago: University of Chicago Press.

Lave, J. (1988). *Cognition in practice: Mind, mathematics, and culture in everyday life.* Cambridge, NY: University Press.

Lave, J., Murtaugh, M., & de la Rocha, O. (1984). The dialectic of arithmetic in grocery shopping. In B. Rogoff & J. Lave (Eds.), *Everyday cognition: Its development in social context* (pp. 67–91). Cambridge, MA: Harvard University Press.

LeBaron, C., & Barney, B. (2002). CD-ROM to accompany the special issue of the *Journal of Communication, 52,* Oxford: University Press.

LeBaron, C., & Jones, S. (2002). Closing up closings: Showing the relevance of the social and material surround to the completion of an interaction. *Journal of Communication, 52,* 542–565.

LeBaron, C., & Koschmann, T. (2002). Gesture and the transparency of understanding. In P. Glenn, C. LeBaron, & J. Mandelbaum (Eds.), *Studies in language and social interaction* (pp. 119–132). Mahwah, NJ: Lawrence Erlbaum Associates.

LeBaron, C., & Streeck, J. (1997). Space, surveillance, and interactional framing of participants' experience during a police interrogation. *Human Studies, 20,* 1–25.

LeBaron, C., & Streeck, J. (2000). Gesture, knowledge, and the world. In D. McNeill (Ed.), *Language and gesture* (pp. 118–138). Cambridge: Cambridge University Press.

Luff, P., Hindmarsh, J., & Heath, C. (2000). *Workplace studies: Recovering work practice and informing system design.* Cambridge: Cambridge University Press.

McDermott, R., & Roth, D. (1978). Social organization of behavior: Interactional approaches. *Annual Review of Anthropology, 7,* 321–345.

McNeill, D. (1985). So you think gestures are nonverbal? *Psychological Review, 92,* 350–371.

McNeill, D. (1992). *Hand and mind: What gestures reveal about thought.* Chicago: University of Chicago Press.

Mead, M. (1975). Review of "Darwin and facial expression" by Paul Ekman. *Journal of Communication, 25,* 209–213.

Mehan, H. (1979). *Learning lessons: Social organization in the classroom.* Cambridge, MA: Harvard University Press.

Moerman, M. (1988). *Talking culture: Ethnography and conversation analysis.* Philadelphia: University of Pennsylvania Press.

Moerman, M. (1990). Exploring talk and interaction. *Research on Language and Social Interaction, 24,* 173–187.

Norman, D. (1993). *Things that make us smart.* Reading. MA: Addison Wesley.

Ochs, E., Gonzales, P., & Jacoby, S. (1996). "When I come down I'm in the domain state": Grammar and graphic representation in the interpretive activity of physicists. In E. Ochs, E. Schegloff, & S. Thompson (Eds.), *Interaction and grammar* (pp. 328–369). Cambridge: Cambridge University Press.

Ochs, E., Schegloff, E., & Thompson, S. (Eds.). (1996). *Interaction and grammar.* Cambridge: Cambridge University Press.

Resnick, L. B. (1991). Shared cognition: Thinking as social practice. In L. B. Resnick, J. M. Levine, & S. D. Teasley (Eds.), *Perspectives on socially shared cognition* (pp. 1–22). Washington, DC: American Psychological Association.

Sacks, H. (1984). Notes on methodology. In J. M. Atkinson & J. Heritage (Eds.), *Structures of social action* (pp. 21–27). Cambridge: Cambridge University Press.

Sacks, H. (1992). *Lectures on conversation.* (2 vols., G. Jefferson, Ed.). Cambridge, MA: Blackwell.

Scheflen, A. (1963). Communication and regulation in psychotherapy. *Psychiatry, 26,* 126.

Scheflen, A. (1973). *Communicational structure: Analysis of a psychotherapy transaction.* Bloomington: Indiana University Press.

Scheflen, A. (1976). *Human territories: How we behave in space-time.* Englewood Cliffs, NJ: Prentice-Hall.

Schegloff, E. (1984). On some gestures' relation to talk. In J. M. Atkinson & J. Heritage (Eds.), *Structures of social action* (pp. 266–296). Cambridge: Cambridge University Press.

Schegloff, E. (1988). Goffman and the analysis of conversation. In P. Drew & W. Wooton (Eds.), *Erving Goffman: Exploring the interaction order.* Cambridge, UK: Polity Press.
Streeck, J. (1983). *Social order in child communication. A study in microethnography.* Amsterdam: Benjamins.
Streeck, J. (1993). Gesture as communication I: Its coordination with gaze and speech. *Communication Monographs, 60,* 275–299.
Streeck, J. (1994). Gesture as communication II: The audience as co-author. *Research on Language and Social Interaction 27,* 239–267.
Streeck, J. (1996). How to do things with things. *Human Studies, 19,* 365–384.
Streeck, J., & Kallmeyer, W. (2001). Interaction by inscription. *Journal of Pragmatics, 33,* 465–490.
Streeck, J., & Knapp, M. L. (1992). The interaction of visual and verbal features in human communication. In F. Poyatos (Ed.), *Advances in nonverbal communication* (pp. 3–23). Amsterdam: Benjamins.
Streeck, J., & Mehus, S. (in press). Microethnography: The study of practices. In K. Fitch & R. Sanders (Eds.), *Handbook of language and social interaction.* Mahwah, NJ: Lawrence Erlbaum Associates.
Vygotsky, L. S. (1978). *Mind in society: The development of higher psychological processes.* In M. Cole, V. John-Steiner, S. Scribner, & E. Souberman (Eds.), Cambridge, MA: Harvard University Press.

APPENDIX A

Assumptions Underlying Microethnographic Research

- It adheres to principles of empirical social science. A particular phenomenon is taken to exist, to the extent that data, analyses, and conclusions are verifiable or reproducible by others.
- It values qualitative analysis. With less concern for coding and counting, analysts seek to understand and explain communicative behaviors through careful and thorough descriptions of their situated occurrence.
- It may proceed inductively or abductively. Through the recording, observing, and analyzing, research claims and conclusions emerge. Researchers recognize that *a priori* theorizing may divert attention from the central task of describing and explaining phenomena based on observable details. Once a research focus has been clarified, analysts proceed abductively—that is, they specifically go looking for additional instances or evidence of some phenomenon toward strengthening or generalizing their findings.
- It privileges subjects' perspectives. Researchers avoid imposing their own theorized views on the social phenomena they examine; rather, they attend to the orientations and relevancies that the research subjects display.
- It acknowledges interpretive aspects of observational work. While adopting and maintaining an empirical stance, researchers are (at least to some extent) members of the social world that they analyze. Researchers do more than document observable behaviors—they appraise the significance of behaviors documented.

- It regards communication as constitutive. Communication is a primary means whereby social realities, microcultures, and meanings are interactively accomplished and experienced. What verbal and nonverbal forms of communication "mean" are what they are being used to do within specific situations.

These descriptions are abstractions from a host of recent microethnographic studies (e.g., Beach & LeBaron, 2002; Button, 1993; Ende, Pomerantz, & Erickson, 1995; C. Goodwin, 1979, 1984, 1986, 1987, 1994, 1995a, 1995b, 1996, 1997, 2000a, 2000b, 2003, in press; M. Goodwin, 1990; Heath, 1986, 2002; Heath & Hindmarsh, 2000; Hindmarsh & Heath, 2000; Hutchins & Palen, 1997; Jones & LeBaron, 2002; Koschmann & LeBaron, 2002; Koschmann, LeBaron, Goodwin, & Feltovich, 2003; LeBaron & Koschmann, 2002; LeBaron & Streeck, 1997, 2000; Luff, Hindmarsh, & Heath, 2000; Moerman, 1988, 1990; Ochs, Gonzales, & Jacoby, 1996; Streeck, 1983, 1993, 1994, 1996; Streeck & Kallmeyer, 2001).

APPENDIX B

Transcription Conventions

The following list was adapted from a transcription system developed by Gail Jefferson (see Atkinson & Heritage, 1984; Ochs, Schegloff & Thompson, 1996).

Symbol	Name	Description
yes	underline	vocal stress or emphasis through increased volume
:::	colon(s)	vocal stress or emphasis through sound stretching
.	period	falling vocal pitch at the end of an utterance
?	question mark	rising vocal pitch at the end of an utterance
-	hyphen	halting, abrupt cut-off of sound
hhh	h's	audible outbreaths
.hhh	period & h's	audible inbreaths
(h)	laugh token	within-speech aspirations (laughter)
(0.8)	timed silence	length of pause by tenths of a second
(.)	micropause	short pause, less than 0.2 seconds
[	brackets	overlapping utterances
0	equal sign	latched utterances, continuing without a gap
( )	parentheses	transcriber doubt
(( ))	double parentheses	paralinguistic or nonvocal behaviors noted

Nonverbal Research Involving Experimental Manipulations by Confederates

Laura K. Guerrero
Arizona State University

Beth A. Le Poire
University of California, Santa Barbara

INTRODUCTION

The goal in experimental research is to manipulate an independent variable (or variables) while controlling for other potential causes of variability in a given dependent variable. Researchers can answer a number of intriguing questions about nonverbal behavior by employing experimental manipulations using confederates. Indeed, experimental manipulations are often essential because they allow researchers to observe the ways people respond to nonverbal communication. By examining such responses, researchers obtain a better picture of the interactional nature of nonverbal cue use.

To encourage valid experimental work, Kerlinger (1986) discussed the *maxmincon principle*. According to this principle, researchers strive to maximize the systematic variability related to manipulated variables (max), minimize error or random variance (min), and control potential sources of extraneous systematic variability to rule out rival hypotheses (con). If researchers hope to meet the first criterion of the maxmincon principle, the manipulations they conduct must be valid, and if confederates are used they must be carefully trained. To meet the second and third criteria, researchers manipulate variables within controlled settings and engage in practices such as using random assignment, including possible mediating and moderating variables in the design, eliminating or counterbalancing potential sources of extraneous variables, making baseline comparisons, and using control groups.

Nonverbal researchers have used various techniques to manipulate independent variables, including the use of stimulus materials (e.g., drawings, photos, or videotapes), environmental manipulations, and confederate manipulations. For example, researchers have manipulated touch in photographs (Burgoon, 1991) or videotaped scenarios (Lee & Guerrero, 2001) to determine how dominant, intimate, formal, and sexually harassing people perceive various types of touch to be. In terms of environmental manipulations, Rind (1996) reported that telling customers it is sunny or rainy can influence the nature of a waiter's tips. Other research has shown that pleasant ambient smells, such as baking bread or roasting coffee (Baron, 1997), and pleasant ambient music (Galizio & Hendrick, 1972) can have a positive effect on helping behavior. Manipulation of these variables can test a host of intriguing hypotheses, but they typically do not impact the communication process as directly and dynamically as the use of confederate manipulations. Thus, this chapter focuses on experimental manipulations of nonverbal cues involving confederates.

In this chapter, we discuss issues related to manipulating confederate behavior, choosing a setting (laboratory vs. field), and designing an experiment. Along the way, we offer practical recommendations regarding how to train confederates and design experiments so that systematic variance is maximized, random variance is minimized, and extraneous variance is controlled. The goal is to provide readers with knowledge of social scientific practices as well as ideas for implementing valid experimental manipulations.

MANIPULATING CONFEDERATE BEHAVIOR

Advantages of Using Confederates

Nonverbal manipulations that involve confederates have several important advantages. First, such manipulations can occur dynamically in real time: Participants perceive the behavior as it occurs as part and parcel of their communicative experience. Second, using confederates enables researchers to examine reactions to specific sets of behaviors that might normally be difficult to observe in their naturally occurring domains. Third, using confederates allows researchers the opportunity to examine communication patterns, as the moves and countermoves of both the confederate and the participant can be observed and measured.

A fourth advantage of utilizing confederates for experimental manipulations is that it allows for the use of within-subjects designs. Frequently, manipulations occur after a set period of time, and they allow researchers to examine each individual participant as their own control. Thus in experiments where involvement (see Guerrero, this volume), for example, is moderate for the first few minutes of the conversation and then manipulated to be high, low, very high, or very low, it is possible to examine four conditions and compare over time *within each condition* to allow each participant to serve as his or her own control prior to the manipulation.

This can be effective in reducing experimental "costs" in terms of decreasing the number of participants required and the number of hours confederates work. In addition, having each individual serve as his or her own control is often the most valid method for determining the influence of the independent variables.

Types of Confederate Manipulations

Two types of confederate manipulations are common in nonverbal research. First, researchers can train confederates carefully prior to interactions to enact particular sets of behaviors with great regularity. Typically, each confederate repeats the manipulation(s) across a number of different participants. We refer to this as the *traditional confederate approach*. Second, to increase face validity, researchers often want to examine behavior within acquainted dyads or groups. In this case, they sometimes train one of the members of a dyad or group to act as a confederate during the course of the experiment. We refer to this on-the-spot training of participants as the *participant confederate approach*.

The Traditional Confederate Approach. There are many examples of the traditional confederate approach in nonverbal research. For instance, Burgoon and her colleagues (Burgoon & Le Poire, 1993; Burgoon, Le Poire, & Rosenthal, 1995) examined the effects of pleasantness and involvement on ongoing communication outcomes and subsequent evaluations. In this research, two confederates of each sex were chosen for similarity in physical appearance and mannerisms (the use of multiple confederates of both sexes also created a need to control for confederate statistically). To control for another source of potential extraneous variance, confederates wore the same clothes for every interaction. Each confederate was cued just prior to the interaction with regard to which set of nonverbal cues he or she was to enact. Pleasantness and involvement manipulations included smiling, head nods, close distances, and vocal warmth (to articulate a few cue complexes). Unpleasantness and lack of involvement included absence of smiling, farther than typical distances, flat vocalic affect, and asymmetrical posturing.

The main advantage of the traditional confederate approach is that, because confederates are trained *a priori*, researchers can instantiate modification that improves the strength and consistency of the manipulation. By training all of the confederates to act the same way within each particular condition, the researcher ensures that manipulations are consistent within conditions. In a study by Le Poire (1994), using one confederate provided consistency across nonverbal behaviors of expressiveness, involvement, anxiety, pleasantness, and interaction management and allowed greater certainty when drawing conclusions regarding the differential types of disclosure the confederate was engaging in within the various "conditions" (i.e., with interactants who were nonstigmatized, gay, and those that had AIDS).

To ensure that this control is achieved, nonverbal researchers can videotape confederates during test runs, have confederate behaviors coded, and then talk about any discrepancies or potential problems with confederates before the actual experiment begins. In fact, training confederates on videotape should be encouraged so that they can observe themselves and the other confederates for similarity across nonverbal elements (and especially enactment of the manipulation). The hours spent in preparation are worth the effort when confederates are found to be similar empirically across non-theoretic variables.

The Participant Confederate Rate Approach. The second type of confederate manipulation—the participant confederate approach—is typically more appealing when researchers want to examine the nonverbal behavior of relational partners and acquainted others. Rather than training confederates *a priori*, this approach usually requires on-the-spot training. For example, Andersen, Guerrero, Buller, and Jorgensen (1998) were interested in investigating how opposite-sex friends reacted to moderate and high increases in nonverbal intimacy. To examine this question, they needed to sample dyadic partners who considered themselves to be friends, but they also needed to manipulate nonverbal intimacy in systematic ways. To accomplish these goals, Andersen and his colleagues separated the opposite-sex friends when they arrived at the research laboratory under the guise that they wanted to give them privacy to complete questionnaires. Unbeknownst to the participant who actually completed a fairly long questionnaire, the other participant was enlisted as a confederate. The participant confederate was given detailed instructions on how to increase immediacy (either moderately or dramatically) at a certain point in the interaction, and then given a chance to practice this behavior on the researcher.

The participant confederate approach is useful when studying in tact dyads. The main advantage of this approach, however, is that the use of acquainted dyads often provides a sense of realism that the use of unacquainted dyads does not. An important disadvantage of this approach is that it is much harder to control confederate behaviors when training is abbreviated. Although randomly assigning participant confederates to conditions helps spread extraneous variance across all conditions in a similar fashion, the strict control that accompanies careful training and retraining is missing. It is also more difficult to train confederates within a short time frame. Additionally, the researcher needs to consider possible effects from the study on the existing relationship.

Researchers have used several methods to enhance the validity of manipulations using participant confederates. Rather than trying to train these confederates to engage in a number of detailed behaviors in a short period of time, researchers generally give them broad instructions and then have them practice the manipulated behavior. For example, when the manipulation involves negative behavior, the experimenter might ask the participant confederate to act more avoidant and withdrawn than normal by engaging in behaviors such as looking away and appearing disinterested. This was the technique Manusov (1990) used in her study of romantic dyads. Then, when the participant confederate practices this behavior, the experimenter can point out some additional behaviors she or he can manipulate.

Another technique for training participant confederates involves showing them a videotape of the type of behavior they should model or showing them their own behavior (videotaped during a first conversation) and suggesting ways of changing their behavior (in a subsequent conversation). Yet another method involves having participants rate their behavior on a scale and then asking them to move it up or down a couple of places for the manipulation (e.g., Floyd & Voloudakis, 1999). These last two techniques can also be combined: An experimenter might show participant confederates videotapes of their behavior and ask them to rate how flirtatious they were on a scale of 1 to 10. If the participant rates himself or herself a 6, the experimenter may ask the participant to move up two notches to an 8, give suggestions for how to do so, and then let the participant practice. In this way, the amount of change from one conversation to another can be controlled to some degree.

Manipulation Checks

Whether using the traditional confederate or participant confederate approach, manipulation checks are imperative for demonstrating validity of the confederates' actions. Not only can manipulation checks enhance the claims of validity of investigations employing confederates (by substantiating claims of consistency), but they can also enhance the internal validity of the experiments as well. For instance, Le Poire and Burgoon (1994) were testing two competing theories of expectancy violations. Both theories offered various predictions based on discrepancies or violations from that which was expected. However, only one theory (discrepancy arousal theory) made predictions based on the size of the behavioral change. Thus, whereas it was expected that high involvement and low involvement changes would be seen as moderate and very high, and very low involvement changes would be seen as large, the manipulation check (which involved measuring global perceptions of involvement across four time periods for both confederates) revealed that the high involvement change was seen as small, the very high involvement change (including touches) was seen as moderate, and the low and very low involvement changes were seen as large and larger.

This manipulation check not only ensured consistency across confederates and maximum variance across levels of manipulations, it also allowed the predictions to be modified to test discrepancy arousal theory's predictions more adequately and fairly than had been done in previous research. Thus manipulation checks are invaluable in both providing tests of internal validity and substantiating claims of controlled variance across conditions and across confederates (in experiments where multiple confederates are employed).

Manipulating Single Versus Multiple Behaviors

As manipulations become more complex, so, too, do manipulation checks. Oftentimes it is helpful to conduct manipulation checks at both a general and a specific level. For example, if a researcher manipulates dominance cues (see Dunbar & Burgoon, this volume), she or he may want to confirm that conditions varied in terms of global impressions of dominance as well as micro-behaviors such as interruptions, voice volume, or forward lean. In such a case, manipulation checks could determine which specific behaviors contributed to the overall impression of dominance, as well as if some behaviors (e.g., interruptions) were successfully manipulated while others (e.g., voice volume) were not. Such information is vital to the proper interpretation of data. In addition to conducting manipulation checks, researchers often check to see whether extraneous variables differed across conditions. When manipulating single behaviors, researchers may wish to verify that only the manipulated variable differed across conditions. When manipulating multiple behaviors, researchers may wish to verify that a set of behaviors was successfully manipulated in a manner that appeared externally valid.

Single Behaviors.   It can be difficult to manipulate only one nonverbal behavior while keeping others constant. As Andersen (1985, 1999) argued, nonverbal behaviors are often encoded and processed as a gestalt. Thus, if someone is instructed to smile warmly at her or his interactional partner, there is an inclination to engage in other warm behaviors such as leaning forward and increasing eye contact. In the same vein, if confederates are instructed to frown, they might very well show other signs of negative affect, such as becoming more posturally tense and averting gaze. When this happens, experimenters cannot rule out the rival hypothesis that other behaviors (such as postural tenseness or averted gaze) are actually responsible for the effects obtained in the study. Thus, whether manipulating single nonverbal behaviors or small groups of behaviors, the experimenter must ensure that all other relevant behaviors (i.e., those that could provide rival hypotheses for effects) are held constant. If a particular behavior, or set of behaviors, is particularly likely to covary with the manipulated behavior, the experimenter should measure the behavior and check for significant differences across conditions. If there are no such differences, the experimenter will be more confident regarding her or his conclusions.

Multiple Behaviors.   It can also be extremely challenging to manipulate multiple behaviors, especially if some of the behaviors contradict. For instance, if an experimenter wants to manipulate some behaviors that show dominance (e.g., lots of interruptions, an intimidating stare) and others that show interpersonal warmth (e.g., smiling, talking in a warm voice), it can be challenging to teach confederates how to engage in such contradictory behaviors in a natural-looking way. In a study on comforting behavior, Jones and Guerrero (2001) manipulated verbal person-centeredness and nonverbal immediacy. For each of these variables, they set up three conditions—low, moderate, and high—so that there were nine cells in the experiment. The confederates had little difficulty manipulating their behaviors when the condition was consistent (e.g., high person-centeredness and high nonverbal immediacy, or low person-centeredness and low nonverbal immediacy), but they initially experienced considerable difficulty when the conditions were inconsistent (e.g., high person-centeredness and low nonverbal immediacy).

To train the confederates, Jones and Guerrero (2001) took one behavior at a time: first person-centeredness and then nonverbal immediacy. For each behavior, they started with the moderate condition, as it best resembled what happens typically in interaction. Then they trained the confederates to move up (for the high condition) or down (for the low condition) from the moderate point. Next, they had the confederates practice consistent patterns of behavior (low/low, moderate/moderate, high/high), followed by the combinations that included a moderate condition with either a low or high condition. Finally, the two most disparate conditions were left for last: the high/low and low/high conditions. By following this type of progression, confederates gained confidence in learning the simpler manipulations before attempting the more challenging ones.

LABORATORY VERSUS FIELD SETTINGS

In addition to developing valid manipulations that maximize systematic differences across treatment groups, researchers using experimental approaches to studying nonverbal behavior must decide whether to conduct their experiment in a laboratory or field setting. When research is conducted in a laboratory setting, "the researcher brings people to a research site, arranges for events to occur, and then measures the effects" (Hecht & Guerrero, 1999, p. 32). Thus, laboratory experiments involve a high degree of control, both in terms of the constancy of conditions and in terms of internal validity (or the careful induction of the manipulation). The setting is constant, and the experimenter has arranged behavior, so a particular independent variable will be introduced at a specific time and in a specific way.

Laboratory experiments are especially useful when it is difficult to manipulate a particular behavior in natural settings or when a researcher wants access to minute behaviors that are best captured on videotape. In general, the more complex the manipulation, the most likely it is that a laboratory experiment using traditional confederates is necessary to produce valid results. For example, if a researcher is interested in investigating reactions to specific dominance-related behaviors occurring during a conflict situation, he or she might determine that it is easier to set up such a situation in a laboratory than in a natural setting. In such a case, traditional or participant confederates might be instructed to engage in submissive behaviors, moderately dominant behaviors, or highly dominant behaviors.

Before starting the interaction, the researcher could stimulate conflict through methods such as having an established couple discuss an issue that they have argued about in the recent past, or finding a controversial issue that strangers or relational partners disagree about. In this way, the researcher has considerable control in terms of setting up the situation. Because the setting is arranged by the researcher and the situation is somewhat contrived, laboratory experiments are typically less externally valid than experiments conducted in natural settings (see LeBaron, this volume). By contrast, when researchers conduct field experiments, they have less control of the situation but more external validity (see Patterson, this volume). With field experiments, the researcher goes to a natural setting and then introduces a manipulation into that setting. To maintain the naturalism of the field setting, it is typically advisable to keep both the manipulation and the dependent behaviors observed fairly simple.

For example, in a classic study on the effects of touch on tipping in restaurants, Crusco and Wetzel (1984) randomly assigned waitresses to one of three conditions: a fleeting-touch condition involving two quick touches, a shoulder-touch condition involving more extended touch, and a no-touch condition. The researchers trained the waitresses so that they behaved the same way across all conditions with the exception of touch behavior. Among other findings, Crusco and Wetzel found that touching increased the amount of tip customers left. In another field study, Sigelman, Adams, Meeks, and Purcell (1986) manipulated physical appearance cues to investigate how children react to disabled individuals. The confederate stood outside discount stores and asked parents if he could interview their children as part of an opinion poll. During the interviews, an observer unobtrusively recorded the children's general behaviors. Half the time, the confederate wore a leg brace and carried a crutch. Sigelman et al. found that children seemed more interested and curious when the confederate appeared disabled. They also found that there were no noticeable differences in negativity based on whether the confederate appeared disabled or not.

Studies such as these illustrate several important points about field experiments. First, the manipulations must be natural-looking enough to fit the setting. In the tipping experiment, for example, the researchers chose a "natural" time for touch to occur: when the waitress was returning the customer's change. Second, in order to reap the benefits of extra external validity, observations must be unobtrusive. In the tipping study, the dependent variable was the amount of gratuity left, which is easy to determine without even observing the interaction. In the study on children's reactions to the disabled, the researchers had an observer stand inside the store where she had a clear view of the children but would not be seen taking notes. By contrast, if it is important to obtain a lot of detailed information about people's reactions to the manipulation, a laboratory situation that allows for videotaping may be more appropriate.

Third, although confederates can be trained to act fairly consistently within conditions, the field setting often introduces variables that cannot be controlled. For example, in a laboratory setting the researcher can control the length of the interaction and keep the interactants isolated so that third parties do not interrupt them. In field settings, these elements are not controlled as easily. Thus, when conducting field experiments, it is particularly important to note any potential intervening variables that emerge during data collection, and then to try and ascertain whether these potential intervening variables could have operated in systematic ways that affected results.

ISSUES RELATED TO EXPERIMENTAL DESIGN

When designing any experiment, including those involving confederates, researchers should be cognizant of the techniques they can use to help them maximize systematic variance while minimizing error and ruling out potential rival hypotheses. Although a complete explanation of various design factors is beyond the scope of this chapter, five issues that are particularly relevant to experiments involving face-to-face interaction are discussed: randomization; posttest only designs; pretest/posttest designs; control groups; and balancing, counterbalancing, and inclusion as methods for ruling out rival hypotheses.

Randomization

The advantage of nonverbal manipulations with confederates is that the minimization of extraneous variance is simpler to achieve through careful training of consistency across confederates and across conditions. However, there are sources of random variance that could evidence themselves potentially in systematic variance and, therefore, skew outcomes. For instance, it is possible that many organismic variables might interfere with communicative outcomes (e.g., participants' mood). Often, however, researchers are not interested in these variables theoretically, so these sources of variance can be eliminated or reduced through random assignment to condition.

To reduce the potential systematic influence of extraneous variables, it is important that all participants be assigned to conditions randomly. Random assignment (Campbell & Stanley, 1963; Kerlinger, 1986) should allow any "errors" in systematic variance to cancel each other out. Thus a potentially systematic source of variance is minimized and relegated to the appropriate source of variance: random error variance. This randomization is fairly simple to achieve in the laboratory setting. By assigning participants to conditions prior to the time they arrive in the laboratory, a researcher can ensure that they are assigned randomly and not based on some demand characteristics. For instance, when Le Poire and Burgoon (1996) executed the second of their experiments, one male confederate was particularly sensitive to instantiating the touch manipulation with other males. Random assignment to conditions within sex-based pairings, however, ensured that all manipulations occurred randomly and were not based on some systematic characteristic.

Posttest Only Designs

A posttest only design is utilized when a researcher wishes to examine the effects of the interaction or stimulus materials on the participants without any measurement of outcome variables prior to the manipulation. In this case, the researcher is only interested in examining differences across conditions and not in how participants have changed due to the manipulation. Many stimulus-only nonverbal research designs are set up this way. For instance, Fortman (2001) was interested in the influence that various emotional expressions had on credibility and trust outcomes. She displayed the emotional expression and had participants make the various ratings following the presentation of the stimulus materials.

Such a design allows comparison of individuals *across* emotional conditions, but it does not allow for a comparison of evaluations of individuals prior to and following exposure to the stimulus materials. Conclusions are limited to a comparison of credibility and trust outcomes associated with the various facial expressions (happiness, sadness, etc.). It would be inappropriate to conclude that facial expressions of happiness decreased ratings of credibility for a particular confederate, but it is possible to conclude that facial expressions of happiness were rated as less credible than facial expressions of surprise, for instance. The advantage of such an approach is that participants are not subject to experimenter expectancy effects in which they can guess the effect the researcher expects to find. Thus researchers can be more confident that their finding is due to the manipulated variable and not due to the demand characteristics of the experimental design.

Pretest/Posttest Designs

To assess the effect of a manipulation, experimenters often make pretest/posttest comparisons, with the pretest occurring prior to the manipulation, and the posttest occurring after the manipulation. There are two common ways of conducting such manipulations when examining actual patterns of nonverbal communication. First, researchers have the confederate manipulate behavior during the course of a given interaction. For example, in some of the work on deception, Buller, Burgoon, and their colleagues manipulated suspicion, using confederates (Buller, Strzyzewski, & Comstock, 1991; Burgoon, Buller, Dillman, & Walther, 1995). Specifically, they told participants in the role of "interviewer" that they should assume that their interactional partners (the "interviewees") would tell the truth when answering questions, as most of the interviewees in past studies had been truthful. They warned, however, that if something seemed suspicious, a confederate would signal them by walking from the back room into the kitchen (a move that would be seen by the interviewer and not the interviewee). The experimenters could then compare the behaviors of both the interviewer and the interviewee before and after the confederate walked through the kitchen. In this way, they could determine whether interviewers inadvertently telegraphed their suspicions to interviewees by changing their nonverbal behavior and if interviewees changed their behavior after interviewers become suspicious.

A second way of setting up pretest/posttest comparisons involves having participants engage in two separate interactions with the manipulation occurring only in the second interaction. For example, Guerrero and Burgoon (1996) had romantic dyads engage in two separate conversations about common relational topics. For the first conversation, romantic partners simply talked to one another about a chosen set of topics. The couple was then separated, supposedly so they could complete questionnaires about the first conversation in private. One of the participants was actually enlisted as a confederate who then increased or decreased nonverbal displays of involvement and affection during the second conversation.

This type of pretest/posttest design has the advantage of negating anticipatory behavior. In other words, because participant confederates do not yet know that they will be manipulating their behavior during the second conversation, their behavior in the first conversation should represent baseline behavior that is free of any influence from the manipulation. In contrast, if confederates knew they would be manipulating their behavior later (e.g., increasing affection), confederates might alter their behavior in the first conversation either intentionally or unintentionally (e.g., by being a little less affectionate than normal so they would have "room" to increase affection later, or by becoming increasingly affectionate during the first conversation to prepare for the second). When using traditional confederates, researchers can minimize anticipatory behavior by keeping confederates "blind" to the condition until after the first conversation has ended.

Researchers can also try to reduce the effects of anticipatory behavior when manipulating behavior within a single interaction. One strategy for minimizing these effects is to give confederates a card they unobtrusively flip over at a certain point in the conversation to determine the type of manipulation they will be performing (e.g., Manusov, 1990, had marked "Trivial Pursuit" cards). Another strategy involves having the experimenter provide some type of signal. Similar to the deception studies that involve manipulating suspicion, experimenters could walk to a certain area to signal to confederates that they are to manipulate their behavior in a particular way. Although random assignment should lead to equivalency in groups (in terms of variables related to demographics, personality, and behavior) when sample sizes are large, when smaller samples are used, equivalency is much less certain. Pretest/posttest designs may thus be particularly important in studies with small samples so that researchers can assess how similar treatment groups were prior to the manipulation. This is an important issue in nonverbal research, as many studies involve intensive coding of many different behaviors (see Bakeman, this volume) and therefore utilize relatively small sample sizes.

Control Groups

When using pretest/posttest designs, the baseline behavior acts as one type of control. Experimenters can compare the baseline (pretest) behavior with the behavior that occurs after the manipulation. However, using a control group provides an even better means of assessing whether or not a manipulation made a difference. Although research methodologists (e.g., Campbell & Stanley, 1963; Kerlinger,

1986; Rosenthal & Rosnow, 1991) recommend that experimenters use control groups with both posttest only and pretest/posttest designs, nonverbal scholars have not utilized control groups very often. Instead, they tend to rely on making comparisons to baseline behavior or other treatment groups.

Using a control group provides many important advantages when interpreting data. One of these advantages involves the ability to rule out "time" or "learning effects" as rival hypotheses. For instance, Guerrero, Jones, and Burgoon (2000) examined how people react to changes in nonverbal intimacy behaviors by their romantic partners. Their experiment involved four treatment conditions so that, in comparison to an initial conversation, during a second conversation participant confederates exhibited nonverbal behavior that showed a large increase in intimacy, a moderate increase in intimacy, a moderate decrease in intimacy, or a large decrease in intimacy. Guerrero et al. also included a control condition wherein neither participant was given any instructions to change their behavior during the second conversation. Thus, this experiment used a pretest/posttest design with four treatment conditions plus a control group.

One of the findings that emerged from their study was that the non-confederate participants engaged in more forward lean in the second conversation (as compared to the first) across all treatment conditions. Had a control condition not been included, the experimenters might have concluded that people respond to increases in nonverbal intimacy by reciprocating and leaning forward, whereas people respond to decreases in nonverbal intimacy by using lean as a compensatory move to try and restore the level of intimacy within a given interaction. Because Guerrero and colleagues included a control condition, however, they were able to see that forward lean also increased when there was no manipulation. Thus, it was more sensible to interpret the data as indicative of a time effect rather than a response to the other's behavior.

Balancing, Counterbalancing, and Inclusion

Several other techniques can be used to control extraneous variance and rule out rival hypotheses. Among these techniques are balancing, counterbalancing, and inclusion via blocking or leveling (Campbell & Stanley, 1963; Kerlinger, 1986). *Balancing* involves assigning participants to cells so that certain characteristics are evenly represented across conditions. For instance, a researcher might want to have equal numbers of men and women within each experimental condition. When trying to achieve this balance, the researcher must also be concerned with random assignment. So if an experimenter has four conditions and wants to balance sex across these conditions, he or she will need to recruit an equal number of men and women and then pull random assignments from within each subset. For example, slips of paper that represent each condition could be placed into different bags for men and women. Obviously, the more variables that one wishes to balance across cells, the more complicated the process of random assignment becomes.

Counterbalancing is used frequently in pretest/posttest designs as a way of ruling out rival hypotheses related to pre-sensitization, time, fatigue, or learning effects (Campbell & Stanley, 1963; Kerlinger, 1986). This technique involves switching the order of the pre- and posttests. For example, imagine an experiment that involves determining how the presence of others affects emotional expression. Specifically, the researcher hypothesizes that people will, say, be more emotionally expressive when viewing a funny movie with someone than alone. The experiment could be set up using a pretest/posttest design with participants asked to watch two 20-minute segments of funny movies. For one group of participants, a confederate (who is introduced as another participant) watches the movie segment with the participant, and then the participant watches the second movie segment alone. For another group of participants, the order is switched so that they view the first movie segment alone and the second movie segment with a confederate. This way, if people showed more emotional expression when with the confederate than alone, regardless of the ordering, the researcher could be confident that the presence of another person was indeed making a difference. If such an experiment was not counterbalanced, a rival hypothesis would be that people become more (or less) emotionally response to funny movies over time. Yet another rival hypothesis would be that one of the movie segments was funnier than the other.

Finally, researchers can rule out rival hypotheses by including potentially important variables in their design. As noted previously, it is challenging to manipulate one or a few nonverbal behaviors while keeping all other behaviors constant. So if certain behaviors are especially likely to covary with those an experimenter manipulates, or are likely to act as moderators or mediators, it behooves the experimenter to include these variables in the design. These variables can be included in the design by *blocking* or *leveling*, which means that they can be included as independent variables, or by covarying them out statistically (Kerlinger, 1986). For example, a researcher who is interested in determining how people react to confederates' flirtatious behavior might consider including the variable of biological sex in her or his design, as sex has been found to influence how people interpret flirtatious behavior (e.g., Abbey, 1982; Saal, Johnson, & Weber, 1989).

SUMMARY AND CONCLUSION

The investigation of nonverbal behavior involves various research designs and approaches; this chapter focuses only on manipulations involving traditional or participant confederates. In line with Kerlinger (1986), the goal in experimental nonverbal research is to manipulate an independent variable (or variables) while controlling for other potential causes of variability in a given dependent variable. If researchers hope to meet the first criterion of Kerlinger's maxmincon principle, the manipulations they conduct must be internally valid and disparate from each other, and if confederates are used, they must be carefully trained and manipulation checks must be conducted. To meet the second and third criteria, nonverbal researchers must engage in practices such as controlling the setting, utilizing random assignment, including possible mediating and moderating variables in the design, eliminating or counterbalancing potential sources of extraneous variables, making baseline comparisons; and using control groups. Indeed, considering all of these issues when conducting nonverbal research utilizing confederates helps ensure the most valid research efforts of this kind possible and allows nonverbal researchers the greatest confidence in their conclusions.

REFERENCES

Abbey, A. (1982). Sex differences in attributions for friendly behavior: Do males misperceive females' friendliness? *Journal of Personality and Social Psychology, 42,* 830–838.

Andersen, P. A. (1985), Nonverbal immediacy in interpersonal communication. In A. W. Siegman & S. Feldman (Eds.), *Multichannel integrations of nonverbal behavior* (pp. 1–36). Hillsdale, NJ: Lawrence Erlbaum Associates.

Andersen, P. A. (1999). *Nonverbal communication: Forms and functions.* Mountain View, CA: Mayfield.

Andersen, P. A., Guerrero, L. K., Buller, D. B., & Jorgensen, P. F. (1998). An empirical comparison of three theories of nonverbal immediacy exchange. *Human Communication Research, 24,* 501–535.

Baron, R. (1997). The sweet smell of … helping: Effects of pleasant ambient fragrance on prosocial behavior in shopping malls. *Personality and Social Psychology Bulletin, 23,* 498–503.

Buller, D. B., Strzyzewski, K. D., & Comstock, J. (1991). Interpersonal deception: I. Deceivers' reactions to receivers' suspicions and probing. *Communication Monographs, 58,* 1–24.

Burgoon, J. K. (1991). Relational message interpretations of touch, conversational distance, and posture. *Journal of Nonverbal Behavior, 15,* 233–259.

Burgoon, J. K., Buller, D. B., Dillman, L., & Walther, J. B. (1995). Interpersonal deception IV. Effects of suspicion on perceived communication and nonverbal behavior dynamics. *Human Communication Research, 22,* 163–196.

Burgoon, J. K., & Le Poire, B. A. (1993). Effects of communication expectancies, actual communication, and expectancy disconfirmation on evaluations of communicators and their communication behavior. *Human Communication Research, 20,* 67–96.

Burgoon, J. K., Le Poire, B. A., & Rosenthal, R. (1995). Effects of preinteraction expectancies and target communication on perceiver reciprocity and compensation in dyadic interaction. *Journal of Experimental Social Psychology, 31,* 287–321.

Campbell, D. T., & Stanley, J. C. (1963). *Experimental and quasi-experimental designs for research.* Chicago: Rand McNally.

Crusco, A. H., & Wetzel, C. G. (1984). The Midas touch: The effects of interpersonal touch on restaurant tipping. *Personality and Social Psychology Bulletin, 10,* 512–517.

Floyd, K., & Voloudakis, M. (1999). Affectionate behavior in adult platonic friendships: Interpreting and evaluating expectancy violations. *Human Communication Research, 3,* 341–369.

Fortman, J. (2001). *Emotional expressions and credibility and trust outcomes.* Unpublished master's thesis, University of California, Santa Barbara.

Galizio, M., & Hendrick, C. (1972). Effect of musical accompaniment on attitude: The guitar as a prop for persuasion. *Journal of Applied Social Psychology, 2,* 350–359.

Guerrero, L. K., & Burgoon, J. K. (1996). Attachment styles and reactions to nonverbal involvement change in romantic dyads: Patterns of reciprocity and compensation. *Human Communication Research, 22,* 335–370.

Guerrero, L. K., Jones, S. M., & Burgoon, J. K. (2000). Responses to nonverbal intimacy change in romantic dyads: Effects of behavioral valence and expectancy violation. *Communication Monographs, 67,* 325–346.

Hecht, M. L., & Guerrero, L. K. (1999). Perspectives on nonverbal research methods. In L. K. Guerrero, J. A. DeVito, & M. L. Hecht (Eds.), *The nonverbal communication reader: Classic and contemporary readings* (pp. 24–41). Prospect Heights, IL: Waveland Press.

Jones, S. M., & Guerrero, L. K. (2001). The effects of nonverbal immediacy and verbal person-centeredness in the emotional support process. *Human Communication Research, 27,* 567–596.

Kerlinger, F. N. (1986). *Foundations of behavioral research* (3rd ed.). New York: Holt, Rinehart and Winston.

Lee, J. W., & Guerrero, L. K. (2001). Types of touch in cross-sex relationships between coworkers: Perceptions of relational and emotional messages, inappropriateness, and sexual harassment. *Journal of Applied Communication Research, 29,* 197–220.

Le Poire, B. A. (1994). Attraction toward and nonverbal stigmatization of gays and persons with AIDS: Evidence of instrumentally symbolic attitudinal structures. *Human Communication Research, 21,* 241–279.

Le Poire, B. A., & Burgoon, J. K. (1994). Two contrasting explanations of involvement violations: Nonverbal expectancy violations theory versus discrepancy arousal theory. *Human Communication Research, 20,* 560–591.

Le Poire, B. A., & Burgoon, J. K. (1996). Usefulness of differentiating arousal responses within communication theories: Orienting response or defensive arousal within nonverbal theories of expectancy violation. *Communication Monographs, 63,* 208–230.

Manusov, V. (1990). An application of attribution principles to nonverbal messages in romantic dyads. *Communication Monographs, 57,* 104–118.

Rind, B. (1996). Effect of beliefs about weather conditions on tipping. *Journal of Applied Social Psychology, 26,* 137–147.

Rosenthal, R., & Rosnow, R. L. (1991). *Essentials of behavioral research: Methods and data analysis* (2nd ed.). New York: McGraw-Hill.

Saal, F. E., Johnson, C. B., & Weber, N. (1989). Friendly or sexy? It may depend on who you ask. *Psychology of Women Quarterly, 13,* 263–276.

Sigelman, C. K., Adams, R. M., Meeks, S. R., & Purcell, M. A. (1986). Children's nonverbal responses to a physically disabled person. *Journal of Nonverbal Behavior, 10,* 173–186.

Author Index

523

C

Cacioppo, J. T., 200, *207*, 313, *315*, 404, 406, 407, *410*
Callan, V. J., 148, *150*, 268, *278*
Campbell, D. T., 515, 517, 518, 519, *520*
Camras, L. A., 349, *355*
Canary, D. J., 255, *258*, 336, *342*
Canli, T., 468, *469*
Caplan, R. D., 474, *480*
Cappella, J. N., 6, 8, *20*, 96, *102*, 149, *149*, 200, 201, *207*, 221, 222, 223, *231*, 309, 310, 311, 312, 313, *315*, 326, *333*, 383, 385, 390, *392*
Caputi, P., 28, *31*
Carlsmith, J. M., 353, *355*
Carlson, J. G., 269, 274, *278*
Carney, D. R., 26, 28, 29, 30, *32*, 110, *111*
Carrell, L. J., 117, 118, *120*
Carrere, S., 163, 165, 166, 167, 168, 169, *170*, 199, *206*, 210, 211, 213, 214, 216, *216*, 282, *288*, 405, *410*, 441, 442, 444, 445, 446, 447, 448, 449, *449*, *450*, 451
Carter, J. D., 484, 489, *491*
Cartwright-Mills, J., 463, *469*
Caruso, D., 29, *31*
Carver, V. H., 151, *158*
Cary, M. S., 432, 435, *439*
Casella, D. F., 30, *31*, 106, *110*
Cate, R., 296, *303*
Caul, W. F., 457, 458, *469*
Cegala, D. J., 222, *232*, 326, *333*
Chadiha, L., 215, *217*, 282, *289*
Chan, A., 28, *31*
Chance, J. E., 47, *54*
Chapin, F. S., 25, *31*
Chapple, E. D., 472, *480*
Charlton, K., 237, 239, 245, *247*
Chartrand, E., 199, 204, *207*
Chartrand, J. A., 309, 310, *315*
Cherlin, A., 209, *216*
Cheshire, J., 317, *323*
Chovil, N., 173, 174, 175, 176, 177, 178, *182*, 206, *206*
Christensen, A., 146, 147, 148, *149*, *150*
Christophel, D. M., 118, 119, *120*
Ciarrochi, J., 26, *31*
Clark, L. F., 281, *288*
Clark, M. S., 151, *158*
Clore, G. L., 406, *410*
Coan, J., 163, 165, 167, 168, *170*, *171*, 199, *206*, 210, 216, *216*, 268, *278*, 282, *288*, 363, *369*, 405
Coates, L., 206, *206*
Coats, E. J., 483, *491*
Cochran, J., 340, *343*

Cochran, W. G., 225, *232*
Cocroft, B., 295, *303*
Cohen, J., 435, *439*
Cohen, J. A., 377, *381*
Cohn, J. F., 310, *315*
Coker, D. A., 114, 115, *120*, 130, 131, 133, *135*, 222, 223, 224, 225, 227, 228, 229, 230, *232*, 251, 254, 255, *258*, 321, *322*, 326, *333*
Coker, R. A., 12, *20*, 130, 131, 133, *135*
Cole, E. J., 30, *32*
Coles, M. G. H., 404, 406, *410*
Collier, H., 163, *171*, 268, *278*, 363, *369*
Collins, N. L., 253, *258*
Colvin, C. R., 349, *355*
Comrey, A. L., 445, *450*
Comstock, J., 516, *520*
Conger, R. D., 480, *480*
Conner, B., 15, *19*
Conrad, A. B., 326, *333*
Cook, M., 437, *439*
Cook, W., 300, *303*
Cooper, H., 237, 239, 245, *247*
Cooper, H. M., 483, *491*
Corbin, S. D., 340, *343*
Corson, R. L., 363, *369*
Costanzo, M. A., 25, 28, *31*
Costanzo, P., 462, *469*
Coussoule, A. R., 116, *119*, *120*
Cramer, L., 336, *342*
Crawfrod, C. B., 61, *63*
Crowell, J. A., 168, *171*
Crowne, D. P., 213, *216*
Crusco, A. H., 514, *520*
Cruz, M. G., 298, *303*
Crystal, D., 317, *322*
Cunningham, J. L., 48, *54*
Cunningham, M. R., 403, 404, *409*
Cupach, W. R., 5, *20*
Custrini, R. J., 35, *40*
Cutrona, C. E., 403, 405, *410*, 480, *480*

D

Dahms, L., 48, *54*
Dakof, G. A., 256, *258*
Daniell, J., 67, 68, *73*
Darwin, C., 472, *480*
Davidson, R. J., 405, *410*
Davis, C. M., 404, *411*
Davis, D., 383, *392*
Davis, E. P., 407, *411*
Davis, J. M., 312, *315*, 348, 349, *355*, 357, 358, 359
Davis, K., 335, *343*
Davis, K. E., 253, *258*
Davitz, J. R., 418, *429*

Foster, D. A., 474, *480*
Fox, J., 48, *54*
Fraley, R. C., 253, *258*
Franceschina, E., 29, *31*
Frank, J. D., 47, *54*
Frank, L. K., 57, *63*, 67, *73*
Frank, M. G., 238, *247*
Fravel, D. L., 282, *288*
Frick, R. W., 394, *400*
Fridlund, A. J., 175, *182*, 462, *469*
Friedlander, M. L., 363, 364, *369*, *370*
Friedman, G. B., 489, *491*
Friedman, H. S., 26, 29, 30, *31*, *32*, 105, 106, 107, *110*, *111*, 237, *248*
Friesen, W. V., 142, *149*, 151, *158*, 164, *170*, 175, 176, *182*, 238, 244, *247*, 267, 269, 270, 271, 273, 274, *278*, 351, *355*, 358, 363, *369*, 400, *400*, 405, 461, *469*
Frijda, N. H., 406, *410*
Fromme, D. K., 67, 68, 72, *73*
Fromme, M. L., 67, 68, *73*
Funder, D. C., 28, *31*, 349, *355*
Fung, H., 281, *289*

G

Gabrielli, J. D. E., 468, *469*
Gada, N., 352, *356*
Galeazzi, A., 29, *31*
Galizio, M., 508, *520*
Gallois, C., 141, 142, 143, 144, 149, *150*, 427, *430*
Garber, J., 441, *450*
Gardner, H., 501, *502*
Ge, X., 480, *480*
Geertz, C., 501, *502*
Giglio, K., 116, 117, 118, *120*
Gilbert, A. N., 175, *182*
Giles, H., 317, 318, *322*, *323*, 383
Gillis, J. S., 312, *315*, 347, 348, 349, 350, 352, *355*, 358
Gladney, K., 72, *74*
Glaser, B. G., 70, *74*
Glover, G., 468, *469*
Goffman, E., 189, 190, 191, *196*, 431, 432, *439*, 500, *502*
Gold, C., 362, 364, *368*
Goldman, C. K., 461, 463, *469*
Goldsmith, D. J., 251, *258*
Goldstein, D., 163, *171*
Gonzales, P., *504*, 506
Gonzales, R., 364, *369*
Goodman, N., 460, *468*
Goodwin, C., 493, 495, *502*, *504*, 506
Goodwin, M., 503, *506*
Gordon, A. H., 107, *111*

Gorham, J., 224, *232*
Gottlieb, B. H., 256, *258*
Gottman, J. M., 3, 6, 15, 16, 19, *19*, *20*, 93, 100, *102*, 151, 152, 153, *158*, 163, 164, 165, 166, 167, 169, *170*, *171*, 199, 201, 204, *206*, 209, 210, 211, 212, 213, 214, *216*, 267, 268, 274, 276, *278*, 282, 283, *288*, 309, *315*, 338, *342*, 363, 367, *369*, 376, 379, *381*, 385, *392*, 404, 407, *410*, *411*, 420, *429*, 441, 442, 444, 445, 447, *449*, *450*, 472, 473, 474, *480*
Grahe, J. E., 312, *315*, 349, *355*, 358
Grammar, K., 309, *315*
Grandpre, J., 244, *247*
Grant, L. J., 175, *182*
Gray, H. M., 15, *19*
Greenbaum, C. W., 200, *206*
Greenberg, D. R., 268, *279*, 474, 480, *481*
Grice, H. P., 237, *248*
Griffin, D., 364, *369*
Griffin, S., 107, *110*
Gross, J., 462, *469*
Gross J. J., 107, 108, 110, *110*
Grotevant, H. D., 282, *288*
Grumet, G. W., 353, *356*
Guerrero, L. K., 6, 7, 11, 16, 17, *20*, 57, 58, 59, 61, *63*, 67, *74*, 85, 86, 88, 89, 90, *91*, 113, *119*, 131, *135*, 190, 192, *196*, 223, 224, 225, 226, 227, 228, 229, 230, 231, *231*, *232*, 253, 254, *258*, 403, 404, *409*, *411*, 441, *449*, *450*, 508, 510, 512, 513, 517, 518, *520*, *521*
Guetzkow, H., 337, *342*
Guilford, J. P., 25, 25, *31*, *32*
Gunnar, M. R., 407, *411*
Gurung, R. A. R., 405, *411*
Guthrie, D. M., 152, *158*
Gutsell, L. M., 115, 117, *120*

H

Haas, S. D., 163, *171*
Habermas, J., 237, *248*
Hahlweg, K., 201, *206*
Hairfield, J. G., 106, *110*
Hairston, R. E., 168, 169, *171*, 214, *216*
Halberstadt, A. G., 109, *111*, 483, *491*
Hale, J. L., 18, *20*, 47, *54*, 97, 100, *102*, 114, *120*, 127, 128, 129, 130, 131, 132, 133, 134, *134*, *135*, *136*, 295, 296, 297, *302*, *303*, 309, *315*, 325, 331, *333*, 363, 365, *368*
Hall, E. T., 114, *120*
Hall, J. A., 25, *32*, 68, *74*, 319, *323*, 483, 484, 489, *491*, *492*

Yonekura, Y., 468, *469*
Yoshimoto, D., *170*, 445, 447, 448, *449, 450*
Young, F., 327, *333*

Z

Zeldin, S., 364, *370*

Zhao, Z., 468, *469*
Zimmerman, J. A., 30, *32*
Zivin, G., 151, *160*
Zuckerman, M., 26, *33*, 105, *111*, 237, *248*, 483, 492

Subject Index